ASIA'S BEST

THE MYTH AND REALITY OF
ASIA'S MOST SUCCESSFUL COMPANIES

Michael Alan Hamlin

PRENTICE HALL

Singapore   New York   London   Toronto   Sydney   Mexico City

First published in 1998 by
Prentice Hall
Simon & Schuster (Asia) Pte Ltd
317 Alexandra Road
#04-01 IKEA Building
Singapore 159965

Prentice Hall, Simon & Schuster offices in Asia: *Bangkok, Beijing, Hong
Kong, Jakarta, Kuala Lumpur, Manila, New Delhi, Seoul, Singapore,
Taipei, Tokyo*

Printed in Singapore

5 4 3 2 1   02 01 00 99 98

ISBN 0-13-080038-4

Simon & Schuster (Asia) Pte Ltd, *Singapore*
Prentice Hall, Inc., *Upper Saddle River, New Jersey*
Prentice Hall Europe, *London*
Prentice Hall Canada Inc., *Toronto*
Prentice Hall of Australia Pty Limited, *Sydney*
Prentice Hall Hispanoamericana, S.A., *Mexico*

CONTENTS

ACKNOWLEDGEMENTS

We are embarrassed to admit that this book has taken two and a half years to write. It should have been out long ago. However, being engaged in business ourselves, we frequently found the attempt to professionally manage our own firm an impatient financial imperative. If not for our managing editor, we might never have gotten our priorities straight.

Lam Wai Ling, who unfortunately has left Simon & Schuster to take up a long-standing calling in community outreach work, has been a wonderful person to know and to work with. We are grateful for her encouragement and faith in our doubtful tenacity. Her former assistant, Nellie Lim, had the patience to listen to our complaints about unreasonable reviewers as well as our increasingly creative excuses for not meeting deadlines. We certainly hope to be more reasonable if we are ever given another chance like this. Christine Chua and Ang Lee Ming have meticulously and thoughtfully taken the manuscript through to the printed book.

Stephen Troth, publishing director of Simon & Schuster, has likewise been a bastion of patience as the years slipped by. Much more important, of course, has been his conviction that we were writing something important, and that we could probably do it better than others who aspired to undertake this task of writing about some of Asia's best companies and their capable managers and leaders. Indeed, our debt of gratitude to Stephen runs deep, in part because of the timing of his expression of confidence – a lonely voice was his. Stephen's conviction rekindled our own, and helped ensure that we would write a better book than we probably would have otherwise.

Renato Ramos, or Totie as he prefers to be called, is principally responsible for the research that went into preparing the book. This was a six-country effort. Much of the information gathered at the beginning of the project had to be updated as the project neared its completion, and the update in itself has been a major effort. Totie also prepared all the survey forms, analyzed the data, and organized the appendixes that appear in the back of the book. Totie managed much of this project while taking on significant areas of responsibility in our principal business. He's a real warrior.

We owe another incredible debt of gratitude to many distinguished friends and associates who have taken their valuable time to read early drafts of the manuscript and provide useful advice. These include Fred Wiersema, coauthor of *The Discipline of Market Leaders* and author of *Customer Intimacy*, who not only offered key insights of his own, but helped us organize the book coherently. It is impossible to convey how important his advice has been. The comments of Daniel R. Stern, the accomplished and energetic president of Leigh Bureau, have been of tremendous value and great encouragement. Danny also kindly showed the manuscript to his colleagues at Leigh Bureau, and we benefited from their counsel as well. In the Philippines, close friend Tony Samson, senior vice president of the Philippine Long Distance Telephone Company, read a few drafts of the manuscript. His feedback came at key moments in the development of the book and was always sincerely appreciated.

There are many members of our staff, former and present, who have assisted us in important ways. They include Mild Calingo, Leng de Mesa, Kin Gatbonton, and Pinky Gallegos. Thank you, ladies. Rhea Roldan, Joji Luna and Katherine David compiled the company surveys as the project drew to a close.

We have received great value from the time we spent with many of the executives who work in the organizations we studied. Much of this time was spent in personal interviews; in other instances, we spoke at length by phone. Most of these exceptional people are identified in the body of the book.

We also benefited from conversations with a number of key management thinkers and authors, including Michael E. Porter, Jerry I. Porras, Gary Hamel, Philip Kotler, Peter Drucker, Adrian Slywotzky and Fred. You will see that we have drawn heavily on the works of these profound authors.

We are grateful for their reactions to our ideas as well as the concept on which this book was first contemplated.

There are many organizations across Asia that supported the program that made this research possible. Principal sponsors have included PLDT, Metro Pacific, Bangkok Bank, Siam Bank, YTL Corporation, Indonesian Banker's Institute, and Neptune Orient Lines. Both *World Executive's Digest* and the *Far Eastern Economic Review* supported the program at different stages. A number of local publications were also exceptionally helpful in communicating information about the program, including the *Hong Kong Standard, Jakarta Post, Business Indonesia, Tempo,* the *Star, Business Times,* the *Philippine Star, Bangkok Post,* and the *Nation.* Thai Airways and Philippine Airlines provided transportation, and Pico Exhibitions assisted us with presentations in each of the countries.

The project, called The Asian Management Awards, started as a corporate communications and data gathering exercise undertaken by the Asian Institute of Management along with other corporate partners, but the actual research for this book was undertaken independently. Originally the manuscript was titled *Asia's Best: Winners of the Asian Management Awards.* A reviewer later suggested that the title should include the underlying theme of myth and reality, and we are grateful for this anonymous contribution.

Although we have benefited in different ways from the kindness of each of these individuals, the shortcomings in the book are ours, and ours alone.

Finally, and most of all, we thank Monette Hamlin, who is our greatest inspiration. The demands of producing a book result in the sacrifice of that most important of life's privileges, time with family. Monette's patience, encouragement, and confidence are the real reason for this book, and we are indebted beyond words. There are no other blessings in life as profound and wonderful as that which Monette and our children have provided.

Michael Alan Hamlin
Manila, Philippines

INTRODUCTION

There is no particular Asian management style.

A number of people who have heard of our work with top Asian organizations have congratulated us on writing a book that – it is assumed – finally and clearly sets forth the unique practices associated with doing business in Asia. We have had to carefully point out in these instances that our findings strongly suggest that there is no such thing. There is no "Asian management style."

Yes, there are cultural influences – well documented by other authors – that help determine how people, including business-people, interact with each other and conduct business. As has so often been reported, there is indeed an Old Boys' Club of sorts at work in the region which is dominated by overseas Chinese. But it really works pretty much like Old Boys' Clubs everywhere. The members help each other out and try to block new competitors. And yes, it is helpful to know people who are politically well connected, but recent developments in the U.S. pertaining to presidential campaign financing show that this is not so unusual elsewhere either.

What of the mystery of consensual decision making? Like companies everywhere, many, but not most, Asian corporations have found that respecting the opinions of workers and getting them emotionally behind a project or an objective is good business. They have also found that handing employees too much power can cause many unhappy moments. Another shared phenomenon with companies everywhere is that no one will make a decision if there is no leadership among a group of "empowered" employees.

Finally, it is important to be polite and not boorish in Asia. Face counts and should be respected. But from our perspective, generally civilized behavior works well everywhere, and cultural sensitivities – or insensitivities –

appear to be as important outside Asia as within. Sensitivity to others' cultural norms is proportional to one's determination and conviction to understand markets, partners, and competitors. It is not proportional to one's "Asian-ness."

We did find that Asian companies, generally, are pretty autocratic, but this is more a function of development state or quality of leadership than cultural practice – or imperative. You will see later on that this is one reason why many Southeast Asian employees prefer to work for non-Asian multinational companies or for expatriate bosses. A good many of the successful companies profiled are run by Asian managers trained in the West. A few Asian companies, as outrageous as it may sound, are actually run by Western managers. Neither nationality nor ethnic origin determines, as far as we can tell, whether management is poor, good, or superior in Asian companies. The ability to adapt to different corporate cultures is important, particularly for managers who have the courage and faith to work for family firms but are not members of the family. This is as true for expatriates as it is for Asian managers. But Asian managers are more affordable.

The Point

The principal point of this book is that we saw a good many instances of just plain excellent – world-class – management by some pretty exciting Asian companies and multinational corporations in Asia. We profile some of the outstanding Asian companies we studied and their most distinguishing characteristics and accomplishments. These accomplishments are extraordinary in that they were the result of exceptionally hard work and frequently brilliant insight. They are ordinary in the sense that they could – and have – occurred elsewhere under similar circumstances.

Second, bigness is not by itself an indicator of management excellence. It can be. But it can, and very often is, an indicator of a profound level of political influence, cronyism, and protectionism. While ethnic Chinese conglomerates are seen by some as a model for patriarchal corporate governance, in this work they are seen as lumbering organizations poorly equipped or prepared to compete on a level playing field. Just as important, they are not seen as breeding grounds of excellence, innovation, or brilliance. This is because they view "loyalty" as the most valued quality, not distinguished performance.

Third, profound changes are taking place in Asia as a result of trade liberalization. This change will require that even very successful companies make profound changes in the way they conduct business. While many companies are working diligently to bring about the changes that are necessary to sustain success and prosperity, the culture of many Asian organizations impedes their transition to globally competitive corporations.

We literally wrote this book all over Asia. The first year of the endeavor took place during preparations for presentations, as well as the actual presentations, in the six countries from which our successful companies were picked. Almost every company was involved in those presentations, and most of our interviews took place during that period. Gathering of data and its analysis took place over the seven years we have been engaged in this project. Not all companies agreed to allow us to present much of the financial or operational efficiency data we were provided – for obvious reasons. They were willing to help out, but they did not want to provide competitors with an unreasonable advantage. Although this information would have helped boost book sales, we understand.

In all, the 95 companies examined in this study were compared over a five-year period to over 600 other Asian companies and multinational corporations operating in Asia. In most instances, they were evaluated by faculty members of an Asian business school and submitted for final selection to six country-specific panels in Hong Kong, Indonesia,

Malaysia, the Philippines, Thailand, and Singapore.

Our findings are presented in two sections, The Myth and The Reality. In the first, we try to dispel any notion of esoteric Asian practices as principal reasons for success. The second has to do with new business paradigms.

Myth #1: A Not-so-uniquely Asian Vision

Harvard Business School professor Michael E. Porter and, conceptually, others argue that the rules of competition are the same everywhere. This study likewise indicates that the elements of corporate vision are as ordinary, and extraordinary, in successful companies doing business in Asia as they are in successful companies anywhere else.

The results of the study do not support the popular thesis that there is a uniquely Asian way of managing a business or purpose in founding and leading a company. There are, however, management practices that are more widely accepted in Asia than they are in a Western environment. These include a greater appreciation for long-term incubation periods for projects and investments, formalized procedures for consensus building, and the fast-fading tradition of lifetime employment.

But these are situational practices, not unique philosophies, techniques, or insights. And these practices are under pressure as equity markets grow, liberalization takes hold, and competition heats up. That pressure is increasing reliance on management principles that are effective in any competitive market.

Myth #2: Technology Transfer

Technology is supposed to make it easier to be competitive, and to add value to products and services, in at least three ways. First, technology lends itself to efficiency, so companies can, with the correct mindset, do more with less money. Gary Hamel and C.K. Prahalad call doing more with less money "corporate stretch." This is most often observed in smaller companies desperately competing with larger companies, and large companies that consistently revolutionize their industries.[1]

Second, technology allows smaller companies to act like larger, better endowed companies in many critical ways, from gathering market intelligence to presenting something as simple as a professional-looking report. Third, technology generates new businesses, products, and standards of service ranging from real-time financial information to instant credit approval for purchasers of cellular telephones.

The transfer of technology to the Asian companies in this study was primarily by outright purchase, rather than by sharing through joint venture agreements or alliances. Wherever possible, these companies sought to own technology to assure full transfer of relevant and leading technologies, after learning the hard way the pitfalls associated with less than outright ownership of technology and the ownership of outmoded technology whose competitiveness was dependent on low labor costs. In some instances, acquisition of technology was originally made possible by protectionism; in others, recognition of opportunity and the determination to capitalize on it was the driving force for technology transfer. More recently, reforms of protectionist policies across the region have made technology sharing more acceptable in joint venture engagements because both partners are full partners and have clearly defined areas of responsibility.

Myth #3: Not Exactly Hotbeds of Innovation – Yet

Neither Asian governments – Japan's included – nor Asian companies have the financial and intellectual resources

---

[1] Hamel, Gary and C.K. Prahalad, *Competing for the Future: Breakthrough Strategies for Seizing Control of Your Industry and Creating the Markets of Tomorrow*, Harvard Business School Press, Cambridge, 1994.

required to do the basic research that creates new industries. And while that will change as prosperity spreads across Asia – along with the awareness that "old" products can only be incrementally improved or even recreated a limited number of times – the emergence of a truly Asian product may be decades away.

On the other hand, it may not. Asia's development cycle has accelerated so greatly that it is imprudent to base development scenarios on historical precedent, especially time lines. And while Asian companies are not hotbeds of basic research, they are becoming experienced innovators in everything – from fast-food fried rice and egg rolls to world-class management consulting.

To deal with new competitive pressures resulting from liberalization of local marketplaces and the need to exploit global markets for newly developed and developing economies, Asia's best companies are pouring increasingly significant percentages of revenue into research and product development laboratories. This is most apparent in the high-technology sector, which regional governments have wisely identified as the high value-added alternative to exporting jobs in traditional export-oriented, labor-intensive industries. But it is also apparent in the consumer appliance industry, dominated by a few large national corporations that must rapidly enhance quality while lowering costs. Service industries, especially financial and advertising services, are responding to the pressures of liberalization by striving for new levels of innovative thinking and development.

Myth #4: Chasing the Market

The typical view of Asian companies is of sprawling conglomerates whose biggest challenge has been deciding what not to do in a sea of economic opportunities available to a few chosen one-time entrepreneurs. While that view has obvious validity, it tends to marginalize other realities.

Asia's best are masters of "niche-manship", taking on with

gusto markets that appear to be either too small or too bothersome to be of interest to larger companies. Take, for instance, deposit-taking companies that have had the region's huge, emerging middle-class consumer finance market largely to themselves while their larger competitors have concentrated on government securities and lending to a select group of elite corporations.

The World Bank reports that incomes in East Asia have almost quadrupled over the past quarter century. That growth has ignited consumer demand, opportunities to fill that demand, and competitors intent on getting a fair share. Competition for market share has benefited the rapidly expanding market, with service quality reaching levels undreamed of just a few years ago.

Customer service is taken most seriously by the region's new, intensely competitive (read cutthroat) telecommunications companies. All over Asia, an executive can purchase a cellular phone and be making calls in about ten minutes – if he or she chooses the right provider, of course. Customer service, or "customer intimacy" as best-selling author and consultant Fred Wiersema puts it, is top-of-mind in boardrooms and showrooms in Asia's best companies.

Reality #1: Growing Talent

Rapid market expansion and increased competition have put new pressure on Asia's best to manage great leaps in expansion, the introduction of new technology, and the recruitment of qualified managers. These changes are having a profound impact on the way Asia's best do business. They are also testing their capacity to preserve culture while trying to learn how to be radically "new" all the time.

Growing organizations face the realization – and the dilemma – that skilled and experienced managers in Asia are in notorious short supply, as are the institutions and professors required to fill the gap. As a result, Asia's best have established some of the finest internal training institutes in the world. Although multinational organizations for the most part lead their Asian competitors in providing world-class training, Asia's best are racing to catch up, and in some instances have done much more.

The issue of Asian management allows us to return to the issue of the Asian-ness of managers in Asia from a corporate culture perspective, separate from the issue of Asian management practice. In an age in which Asian values and Asian management styles are held up to both inspire and preserve a way of life imperiled by the relentless pace of spreading prosperity, Asian employees find that they frequently prefer to work for non-Asians and for companies whose management culture compares favorably with global standards rather than local practice.

Asian employers find that expatriates can run Thai and Indonesian companies, and that the best employee is the person best qualified for the job, irrespective of his or her citizenship, sex, experience in Asia, or political correctness. And although the quality of the region's universities and business schools has reached impressive heights, the preferred MBA is still one from the West.

Reality #2: The Productivity Urge

Asian consumers for years had no alternative but to purchase relatively shoddy, overpriced goods. Liberalization has already produced a hard-core concern for value for money in pricing strategy. From Singapore's Orchard Road to Manila's shopping and entertainment megamalls, aggressive pricing benefits consumers purchasing electronic components, computers, cellular phones, groceries, or athletic wear.

Rising prosperity and better times for Asia's consumers are making life much more difficult for Asia's manufacturers and retailers. Providing and communicating value have replaced gimmickry and poor or nonexistent after-sales service in housing, appliances, and financial services. Customer loyalty to brands – in Asia, like everywhere else – is only as good as the product's capacity to fulfill promises better than the competition.

Reality #3: Bringing Focus to Asian Conglomerates

Hamel and Prahalad popularized the notion of core competence;[2] more of Asia's best must learn to practice it. Hamel and Prahalad have been criticized for suggesting that industry leaders should rely on a single overriding core competence to sustain leadership. Porter believes that a related set of business activities is more effective in sustaining competitive advantage because it is far more difficult to emulate a set of activities than to benchmark a single core competence.

We suggest that core competence is probably best taken as a notion involving a set of related activities, rather than an altar to a single overpowering technology or expertise. Not many of Asia's best were found to be concentrating on either core competence or refining the efficiency and productivity of a set of operational activities. For those that are doing so, however, it is paying off.

Reality #4: Alliances and Joint Ventures

Asian conglomerates have not done well at either forging or sustaining strategic alliances, despite the common perception of powerful alliances among their founders. Although intra-Asian alliances are on the rise, we believe they are primarily marriages of convenience and do not represent strategic efforts to enhance competitiveness or establish industry leadership.

The real problems, however, are found in attempts to form "legitimate" alliances by large Asian and multinational firms. Culture clashes, inexperience managing across borders, and

---

[2] Hamel and Prahalad.

unrealistic expectations are the unfortunate norm. However, alliances are not the exclusive purview of the conglomerates and large national organizations. There are young, aggressive firms capitalizing on their own expertise and capacity to skillfully manage alliances to accelerate growth and enhance competitive advantage.

Reality #5: Competing for the Future

Just when things were going so well, Asian business came face-to-face with a reality check in 1996. Across the board, exports fell and pessimists happily pronounced the imminent end of the Asian miracle due to structural infirmity. Thailand's economy appeared to disintegrate in 1997. Asian stalwarts attributed the wake-up call to the cyclical nature of the country's principal exports. The reality was both. While productivity in Asia has been rising, very little purely Asian technology has accounted for the increase. As the region enters a new era of liberalization and intense competition, its reliance on Western technology and low value-added exports is dangerously high. Worse, not enough investment has been made in education and the development of research centers necessary to support the creation of indigenous, productivity-enhancing technology. Massive public and private investment in educational infrastructure will be required to sustain the rapid growth in Southeast Asia.

Practical Considerations

Who will benefit from reading this book? We would like to think just about everyone. However, that is probably not the case. It is fair to say that anyone who knows absolutely nothing about Asia will learn a great deal about Asia and Asian companies. Those who work in Asia and are familiar with some or all of the firms will enjoy reading about their friends and competitors, and learning more about why they are successful and what their chances may be of remaining successful. Asian managers may recognize similarities in their own firms and be alerted to important warning signals as well. This is a time of great change in Asia, and information such as we provide in this book will be of value as managers ponder the implications of vast change in the business environment.

It is also likely that students will enjoy and benefit from reading about these companies. A number of them have competed very well with some tough world-class competitors. Not only have they competed well, they have staked out territory at the top of their industries. These are competitors to reckon with, and today's students may have the opportunity to do so in the future.

Finally, there are many examples that managers and students alike may find of use in their current assignments or studies. We have tried to relate what we have observed to the thinking of some of the world's top management thinkers, both as an evaluation and a validation of business practice and theory. We have attempted to use these frameworks to suggest what needs to happen over the next decade or so for successful companies in Asia to sustain their success. The exercise was fascinating and useful in our own work, and we certainly hope that managers everywhere will find this a valuable exercise, too.

Part I
THE MYTH

Chapter One

☆

WHERE EXCELLENCE RESIDES

Think about this. Asia's most efficient, quality-driven, customer-conscious transportation company operates 3,800 taxis, buses, and trucks – in Jakarta. No matter where in Jakarta and no matter what the time, customers who call for a cab or limousine can reasonably expect to be picked up promptly by an intelligent, friendly driver in a late model Japanese or European automobile in great condition in a matter of minutes. Even during rush hour.

Nowhere else in Asia – not in Tokyo, Singapore, or Hong Kong (and certainly not Seoul or Taipei) – is this quality of service by a taxi company available. It is necessary to go to Indonesia, with a per capita income of less than US$1,000 per year, to avail of this standard of customer-intense service. Blue Bird Taxi relies heavily on up-to-date communication and information technology.

Joggers who purchase a pair of tennis shoes in a Singapore sporting goods store designed to provide the atmosphere and excitement of a sports stadium are showered with goodwill and a genuine desire to be of service. The store boasts teams of sales assistants trained in Asia's only retail sales training institute. The headquarters/distribution center of the chain, which includes stores in three other ASEAN countries, is as

3

futuristic as any Silicon Valley firm and is replete with product displays, even in the elevators. The company is considering the installation of computers in its trendy stores to provide customers access to the Internet.

Try telling a shoe salesperson anywhere else that you are an "over-pronator" and see what happens next – and expect nothing. At Royal Sporting House, you will be provided with a product designed to fit your need.

The founder of Thailand's leading high-technology components manufacturer is building two silicon wafer fabrication plants against daunting odds exacerbated by a severe downturn in semiconductor prices and the sudden crumpling of the Thai economy. Yet this determined entrepreneur supplies 12 of the top 30 manufacturers of computers and computer peripherals with about US$1 billion worth of semiconductors and other components every year. His goal is to be the Samsung of Thailand.

The first silicon wafer plant being built by an Asian technology company has benefited from connections. Asian connections helped finance Alphatec's start-up, but the network of its cadre of experienced Western managers has been instrumental in providing an impressive group of clients drawn from the world's top technology companies. But it is yet to be seen whether those connections and experience will save the company from profound setbacks in construction and an ill-fated alliance with a multinational partner. Success may not beget success for this ambitious company and its visionary founder, Charn Uswachoke.

Hong Kong's largest financial services network is operated by a deposit-taking consumer finance company that traces its roots no farther than Kuala Lumpur, not London or New York. It has a capital adequacy ratio of 57% – the minimum is 16% – and a liquidity ratio that is an astounding 66%. Annual growth in profits ranges upward from 41%. Its customer: the lower middle-class consumer.

Looking for a niche in the competitive Hong Kong market, J.G. Finance specializes in mortgaging older homes. While the taipans stay focused on development, this innovative consumer finance company is focusing on redevelopment.

In the Philippines' fast-food industry, McDonald's must content itself with the number two position: a local upstart enjoys a 70% share of the hamburger business. This Asian competitor has forced the global fast-food leader to do the unthinkable – add spaghetti to its menu – to remain competitive. While McDonald's walks away with media and advertising awards around the world, its competition home grown in the Philippines gets the attention – and respect.

Not content with beating McDonald's on its own turf, Jollibee Foods Corporation is expanding overseas and winning accolades from media and peers while its erstwhile global competitor reduces prices in hopes of revitalizing its business.

Kuala Lumpur's leading stock brokerage – and the fastest growing in Asia – is neither politically connected nor part of an international banking group. It is run by a Chinese entrepreneur who named the company using the initials of his own and his wife's first names. The company has expanded into Hong Kong, Australia, the Philippines, and Sri Lanka and boasts major property holdings at home and in North America.

And the founders of TA Enterprises started from scratch. The founders may not be well appreciated in politically correct circles, but they have created a powerhouse with significant impact on the development of Malaysia's capital markets.

These companies shatter the usual stereotypes about Asia, Asian conglomerates and business, and the capacity of Asian firms to compete with some of the world's finest corporations. Seeing through those stereotypes is important for anyone doing business in Asia. Overseas, relationship-based networks; politically-connected, massive conglomerates; and under-the-table connections may have been a fixture of development for 50 years, but Asia is evolving. Fast.

Access to and the capacity to develop technology and ideas are becoming the principal opportunity generators, not the good old boys' network. Political concessions are apparent, but they are increasingly scrutinized and subject to criticism in the media as well as in business circles. While it is always possible to find someone willing to take a bribe, it is no longer certain that the bribe will make a difference.

Asia – and Asian companies – are becoming market driven. And there is no turning back.

The six corporations cited above are drawn from the 95 mostly Asian corporations in Hong Kong, Indonesia, Malaysia, the Philippines, Singapore, and Thailand that agreed to participate in the research that made this book possible; the latter have been cited in one or more regional surveys or awards in the past five years as companies where excellence resides. The largest group of companies is indigenous and dominates national industries from natural cosmetics to DRAM (dynamic random access memory) chips.

There is a much smaller, but reasonable, number of state-owned enterprises, multinational corporations, and conglomerates, which demonstrates that big companies in Asia can be enlightened, innovative, and entrepreneurial, too. But the story to be told here is principally about visionary Asian companies – and their founders and managers – that set out to become world-class organizations and are succeeding. Just as important, it is about what they must do to sustain competitiveness and their success.

Likewise, a number of not-for-profit organizations and government agencies were examined. They clearly demonstrated, often in a profound manner, that the qualities of excellent organizations characterize more than just private-sector institutions.

Old – and Dangerous – Clichés

As students and entrepreneurs back in the days when Japan was only approaching Ezra Vogel's proclaimed status as Number One, we, along with other champions of Japanese business and culture, were lonely voices.[1] Ten years later

---

[1] Vogel, Ezra, *Japan As Number One*, Tuttle Tokyo.

Japanese production management methods had taken the business universe by storm and made W. Edwards Deming the renowned authority he always deserved to be.

But as is the case with most success stories over time, things went too far. They went too far because: 1) the Japanese had begun to believe they were invincible and of course they were not; 2) their production techniques were being fairly easily adopted, or adapted, by non-Japanese competitors despite warnings of glass and cultural ceilings; and 3) there were many things Japanese companies were inept at, such as running the administrative side of their business, managing overhead, fostering original research, and providing after-sales service.

Nothing was more dangerous, of course, than the Japanese allowing themselves to be lulled into a sense of complacency by all the hype the highly respected Vogel kicked off. In doing this, Japanese companies and their managers became exactly what they derided in their American competition: soft. Frank Gibney had it right when he proclaimed Japan the fragile superpower.[2]

The popular literature on Asia and Asian development promotes a similar myth, this time about Asia and its three billion or so people and their values. In the same way that Vogel's *Japan As Number One* spawned a two-decade stretch of books that more or less worshipped the Japanese business model, with future caster John Naisbitt's new book *Megatrends Asia* – reviewed by most old Asia hands with the warmth old Japan hands accorded Vogel – we seem destined to endure a decade or two of business books extolling esoteric, or quaint depending on the perspective, Asian values and business practices, endless projections of and debates centered on Asian market potential, and the promotion of the mystical and fundamental role of and reliance upon *guanxi* to enter this actually less than inscrutable market.

This is dangerous for Asians as well as non-Asians coming

---

[2] Gibney, Frank, *Japan: The Fragile Superpower*, Tuttle Tokyo.

into the region. For Asians, it could lead to the complacency that so recently wrought a painful descent to hard earth for Japan, or that of the Americans a decade before who thought no nation could match their industrial output. It is dangerous for new market entrants, as so many have found, because success in Asia requires a fundamental appreciation of Asian realities, not the happy myths.

So the reader of this book will probably find – and we certainly hope this to be the case – that the companies and practices profiled here pretty much broke all the stereotypes that will be fostered upon you in the next two decades by Asian experts.

Mythical Models

Porter has presented similar conclusions with respect to Japanese business. Porter found that companies that fitted the fabled "Japanese model" were actually for the most part uncompetitive. These are companies in the aircraft, chemical, software, financial services, consumer package goods, prepared foods, and apparel industries. According to Porter, revolutionary Japanese companies producing such things as automobiles, VCRs, robots, facsimile machines, carbon fiber, air conditioners, and even sewing machines, broke most of the rules inherent in the Japanese model on the road to industry leadership.[3] Hong Kong banker David K.P. Li recently reported the results of a survey that found 87% of Japanese business to be globally uncompetitive. "Let me say that number again," Li said for emphasis, "87 percent. And this is the region's most advanced economy?"[4]

Jerry I. Porras and James C. Collins in their immensely popular book, *Built To Last*, remind us that the inspiration for

---

[3] Porter, Michael E., A presentation entitled, "Global Competitive Advantage", March 8, 1996.

[4] Li, David K.P., "Tomorrow's Asian Management Style: The Challenge of Mastering Today's Conflicts," a speech before the AAMO-12 International Management Conference, Singapore, November 7, 1996.

Sony's walkman was the image of the music-mad Masaharu Ibuka hauling a large tape recorder around headquarters on his shoulder, not government targeting of strategic industries.[5]

There are those who feel that any positive attention Asia gets is good. Richard Halloran, for example, has lived in and written about Asia for the *New York Times* for 20 years. Writing in *Foreign Policy*, Halloran proposes that "John Naisbitt captured the new reality of Asia in his 1995 book *Megatrends Asia*, writing, 'What is happening in Asia is by far the most important development in the world. Nothing else comes close, not only for Asians but for the entire planet. The modernization of Asia will forever reshape the world as we move toward the next millennium.'"[6]

Halloran believes that benign neglect of the "revolution in Asia" by American politicians and businesspersons is a great disservice to his country. Lester Thurow, Paul Kennedy, and Paul Krugman, Halloran frets, perpetuate this neglect in their work and public statements and thereby contribute in a mighty way to keeping Asia and opportunity in Asia in the background of the American mainstream.

While Halloran's concerns with the American mindset toward Asia have much merit, anyone who has done research on Asia and Asian business – in preparation for writing a book, for instance – knows that there is an incredible amount of information available in the Western and regional press. Institutional and academic research data is provided in virtual knowledge repositories all over the world and increasingly in Asia. These are easily and quickly accessed via the World Wide Web.

What cannot be found is much information on Asian companies outside of the top, major domestic corporations, although regional media such as the *Far Eastern Economic*

---

[5] Collins, James C. and Jerry I. Porras, *Built To Last: Successful Habits of Visionary Companies*, Harper Business, New York, 1994.

[6] Halloran, Richard, "The Rising East," *Foreign Policy*, No. 102, Spring 1996.

Review, *Asian Business*, and *Asia, Inc.* have begun addressing that information gap in a fairly competent and relevant way. Surprisingly, financial analysts frequently seem the most backward, perhaps reflecting the still embryonic stage of most Asian capital markets and the tightly held majority stakes of most "public" Asian companies. So do not bother checking out the companies profiled here in the Dunn & Bradstreet database. You will find very few outside Singapore and Hong Kong.

Despite the rigor and competence with which international and regional media and academia have begun to examine Asian businesses, no comparative study of outstanding Asian organizations seems to have been undertaken with a view to understanding how innovative these companies are, why they are successful, and what their chances of remaining successful might be. And that, happily, is the task undertaken here.

Transitioning

Porter recently presented to Asian audiences the results of his research into successful Asian companies and the challenges they face in transitioning and adapting to new, free-market standards of competition. Porter suggested that most Asian business groups are widely diversified and that there is little corporate value added to the whole.

Asian business has been busy responding to opportunities (i.e., it is opportunistic rather than strategic), but it has not created opportunity, or true competitive advantage, or value. Not surprisingly, many Asian managers and academics have reacted critically to Porter's views.

Because access to inputs is so very nearly universal, Porter argues that in a competitive marketplace the challenge to Asian companies will be the value they add to inputs, or "the capacity to use inputs productively."[7] Developing the capacity to use inputs more productively than competitors requires

---

[7] Porter.

that companies become more innovative in developing business systems, products, and strategy. This is what economists like to call Total Factor Productivity, or the value of a product or service less capital and labor. We call this value-added.

Put another way, Porter argues that Asian companies must be smarter, more energetic, more restless, more single-minded, and more resourceful than the competition. While competition within Southeast Asian markets has frequently been strong among small and medium-sized firms, it has seldom been world class. The companies profiled here are showing that it can be.

It is not Asia's conglomerates for the most part, however, that are demonstrating Asian competitiveness. Few have ever been subjected to anything approaching real competition in a free market. This is worrisome because, with few exceptions, Asia's conglomerates and their founders appear determined to ignore the new realities before them or write off warnings of poor preparedness for competition as the product of a Western intelligentsia that does not understand Asia. The reality is that competition in Asia will make it very difficult to attain industry leadership in a single core business let alone a myriad of wholly and even marginally unrelated business interests. Benign neglect, for whatever reason, of that reality means that strategic investments designed to position core businesses competitively in their industries are not being made. More retail development, food processing plants, or breweries alone will not make Asia's conglomerates internationally competitive, because competitiveness no longer evolves from having the most and the cheapest resources. Rather, it evolves from putting resources in the right place. The right place will increasingly be in areas enhancing productivity and value, and not merely wrestling opportunity to the ground first.

What is Asia?

Approaching Kuala Lumpur from Subang, commuters gaze

through their windshields at a dome of dust, dirt, and hydrocarbons that has become a fixture over what is still one of Asia's greenest cities. Near the center of that dome are purported to be the two highest buildings in the world, rising amid public controversy, political intrigue, and historic prosperity.

Yet it was not long ago – just over a decade – that this same bustling economy was reeling from the effects of a severe, closed-market, import-substitution induced recession. Foreign investment and a stable, pro-business government pulled the Malaysian economy out of its tailspin and stimulated the very high growth rates that have characterized the national economy since that time and made the country – along with Thailand and Indonesia – one of Asia's direct investment darlings. Spurred by its success in attracting foreign investment, government identified and pressured key business leaders to successfully undertake a series of projects deemed critical to national development and growth.

The World Bank, Halloran reports, indeed says, "pragmatic policy, not ideology, has been largely responsible for Asia's economic growth." As a result of this pragmatic development policy, Central Intelligence Agency and World Bank estimates project that by the year 2020, Indonesia will boast the world's fifth largest economy; and Thailand, temporarily floundering, the eighth, right behind Germany and ahead of France. Malaysia, with a population only about a third of Thailand's, will not reach the top ten.

As prosperity spreads and national confidence and technological competence rise, nationalist and frequently racial sentiments have begun to wane. Despite the occasional criticisms of Western media, business and governments, the perception of the West as the exploiter of Asian wealth is not much on the minds of the average Asian wage earner or executive. Instead, regional governments have shifted their concerns to managing prosperous societies and the new set of problems that reality presents. Asia's very young, untested, and restless population makes that a daunting task.

Asian leaders – notably Malaysia's Prime Minister Mahathir Mohamad – frequently seem reduced to blaming the problems of enhanced prosperity on Western influences. The West's problems in dealing with the dark side of prosperity provide an opportunity for Asian governments to avoid some of the mistakes made in the West, such as creating welfare states that ultimately bankrupt national coffers and probably enhance the deterioration of ethical and moral values and standards. But as Asian corporations face the challenge of revolutionary market economies, they will increasingly do so with an intellectual and emotional capital that does not know or understand the crushing burdens of poverty, war, or hunger, and as a result will not demonstrate the burning passion for a better life that characterized the last half century of Asian growth.

Prosperity, and the emergence of China as an involved player in the regional economy, have made it easier for the region's 51 million overseas Chinese to participate more overtly in regional development. *The Economist* recently reported that overseas Chinese control about half the total foreign direct investment in China and are responsible for over half the wealth in Indonesia, Malaysia, and the Philippines.[8] And so it is popular to focus on Chinese business in the popular literature. But it should be just as important not to forget the other near-half of the region's business community, which is distinctly non-Chinese.

Travel around Asia is fast and convenient and quickly brings home the vast contrasts prevalent in Asian societies. For that is what Asia is, a working network of Asian societies, but certainly not a society. The contrasts in speech, food, and customs obvious across China are magnified across Asia. Hong Kong and Singapore are two vastly different "nations," as different as London and New York or New York and Dallas. Traveling from either city to Kuala Lumpur, Jakarta, or Manila, one can experience the contrasts and similarities

---

[8] _____, "A Survey of Business in Asia," *The Economist*, March 9, 1996.

prevalent in the religions and ideologies that have shaped their present character: the devoutness of Islam, the passion of Christianity, and the simple sophistication of Buddhism.

A recent *Asian Wall Street Journal* report explained the financial contrasts of these markets:

- In Singapore, the 33% of middle-class households with the highest incomes each earn at least US$3,200 a month. In Indonesia, the middle class only has to earn US$260 a month to make the top 33%.
- Reflecting differences in tastes and lifestyles, the middle class is twice as likely to live in air-conditioned homes in Hong Kong as in equally affluent Singapore, where the climate is hotter.
- Despite growing affluence, Asia remains a telecommunications backwater. In Thailand, middle-class households with cars outnumber those that have telephones.

"To say middle class implies an easily defined group. It is a bit of a misnomer in Asia because, for us, it means little more than somewhere between the top and the bottom," says Steve Garton, a director of Survey Research Hongkong Ltd., a Nielsen SRG unit," according to the report.[9] Incidentally, the report showed the largest middle class to be in Vietnam: 54%.

As the middle class swells, it seems to defy definition or categorization. When one considers what the middle class in Asia does for a living, what they earn, and what they own, the contrasts are profound: "If cars were the sole measurement of middle-class affluence, then Malaysia, where 62 percent of households own at least one set of wheels, would be at the top. And Hong Kong, where government measures to curb congestion have kept car ownership at 15 percent, would be near the bottom. Only middle-class households in the Philippines, China, and Vietnam are less likely to own a car."[10]

---

[9] Wong, Jesse, "Asia's Middle Class Defies Definitions," *The Asian Wall Street Journal*, Vol. XX #85, December 30, 1995.

[10] *Ibid.*

These facts help demonstrate why it is impossible to generalize about Asia or Asians. This is a vast region of sharp differences in political, religious, and social perspective. While prosperity and trade liberalization will strengthen financial and trade networks, it is likely that regional specialization, within as well as among nations, will become increasingly prevalent as corporations and nations seek to capitalize on distinctive competencies and competitive strengths.

In the end, however, Asia must soon deal with the new realities of prosperity, whether they be a smog-induced dome of grit over a city center or sustaining near double-digit growth, as Thailand, and the region, have just learned. The capacity to deal with these challenges, and perhaps the willingness to do so, will determine how successfully the Asian network handles its profound development success, "having compressed into 50 years the industrial revolution that the West took 200 years to accomplish."

This examination of how some of Asia's best companies helped accomplish that phenomenal task, and are preparing for increased competition in the new global marketplace, shows that they can be well up to the task. They will have to be.

Chapter Two

★

A NOT-SO-UNIQUELY ASIAN VISION

When *The Asian Wall Street Journal* celebrated its 20th anniversary, a special supplement illustrated the contrast between 1976 Asia and 1996 Asia in two drawings. The first showed a young Asian boy working in a flooded rice field. The second showed a young businessman talking on a cellular phone surrounded by an impressive high-rise skyline.

Within 1976 Asia, economic disparity across borders reflected cultural contrasts as dramatic as the contrasts in development status that would be apparent 20 years thence. Singapore's 2.3 million citizens generated a per capita GNP of US$2,860. At the opposite end of the economic spectrum, Indonesia's 139 million-strong population boasted a per capita GNP of just US$270.

Table 2.1 illustrates a number of important facts. First, despite progress in each country, the disparity between countries remains pretty much the same. Second, some countries have developed faster than others. Malaysia and Thailand have developed faster than Indonesia and the Philippines. Of course, it is much harder to make 190 million people prosper than Malaysia's 20 million or even Thailand's 59 million. But the Philippines should have been able to keep

Table 2.1

	1976	1996
Hong Kong		
Per capita GNP (US$)	2,790	21,650
Population (million)	4.4	5.8
Indonesia		
Per capita GNP (US$)	270	880
Population (million)	139	189.9
Malaysia		
Per capita GNP (US$)	950	3,520
Population (million)	12.5	19.5
Philippines		
Per capita GNP (US$)	410	960
Population (million)	44	66.2
Singapore		
Per capita GNP (US$)	2,860	23,360
Population (million)	2.3	2.8
Thailand		
Per capita GNP (US$)	380	2,210
Population (million)	43	58.7

up with Thailand.

Third, market conditions for corporations operating within these countries also varied significantly across borders. Despite these contrasts, the overseas Chinese conglomerates followed pretty much the same development path from small trading firm to diversified conglomerate,[1] regardless of location of their transplanted roots, and Indonesia, the least wealthy country in terms of per capita income, produced three of Asia's largest overseas Chinese conglomerates, including the largest by far. Sales of the Salim Group in 1992 reached US$10 billion compared to the next largest conglomerate, Formosa Plastic of Taiwan, at US$6.7 billion.

---

[1] Lasserre, Philippe and Hellmut Schütte, *Strategies for Asia Pacific*, MacMillan Business, 1995.

The third largest group is Thailand's Charoen Pokphand, with 1992 sales of US$5 billion.

While economic, infrastructure, and sociopolitical conditions vary within the six countries involved in this study, the aspiration seems to have been remarkably similar, at least among the region's biggest firms. Their vision was to be big and diversified. Twenty years later, they are. Now, it is time for priorities and visions to change.

To their credit, Asia's lumbering conglomerates and multi-nationals are demonstrating a new concern about professionalizing management and developing strategic foresight. As they follow through on those concerns, will they ultimately more closely resemble Western multinationals than their heritage? "Increased competition from established multinationals – as well as a trend toward more open markets in Hong Kong, Taiwan, and Southeast Asia – will hurt players that fail to alter their traditional paternalistic management style," a recent survey observed, suggesting that radical change is inevitable.

"For years, Asian companies have succeeded by riding on a wave of double-digit economic growth. Overseas Chinese entrepreneurs who dominate the region's economies, for example, hold liquid assets conservatively estimated at US$2 trillion. For them, constantly rising land prices, the ability to tap large pools of cheap labor, and an extensive network of personal connections were more important than advanced management methods.

"But that era is fast ending."[2]

Former director of the University of Hong Kong Business School S. Gordon Redding argues, "If they (the conglomerates) can't decentralize real decision-making in their organizations, then they can't be multinational."

Large conglomerates with no clear indigenous or acquired expertise contributing to competitive advantage must soon face up to new competitive threats by becoming more

---

[2] _____, "Asia's New Giants," *Business Week*, November 27, 1995.

strategy driven than opportunity driven. Liberalization, increased competition, and a new generation of managers that puts priority on the deal – rather than deal making – have made it easier for the founders and managers of Asia's unwieldy conglomerates to think seriously about what it will take to achieve the efficiency the best multinational corporations have capitalized on to dominate industries.

The profound change that is already taking place has not made it any easier to consolidate core businesses. For instance, the Salim Group has had difficulty in pushing decision-making down the hierarchy, despite the determined efforts of Anthony Salim, third son and chosen successor of founder Liem Sioe Liong. Salim's resolve in streamlining decision-making is nevertheless evident in its Hong Kong affiliate First Pacific, itself an increasingly impressive group of companies. First Pacific has been left virtually to itself despite significant birthing pains that spanned a decade. Partly as a result of that autonomy, First Pacific is thriving and has become "part of Hong Kong's benchmark Hang Seng Index."[3]

There are other large national companies – such as virtual icons Sime Darby in Malaysia and the Ayala Group in the Philippines – as well as budding multinationals such as upstart First Pacific, that are demonstrating a new dynamic as young, professional managers are brought on board to consolidate diverse businesses. Even so, focusing on core competencies is hard when the companies these organizations control are found in a bewildering array of industries spanning the trade, property, technology, manufacturing, and financial sectors. Focusing is made even more difficult when these businesses are anchored in an opportunity-rich mindset that in the past required little expertise or value-added.

Smaller, newer, and less entrenched Asian companies also face new, competitive challenges but are growing very differently and may ultimately be better prepared for the new

---

[3] *Business Week*, September 2, 1996.

competition. They are unrestrained by paternalistic or affiliated networks, outdated corporate cultures, and what has passed as "honor-driven" management systems.[4] These companies are value-driven, value-added obsessed, and market-intimate. They can be intimidating and ambitious competitors willing to take their fair share of calculated risks, even when it means betting the company to achieve extraordinary goals.

They have had little choice. The old boys' network is not accessible; neither are the political favors the network can cultivate. Doing business in a radically different way is the only viable development strategy available.

The connections these companies rely upon, therefore, are needs-based and rooted in the logic of the marketplace. Managers and employees are concerned more with how the company runs than who runs the company. Focus allows them to maximize returns on extremely scarce resources and to accomplish more with less of everything: people, financial resources, and breadth of product line.

Not surprisingly, these newer and more focused companies – independents and independent subsidiaries both – have a good feel for what they ultimately are as businesses, and where they want to be in ten or 20 years. It is easier to say that a company sees itself as a high value-added original designer and manufacturer of logic chips, say, than a company that aspires to be an industry leader in, well, everything. Not that it cannot be done, a goal General Electric CEO Jack Welch institutionalized with the vision statement "To become #1 or #2 in every market we serve and revolutionize this company to have the speed and agility of a small enterprise." But it is very rare.

Becoming Visionary

Collins and Porras say that the idea of companies becoming

---

[4] Hamlin, Michael Alan, "Whither Asia's Business Dynasties?" *Business Times*, December 29, 1993.

visionary through "vision statements" is a myth. Rather, "visionary companies attained their stature not so much because they made visionary pronouncements," but because they undertook that step with thousands of others.[5]

Hamel and Prahalad prefer the word foresight to vision, but agree that it must be undertaken with a large cross section of a company's employees. "Vision connotes a dream or an apparition," they argue, "but there is more to industry foresight than a single blinding flash of insight. Industry foresight is based on deep insights into the trends in technology, demographics, regulation, and lifestyles that can be harnessed to rewrite industry rules and create new competitive space."[6]

Given this, where do Asia's Best see themselves now, and where are they going?

For Asia's Best, vision or foresight evolves from eight not-very-unique principal concerns, which we will call vision components. Collectively, they can easily provide the basis for forming deep insights. Individually, they are much more complex than simply getting big and diversified in an opportunity-rich environment.

- Market intimacy – For some companies over the last decade, this has meant conforming to local norms. But over the last decade, the local norm has been rapidly globalizing, increasingly universal, and constantly changing.
- Cost leadership – Technology is becoming more than a way to manufacture something new; it provides a more cost-effective way to do business. That is important because labor and other cost advantages are eroding. However, the newest technology may not always provide the "best" strategy for market development: it may be too expensive or simply inadequate during development.

---

[5] Collins, James C. and Jerry I. Porras, *Built To Last: Successful Habits of Visionary Companies*, Harper Business, 1994.

[6] Hamel, Gary and C.K. Prahalad, *Competing for the Future*, Harvard Business School Press, Cambridge, 1994.

- Empowered employees – The other hand of eroding cost advantage is an empty hand signifying a shrinking pool of qualified workers. Increasingly prosperous employees are seeking enhanced psychological satisfaction from work. Most often, that means the capacity to influence the way they do their jobs.
- Customer service and satisfaction – The days when customers had no choice but to stand in line to buy a car, obtain a phone, or make a deposit are gone. Whether it is assembling and testing semi-conductors or providing on-line banking services, doing it on time and better than anyone else is not just a competitive advantage, it is a basic requisite of industry leadership.
- Value – Because outstanding service is not enough, value for money has become a key component of competitive advantage. Bells and whistles count, because loyalty is increasingly proportional to customer delight, not "mere" satisfaction.
- Value-added – As costs rise in Asia, so does value-added. Advanced technology is in demand. But will it be created in Asia?
- Regional and global expansion – In a bid to sustain Asia's rapid growth, with their own markets maturing, Asian companies are expanding throughout Asia, Europe, and the U.S.
- Aversion to complacency – There is an acute, and frequently painful, realization that industry leadership is a goal that has to be met every day no matter how brilliant past accomplishments may have been.

To illustrate how Asia's Best rely on these principles, let us visit a few.

Market Intimacy and Empowered Employees

Asia's fast-food industry provides a superb example of market intimacy and energetic, empowered employees. Throughout the region, indigenous companies have outperformed such world-class industry leaders as McDonald's and Wendy's. Much of their success can be attributed to determined efforts to cater to local tastes, something the global industry leaders have tried not to do to maintain consistency globally.

The successful Asian companies have also capitalized on family values, making their restaurants family-oriented virtual theme parks. Staying close to changing tastes as well as value has been made easier by giving employees a significant stake in the success of the company and providing effective programs to capitalize on their feedback.

Step, for instance, into any Ah Yee Leng Tong – a Hong Kong chain of Chinese restaurants serving soup and specialty dishes – and you may sample the pleasures of the popular "Sweetened Ginseng, Red Jujube, Lotus Seeds and Fat of Snow Toad." Or if you are on the run, duck into a corner Café de Coral for "Soup Earthen Hot Pot or Hot Pot Rice" served in an efficient, customer-friendly cafeteria-like environment. Of course, for less exotic fare, one can always sample "Spanish Gambas Al Ajillo" at The Spaghetti House.

Café de Coral is a Chinese-Occidental fast-food chain operating 140 outlets, including 12 in China, with a 25% market share in the Hong Kong fast-food segment. Including 15 Ah Yee Leng Tong outlets and 20 The Spaghetti Houses, the chain enjoys the patronage of about nine million diners a month, or nearly one and a half times Hong Kong's population. By way of comparison, McDonald's has a 20% share of the market.

Unaided brand awareness measured in company surveys paints an even clearer picture of the Hong Kong company's success at getting into the minds of its customers. Total unaided brand awareness measured in 1993 was 85%. Local competitor Fairwood Fast Food came in second at 75%, with McDonald's a distant third at 46%.

"The moon mission didn't need a committee to spend endless hours wordsmithing the goal into a verbose, meaningless, impossible-to-remember 'mission statement,'" Collins and Porras dryly observe.[7] Likewise, Café de Coral's –

---

[7] Collins and Porras, pp. 94–95.

the Chinese characters used in the name mean "Happy Together" – managing director, Michael Chan Yue Kwong, does not seem to need stirring statements of purpose to provoke quality service and innovation out of his employees.

The company has been the market leader for two and a half decades in part because of obsessive cost controls, which are characteristic of the fast-food industry and therefore basic requisites of successful operation. Market leadership can be more correctly credited to a penchant for market intimacy, and to employees who are stakeholders by way of a profit-sharing scheme at the unit level and share option incentives.

Another measure of the success of the firm is the rapidity with which its menu items and packaging materials are emulated by the competition. Consistent concern for professional appearance as well as environmental consciousness have led to a series of innovative packaging alternatives. Innovation is also seen in the menu itself, which is widely copied by other indigenous fast-food start-ups. Café de Coral is setting the fast-food industry rules in Hong Kong and China, and everyone else is following.

Customer Service, Product Innovation, and Cost Leadership

Admittedly, Hong Kong media tycoon and recent Silicon Valley venture capitalist Jimmy Lai is an unusual businessman. But there can be only one industry leader, so it is probably safe to suggest that there are important lessons to be learned from exceptional businesspersons and their companies.

Lai founded the Hong Kong retailer Giordano, where value for money, customer service, and quality are the operating principles and the key components of its success. "The chain's ability not only to read customers but react quickly has made it a model Asian retailer," according to one published report.[8] "Giordano shops don't run out of product, and if a product

---

[8] *Far Eastern Economic Review*, June 8, 1995 p. 47.

isn't moving, they cut the price to get rid of it," the author gushed.

That is because "the group aims to offer its customers quality products at affordable prices in order to ensure a high level of turnover as well as to promote customer loyalty." Outside consultants have been appointed "to advise the group on ways to improve customer service. All sales personnel, including staff working in franchise outlets, receive extensive training on service and product knowledge."

"Furthermore," company spokespersons note, "goods purchased may be exchanged at any Giordano outlet."

The company believes that the highly fragmented apparel markets in Hong Kong, Singapore, Taiwan, and even Japan provide the group's competitive edge: the opportunity to sell on the basis of basic values. Sales of US$450 million in 1995 – up 22% over the previous year – and profits after taxes of over US$26 million suggest the value system works.

The service is so good at Giordano, it can be frightening for old Asia hands accustomed to bureaucratic, disinterested service. It is frightening because it is so easy to buy clothes at Giordano – and it feels so good – that customers find it difficult to resist purchases entirely unnecessary. Prices are competitive because the company designs, manufactures, distributes, and retails its products.

But for founder Lai, a real-life street urchin who still displays street characteristics, retailing became too tame, and in 1989 Peter Lau was appointed chairman and CEO. As a media tycoon, Lai shook up the Hong Kong publishing industry in the same manner he rewrote the retail rule book with Giordano: providing value – he started a price war; substance – he doesn't pull any punches, even with the Beijing leadership; and product focus – he sensationalizes.

Not that Lai will not walk away from a fight under the right conditions. His escalating war of words with Beijing was reported tirelessly. As a result of "vitriolic comments about Chinese premier Li Peng"[9] in the Chinese weekly *Next*, which

---

[9] Reuter, April 29, 1996.

Lai publishes along with *Apple Daily*, the charismatic founder found it prudent to divest his holdings in Giordano, which has 102 outlets in China. Sixteen of those outlets were closed by authorities, and the company believes that its association with Lai is the reason. Lau says, "We adapt to crises," and the divestiture occurred subsequent to Lai's most notorious characterization of the Chinese leadership and almost immediately after published reports of the Giordano outlet closings.

Giordano went to the extent of hiring a respected law firm to audit shareholdings to prove to the Beijing leadership that Lai had nothing to do with the company, which is already counting on the developing China market to sustain growth. Lai's penchant for stirring up political crises has likewise left its mark on the popular *Apple Daily*. The company is unable to find an investment bank willing to underwrite its initial public offering. None of this, of course, changes the fact that Giordano introduced new competitive pressures – quality, value, and service – to an already dynamic marketplace, and its founder established a value system that has allowed the chain to flourish.

Like Café de Coral, Giordano sets the rules.

Value Lessons

Increasingly prosperous and demanding consumers, coupled with enhanced competitive pressures, have finally made value for money a key competitive component of product and service retailing. For Café de Coral, value has to do with providing what Wiersema would call the best total solution: service, good food, and convenience. In every Giordano outlet, value is provided in terms of best product. The company's factories churn out trendsetting garments faster than the competition.

The Philippines' Ayala Group has long been obsessed with the idea of value. Ayala is a much older company than either Café de Coral or Giordano, tracing its roots to a partnership between Don Domingo Roxas and Don Antonio de Ayala consummated in 1834 as Casa Roxas, a distillery.

This highly respected company – it consistently appears near the top of surveys purporting to identify Asia's most admired companies – has endured natural calamities, two world wars, and the region's most spectacular sociopolitical debacle which decimated the Philippines, Asia's most promising post-World War II economy, because its name has been synonymous with value. Its success – beginning with early diversification into coal mining, sugar cultivation, and land acquisition and management to its present interests in banking, food processing, real estate development, insurance, telecommunications, and semiconductor assembly – the company says, is because "Ayala's foundations have been carefully laid out by visionaries who guided the conglomerate generation after generation."

In reality, it is probably not the visionaries who have been the key, but the visionary values held close by generations of managers.

"The Ayala Group has nurtured big corporations which have emerged as leaders" and "a solid group of companies which sees itself as Government's partner in building the nation," according to company spokespersons. It has been an interesting partnership.

The company sees itself as "one of the country's better managed conglomerates." Don Jaime Zobel de Ayala became chairman of the conglomerate two months following the assassination of former senator Benigno S. Aquino in August 1983, with the nation and the economy "in a situation that baffled even the evil mind that created it,"[10] Ayala wrote in May 1995.

Ayala took the dangerous step of publicly opposing former president Ferdinand E. Marcos when "management and staff had taken to the streets with the rest of the great Filipino nation in a dramatic assertion of their inalienable rights. Close family members were at the forefront. The Ayala plane

---

[10] De Ayala, Jaime Zobel, *The Golden Decade of Ayala*, May 1995.

carried the standard-bearer of the opposition in her sorties. And I could not repress my pride over this uncharacteristic outpouring of political commitment," Ayala wrote.

"Nor could I refrain from expressing our joy over the triumph of the popular will and the peaceful restoration of democracy, to which I affirmed the company's commitment as the best and safest way to change."

The visionary values that made possible the hard decision to support political change are not, unfortunately, seen across many of Asia's Best, but that may be because few companies outside of the Philippines have had to face that sort of decision in the last 20 years. Certain Thai companies may have, such as Saha Union, chaired by former prime minister Anand Panyarachun, but changes in Thai politics have not brought about the profound transformation of the political system seen in the Philippines.

Holding fast to those values has created for Ayala a reputation as the quality leader in housing and retail property development, and those values also influence how business is done in other new businesses, such as in the technology sector. The company's joint venture with Singapore Telecommunications, Globe Telecom, is based on digital technology and boasts the most extensive international roaming agreements in the market.

The company also offers access to the Internet. Like other telecommunications companies profiled in subsequent chapters, Globe provides near instant access to customers. We received first hand an exceptional example of Globe's value standards when recently in need of a PCMCIA computer card. This card enables wireless connection from a laptop computer to the Internet via a cellular phone.

An inquiry revealed that the card was not yet available to customers, but that the service was indeed operating and undergoing final testing. Instead of being turned away when insisting that we needed the card immediately, we were put in touch with a representative during lunch hour. She said she could go ahead and give us a card and initiate the service. We did have to go to her office, but it was worth the trouble.

Once there, the PCMCIA card was brought out and we paid for it with a slightly less exotic credit card, but not before leaping over a slight hurdle: there were no forms to document the purchase or facilitate programming the service into the computer, because it was not being sold yet. That problem was quickly solved using a standard cellular phone form. We also used the form to apply for a credit limit increase. Next, we learned that it would take 48 hours to turn on the service.

That was not bad for a service that would not officially be available for several more weeks, but we insisted on having it immediately. The representative swallowed hard and said she would take care of it.

She did. As promised, within two hours she had called us on our cellular phone and we were surfing the Net. That was service value. But the most impressive feature of Ayala is its unsurpassed quality. Ayala sets the standard for best product and, in this case, superb service far beyond the call of duty. Unfortunately, superb service has not translated into superb profits for this particular Ayala subsidiary, as we shall see later.

Transformation

Ayala Corporation says it is consolidating its strengths to attain focus on profitable operations and capitalizing on expertise honed over generations. It is also betting big on technology, from cellular communications to semiconductor manufacturing. Another large national company, this time in Malaysia, is also betting on technology and a lot more as it aggressively diversifies while expanding internationally. A long history of success coupled with the inherent risks of bureaucratization during rapid and far-flung expansion have put the company on guard against complacency.

Sime Darby is a legend. A great agricultural company founded as a rubber and trading enterprise, Sime Darby was established in Malaysia by a Scots planter and an English banker in 1911. Prominent Malaysians eventually won control of the firm in a series of astute moves that would bring a smile to the lips of the most cold-hearted arbitrageur. Today the group operates over 200 companies. Plantation-based revenues accounted for only about 10% of total revenues in 1995.

The company in recent years has diversified from food processing and light manufacturing into heavy manufacturing, property development, and, most recently, satellite-based telecommuni-cations. Sime Darby has over 32,000 people working in seven industry sectors in 22 different countries, according to group chief executive Datuk Nik Mohamed Yaacob. The company believes it is Asia's most important and impressive indigenous multinational.

"If I were pressed to give a one-line answer on how the Sime Darby Group has managed to perform well consistently, I would say that it is the firm commitment of its manpower towards common objectives, without losing sight of important basic values such as integrity, a sense of duty, trust through professional conduct, and the good, old-fashioned belief in hard work," Datuk Nik has said. But the group chief executive believes that continued success will be driven as much by the company's capacity to read and satisfy the market as its diversification-internationalization strategy.

"We have to be more market driven and devote our energies to reaching out to get the customers and keep them satisfied.

"You only have to look at the banking industry to see an illustration of this change in approach. Not many years ago, bankers anointed themselves as keepers of other people's money and customers were usually treated as a necessary evil.

"Today, however, we see a proliferation of new products and services, all designed to woo customers who have suddenly become more discerning and elusive. Bankers will now even buy you lunch get your business! The point I am making here is that gone are the days when a person can be desk-bound doing a white collar administrative type of job.

"To be successful, he or she has to be more ambitious and not be satisfied with his or her lot. From the Group's perspective, he or she will have to be what I would term as a 'well-rounded international executive.'"

Datuk Nik's concern that his executives themselves be market driven is a reflection of the group's dramatic transformation. The group has expanded especially aggressively since Datuk Nik assumed his position in 1992, and he is wisely concerned that the company must make a conscious effort to stay close to its customers while growing – and diversifying – dramatically.

In less than four years, the company acquired positions in 66 companies in 12 countries in Asia, Europe, and North America. Expansion has made Sime Darby a player in everything – from the manufacture of tractors, buses, cars, and tires to power generation, property development, satellite communications, and now, banking services. In 1995 the company acquired a 60% stake in the homegrown United Malayan Banking Corporation Berhad, the fifth largest banking group in Malaysia.

The impact of the group's diversification on its character is profound. Just the bank was expected to contribute a huge 29% of group profits in 1996!

Sime Darby has twin objectives under Datuk Nik. First, it is expanding outside Malaysia to sustain growth; and second, it is diversifying into profitable sectors to reduce reliance on income streams from mature sectors.

New market realities, Datuk Nik believes, have made this strategy possible as well as necessary. Liberalization, he says, "brings many implications, positive and negative, to industries here in Malaysia. On one hand, AFTA (Asean Free Trade Area) will mean access to a market of more than 300 million people instead of the 18 million that make up the domestic market. On the other hand, this development will put a lot of pressure on the companies which have not taken the necessary steps to ensure that their products and services are internationally competitive."

Clearly, for Datuk Nik, being competitive and sustaining the Group's premier status means acquiring the reach and market clout to compete with Western multinationals. Whether it also requires the focus that most multinationals operating in Asia demonstrate remains to be seen. The induction of professional managers and management systems into the Group – and a high level of autonomy – suggests that the operating units are intent on become increasingly focused while contributing to the group's aggressive vision.

Value, Market Intimacy, and "Old" Technology

While major European and U.S. companies find themselves refocusing on core businesses and strategies, the notion that companies must be less driven by deals and develop truly competitive strategies is new in Asia and not too readily accepted. So there are few instances of strategy focused on a single core industry and related activities with the ultimate objective of becoming a global industry leader on the basis of innovation and value-added. Within the conglomerates, however, there are plenty of examples of companies that have learned to focus on customer service and value for investment. The Philippines' Smart Communications[11] is one of those companies.

Smart is owned by Metro Pacific Corporation – the holding company that was originally funded by Indonesia's Salim Group – Japan's cumbersome giant Nippon Telephone and Telegraph, the largest telecommunications company in the world (after the breakup of AT&T), and founders Orlando Vea and David Fernando. Smart itself, largely as a result of the entrepreneurial zeal of the founders, has managed to successfully pursue a culture that is blazingly responsive to market realities. In the Philippines that means, first and foremost, value for money.

The company "envisions itself to be the premier provider of

---

[11] Smart Communications is not one of the 95 companies that participated in the formal study.

integrated telecommunications services in the Philippines, giving the public access to telecommunications services that are efficient, reliable, and affordable." It believes its mission is, first, to "distinguish ourselves as a customer-driven company offering a broad and integrated range of domestic and international telecommunications services that are efficient, reliable, and affordable."

Competing in what has suddenly, and rather unexpectedly, become one of the most competitive telecommunications markets in the world, Smart in less than four years has gone from zero to US$32.5 million in revenues – with US$4 million in profit – and the number one position in the cellular communications sector, with a 34% share of the market. An independent survey conducted in December 1995 shows that the company leads the market in terms of perception of overall excellence. Smart has shown in Asia's most cost-conscious, yet communications hungry, market that long gestation periods for major infrastructure investments do not have to be a fixture of development.

"Instead of waiting for consumers to come to it, Smart went to the consumer and thus made the product and service accessible," the company says. Third party retail agents and a program to sell through a fleet of roving vans helped the company achieve its phenomenal first year results. The company's marketing efforts emphasizing value and quality were made possible largely because the company made the conscious decision to base its cellular network on older and cheaper analog technology, while other companies moved on to newer digital technology. Smart believes that analog is also more reliable, easy to set up, and cheap to maintain compared to digital technology.

It is hard to believe that Smart did not have the future in mind, however, when it made the decision to enter the market with analog technology. Five years from now, the company can begin to move its loyal customer base over to digital technology and sustain its rapid rate of growth.

A Quest for High Value-added in High Technology

Thailand's Alphatec Electronics "is guided by a clear long-term vision: to create and develop Thailand's first one-stop semi-conductor-industrial site." That vision began with semiconductor assembly and testing in 1988. Today, despite serious setbacks in obtaining financing and the dissolution of a major strategic alliance, the company is building two wafer fabrication plants at a site widely known as Alphatecnopolis, a high-tech industrial park envisioned by Charn Uswachoke when he founded the company. Charn has announced plans for Alphatec to produce its own brand of semiconductor by the year 2000.

Charn's gamble comes as close as any – except, perhaps, for recently troubled Singapore-based Creative Technology's Sound Blaster – to the eventual promise of original Asian technology. By providing the basic building blocks and what the company calls a one-stop industrial chip park, Charn has assembled all the components required to both design and manufacture logic chips. Importing world-class talent to train a new generation of Thai and Asian hardware scientists and engineers may well be the catalyst that turns vision into reality. And that is the next step to achieving Charn's vision.

However, Charn's problems of financing the factories and the pullout in 1997 of Texas Instruments from the alliance formed to build them have put extreme pressure on that vision. As a result of the subsequent cash-flow crunch, some employees have not been paid for eight months, and suppliers are owed at least US$450 million. Charn's early and commendable success did not ensure the smooth development of his vision. His failure to adopt his once successful strategy may very well have doomed his ambitious plans. Alphatec appears to have gambled and lost, because as one analyst said, "Charn began to believe the hype." When that happened, Charn chose to forget that his strategy was based on a vibrant semi-conductor market. When prices began to fall, Charn stubbornly stuck to his plans despite very substantial changes in the market fundamentals he had based his strategy upon. The question now is whether the company and its founder will demonstrate a capacity to draw on past strengths and experience to find a way to regroup.

Meanwhile, Philippine companies allied with international partners are giving Charn a run for his investment. For instance, Intel assembles and tests its top-of-the-line Pentium chips in the Philippines and Gateway Property Holdings developer Geronimo de los Reyes recently pointed to a computer-chip wafer set in a gold frame and told a visitor, "That's what I want to make."[12]

Intel has built a US$523 million plant in Gateway, and nine other high-tech manufacturers from Europe, the Philippines, and the U.S. account for the sale of 85% of the park. The Intel site, according to general manager Jacob Pena, "is one of Intel's biggest facilities in the world."[13]

The nine foreign plants going up in the park represent about 60% of total semiconductor investment in the country in 1995. "Next on de los Reyes' wish list: A wafer-fabrication plant, to help the Philippines catch up with its more advanced neighbors." He hopes to be producing wafers within two years, not long after Charn's new plants were originally scheduled to come on line. Charn's vision is also being challenged in Malaysia by arguably Asia's most respected leader, Mahathir Mohamad, the charismatic Prime Minister of Malaysia. Mahathir has recruited the world's top technology companies to help build an ambitious super corridor of technology companies.

Success can Cause Failure

Charn's present problems help explain why for James Riley, the identification of Singapore-based Cycle & Carriage as a well-managed company is, well, dangerous. The group's finance director feels that such honors can induce a sense of

---

[12]"Field of Dreams," *Far Eastern Economic Review*, April 4, 1996, pp. 50–51.
[13]*Ibid*.

complacency, and that worries him. In a company in which "customer service is the single most important success factor," Riley's concern is real.

So far, though, Cycle & Carriage has managed to remain determinedly uncomplacent. As a result, the company has received three international awards for management excellence, one in each of the past three years.

The 13th largest company on the Singapore Stock Exchange, Cycle & Carriage calls itself "a diversified Group involved principally in three core business areas: motor vehicles, properties, and food and retail."[14] The company was founded by the Chua brothers in Kuala Lumpur in 1899, long before Singapore was effectively ejected from the Malaysian Federation. The company was a small family business known as Federal Stores and dealt in bicycles, carriages, and haberdashery.

Cycle & Carriage was later incorporated and moved its headquarters to a branch on Orchard Road in Singapore in 1926. During the depression of the 1930s, business became so bad that operations ceased everywhere but in Singapore, and the company completely shut down during World War II. But by 1951, with the acquisition of the Mercedes-Benz dealership and the reopening of its Kuala Lumpur branch, the company was again booming. It began producing Mercedes-Benz automobiles in 1965, and by 1968 its Johore plant was also spitting out Mitsubishi products and turnover reached US$80 million.

Like Sime Darby in Malaysia, Cycle & Carriage, which is now part of the Jardine Group, has become widely diversified. Like Sime Darby, it has also acquired a bank – Malayan Credit Limited – and this acquisition likewise threatens to redefine the character of the company. Following the acquisition in 1992, the company launched a new corporate identity program.

Malayan Credit provided the group a land bank including

---

[14] *Cycle & Carriage Limited: Heritage & Vision.*

"some of the choicest residential sites in Singapore and Malaysia. The acquisition put the Group in the forefront of the property industry," the company says. "It also provided an opportunity for the Group to play an active role in this area of regional development."

Regional development is a key goal. Riley candidly says that the group's success to date is due to its 25–30% automobile market share in Singapore, despite its 80 subsidiaries and associates with operations in Singapore, Malaysia, Australia, New Zealand, Thailand, Vietnam, Myanmar, and China. Of its three core businesses, automobiles and property in Singapore and Malaysia account for the lion's share of revenues and profit.

The group's foray outside Singapore reflects the realities of a mature market and the company's – along with the Singapore government's – desire to sustain growth. "The future depends on exposure outside Singapore," Riley notes. Outside Singapore and Malaysia, that exposure is going to come principally from the core business closest to the company's original product line, automobile distributorships.

Product and customer service will determine how well the company succeeds in sustaining growth and profitability regionally. With regional governments liberalizing, markets are increasingly competitive. Even in Vietnam, the market has opened to 11 manufacturers who dream of selling cars to 70 million Vietnamese who some time in the future will boost their annual incomes from the current US$250 per capita to around US$3,000. That sort of growth will not be rapid, but it is certainly long term.

Cycle & Carriage is hard to beat when it comes to assembling and selling automobiles, but diversification into property development appears to be principally intended to sustain revenue growth, and the food processing venture to reduce dependence on the company's core business. The logic of diversification into food processing is hard to follow – barriers to entry are low, competition is already fierce, and margins are thin – and it will be interesting to see how that business fares. Property development is hardly an innovative diversification strategy, and comes late in the Asian property boom.

Bank Branches as Sales Outlets

Riley's dread of complacency is shared by Alexander S.K. Au, the vice chairman and chief executive of Hang Seng Bank Limited, Hong Kong's second largest locally incorporated bank. The bank started business in 1933 as a money-changing shop with 11 employees. From the beginning, Hang Seng Bank Limited was involved in three key areas of business: gold trading, money changing, and remittances.

The bank, now part of the HSBC Group of Hongkong Shanghai Bank fame, has 138 branches and is the fifth largest listed firm on the Stock Exchange of Hong Kong. It is also "Asia's 49th largest commercial lender in assets" and "the region's third most profitable financial institution."[15]

It is ironic that anchoring Asia's most freewheeling market has been a highly regulated banking sector. Experiments with liberalization are characterized by their temerity. Nevertheless, Hong Kong's banks see the writing on the wall and are gearing up for intense competition in a liberalized market despite much public kicking and screaming. Hang Seng's specialty is retail banking, and it is probably better prepared for competition than most banks. But Au is taking nothing for granted.

"In the present competitive environment," he said recently, "it is not enough that we are a well-managed bank with a string of successes behind us. We cannot afford to rest on our laurels. That is why the Bank has adopted a series of new strategies, and totally restructured and repositioned itself to capture an even larger market share. This has involved the creation of a brand new image for the Bank and the development of a wider product range. Previously considered

---

[15]Fletcher, Matthew, "Prudence and Profits: Hang Seng Bank Looks Beyond Conservatism," *Asiaweek*, December 6, 1996.

low profile and conservative, we are now moving towards the image of a modern and dynamic bank."

Retail banking in Hong Kong is already competitive in terms of service, since interest rates have been regulated. Au notes, "banks in Hong Kong provide more branches and automated teller machines per 10,000 people than those provided in the U.K. and the U.S." The former British colony's 183 licensed banks will soon "discover themselves engaged in a new battleground: an intense war on service quality," Au predicts.

Au believes that competitive advantage for retail banks in a liberalized environment will be determined by three factors: technology, sales, and cost leadership. That does not sound much like a bank. Especially an Asian bank.

By technology, Au does not mean more ATMs. ATMs, he believes, are like the fax machine, a passing craze. For non-cash transactions, "phone banking" will replace ATMs, Au says, and "because of a greater acceptance of automated products by customers, we expect that the introduction stage will be much shorter and the growth curve in the product life cycle much steeper."

Cash transactions will also disappear. "The introduction of smart cards, or electronic wallets, will obviate the need to carry cash. There would be no need for customers to visit bank branches or even ATMs for their banking needs." "Hence, branches will need to be adapted to become sales outlets," Au adds. These outlets would sell services and, one suspects, may themselves very well become virtual sales centers easily accessed through dial-up connections or via the Internet.

While technology will make life easier for the bank's customers, life will get harder within the bank – indeed, all banks. As a result, Wiersema's value proposition[16] – which assumes that companies must decide whether to offer the best service, best product, or best total solution to be

---

[16]Treacy, Michael and Fred Wiersema, *The Discipline of Market Leaders*, Harper Collins, 1995.

successful – will assume great importance. For Hang Seng, the proposition appears to be best total solution.

Foresight and Vision

We have tried to make two important points. First, Asia's Best know and understand that two decades of opportunity-driven growth have ended. The end of that era requires a transition to strategy-driven growth characterized by operational excellence, market or customer intimacy, and focus on core competencies contributing to enhanced capacity to deliver on value propositions.

Second, Asia's Best embrace, to varying degrees, the eight principal concerns or vision components we have proposed. These concerns are far from unique, and they have been adopted principally in response to market realities rather than some high-minded "vision" or dream, although companies such as Ayala appear to hold such dreams close to their corporate hearts, and have for many years.

Finally, we have seen that contrasting economic states across political boundaries do not always suggest that there are similar contrasts in corporations across borders. However, it has been more difficult in this study to identify firms in Indonesia and Thailand that demonstrate the sense of urgency to adapt to changing market conditions than in the four other countries.

In Indonesia, perhaps this is so because Indonesia's economy is dominated by firms "built through the exploitation of exclusive licenses for the import or manufacture of goods for the domestic economy."[17] For these firms – and any firm reliant on artificial controls to sustain viability – liberalization and increased competition is an ominous threat indeed.

Similarly, in Thailand there has been little need to allocate resources toward productivity enhancement and brand development. Development has been a mad dash for

---

[17] Lasserre, Philippe and Hellmut Schütte.

opportunity – any opportunity – by many banks, developers, and manufacturers. Asia's Best, however, are determined to meet the challenge of liberalization and competitive marketplaces and, in some industries, are setting the standards for the global economy. These are companies with global – not Asian – vision and foresight

Chapter Three

☆

TECHNOLOGY:
THE GREAT EQUALIZER

One Moment in Time

"Asian companies," says energetic Acer chairman and CEO Stan Shih, "have to continuously explore new technologies, enhance management capabilities, focus development on certain strategic product lines and become regional or global market-segment leaders. Only by working in this direction will we have an opportunity to continue maintaining our pace of development into the 21st century."

Over the last half century, how inputs are processed has become more important than mere access to inputs. Technology – its access and application as well as the capacity to develop innovative technology – has become a key component of competitive advantage. Technology's role as a productivity tool and provider of value-added emerged over three distinct political and economic development periods for Southeast Asian companies.

Japanese and Western companies exported second and third generation technology to ASEAN during the region's disastrous dalliance with import substitution and highly protected markets for close to three decades after World War

II. These policies were reactionary and intended to help redistribute wealth and opportunity from former colonists to the citizenry. They favored elite, politically-connected families and discriminated against entrepreneurs, small businessmen and exporters, and large minority populations of overseas Chinese, who through sheer hard work and fear of poverty had managed to gain control over substantial portions of economies throughout Asia.

Dated, inefficient, but affordable technologies worked fine for local companies whose purpose was to sell to, or exploit, local markets or to export production to developed economies by exploiting local low-cost labor advantage. There were no superior products to compete with, and the citizenry had little or no choice but to accept increasingly shoddy workmanship and generally insolent service both before and after the sale. Foreign "investment" was principally in the form of contract runs or local majority-owned joint ventures for labor-intensive, low value-added assembly of appliances and accessories with 100% of production exported.

As it became apparent that limited domestic investment capacity could no longer create many jobs; domestic manufacturers could not sell products internationally because of their high internal, small scale costs and poor quality; and natural resources began to give out even while commodity prices plunged, Southeast Asian governments – with the notable exception of the Philippines under former president Marcos – began to rethink the logic of providing generous opportunities in the form of protected markets to elite local industrial groups. These groups had replaced the former colonists, it seemed, but had not contributed much to nation building or enhanced prosperity, except, of course, for their own.

Sadly, local industrialists would lead development only if they had no choice. Performance, along with loyalty, became an important criterion for government support. However, performance was seldom evaluated on the basis of world-class standards, but, rather, on the capacity to turn a profit on an uneven playing field. Not much of a quality standard, that.

It was unfortunate that regional governments began to think about the benefits of more open markets so close to the time Japanese automobile, appliance, and electronics manufacturers were becoming worried about competition out of Korea, where they had in fact transferred much leading-edge technology. Asia's dominant economic power and soon-to-be principal investor was becoming, understandably, reluctant to export world-class technology and create more competition just when Southeast Asian officials realized that was exactly what they needed.

Rising costs in Japan, nevertheless, made it imperative to move work, especially labor-intensive work, offshore as competitive pressures increased between Japanese manufacturers and new, emerging Asian competitors. As a result, Southeast Asia found itself, in the enviable position of being able to attract billions of dollars of foreign direct investment year after year, led by Japanese and U.S. multinationals and large corporations. From 1987 to 1992, Indonesia, Malaysia, the Philippines, and Thailand received over US$32 billion, according to Asian Development Bank reports, with almost half, US$13.3 billion, going to Malaysia alone. Singapore received more than twice that amount – close to US$25 billion – in foreign direct investment during that same period.

Most investors, however, kept their newest technologies at home. This was due, in equal measure, to insecurity; concern about the capacity of Southeast Asian firms to handle advanced technology; and the obvious economic considerations. High value-added manufacturing was still financially viable in high-cost-production environments. Singapore, with different economic and resource conditions from its neighbors, undertook reforms and infrastructure development that would ultimately make it an attractive location for the regional offices of multinational corporations and increasingly high value-added manufacturing.

In one three-year period, it was said that a new Japanese

factory began operations every week in Thailand. Thailand, Malaysia, and Indonesia recorded total foreign direct investment of US$1 billion up to over US$4 billion each in a single year in the early 1990s, as Japan became the region's largest investor and Taiwanese and Korean companies, also feeling cost pressures, began moving production off shore. Many observers in Asia began to feel that the U.S. was missing the boat in the Asian investment race.

The determination of Southeast Asian governments from the mid-1970s to develop export industries to exploit non-Asian markets – bringing in foreign exchange and investment capital and creating jobs – brought pressure, particularly in the last half decade, to bear for equal opportunity within their own markets. As the effects of sustained foreign investment – and intense competition for foreign investment – coupled with increasing export revenues transformed regional economies into rapidly developing, increasingly prosperous societies, tariff reductions and market liberalization became not only politically tenable but attractive.

In recent years, almost half the total foreign direct investment in Asia – and the transfer of technology, loosely defined – has been generated internally, further enhancing the attractiveness of open investment and trade policies. Intra-Asian investment, however, is principally from large infrastructure and property development companies and low value-added, labor-intensive manufacturers. Asian companies like Acer, which now exports high value-added jobs and technology along with assembly work, are the exceptions to the rule.

The overall character of direct foreign investment, nevertheless, has begun to change as costs within Southeast Asia have increased with prosperity. Energy and telecommunications costs are high throughout Asia, and as the advantage of low-cost labor – and in Singapore and Malaysia, labor period – has faded, so naturally have certain types of foreign direct investment. As workforces have become more prosperous, they have also become more educated, and more value-added aspects of production – and more advanced technology – have shifted to these former low value-added assemblers.

Getting Technology and Knowing When to Capitalize on Good Fortune

There are three principal ways to acquire technology. First, it can be licensed directly or through a joint venture. Second, it can be purchased outright. Third, it can be developed. Frequently, companies employ all three alternatives – reflecting their state of development – as they grow and environmental conditions change. Following are some examples taken from among Asia's Best.

Malaysian food processing company Kumpulan Barkath was founded in 1945 as a "family-run sundry shop" and trading company that traded primarily with airmen of the Royal Australian Air Force at Butterworth Field. Kumpulan supplied mostly imported goods and processed foods to the airmen, acquiring much knowledge and expertise in the import and small scale distribution of food and sundry products. That expertise provided a launchpad that hurled the small company along a five-decade period of rapid growth and expansion from modest trading firm to international food processing company.

The company's late founder, Haji Abubacker bin Mohd. Hussain, imported the British confectionery Hacks during the 1950s for distribution in Malaysia, Singapore, Indonesia, and Thailand. Protectionist market policies – high tariffs and an intrusive bureaucracy – by 1965 had created conditions ripe for local production, and Abubacker successfully negotiated the company's first production license covering all four countries. Production was handled by a joint venture company 60% owned by Kumpulan.

The expertise gained in the production of Hacks provided three important opportunities. First, the company eventually developed a range of indigenous products, including a new but related product, cough drops, and honey lemon sweets for export. Second, production success in Malaysia provided the impetus for new production sites, and by 1967 the joint venture production company had expanded into Singapore. Third, the company became a serious contender for distribution rights of other international products. In 1970, Kumpulan began processing Sunquick concentrate, setting the stage for another future joint venture arrangement.

By 1987, Kumpulan bought over in perpetuity the Hacks trademarks for Peninsular Malaysia, Singapore, Brunei, and India. Its relationship with Sunquick developed into a 51% Kumpulan-owned joint venture that enjoys a 40% share of the domestic fruit juice market. The group – consisting of 22 production and distribution companies – currently produces a wide range of food products exported throughout the region, the Middle East, Europe, and the U.S. With over US$40 million in turnover, the company has just started research intended to develop new products and packaging materials. The company expects to export its expertize and technology to China.

Kumpulan's managing director and group chairman, Haji Barkath Ali, is the eldest son of the founder. He readily admits that the company's initial good fortune grew out of a highly regulated environment. That environment provided the opportunity to license important technologies that would ultimately provide the foundation for a diversified group of food processing companies. But Barkath also makes the point that the company continues to grow on the basis of emerging market realities.

Barkath believes quality will be more important than price or special offers in a liberalized environment, along with an immediate supply of goods. The technology incorporated in his joint venture production agreements provides world-class manufacturing capacity of quality products, from the production of fruit juice and frozen foods to seafood processing. However, Porter's research suggests that quality will increasingly be a requisite to successful operation, not an advantage that clearly distinguishes the company from its competition.

The reliance on joint ventures to access modern technology is offset by Kumpulan's impressive distribution and warehousing network. The alliances have worked well for the company, in part because of the strong brand names of the company's partners. For Barkath, the principal challenge will be sustaining these alliances in a liberalized marketplace in which his partners can own 100% of their manufacturing, and even distribution, capacity. In fact, as Porter argues, it may be this particular mix of key activities that provides Kumpulan its advantage in the marketplace.

The Quest for Value-added High-tech Footholds

Thailand's Alphatec originally set out to prove that liberalization does not have to be a threat to the viability of Southeast Asian joint ventures. Like Kumpulan, this once rapidly growing company worked to access technology through joint venture agreements with Texas Instruments (TI), but the result was not what the company had in mind, or even mildly successful. Prior to the ventures with TI, the company purchased technology outright by buying over operating production capacity in Thailand. And it recruited top management from the world's best technology companies to oversee the company's growth and manage production. Of the top ten executives, only the founder, Charn Uswachoke, is Thai.

Another early critical success factor was the company's talent for negotiating agreements to sell the output of purchased capacity back to its original owners. The former owners were released from the burden of carrying excess production capacity during lean times, but they were assured of consistent supply in times of demand. This works the other way around, of course, for the new owners. Although Alphatec's timing was extraordinary in this respect for several years, the group's luck changed.

Since its founding in 1988, Alphatec has grown into a group of nine companies that collectively posted sales of

US$1 billion in 1994 and earned US$60 million. Alphatec recently admitted overstating financial results (refer to the appendix for details). Even in an industry characterized by sudden and rapid growth, Alphatec has been viewed as a phenomenon. President and chief operating officer of the group Robert E. Mollerstuen says that there is no development curve in the semiconductor industry. Production must be, from the very first chip, up to the world-class standards demanded by customers.

That is a standard everyone in the industry has to match, and it is a basic requisite of doing business. Alphatec was able to meet that standard and become the leading IC company in Thailand and the darling of the local bourse in less than a decade largely because it started with proven production technology, capable executives, and a firm customer.

The Alphatec saga began with the acquisition of Signetics, the local hermetics division of Philips Electronics. As part of the deal, Philips agreed to continue buying Signetics output. Two years later, the company bought the Thai operations of U.S.-based Cypress Semiconductor, under a similar arrangement. The company presently sells to 12 of the top 30 purchasers of semiconductors worldwide, including TI, IBM, and Philips. Talks are on with three leading Japanese technology companies, even as the Asian market for semiconductors threatens to outpace that of Japan, despite the recent downturn.

Charn is an industry veteran, who worked for several multinational electronics companies in the U.S. after obtaining an MBA from North Texas State University. He set up Honeywell Synertek and served as a director of AT&T's Thai subsidiary. Charn founded Alphatec with the intent that it ultimately become a high value-added technology company that would produce its own brand of products by the year 2000.

"Alphatec has already bought up a slew of local operations owned by U.S. companies, and picked up a strong team of American technicians along the way," *Asian Business* recently reported. In 1994 and 1995, the company acquired National Electronics in Thailand and Indy Corporation in California, "to make prototypes there for our customers," Charn says.

The year 1994 was also a big one because the company established Alphatec Electronics Corporation of Shanghai, a US$50 million chip-testing and assembly facility. As in the past, this deal was driven by customer need. Mollerstuen says the 51% Alphatec-owned joint venture is in partnership with a major client that projects strong local demand for the plant's product. "Northern Telecom is building switches there, and the government needed an adequate testing facility."

Mollerstuen is happy to be in China for another reason: access to technical talent. "Chinese engineers have a very good technology education," he says, "but China hasn't had the industrial structure to absorb this talent." Alphatec is bringing 90 Chinese engineers to Thailand, enhancing the firm's pool of intellectual talent and future capacity to develop new technologies.

"Can Asian companies develop technology on their own?" *The Economist* recently asked. Alphatec has concentrated on higher value-added expansion through joint ventures and public domain technology with the intent that it eventually acquire the capacity to develop indigenous technologies. The company broke ground late last year on the first phase of what was originally its IT joint venture plant – Alpha-TI. When it is completed – well behind schedule, in 1998 – the US$1.2 billion plant will produce wafers for dynamic random access memory chips.

Construction on Thailand's first logic chip silicon wafer production plant – considerably raising the value-added stakes – also started late last year. Dubbed Submicron, this former TI joint venture is presently 87% owned by Alphatec Group. The group is putting up two other US$400 million plants nearby, in what is becoming Charn's visionary Alphatecnopolis – Thailand's first high-technology industrial park, which the founder hopes will be a hotbed of Asian technology. Perhaps that vision will look more attainable when the semiconductor cycle begins its inevitable upswing, but the company must survive a series of crucial challenges in the meantime.

Technology has not come cheap, financially or in terms of financial risk, for Alphatec. *Business Week* reports that the allure for Texas Instruments in originally setting up joint ventures in Japan, Singapore, Taiwan, and now Thailand comes from the "opportunity to sink even deeper roots in Southeast Asia – the world's fastest-growing semiconductor market and production base." But TI's joint ventures are "set up so that TI can pass off most of the huge investment burden, reap profits as long as the chip market is strong, and shrug off the damage if the market tanks."

That is exactly what has happened. Although Alphatec was funding 74% of the Alpha-TI project, TI announced in May 1997 that it was pulling out of both its joint ventures with Alphatec. The group had failed to raise the necessary funding to get the ambitious projects off the ground.

Timing is a big part of Alphatec's problem. After five years of healthy sales in the semiconductor industry, demand has fallen dramatically, primarily as a result of lower-than-expected sales of home PCs to consumers in the key U.S. market and what appears to be a glut in manufacturing capacity. The semiconductor industry's five-year-strong record of robustness was in part due to a sellers' market in the late 1980s. Diminished capacity following a severe downturn in demand found Japanese manufacturers the sole source of lower-end memory products. The clout these companies exerted over the world's top technology companies prompted Shintaro Ishihara and Sony founder Akio Morita to argue that Japanese technology companies even had the American defense complex on a short leash. The likelihood that supply will contract as drastically again may be remote, but that prospect has severely curtailed Alphatec's development strategy.

The situation will not improve in the near future. As this

manuscript was being finalized, wholesale prices for memory chips had fallen 50% from the year before, and the Thai government was conducting discussions to buy stakes in both Submicron and Alpha-TI. The government was also helping the group look for new investors, with sometimes embarrassing results. The announcement by Thai Industry Minister Korn Dabbaransi that Motorola was interested in acquiring a stake was quickly denied by a surprised Motorola chairman, Gary Tooker. "We haven't agreed to anything," he said in response to news reports.[1]

Submicron was also in arrears to suppliers to the tune of US$190 million after postponing its IPO in the wake of the meltdown of the Thai stock market, and Alphatec had twice failed to make US$45 million in bond payments. Both companies have delayed openings of their new plants.

Alphatec's capacity to fund its early expansion originally came from Charn's close ties to three wealthy Sino-Thai families, including the Wanglee family, which controls Nakornthorn Bank and Poonpipat Finance and Securities. The families are also close to Bangkok Bank and Thai Farmers Bank. Charn's friends are believed to have come up with as much as US$600 million for publicly listed Alphatec's expansion since 1988.

Although the company's expansion strategy and unfortunate timing have put the group in a precarious – and embarrassing – position, Charn has made Alphatec the most important high-technology manufacturer in Thailand, and certainly in Southeast Asia. He has also established a record of success in managing multi-national technology companies as well as in the development of a Thai technology company few expected to grow into a high value-added, sophisticated industry leader less than a decade ago. It may not be far fetched to imagine Alphatec following in Acer's steps as an Asian technology company, as it approaches its tenth anniversary. It was not too long ago that observers wondered

[1] _____, *The Asian Wall Street Journal*, May 22, 1997, p. 3.

whether Acer would survive its race into the American market when the company's goal was to become a US$1 billion company. Then, Acer suffered from setbacks similar to those being experienced by Alphatec. But last year, Acer's revenues came to US$5.7 billion, and Shih intends to reach the US$15 billion mark before the end of the century.

"I expect that within five years of the start of operations at Submicron, you will witness tremendous changes in Thailand's electronics industry," Charn predicts. "In Thailand today, we don't have any design houses. We don't have any engineers who want to set up their own companies here. But if you have a wafer factory in the country more and more engineers will want to set up their own ventures here."[2]

But as Mollerstuen himself says, Alphatec's competitiveness is technology dependent, and delays in construction raise the specter of its new plants opening with dated – or soon-to-be-dated – technology. It must also cope with the current financial squeeze operationally, and the reported defection of key personnel and technicians recruited by competing technology firms throughout the region. The company must also cope with negative media reports on its setbacks, which can severely impact Alphatec's capacity to interest financiers and investors in coming to its aid. Mollerstuen, whose professional credibility has been an important factor in establishing Alphatec's early credibility with customers, looks set to ride out the present setbacks, and attempts to lead the company back to the point where it regains credibility and financial health.

The not-too-distant boom times in the semiconductor industry did not guarantee profit either, as the Philippines' Integrated Microelectronics Incorporated (IMI) found. Although this company was the first Philippine company to receive ISO 9000 certification and has received a number of quality awards from such international technology giants as NEC Technologies, profit, despite impressive growth in

---

[2] *Asian Business*, June 1995, pp. 9–10.

revenues after selling or closing unprofitable but higher technology divisions, was elusive until 1995.

IMI has been around much longer than Alphatec, but it had to endure the dark closing years of the Marcos administration as well as severe recession and loss of confidence internationally just when Thailand was demonstrating a capacity for consistent growth. Aside from revenue and profits – IMI's 1994 revenues were roughly equal to Alphatec Electronics' profit for that year – it differs in at least two other ways from Alphatec. First, IMI started business as a contract assembler for a large Japanese telecommunications company. Alphatec is only now negotiating with Japanese companies.

Second, Alphatec has been managed by a well-connected group of expatriate, primarily American, executives who are known and respected in their industry. Charn believes that this has been a key factor in establishing credibility and confidence among major American technology companies. Occidental *guanxi*? After restructuring and benefiting from vastly improved confidence in the Philippines, IMI almost doubled revenues in 1995 to US$41.6 million, posting a profit of US$3.6 million, and had another record year in 1996. While small in the industry, as part of the Ayala Group of companies IMI can probably generate the financial backing required for expansion into high value-added manufacturing. However, IMI must compete for development funding with other companies in the Ayala Group, including a costly joint venture with Singapore Telecom. Given the risk of investment in the capital-intensive high-technology industry, Ayala is likely to think twice before increasing substantially development funding for IMI.

Technology, of course, is not always high tech or hardware.

Soft Tech

Asia's most successful franchisor – not franchisee – began its corporate history as a two-branch Manila ice cream parlor franchise of Magnolia Ice Cream in 1975. By 1977, when

McDonald's entered the Philippine marketplace, "it was quite evident that the parlors were being sustained by hot sandwiches, particularly hamburgers, instead of ice cream," according to the company. The threat of competition from McDonald's almost resulted in the premature demise of the young company. Anyway, founder Tan Caktiong (Tony) had a fallback: he would start a hardware store.

Fortunately for Tan, Manila is shy by at least one prospective hardware store. Meeting with brothers William and Ernesto along with American consultants Paul Rosenburg and Smitty Lanning, Tan began to think about the basics of his operation, his strengths and weaknesses compared to established foreign competitors like McDonald's and Wendy's. That seemed presumptuous then. But it was not.

The American franchisors, Tan reasoned, served the same hamburger with the same taste to customers in widely divergent cultures and societies all over the world, and it was, well, bland. "Very bland." So, "we saw an advantage in food. In other words, in terms of food, we positioned our product to cater to Filipino tastes," vice president for finance Raffy dela Rosa says.

"Asians – Filipinos and Chinese and all the rest – like their hamburgers to have a 'cooked-in' taste. In other words, not bland but spicy. We tailor-fit our taste to the Filipino taste."

De la Rosa says that making their hamburgers "Filipino" was the single most important decision in the history of Jollibee Foods Corporation. The idea of a spicy hamburger has driven the company's rapid expansion, as well as its marketing and advertising programs. But the company had other strengths as well, including a firm hold in the B, C, and D markets, while McDonald's was seen to target the well-heeled A segment; a franchise with children, providing a family environment versus the competition's yuppy crowd; and the superior service Filipinos are known for, as opposed to "what you see is what you get."

Advertising featuring Filipinized hamburgers, a family environment, and superb service popularized Jollibee Foods

Corporation. The name is derived from "jolly" and "bee" and was meant to incorporate two ideas: jolly workers, busy as bees. It may sound corny, but it works. The orange, rather odd-looking Jolly Bee mascot is a favorite among children.

By 1981, the small chain consisted of 14 outlets with revenues of P37 million (US$1.5 million), which put it in the ranks of the Philippines' top 1,000 corporations.

Langhap-sarap is a Filipino term that roughly implies a mouthwatering aroma and great taste. In 1983, considered by many to be the Philippines' darkest hour following the assassination of Benigno Aquino in August, the company launched a powerful advertising campaign built around this term. During the gravest economic and political time in the nation's history, Jollibee became one of the Philippines' top 500 corporations and the market leader in the fast-food industry.

The company did even better in better times, increasing revenues to US$37 million and the chain to 38 stores in 1989. In 1994, *Far Eastern Economic Review* readers ranked the company as the seventh most admired company in Asia, and number two after San Miguel Corporation in the Philippines. That year, revenues reached US$45.9 million.

Jollibee's homegrown technology was likely borrowed in part from McDonald's, but that is probably true for every Western fast-food franchisor. Like many of those franchisors, Jollibee differentiates itself by its food and competes to equal or exceed quality service. Like the world market leader, the Jollibee operation is now highly computerized, and like its biggest threat, it is always on the lookout for new products.

The company is parlaying its expertise in food into related businesses, including a chain of doughnut shops and delicatessen restaurants. It will also soon reenter the ice cream business – again as a franchisee – with Royal Copenhagen Ice Cream Cone.

"Exotic Technology"

Indonesia's Mustika Ratu – originally a hobby, then a small

family business – has transformed itself into a leading consumer products company in less than two decades, outperforming some of the world's most fiercely competitive multinational corporations in the process.

The company boasts diversified interests in the manufacture and distribution of cosmetics, toiletries, herbal medicine, health drinks, and mineral water, but focuses on traditional cosmetics and *jamu*, or herbal products. President Director BRA Mooryati Soedibyo is a princess from Central Java who has built a primitive technology into a consumer powerhouse.

That technology involves "blending of ingredients to make *jamu* and other preparations for health and beauty care," according to company spokespersons. The company now has 500 cosmetic products, a 70% market share in Indonesia, and growing exports to Singapore, Malaysia, and Brunei. In 1994 the company reported revenues close to US$45 million, and in 1995 it went public as a strategy to fund operations and distribution into regional markets.

Expanding Competitive Boundaries

Singapore, as we earlier noted, received more than twice the foreign direct investment in 1987–1992 that the rest of Southeast Asia did – with just a fraction of the population. The respected but frequently controversial city-state rapidly developed the transportation and communications infrastructure required to make it Asia's trans-shipment port, a position it competes for vigorously with Hong Kong. Hong Kong currently leads the race as the busiest container port in the world.

Adjusting to new realities, Singapore is now seeking competitive advantage in attracting higher value-added industry, especially of the high-tech variety. Where a world-class port built by the colonial government provided the small nation's impetus for growth after World War II, separation from the Malay Federation and independence, com-munications, and a highly educated population are the central components of a strategy to take Singapore into the 21st century and assure it of a key role in Asian trade.

Over 4,000 multinational corporations have made Singapore their regional headquarters. Its communications infrastructure, which was rated top in the world four years in a row by the *IMEDE World Competitiveness Report*, was an important consideration of these companies in selecting Singapore. "In the next five years, Singapore Telecom will spend over US$2.2 billion to complete a program that will wire every building and residence in Singapore in a fiber optic network and enhance its mobile network system, which already boasts the highest density in the world at eight phones per 100 residents.

"We want to be in the forefront of technology, so we try to bring in new services fast to enhance our network to provide new applications," according to Lim Toon, EVP for network services. "This way we are giving our customers a lot of choice, especially for business customers; this is important."[3]

Partly privatized and publicly listed in 1993 with a capitalization close to US$40 billion, Singapore Telecom has undertaken an impressive global expansion program and has operating subsidiaries or joint venture investments throughout Asia and in the U.S. and Europe. These operations include land lines, cable television, paging services, data communications, and cellular telephone service.

Singapore Telecom has no competition domestically. Other than mobile services which were opened to competition in 1997. National and international telecoms will be open to competition in the year 2000. But the company has been an important component of the city-state's competitive strategy in attracting foreign direct investment. By expanding its communications network globally, it is extending that competitive advantage through the capacity to service clients anywhere in the world, and it is making large strides toward offering the convenience of full integration through one service provider and its global partners.

---

[3] *Comamunications International*, December 1993, Vol. 20 No. 12, pp. 44–49.

Clearly, Singapore Telecom has more on its mind than wiring one island, and for two reasons. First, there is nowhere to grow domestically. The market is mature. Second, according to competitor Hongkong Telecom's Andrew Mutch, director of corporate markets, "Telecommunications is becoming increasingly important in terms of deciding where to put your regional headquarters."[4]

That is understandable. Multinationals are estimated to account for 60% of global traffic.[5]

"We intend to provide the best possible hubbing services, so that various multinational customers are more likely to come here," Mutch says in the way of a battle cry. Hongkong Telecom's domestic network became 100% digital in 1993, "probably the first major network in the world to do so."[6] Hongkong Telecom is 58% owned by Britain's Cable and Wireless.

With China at the back door, Hongkong Telecom is less worried about sources of new revenues than its erstwhile competitor – 20% of the firm is held by the mainland's investment holding company – but attracting regional business headquarters is critical to sustain confidence in Hongkong after its reversion to China in July 1997. So far, both markets are expanding rapidly.

"Between 1988 and 1993 total leased-circuit capacity into Hong Kong increased over seven-fold, while Singapore's outgoing telephone traffic tripled in the five years from 1986 to 1991. As Malaysia, China's Guangzhou Province, and others vie for the title of Fifth Dragon, two natural telecommunications hubs are forming in response to economic growth and the needs of multinational corporations: Hong Kong and Singapore."[7]

With AT&T, MCI, and British Telecom all looking for a piece of the action in Asia, competition for the much smaller

---

[4] *Ibid.*

[5] *Newsweek*, April 15, 1996, pp. 41–43.

[6] *Communications International*, December 1993, Vol. 20 No. 12, pp. 44–49.

[7] *Ibid.*

Singapore Telecom will be a ferocious challenge despite the size of the US$500 billion global telecommunications market. They are all "especially eager to serve huge, multinational companies frustrated with the world's patchwork quilt of products and pricing."[8]

Singapore Telecom is responding to increased competition in Asia by spreading its bets in other markets. The company is making a US$1 billion investment in the Belgian state telephone company, part of a US$2.47 billion bid of a consortium led by Ameritech Corporation for a near-50% stake in Belgacom.[9]

Open Market Overdose

Meanwhile, Malaysia liberalized its telecoms sector earlier than either Singapore or Hong Kong. It is a bit of irony that the emerging dragon may have "too many telecommunications companies"[10] in Asia's until only recently highly protected telecommunications sector. The Philippines has also suddenly experienced a healthy dose of intense competition in the telecoms industry. Singapore Telecom, in fact, owes its biggest overseas foothold, a 38% equity position in the Philippines' Globe Telecom, to liberalization of telecoms in the Philippines. (As mentioned earlier, Globe is an Ayala Group company.)

The liberalized Philippine environment is probably the toughest place to be for telecommunication firms in Asia, with four other competitors in the provision of cellular services, eight in the provision of international gateways, and ten fixed line/local exchange providers. In 1995, Globe Telecom had 8% of the cellular market, making it fourth in a field of five.

Entering the market, Globe marketed its service on the basis of advanced digital technology and superior service. Its

---

[8] *Newsweek*, April 15, 1996, pp. 41–43.

[9] Reuter, April 17, 1996.

[10] *Far Eastern Economic Review*, November 16, 1993, p. 106.

principal competition – aside from the entrenched subsidiary of PLDT – was new market leader Smart Communications, a joint venture between Metro Pacific Corporation, a subsidiary of Hong Kong-based First Pacific Group, and Japan's giant Nippon Telegraph and Telephone Corporation, the largest telecommunications company in the world.

Smart entered the market, as we have previously seen, as a low-cost analog cellular service provider. To the average consumer in the Philippines – far behind on the prosperity scale compared to his neighbors in Hong Kong, Malaysia, Singapore, and Thailand – the very low-cost analog technology was a godsend. Extremely aggressive pricing of airtime coupled with subsidized sales of handsets rapidly catapulted Smart to a 27% market share and 120,378 subscribers. By 1997, Smart was the market leader with over 500,000 subscribers.

Advanced technology has its limits, particularly when its advantages – value-added – is difficult to communicate. Whether those limits are short term or long term for Globe is yet to be seen. In another fitting piece of story, Smart may well capitalize on digital technology as well as sustain growth by encouraging newly prosperous subscribers to "upgrade."

Hot competition in Malaysia provoked Cellular Communications Network (Celcom) to focus indigenous technology on customer service. By providing on-line credit approval, the market leader in cellular communications provided its broad dealer network the capacity to activate new phones within 15 minutes of registration.

It is ironic that in an age of wireless communications, actual connection is seldom less than 48 hours in coming.

For a while, it seemed that the benefits of fierce competition could be short-lived in Malaysia, in part because the government felt that too many licenses – to nine companies – have been issued, and called for three of five international gateway operators to defer development until 1999. Wisely recognizing the impact of suddenly changing the rules, the government has now canceled that call. Since then,

Sime Darby has announced its entry into the wireless communications fray in a tie-up with AirTouch Communications.

An Asian Technology

Singapore's Creative Technology – not one of the companies participating in the survey – is best known for its Sound Blaster technology. It is hard to find another company in the region that can match Creative's success in developing indigenous high technology, but Creative itself is experiencing difficulty sustaining innovation, and has only recently returned to profitability.

Taiwan's Acer has succeeded in packing its "boxes" with value, but not in the introduction of original technology, although the company has tried to make a name of its server technology. Servers are computers that link networks within companies, now popularly known as "intranets."

But it is not hard to identify companies that have capitalized on opportunities that are technology driven, although those technologies are not always sophisticated or significantly value-added. When they are coupled with innovative marketing and entrepreneurial zeal – and some good fortune – they do pay off.

The Asian companies profiled here have shown that they have the capacity to compete with global industry leaders. Their challenge now is to push their technologies forward.

Chapter Four

★

NOT EXACTLY HOTBEDS
OF INNOVATION

Researchers in the U.S. produce more basic scientific papers than Britain, Canada, Germany, France, Italy, and Japan combined.[1] Japan, which produces less than a quarter of the scientific papers generated in the U.S., recently announced that it would spend US$155 billion over five years to boost basic research. That would put spending on basic research at about 1% of gross domestic product, a level roughly at par with the U.S.

By that standard, basic research throughout Asia, despite rapid, sustained growth over two decades as shown in Table 4.1, is virtually nonexistent. Although it may not seem fair to evaluate Asia's developing economies by the same standard as that applied to developed countries, just about any standard will yield the same conclusion.

That is beginning to change, but it will be an uphill battle. Many local and multinational companies – such as Intel and Motorola – have begun to develop the design capacity of their Asian production facilities. However, these research efforts

---

[1] Institute for Scientific Indicators.

63

Table 4.1 On the fast track

GDP Growth (%)			
	1995	1996	1997
Bangladesh	4.1	3.6	5.5
China	10.2	8.0	9.0
Hong Kong	4.6	4.5	4.5
India	6.2	6.4	6.6
Indonesia	7.6	7.8	7.7
Malaysia	9.3	8.5	8.0
Pakistan	4.7	5.5	5.8
Philippines	4.8	5.5	5.7
Singapore	8.9	8.0	7.5
South Korea	9.2	7.5	7.0
Sri Lanka	5.6	5.2	5.5
Taiwan	6.3	6.4	6.3
Thailand	8.6	8.3	8.0
Vietnam	9.5	9.8	9.9

Source: Asian Development Bank.

are directed principally at adaptation of proven technologies for local application or incremental product enhancement. In less technical fields, much of the local development effort is directed at refining products for local use, such as providing diapers that properly fit Asian babies, and cost reduction in manufacturing processes. Examples of original technology such as those provided by Creative Technology and, arguably, Acer are very new developments, and still extremely rare. But it would be reasonable to suggest that these examples do demonstrate that Asian companies can – with the right combination of R&D investment and vision – develop thoughtful new products that are received exceptionally well in both domestic and international markets.

More important, the success of these companies should be properly viewed as the first ripples preceding an eventual wave of Asian innovation. Increasing market liberalization will help catalyze creativity as Asian companies look for ways to become truly competitive.

Pouring money into R&D, however, will not alone provide the basis for developing the creative edge required to realize new Asian strategies for development. Even more basic is the matter of the intellectual resources required to make such investments prudent. While companies can frequently provide basic training for managers – as discussed in Chapter Seven – they cannot rapidly train scientists and engineers. "It takes only two years to build a new factory," Enrique Subercaseax, former director of the Pacific Economic Cooperation Council, says, "but it takes at least five years to train a specialist engineer."

It has been estimated that Thailand alone will need 400,000 skilled workers by the year 2000, but only 12% of its workforce is educated beyond the secondary level. Singapore imports 30% of its 18,000 information technology professionals from India, Australia, the Philippines, and China, and is trying to reverse declining enrollment in technical subjects. Malaysia needs 10,000 new engineers every year, but it produces only 5,700.[2]

Southeast Asia – particularly Southeast Asian governments – have belatedly begun to address this need, but they will be playing catch-up for years. Further complicating the effort to remedy the shortfall is increasing demand for engineers of all types in North America. So important a resource is engineering talent there that technology companies have formed an odd alliance to thwart moves in the U.S. Congress to limit immigration of technology specialists and engineers. So Asia is not only in a race to develop, it is increasingly in a race for talent.

Similar but less critical shortfalls in the supply of management talent are being experienced throughout Asia, although

---

[2] Tripathi, Salil, "Skills Wanted," *Asia, Inc.*, December 1995.

the region has a bevy of impressive business schools that churn out both respected MBAs and short-course certificate holders. And in the financial and marketing sectors, particularly, the region is beginning to enjoy something of a reverse brain drain, as pressure on middle management in the West increases while new opportunities open in Asia. New waves of would-be expatriates invade Hong Kong monthly and generally find jobs in a matter of weeks. Asian investment bankers and marketing whiz kids are packing their bags on Wall Street and heading for the new skyscrapers in Manila, Kuala Lumpur, Bangkok, Jakarta, and Singapore.

But meanwhile, the dearth of basic research and short supply of engineers, scientists, and technicians account for the low levels of technological innovation in Asia. Alphatec's Charn, as we have noted, has worked to provide a veritable engineering paradise to attract talent to the region. That will take time to do, and it will take more time to make that talent productive. In a recent interview Charn said, "We have all the facilities now. The only thing we need is the engineers to design the product." That is what everyone else needs, too.

Innovation in Southeast Asia, therefore, is presently limited to innovation in the context of management disciplines – marketing, financial services, service quality, manufacturing – and it becomes increasingly prevalent in competitive industries. The development threshold is naturally lower than that for basic technological innovation; management infrastructure is much more developed and battle proven, and as we know markets are more competitive, sparking management innovation.

All in a Day's Work

Difficult market conditions are usually associated with competition and economic health. Regulation can also raise major hurdles, as Singapore's Cycle & Carriage knows well. The Singapore government has made quality of life a major development objective. One indicator of quality is roads that are not clogged with automobiles, a daily scene everywhere else in the region.

Taxes, along with what is called a Certificate of Entitlement – the right to purchase a car, in effect – push the price of a new E-class Mercedes-Benz upward of US$150,000 without options. A car that retails for US$20,000 in the U.S. would sell for around US$75,000 in Singapore, making an automobile a very valuable possession, indeed, and a prized but mostly out-of-reach status symbol for the prosperous city-state's population.

Japanese, Korean, and European manufacturers fight fiercely for a share in the artificially controlled market. Cycle & Carriage sells Mercedes-Benz along with Mitsubishi and Proton (Malaysia's "national car," based on the Mitsubishi Lancer platform) automobiles in Singapore. Competition with BMW is particularly intense, and is increasingly characterized by splashy direct mail brochures and rollouts that look like Las Vegas productions.

To launch the E-class Mercedes-Benz, Cycle & Carriage spent US$260,000 on a television presentation – A Touch of Class – featuring local superstars, a press lunch, and a mass delivery of 300 of the luxury automobiles. But that is just half of what the company spent to launch the S-class five years earlier: US$520,000. Singapore buyers eventually purchased 13,600 of those automobiles.

In addition to the 300 E-class cars delivered at the model's debut, Cycle & Carriage had 2,000 more orders on the books, which would take almost a year to fill. These numbers are important, for two reasons.

First, because of government regulations limiting the number of cars allowed on Singapore's roads, the market does not expand. A purchaser must trade in an earlier model – and other government regulations encourage upgrading by making it financially imprudent to maintain an older car – or the market niche must grow. People driving Toyotas and Hondas must develop the financial wherewithal to buy their long-dreamed-of Mercedes-Benz – or BMW for the luxury car market to expand.

Second, they are important because they illustrate successful, innovative marketing in an extremely difficult environment: there is a ceiling on market sales, growth is slowing in industrially advanced Singapore as is expansion of the upper income bracket, and the cost of living is increasing, resulting in additional pressure on automobile prices. And the competition is good.

Under these conditions, increasing the number of units sold annually, not just overall sales, requires some hardball marketing. Cycle & Carriage approaches this challenge from a number of fronts. Particularly notable among them, is what might be called "event marketing." As the return on traditional forms of advertising declines in one of the world's most static markets, convincing other brand owners to switch loyalties – and prospective customers to buy a little more car than perhaps they really should – has become a critical factor for sustaining sales growth. Delivering 300 automobiles in a grand ceremony is more than a "drum-beating exercise" as some critics claim. It is a way to burn the success of the product into consumers' minds.

Cycle & Carriage is not the only automobile distributor that has seized on events as powerful advertising tools. "News is more credible than advertising," said Terence Cheng of Hong Kong's MD Motors. Indeed, the story of Cycle & Carriage's mass delivery was front page news in Singapore. If the company can sustain that kind of impact – coupled with the high standards of service quality for which it is known – it will very likely continue expanding market share in a near impossible-to-expand market. Cycle & Carriage depends on marketing innovation to sustain growth in the world's most artificially controlled market.

Cerebos Thailand – best known for its Brand's Essence of Chicken – has also relied heavily on event-based promotion to generate media attention and goodwill. Cerebos Pacific, which is an affiliate of Japan's giant Suntory distillery, has poured millions of dollars "into research and marketing to back up centuries-old folklore about the benefits of essence of chicken."[3] Those efforts were designed to bolster consumption among younger consumers infatuated with Big Macs and Coke.

No independent study has ever been made to back up the findings of Cerebos-funded research indicating the nutritious benefits of consuming Essence of Chicken, but communicating their own findings has helped boost group profits to US$103.8 million on revenues of US$503 million. The group has also developed new products, such as a watered down version of Essence of Chicken for children.

The third breakthrough for the Thailand affiliate – following dissemination of the company-funded research results and introduction of new products – in recreating the 160-year-old Brand's image was what the company calls Brand's Summer Camp, according to deputy managing director Lackana Leelayouthayotin. First held in 1990, the program tutors high school seniors preparing for university entrance exams.

Lackana says the program has become an annual event, "attracting thousands of school students who would not have an opportunity to attend a university without Brand's assistance. This event has helped Cerebos win Thailand's Marketing Award for socially responsible marketing, and elevated Brand's awareness to a high level of 97% among all adults age 15+."

Responding to More Regulation

We have noted the irony of Hong Kong's highly regulated financial sector, particularly, the banking sector. Although the regulatory environment does not actually regulate the size or value of the marketplace, it places severe restraints on how

---

[3] Warner, Fara, "Cerebos's Recipe for Growth: More Than Chicken Essence," *The Asian Wall Street Journal*, April 16, 1996, p. 1.

deposit-taking finance companies – akin to savings and loan associations – operate compared to licensed banks, which cater principally to the corporate market.

JCG Finance Company – originally an affiliate of a Japan-based group – opened its first branch in the Central District of Hong Kong in 1997. Its principal business was accepting term deposits and providing personal loans and overdrafts, primarily to individuals in the middle to lower income brackets. The company was purchased by Malaysia's Public Bank Berhad in 1990.

Since its incorporation, JCG has built a network of 35 branches in Kowloon, the New Territories, and on Hong Kong Island. It has also expanded its service product range to include leasing, property mortgages, credit cards – and overseas real estate development and sales, a useful investment for Hong Kong citizens seeking a second passport.

JCG has had to compete fiercely, principally to develop markets that it could exploit without attracting the interest of the licensed banks. As a deposit-taking company, JCG cannot offer the attractive rates licensed banks offer to their best customers. Identifying niche markets, then, has been JCG's most important challenge. By focusing on specific market niches, the company has prospered by providing efficient and personalized service to an income group not usually accorded much deference.

One excellent example of JCG's soaring expertise at nichemanship is its targeting of an unusual subsegment: financing "older" properties. Clearly not a priority for many banks or financing companies. However, focusing on older properties in a virtually competition-free subsegment of the lower income niche provided JCG an opportunity to expand its mortgage business rapidly while benefiting from the premium interest rates the company was able to charge.

With the winds of liberalization and enhanced competition sweeping Hong Kong, licensed banks have recently begun to warm to the idea of competing with companies like JCG. The corporate market is becoming more difficult, and returns are diminishing. As a result, the wider margins available in consumer financing are becoming impossible to resist. So for companies like JCG, innovation in nichemanship has been and will continue to be a constant requisite of success as their principal competitors seek positions in the markets the finance companies created.

Roving Assumptions

Innovative adaptation to new market realities is something JCG is used to, and banks concerned with strategic development should take note of the company's ability to bend itself to new conditions. "Our basic assumptions and previous successes are no longer valid or relevant," says Larry Gan, country managing partner in the Malaysian office of Arthur Andersen. Gan is talking about the environmental changes all Asian companies must respond to, but he zeroes in on banks.

"Bank branches are no longer necessary. A virtual network of branches has been made possible by technology" (and the lack of tellers to staff them). For Gan, such change means that virtual location has become more important than location, location, location. Similarly, other tried and true basic assumptions for business and success may no longer be the sound pillars of business practice or competitive advantage they once were. Companies that recognize this reality are the organizations Gan believes should be his customers. He says they have three qualities: they want to be industry leaders; they are small and want to be big; and they want to break away from the pack.

Counterpart Willie Cheng in Singapore echoes Gan's virtual theory of future competitiveness. "Our business is to help companies continually transform and re-create themselves."

Change is something both Cheng and Gan know a lot about, because they have been leading change – in response to new environmental assumptions – in their own organizations. A great deal of that change has to do with understanding how companies internationalize, manage across cultures, and learn the new rules of competition.

Their approach to understanding the process of internationalization has been to, well, internationalize. For a worldwide group that does not seem much of an innovation, but in the Asian context, where local cultures are rich, dramatic, and varied, it is an ambitious goal designed to produce synergy across cultures and areas of specialization. Andersen has pumped US$300 million into the effort – dubbed Asian Dynasty – which is intended to achieve four key objectives:

- Growth: create new markets by shaping buyer values, stimulating demand, and then dominating;
- Leader structure and capacity: reorganize to transform business and facilitate significantly greater growth;
- Business integration capacity: instill the skills necessary to be a complete provider of business integration services throughout the area;
- Knowledge transfer and international mobility: strike the right balance between area and worldwide resources to deliver highest quality services.

Of the four objectives, international mobility is striking. Andersen believes that to dominate its industry, it must reach "the customer first and give the customer what he wants, when he wants it." To do that, the firm believes talent and resources must be pooled across national borders. The capacity to do this creates a competitive synergy that provides the firm the agility to respond quickly with the most appropriate team to a customer's request. Just as important, it provides the capacity for the team to work with an intimate understanding of the varied cultures its Asian customer base exemplifies – because that is the norm within the firm itself.

Exporting Applied Technology

While Arthur Andersen looks for innovative ways to adapt its organization and expertise to new Asian realities, a number of the region's multinational corporations have developed impressive levels of applied technological innovation, particularly in the areas of manufacturing processes and new product development. Among them is Johnson & Johnson Philippines, whose engineering group "is recognized as the center of excellence in engineering in the ASEAN region," according to corporate planning and development manager Jess San Mateo.

The engineering group, he says, has distinguished itself with a propensity for designing and fabricating completely new manufacturing equipment as well as improving on commercially acquired machines. The group has saved the company millions of dollars. In just one instance, engineers saved US$1.5 million adapting what San Mateo calls an "old economy machine" to manufacture a brand of sanitary napkins incorporating a new design. The modifications were made with primarily locally fabricated parts, but critical components were imported.

Practically all packaging equipment is locally designed and built. Most recently, the engineering group broke its own record by developing a new design for packaging equipment to replace its own earlier design. The new machine packages 21 product bags per minute at close to 90% efficiency compared to its predecessor, which ran 18 bags per minute at just 75% efficiency. And coupled with another device, called a stacker, the engineering group managed to reduce the packaging crew from three to just one line worker.

The group has an impressive list of accomplishments that include a device accurately called a bottle unscrambler. Not exactly exotic technology, perhaps, but the device has enabled the company to automate its liquid filling lines and reduce head count. They increased the speed of one wrapping machine to the extent that a second was no longer needed, resulting in productivity gains and lower running costs. Other accomplishments include a re-layout of production lines and automatic fillers and cappers for bottled products.

The Philippine subsidiaries of Kimberly-Clark and Procter & Gamble demonstrate similar proclivities. Marino Abes, director of human resources at Kimberly-Clark, says upgrading equipment and manufacturing technology is key to meeting new competitive challenges. Like Johnson & Johnson, its engineers have helped increase productivity and reduce costs by developing original equipment designs as well as the technology to enhance existing equipment. Both companies export their homegrown innovations to affiliates throughout the region.

These companies are impressive for other reasons, too, particularly those that have to do with innovations evolving from the necessity to adapt products to local conditions. For Kimberly-Clark, this meant learning the business of baby-care toiletries from scratch; in Procter & Gamble's case, the challenge was "to bring world-class products to the Philippines and still make them affordable to the vast majority of Filipino consumers," according to company spokespersons.

"For example, when we introduced Whisper sanitary napkins, our consumers initially could not afford to buy the entire pack of 20 pads, which is the common size in other countries. We had to reduce the pack count to 8s and 4s to make the product affordable."

"Even this was not sufficient. We eventually had to sell Whisper in single pieces, particularly to the sari-sari (small, neighborhood general) stores in order for the product to be affordable. Selling in single pieces, of course, increases our cost of production because of the extra packaging material and labor costs. We had to develop new technologies to drive the cost down in order to give our consumers superior value from our products."

Those early innovations helped prepare the company for bigger challenges ahead, such as streamlining a bulky, difficult-to-manage sales network. "We reduced our direct customers from 1,700 in 1991 to only 150 in 1994," says Lirio O. Mapa, Procter & Gamble's HRD group manager. "At the same time we increased coverage from 33,000 stores to 125,000 stores. We were able to lower our cost of distribution because the entrepreneurial distributors have much lower overhead than we do."

The company also centralized warehousing because of problems with incomplete and late deliveries. Eight regional warehouses were consolidated in Manila. Mapa says this "allows us to serve our customers better. Perfect orders increased from 9% in 1991 to 50% in 1994."

Innovation – and world-class development standards – are not limited to manufacturing and distribution. "Procter & Gamble Philippines piloted the 'megabrand' concept of building on and constantly improving an already established brand instead of trying to introduce a new but similar product and thus killing one's market.

"This megabrand concept emerged with Safeguard, the leading toilet soap brand with a 48% share of the market. The introduction of a new laundry product form called compacts (compact detergent packages – perhaps reflecting the same economic realities earlier discussed) has allowed Tide to achieve a similar market leadership (position) greater than all seven brands of the number two detergent company combined. These two megabrands, Tide and Safeguard, have since become the company's success model for worldwide expansion," Mapa elaborates.

Building a Brand

Market innovation is hardly the preserve of multinational subsidiaries or consumer product companies, as Singapore's Excel Machine Tools demonstrates. Group general manager Wee Yue Chew says, "The main factor contributing to our success is our creative use of marketing innovations. We started Excel with only a capital of S$150,000 (US$93,750)," he says.

To sell precision milling and grinding equipment profitably, the company knew that it would have to rely on overseas markets. So it started business by interviewing major machine tools distributors and users in the U.S., Europe, and Japan. Its first products reflected the lessons learned in that early research effort, but the company had to rely on a network of distributors to get the product to the customers.

Wee says their edge with distributors is the company's commitment "to support them in terms of after-sales services. We are prepared," he says, "to dispatch our engineers to any part of the world if we need to give our customers the best support services."

Today the company still relies on its willingness to take the risks involved in developing innovative products in response to customer requests as its most important competitive edge – outside of the essential high quality of the product. The company is about one-third the size of the two companies it considers its most important competitors, but it exports to 22 countries and, with the support of the Singapore government, is investing in manufacturing capacity in Hungary.

Also expanding overseas is a very different company that shares Excel's concern for what the customer wants: the Philippines' erstwhile hamburger franchisor, Jollibee. The company has 16 restaurants in Southeast Asia and the Middle East, including its most recent opening in Hong Kong. Stores are also planned on the U.S. West Coast. In the meantime, Jollibee has outpaced McDonald's in other Southeast Asian markets outside the Philippines by consistently adapting its product to local tastes. Hong Kong's Café de Coral likewise boasts a menu regularly enhanced by new product offerings reflecting recent feedback from the marketplace – as well as such staples as its original fried rice and egg rolls.

These companies are constantly getting better. But getting better with new and innovative product ideas is solidly anchored in rigorous market research as well as a driving passion to give the customer exactly what he or she wants –

whether it is a spicy hamburger or a world-class precision instrument.

Building on Strengths

Although much of Asia is mesmerized by high technology and the promises of the future that technology seems to hold, there are, among Asia's Best, companies that have used technology to capitalize on existing strengths rather than to capitalize on new opportunities. Among those companies is Thailand's Asia Fiber.

Like Alphatec, Asia Fiber relies on leading-edge technology and manufacturing processes to sustain competitiveness. Unlike its chip-manufacturing contemporary, however, it relies on local talent to understand, acquire, and implement those technologies. Vice president Chen Namchaisiri says, "Technology transfer is becoming more expensive and, depending on the recipient, not always effective. Smaller companies with less qualified staff may not fully master the technology.

"In our case, our staff was mostly involved with the process from the start, and the technology was mostly from the equipment manufacturer (rather than a foreign partner). We therefore received full transfer at a much lower cost." What makes the technology transfer innovative – aside, perhaps, from its decision not to rely on a foreign joint venture partner – is Asia Fiber's position as the technology leader in Thailand and much of Asia. The US$73 million company was the first to introduce a number of new nylon-based technologies that have expanded overseas opportunities and made the company the largest domestic supplier of nylon chips.

Unfortunately, technology-based gains have not increased profitability, but they have kept the company profitable, unlike its two largest competitors. The company attributes lower profitability to increased costs of raw material and increased competition. Asia Fiber's biggest challenge will be to consolidate its technological strengths to restore profit margins. However, operational efficiency, as Porter warns, will ultimately be insufficient to sustain industry leadership or profitability. Some time soon, Asia Fiber will need to determine a new and distinctive competitive strategy.

Changing Nature of Direct Foreign Investment

Most early foreign direct investments in Southeast Asia was intended to capitalize on low cost factors: low wages, operating costs, and government incentives. As economies grew and costs of operation increased, those early operations have had to either close down – or will soon – or transform themselves into organizations that compete on something other than low cost. While costs in Southeast Asia are substantially below those in Japan, Taiwan, Korea, and other developed countries, they are substantially higher than those enjoyed by similar operations in Vietnam and China, for example.

Thailand's Kang Yong Electric is an example of a firm that is in the process of transforming itself from an assembly operation into an original equipment manufacturer and exporter. Corporate planning department manager Preecha Thiengburanathum says the company has "begun the process of self-development by designing certain lines of products itself," and that the company expects to expand the product line locally developed very soon.

Kang Yong manufactures everything from electric fans to refrigerators under the Mitsubishi label. Like so many other Asian companies, it looks to sustain its growth through exports. The Philippine Appliance Corporation (Philacor) has similarly manufactured General Electric, Hotpoint, and White Westinghouse appliances for over three decades for the export market, as well as a domestic brand.

Like Kang Yong, the company is responding to market liberalization by enhancing its capacity to compete internationally. Those efforts include ISO certification and advanced product development. Marsha S. Hilker, senior vice president for corporate planning of the Philippine firm, notes,

"Philacor's own technical group translates/modifies foreign technology to adapt to local conditions. Additionally, Philacor engineers design and develop the equipment and tools necessary on the production lines."

One of the most aggressive – and enlightened – examples of an Asian company preparing for market liberalization is also found in the Philippines. Concepcion Industries – not one of the companies participating in the formal study – is also an appliance manufacturer that has transformed itself rapidly from an assembler of appliances based on dated technology to a technology innovator. To do this, the company established a US$20 million research and development facility that is proud testimony to the wonders of market liberalization.

To decrease reliance on imported components and overhead, the company has also implemented a strategy to develop a network of subcontractors. Senior, loyal employees are invited to set up their own companies with backing from Concepcion. The company itself has only about 500 employees, but 50 supplier companies set up by the manufacturer employ almost 5,000 people.

On to High Technology

Malaysia, the Philippines, Singapore, and Thailand have all identified high technology as a key strategic industry. All have constraints. For Malaysia, educational infrastructure is inadequate and it shares an acute shortage of skilled workers, engineers, and technicians with Singapore. Likewise, Thailand is short of engineers, but visionaries like Alphatec's Charn are working – despite setbacks – to overcome obstacles to development, which are substantial. The Philippines' physical infrastructure is very poorly developed, and while it has a more plentiful supply of engineers, they are not specialists.

How quickly these nations address such resource issues will likely determine which nation becomes the dominant technology center in Southeast Asia. The Philippines' talented software engineers give it an added advantage, but Singapore has the technical and infrastructure lead. And it is a long lead. Malaysia has the political will that Singapore has demonstrated, and a budding technology oasis in the state of Penang, where advanced engineering processes are being introduced, and now the country is building a technology super corridor outside Kuala Lumpur. This is one of the few large infrastructure projects Malaysia has said it will move forward with after canceling a number of other trophy projects in the wake of the recent downturn.

Intel is producing its most advanced chips – the Pentium II – in the Philippines, and expects to rapidly increase the level of engineering undertaken locally. As the technology companies put more responsibility on local talent for original product development, they will be making an important – even vital – contribution to the development of the intellectual resources the region requires to undertake basic, innovative research. They will also be sharply enhancing demand for world-class education and training centers, providing yet another opportunity for Southeast Asia's governments and the private sector to capitalize on technology-based development opportunities.

But as many of the companies among Asia's Best have demonstrated, innovation is far from just technology innovation in the usual comtemporary sense. Innovation in adapting processes, products, and technology to Asian conditions is thriving, and Asia's marketers have become some of the most sophisticated anywhere.

Chapter Five

---- ☆ ----

CHASING THE MARKET

An old Asian proverb goes, "A man without a smiling face ought not to open a shop."

There are more and more smiling faces in Asia. And these are the faces of Asian corporations, not just their sophisticated multinational competition out to conquer the region's robust economies. Increased competition is proving to be a great thing for Asian consumers. Long-cuddled local corporations may be less than enthusiastic in their welcoming embrace of market reform, but it is revitalizing their organizations while squeezing profit margins.

Fortune magazine recently reported, "Asia's growth is spawning a new batch of homegrown competitors, increasingly ready to take on established heavyweights from the developed economies. Evidence: Between 1990 and 1994, the number of non-Japanese companies in Asia with a market capitalization of more than US$1 billion soared from 90 to 268."[1] For the most part, there is plenty of pie to fight over, depending on the industry. Take automobiles, for instance. One analyst "predicts that car purchases in East Asia alone will double in 10 years, to more than 8.5 million. By contrast,

---

[1] Jacob, Rahul, "Where to Invest in Asia," *Fortune*, October 30, 1995.

81

6.6 million cars were produced in the U.S. last year – about the same as in 1975."[2]

The changes taking place in Asia's markets and companies can be roughly classified into five:

- First, there is the switch to a consumer-driven economy, and a refocusing away from mass market precepts to niche markets. Stan Davis has coined an appropriate term for this phenomenon – "mass customization."
- Next, *where* is becoming as important as *what* to consumers.
- Third, for this and other reasons brand equity is diminishing in value, especially with the emergence of young, dynamic Asian corporations.
- Fourth, the capacity to innovate is rapidly becoming a basic requisite of success, as well as a determinant of market leadership. While Southeast Asia has not produced a Sony or Nike yet, its companies are demonstrating innovative thinking and product development in fields as varied as software development and selling fast food.
- And finally, the notion of value for money has begun to supersede quality in purchase decisions.

Racing through "Recession"

Strolling down Singapore's Orchard Road recently, we observed major refurbishing taking place in the Lane Crawford department store. Only it is no longer a Lane Crawford.

Prosperity in the city-state has come with a price for many retailers, and Lane Crawford is testimony to the perils of not adapting quickly enough to new market realities. With high labor and real estate costs, Singapore is no longer the low-priced shopping paradise it was just a few years ago. Slower growth in the economy has further contributed to the retail sector's woes.

During the retail downturn the Orchard Road store was downsized, and freed-up space was rented to tenants.

---

[2] Spaeth, Anthony, "Asia Takes the Wheel," *Time*, October 16, 1995.

Downsizing did not do the trick, however, and the store has closed completely.

Just a few blocks away, meanwhile, at Royal Sporting House – a trendy athletic shoe, apparel, and equipment retailer – sales are booming. "Hard work, persistence, and luck" account for the success of the group during generally hard times for retailers, according to chief executive V.K. Gomber. Gomber originally got into the business, he says, because retailing provided a great career opportunity. Retail was not a "sexy" industry compared to finance and marketing, he explains. So there was a dearth of talent, and little innovation. That left plenty of space for a talented former multinational banker anxious to break some rules.

Not all of Gomber's marketing programs have been "sexy," however, or necessarily oozed with talent-inspired innovation. Some have just been "gutsy."

Take his response to a strengthening Singapore dollar coupled with the downturn in retail sales. His Golf House outlets – whose products are almost exclusively imported – shocked and trounced the competition when prices were suddenly discounted by as much as 40%. Gomber says the move was both "sincere and calculated." It was sincere because the group was passing on foreign exchange breaks to customers; it was calculated to seduce hard-nosed enthusiasts, and it worked, boosting weekly sales to five digits for the first time.

Reflecting complex market realities, the group has diversified by niche, and calls its various outlets boutiques, supermarkets, superstores, stadiums, and even warehouses (appropriately dubbed Why Pay More?). It was the first company in Singapore to put an athletic goods retail shop in a major shopping center, and it has kept the pressure on ever since to continue coming up with firsts.

Most outlets, however, do not target the cost-conscious consumer. In a recent letter, the Singapore Army's chief medical officer, Lieutenant Commander Low Wye Mun explains what brings customers back:

"I recently visited Royal Sporting House in Marina Square where I was attended to by Ms. Alice Tan, the shop manager. As a fitness enthusiast who happens to be a doctor trained in sports medicine, may I say that I have not been impressed by any of the sports shoe personnel I've encountered in Singapore sports shops. They have little knowledge of the foot, sports, or the features of different sports shoes on the market. They are usually interested only in selling the products they have and, amidst the great local competition in this area, spend little time trying to help their customers.

"In this light, may I place on record my appreciation of the services which Ms. Tan so professionally provided during my visit. Apart from a sparkling personality, I was very impressed with her knowledge not only of the foot but of the different shoes she had available. I only mentioned to her that I was an 'over-pronator' before being brought three different pairs of shoes that would correct my problem as I ran. Having a personal interest in this area, I was fascinated at how comfortable Ms. Tan was in talking about the technical aspects of running shoes right down to her shoe lacing techniques."

It is not just the service that makes a difference at Royal Sporting House, it is educated service. Devoting substantial resources to training and educating personnel has turned what Gomber considered a boring industry into an exciting, customer-intimate career. Gomber is the first Asian retailer to have set up a training institute for his retail front liners. Trainees learn their product and trade, and they are given tools to deal with situations ranging from greeting the customer to avoiding hard selling or embarrassing customers whose credit cards are declined.

A good part of the enthusiasm that must be generated to develop the level of interest the group's salespeople exhibit, however, evolves from Gomber's insistence that his managers "walk the talk." Gomber does quite a lot of walking himself.

Corporate services administrator Lim Yin Cheng says, "Every month, each manager spends a full day working on the shop floor. He is assigned normal shop floor duties, such as serving the customer, packing goods, working the cash counter, or price tagging, as deemed fit by the respective shop manager."

"This unusual move made headlines in *The Straits Times*, our main English newspaper, and served to impress upon the public our commitment to knowing and serving our customers better. Our chief executive officer, Mr. Gomber, led the way by fulfilling the normal work routines of a customer service associate."

"In addition, the move helped to boost the morale of our front-end staff when our management displayed its genuine desire to fight the retail battle together with our sales staff. The deployment of management to the shop floor has drawn managers closer to the sales staff and has helped to create an understanding between both parties. More important, it has given our management staff better knowledge of the customer's needs and buying behavior, and it has helped our company to keep a finger on the pulse of the retail market."

Gomber says that his experience in the retail industry has convinced him that the day when being a good marketer is synonymous with being a good retailer is not far off. If the exciting growth of his group and the enthusiasm of his people are an indication, odds are that he is correct.

From Innovative Middleman to Social Investor

Not too long ago, Bangkok business circles were smiling over a homegrown anecdote. Apparently an extremely high-level senior official of the upstart Bank of Ayudhya was observed "paying cash for the privilege of copying personal documents on a bank copying machine." While that may not be the banking equivalent of fitting shoes on customers, it certainly is setting an example.

Setting an example is something the bank has had to be good at in order to grow past its provincial roots. The bank of Ayudhya is the first Thai bank to commence operations outside the capital, although it soon found it prudent to have a presence there as well, and to call that presence a head office. As a countryside bank, the company thrived despite small average deposits because those deposits provided a ready source of funds for investment and lending to large national corporations.

However, the bank has also found that it can function as a sort of financial intermediary between other banks and their customers in the countryside. For example, the bank collects credit card payments for Citibank. Similarly, there are other sources of income, such as the collection of tuition fees for the respected Sukhothai Thammathirat Open University, which seeks to broaden the nation's educational base through an array of extension study courses.

Increased competition and creeping prosperity in the countryside have brought with them new competitors. In response, the bank has decided to "go retail and serve our country." Serving the country has to do with enhancing the quality of life, and the bank believes it can make an important contribution to that end by actually managing its depositors' funds, rather than simply keeping them safe. So the Bank of Ayudhya is becoming a mutual fund manager for very small investors.

Armchair economists who have studied the way central commercial districts of a developing nation suck up cash from the countryside to fund infrastructure and private sector expansion will recognize the bank's strategy as a sound one. It may even be an equitable one, and it will almost surely become a controversial strategy if the bank somehow fails to provide an adequate return to hopeful farmers and other provincial folk.

Either way, the provincial folk may understandably take comfort in the fact that the commissions they pay will not be misapplied to such things as personal copy making by executives.

Surprising the Customer

Using company property for personal business is one thing, but at Indonesia's PT Blue Bird, customer complaints about service quality are considered a sin. Operations director Purnomo Prawiro says, "Satisfied customers are not necessarily loyal customers nor repeat customers. As Blue Bird's target is to have long-term relationships with customers, we developed a new program that goes beyond just customer satisfaction. The program is called Surprising the Customer.

"Surprising the customer means going out of our way to exceed customer expectations and needs, stated or unstated, at no extra cost or delay. Blue Bird believes surprised customers are not just loyal customers, they also become our most dedicated and effective salespersons and advertisers."

The company – whose fleet includes a total of 3,800 taxis, limousines, buses, and trucks – has invested heavily in technology and training to surprise its customers. A current customer need only give an operator his phone number, the locations of his office and home, and automobile preference, and his account history is almost instantly displayed on the operator's computer screen. If the customer has had a complaint in the past, it is also displayed on the screen so that the dispatcher can assure him it will not happen again – as well as warn the driver.

"All of Blue Bird's policies, Prawiro explains, are driven by customer needs and not by internal perceptions. Blue Bird introduces its product as 'The Reliable Transportation Partner;' therefore, every strategy and operation is focused on the achievement of service reliability."

New drivers go through an initial training program designed to make them "part of the total machinery" and periodically attend refresher programs. These programs are "conducted for old and new employees to bring them up to date with the latest developments and innovations within the company," Prawiro says, "in order to give them a broader view of the company."

"We want the employee to know how important he is, and how his involvement affects productivity and the improvement of the whole company. This program is carried out through seminars and workshops. We invite other companies and government officials to participate as guest speakers in the seminars."

The seminars are intended to keep customer surprise as the priority objective of the entire company. To make certain that customers do not have to wait longer than 10 minutes for their ride, Prawiro has positioned his fleet in nine depots across Jakarta, including all major five-star hotels. Coupled with installation of a state-of-the-art "automatic number identification bid select system," the company has nearly doubled the number of cars dispatched daily from 2,500 to 4,600.

This system allows drivers to "bid" for reservations electronically by pushing one of three buttons installed on the automobile's console. Pushing the bid button transmits a signal to the operator's computer that causes the taxi's number to be displayed on the screen. The operator then communicates the details of the reservation and the driver pushes another button to signal that he has received the information.

This level of service has been attained by benchmarking transportation companies in Australia, Singapore, Japan, and the Netherlands, not the local competition. It has also come from listening to customers.

Blue Bird introduced a service it calls Silver Bird, in response to customer recommendations. The service was intended to fill a gap between the standard subcompacts the company uses as taxis and its top-of-the line European limousines. Some customers – mostly executives – were willing to pay a higher rate for larger automobiles, but were reluctant to pay the price of a luxury European automobile.

Silver Bird is a larger Japanese sedan with more legroom and a more comfortable ride compared to the company's well-serviced but somewhat cramped subcompacts.

Blue Bird exemplifies the world-class qualities Asian companies attain. It is a remarkable example in part because the quality of operations and drive to be a customer-intimate company did not come about as a result of intense competition or liberalization. This company became world class because its executives were determined to be nothing less than the best.

"Blue Bird believes that continuous improvement is very important with today's more competitive environment and with increasing expectations of customers," Prawiro elaborates. "We always try to think ahead of time so that we can provide services that are unique and surprise our customers."

Another Surprise

But a bureaucracy that surprises customers . . . er, constituents?

"The company's thrust is to reach out to its members with its services," says deputy administrator of the Philippines' Social Security System (SSS) Horacio Templo, "rather than ask its members to reach out to us for their benefits."

It is significant that Templo regards his organization as a company. That helps explain why reaching out to its customers includes downright incredible productivity and service enhancements. For example, pension processing has been reduced from 22 days to two, and "productivity has more than tripled from an average of 100 to 450 claims processed daily. Manpower has been reduced by 75% from 163 to 42 (in that department)." That is another unusual phenomenon, a *shrinking* bureaucracy.

Templo adds, "tracking and monitoring of claims now takes a few seconds, enabling us to pinpoint an application at any given time. Work and storage areas have been decreased from 710 to 267 square meters. We have likewise saved US$700,000 annually in operational expenses such as manpower, work and storage spaces, supplies, filing cabinets, etc."

Those gains came about as a result of "the company's" two-pronged development program. The first component of the program involved vast decentralization. "We focused our efforts on expanding our network of branches nationwide and improving existing offices," Templo explains. "The target in the next two years is to establish at least one branch in every city or province, or about 100 full-service and fully computerized branches."

And that is not all SSS has planned. Its "Action Center concept has been institutionalized as the Company's response in times of crises such as natural and man-made calamities. Mobile units equipped with on-line computer facilities are fielded at the Action Centers. This is the Company's way of bringing its services promptly to the members," Templo says.

The second strategy component was turning "the company" into a wired organization. "Under our computerization program," Templo explains, "we have placed our data and computing resources where they are most needed – right at the fingertips of our front-line staff. A distributed processing scheme was adopted where mission-critical application systems and databases were moved from the centralized mainframe systems at the main office to smaller networked workgroup servers distributed in all branches nationwide.

"We also installed innovative and state-of-the-art technology such as the Document Management System, using optical disk and imaging technology." The scale of the computerization effort at SSS is substantial, and "the company" now boasts the largest Oracle relational database installation in Asia, and the fifth largest in the world.

Technology has improved customer service in other ways as well. Pensioners can now withdraw their benefits from the nearest ATM. Employers transact business on-line, and "the company" is linked to hospitals, making immediate confirmation of benefit eligibility routine. This does not sound like a developing country government agency.

Not all of SSS's efforts to reach out to its market involve technology. There is a good dose of well-intentioned common sense as well. SSS has extended benefits to unemployed housewives based on their employed husbands' contributions. "The company" has also extended services to the Philippines' informal sector, which accounts for a disproportionate share of the economy. The capacity to convince this sector to pay premiums is powerful testimony to the perceived value of "the company's" services.

Media Lab founder Nicholas Negroponte has said that technology is, in part, good because it flattens organizations. SSS is an example of how positive technology's impact can be, both in terms of leveling the organization and bringing it close to the market, as well as enhancing the capacity of a once ungainly, inefficient government agency to fulfill its mandate by metamorphosing into an icon of excellence.

The Weakest Link

Singapore Airlines (SIA) is a well-known Asian icon of excellence, yet this hugely profitable airline has been consumed with finding – and fixing – the weak link in its customer service standards that could endanger its leadership in an increasingly competitive industry.

Senior public affairs manager Rick Clements said recently, "What we've done there (in service) is, well, some years ago we came to the conclusion that no matter how good your service was, it was only as good – no matter what you did in the cabin to make the journey more pleasant to passengers – as the weakest link. So we looked at the weakest link, and at that time, it was on the ground. The ground service didn't measure up," he says matter-of-factly.

"The first point of contact (with passengers) is on the ground: in the ticketing office, at the check-in counter; they might not be eligible to use the lounge. All of these contacts are on the ground, and by the time the passenger gets on board (if he's had a lousy experience), you won't see him again."

"As a result," Clements says, "we are now pushing the total service concept. There's no point in having the greatest fleet in the world – no matter how technically superior it may be compared to other fleets – if at the end of the day, the customer really doesn't feel he's being listened to or being taken care of."

SIA has long sought to project its services as both top value and world class. Early in its history, the airline stayed out of the International Air Transport Association so that it could offer features that member airlines were prohibited from providing. Those services, now standard on most airlines, included free drinks, choice meals in economy class, and free headsets (Remember when we paid for these things?).

"There was this slogan," Clements chuckles, "that we were the airline that other airlines talked about. Well, they did, but it was not always flattering."

New competitive pressures continue to make SIA the airline others talk about, and it is still not always flattering. The airline's employment policies for cabin staff, particularly stewardesses, have occasionally come under scrutiny. Until recently, once a stewardess had children, her career was over. Now, she can return to work at the same seniority level up to two years after beginning maternity leave.

Still, the airline has found it harder to recruit cabin staff in Singapore that meet its exacting standards, and now it "recruits outside Singapore to sustain standards rather than compromise by recruiting people in Singapore we would not have taken previously," Clements says. But providing the best in service does have a price.

"We continue to compete on service as well as price, but we're not going to be the cheapest airline in the market, that I'm sure. Passengers will be prepared to pay, if they feel they're getting a better quality product or service."

SIA is proud of its technologically advanced aircraft, its status as the youngest fleet in the world, and the perks it offers both on the ground and in the air. But it also knows that its most distinctive competitive advantage is its people, and it will go wherever it has to in order to get the best.

The Five Changes in Asia's Markets and Companies

This brings us back to the five major changes taking place in Asia's markets and companies. The first was the switch to a consumer-driven economy characterized by niche marketing. We have seen that Singapore's Royal Sporting House has remained focused primarily on the sale of athletic shoes, although it also retails apparel and dress shoes in its branded boutiques, and has developed a range of outlets ranging from the expensive and trendy to the low-cost and bargain-filled. Like SIA, it relies on highly trained personnel working in state-of-the-art facilities to cater to consumers looking for more than best price. However, its Why Pay More? warehouses offer little in the way of service for customers intent on capitalizing on the best bargains they can find. Royal Sporting House is unusual among the companies we have examined, because it is so far successfully servicing more than one market niche. Its success is probably explained by clearly differentiating the outlets catering to different market segments while staying very close to its basic core business.

Similarly, Blue Bird has excelled in providing the best product to its target market – well-heeled consumers, tourists, and executives – by offering service far beyond comparison in its market, and clearly better than some of the most advanced markets in the world. Other companies previously discussed, such as Giordano, Jollibee, and Café de Coral, have excelled in highly competitive industries with multinational players because they have actively catered to customer preferences. The Bank of Ayudhya has been successful because of its capacity to understand and cater to its provincial customers' unique needs and requirements.

The second change is the importance of *where*, and this has to do with convenience. The Bank of Ayudhya is where its customers are, in the countryside. The Philippines' SSS is seeking to be everywhere, because that is where its customers are. Royal Sporting House positions its outlets demographically by market niche. Like SSS, Blue Bird is all over, and no-where more than 10 minutes away.

Next, brand equity has given way to other priorities. The shoes Royal Sporting House sells can be purchased in hundreds of stores along and near Orchard Road. Customers go to Royal Sporting House's trendy outlets because they know they will get the shoe that is right for them with the help of knowledgeable sales assistants and store managers.

Successful Asian corporations are demonstrating that the value of a brand name is only as good as the service and quality behind that name today. The first time service and quality suffer, so does the brand. Reputation rests on standards of service; in other words, reputation evolves from promises of quality and service that are kept day in and day out. Name is only as good as the offer, and every offer had better be good.

Fourth, innovation is becoming a fixture of market leadership as we have seen in this as well as the previous chapter. Royal Sporting House has adapted in innovative ways to harsher market realities, from introducing discount warehouses to providing mobile repair services for golf enthusiasts. Likewise, SSS has developed computerized mobile action centers to provide the capacity for near instantaneous service where and when it is most critically required. Where else but Jakarta will Asia's business executives find a taxi service that tracks and studies its customers as carefully as a world-class airline like SIA does?

Finally, the notion of value for money has superseded quality in purchase decisions. As Porter argues, quality of products has become a basic standard of salability. Quality must be built in. Assuming that all leading brands provide quality products, the priority understandably becomes value: What purchase makes the most sense?

Royal Sporting House approaches this problem most frequently by making sure that customers get the shoes that are best for them. This is accomplished by providing training to sales personnel that enables them to find out from the customer the priorities leading to his purchase: style, activity, and even physical characteristics or handicaps.

SSS has undertaken the challenging task of enlisting members from among the informal sector, a cynical customer base that has been convinced the agency can do a better job providing for future risks than it can. SIA promises a premium travel experience for a premium price, and Blue Bird offers both personalized and safe, dependable service.

The Challenge of the Market

Acer's Shih said in a recent interview that his "immodest goal" was to challenge "Japanese dominance of consumer electronics."[3] We have seen SIA challenge Japanese, European, and American airlines for dominance in local markets, and Jollibee and Café de Coral successfully challenge companies like McDonald's. The Philippines' SSS has become an agency whose standards of operation rival those of the best of the private sector. Avis or Singapore's Comfort taxis would be hard pressed to compete with Blue Bird, and not many banks anywhere in Asia or the world would be anxious to follow the Bank of Ayudhya into the countryside.

Asia offers vast opportunities for companies the world over, but those opportunities are not just there for the taking. Grinding through a corrupt bureaucracy is no longer the chief challenge for multinationals expanding into this region. The real battle will be chasing the market by battling many other smiling faces for industry dominance and product leadership.

---

[3] Kraar, Louis, "Acer's Edge: PCs to Go" in *Fortune*, October 30, 1995.

Part II
THE REALITY

Chapter Six

☆

WHERE ARE THE MANAGERS AND SCIENTISTS?

Asia has long been sensitive to the issue of exploitation of its resources, markets, and new business opportunities by Western countries and Japan – and for some good reasons. But exploitation by local industrialists and politicians can be – and not infrequently has been – worse. Neither consumers in general nor resources in particular have fared well in highly protected markets, regardless of who is doing the exploiting.

Perhaps somewhat ironically, it can be fairly easily argued that an important Asian resource has been exploited with much success – within Asia and without – generally with the enthusiastic support of Asian governments, because this resource has been a stable source of foreign exchange. So while activists, provocateurs, and advocators have focused much attention on environmental issues, level playing fields, and the benefits of market liberalization, comparatively little has been said about the important role skilled Asian labor – engineers, scientists, and managers – play in developed countries everywhere. That role was briefly highlighted recently during a national debate on immigration policy in the U.S.

Leading technology companies such as Microsoft and Intel

lobbied vigorously against tightened restrictions on the granting of work visas and permanent residence to engineers and scientists recruited overseas. The logic of these companies was that the best and the brightest do not reside exclusively in the U.S. To remain world leaders in their industries, these American multinationals believe that it is imperative to hire the very best people in the world, regardless of their nationality. And there is much obvious merit in this argument, as their employees' profiles show. Andrew S. Grove, chairman of Intel and one of the firm's three original founders, was born in Hungary.

However, this argument also raises the curious but real problem of less economically developed countries providing developed countries with many of their most important people. That means that the substantial portion of the investment in their training is made in the place that can least afford either that investment or the loss of some of the world's top talent. That is exploitation, especially at a time when human minds are increasingly seen as the single most important success factor in a competitive, knowledge-based market environment. And at a time when Asia needs trained minds more than any other resource.

"In Thailand, every year Japanese car factories lose roughly one in four managers they train,"[1] according to one recent report. Motorola's Malaysian operation bravely submits that even though its engineers are frequently recruited by local and international competitors, it continues to view training them as an investment – not just in the company, but in the nation. Turns out, other nations, too.

It makes sense for Western multinationals. After all, a recent "worldwide math-and-science study shows that Asian kids outrank their peers in America and Western Europe."[2] But it does not make sense for Asia, which does not have the advanced educational infrastructure required to produce the

---

[1] _____, "Business in Asia," *The Economist*, March 9, 1996.

[2] _____, "At the Top of the Class," *Newsweek*, December 2, 1996, p. 57.

100   The Reality

large number of engineers, scientists, and managers it requires on its own, let alone to supply the West. Interestingly, some of the more rapidly developing Asian economies – such as Singapore and Malaysia – are in turn now importing skilled labor, engineers, and managers from India, the Philippines, and Eastern Europe. These new competitors for Asia's best human resources have intensified human resource shortfalls within Asia just as governments have belatedly acknowledged the need to improve tertiary education. These countries may well find themselves producing more brainpower for competing economies that can afford to pay a premium for top people. Ironically, tight restrictions on imported brainpower into Asia remain in place in Indonesia, Malaysia, the Philippines, and Thailand on the premise of protecting Asian jobs for Asians. Thus, these developing economies find themselves unable to retain many of their best minds and unwilling to import those produced somewhere else.

Educating Managers

A number of established business schools provide an excellent graduate education for managers whose priorities include cost and proximity. These schools and their students also argue that attending an Asian business school boosts networking opportunities and that the curriculum is more relevant to managers intending to do business in Asia. However, "despite major investments in gleaming school buildings and talented faculty, the best Asia-Pacific schools remain poor cousins of their Western counterparts. When Asia, Inc. listed the top 25 business schools in the world for Asian students, the Melbourne Business School was the only one outside North America and Europe to creep into the reckoning (in 25th position)."[3]

One reason for this may be that there is no universal accreditation system for the region's business schools. Local

---

[3] Tripathi, Salil, "Masters of Their Own Destiny," *Asia, Inc.,* September 1995.

demand, nevertheless, is so great that applications far outweigh places. For example, the prestigious Indian Institute of Management school in Ahmedabad receives nearly 25,000 applications every year for its 200 places. Lee Kam Hon, dean of the business school at the Chinese University of Hong Kong, adds, "Asian MBA programs can be competitive but they are overwhelmed by local demand." Unfortunately, a seller's market rarely fosters excellence, and there is a good chance this is as true for business education as it is for business. And the value of networking likely evolves first from quality, not quantity.

Demand for Western management skills has also been enhanced by the transition of Asian family firms to professionally managed organizations, a phenomenon discussed earlier. Young Kuan-Sing of Korn/Ferry International says, "Demand from Asian family companies has surged in the past couple of years. Many such companies want more sophisticated management systems and need help expanding abroad, he says. Those that raise money by selling shares in some of their subsidiaries require managers able to schmooze with foreign investors."[4]

Table 6.1 shows how hot the competition for top executives has become in Asia. It is clear that "the greatest demand of all is for general managers – people with a rough grasp of finance, marketing, and organization."[5]

It is worth noting that the table also makes clear that while most of the rest of Asia has placed premiums on engineers, architects, and computer professionals, in the Philippines there appears to be an over supply, and relatively speaking, they are poorly paid. Since the salaries of people in other positions are roughly at par with and sometimes even higher than salaries paid in other countries, the low salaries for these professionals do not strictly reflect disparities in economic development. In fact, as this book was being written, indus-

[4] Hagerty, Bob, "Asian Family Firms Stalk Western-Trained Managers," *The Asian Wall Street Journal*, May 20, 1996, p. 6.

[5] "Business in Asia".

Table 6.1

Position	Hong Kong	Indonesia	Malaysia	Philippines	Singapore	Thailand
Corporations			Median Pay (US$)			
CEO (Mfg. $50 m)	19,900	13,108	7,075	10,299	17,110	12,705
CEO (Mfg. $25m)	15,927	10,833	7,650	7,373	13,380	8,144
CEO (Mfg. $9m)	12,225	8,953	5,133	7,134	11,702	5,210
Head of Engineering	7,976	3,562	2,732	2,363	5,389	3,139
Head of Finance	7,380	4,063	3,012	3,575	6,626	3,281
Head of HR	7,847	3,182	3,012	3,179	6,458	3,192
Head of Info System	7,644	3,606	3,073	2,339	6,264	3,312
Head of Production	7,950	2,634	2,842	3,558	6,034	2,965
Systems Analyst	3,459	1,328	1,231	763	2,629	1,363
Comp Programmer	2,563	1,018	848	535	2,069	927
Production Superintendent	2,313	682	1,010	686	2,261	685
Skilled Production	1,169	245	269	276	803	246
The Professions			Top Pay (US$)			
Investment Banker	24,256	20,000	6,000	4,954	8,000	9,839
Fund Manager	21,022	8,000	2,600	2,287	12,000	5,903
Stockbroker	17,788	20,000	1,600	5,640	4,255	3,935
Architect	9,702	1,200	3,200	762	4,255	5,903
Architecture Partner	32,342	5,000	4,000	7,622	14,184	3,935
Creative Director	10,349	7,240	2,800	1,143	14,184	3,935
Chemical Engineer	4,851	5,700	1,800	457	4,397	2,361
Mechanical Engineer	5,929	5,700	1,680	457	4,397	1,968
Industrial Engineer	5,929	5,700	1,680	457	4,397	2,361

Source: AsiaWeek Corporations based on a 1996 survey by Corporate Resources Group. Professions based on an AsiaWeek survey of management consultants, professional associations, human resource managers, and employees.

Where Are the Managers and Scientists? 103

tries requiring all three areas of expertise were enjoying unprecedented growth. It may actually make sense, therefore, for the Philippines to capitalize on its position as a bank boasting a vast supply of qualified engineers, architects, and computer professionals by making them virtual export industries. Indeed, "many of the top engineers and technicians in Malaysia and Thailand and even in Taiwan are Filipinos, and these are the people who left the country during the crisis years," according to Andy Galderon, vice president of Gateway Electronics.[6]

But developing a qualified pool of engineers is so important to companies like Motorola Malaysia that they have developed programs to turn technicians into full-fledged engineers with the assistance of local colleges. Former managing director Roger Bertleson says that the company "believes in working with external training institutions to tailor programs that meet the company's requirements and which make programs compatible to the company's training needs."

Technicians selected for Motorola Malaysia's engineering course attend classes at Kolej Damansara Utama for three years. Other programs provide a Bachelor of Science in Manufacturing Management and even a Masters of Electrical Engineering. How seriously top multinationals and other organizations take training is demonstrated in Table 6.2. The organizations shown have received at least one international award in recognition of the quality of their training programs.

All spend substantial funds on training and, as a percentage of budget, a sum worthy of any marketing or advertising manager's attention. Each of these organizations also requires that top management undergo formal training every year (see Table 6.3).

---

[6] Tiglao, Rigoberto, "Field of Dreams," *Far Eastern Economic Review*, April 4, 1996, pp. 50–51.

Table 6.2 Training Expenditure Per Employee Per Year (US$)

Year	Motorola Malaysia	TI Phil	Yaohan HK	Intel Phil	SIA Sing	Mount Elizabeth Hospital Sing	Caltex Pacific Indo
1993	385	378	n/a	909	3,583	n/a	992
1994	n/a	517	620	1,018	3,401	535	1,100
Number of Employees							
	12,000	2,009	7,740	2,289	23,500	1,560	6,307
Total Expenditure in 1994 (1993 for Motorola) (US$)							
	4,620,000	1,038.653	4,798,800	2,330,202	79,923,500	834,600	6,937,700
Percentage of Budget (US$)							
	n/a	1.3	5.9	3.17	1.2	3.74	1.96

Table 6.3 Hours of Training Per Year – Top Management

Year	Motorola Malaysia	TI Phil	Yaohan HK	Intel Phil	SIA Sing	Mount Elizabeth Hospital Sing	Caltex Pacific Indo
1993	100	69	n/a	146	48	n/a	77
1994	n/a	83	208	n/a	48	10.2	78

Filling the Gaps

Gaps in Asia's educational infrastructure are being filled by the private sector, using in-house resources, consultants, and academics, often from the world's top schools, and outside institutions within Asia and in the West. Figure 6.1 provides a perspective of the standards of education in the organizations participating in this study.

Most of the companies profiled in this chapter are Western multinational corporations. There are two notable exceptions: Mount Elizabeth Hospital and Singapore General Hospital, the only hospitals to take part in the study. The critical role of education and training in health care is obvious. One other company which has been profiled earlier, is also briefly referenced, Royal Sporting House, a Singapore company with regional operations. Yaohan was originally a Japanese retailer but has moved its international headquarters to Hong Kong, although it continues to operate in Japan. Interestingly, losses by the Japan unit have led to a scaling back of plans for expansion in China (the Japanese company filed for protection from creditors while reorganizing its operations).

Figure 6.1   Standards of Training and Education

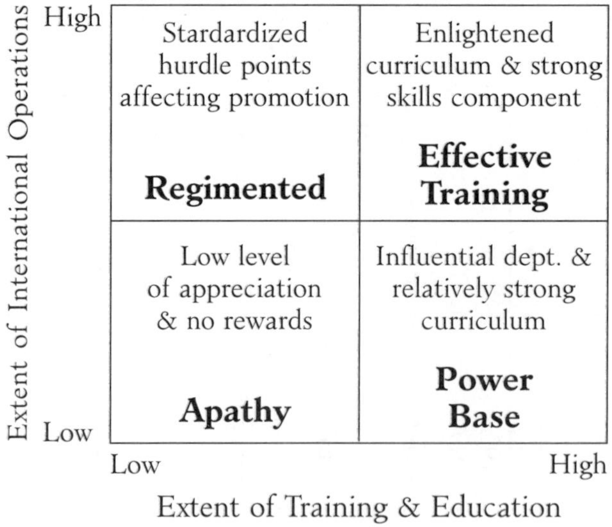

	Low ———— Extent of Training & Education ———— High
High Extent of International Operations	Stardardized hurdle points affecting promotion **Regimented**	Enlightened curriculum & strong skills component **Effective Training**
Low	Low level of appreciation & no rewards **Apathy**	Influential dept. & relatively strong curriculum **Power Base**

Extent of Training & Education

Role of Education in the Organization

As an organization grows, its reliance on education appears to increase. Not always, however, in positive ways. For example, education and personnel departments may become more notable for their political clout in an organization than the quality of their curriculum – and frequently, not many insiders would care to openly comment on the curriculum. Other companies may find that their educational departments become de facto evaluation bureaus or certification centers.

The companies profiled here have developed education and training programs that are of direct relevance to operations and organizational issues, and which provide for advanced leadership and strategic training for senior managers.

Good Habits

At Texas Instruments, in Baguio, the Philippines, the training curriculum ranges from operations, safety, and technology to leadership skills. Mark Go, human resources director, says leadership skills begin with basic supervisory knowledge and ultimately lead to discussions of strategic leadership. In between, employees are introduced to Stephen Covey's *Seven Habits of Highly Effective People and Principle Centered Leadership*. Developing creative people is central to meeting the company's biggest challenges: recruiting and training enough people to maintain a seven-day workweek in response to market demand.

TI measures the effectiveness of its training programs at four levels. The first consideration is the reaction of employees: How do participants feel about the training? Did they feel it was worth their while? Second, the company measures learning: How much did participants effectively absorb?

Next come the meaty issues. TI observes the behavior of the participants and asks how what has been learned is reflected in the workplace, to determine its practical relevance – and the value of the investment. Finally, the company wants to determine how training contributes to the overall objectives of the company, which include quality, productivity, and profitability.

While quality and profitability are determined by the usual indicators, employee productivity is measured by the formula NUB/DLH. NUB stands for Net Units Billed, or total number of units billed and shipped. DLH is Direct Labor Hour, or the actual number of man-hours worked. TI also uses this measure to determine annual increases in productivity.

New Heights

The biggest challenge for Intel Philippines, according to president and general manager Jacob Pena, Jr., is working to move to the next level of technology, such as product design and application. Its parent company is the world's largest microprocessor maker and has grown locally by just completing a US$523 million assembly and test plant for its top-of-the-line Pentium processors. Pena says the new plant is "one of Intel's biggest facilities in the world."[7]

The company averages 146 hours of training annually for each technical employee, leading the other companies profiled in this chapter. That is equivalent to US$1,018 per employee. Among the companies surveyed, only Caltex Pacific at US$1,100 and Singapore Airlines at US$3,401 – reflecting the high costs of equipment and operations – spend more. But the pride of Intel's people management and development program is its five guiding principles.

Training and Development. Training and development at Intel is "a never ending pursuit." Cute, but the company boasts 33 professionals in the training department whose backgrounds provide the basis for both functional expertise and customer focus. The training program for every employee

---

[7] *Ibid.*

has three components: assimilation, development, and rewards and recognition. Technical personnel receive an average of 146 hours of training annually. Non-technical personnel receive an average of 67.

Open Communication. Intel chairman Grove makes much of the necessity for open communication, so it is not surprising to find it a mainstay of employee development in the Philippines operation. Pena says, "Open communication is a policy. A wide array of upward, downward, and lateral communication programs are structured to make this program work." Year-round, family-oriented recreation programs are used as communication venues and to foster camaraderie.

Total Compensation. Like most top technology companies, Intel believes that top money is required to get top people – even though the challenge and prestige of working for a company like Intel may ultimately override other considerations in evaluating job opportunities. As we have noted, engineers are considerably more affordable in the Philippines than in other Asian countries, but those employed at Intel Philippines are among the best compensated in the industry locally.

The company's "T-Comp," or total compensation program, is a meritocracy that is "equitable, administratively efficient, and provides discretion to recognize good performance," according to Pena. The program provides competitive and "cost effective" benefits for all employees based on market competitiveness. It also addresses concerns for catastrophic needs, employee demographics, and lifestyle requisites.

Health and Safety. "Think, breathe, and sleep safety" may sound trite, but it is a prime concern at Intel. Interestingly, this high-tech company includes concern for the environment as a health and safety concern. "Intel's philosophy reflects (the fact) that we protect the community (in) which we operate, comply with all related regulations, and anticipate changes in technology (and their effect on the environment)," Pena says.

Community Service and Involvement. People development and management also includes social responsibility. The company's involvement in the community and academic development builds relationships, is good public relations, and helps provide for a skilled pool of new talent. Intel in its expansion continues to be socially and academically responsive locally, despite the fact that its customers were all until recently outside the Philippines.

And it all pays off. Intel Philippines employees "can now be found occupying sensitive positions at both the administrative and technical levels in the U.S. and other international sites," Pena says. And when this project commenced the company was the only multi-national in the Philippines with an all-Filipino management team.

A Focus on Generic Skills

Singapore Airlines' whopping training tab – almost US$80 million annually – does seem to suggest that it is mighty expensive to train pilots and cabin crew. And that training is focused on specific functions and technical skills.

Not necessarily so, according to Clements. The airline's impressive Management Development Center focuses on generic skills. That focus has helped the airline strengthen what Clements called its "weakest link" – customer service on the ground. It has also helped the airline find the right management recruits to oversee the customer-centered service the airline is famous for, train and motivate them, and retain their services in the increasingly competitive Asian airline industry.

The Management Development Center's programs are divided into three broad categories: management development, manage-ment skills, and self-development. Management development courses are generalist and keyed to rank within the organization. "As the manager moves up the corporate ladder, the programs provide deep insight into the different challenges faced," according to Clements.

Management skills courses, on the other hand, are specific and functionally focused, and are designed to meet particular route needs, such as negotiating skills and intercultural understanding. Self-development is intended to help the manager improve – or upgrade, according to the company – himself or herself as a manager. So courses include social etiquette, stress management, and speed reading.

This intense training schedule has produced an empowered management group. "Even low-level management are empowered and encouraged to take decisions according to their own reading of the situation," says Clements, "without referring to their superiors or consulting a manual. This philosophy of empowerment and delegation of authority runs right through the SIA organizational structure."

The center has also begun offering its executive programs to organizations throughout the region on a cost-sharing basis – a move similar to that of Royal Sporting House's retail academy. "The rich mix of participants brings about interaction and an exchange of ideas among corporate executives from different companies in the region," Clements notes. He also says this set of programs – which generate valuable content for the center – "is a notable ingredient in the Center's continuing success." The faculty is drawn from institutions in Europe, the U.S., Australia, Japan, and Singapore.

The airline also boasts seven functional training departments in its line divisions, and these are mostly found in the US$57 million Training Center, which was opened in 1993. "The four-story building features a 200-seat auditorium, a 50-seat theatrette, flight simulators, a cabin evacuation trainer, a wave pool, cabin mock-ups, and nearly 50 classrooms. The building houses the Management Development Center and a number of other flight and functional training schools."

However, "the Engineering Training School, by necessity," Clements notes, "remains at Airline House, where trainees gain 'hands on' experience in the hangar." Interestingly, financial training is also located at Airline House. Presumably a close-up view of the company's capital investments in the hangar is a powerful inspiration.

Subsidized Customer Care

Like SIA and Royal Sporting House, Singapore General Hospital provides the benefits of its own training infrastructure to other organizations. One of Singapore's top ten employers, the hospital is the largest acute care facility in the city-state, with 1,664 beds – equivalent to 87% of total beds available in the private sector and 31% in the public sector. It boasts 27 specialty departments, and its physicians and surgeons have garnered international recognition for procedures as varied as pediatric surgery to reconstructive surgery.

Patients who say they would recommend SGH to their friends increased from 77% in 1990 to 98% in 1991. Training manager Chua Yan Hong attributes this success to "a change in employee mindset."

It was the need for an employee mindset change that spurred the restructuring of the hospital to provide autonomy, flexibility, and responsiveness to rapid change, liberating SGH from direct government oversight. "Beginning in 1991, Chua says, the hospital launched an organization-wide service training program (that was) specially developed and conducted at SGH at a cost of more than US$178,000. Its focus was creating a more service-oriented employee."

At SGH, known as the "people's hospital," 85% of all patient care is subsidized. Subsidies vary from 20% to 80% of costs, depending on the patient's financial status. SGH is also a teaching hospital.

Despite the subsidies offered by the hospital, SGH strives to offer its patients a higher level of service quality in terms of improvements to its systems and procedures and the enhancement of its employees' service delivery, according to Chua. "The goal is to offer patients efficient service as well as service that is warm, caring, and helpful," he says. Here are some of the principal – and revolutionary – changes this customer-driven facility provides.

One-stop Services for Patients' Convenience. Patients can now receive one-stop services at all of the hospital's outpatient service counters, for example, the Specialist Outpatient Clinics and the Diagnostic Radiology Department. This means that patients can register, make payments, and arrange for subsequent appointments at the same location, saving time and making the patient's visit a more friendly experience.

Decentralization of Pharmacy Services. Previously, all patients – outpatients and inpatients – had to collect their medications at the Central Pharmacy. That can be quite a chore in a hospital that encompasses 12.9 hectares housed in a facility of 183,000 square meters. To make pharmacy services more accessible, SGH created satellite pharmacies and a discharge pharmacy near the wards for patients being discharged.

Shortened Waiting Times and Faster Turnaround Times. In laboratories now, the turnaround time for test results is one day, a 60% improvement from three days. Waiting time for elective surgery has dropped from 14 days in 1989 to eight days in 1991. Hospital bills for patients are dispatched within five days of discharge – they let you out of the hospital without paying the bill!

Improved Information Services. The hospital actually has patient relations assistants move around to look for patients who may need assistance. Patients staying in single or two-bed rooms now have a choice of meals.

The training program that made these enhancements possible featured three principal components. First, a strong Train-the-Trainer orientation for both in-house dissemination of skills and knowledge as well as technology transfer. Next, training was three-tiered, involving staff, managers, and doctors. Specialties and career paths were mapped out in these sessions, including opportunities for advanced, formal education. Finally, the program developed a proactive communications perspective and recognition program. Service began to pay off.

As a result, everyone at SGH is a customer: outpatients, inpatients, staff, doctors, and technicians. This is because everyone is doing something for someone else.

One of SGH's smaller, private sector "competitors" is Mount Elizabeth Hospital. This 505-bed private hospital boasts a total quality management program involving "the entire company from the chief executive officer to the rank and file," and features a regular TQM (Total Quality Management) Awareness Workshop. "Management trainees" – residents – are exposed to cross-functional training in all departments. Externally, the hospital relies heavily on its U.S. parent to conduct training courses and workshops. One example is the series of courses in rehabilitation nursing and management. Courses like these are the first and only ones of their kind available in the region. They are especially worthy because they are available to other participants: not only restructured government hospitals and nursing homes in Singapore, but facilities in Malaysia, Brunei, Indonesia, and Thailand.

Attracting, Retaining, and Developing Talent

"Expatriates, no matter how skilled, need special training," wrote one of the region's first Asians to head a Western multinational corporation. "Most foreigners in the developing world know nothing about their host country's history, culture, and government. If expatriates are to participate in the transfer of competency, they must learn. In Indonesia, Americans frequently misread signals. For example, when Javanese listen, nod, and say nothing, it means they hear you, not that they agree. When they say 'y-e-e-s-s-s,' it means they question what you are saying and may already have decided it is not acceptable. If you ask Indonesians to do something and they reply with a 'perhaps' or 'maybe,' they are not being tentative. Answering a question with a direct yes or no is considered immodest," he said.[8]

That might seem to some like a rather basic training lesson. It is not. The author, Julius Tahija, was Caltex Pacific Indonesia's first Indonesian chairman of the managing board. Since that time, the chair has continued to be held by an Indonesian, Caltex was the first international oil company to have an Indonesian as its chairman. Tahija led the company's Indonesianization program, which reduced the number of expatriates from 600 in the late 1950s to 121 today. Tahija remarks that in his early years at Caltex, even the bulldozer operators were expatriates.

Like Hong Kong's David Li, however, Tahija does not believe that filling a position with an Indonesian is an appropriate objective. "It is always a mistake to promote nationals simply because they are not expatriates," he writes. "To promote people because they are Indonesian, or to be biased in their favor, is to lower standards. Once word gets out, expatriates and the local people they are training will take the transfer of competence less seriously. If anything, local workers should be better qualified than the expatriates they replace. I am harder on Indonesians than I am on Americans because Indonesians are the ones who will be around when the Americans go home."

Current president and chairman of the managing board Baihaki H. Hakim says that this philosophy of Indonesianization has been singled out by the Indonesian government as a model for other multinational corporations. Its primary goal was to attract, retain, and develop quality employees. To help accomplish that task, the company in 1972 first set up its long-running management development program. And it was

---

[8] Tahija, Julius, "Swapping Business Skills for Oil," *Harvard Business Review*, September–October 1993.

the first company in Indonesia to develop non-petroleum engineers into production engineers.

Hakim says that there are four guiding principles to the company's approach to people development and management. First, employees are trusted. They are considered honest, mature, and capable of correct decision-making. Second, employees derive satisfaction from continuous improvements based on clear criteria for success and performance measures. In fact, the company boasts an impressive and sophisticated performance agreement titled "Performance Agreement for Excellent CPI Teamwork," which provides for the development of clear goals, assessment, and rewards. Third, the company's profitability is believed to be the route to employment security. Fourth, capable team leaders and managers are viewed as key to the company's success.

"A developing nation needs all the social and economic competencies that are so plentiful in the developed world. And although these are the very competencies that the governments of developing societies are ill equipped to disseminate – even with international aid – they are precisely the competencies that transnationals possess in abundance and can provide, teach, and encourage with relatively little extra effort or expense simply by paying greater attention to the way they conduct business," Tahija says.

The goodwill that results, Tahija argues, provides important short-term as well as long-term benefits. The most important short-term benefit is the goodwill that attracts the best workers and earns their loyalty. Although Asia has developed rapidly and changed radically since the time Tahija was wondering why expatriates were working oil rigs and driving tractors in Sumatra, the benefits of goodwill are unchanged. So is the role of multinational companies in providing real and effective transfer of technology to a knowledge-hungry Asia.

A Tidy Investment

Back at Motorola, learning is taking place in two directions. There is the transfer of competence and the training and education of engineers, technicians, and managers. And then there is the knowledge acquired by top management from employees. Part of the company's training and empowerment initiative includes what is called the "I Recommend" program. The program provides a formal, institutionalized mechanism for capturing employees' insights and recommendations. Total submissions to the program rose like a rocket from 633 in 1985 to 98,607 in 1992. Impressive.

But wait for this. Improvements that result in cost savings for the organization are rewarded through cash payouts. In 1990, rewards amounted to US$183,000. In 1992, rewards reached a staggering US$985,000 but fell back to US$492,000 in 1993. What value lies behind these payouts, one might ask. Simple greed? A genuine desire to contribute? The acute shortage of engineers and increased turnover across industries make that question even more acute. Whatever the answer may be, it is probably true that rewarding exceptional intellectual contributions with a monetary payout is an idea that works as well at the top management level as at any other.

What we do know for certain is that the more successful a company becomes, the more it trains and educates, develops concern for goodwill in the community and among employees, and chases after top talent. It might have become good before it could afford the investment in people, but staying good requires new talent. To get it, doing good things – training, educating, motivating – pays off. And this is particularly true in an era, and a market, where everyone is looking to recruit the best brains.

Chapter Seven

☆

THE PRODUCTIVITY URGE

"It was trade," Hong Kong's last British governor, Christopher Patten, wrote in the final months before Chinese sovereignty, "which gave Asia its big break." In another decade, a judgement will be in order for free trade and liberalization in Southeast Asia.

The members of the Asia-Pacific Economic Forum (APEC) have made historic commitments to removing informal barriers to free trade. Reform has begun, and if the admittedly fragile multilateral commitments take hold, by early 21st century Asia will be the world's largest – and most liberated – marketplace. In response to early liberalizing reforms and in preparation for what is to come, both governments and corporations are changing the way they do business, despite the inevitable efforts to delay or side track change within the established private sector.

For governments, reform and liberalization means getting out of business. The world's best examples of privatization working are found in Asia. Asia's newest emerging economy, the Philippines, boasts the world's largest privatization project: the water utility. In early 1997 the government auctioned off the rights to rehabilitate and operate a system that loses almost half the water it sends through its network while leaving vast areas of Metro Manila unserved.

Early in the Ramos administration, the government set a new standard for Asian privatization when it liberalized the power sector in the midst of a severe energy crisis characterized by daily brownouts in business districts of up to eight hours. Under liberalized investment guidelines, developers/operators built new fixed power plants and even floated generating facilities on barges up rivers to service the countryside and inland cities.

Malaysia, likewise – itself beginning to experience crushing demand in its second decade of near double-digit growth – embarked on an impressive build-operate-transfer program for financing and putting on-line new generating capacity. Indonesia and Thailand have refined build-operate-transfer programs of their own for the provision of transportation infrastructure as well as energy generation. For governments that began independence intent on becoming welfare states, the contrast with present-day public policy illustrates a profound shift in the perception of government's role in economic development from principal participant to catalyst-manager-arbiter, and the private sector's beneficiary status to responsible wealth generator. Foreign investment is, despite the occasional setback, seen as the most viable path to job creation on the scale required to bring prosperity to anywhere from 20 million citizens, in the case of Malaysia, to over 180 million in Indonesia. Regional governments view themselves as competitors for foreign investment, and they lobby hard for companies in industries that provide the prospect of leading technology transfer, high value-added manufacturing, and investment in new research capacity in Asia.

For Asian governments, this is an era in which the interests of the Asian consumer are finally, and definitively, taking precedence over those of the Asian manufacturer. As a result, Asian companies are focusing on building brand value and awareness as never before – to both attract new customers and safeguard their established retail base which was for many years used to having very little alternative in purchasing decisions. Needless to say, that is frequently not an easy task, with new domestic and international competition reminding consumers of the abuse they endured when monopolistic practices were perpetuated in the name of growing domestic industry and protecting the Asian industrialist from foreign competition.

Yet as the Asian economies first took off two generations ago, to many in the private sector in a newly opportunity-rich environment, enhanced consumer prosperity in protected marketplaces frequently presented the illusion that business could pretty much do anything it wanted and prosper. In fact, this is what the conglomerates did – everything. The liberalization of the 1990s has brought about a new reality: fierce competition everywhere and opportunities that do not always pay off.

As a result, Asian companies have found that the need for strategy and focus discussed earlier is fundamental to success, and that resources must be allocated in a manner that contributes to the competitiveness of the firm rather than merely to service exclusive opportunities. For many companies in Asia, this has also meant undertaking a commitment to vast change in the firm's business model.

New Realities

The benefits generated by low-cost manufacturing and assembly include a wealthier working class. As workers begin to enjoy their newfound prosperity, they take on more liabilities that enhance the quality of life materially. As demand for such things as better homes, appliances, and automobiles increases, prices likewise move upward. Increased monthly expenses and taxes make workers anxious to enhance their income, and the economy begins the transition from low-cost manufacturing to higher value-added manufacturing and export in order to pay for higher operating costs.

However, this transition requires that the workforce be better educated – not just well heeled. As discussed in Chapter 6, most Southeast Asian governments in their enthusiasm for economic reform have failed to invest substantially in enhancing educational infrastructure. Because that infrastructure is critical to high-value growth, the private sector has assumed a significant role in educating and training higher-value workforces to keep pace with new investment in value-added manufacturing, services, and export. We have also noted the irony of Southeast Asian economies and companies educating and training people in high value-added skills only to lose them to developed economies and multinational corporations.

This presents an intense dilemma for national firms that do not have the resources to train their own workforces and have difficulty competing with multinational corporations for the best people. The lack of an educated human resource pool leaves them at a significant disadvantage. Governments have instituted effective energy, transportation, and telecommunications infrastructure build-operate-transfer programs to rapidly overcome major hurdles to development. Similarly, educational infrastructure requires a radical and effective program to bring educational standards to the level at which that infrastructure can be reasonably expected to support high-value manufacturing and business services.

In the meantime, Asian business has to learn to compete with its wealthy multinational and regional competitors. Arthur Andersen's Singapore office says, "Increasingly, clients are calling on us to create transformational change. Not incremental change, but deep, fundamental change which catapults an organization ahead of its competitors." Business processes is the fastest growing segment of the consulting firm's business, which shows that fundamental change is critical in developing the processes – and the perspective – required to succeed and prosper in a competitive environment.

Three Qualities

There are three qualities of such fundamental change: quality, productivity, and value. Asian companies, like profitable companies everywhere, began to hop on the Japan-inspired quality bandwagon in the early 1980s. Manufacturing companies began to focus on zero defects, reduction of customer complaints, the 5-Ss (Japanese efficiency/quality work performance) and other manifestations of the quality urge so familiar to the global business community today. And, like their Western counterparts in that community, their quality quest has over the last two decades transitioned from fundamental component of competitive advantage to basic requisite of profitable operations. As an indicator of quality-focused operation, Asian companies have broadly embraced the ISO 9000 standards of operations to the point that this certification itself is a de facto requisite of doing business.

The second quality is productivity. Productivity is a mid-point of sorts in the transition of Asian firms from national corporation to globally competitive manufacturer. With quality a basic requisite of business, and labor costs on the rise, competitiveness is derived from efficiency of operations and automation. Reengineering has of late been heavily criticized as a brilliant excuse to "downsize" personnel in the West. In Asia, it has been frequently argued that reengineering has a kinder, gentler veneer. Whether it actually does, of course, is an interesting question. What can be said of the reengineering effort in Asia is that it has provoked the same phenomena of job insecurity, management upheaval, and increased profitability through attrition that it has elsewhere. Indeed, protected markets contribute greatly to corporate bloat, and competitive pressures have made pruning inefficient operations critical but never pleasant.

Many of Asia's cultures have had to deal with customs – or bad habits – that made excuses for low productivity acceptable. For example, the attitude still prevalent among laborers and low-ranking white collar workers in the Philippines, Malaysia, Indonesia, and Thailand that tasks can wait until tomorrow – or, even worse, that problems will take care of themselves – clearly cannot withstand the onslaught of liberalized competition. Benchmarking productivity against international industry leaders has become a popular method of both communicating by example to workers the importance of higher productivity to job security as well as setting operating objectives that companies use to determine their competitiveness. Productivity indicators include such indexes as cost of goods/finished goods, cost of goods/work in progress, and cost of goods/raw materials as well as standard indicators providing revenue and profit per employee. As in the case of quality indicators, Asian companies are finding that they can match and exceed industry standards for productivity. OEM manufacturers of everything from athletic shoes to computer motherboards know this and understand the price required to meet those goals: revitalizing corporate culture, substantial capital investment in productivity enhancing equipment, and continuous enhancement of operations.

Like quality, however, productivity benchmarking can go only so far in terms of providing competitive advantage. Ultimately, high productivity will also become a basic requisite of being in business in Asia. Both will be fundamentally important, but they will not provide competitive advantage. Competitiveness, then, must ultimately come from some other source of sustainable competitive advantage. And it is likely that the source of competitive advantage will increasingly be derived from the perception of value. That raises the question of where value resides.

Intel's European chief, Hans Geyer, say, "Competitiveness today means speed."[1]

Another executive echoes, "The 1990s will be a decade in a hurry, a nanosecond culture. There'll be only two kinds of managers: the quick and the dead." Whether in the case of products or services, these managers believe speed of intelligence, speed of innovation, and speed to market, will determine competitiveness – and value – in a liberalized

---

[1] _____, *Fortune*, March 17, 1997, p. 20.

marketplace. Peter F. Drucker put it this way, "The productivity of knowledge workers is the chief determinant of success." For Drucker, value is derived from highly productive innovators who provoke "quantum leaps" in the value of products and services.

For others, the classic view persists that value is not just intrinsic, but perceived. William H. Davidow argued, "While great devices are invented in the laboratory, great products are invented in the marketing department."

The legendary Walter Landor said the same: "Products are made in the factory, but brands are created in the mind."

Smart Communications in the Philippines again provides an interesting illustration of value, and the value of timing. You will recall that Smart's entry into the telecommunications sector was controversial because the company intended to build its network around "old" technology. Its elite competitors trumpeted and continue to trumpet the advantages of digital "unclone-able" technology. Smart is not the leader in technology, but it is first in innovative marketing and network development in far-flung areas of the country.

While its competitors sat back and relied on the advantages of new technology or an old, established network inherited from a monopolistic past, Smart was sprouting cells throughout the land. A series of brilliant full-color, half-page advertisements boasted that Smart technology meant you were never out of touch, whether you were vacationing on an exotic island, building business in the North, or managing a shrimp farm in the South. And the only way you could stay in touch was with Smart.

As a result, Smart now boasts over 500,000 subscribers and has overtaken the former market leader. Its high-tech competitors remain unprofitable and network expansion has not been impressive. For one competitor, euphoric sales of their phones were revealed to be substantially fraud-ridden, and that company took a P441 million (US$17.6 million) write-off as a result and remains unprofitable.

Smart's example shows that speed to market with new

technology per se, while not without value, can be costly. The correct value in the Philippine market was access and reliable service. Speed had to do with rapid development of a national network, not high technology.

Perception of Value

So important is the perception of value that David Packard said, "Marketing is too important to be left to the marketing department," suggesting that marketing was the responsibility of the entire company.

George Gilder says, "In an era of acceleration, the rule of success will be self-cannibalization," in support of the notion of continually reinventing the firm and its products.

Another executive once noted, "Great ideas need landing gear as well as wings,"[2] again suggesting the notion of a continuum, or product life cycle and continuous regeneration and re-creation of products and services.

These statements should be read as challenges to Asian companies – indeed, to companies everywhere. But they are particularly relevant to Asian firms for two reasons. The first is their development cycle. Asian manufacturers are in transition from quality-focusing firm to high-value firm. The halfway mark in that transition is the transformation into high-productivity manufacturer. As Asian companies increasingly focus on value they should evolve from OEM manufacturer or local-brand manufacturer to manufacturer of global Asian brands; that is where long-term growth opportunities will lie, because these companies will no longer be able to manufacture products for the lowest price. The second reason these notions are particularly important to Asian firms is the pace of the transition. Just as Asian economies are the fastest developing economies in history, Asian companies are changing and developing at a blazing

---

[2] These quotes are from a presentation by Dr. Philip Kotler entitled, *"Marketing for the New Global Economy"* organized and presented by TeamAsia in Singapore and Manila in 1997.

pace in response to both opportunity and competitive threats.

That pace is likely to be sustained and should increasingly reflect higher levels of productivity and value. "In theory, *The Economist* recently reported, East Asia's growth can remain faster than rich economies for decades because the need to innovate, instead of copy, limits growth," but "higher wages or rising exchange rates provide an incentive for firms to move into more productive, higher-value activities."[3] In fact, predictions of slower growth in the emerging Asian economies following a 1996 slowdown in Singapore growth and a severe downturn in the real estate and banking sectors in Thailand are widely accepted to be temporary setbacks.

For instance, Kay Hian's senior economist Yang Sy Jian said recently one indication of robust performance in Singapore's financial services sector is that, "15 initial public offerings were launched in the first quarter of 1996, compared with 10 for the same period in 1995. Moreover, the 15 IPOs raised net proceeds that were about 40% higher than in the same period of 1995." Although semiconductor sales were depressed in 1996 and early 1997 and the drop in non-oil exports "showed new areas of weakness that rattled even economists who warned of monthly volatility."[4] Other economists said that Singapore's commercial sector has been boosted by technology sales both domestically and internationally. Indeed, exporters reported improved revenues. For instance, "ST Electronics & Engineering said 1996 sales were boosted by export revenue, which grew 21%."[5] The company said net profit advanced 46%. Early in 1997, IBM announced significant new investments in disk manufacturing capacity despite reports of a downturn in disk-drive exports. Meanwhile in Thailand, trouble in real estate and banking has been somewhat offset by news of investment

---

[3] _____, "The Asian Miracle," *The Economist*, March 1, 1997, pp. 23–25.

[4] Rajendran, Joseph, "Singapore Edgy Amid Decline In Its Exports," *The Asian Wall Street Journal*, March 21–22, 1997, p. 1.

[5] _____, "Singapore Companies Report Better Results," *The Asian Wall Street Journal*, March 18, 1997, p. 3.

in higher value-added electronics and automobile parts manufacture. Property and banking may be DOA for the moment, but exporters are delirious.

While the economic momentum in the region may in fact provide the prospect of sustained high growth without the need to innovate – and the pace of development makes that notion a potentially dangerous one – the rapid and pervasive introduction of competition in Asian marketplaces does require innovative and effective marketing.

A Decade in a Hurry

Most of Southeast Asia has been in a hurry to develop for considerably more than a decade. Yet it is difficult to visualize its sprawling conglomerates as ever acting with a sense of corporate urgency. These conglomerates simply have not had to be in a hurry for most of the past three decades in anything much other than opportunity snatching. Market liberalization and new competitive pressures – as well as the old age of their founders – are, however, forcing fundamental changes in the way these companies operate. Nevertheless, warnings by Western academics and management experts, such as Porter, that Asian companies must become more focused frequently provoke rebuttal by Asian managers and management experts who suggest in an un-Asian manner that the former do not know what they are talking about. Of course, Porter, like all gurus, has plenty of detractors outside Asia as well. However, the skeptical criticisms leveled by Asian critics are exceptionally shallow, suggesting that the dynamics of a sprawling conglomerate are appropriate in an Asian context and reflect Asian "values." But the reality is that on a level playing field the sprawling conglomerate is no match for an aggressive, focused firm no matter where it traces its roots. And the playing field in Asia is becoming more level every day, despite the occasional and inevitable setback.

It was Bill Gates who replied, in response to his major detractors' efforts to reduce Microsoft's domination of the desktop software market, that it was not the major firms that worried him. It was the single-minded guys in their garages. Netscape showed that Gates' paranoia was well placed when the start-up forced Gates and Microsoft to rethink the future of desktop software and the impact of the Internet on personal and corporate computing.

Asia's principal conglomerates would do well to ponder the effects of determined entrepreneurs and national corporations as well as Western multinationals on their own operations. Like Microsoft, they have the financial strength to respond effectively to new sources of competition, once recognized. But also like Microsoft, new competition can force a radical change in market values and, as a result, in the way Asian conglomerates operate. Whether Asian conglomerates have the leadership – or the corporate will – necessary to undertake fundamental change at a time when many second generation family members are assuming control is the big question. But there is no question that Asian corporations are in a hurry to grow and prosper. And many Western corporations are only now being given the opportunity to demonstrate just how aggressive they can be in a competitive Asian marketplace.

Thailand's Alphatec was, until recently, one of the young Asian companies setting new standards of operation in its industry – although it is facing enormous financial and development problems unrelated to its original assembly and testing operations. The company relied heavily on expatriate management expertise to open marketing and distribution channels, as well as engineering expertise. However, one of the most important side effects of its expansion to China was access to a large and impressive pool of highly educated engineers, in short supply in Thailand and most countries of Southeast Asia. Acquiring that expertise potentially provides Alphatec the opportunity to undertake high-value services for customers, and certainly enhances its capacity to offer value at competitive rates. "By eliminating the need to manufacture silicon chips outside Thailand and then import them for assembly, CEO Charn aims to cut production time for chips from three months to as little as three weeks, while slashing inventory and transportation costs."[6] Unfortunately, for Charn and despite his early success if he does not complete the new plants quickly, his technology may be outmoded before it is put to work. But even if Charn eventually fails as a result of his financial travails, he will have succeeded in demonstrating in a dramatic way that new boys on the block can come out of nowhere and have a major impact on their industries and their countries.

Following a difficult start, IMI in the Philippines reported record operating profits in 1996 – particularly significant because of the vast depreciation in semiconductor prices that year. IMI says that it has learned to differentiate itself from the competition by emphasizing quality, cost competitiveness, on-time delivery, customer service, and manufacturing flexibility. Although IMI has not recruited the western expatriates with a worldwide network of valuable contacts in leading technology companies that Alphatec has, IMI has succeeded by enhancing, its capacity to produce value-added products and nurturing ties with predominately Asian manufacturers.

Competition and Transformation

IMI is part of the Philippines' Ayala Group. Another Ayala company, Ayala Land, has also gone through a significant transformation over the last half decade of rapid economic growth in that country. Once seen as a fairly stodgy, set-in-its-ways near monopoly because of its domination of the Makati financial district, the company has started redeveloping itself as well as the business center for which it is best known. That redevelopment includes transforming the Makati retail area into Asia's most dramatic – and largest – commercial shopping mall, in a bustling metropolis brimming with huge, world-class shopping districts.

---

[6] Austria, Cecille, "Dominate Your Niche," *World Executive's Digest*, December 1995, pp. 16–22.

The redevelopment has helped foster a surge in real estate values – along with the Fort Bonifacio development led by rival Metro Pacific Corporation across the famous EDSA artery – by as much as 100%. It has also encouraged this bastion of conservatism to experiment in more speculative developments such as high-end residential condominiums. To this new sector Ayala brings the extremely high level of prestige associated with its name and the exclusive developments it has been building for over half a century. Its task now is to sustain and enhance that perception of exclusivity in a competitive marketplace that uses international standards of development to measure its competitive forces.

Some of the most startling corporate transformations wrought by competition in Asia are in the financial sector – specifically, consumer banking. In some cases, the changes evolve from the opportunity presented by technology. Bangkok Bank and the Hongkong & Shanghai Banking Corporation are two good examples. As the financial sector liberalizes across the region, both banks are using technology to expand their networks by relying on automated teller machines (ATMs) and desktop banking to reach new retail customers rather than traditional brick and mortar branches and human branch managers and tellers. As Andersen's Gan said, who needs branches?

Technological innovation in consumer banking begins with ATM networks, but these networks are only the beginning. Hongkong Bank's Midland Bank subsidiary, for example, has pioneered a direct telephone banking system that will be used in Asia. "You can ring them up at two in the morning and arrange to pay your gas bill, [order] traveler's checks, or arrange a loan," according to a company executive.[7] The system represents "a new focus on customer relations" that permeates the bank's operations throughout the region.

---

[7] Leung, James, "Hongkong Bank Extends Personal Touch," *Asian Business*, February 1997, pp. 22–27.

There are at least two evolving market factors that explain Hongkong Bank's transition from principally corporate banker to retail champion. The first has to do with the opportunities already discussed. Liberalization has made retail banking an attractive and opportunity-rich alternative for expanding business. Asia's burgeoning middle class is enjoying the privileges of unencumbered credit and the luxury of home and automobile ownership. "The profitable credit-card business done by the group's subsidiaries in Britain and the U.S. helped convince management to push for the development of personal banking and its cross-selling spin-offs in Asia"[8] just a year after executives said in interviews for this book that the bank would continue to focus on corporate banking. Second, Asian corporations – after decades of enduring unreasonably high credit hurdles – have discovered the capital markets, reducing the need to finance operations and expansion through debt.

The bank's Asset Vantage program focuses on customers who have more than one account. It is an "all-in-one that combines checking, savings, time deposits, insurance, money market and other investments, making it easier for customers to track their available balances in different accounts and to switch them from one account to another and to obtain the highest rate of return."[9]

To further enhance standards of customer service, the bank has introduced what it calls Hexacon, a system that allows customers to conduct a wide range of bank transactions from their own desktops. Hexacon allows customers to transfer funds between accounts, open new lines of credit, and take an active hand in managing their investment portfolios.

Concerned with the need to innovate to attract and retain customers, the bank has obtained the Mondex – smart cards used for direct debit of accounts – franchise for the region. Given its vast network in 22 countries, the bank's ATM and

---

[8] *Ibid.*
[9] *Ibid.*

Mondex smart-card tandem provides significant benefits for increasingly mobile Asian travelers.

The Value of Brands

Helping many banks transition from financial repository to dynamic provider of retail banking services is Arthur Andersen Consulting. It is not hard to argue that Arthur Andersen is the preeminent systems integrator in the world. In Asia, where technology is seen as both competitive edge and playing field leveler, its business potential is outstanding. A 1995 survey showed, "Andersen is the only organization to be rated above average in three crucial areas: client/server development, groupware, and object technology. These are the three most critical areas for integrating regional financial networks," according to the firm.

In Singapore, Arthur Andersen's revenue per partner is almost twice that of Arthur Andersen worldwide, and in recent years the firm has enjoyed 25% annual growth in what it calls "client relationships."

To sustain growth, Arthur Andersen has undertaken a global branding campaign with the apparent objectives of broadening its franchise in systems technology and retaining its solid client base. The firm is touting its "customer intimacy" and the confidence of providing to customers the "best total solution" to meet their development objectives. That intimacy has a price, though, and it is high, or, as Philip Kotler says, "more for more."

The campaign is based on a solid footing. "A five-percentage point advantage in customer retention leads to a doubling of company size in 14 years," according to Kotler. By transforming the Arthur Andersen "brand" from a relatively esoteric dimension in terms of top-of-mind, particularly with respect to the principal business of the consulting firm, Arthur Andersen appears to be staking out and defending its turf on the basis of depth, experience, and speed.

Similar trends are seen across industry borders. Singapore's

Excel Machine Tools has undertaken what is clearly an aggressive corporate communications program with government support intended to project the quality specialty tools manufacturer as an exporter of jobs and opportunity as far away as eastern Europe. Neptune Orient Lines (NOL), it may be argued, is building its brand by projecting its expertise in information technology and customer service, and not merely number of ships. Like its cousins in the document and package courier business, NOL has invested heavily in information and tracking systems in order to develop the capacity to communicate the exact location of a customer's shipment, 24 hours a day.

Hong Kong retailer Theme International says that in a competitive market it is building a value-added image promoting the innovative character of the chain and its value proposition. Malaysia's Kumpulan Barkath is a manufacturer and distributor of processed foods, but first and foremost it considers its business to be merchandising. Indonesia's Mustika Ratu is working aggressively to build an image of supplier of exotic products designed for Asian skin and hair.

The Capitalist Cooperative

Turning a union cooperative into a trendy retailer is clearly an unusual business undertaking. Singapore's National Trade Unions Congress (NTUC) has grown accustomed to undertaking the unusual. Its NTUC FairPrice stores have become a fierce competitor in the best capitalist tradition. Its success, the cooperative says, comes from "carefully identifying the appropriate product quality and service level that will be perceived by the customer as superior relative to price and more so when compared with the competitor's offering."

This unusual retailer has devised a retail pricing benchmark from a basket of essential items for comparison against the competition – not unusual. However, its objective is to be the lowest average cost retailer in every single market survey taken. So the cooperative's brand value has emerged as the retailer providing value for less. It is able to sustain that perception by delivering on its promise. It delivers by identifying cost drivers throughout the value chain and working with suppliers to provide "the lowest cost formulation" in the market.

The Bottom Line

Like everything else the region has accomplished in the past 25 years, Asia is learning to compete very quickly. While there are instances of concessions awarded as a result of political lobbying, the average Asian company's operations are subject to nothing more – or less – than market forces. Companies in the manufacturing, telecommunications, energy, and infrastructure industries that have obtained public concessions have found that political connections will not sustain them, whether they manufacture national cars in Indonesia or provide cellular phone service in Malaysia. Ultimately, they must make the best deal, as well as provide the best value proposition and live up to its terms.

Making the best deal will increasingly demand the capacity to provide the highest level of productivity. Drucker argues that labor content will shrink to 20% early in the next century for virtually all products and services. That presents an enormous problem for Asia. For despite the huge population, it does not have the highly productive knowledge workers to provide that 20% value in a competitive global marketplace.

For Asia, the race to higher productivity and value is a race to enhance educational infrastructure and create conditions to help retain the workers who will provide the competitiveness of 21st century corporations.

Chapter Eight

───────────────── ☆ ─────────────────

BRINGING FOCUS TO ASIAN CONGLOMERATES

Focus and core competence lie at the heart of a firm's competitiveness. Focus means developing the capacity and expertise to consistently perform a series of usually complex, interrelated activities to provide a product or service. The idea is that it is harder for competitors to emulate a series of complex activities than a particular core competence. Focus requires discipline and the ability to resist the temptation to expand into related business activities – because expansion will impinge on the efficiency of the system. Competitive advantage, then, is derived from a set of synergistic competencies, some of which may be core competencies, and not just the capability of producing the best, the cheapest, or the most practical product or service. Porter is the primary exponent of focus, although his critics argue that Jack Trout and Al Ries have put forth a similar argument for years.[1]

Figure 8.1, developed by Porter, shows a business system – in this case, IKEA's – consisting of various activities that alone are not difficult to emulate. However, IKEA's competi-

---

[1] Milunovich, Steve, "Strategic Thoughts: Michael Porter Reinvents Trout & Ries," a paper published by Morgan Stanley, November 12, 1996.

Figure 8.1 IKEA Activity System

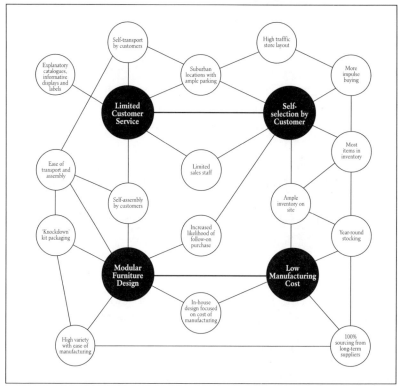

Source: Michael E. Porter

tive advantage comes from the synergy thrown off by these activities when they function as a system. Such a system, Porter argues, is difficult for competitors to emulate, and perhaps even impossible, unless the competitor enjoys very similar circumstances to IKEA's in terms of such things as market focus and even corporate values, mission, and culture.

Core competence, on the other hand, is most frequently expressed as the idea that a company must develop a particular capability that differentiates the company from its competition and provides the opportunity to change the rules of competition. Hamel and Prahalad in *Competing for the Future* suggest that Matsushita's successful development of the VHS video format, for instance, and Swatch's rebirth as a trendy, low-cost manufacturer of watches are instances demonstrating the development of core competencies that changed the rules of competition in their industries. Since these companies changed the rules, it follows that they were setting standards of competition for others to benchmark and try to exceed.

Both focus and core competence proponents accept the need to constantly keep improving to sustain competitive advantage. For Porter, "long-term success is based on a dynamic strategy for the creation, destruction, and re-creation of short-term advantages evolving from a system of competencies."

Hamel and Prahalad argue that an organization must continually wager its future on the strength of its capacity to develop new core competencies that change the rules of competition. To sustain leadership, companies must continually "revolutionize" their industries by developing new sets of core competencies that set them apart from the competition.

Companies may become focused as a result of the development of a core competence, or core competence may evolve from focus. Federal Express developed its competencies, for example, as a result of its focus on the efficient delivery of documents and packages. Sony became focused on audio-visual equipment because one founder got tired of seeing another carrying a large radio around the offices on his shoulder and started work on miniaturization. Federal Express is the global industry leader, but companies like DHL and UPS have shown that the whole system can be emulated. Sony developed a system of core competencies, but found that its Asian competitors can quickly and successfully emulate new technological breakthroughs nevertheless. However, Sony has many more competitors than Federal Express does. There is more pressure for revolutionary change on companies that rely on particular competencies rather than systems of competencies.

We said that focus requires that activities be improved – or even revolutionized – while avoiding the temptation to undertake attractive opportunities that will cause an erosion of the system. In IKEA's case, such a temptation might be retailing furniture for the well-to-do, since traditional furniture manufacture and retail would seem to be a natural extension of its core competence; that is, retailing furniture and furnishings for up-and-coming young adults. For Porter, this would be disastrous because of the disruption of the well-oiled systems IKEA has developed for retailing its product line. Customers carry their purchases away from IKEA to be assembled in their homes, while traditional furniture comes assembled and must be delivered, for example. The result would be system imbalance and lost efficiency as resources and attention were focused on new systems for new products built for a new market segment.

It is interesting to point out here that from a marketing perspective, Kotler believes that a strong brand name can be effectively used to develop related product lines. He uses as an example Marriott's foray into several chains of motels, inns, and hotels to cater to different economic classes. Marriott does not use its name at the low end of these chains, but presumably capitalizes on its knowledge of operations in the industry to efficiently run motels. Porter would likely argue that while the brand name can be effective in promoting related businesses, it is difficult for the systems that profitably operate a five-star hotel chain to provide the competitive advantage necessary to successfully operate a chain of cost-effective motels.

Asian Conglomerates

As these gurus have made presentations throughout Asia in the past few years, they have sparked much debate as to the applicability of their notions to Asian conglomerates. Reaction to Porter's straightforward pronouncements that the conglomerates are entering an era in which they will no longer be opportunity driven but market driven has been especially noisy. Acknowledging that his statements are intended to provoke such arguments, Porter asserts that Asian conglomerates must dismantle themselves to allow their separate parts to focus on developing systems that provide competitive advantage in specific industries but will not contribute to the competitiveness of the present whole.

"For the moment," it is reported, "most Asian businessmen believe the conglomerate is well suited to the region. Skepticism about the value of core business is particularly rife among the ethnic Chinese who migrated to East Asia from the mainland. They founded most of the region's largest conglomerates, and many still run the companies they created. These so-called 'overseas Chinese' dominate the ranks of the region's billionaires. They control eight out of ten of Indonesia's top companies, for instance; a similar proportion of Thailand's leading firms; and numerous corporate giants in the Philippines. They are also the biggest investors in China."[2]

The financial reach of the conglomerates far outstretches their ethnic proportion of the population. "In the Philippines, the overseas Chinese make up only 1% of the country's population, but control over half the stock market. In Indonesia, the equivalent proportions are 4% and 75%, in Malaysia 32% and 60%. Hellmut Schütte, coauthor of *Strategies for Asia Pacific*, and a management professor at INSEAD's Euro-Asia Centre, reckons that by 1996 the 51 million overseas Chinese controlled an economy worth US$7 billion, roughly the same size as that of the 1.2 billion mainlanders."[3]

Conglomerate founders and managers support their argument that their present structure is better suited to Asia by pointing out that Asian businesses are run on the basis of relationships, something many management experts say is a basic requisite of successful operation anywhere. Those same

---

[2] _____, "Fissiparous fortunes and family feuds," *The Economist*, November 30, 1996, p. 69.

[3] Micklethwait, John and Adrian Wooldridge, *The Witch Doctors*, Times Books, New York, 1996, p. 261.

experts would quickly add that relationships alone are not enough in a competitive marketplace with a level playing field. Ultimately, the company that makes the best deals will be the industry leader, and its capacity to make attractive deals will be determined by its operating efficiency and effectiveness, not by relationships.

Another advantage of the family-run conglomerate, it is argued, is rapid decision-making. In fact, operationally, nothing could be further from the truth. Because the founder/owner makes all the important decisions, decisions that are not opportunity-based but rather have to do with improving operations, must wait because of the sheer volume of decision-making the chief executive has to undertake. It is also argued that the conglomerates are suited to exercising political power, something still very important in Southeast Asia. However, as the region's economies step up their competition for foreign investment, there will be a power shift because the political liability associated with favoritism toward national conglomerates will reduce the attractiveness of the country for the most important type of investments, those that are high value-added and require the transfer of proprietary, leading-edge technology.

But conglomerates have other problems. Particularly because they are opportunity- and development-based, they are not value-rich. They generate speculative profit – or profits evolving from monopolistic franchises – and do not create value in terms of new proprietary technology or products. "Trevor MacMurray, a consultant at McKinsey, argues that too many overseas-Chinese businesses are 'structurers' as opposed to 'builders.'"[4] That is a criticism the conglomerates are sensitive to, perhaps because it is difficult to argue with. It would be a mistake to suggest that the conglomerates have not made important contributions to the region's development. At the same time, it would be legitimate to ask whether they could have done more had

---

[4] *Ibid.*, p. 265.

they been made to compete for opportunity in ways besides political patronage.

The success – and the ages – of the founders of Asia's conglomerates, not surprisingly, create hurdles to dramatic change. It is hard to argue with success, and age does dampen the entrepreneurial risk-taking edge. While investment is still opportunity driven, it is with the intent of consolidating positions and strength, not staking the family fortune, or betting the company as Hamel and Prahalad put it, to attain industry leadership. The objective for Asia's conglomerates seems clear: it is sustaining great size.

Raymond W.Y. Kao in *Entrepreneurship: A Wealth-Creation and Value-Adding Process* relates two charming stories which we believe convey the dilemma of the conglomerates. The first is the Bicycle Story:

> This story tells of a person who purchased a new bicycle. He cared about the bicycle so much, he washed, cleaned, and polished it on a daily basis. He was worried that the road might dirty it, and there might even be a slight chance the bicycle would accidentally be damaged. He loved the vehicle so much that he decided to preserve it as long as he could, so he decided not to ride on it to work, but carried it on his shoulder instead.

The second story is the Fan Story:

> This is another interesting story about an old man who loved his newly purchased fan made of bamboo and paper that could be folded or opened. Three years later, his friend saw him with the same fan in his hands but as fresh and new as before. His friend asked him: "Why is your fan so new when mine, which I acquired only a few months ago, is already out of shape and partly ripped?" The old man told his friend: "Oh, it's simple. I keep it so well, and I will show you how." He opened his fan, but instead of moving his fan left and right, he held his fan still and moved his head.[5]

---

[5] Kao, Raymond, W.Y., *Entrepreneurship: A Wealth-Creation and Value-Adding Process*, Simon & Schuster, Singapore, 1995, p. 122.

The founders love their conglomerates so much, in other words, that it is highly unlikely that they would ever allow them to undertake the risks required to become truly great companies instead of great opportunists. The succeeding generation may come closer, as evidenced by Richard Li, the youngest son of Li Ka-Shing, probably the best-known of the Asian *taipans*. "The younger Li is credited with founding and building up Star TV before selling it in 1993 to media mogul Rupert Murdoch."[6] But even then, Richard was hardly betting the company; he was betting more his credibility. And he has found his second big deal to be elusive.

It is important to note here that work by Porras and Collins, authors of *Built to Last,* and de Geus, author of *The Living Company,* shows that to survive, companies must evolve to reflect new market realities. Many times, they must be the driver of industry change. And in every instance, they must undertake revolutionary change to maintain industry leadership. De Geus writes, "By 1983, one-third of the 1970 *Fortune* 500 companies had been acquired or broken into many pieces, or had merged with other companies."

He argues that the natural life span of a company should be two or three centuries or even more. Of course, very few endure for that period. Those that do exhibit four "personality traits" that de Geus says explain their longevity.[7]

- Conservatism in financing
- Sensitivity to the world around them
- Awareness of their identity
- Tolerance of new ideas

We would argue that Asian conglomerates do not reflect these four personality traits, although conservatism in financing would in at least some instances be open to debate

---

[6] _____, "Who's Who in Hong Kong," *Asia, Inc.*, Special Issue February 1997, p. 36.

[7] De Geus, Arie, "The Living Company," *Harvard Business Review*, March–April 1997, pp. 53–54.

at least until fairly recently. There is little room for debate elsewhere. First, if the conglomerates were sensitive to the changes taking place in the marketplace, they would be reacting or driving change rather than trying to preserve gains and positions. Second, the identity of the corporations is that of their founders, who overshadow their organizations. And as widely diversified conglomerates, it would be difficult indeed to project any other sort of unified, consistent corporate identity. Third, there is little tolerance for new ideas. The conglomerates continue to use the same models to exploit opportunities, and the pressure of market forces and competition are not yet great enough to force change. De Geus' work, which included companies from North America, Europe, and Asia, suggests that if the conglomerates are to survive, radical changes in the values and culture of these sprawling organizations will be required.

Hamel and Prahalad argue that "any company that doesn't today derive at least 20% of its revenues from Southeast Asia (not including Japan) is, by definition, losing world market share. European and U.S. producers of automobiles, consumer electronics, and many industrial products must work hard to ensure that fast-growing Asian markets are not ceded to Japanese rivals."[8] It is clear that pressure to develop the capacity to exploit fast-growing Asian markets is intense, and will grow more intense. Asian conglomerates must start working hard to be worthy competitors in these fields of European, U.S., and Japanese companies.

The Other Side of Asian Business

Despite the awesome share of the economic pie held by Asian conglomerates – which are principally but not entirely dominated by overseas Chinese – most Asian businesses are not part of a conglomerate. Many of the companies that agreed to participate in this study were not part of a larger

---

[8] Hamel, Gary and C.K. Prahalad, *Competing for the Future*, Harvard Business School Press Cambridge, 1994.

group of companies. Although a number are relatively new companies, there is at least one in each of the six countries involved in the study that appears to demonstrate the four personality traits identified in de Geus' group of "long-living" companies (see Table 8.1).

Table 8.1

Hong Kong	Indonesia	Malaysia	Philippines	Singapore	Thailand
Café de Coral	Blue Bird Taxi	TA Enterprises	Jollibee	Royal Sporting House	Bangkok Bank
Theme Int'l	PT Giant Pineapple	Kumpulan Barkath	Philacor	Excel Machine Tools	
Giordano	Mustika Ratu	Tan & Tan Developments		Singapore Airlines	

All of these companies are managed in a financially sound manner. Alphatec is not on this list because it leveraged its future on demand for products that are frequently subject to volatile cycles of demand and unsound strategic alliances. To some, Alphatec's financial strategy is typical of high-technology investments – risky. It is also been recently received that Alphatec has been financially imprudent in other ways, as explained in the appendix.

As for sensitivity to the world around them, Giordano probably fails to meet this criterion because it is widely believed to be in serious trouble as a result of persistent problems in China due to the rocky relationship between key government officials and founder and former chairman Lai. Without access to the China market, it is believed that the aggressive retailer will be unable to sustain growth. However, Giordano's political problems are just that: political. They are not market or competitive problems that came about as a result of the company's failure to stay close to the market. On the contrary, we have already seen that Giordano is a leader in reading its market and keeping it satisfied. Its China stores are doing poorly because they have been closed by government order, not as a result of poor demand. Nevertheless, it cannot hope to endure if it does not find a way to effectively adapt to political realities in its principal growth market. Café de Coral has been much more astute in this respect, and it is expanding aggressively.

Blue Bird Taxi has capitalized on its close relationship with the Indonesian government to consolidate its market position, but it has stayed close to the market, as seen by its expanded product offerings resulting from customer feedback. TA Enterprises brought Malaysia's capital markets to the middle class, and its aggressive expansion has on occasions attracted the attention of key government officials. However, the company deftly managed those relationships to help send it rocketing to the pinnacle of its industry. Royal Sporting House has raised the "profession" of retailing to an art form, and it has responded to the government's call for expansion overseas by opening outlets – and even a training school – throughout the region. Bangkok Bank in Thailand is a source of pride, and a reassuring bastion of strength in a time of great challenge.

De Geus says, "No matter how broadly diversified the companies were, their employees all felt like parts of a whole,"[9] so that the corporation as that whole was aware of its identity. We have said that it is difficult to establish a corporate identity when the identity is that of its founder's. Of course, there are excellent U.S. multinationals that are identified with respected founders, such as Hewlett Packard, and Japan has the legendary Konosuke Matsushita. But in the case of Hewlett Packard, the founders worked hard to develop a sense of company, not of following. This is also true for Matsushita. There is another important difference between these companies and the typical Asian conglomerate. That is that companies like Hewlett Packard

---

[9] De Geus, Arie, p. 54.

and Matsushita were established on principles, not opportunity. They were chasing dreams, not franchises. Perhaps most important of all, these companies were dedicated to producing original products and new technologies. Among the Asian conglomerates, there is not a single instance of a new technology even being thought about, let alone developed. All of these reasons are why the Asian conglomerates – for as long as they are around – will be an extension of the personalities of their founders instead of great companies.

We should note that despite the attention its charismatic chairman generates, Giordano succeeded in the marketplace because of savvy marketing and brand recognition development. Café de Coral, on the other hand, has achieved a high level of internal awareness of its identity because its principals have chosen to develop a community of workers who are stakeholders in the company's success. Every driver at Blue Bird Taxi is in uniform and takes great pride in the near fabled reputation of this highly service-oriented company and its dedication to customers. The sense of family that Jollibee seeks to establish in each outlet begins with its employees and store managers. While its principals are well known and respected, they are nowhere near as well known as the company's Jollibee mascot. The level of service the company achieves would simply not be possible if staff did not feel that there was more at stake in their work than a good performance evaluation. Excellent service is a personal standard, borne out of respect for each individual and appreciation for his contribution. This same sense of high personal standards is seen at Royal Sporting House, the only shoe store in Asia where buying shoes is an educational experience. At Bangkok Bank, stability and reliability are a mission. That mission and its openness to new ideas has made the bank one of Asia's fastest growing despite profound problems within the banking industry in Thailand.

"The long-lived companies in our study tolerated activities in the margin: experiments and eccentricities that stretch their understanding. They recognized that new businesses may be entirely unrelated to existing businesses and that the act of starting a business need not be centrally controlled,"[10] de Geus reports. While control remains much more centralized in Asian companies, the extraordinary reliance on employees demonstrated in these companies is reflected in a similarly high level of decision-making authority at relatively low levels. Alphatec's Charn is the driving force behind the company, but it is run by professional managers, and this accounts for its initial success. A manager at Royal Sporting House is said to have left the store to purchase a pair of shoes from a competitor at a higher retail price for a customer because the customer's size was out of stock – and then resold the shoe to the customer for a lower price. Likewise, Jollibee, TA Enterprises, Blue Bird Taxi, and Giordano expect and encourage their employees to exercise their best judgement to take care of business according to the standards these companies have said are important. As a result, employees work in the best interest of the companies as well as customers.

Focus and Core Competence

Hamel and Prahalad say, "For more and more companies today, the ratio of market value to asset value is 2:1, 4:1, even 10:1. The difference between asset value and book value is not goodwill, it is core competence – people-embodied skills. Protecting core competencies from erosion takes continued vigilance on the part of top management."[11] Each of the companies profiled here has benefited and grown because of enlightened management, management that is always looking over its shoulders.

Café de Coral understands that every product innovation it introduces will be replicated by the competition within days.

---

[10] *Ibid.*, p. 54.
[11] Hamel, Gary and C.K. Prahalad, *Competing for the Future*, Harvard Business School Press, Cambridge, 1994.

There is incredible pressure to sustain growth not just by building more stores, but by building volume in each one. Maintaining standards and generating new product ideas is simply too awesome a task to be dictated from above; it must be lived and breathed from below, where constant interaction with customers breeds creativity and fosters innovation. To continually delight its customers technologically as well as in service quality, Blue Bird relies on the goodwill of its drivers, because technology ultimately is only as good as its application. It is the drivers who know what their customers want and who feed this information back to management. Management, in turn, listens – and acts.

TA Enterprises' Tony Tiah makes it a point to have lunch with his brokers practically every day that he is in town, because that is how he stays close to the marketplace. He also knows that it is his brokers who will tell him what has to happen to make sure they sustain and grow core competence. As customer preferences evolve in the Philippines and other markets, Jollibee's capacity to adapt products to local conditions is directly proportional to employees' capacity to understand and translate those preferences into new product standards. In each of these companies, people are the principal asset and the source of core competence – Alphatec because of the network its managers maintain and grow, and Royal Sporting House because its employees are practitioners of the art of retailing.

If we accept that these companies demonstrate impressive core competencies that evolve from their people, perhaps we can now establish the relationship of competence to focus in these firms. To us, core competencies have evolved from the determination to focus on particular products and services; focus has not evolved from a particular core competence.

Take, first, Alphatec, for the reason that Charn did make a profound impact on Thailand and Asia, and may well continue to do so depending on how he responds to the challenges he faces. Although Alphatec is a technology company seeking to produce increasingly higher value-added products, it is a service and sales company. It tests and manufactures products according to high international quality standards that are available from many other sources. Its core competence includes technology, but its principal competence is its people who network with clients around the world. That network is fairly narrow: it is focused on buyers of semiconductors. Its core competence, then, keeps the company focused on developing and refining systems to serve that network. Other competencies serve to keep that network satisfied: quality products, high-value manufacturing, impressive engineering. If Alphatec were to begin manufacturing computers, the value of that network would erode in terms of its capacity to contribute to generating profit. Alphatec, therefore, has very good reason to stay focused and resist any temptation it may be presented with to broaden its product line into related, but different, product categories.

Royal Sporting House, on the other hand, has expanded up and down the value chain as well as deepened its focus on retailing high-end clothing and shoes. But it has not used the Royal Sporting House name to achieve recognition – or confuse the marketplace – to bolster its expansion. It is seeking to capitalize on its expertise in retailing high-end items other than sports-related products because that is exactly the same market that it principally serves anyway. Its move away from that market to discount outlets – and the blurring of its focus – was in response to the souring of the high-end market as prices rose above the boundary of practicality. So it has sought to rebuild sales by deepening its focus on retailing as well as broadening its offerings on the value chain. Of the two parts of the strategy, it would seem that the deepening initiative is the more promising, because it maintains the same values, niche, and philosophy as the principal business of selling high-end sports apparel and shoes. Nevertheless, the company did respond effectively to new market conditions, and despite Porter's pronouncements advising against blurring the focus of the company, there are conglomerates that are successful and much more highly diversified. However, they are few in number. And, Royal Sporting House is firmly focused on retail, and it is unlikely that Gomber would even momentarily consider manufacturing what he sells, as Giordano does.

TA Enterprises has recently begun to expand into related fields and some not so related. In addition to brokerage services, the company now sells life insurance and invests in real estate. McDonald's founder Ray Krock is often quoted as saying that his real business was real estate, and that selling hamburgers was his career. It is hard to imagine selling securities as TA's career and its business evolving into real estate development. One could even speculate about the soundness of an investment firm selling insurance, which is certainly a short-term hedge. The competencies required to do these three things are very different, reflecting different market niches and their value systems. Focus on a single core competence brought TA Enterprises to where it is today, and we wonder whether the blurring of that focus will serve the company well. As Kotler has said, the principal cause of failure is success, suggesting that it becomes too easy for companies to believe that whatever they do, they will be successful. This is a lesson Alphatec's Charn knows well.

Blue Bird Taxi, meanwhile, remains one of the most focused companies examined in this study. It does nothing but provide ground transportation services to its clients, who are at the very least fairly well off to be able to afford being chauffeured around Jakarta. Like Royal Sporting House, Café de Coral has expanded up and down the value chain, with varying degrees of success. Clearly, however, its principal business will remain Chinese fast food served at Jollibee-like stores. These examples show that while success provides many opportunities for growing business, it also presents many temptations. Hamel and Prahalad's warning that managers must be constantly vigilant in maintaining the integrity of their core competence could well be expanded to include vigilance with respect to focus.

Not a New Company Preserve

It should not be assumed that companies that belong to a conglomerate are always less competitive than companies that have grown up independent of any of the major conglomerates. While it is true that it is much harder to find a dynamic company within most conglomerates, they are out there. We have referred to Hong Kong's First Pacific Group, run autonomously by Asia's largest conglomerate, the Salim Group. First Pacific's Smart Communi-cations in the Philippines is one of the most market-savvy companies in the region. At one time, the Shangri-La Hotels set a standard for world-class hotels all over the world to benchmark. Sadly, that luster is beginning to fade.

Cycle & Carriage is part of the Jardine Group and one of the tightest run companies in this study. That is not hard to understand, given the extraordinarily difficult conditions under which Cycle & Carriage sells automobiles. The company is also mostly focused, although it would like to think of itself as diversifying into real estate and food products, perhaps because, as de Geus notes, new businesses may be completely unrelated to the current business. Indeed, in the study by Porras and Collins, many of the visionary companies started off doing something quite different from what they are doing today. Nevertheless, there is considerable room for expansion in Cycle & Carriage's core business, and it is unlikely that its present expertize will lend itself to such diversified activities as real estate development – more an opportunity than a strategy, in fact – and food processing.

Protecting Core Competence and Preserving Focus

We have taken the concepts of core competence and focus and suggested that they are more than complementary; indeed, in the firms taken up in this chapter core competence is a product of determined focus. Focus has evolved into a complex system of competencies, some of which are core competencies. We agreed with Hamel and Prahalad that core competencies evolve from people, and that these enlightened firms realized this very early in their development, taking the steps that would preserve that competence by creating a sense of mission and community among employees.

We have also suggested that a number of the companies in this study presently demonstrate the four qualities de Geus identified in enduring corporations. At the same time, we have said that we are not sure these companies will maintain their focus or the personality traits of enduring companies. Indeed, there are danger signs as cor-porations succumb to the temptation, most frequently, to participate in Asia's real estate love feast. Real estate – with the possible excep-tions of Jollibee and Café de Coral – operates on completely different systems from those that made these six companies the successes they are. For these two, real estate for operations is a key success factor in fulfilling the promises they have made to their customers.

Of these companies, only Alphatec faces immediate, serious threat, although there are threats to continued high growth rates. For Cycle & Carriage, that threat evolves from government regulation; for Alphatec, it is the volatility of the global semiconductor market. All of these companies have revolutionized their industries in ways encompassing new product development to the marketing of semiconductors. With Asian economies hot but showing the strain of sustaining high growth, they must now begin to think about what it will take to protect their core competencies and preserve focus. Hamel and Prahalad suggest that their goal should not be to "'hardwire' the core competence into the organization through structural changes, but to 'softwire' the perspective into the heads of every manager and employee. This means 1) establishing a deeply involving process for identifying core competencies; 2) involving strategic business units in a cross-corporate process for developing a strategic architecture and setting competence acquisition goals; 3) defining a clear set of corporate growth and new business development priorities;

4) establishing explicit 'stewardship' roles for core competencies; 5) setting up an explicit mechanism for allocating critical core competence resources; 6) benchmarking competence-building efforts against rivals; 7) regularly reviewing the status of existing and nascent core competencies; 8) building a community of people within the organization who view themselves as the 'carriers' of corporate core competencies."[12]

That sounds rather complex, and it is. Perhaps it can just as well be said that successful companies like the above must begin to build an awareness of what made them great among their employees and other stakeholders. An important part of that awareness will be: 1) understanding that success does not beget success; indeed, quite the opposite; and 2) that there will always be the need to re-create success, because the global marketplace is not static. As Porter suggests, every advantage is a temporary one. Strategic advantage requires a well thought out series of temporary advantages that will continue the revolution these companies began.

---

[12] *Ibid.*, p. 235

Chapter Nine

☆

ALLIANCES AND
JOINT VENTURES

"Asian companies," according to Asia's legendary advisor and investment counselor Washington SyCip, "have been practicing the art of the virtual corporation for years. It is not new, it is business as usual." He was referring, of course, principally to joint ventures between the region's conglomerates. As we pointed out in the last chapter, none of these conglomerates has ever on its own invested in original, value-added technology. When SyCip talks of alliances between Asian conglomerates, he speaks of opportunistic marriages of convenience, not strategic development or value-added manufacturing and services.

As SyCip correctly argues, the Asian Development Bank in its *1996-1997 Asian Development Outlook* report identifies a bias for intra-Asian investment among Asian corporations, with direct foreign investment flows from Indonesia and Malaysia even more strongly intra-regionally biased than flows from Hong Kong and Singapore.[1] Overall, the report states, "the share of intra-Asian foreign direct investment

---

[1] _____, *1996–1997 Asian Development Outlook*, Asian Development Bank, 1996, p. 197.

(FDI) in total Asian FDI has increased. This increase is partly a result of the liberalization of FDI in the region and partly the result of the opportunities for investment created by high rates of growth. It is also partly the result of the liberalization of trade in goods and services which has encouraged the transfer of some productive activities to new, more competitive locations."[2]

The ADB says that it is impossible to analyze these investments by industry, but Victor Fung, chairman of Li & Fung and the Hong Kong Development Council, says, "We're seeing a new kind of networking going on in Asia among the overseas Chinese."[3] By new, it is suggested that these investments represent "support alliances," rather than investments intended to convey a controlling interest. "The push (for these alliances) came from rapid economic growth, which led many Asian firms to outgrow their traditional markets. The pull, from new opportunities to expand into previously closed markets."[4] Clearly, this is the type of investment of which SyCip speaks.

We argue that a supporting alliance is not a strategic alliance, particularly if it is outside the corporation's core business. It is, rather, an investment, facilitated by liberalization of trade and FDI. A strategic alliance should provide competitive benefits and be undertaken to position the partners in an industry.

If we accept the notion that strategic alliances are intended to generate focused opportunity rather than exploitation of diversified opportunity, it would be safe to say that there are few true strategic alliances among Asian firms. (We do not consider investments in low value-added, labor-intensive manufacturing strategic alliances.) There are even fewer that work, but this appears to be the pattern outside Asia as well.

---

[2] *Ibid.*, p. 201.

[3] Perton, Mark and Stephen Stine, "Here Comes Chinese Capital: A New Era for Asian M & A," *Asia, Inc.*, March 1993.

[4] Perton, Mark and Stephen Stine.

Indeed, "the mere convergence of strategic objective is not enough to make a cooperative venture work," Philippe Lasserre and Hellmut Schütte observe.[5] Neither is it sufficient to constitute a true strategic alliance.

Name an Alliance

"Quick, name an alliance that has been a spectacular success," Ries asks. "The truth is, most alliances have been disappointments to their principals. They drain money, resources, and management time into unproductive areas. Alliances unfocus a corporation."[6] Ries cites the example of IBM, Apple, and Motorola and their PowerPC chip. The chip has done little for Apple, disadvantaged IBM by forcing it to support two separate technology standards, and "helped Motorola sell a few more chips," despite great fanfare when the alliance was launched. There are exceptions – "At Hewlett Packard, the saying is now mantra: 'Partner or die'." Still, happy experiences such as H–P's are rare. "A highly hyped pairing of MCI Communications and Rupert Murdoch's News Corporation, for instance, hit the skids the moment MCI agreed to merge with British Telecom. US West's three-year-old marriage with Time Warner produced a nasty lawsuit over the Time Warner-Turner merger and now seems on the verge of dissolution. And in the transportation world, USAir was stunned when its bedfellow British Airways went behind its back to arrange a virtual merger with rival American Airlines."

"When someone says they're interested in a strategic alliance, says Robert C. Miller, chairman and president of computer-maker NeTpower, what they really mean is how do I convert your assets to my cash flow."[7]

The record for outright mergers is also mixed. "A survey of

---

[5] Lasserre, Philippe and Hellmut Schütte, *Strategies for Asia Pacific*, MacMillan Business, 1995.

[6] Ries, Al, *Focus: The Future of Your Company Depends on It*, Harper Collins, 1996.

[7] Thomas, Jr., Emory, "Bitter allies: partnerships for the '90's, MSNBC, 1996.

more than 300 big mergers over the past ten years by Mercer Manage-ment Consulting, a consultancy based in New York, found that, in the three years following the transactions, 57% of the merged firms lagged behind their industries in terms of total returns to shareholders. The long-run failure rate appears to be even higher."[8]

Nevertheless, in the past two years, top U.S. corporations have "formed more than 6,000 alliances – defined as something less than a merger and more than a client-supplier relationship. About 15% of the revenue generated by the top 1,000 public companies in the country now comes from alliances,"[9] and the number is growing about 20% a year.

"Experts cite several reasons for the trend: Technologies are growing and converging so quickly that no single company can be expert in multiple areas; research and development is often too expensive to do alone; a company needs a cash infusion; globalization means companies need allies that know the lay of the land in foreign countries."[10] Most alliances fit neatly into three categories:

- A Love-Hate Relationship, typical among strange bedfellows with common enemies;
- Hedging Bets, or shots in the dark in hopes of dominating emerging trends and technologies; and,
- One In a Million, that rare worthwhile relationship.

These three relationships may involve non-transactional agreements to cooperate, joint venture agreements, and joint development of technology. However, Lasserre and Schütte argue that foreign investors appear to be driven by three major forces in choosing partners in Asia, all mundane. "The first is a political imperative (the will of local governments); the second is a competitive imperative (the need to acquire local resources, assets, and competencies in order to compete

---

[8] _____, "Why too many mergers miss the mark," *The Economist*, January 4, 1997.

[9] Thomas, Jr., Emory.

[10] *Ibid.*

more effectively); and the third is a risk-sharing imperative (to hedge against adverse conditions when the stakes in the investment are high)."[11] None of these reasons provide the basis of a strategic alliance, because they are intended to address artificial hurdles to business and not to contribute to sustainable competitive advantage.

Lasserre and Schütte also provide an analysis of strategic fit, as shown in Table 9.1. Please note that this analysis is based principally on joint venture alliances between Asian and Western firms. It is doubtful, however, that the analysis would vary substantially in the case of intra-Asian investment. This would be particularly true in the case of Japanese or Korean investment, for example, in an ASEAN-member nation. Diversity of culture and development status within ASEAN itself also suggests that the basic framework presented will hold.

As in the case of the Western alliances cited above, Lasserre and Schütte observe, "when the motivation of both partners is to gain access to the other partner's resources, assets, or competencies (two extractive motives), the stability of the joint venture is a function of the length of time that the partners take to absorb or extract what they need from one another. When this process is complete, interest in continuing the collaboration often wanes."[12]

The One In a Million alliance comes about when "the long-term objectives or motives of the partners are compatible. In this case, firms pool some of their assets, resources, and competencies in order to reach goals which they could not attain individually."[13]

The prestige and quality of the organizations involved does not seem to strengthen relationships entered into as a result of political imperative or short-term access and gain. Take, for example, the joint venture between two of the region's top

---

[11] Lasserre, Philippe and Hellmut Schütte, p. 172.

[12] *Ibid.*, p. 184.

[13] *Ibid.*, p. 172.

Table 9.1

		Foreign Partner		
		Build New Business (Venturing Motive)	**Extract Market Knowledge** (Extractive Motive)	**Comply with Law to make a 'Deal'** (Opportunistic Motive)
Local Partner	**Build New Business** (Venturing Motive)	Child Strategy Basis for long-term success is present	Stable in the short term Potential conflicts arise very rapidly	Asian partner may feel frustrated by lack of clear vision support from partner
	Extract Technology (Extractive Motive)	Stable in the short term Potential conflicts arise very rapidly	Short-term stability Conflicts will arise when a 'learning' period is over	Conflicts will appear very rapidly
	Benefit from Political Rent (Opportunistic Motive)	Can be successful if the Western partner is self-sufficient High risk of frustration	Western partner may feel frustrated by lack of operational support from partner	High risk of frustration and misunderstanding
	Financial Investment (Opportunistic Motive)	Can be successful if the Western partner is self-sufficient	Chances of failure are high, especially if the Western partner is not familiar with the environment	Chances of failure are high, especially if the Western partner is not familiar with the environment

companies in this study, Ayala in the Philippines and Singapore Telecom. Ayala is the largest conglomerate in the Philippines and is highly respected. Singapore Telecom has long set the standard for quality, as we learned much earlier. Near market saturation in Singapore, the introduction of competition, and the government mandate to sustain growth through international investment were the motivation for the company's major expansion initiatives in Indonesia and the Philippines.

Ayala Corporation, seeking to diversify into new, value-oriented technology industries – a strategy we have raised strong concern over – provided the second half of a classic extractive relationship. Ayala and Singapore Telecom each own 38% of Globe Telecom, a full service telecommunications company and one of three new cellular communications providers allowed to operate in the Philippines following industry deregulation in 1994.

Unlike Smart Communications, Globe chose to compete on the basis of quality of service and technology, and introduced digital cellular technology to the Philippines. The company has promoted itself on the basis of its "uncloneable" technology and "strong sponsorship technically and financially," as a result of the alliance between Ayala and Singapore Telecom. The company also offers long-distance services, and has made significant investments in various submarine facilities to link the company's network to ASEAN, Taiwan, Korea, Australia, and Japan, as well as North America and Europe. The partnership has been an interesting case study in intra-Asian relationships, primarily because it held such promise but has lost so much money.

Globe's losses in 1996 increased 383% to P751 million (US$30 million) from P155 million (US$6.2 million) in 1995. Although the company's phones are immune to cloning – a problem that older technology cellular networks are plagued with – the company proved to be particularly susceptible to subscriber fraud. Financial controls and account approval procedures were no match for ingenious thieves opening accounts – and running up huge bills – under fictitious names. As a result, the company took a P441 million (US$17.6 million) write-off in 1996.

Those controls were supposed to be part of Singapore Telecom's contribution to the partnership. As an experienced cellular operator, Singapore Telecom was expected to provide the financial expertise and systems required to qualify customers and track calls for billing.

That expertise has proved wanting, not only in terms of subscriber fraud resulting in huge write-offs, but also in tracking calls, particularly regional roaming and fax and data calls. In April 1997, for instance, subscribers were receiving bills for calls made a year earlier.

Both Ayala and Singapore Telecom have received numerous awards for their management and quality of operations. In many ways, those qualities – service is excellent, for instance – have translated into the Globe-Singapore Telecom joint venture. However, the quality of these firms has not translated into market leadership in the Philippines. In fact, Globe has just 5% of the market, while its competitor Smart Communications has zoomed from zero to market leader, even displacing the long-entrenched market leader. Of the 112,000 land lines Globe has installed, only 12,000 have been subscribed. Despite Globe's substantial losses, under the terms its license was granted it must continue to install land lines. By the first quarter of 1998, the joint venture must roll out another 688,000 lines, requiring further and substantial investment on top of mounting operating losses.

Happy partnerships are always characterized by profitability. Unprofitable partnerships are almost always unhappy. It was not surprising when media reports in early 1997 were beginning to suggest that the Ayala–Singapore Telecom tandem was not a happy affair. Although top management of Ayala immediately and forcefully denied these reports, Singapore Telecom was believed to be unhappy with the prospect of further investment in the hugely unprofitable venture. Ayala, meanwhile, was concerned that it maintain its reputation for integrity, including meeting its commitments to the government to add new land lines. Both companies, understandably, were unhappy with the negative publicity. However, Ayala has many other profitable companies in industries spanning real estate to semiconductor manufacturing, and all are highly competitive. Singapore Telecom is still a virtual monopoly. As this manuscript was being finalized, cellular communications in Singapore had just been opened up to two other operators. Fixed lines remain a monopoly until the year 2000. Skeptism in Singapore about the capacity of Singapore Telecom to withstand competitive pressures has caused the stock to take a beating.

Failure of Mergers and Alliances

The Singapore Telecom alliance is not Ayala's only unhappy experience with international joint ventures. Ayala's overseas arm is selling its 50% interest in PT Sinar Purefoods International, owned with Indonesia's PT Sinar Mas Tunggal. That operation has managed to break even in only one year since 1991.

A recent report on the failure of mergers suggested that frequently the acquirer was obsessed with making the deal but paid too little attention to what happened next. That could very well explain many of the problems Globe has experienced. Ayala, market tested and proven, should not have experienced the indignity of seeing Smart in little more than three years become the dominant cellular provider, leaving Globe with substantially less than 10% of the market. Perhaps it was the obsession with doing business with the highly respected Singapore Telecom that deflected attention away from the realities of a competitive marketplace. For Singapore Telecom's part, liberalization on the horizon and pressure to sustain growth could have given rise to obsession as well. The Philippines was a vacuum. The dominant industry player was lethargic and poorly managed. The only other player was rumored to be owned by the same family that controlled the industry leader. Two new competitors – Smart and Islacom (originally a joint venture between a local Philippine firm and Thailand's Shinawatra) – could draw on experience in Hong Kong and Thailand, but neither could come close to rivaling the reputation of Singapore Telecom. Ayala was the Philippines' largest conglomerate. Who would not be obsessed?

Obsession, unfortunately, creates tunnel vision and overconfi-dence. Success does not evolve from the assumption of success, and it frequently contributes to failure. It has been a factor contributing to Globe's difficulties: 1) Two great companies; 2) little competition; 3) "superior" technology. But having all the right parts in the right place is of little value when some or all of the assumptions turn out to be wrong. Smart, despite its reliance on analog technology already available in the marketplace, became a formidable competitor and learned to change the rules of competition in the industry. Globe's superior technology produced a false sense of security, allowing other financial controls to lapse. Ironically, the security features provided by digital technology against eavesdropping have also recently come into question.

Smart, on the other hand, appears to have been as successful at managing relationships as it has been in managing the marketplace. Japan's giant NTT owns just 15% of the company and brings the expertise and technology Smart required to develop its land lines network. NTT will help Smart introduce a new line of multimedia services in 1998, which include video conferencing and Internet access. Of course, it is still much easier to manage relationships when the bottom line is in good shape.

Proton and Mitsubishi

Another high-profile Asian partnership is that between Malaysian car manufacturer Proton and Mitsubishi of Japan. Proton's first model was based on a Mitsubishi design, and all major components were provided by the Japanese company. Over the years, local content has increased, but the technology required to manufacture major components, the engine and the drive train, remain locked away from Proton and safely in the hands of Mitsubishi.

Malaysian Prime Minister Mahathir Mohamad, widely revered in Japan, grew so weary of trying to convince Mitsubishi to transfer valuable technology to Proton that he helped forge a partnership between the Malaysian carmaker and France's Citroen. Unfortunately, that partnership has been hounded by the very same problem. The company's former chairman, Yahaya Ahmad, who died tragically in a helicopter crash in 1997, purchased 80% of British carmaker Lotus in October 1996, in order to leap the technology hurdle. "Several Lotus engineers are currently attached to

Proton's R&D division," according to Yahaya's successor, CEO Saleh Sulong.

Across the region, partnerships and alliances are mostly troubled, and although the reasons vary, ultimately rocky relationships are traced to the partners' overriding concern with what they are getting out of – and giving up for – the relationship. In Indonesia, for example, no foreign company can be legally registered. Companies that want to do business in Indonesia must find a local partner, which may be real or may be a front. While most of the companies in Indonesia may actually prefer to have a local partner, the fact that they have no choice is not a very positive basis for a relationship. Japanese companies are particularly notorious for withholding technology and benefits from affiliates.

Take Indonesia's huge automobile assembler and manufacturer Astra, for example. To finance the import of key components into Indonesia, the company obtained yen-denominated loans from its Japanese partners, principally Toyota. When the yen began to appreciate, Astra faced severe foreign exchange losses. Its Japanese partners resisted pressure to reduce Astra's obligation and enjoyed windfall profits. Only when the company's predicament made international headlines did its Japanese partners reluctantly agree to a conservative refinancing of the giant assembler's obligations.

As foreign investment liberalizes, Asian companies sometimes may also find themselves being taken over by their overseas partners, such as Matsushita Electronics' operations in the Philippines, originally called Precision Electronics. Although the Filipino founder, upon retirement, enthusiastically entered the agreement conveying his interest to the Japanese manufacturer, other companies in Asia may find themselves takeover targets as restrictions against majority-held corporations are eased. It is difficult to imagine Kumpulan Barkath, for instance, making the licensing deals it made at the apex of import substitution today. Its existing agreement and distribution network will act as a barrier to takeover for a few more years, but there is little long-term value for Sunquick, for example, to continue to share profits with the company. Likewise, more Japanese, North American, and European companies will find themselves takeover targets as restrictions there ease as well. There are already a number of instances in which Hong Kong and Singapore companies have acquired control of Japanese firms, such as Hong Kong's Semi-Tech's acquisition of bankrupt Sansui Electric.

The Nature of Alliances

Alliances in Asia will likely give way to a wave of mergers and acquisitions in an expanding, liberalized Asian economy. Vibrant, developing capital markets provide an alternative to both traditional debt financing as well as bringing in deep pockets from within Asia or internationally. For international firms, always hesitant to truly transfer leading-edge technology, the precedence that job generation and export growth have increasingly taken over nationalist interests now provides the opportunity to establish wholly owned corporations in most of Southeast Asia. While the value of political connections may continue to encourage alliances with local partners, the importance of those connections will also continue to decline in importance across the region, although the pace of reform will vary.

Sustained high levels of foreign investment in the U.S. suggest that as the Asian economy continues to grow, foreign investment will likewise flourish in a liberal environment. The example of Japan, where trade barriers have kept foreign investment a fraction of that in the U.S., further suggests that to sustain high levels of foreign investment, restrictions regulating investment must be liberalized. Unlike Japan, which received preferential treatment by the U.S. after World War II, Southeast Asian companies cannot expect to have the privilege of direct investment in the U.S. unless they provide reciprocal privileges in return as their local economies strengthen and the companies themselves grow. For governments to sustain high levels of growth, it will be critical that their private sectors export themselves to develop other Asian, North American, and European markets.

The difficulty in achieving the elusive One In a Million alliance further suggests that foreign direct investment in Southeast Asia will be increasingly outright mergers and acquisitions so long as Southeast Asian governments continue to liberalize. Pressure to liberalize will increase as Southeast Asian companies seek alternatives to sustain growth, and increasingly find those opportunities in other Southeast Asian countries and the global marketplace. Pressure to expand operations outside of principal domestic markets will also stimulate other changes. For example, Asian conglomerates will find it difficult to sustain highly diversified operations and investments unless they somehow learn to emulate the success of General Electric, which very few companies anywhere have been able to do. As Asian companies are forced to continually seek out sources of competitive advantage, they will find it impossible to spread financial and intellectual resources relatively thinly across highly diversified divisions. Investment will, therefore, be increasingly directed toward evolving core businesses that present new market development opportunities, the promise of technological advancement, and the recruitment of Asia's best minds.

The Future of the Deal

While deal making is as old an art in Asia as anywhere else, the nature of deals will change. Alliances will continue to flourish and be directed toward achieving short-term advantages or capitalizing on opportunities. However, strategic alliances are destined to be primarily acquisitions. The Asian psyche will hold off mergers for a good many years to come, but ultimately resource limitations and shareholder value concerns will make them more attractive to the generation of managers that takes over family conglomerates and businesses from their founders.

The danger to Asian companies here is what they will bring

to the table in terms of competitive advantage. That danger falls into two categories: 1) original technology; and 2) minds. As we have previously noted, the investment in fundamental, original Asian technology is practically nonexistent. Both Asian companies and governments must address this deficiency, because they will no longer be protected by artificial barriers to foreign competition and technology. Because there will be no barriers, the value of political connections will diminish greatly. While some countries, such as Indonesia with its very large population, may try to delay liberalization, these countries will feel severe pressure to open markets and reduce regulation, because this will be requisite to full participation in the global economy. Limited foreign direct investment will simply flow elsewhere, and this will restrict domestic growth. Exports will be limited from countries that do not reciprocate low global tariffs.

Seventy-nine percent of Asian FDI went to Indonesia, China and Singapore in 1996. However, investment in Indonesia and China contracted sharply when those governments began to actively intervene or reduce incentives. As a result, both governments have acted to restore their "investor-friendly" policies. Meanwhile, Singapore remains a high-value FDI destination.

Asian companies that do not have much to offer in terms of technological expertize will increasingly find themselves unable to compete despite established distribution networks, and will be perfect targets for acquisition. While research and development is expensive and takes time to develop, the alternative for Asian companies and governments is an economy dominated by multinational companies supported by networks of subcontractors and suppliers.

The second area of concern is people. With the exception of the top corporations in each country, the best people do not work for Asian companies. They try very hard to work for multinational companies, for a variety of reasons ranging from remuneration to workplace environment. We often note the dearth of management speakers in Asia, for example.

While there are many excellent professors and teachers in Asia, they have very little money available for original research compared to their North American and European counterparts. Because there is little original research, there is little original thought that comes out of Asia's academic community other than anecdotal recitation or esoteric murmuring about some supposed Asian way of doing business or Sun Tzu's battlefield techniques.

Critics will respond that management technology is communicated informally much more efficiently in Asia, in the same way that Asia's mysterious deal making takes place on the basis of friendship and a handshake. That is just wishful thinking. The fact is simply that research does not take place, and most of the credible research taking place in Asia is undertaken by international consulting firms. Management schools rely predominantly on Asian cases, though they pretend not to. In fact, they do not have the funds to do real case research. Harvard Business School's Asian cases would put any Asian business school's cases to shame. This is why we find Asia's top academic minds in America. That is where the support is; that is where the money is.

Likewise, domestic firms will have to compete for the best people on a level playing field with multinational corporations. The global marketplace is characterized by competition and the value of knowledge. Ultimately, all competitive advantage will reside in what people are about to do, not the technology they have already created. While a Filipino manager may want to return to Manila because it is home, he or she would have very little hesitation before going to work for a multinational bank, technology firm, or consumer products company. Loyalty resides in the Philippines but not for Filipino companies.

Many firms are scampering around in Malaysia, Indonesia, Thailand, and elsewhere in Southeast Asia consolidating industry footholds through new acquisitions, development of consortia, or government licenses. None of these will protect them from competition as liberalization continues its spread through the region. Companies like Thailand's Alphatec and the Philippines' Concepcion Industries have begun to develop the resources, culture, and people required to develop original technology, but it is a safe bet that most large Asian companies are nowhere near ready to truly compete.

It is those companies that will very soon find themselves involved in Asia's new wave of mergers and acquisitions, and it is quite unlikely that they will be doing the acquiring. Some of Asia's best have put together impressive alliances to both take advantage of new opportunities in just deregulated markets as well as consolidate their position within established industries. However, their record in forming successful alliances in competitive markets is spotty at best, and while they may provide limited short-term benefits, it is unlikely that many will provide long-term strategic benefits. Rather, it will be acquisitions that characterize industry shakeouts in a newly competitive Asia.

Chapter Ten

─────────── ☆ ───────────

COMPETING FOR THE FUTURE

The title for this chapter is borrowed from the management best-seller *Competing for the Future* by Hamel and Prahalad, two of this decade's most profound thinkers. As we have said, Hamel and Prahalad argue that industry leadership is held by companies that successfully change the rules of competition. To sustain success, companies must continually change the rules of competition in their industries. They change the rules by continually developing and nurturing core competencies that challenge the competition by raising standards of performance, quality, or value.

Asian companies and Southeast Asian countries are both competing vigorously for the future. As the 20th century draws to a close, it is also clear that the entire world seems to have awakened and decided to compete for the future at the same time. In Europe, South America, and even Africa we see signs of dramatic, profound reform in economic policy leading to liberalization of marketplaces, enhanced productivity, and prosperity. In these regions there is fierce competition for foreign direct investment – the capital funds required to catalyze economic development – among nations and among geographic-based trade blocks. Even in the U.S., characterize Asian business practices. And, while there are distinct business practices in Singapore, Malaysia, Thailand, Indonesia, Hong Kong, and the Philippines, they are just that: distinct from one another. What has been described as Asian values is a smoke-screen intended at times to project a specific agenda and at others merely business as usual. In reality, corruption, red tape, and dishonesty have also been fixtures of doing business in Southeast Asia, but we would hardly suggest that these practices, found in many different environments, evolve from Asian values. In the same manner, integrity, hard work, and family are not the exclusive distinguishing qualities of Asian countries, families, and businesses, although they do exist in abundance.

Second, conditions in Asia now and 30 years ago provide a remarkable contrast. During those three decades, Southeast Asia has transitioned from a war-torn, "economically protected," ethnically troubled region of great poverty and despair to a tremendously vibrant, economically prosperous, intellectually cosmopolitan marketplace that is setting world records for privatization and liberalization. Business practice – and culture – will obviously have to keep pace. A new generation of business leaders seems to be working hard to haul their diversified organizations and interests into a new era. Perhaps Anthony Salim best represents this new generation, and it is comforting that this unique and visionary leader is the product of the region's largest conglomerate.

Third, "If there's one message that Asia's economic miracle brings to the developing world, it's that liberalization works, competition works," according to Ms. Lee. To get to where it is now, Asia has competed on the basis of cheap labor, government incentives, and low operating costs. Development, and the awakening of Indochina and Eastern Europe, have erased those advantages. Asian governments and business in general have accepted the new reality that competitiveness will increasingly reside in what economists call Total Factor Productivity, regardless of whose definition they view with the greatest affinity. They are also finding that

the decade-long obsession, and despair, with Japanese competitiveness has given way to celebrations of technological leadership in many of the industries of the future: computer software, communications, and many areas of business and financial services.

Asia is largely responsible for this awakening. Sustained and rapid growth of Southeast Asia and Asian companies, particularly, has demonstrated to the global community that foreign investment, liberalization, and pro-business public policy dramatically change the circumstances of nations and their citizens. "Hong Kong and Singapore are both richer than Britain. China, Indonesia, Malaysia, and Thailand have started to chase the leaders' tails."[1] And, as happens in a free market environment, there is no shortage of die-hard emulators who know a good thing when they see it, especially when they see it so clearly. Among the problems of success that Southeast Asia is facing, therefore, is the threat of its admirers who want to do even better and are competing vigorously for foreign investment and opportunity.

That is a threat that M.I.T. economist Paul Krugman has done a great deal to bring to the forefront of Asian thinking. Although Krugman's ideas have been hotly debated and generally contested within Southeast Asia, that is not evident from the public policy actions of Southeast Asian governments in the wake of his 1994 *Foreign Affairs* article titled "The Myth of Asia's Miracle." Krugman argues in that article that Asian growth has been fueled by resource mobilization, capital, and labor, not enhanced productivity, or what economists call Total Factor Productivity. To illustrate his argument, Krugman suggests that the Singapore economy has developed in much the same way that the Soviet economy developed after World War II. More capital and increased labor utilization stimulated economic growth. However, the efficiency with which such factors as money, land, and technology were being used remained low. In other words,

[1] _____, The Asian Miracle: Is it over? *The Economist*, March 1, 1997, pp. 23–25.

more value could have reasonably been obtained from these factors as the economy grew.

Krugman's comparison was, not surprisingly, viewed as a public relations problem by the Singapore government. But while publicly refuting Krugman's arguments, Singapore, along with other Southeast Asian governments, is taking important steps to improve Total Factor Productivity. Singapore's Senior Minister Lee Kuan Yew told Krugman in a recent meeting, "Our Total Factor Productivity growth will be much higher in the future because of the investments we're making in education."[2]

Many economists believe Total Factor Productivity has been far greater than Krugman argues. That is because Total Factor Productivity is hard to measure: its measurement is "a black box exercise," according to Singaporean economist Lee Tsao Yuan. Krugman himself has evaluated Ms. Lee's work approvingly.[3] As reports by the World Bank and Swiss bank UBS have shown, Total Factor Productivity often depends on the return largely provided by "heroic assumptions" on the return on capital investment. World Bank economists provided a low return based on an average provided by 113 countries, which produced a high Total Factor Productivity value. "Mr. Krugman points to a section of that report that recalculates the results using a higher return on capital. Under that calculation, only Hong Kong, Japan, and Taiwan were catching up with the advanced world"[4] in Total Factor Productivity.

Krugman may be underestimating Total Factor Productivity for another reason: capital investment may, in fact, be financing increased productivity through the acquisition of new technology. However, Krugman's detractors cannot argue that education and original research and development work in Southeast Asia are sufficiently

robust to continue to provide sustained high Total Factor Productivity, even if their arguments against Krugman assumptions are accepted. "The country (Malaysia) will have to shift from an input-driven to a productivity-driven economy . . . by enhancing the contribution of Total Factor Productivity to growth," tycoon and top government advisor Daim Zainuddin recently said.

Singapore Trade and Industry Minister Yeo Cheow Tong worried about "our weaker R&D capabilities compared with developed countries and some NIEs."

Former Thai Deputy Prime Minister and Finance Minister Amnuay Viravan concurs: "No country can stand still. We have to keep upgrading and it gets harder as you go up."[5]

Based on the information provided by the companies that agreed to take part in this study, we have argued that they have succeeded as a result of hard work, astute marketing, quality of operations, and innovative approaches to developing their businesses as well as their markets. As is the case with many companies, a good portion of their fortune resides in luck, or being at the right place at the right time and having both the courage and the intelligence to recognize and exploit opportunity. We have also argued that past success is rarely a precursor of future success, and may in fact hinder success because of dangerous comfort levels with old ways and habits. An extraordinary number of Asian businesspeople and academics have tried hard to argue that the manner of doing business in Asia is suited to business as usual in response to arguments that Asian companies must change the way they operate to keep up with new business realities. We have, with a large dose of temerity, principally rejected those arguments on several grounds.

First, there is no *Asian* business culture. While there has definitely been a business culture evident among the large-sized but small number of Chinese conglomerates operating in Asia, it is simply wrong to suggest that those qualities

[2] Lehner, Urban C, "An Economist's Provocative Views Stir Anger and Debate Across Asia," *The Asian Wall Street Journal*, October 9, 1995.

[3] *Ibid.*

[4] *Ibid.*

[5] Saludo, Ricardo, "The Next Era," *Asiaweek*, January 10, 1997, pp. 34–42.

just as investment in physical infrastructure was insufficient in some Asian economies, investment in educational infrastructure has been insufficient to provide the growth in Total Factor Productivity that the countries require to sustain high growth.

Although belatedly, Asian governments are responding. In Singapore, for instance, "the government aims to equip 60% of the workforce with a post-secondary education, to raise R&D spending to 1.6% of GDP, and increase the number of scientists and engineers to 65 per 10,000 population. Singapore also plans to spend more than US$1 billion over five years on programs for creative thinking."[6]

The suggestion that educational infrastructure in Asia is inadequate is surprising, given how highly valued education is among Asian parents and how well Asian students perform academically. However, it may well be that the difficulty of obtaining an education, due to limited infrastructure, is in large part responsible for that premium. Limited opportunity also serves to widen the gap between the educated and the relatively uneducated. The other problem with educational infrastructure is that education has frequently been used as a political or cultural tool. During bouts with nationalism, Malaysia and the Philippines, for instance, promoted the use of national languages over English. Whether such policies actually increased the sense of national pride among citizens is hard to measure, but it clearly diminished the competitiveness of both countries and brought about conditions where there is a profound shortage of executives and workers who speak English comfortably as well as a dearth of competent English instructors.

But the biggest gap in educational infrastructure is in the capacity to teach the hard sciences, and to provide the faculty and facilities necessary to undertake original research. It is the capacity to undertake and capitalize on such research in the private sector that will ultimately determine whether

---

[6] Ibid.

Southeast Asian countries and companies will sustain growth. While we accept the premise that much of Southeast Asia has enough catching up to do with its better-off neighbors and trading partners to sustain rapid growth for another decade, it will take a decade of investment and development now, in areas that will increase Total Factor Productivity, to sustain growth thereafter. These are investments that cannot wait.

Fourth, there is no Asian management style or characteristic that is notably distinguishable from managementstyle – good or bad – anywhere else. There are transitory business practices that reflect local culture and the state of economic development – or, more accurately, individual prosperity. We have suggested that those practices, which largely evolve from the persona of company founders, are not necessarily more effective in terms of managing people and operations than the practices of Western managers. The mystique of Asian business practices frequently serves to protect Asian businesses from intruders within and without Asia. While relationships are important in transacting business, they are important in terms of demonstrating competence and performance rather than loyalty. Ultimately, the quality of the deal determines whether the deal prospers.

Fifth, the history of highly diversified corporations – with just one or two unique exceptions – in competitive environments shows that they perform poorly overall. This becomes an even more important consideration in Asia because none of the major conglomerates is an industry leader as a result of technological advances, innovative marketing practices, or original product development. None.

That does not mean they have not worked hard and done well. But it does mean they are vulnerable in every industry in which they operate. It also means that competitors will pick up on this vulnerability and exploit it. Asian conglomerates must, therefore, consolidate resources and look for ways to make, themselves, distinctly competitive in the industry in which they have the greatest strength.

Asia's Best

We have seen that Asia's Best have some extraordinary strengths, and some truly phenomenal accomplishments. They also have a great many challenges on the way to the future. If their performance in the past is any indication, they are clearly capable of recognizing and capitalizing on new opportunities. Most of them have the will to do so, and it is likely that many of these excellent organizations will continue to excel.

Excelling in the future is going to be every bit as hard as it was in the past. In fact, it is going to be harder. Providing Asia's Best match their past performance – or better it – over the next decade, what can we expect in the year 2010?

Most of the companies we have examined will be operating regionally and internationally to a much greater extent than they are now. Retail operations will likely be concentrated in Southeast Asia, although there will continue to be development in China, principally by the Hong Kong retailers such as Theme and Giordano. Companies like Royal Sporting House will grow aggressively throughout Asia, while low value-added manufacturing will largely be moved to Indochina and China. Thailand and Malaysia will form the core of the automotive industry, while Singapore and Malaysian firms will emerge as new hard technology developers and high value-added manufacturers. Alphatec will be the exception for Thailand and will – if it survives its current financial problems – become even more of an international than a Thai firm. Philippine companies will demonstrate leadership in service industries, including fast food, entertainment, and publishing. The country's large pool of engineers will provide the opportunity to challenge Malaysia as a high-technology manufacturing center, with companies like Intel and component manufacturers establishing some of their largest facilities in the country. Software development and manufacturing will also be a mainstay, provided Philippine companies can convince software engineers to stay put.

Hong Kong companies will continue to grow from the synergy of China's development but, ironically, will not make the technological advances that most of their counterparts in Southeast Asia must. The sheer volume of growth in China will preclude that necessity over the next decade, and sustain low value-added manufacturing of toys, appliances, textiles, and low-end semiconductors.

However, there are moves in Hong Kong to encourage government incentives for high-value added research and manufacturing. Poor educational infrastructure, however, will hinder these moves.

Indonesian companies will also find themselves displaced from low-end manufacturing as prosperity spreads. Companies like textile manufacturer Texmaco will seek to exploit the high end of their industries and will make significant investments in technology. To do this, they will need government support for overturning policies that favor labor-intensive industries. Government must also provide enhanced educational infrastructure for its huge population. Other than by the conglomerates, it is unlikely that much overseas expansion will take place. Although non-oil exports from Indonesia are on the rise, these are principally low value-added and agricultural products. Most companies will continue to look for ways to exploit the nearly 200-million strong market.

The most remarkable changes, though, will likely be in how much more like their Western counterparts all of the companies become. First, there will be fierce competition for the best minds. Because of limited educational infrastructure, it is likely that pressure will build to recruit managers and scientists from around the world, as companies in both Singapore and Malaysia have already started to do. Alphatec has raised the practice to an art form, importing both Western expatriates and Chinese engineers.

Second, decision making will be pushed down the line to enable companies to respond quickly to rapidly changing market conditions. This will require a huge change in culture and values, as companies go horizontal.

Third, there will be even bigger investments in education internally, as companies wait for increased government investment in educational infrastructure to mature and pay off. There will be great opportunities for management educators and trainers, although it is doubtful that business schools will have the financial resources required to put them on par with their western counterparts. Technology will make a western MBA more accessible to Asian students.

Fourth, much of that investment in education will be directed toward the development of original technology leading to new products.

Fifth, as a result of the emphasis on new product development, companies will try to learn how to market and advertise original Asian products as world-class brands in the way that Giordano has set the pace in apparel and Acer is trying to do with personal computers.

Sixth, there will be heavy reliance on technology to market products. The ordinary businessperson may never have to set foot in a bank, instead transacting business from the comfort of his office or hotel room via computer. Exporters will increasingly make their product catalogue available over the World Wide Web, updating it daily if necessary. There will be fewer support personnel as organizations link themselves electronically, bypassing the secretarial pool.

Seventh, there will be much greater individual accountability, commensurate with the high wages paid to recruit top minds. The chances of flame out will be greater and the effects more profound on the executive's career.

Eighth, executives will be expected not just to be accountable, but also to be more productive. Revenue and cost per employee will become key indicators of profitable operations, as well as return on cost of sales and investment.

Ninth, there will be much more loyalty to the firm. Retaining the best minds will be a matter of one part remuneration and one part inspiration and challenge. Ultimately, there must be something better than money, because someone will always be willing to pay more.

Final Thoughts

When this project first started seven years ago, a group of very successful, highly respected businessmen from around the world gathered to review our plans for searching out Asian companies that had distinguished themselves in the development and the quality of their operations. Many of this group said that the project would wind up focusing on multinationals, since few Asian firms could match their management expertise or volume. Others suggested that the Asian business community was still a bit of a frontier town, and it could be embarrassing to pick out an organization and hold it up as an example of excellent management in Asia. And indeed, a number of the companies that took part in the program suffered a reverse in fortunes to varying degrees after their recognition. As Tom Peters remarked of the companies profiled in *In Search of Excellence*, the principles still applied, the companies just forgot them. Others were unable to deal with changing circumstances politically, in the marketplace, or with the founding families.

While no company is perfect in every way, the companies involved in this study were all excellent in some important way. Among them are companies such as Mustika Ratu and Alphatec, which have proved worthy competitors to some of the world's top companies in their industries. There is Blue Bird Taxi, which is remarkable in that it provides what should be a straightforward service better than any other company in Asia. Royal Sporting House distinguishes itself by making merchandising a profession, and innovation a standard business practice. Giordano was founded by a legendary and controversial marketer who revolutionized the boutique retailing industry and left behind managers capable of dealing with great challenges. Companies like Smart Communications have proven that a strong founding vision and entrepreneurial zeal can provide the energy required to do simply extraordinary things, while a conglomerate like Ayala still sets the industry standard, a standard founded on integrity and value. Cycle & Carriage has prospered in

Singapore under the harshest regulations an automobile retailer could imagine, and Kumpulan Barkath first turned adversity to advantage through the acquisition of technology and market rights. It went on to develop a distribution and marketing network impressive by any standard.

Watch these companies. This is a determined lot. No doubt there are many more out there that demonstrate a similar passion to succeed. And note that none of them succeeded by common myth. They earned every success they have. And for the most part, they are competing for the future.

APPENDIX

THE COMPANIES

Brief company summaries are provided in this section. Each of the companies or agencies profiled was a formal participant in the study. The information contained in the summaries was provided by the companies and verified at the time of submission by our research team. Over the course of the study, many changes took place in these organizations, and we have attempted to bring this information up-to-date as of the time the final manuscript was submitted to the publisher. Last minute updates were included as the book was going to press.

Where appropriate or necessary, we have provided additional comments. The best example of this is the first company in the summary, Alphatec. Alphatec was moving through a very serious period as this project wound up, and it was not clear whether the company would be able to successfully restructure itself and "get back on the track." The company illustrates beautifully one of the principal themes of this book: success does not beget success. It is hoped that eventually it will illustrate another: although the "Asian growth miracle" is not a guarantee of sustainable success, companies that eventually make the right decisions after major setbacks can recover and become successful.

Alphatec Electronics Public Co. Ltd.

Founding Concept: To establish an organization that would become Asia's leading semiconductor manufacturer and assembler.

Country of Operations: Thailand

Description of Operations: Alphatec is the largest and leading integrated circuits (IC) assembly and testing company in Thailand. Its business portfolio recently expanded to include semiconductor assembly and manufacturing, and the company is attempting to complete two wafer production facilities.

Address: 17/2 Moo 18, Suwinthawong Road, Tambon Saladang, Amphur Bang-num-priow, Chasoengsao 24000, Thailand
Tel: (662) 229-4670/229-4680-84
Fax: (662) 229-4675/229-4677

Date Founded and History: The company was founded in 1988 by Charn Uswachoke, who resigned as CEO in July 1997 following reports by auditors of phantom profits. He remains a director of Alphatec and chairman of the Alphatec Group. The company began operations in 1990 with the assembly and testing of hermetic IC packages. The company is building two semiconductor wafer production plants, a dynamic random access memory plant, and a high-tech industrial park, all of which are firsts in Thailand.

Current Leadership: Robert Mollerstuen, President and Acting Chief Executive

Significant Events: Two years after beginning operations, the company began assembly and final testing for plastic IC packages. Between 1992 and 1994, it acquired the local operations of National Electronics in Thailand; also acquired Alphatel (a local subsidiary of AT&T); and established Alphatec Electronics Corporation of Shanghai. In 1995 it entered into a number of significant ventures: the acquisition of Indy Corp. in California; the start of construction of a $1.5 billion semiconductor wafer fabrication plant called Submicron, the country's first – in a joint venture with Texas Instruments; the start of the first phase of its US$1.2 billion dynamic random access memory (DRAM) plant, also with Texas Instruments; and the construction of Alphatechnopolis, the country's first high-tech industrial plant. In 1997 Texas Instruments withdrew from its partnerships with the company, following difficulty arranging financing for the projects. Analysts expressed doubts in August 1997 that the once successful company would survive its current troubles intact. However, the company has convinced bondholders not to declare the company in default pending submission of a restructuring plan.

New Markets or Products Being Pursued: Prior to the crisis brought on by plummeting semiconductor prices and TI's withdrawal from the Submicron partnership, Alphatec had initiated expansion to wafer production technology, in order to fulfil its vision of becoming a one-stop center for semiconductor companies. The company had hoped to become a production-testing-research and development center for semiconductors.

*Gross Sales: 1994   US$353 million
1995   US$432 million

AMMB Holdings Berhad

Founding Concept: To sustain the collective position of its operating companies as a premier financial services group providing innovative products and services.

Country of Operations: Malaysia

Description of Operations: A fully integrated financial company that includes Malaysia's largest merchant bank and the third largest finance company, AMMB Holdings boasts investments in insurance, stock brokerage, and leasing.

Address: 22/F Bangunan Arab Malaysian 55, Jalan Raja Chulan, 50200 Kuala Lumpur, Malaysia
Tel: (603) 238-2633
Fax: (603) 238-2442

---

*An audit by Price Waterhouse in July 1997 "found that Alphatec had created fake purchase orders to show profits that never existed. The company overstated its 1995 and 1996 profit by 1.8 billion baht each year, and 1997's first quarter earnings by 500 million baht. But Alphatec, in fact, had losses totaling 2.88 billion baht for those periods." (*The Asian Wall Street Journal*, July 29, 1977, p. 1.)

WWW: http//www.jaring.mylat-asia/ambg.html
http//www.mol.com.my/ambg/ambg.html
http//www.mol-USA.com/ambg/ambg.html

Date Founded and History: The company was incorporated on August 15, 1991, to implement the corporate restructuring of Arab Malaysian Merchant Bank (AMMB). It was created through a "scheme" involving the acquisition of the entire issued and fully paid shares of AMMB. Today, it manages 22 subsidiaries and six associated companies.

Current Leadership: Tan Sri Dató Azman Hashim, Chairman
Dató Azlan Hashim, Deputy Chairman

Significant Events: The formation of the holding company has strengthened the group's capital structure and created a sound, flexible financial base to support growth and diversification. This move eased pressure on AMMB Holdings to provide funding for the expansion of its subsidiaries. As a result, AMMB has been able to improve the stream of dividends to shareholders while increasing its flexibility in raising capital for the operating companies.

Gross Sales: 1994   US$644.2 million
1995   US$704.3 million

Andersen Consulting Sdn. Bhd.

☆

Founding Concept: To provide Malaysian companies with competitive consulting services and to facilitate their corporate structural changes.

Country of Operations: Malaysia

Description of Operations: Andersen Consulting Sdn. Bhd. is a management and information technology consultancy firm, principally focused on business integration.

Address: 26/F Menara Tun Razak, Jalan Raja Laut, 50350 Kuala Lumpur, Malaysia

Tel: (603) 293-5133
Fax: (603) 293-5360
WWW: http://www.ac.com
http://www.jaring.mylackl/html/i-itr-5.htm

Date Founded and History: Andersen Consulting Sdn. Bhd. traces its roots to a firm of five staff members established in 1979. Then known as Administrative Services Sdn. Bhd., it subsequently underwent a merger with Samad and Co., an audit firm. The firm was later known as Management Information Consulting Division, Arthur Andersen & Co. In 1989, it became Andersen Consulting.

Current Leadership: Larry N. L. Gan,
Country Managing Partner
Michael Henry, Manager

Biggest Challenge: The astounding growth of the Asia Pacific region paved the way for rapid growth of the consulting sector. The rise of small upstarts with expertise in specific technologies, combined with a serious shortage of skilled manpower, has posed a major challenge to the company. In response, the company has continually sought to strengthen its ability to deliver integrated business solutions. The company initiated a Career Development Model – a program designed to enhance people management, from recruitment to training to compensation. This effort was undertaken to assure that the firm attracts and maintains the best people with broader, deeper and more focused skills in delivering business integration.

Andersen Consulting Singapore

Founding Concept: To provide competitive consulting services and to facilitate corporate structural changes for companies to become more successful.

Country of Operations: Singapore

Description of Operations: Andersen Consulting

Singapore is a management and information technology consultancy firm, principally focused on business integration.

Address: 152 Beach Road, #18-01/04, Singapore 189721
Tel: (65) 290-8943
Fax: (65) 291-7177

Date Founded and History: Andersen Consulting Singapore is one of the earliest information technology (IT) consulting firms in the city-state. It was founded in 1975 and is a member of Andersen Consulting, the global management and IT consultancy.

Current Leadership: Willie Cheng,
Country Managing Partner
Corinne Tan, Marketing Manager

Significant Events: Andersen Consulting Singapore was the first consulting firm to receive ISO 9000 certification in the country. Most of its information technology programs have received citations or awards from national and regional bodies.

Asia Fiber Public Public Company Limited

Founding Concept: To become the country's largest and leading producer of textile products.

Country of Operations: Thailand

Description of Operations: Asia Fiber Public Company is the largest and most integrated textile manufacturer in Thailand.

Products: Nylon chips, nylon filament and textured yarns, filament woven fabrics

Address: 27/F Wall Street Tower, 33/133-136 Surawongse Road, Bangkok 10500, Thailand
Tel: (662) 632-7071
Fax: (662) 236-1982
E-mail: afenyg@kse.th.com

Date Founded and History: Asia Fiber Public Company was formed through the merger of Asia Fiber Co., Ltd. and Asia Synthetic Textile Co. in 1975. Its aggressive expansion has made the company the largest manufacturer of nylon since 1990.

Current Leadership: Snit Viravan, Chairman
Pipat Sirikietsoong, Vice Chairman
Namchai Namchaisiri, Vice Chairman
Akadej Prathuangsit, President

Biggest Challenge: Competition, particularly in the manufacture of nylon woven fabric, Asia Fiber's principal product, has dented profitability. Performance has been further hampered by Thailand's severe economic downturn. Despite weak market conditions, the company has successfully expanded export markets and shifted production priority to nylon chips. This shift has helped the company weather the effects of the devaluation of the Thai baht.

Significant Events: The company is the industry leader in new technologies and, consequently, new products in the Thai market. Among the products the company pioneered were nylon pre-oriented yarn, nylon fully-drawn yarn, nylon-drawn texture yarn, and nylon-woven fabrics manufactured with water jet looms. Most, if not all, of these products are being produced using high-efficiency, high-productivity, and step-reduction process technology with equipment developed by the company's in-house research and development group.

Gross Sales: 1994   US$64.1 million
1995   US$70.0 million
1996   US$67.1 million
1997   US$72.8 million

Asian Institute of Technology

Founding Concept: To provide advanced education and research skills in engineering, management, planning, science and technology, and the interfacing of these specializations, to serve the economic and social needs of the region, with the ultimate goal of environmentally, socially, and economically sustainable development.

Country of Operations: Thailand

Description of Operations: The Asian Institute of Technology (AIT) is an international, autonomous graduate school established in 1959, providing education conducting research and offering outreach through its four schools: Advanced Technologies; Civil Engineering; Environment, Resources and Development; and Management; and in seven centers, two of which are located in Vietnam.

Address: 58, Mu 9, Phahonyothin Road, Tambon Khlong Nueng, Khlong Luang District, Pathumthani 12120, Thailand
Tel: (662) 516-0110/524-5002
Fax: (662) 516-2126/516-1418
WWW: http://www.ait.ac.th

Founders: South East Asia Treaty Organization member countries

Current Leadership: Roger G. H. Downer, President
Karl E. Weber, Vice President for Academic Affairs
Pisidhi Karasudhi, Vice President for Development

Significant Events: Initially, AIT had students from only three countries. Today, the institution has served over 8,500 alumni from more than 50 countries worldwide and many more in its non-degree programs. AIT offers more than 30 different fields of study.

Gross Sales: 1994   US$25.2 million
1995   US$28.5 million
1996   US$31.5 million

Ayala Corporation

---✩---

Founding Concept: To become a highly diversified yet efficient and highly respected company.

Country of Operations: Philippines

Description of Operations: Ayala Corporation is a diversified corporation with development and significant presence in real estate, banking, food manufacturing, electronics, telecommunications, automotive, and infrastructure.

Address: 341F, Tower One, Ayala Triangle, Ayala Avenue, Makati City, Philippines
Tel: 848-5643
Fax: 848-5846
WWW: http://www.ayala.comp.ph

Date Founded and History: Ayala Corporation was established through a partnership forged by Don Domingo Roxas and Don Antonio de Ayala. In 1834 they formed Casa Roxas, which started as a distillery and later moved into coal mining, sugar cultivation, and land acquisition and management. By the turn of the century, Ayala Corporation had built a diversified business portfolio and invested in the three areas that now comprise its main interests.

Current Leadership: Jaime Zobel de Ayala,
Chairman and CEO
Jaime Augusto Zobel de Ayala II,
President

Significant Events: As a result of the company's intensive efforts to expand and diversify, Ayala Corporation has formed alliances with a number of respected names in various industries. Among these are Mitsubishi Corporation, Honda Motor Co. Ltd., Singapore Telecom International, Hong Kong Land, Bechtel Enterprises MWSS Holdings Ltd. and United Utilities of the U.K.

Biggest Challenge: The prime challenge for Ayala

Corporation is focusing on priorities and expanding at the international level, especially with the opening of markets in the ASEAN region. Ayala Corporation formed Ayala International Pte. Ltd. in Singapore, whose sole task is to explore international business opportunities by identifying possible synergies and tie-ups with other business organizations outside of the Philippines. As the group evolves from a primarily real estate business into a major, diversified corporation, Ayala faces the challenge of emerging conglomerate-competitors, most of which have real estate business in their portfolio. In addition, the company faces the problem of foreign players' entry into several of its businesses. Ayala faces such challenges by balancing its efforts in investment and expansion for new businesses, and establishment and maintenance of leadership in its current businesses.

New Markets or Products Being Pursued: Most of the companies under the Ayala umbrella are projecting new market segments: Pure Foods, its subsidiary in the food processing business, recently ventured into flour milling, and fast-food franchising; Ayala Land, Inc., its real estate arm, has entered the mass housing market. Ayala Corporation is currently planning to expand its participation in the automotive business and is opening up opportunities for entry in infrastructure development.

Gross Sales: 1994   US$902.2 million
               1995   US$974.3 million
               1996   US$1.185 billion

Badan Koordinasi Keluarga Berencana Nasional

Founding Concept: To provide a national family planning program that would play an integral part in the country's national development.

Country of Operations: Indonesia

Description of Operations: The Badan Koordinasi Keluarga Berencana Nasional (BKKBN), otherwise known as the Indonesian Family Planning Coordinating Board, is a government organization charged with the implementation of family planning projects. It covers all the provinces of Indonesia.

Address: Jl. Letman Jend. Haryono, Mt. Kav 9-11, Jakarta, Indonesia
Tel: (6221) 819-3083/819-4650/819-4372
Fax: (6221) 819-4532
WWW: http://www.bkkbn.go.id

Date Founded and History: BKKBN was founded through Presidential Decree No. 8 in 1970. It was formed mainly to facilitate the implementation of family planning programs throughout the country. It has implemented strategic programs that are clearly visible: it has been able to bring down the fertility rate of women to 40%, and the majority of the country's female population (95%) is now familiar with modern contraceptive methods, despite limited financial resources compared to similar programs in the region.

Current Leadership: Haryono Suyono, State Minister of Population and Chairman, BKKBN
Loet Affandi, Vice Chairman

Significant Events: Strong political commitment, community support, and networking have permitted the agency to maintain a wide, effective network of community organizations that provide contraceptives and information, education, and communication services.

Biggest Challenge: The greatest challenge for any organization in Indonesia striving for an effective national operation is the country's geography: it consists of 13,600 islands spread over two oceans. For BKKBN, this challenge was taken very seriously because its mandate requires implementation of its programs in every community in the nation and, further, full community participation. The agency plays an important role in "developing prosperous families and in poverty alleviation."

Bangkok Bank Public Company Limited
——————————— ☆ ———————————

Founding Concept: To become Thailand's premier financial institution and leading commercial bank, catering to the corporate, commercial, and consumer banking sectors.

Country of Operations: Thailand

Description of Operations: Bangkok Bank is the largest commercial bank in Thailand, accounting for nearly one-fourth of the total domestic bank loans and deposits. It maintains leading positions in trade financing, treasury services, credit card services, custodian services, and private banking services, and operates in 15 countries outside Thailand, including China, Hong Kong, Japan, Singapore, the U.K., and the U.S.

Address: 333 Silom Road, Bangkok 10500, Thailand
Tel: (662) 230-2330/230-1730
Fax: (662) 236-8983/236-8288
WWW: http:www.bbl.co.th

Date Founded: December, 1994

Current Leadership: Chartsiri Sophonpanich, President
Piyapan Tayanithi, Vice President

Biggest Challenge: The current liberalization of the Thai financial market will eventually lead to a very diverse and very competitive sector. New banks, be they small local upstarts or big international banks, will enter the country and pose serious challenges to Bangkok Bank. Despite these challenges, the bank is counting on its financial strength, professional management, extensive branch network, and broad customer base to sustain high growth with quality.

Gross Sales: 1994   US$3.6 billion
1995   US$4.6 billion
1996   US$5.2 billion

Bangkok Insurance Co., Ltd.

―――――――――――――――― ☆ ――――――――――――――――

Founding Concept: To become the country's leading insurance company.

Country of Operations: Thailand

Description of Operations: Bangkok Insurance Co. was established in 1947 as a marine, fire, and motor insurance provider. Its services now include other miscellaneous insurance services.

Address: 302 Silom Road, Bangkok 10500, Thailand
Tel: (662) 237-8237
Fax: (662) 237-8211
WWW: http:www.bki.co.th

Current Leadership: Chai Sophonpanich,
Chairman and Managing Director
Voravit Rojrapitada,
Assistant Managing Director

Significant Events: In March 1997, the company became the first insurance company in Southeast Asia to receive ISO 9002 certification.

Biggest Challenge: The liberalization of the country's insurance industry is seen as the current biggest challenge to the company. As a result, it has reviewed its current corporate strategy and is implementing programs that seek to strengthen the company's hold on the market. Among these are: an effective people management policy that strives to recruit, train, and maintain the best possible staff; the creation of flexible yet innovative solutions for individual clients; diversification into new markets; and investment in technological applications in communication and on-line servicing.

Gross Sales: 1994   US$124.0 million
1995   US$161.0 million
1996   US$188.5 million

Bank of Ayudhya Public Company Limited

——————————— ☆ ———————————

Country of Operations: Thailand

Description of Operations: Bank of Ayudhya is one of Thailand's leading commercial banks.

Address: 1222 Rama III Road, Bang Phongphang, Yan Nawa, P.O. Box 491, Bangkok 10120, Thailand
Tel: (662) 296-2000/683-1000
Fax: (662) 683 1304
WWW: http://www.bay.w.thlhtml

Date Founded and History: Bank of Ayudhya was the first commercial bank in Thailand to commence operations outside of the capital, Bangkok. The bank was founded on January 27, 1945, in Ayudhya province and started operations on April 1 the same year. It initially had one million baht as capital. Over its first half century of operations, the bank has grown immensely, becoming a leading financial institution, with a paid-up capital of over four billion baht.

Current Leadership: Krit Ratanarak, Chairman
Somchai Sakulsurarat, President
Mitraparp Jalanugraha,
Senior Executive Vice President
Dr. Jamlong Atikul,
Senior Vice President and VP,
Office of the CEO

Biggest Challenge: The deregulation of Thailand's financial sector, especially the banking industry, posts the challenge of new competition from both local and foreign banks. In response, the bank of Ayudhya has embarked on programs designed to capture and maintain the best possible staff for its operations. As of June 1997 the bank had 400 domestic branches and three overseas branches in Hong Kong, Vientiane, Lao PDR, and the Cayman Islands. Three representative offices have been opened in Myanmar, Vietnam, and the People's Republic of China. The bank is pursuing expansion into new businesses, particularly retail banking, to generate more fee income.

Gross Sales: 1994   US$26.105 million
1995   US$40.935 million
1996   US$47.310 million

Café De Coral Holdings Limited

Founding Concept: To establish a network of restaurants throughout Hong Kong with a view to strategic expansion in China covering the principal commercial and residential areas in central business districts and new town developments.

Country of Operations: Hong Kong

Description of Operations: Café de Coral is principally a chain of 182 restaurants operating under the trade names of Café de Coral, Ah Yee Leng Tong, and Spaghetti House in Hong Kong and China. It also has investments in institutional catering, serving various organizations in Hong Kong.

Address: Café de Coral Center, 5 Wo Shui Street, Fo Tan, Shatin, NT, Hong Kong
Tel: (852) 2061-7888
Fax: (852) 2609-4529

Date Founded and History: 1968. Opened its first restaurant in 1969 and now operates close to 200 restaurants in Hong Kong and China. The company was the first fast food operator to open restaurants in a public housing estate and the first in its industry to be publicly-listed. The group's market share of Hong Kong's "eating out industry" is close to four percent.

Current Leadership: Lo Kai Muk, Chairman
Michael Chan Yue Kwong,
Managing Director

Significant Events: A food processing plant in Guangzhou,

China, commenced production in 1995. Centralization of the Group's PRC material sourcing, food production, and distribution facilities provides synergistic benefits to the Group.

Biggest Challenge: In order to remain the undisputed market leader in the fast food and leisure dining industry in Hong Kong, the company strives to create innovative new products, and marketing excellence with uncompromising standards of quality, unconditional service to customers, and undivided commitment to excellence. The company's corporate motto is "A Hundred Points of Excellence."

Gross Sales: 1994   US$234.5 million
1995   US$246 million
1996   US$258.5 million

Cellular Communications Network Sdn. Bhd.

Country of Operations: Malaysia

Description of Operations: Cellular Communications (Celcom) is Malaysia's first privately owned cellular communications. It is the market leader in cellular communications in Malaysia, providing both analog and digital mobile services. Celcom also provides fixed line services, multimedia applications, voice information services, trunk radio, wireless data and paging services and satellite services. The company has a license to provide international gateway services.

Address: 23/F Menara TR, 161B Jalan Ampang, 50450 Kuala Lumpur, Malaysia
Tel: (603) 262-3900
Fax: (603) 262-3331
WWW: http://www.celcom.com.my

Date Founded: 1989

Founder: Tajudin Ramli

Current Leadership: Tajudin Ramli, Chairman and Chief
Executive
Wan Aishah Hamid,
Group Executive Vice President

Significant Events: In 1996, Celcom's holding company, Technology Resources Industries Berhad (TRI), sold a 21% stake in the company to Deutsche Telekom A6 to accelerate the acquisition of technology and expertize. *World Link*, the official magazine for the World Economic Forum ranked TRI as the world's seventh fastest growing company in its March 1997 issue.

Biggest Challenge: The company's "struggle has been to remain buoyant in an increasingly liberalized sector since it lost its national monopoly about three years ago."[1] The company experienced an exodus of senior executives in 1996, including Rosli Man, the president, after Ramli acquired Malaysia Airlines.

Cerebos (Thailand) Ltd.

Founding Concept: To nurture a brighter tomorrow through caring for people today.

Country of Operations: Thailand

Description of Operations: Cerebos is Thailand's leading health and natural supplement products manufacturer. Among its products are Brand's Essence of Chicken and Bird's Nest, Veta Prune Concentrate, and Veta Carrot Concentrate, all of which are marketed locally and abroad.

Address: "M" Floor, Kian Gwan I Building, 140 Wireless Road, Lumpini Pathumwan, Bangkok, Thailand
Tel: (662) 651-4211/651-4207718 Ext 221
Fax: (662) 253-7398/254-1711
WWW: http://www.brands.cerebos.com.sg

---

[1] Shameen, Assif. "Fasten Seat Belts!" (*Asiaweek*, April 25, 1997)

Date Founded: August, 1974

Founders: Cerebos Pacific and Diethelms

Current Leadership: Lackana Leelayouthayotin, Managing Director

Biggest Challenge: The current economic downturn.

New Markets or Products Being Pursued: Indochina

Citytrust Banking Corporation

Founding Concept: To create financial products and services suited to its customers and to become an active partner in the country's economic development.

Country of Operations: Philippines

Description of Operations: Citytrust Banking Corporation was a Philippine universal bank offering both traditional and non-traditional services until its absorption by the Ayala-controlled Bank of the Philippines Islands (BPI). Prior to the BPI takeover, Citibank was a major shareholder. It served three clearly defined markets: the individual or consumer segment, institutional or corporate segment, and investment banking segment.

Address: Citytrust Building, 379 Sen. Gil Puyat Avenue, Makati City, Philippines

Date Founded: 1961

Founders: Salvador Araneta, Victoria de Araneta, Jose Concepcion, Sr., Leonardo Gregorio, and Gregorio Zara

Most Recent Leadership: Jose R. Fucundo, President

Significant Events: The company was acquired by BPI in 1996 when Citibank announced it would sell its interest in the institution.

Gross Sales: 1994   US$112 million
1995   US$136 million

Community Chest of Hong Kong

—————————————— ☆ ——————————————

Founding Concept: To obtain donations for charity and social welfare services.

Country of Operations: Hong Kong

Description of Operations: The Community Chest of Hong Kong is involved in charity and related services. Its main activity is the raising of funds for charity and community development activities.

Address: 18/F, NatWest Tower, Times Square, Causeway Bay, Hong Kong
Tel: (852) 2599-6103/2599-6111
Fax: (852) 2566-1201
WWW: http://www.hkstar.com/~chest

Date Founded and History: The Community Chest of Hong Kong was established in November 1968 to act as a coordinating organization in raising funds for charity and welfare services. Back then, welfare services were still dependent on overseas aid. Today, the Community Chest allocates funds to more than 140 social welfare agencies providing family and child care, activities for children and youth, rehabilitation, aftercare, care for the elderly, and community development services.

Current Leadership: Darwin Chen, Chief Executive
Cecilia Li, Director of Campaigns and Donations

Significant Events: In its first year of operation the organization was able to raise US$0.79 million, and in a span of 29 years it raised this figure to US$29.5 million. The number of welfare agencies it supports has increased from the initial 43 to 140, serving more than 700,000 people in need every year.

Biggest Challenge: The biggest challenge currently facing the organization is to identify potential donors and to develop marketing strategies to appeal to them. To meet this challenge, the Community Chest has launched a large-scale program to get more people involved in voluntary community services and charity work. Dubbed "Friends of the Chest," the program aims to expand the organization's support base by gaining donors through membership incentives. As "Friends of the Chest," donors have the chance to visit the recipients of their generosity and to gain a firsthand account of the services they help fund.

Cycle & Carriage Limited
— ☆ —

Founding Concept: To take advantage of the growth potential in the vehicle industry.

Country of Operations: Singapore

Description of Operations: Cycle & Carriage is a diversified group with a focus on Asia-Pacific markets. With a capitalization of US$2.5 billion at the end of 1996, the Group ranks among Singapore's top R20 listed companies. Its core businesses are concentrated in motor vehicles and property. While developing and strengthening these core businesses, it strives to expand regionally to achieve a broad earnings base for its investors. Its major shareholders are Jardine Strategic Holdings, Edaran Otomobil Nasional, and Employees Provident Fund.

Address: 239 Alexandra Road, Singapore 159930
Tel: (65) 473-3122
Fax: (65) 475-7088

Date Founded and History: Founded by brothers Chua Cheng Liat and Chua Cheng Bok in 1897, Cycle & Carriage began operations in Kuala Lumpur as a small family business dealing in bicycles, carriages, and other merchandise. The company has since grown to become a large, diversified group with core businesses in motor vehicles, property/food, and retail, comprising 90 subsidiaries and affiliates with operations in Singapore, Malaysia, Australia, New Zealand, Thailand, and Vietnam.

Current Leadership: Philip Eng Heng Nee, Group Managing Director

Biggest Challenge: To maintain its position as a premier motor vehicles and property group, providing the highest-quality products and services.

New Markets or Products Being Pursued: The company is expanding its businesses in the region.

Gross Sales: 1994 US$1.6 billion
1995 US$2.1 billion
1996 US$2.1 billion

DBS Land Limited

Founding Concept: To become the largest and best-managed property and hotel group in Singapore.

Country of Operations: Singapore

Description of Operations: DBS Land Limited is the leading property and hotel group in Singapore. It has 56 subsidiaries located in Singapore and eight other Asia Pacific countries.

Address: 68 Orchard Road, #06-01 Plaza Singapura, Singapore 238839
Tel: (65) 536-1188
Fax: (65) 533-6133

Current Leadership: Lim Joke Mui, General Manager

Significant Events: The company takes pride in its image as the trendsetter in Singapore for innovative real estate developments. DBS was the first Singapore developer to conceptualize and develop projects involving condominium housing, suburban shopping centers, family shopping centers, a city-within-a-city, and a festival village.

Biggest Challenge: The expected growth in tourist and business travel in the Asia Pacific region has prompted the group to expand its hotel operations. In addition, the group has reorganized all of its hotel and resort investments into a single management unit, Raffles Holdings, to address and capitalize on the opportunities presented by the region's growth.

New Markets or Products Being Pursued: The company is presently pursuing the development of its own hospitals as its newest strategic investment in health care. It has also entered the Australian residential property market through the acquisition of a 60% stake in Australian Housing and Land Group (AHLG). AHLG is one of the largest and best-established suburban housing developers in Australia.

Gross Sales: 1994   US$141.4 million
1995   US$156.7 million

Development Bank of The Philippines

Founding Concept: To provide banking services principally to cater to the medium- and long-term needs of agricultural and industrial enterprises, particularly in the countryside, with emphasis on small- and medium-scale industries.

Country of Operations: Philippines

Description of Operations: Development Bank of the Philippines (DBP) is a government bank tasked with the coordination and management of government trust funds. It provides lending services for housing, agriculture, and small- and medium-scale industries.

Address: 8/F DBP Building, Makati Ave. cor Sen. Gil Puyat St., 1200 Makati City, Philippines
Tel: (632) 818-9511
Fax: (632) 812-8099/816-4105
E-mail: dbpinfo@ibminet
WWW: http://www.orim2000.com/philippi/dbp/dbp.html

Date Founded and History: In 1935, the National Loan and Investment Board was created to coordinate and manage government trust funds. This organization ultimately evolved through various government reorganization exercises into the Development Bank of the Philippines in 1958. In 1995, DBP was granted a universal or expanded commercial banking license.

Current Leadership: Alfredo C. Antonio,
Chairman and CEO
Francisco F. Del Rosario,
Vice Chairman and CEO

Significant Events: Successful US$175 million Eurobond flotation reintroduced DBP to the international voluntary market without government guarantee; created Philippine Strategic Investment (Holdings) Ltd., a closed-end investment company with Clemente Capital Inc; and, provided an aggregate US$174 million in loans to two "fast-track" Build-Operate-Transfer projects of the National Power Corporation.

Biggest Challenge: Increase from P5 billion to P50 billion in authorized stock; exemption from Salary Standardization Law and adoption of a compensation plan comparable to the private sector; and, authority for corporate reorganization.

New Markets or Products Being Pursued: Small and medium enterprises; local government unit financing; financial institutions; capital market development; and, environment financing.

Gross Sales: 1994   US$289.99 million
1995   US$280.31 million
1996   US$320.19 million

DHL International (Singapore) Pte. Ltd.
—————————————— ☆ ——————————————

Country of Operations: Singapore
Description of Operations: A branch of DHL Interna-

tional, DHL International Singapore provides door-to-door delivery to individuals and corporations. It serves 218 countries worldwide.

Address: 1 Tai Seng Drive, DHL Air Express Centre, Singapore 535215
Tel: (65) 288-4922
Fax: (65) 288-6855/383-4692
Current Leadership: Charles Chia, General Manager
Gross Sales: 1994   US$47 million

DuPont (Thailand) Ltd.

Country of Operations: Thailand

Description of Operations: Established in Thailand in 1971, DuPont Thailand repacks and formulates agrochemicals and markets chemicals, polymers, fibers, automotive paints, filaments, electronics, and petrochemicals to the Thai market.

Address: 9/F Yada Building, 56 Silom Road, Surlyawongse, Bangkok 10500, Thailand
Tel: (662) 236-0026/238-4361
Fax: (662) 236-6798/238-4396
WWW: http://www.es.dupont.com

Date Founded: 1971

Current Leadership: Thirachai Ongmahutmongkol,
                         President

Significant Events: Opened the Bangpoo pesticide repacking and formulating plant in 1982. The plant operates on the same safety standards as any DuPont plant anywhere in the world, and has won several environmental and occupational safety awards. It is ISO 9002 certified. Over the years, DuPont has developed and sustained a group of strong core businesses including agrochemicals, chemicals, polymers, refinishes, fibers, electronics, and petrochemicals.

Biggest Challenge: To provide full customer satisfaction. The company believes that it is essential to have a well-trained staff that will deliver excellent customer service by utilizing all available support from local, regional, and worldwide resources. DuPont's training programs are intended to support this objective.

Gross Sales: 1994   US$39.3 billion
              1995   US$42.2 billion
              1996 (Globally)   US$43.8 billion

Eastern Telecommunications Philippines, Inc.
———————————————— ☆ ————————————————

Founding Concept: To serve the telecommunications needs of the country using the most appropriate technology available coupled with quality service.

Country of Operations: Philippines

Description of Operations: Eastern Telecommunications provides a range of international telecommunications services, including international telephone service, Eastern International Payphone and Phone Card, managed facsimile service, global managed data service, teleprinter exchange service, international private leased circuit, packaged switched data service, and local exchange service.

Address: Telecoms Plaza, 316 Sen. Gil Puyat Avenue, Makati City, Philippines
Tel: (632) 816-0001/815-8921
Fax: (632) 817-9742

Date Founded and History: 1878 as a merger between Eastern Extension Australasia and China Telegraph Company. China Telegraph was subsequently absorbed by Cable and Wireless Plc. In 1974 Eastern Extension was privatized and renamed Eastern Telecommunications. Cable and Wireless retained its 40% interest. The 60% interest held by Filipinos was sequestered after the fall of the Marcos administration by the government.

Founders: Eastern Extension Australasia and Asia Telegraph Company

Current Leadership: Melquiades C. Gutierrez, Chairman and President

Significant Events: Smart Communications acquired a 9.8% interest in the company in August 1996 and stated its objective of obtaining an additional 40% interest subject to litigation pertaining to the sequestration of those shares by the Philippine government.

Gross Sales: 1994   US$93.884 million
1995   US$93.159 million
1996   US$105.162 million

Excel Machine Tools Pte. Ltd.

Founding Concept: To be recognized as one of the world's leading high technology and high value-added precision machine tools manufacturers with state-of-the-art manufacturing technologies.

Country of Operations: Singapore

Description of Operations: Excel Machine Tools is engaged in the manufacture and sale of machines used for metal cutting, welding, and soldering to manufacturing companies in 30 countries worldwide.

Address: 88 Second Lok Yang Road, Off International Road, Jurong, Singapore 659544
Tel: (65) 268-6288
Fax: (65) 261-7388

Date Founded and History: Founded in 1986 by Robin Lau, its current chief executive, with a paid-up capital of only US$100,000, Excel Machine Tools has grown into a solid, full-scale heavy equipment manufacturer. During its initial year the company offered only machine maintenance service. In its second year, it received a loan grant, which financed the development of its first original design. Since that time it has continued to grow, developing machines used for metal working. Today it offers machines for metal trimming, welding, and soldering using laser-cutting technology (developed by the company's researchers, along with associates in Singapore and China).

Current Leadership: Robin Lau, CEO
Wee Yue-Chew,
Group General Manager

Significant Events: Since its creation, Excel Machine Tools has won several citations for its innovativeness. Among these are Singapore's National Productivity Award in 1991, Britain's International Quality Design Award in 1993, and the Entrepreneur's Excellence Award in Singapore (for Robin Lau) also in 1993.

New Markets or Products Being Pursued: The company has developed a laser-cutting technology for metal sheets and products, and is currently seeking opportunities to exploit this technology internationally.

Genting Berhad

Founding Concept: To develop and establish a world-class resort that is easily accessible and affordable to Malaysians.

Country of Operations: Malaysia

Description of Operations: Originally involved in hotel and resort activities, Genting Berhad has since expanded to plantations, property development, hydrocarbon exploration, and power generation.

Address: 24/F Wisma Genting, Jalan Sultan Ismail, 50250 Kuala Lumpur, Malaysia

Tel: (603) 261-2288
Fax: (603) 261-5304
WWW: http://www.genting.com.my

Date Founded: Founded in 1965; incorporated in 1968

Founders: Lim Goh Tong and Mohammed Noah bin Omar

Current Leadership: Lim Goh Tong, Chairman and Joint Managing Director
Mohammed Hanif bin Omar, Deputy Chairman
Lim Kok Thay, Joint Managing Director

Significant Events: From earnings of RM2.4 million in 1971, Genting now generates a turnover of RM2.4 billion in pretax profit.

Gross Sales: 1994   US$930 million
1995   US$975.8 million
1996   US$1.015 billion

Giordano Holdings Limited

Founding Concept: To engage in the manufacture and retail of basic and casual apparel.

Country of Operations: Hong Kong

Description of Operations: Giordano is engaged in the manufacture and retail of casual apparel and leather goods, focused on a "value-for-money" strategy. It has well-positioned outlets throughout the Asia Pacific region, including Taiwan, Hong Kong, China, Malaysia, the Philippines, New Zealand, and Japan.

Address: 5/F Tin On Industrial Building, Kowloon, Hong Kong
Tel: (852) 744-5010/746-5168
Fax: (852) 743-0440/785-0343

Founder: Jimmy Lai

Current Leadership: Peter Lau, CEO

Significant Events: An editorial criticizing the Chinese government and its leaders, authored by Lai, resulted in his divestment and the subsequent closure of a number of Giordano outlets in China.

Biggest Challenge: Giordano's challenge is to sustain growth. The retail apparel industry has a large number of operators competing against each other. Giordano responds by providing quality products and emphasizing customer service.

New Markets or Products Being Pursued: The company is planning to establish a wider network of Giordano shops throughout Asia.

Gross Sales: 1994   US$370 million
1995   US$450 million
1996   US$460 million

Hang Seng Bank Limited
☆

Founding Concept: To provide gold trading, money exchange, and remittance services.

Country of Operations: Hong Kong

Description of Operations: Hang Seng Bank employs over 8,000 staff in its 147 branches in Hong Kong, a branch in Guangzhou, and representative offices in Shanghai, Shenzhen, and Xiamen. The bank offers a full range of commercial banking services to its customers.

Address: 83 Des Voeux Road, Central, Hong Kong
Tel: (852) 2825-5111
Fax: (852) 2845-9301
WWW: http://www.hangseng.com

Date Founded and History: Hang Seng Bank started its operations in 1933 as a money-changing shop. In 1952 it was incorporated as a private limited company with a new focus on commercial banking. During a bank run in Hong Kong in 1965, the bank sold a 51% interest to Hongkong Bank and became a member of the HSBC Group. Hongkong Bank's interest in Hang Seng was subsequently increased to 61.51%. Hang Seng is now the second largest locally incorporated bank and among the five largest listed companies in Hong Kong.

Founders: B.Y. Lam, S. H. Ho, C.W. Leung, and T.L. Sheng

Current Leadership: Lee Quo-Wei, Chairman
Alexander S.K. Au,
Vice Chairman and Chief Executive

Significant Events: With consolidated assets of HK$398 billion at the end of June 1997, Hang Seng Bank reported a profit attributable to shareholders of HK$4.98 billion in the first half of 1997 and HK$8.49 billion in 1996.

The bank's shares have been publicly listed in Hong Kong since 1972, and are now traded on the Stock Exchange of Hong Kong Limited and the London Stock Exchange. The bank has also offered investors in the U.S. a Sponsored Level-I American Depository Receipts Program through the Bank of New York.

Biggest Challenge: Although competition is expected to continue to intensify in the Hong Kong banking sector, Hang Seng is well placed to take advantage of business opportunities in the expanding economy. To extend its market leadership, the bank is building on its high liquidity, strong capital base, and lean cost structure. It is leveraging its strong customer franchise, widening its range of innovative products, expanding its network of branches, and continuing to invest in new technology.

New Markets or Products Being Pursued: The bank's core business focus is on Hong Kong and mainland China, and its core businesses are retail banking, corporate banking, and treasury services. These are supplemented by new and developing businesses, such as private wealth management and investment services, reflecting the bank's aim to diversify earnings and to become a modern and dynamic financial services supermarket.

Its life insurance subsidiary, Hang Seng Life Limited, a

joint venture with HSBC Life Holdings Limited, is set to tap the growing retirement benefits and life insurance markets in Hong Kong. Under planning, for launch in 1998, is home banking. The bank's strategy is to offer value-added products supported by premium customer service.

Hong Kong's reunification with China on July 1, 1997, will lead to closer economic interdependence and provide further impetus for growth in Hong Kong and the mainland in the long term. The bank upgraded its representative office in Shanghai to a branch in Pudong in 1997, and this significantly strengthened its presence on the mainland. Its Guangzhou branch was relocated in mid-1997 to larger, purchased premises in CITIC Plaza, Tien He district, to accommodate future business expansion.

Hongkong & Shanghai Banking Corporation Limited
☆

Founding Concept: To provide trade finance services.

Country of Operations: Hong Kong

Description of Operations: Hongkong & Shanghai Banking Corporation (HSBC) is a leading international bank providing a wide range of retail and commercial banking and related financial services. Along with its subsidiaries (the Hongkong Bank Group), it has more than 600 offices in 21 countries and territories in the Asia Pacific region.

Address: 1 Queen's Road, Central Hong Kong
Tel: (852) 2822-4929/2822-1111
Fax: (852) 2845-0113/2822-1646
WWW: http://www.hsbcgroup.com
　　　　http:/www.hongkongbank.com

Date Founded: 1865

Current Leadership: John Strickland, Chairman
　　　　　　　　　　　　David Eldon, Chief Executive

Significant Events: HSBC, Hongkong Bank's holding company, relocated to Britain after acquiring Britain's Midland Bank in 1992.

Biggest Challenge: The company is threatened by competition from institutions affiliated with the Chinese government and the mainland as well as aggressive international competitors. Growth in Hong Kong has been slow, despite the high overall profitability of the group. Rising costs are another principal concern.

New Markets or Products Being Pursued: Personal banking in the Asia Pacific region.

Hong Kong Productivity Council

Founding Concept: To promote increased productivity and the use of efficient methods throughout Hong Kong's business sector.

Country of Operations: Hong Kong

Description of Operations: The Hong Kong Productivity Council provides a diverse range of services in product development, consultancy, and training and operates a technology center serving both the industrial and commercial sectors of Hong Kong.

Address: HKPC Building, 78 Tat Chee Avenue, Yau Yat Chuen, Kowloon, Hong Kong
Tel: (852) 2788-5678
Fax: (852) 2788-5900
WWW: http://www.hkpc.org:8080/index.html

Date Founded and History: The Hong Kong Productivity Council was established by statute in 1967 to boost productivity and increase the use of more efficient methods throughout Hong Kong's business sector. Between 1979 and 1991 the council increased its staff threefold and income 16 times. Today, this multidisciplinary organization provides a wide range of services in people, product, and process development to over 4,000 companies each year.

Current Leadership: Thomas Tang, Executive Director

Significant Events: The Hong Kong Productivity Council was the pioneer consultancy organization to help local companies implement and acquire certification to the ISO 9000 standards. It is considered the major ISO consultancy provider in Hong Kong.

Biggest Challenge: The Hong Kong economy is moving away from assembly operations to higher value-added production. Hence, a constant flow of creative, applied technology is essential to stay ahead in competitive global markets. To fulfill its role, the council has invested heavily in new technology and in-house training to upgrade the value-added performance of its workforce.

New Markets or Products Being Pursued: The council is positioning itself to further extend its expertise to the service industry sector. It has formulated a strategy that aims to expand its support and productivity promotion programs to the increasingly important service sector.

Hongkong Telecommunications Limited

Country of Operations: Hong Kong

Description of Operations: Hongkong Telecoms provides local and international telecommunications products and services, including high-frequency radio, telephones, telex, telegraph, microwave, international television, video-conferencing, and facilities management.

Address: 42/F, Telecom Tower, Taikoo Place, 979 King's Road, Quarry Bay, Hong Kong
Tel: (852) 2888-2888
Fax: (852) 2877-8877
WWW: http://www.hkt.com

Date Founded and History: Hongkong Telecom's major shareholders are Cable and Wireless at 54%, China Everbright Holdings Company Ltd. at 7.6%, and China Telecom at about 5.4%. The remaining shares are public.

Current Leadership: Linus Cheung, Chief Executive

Significant Events: The company's exclusive license to provide local telephone services expired in mid-1995, though the company retains the exclusive license to provide international services until 2006. In 1996, *Asian Business* magazine named the company the top telecommunications company in Asia.

Biggest Challenge: New competition, especially from China, although China is Hongkong Telecom's single largest telecoms partner, according to the company, and the Hong Kong–China route is the fourth busiest in the world. The company focuses strongly on quality of service and product to protect its position in the marketplace, and has undertaken significant infrastructure investments of more than US$3.7 billion in the past decade.

New Markets or Products Being Pursued: Like most regional telecommunications companies, the company seeks to extend its operations significantly as the Chinese economy continues to develop. It is racing to develop products and services, including interactive multimedia services.

Gross Sales: 1996   US$4.2 billion

Housing and Development Board
————————————— ☆ —————————————

Founding Concept: To provide quality and affordable public housing in Singapore.

Country of Operations: Singapore

Description of Operations: Formed initially to provide affordable public housing mainly for rent, the Housing and Development Board (HDB) now has interests in mortgage financing, selling of flats, commercial and industrial properties, car parks, and markets. It houses 86% of Singapore's population.

Address: 3451 Jalan Bukit Merah, HDB Centre, Singapore 159459
Tel: (65) 273-9090
Fax: (65) 278-0144
WWW: http://www/hdb.gov.sg

Date Founded and History: HDB was formed in February 1960. Its initial task was to provide low-cost housing for rent. Over the years HDB's main activity shifted from renting to selling flats. It also deals in the construction and management of commercial and industrial properties, car parks, and markets.

Current Leadership: Tan Guong Ching, CEO

Significant Events: From the construction of one- and two-room flats, HDB now plans and builds estates and towns within a total living environment. Each estate or town is planned such that it is self-sustainable, with its own social and recreational facilities (playgrounds, stadiums, swimming pools) as well as educational, medical, commercial, and industrial facilities to meet the daily needs of residents.

For its achievements and dedication in providing world-class public housing through advanced technology and strong people-centered practices, HDB was recently awarded the 1997 Singapore Quality Award, the republic's top prize for business excellence.

Biggest Challenge: As Singapore's public housing authority, HDB's biggest challenge is meeting the expectations of Singaporeans for quality and affordable housing, as well as maintaining existing properties and services. To meet these expectations, HDB continues to develop and construct quality housing units at the lowest possible cost within the shortest possible time. It also implements policies and programs concerning the maintenance, upgrading, and redevelopment of established estates.

New Markets or Products Being Pursued: As the leader in Singapore's construction technology, HDB continues to adopt innovations that increase productivity and quality. Prefabrication technology, currently being used and improved on by the board, has contributed significantly to meeting housing demand.

Gross Sales: 1994/95 US$4.232 million
1995/96 US$4.793 million
1996/97 US$4.925 million

ICI Paints (Malaysia) Sdn. Bhd.
———————————————— ☆ ————————————————

Founding Concept: To manufacture high-quality paints and surface coatings.

Country of Operations: Malaysia

Description of Operations: ICI Paints Malaysia manufactures and supplies high-quality paints and surface coatings for decorative, refinish, motors, coils, packaging, powders, marine, and general industrial markets.

Address: Jalan 205, P.O. Box 78, 46700 Petaling Jaya, Selangor Darul Ehsan, Malaysia.
Tel: (603) 791-2322
Fax: (603) 791-4846

Date Founded and History: ICI Paints Malaysia was established in 1959 to manufacture and supply high-quality paints and surface coatings. Since its inception, the company has made steady progress and is now the number one paints company in Malaysia. The company is currently the fourth largest contributor of profit to the ICI Paints World Group and the biggest ICI Paints operation in Asia.

Current Leadership: Syed Salleh Othman,
Managing Director
Ahmad Zamani Alip,
Business Process/Planning Manager

Biggest Challenge: Customers are becoming more discerning in their tastes and requirements. The company answers their needs by acquiring feedback through surveys and third party organizations. It is also continuously formulating strategies to improve its products and services.

New Markets or Products Being Pursued: The company intends to contribute to the protection of the environment by phasing out traditional solvent-based products. It is planning to manufacture water-based products that will minimize VOC emissions into the environment.

Integrated Microelectronics Inc.
☆

Founding Concept: To establish a pure IC assembly plant, but later modified to include contract manufacturing of electronic components.

Country of Operations: Philippines

Description of Operations: A member of the Ayala group Integrated Microelectronics Inc. (IMI) started operations as an integrated circuit assembly plant. It has now diversified its business, with several manufacturing plants located in Metro Manila, Laguna Technopark, Muntinlupa, and Paranque.

Address: KM. 22 East Service Road, South Expressway, Cupang, Muntinlupa, Manila, Philippines
Tel: (632) 842-2247/842-0534
Fax: (632) 842-1368
E-mail: imistrat@globe.com.ph

Date Founded and History: IMI started operations on August 26, 1980, as a company assembling integrated circuits. Through the years it has grown and diversified into contract manufacturing of electronic products. The company has several manufacturing plants, and is servicing such major clients as Yamaha, Philips, Toshiba, SSO, and NEC.

Founders: Major shareholders are Ayala Corporation, and

Resins, Inc. Japan Asia Investment Co. Ltd., Mitsubishi, and Yamaha are also shareholders.

Current Leadership: Francisco I. Ferrer, Group President
Gerardo B. Amisola
Head, Strategic Planning and
Business Development

Significant Events: IMI suffered loses until 1981 but recovered shortly after. The knowledge it acquired in the market helped it achieve substantial customer influx. At present, it is focused on contract manufacturing and on strengthening its own quality and productivity.

Biggest Challenge: The increasingly competitive electronics industry prompted the company to form key strategies for its future growth and profitability. The strategies are: focused approach in identifying and pursuing new markets, companies and products; ensure space for expansion of existing businesses and for new businesses; adopting a progressive organizational development program; and pursue quality leadership in our business.

New Markets or Products Being Pursued: The company is currently investing heavily in facilitated production plants and the development of its human resources to keep pace with increasing competition.

Gross Sales: 1994   US$25.3 million
1995   US$46.1 million
1996   US$79.4 million

Intel Philippines Manufacturing Inc.

Founding Concept: To establish a reliable semiconductor assembly plant in Manila.

Country of Operations: Philippines

Description of Operations: Intel Philippines is involved in the assembly and testing of semiconductor devices. It serves original equipment manufacturers of PCs, cellular phones, and automotive electronics.

Address: 1321 Apolinario Street, Bangkal 1233, Makati City, Philippines
Tel: (632) 841-7316
Fax: (632) 816-2811
WWW: http://www.intel.com

Date Founded and History: Intel Philippines started operations in 1974. From a semiconductor assembly plant with 141 employees, the company expanded to include a test plant and components warehouse. At present Intel employs 2,500 workers and is considered the leader in the semiconductor industry.

Founders: Intel Corporation (worldwide)

Current Leadership: Jacob A. Pena, Jr.,
President and General Manager

Significant Events: Initially an assembly plant for semiconductor components, Intel Philippines employed talented and highly motivated professionals to facilitate the development of a test plant and components warehouse. The company has just completed a new production facility that is among the largest Intel facilities in Asia.

Biggest Challenge: Considering the volatility of the semiconductor market, Intel's biggest challenge has been to continuously transform the organization to meet the demands of new product technologies, increase the level of current technology, and bring in new microprocessor products. Intel addresses this challenge by developing and promoting new methods of manufacturing current and new products, building a culture that embeds emerging technical skills with new ways of management, and motivation.

New Markets or Products Being Pursued: As a subsidiary of a worldwide manufacturer of semiconductors, Intel Philippines' new products and market targets are dictated by the product developments of its mother company.

JCG Finance Company Limited

— ☆ —

Founding Concept: To engage in the business of accepting term deposits and providing personal loans and overdrafts.

Country of Operations: Hong Kong

Description of Operations: JCG Finance is the largest among all deposit-taking banks in Hong Kong, with 36 branches in Kowloon, the New Territories, and on Hong Kong Island. Its services include the acceptance of term deposits, personal loans and overdrafts, hire purchase and leasing, property mortgage loans, share margin financing, and the issuing of credit cards. JCG has the largest branch network among all deposit-taking companies in Hong Kong.

Address: Room 1105-1107 Wing On House, 71 Des Voeux Road, Hong Kong
Tel: (852) 2526-6415/2868-3211
Fax: (852) 2877-9084

Founders: Teh Hong Piow, Tan Yoke Kong

Current Leadership: Teh Hong Piow,
Chairman of the Board
Tan Yoke Kong, General Manager

Significant Events: In 1996 JCG Holdings Limited, the holding company of JCG Finance, acquired a controlling interest in Winton Holdings (Bermuda) Limited, a company listed on the Stock Exchange of Hong Kong Limited, engaged in taxi license financing in Hong Kong.

Biggest challenge: As a deposit-taking company, the cost of funding is much higher than for licensed banks. JCG does not have the competitive advantage to compete with the banks in terms of pricing its services and products. To keep up, the company constantly identifies new niche markets and provides efficient, personalized services.

Johnson & Johnson (Phils.), Inc.

— ☆ —

Founding Concept: To manufacture health care products.

Country of Operations: Philippines

Description of Operations: Johnson & Johnson Philippines manufactures and markets baby and adult toiletries, feminine hygiene, oral care, and over the counter pharmaceutical products.

Address: Edison Avenue, Bo. Ibayo, Parañaque, Manila, Philippines
Tel: (632) 824-0543
Fax: (632) 824-0171
WWW: http://www.jnj.com

Date Founded and History: Established in February 1956, Johnson & Johnson Philippines' initial business was mainly the manufacture of baby powder.

Current Leadership: Godofredo Rodriquez,
President and Managing Director
Perpetuo M. de Cearo,
VP-Sales and Marketing
Balbino K. Herando, VP-Operations

Significant Events: From a four-man operation in 1956 producing Johnson's baby powder, the company has grown into a P2 billion manufacturer. The company received Johnson & Johnson's Signature of Quality Award at the "silver level" – one of two companies worldwide to be so recognized. It produces and markets baby and adult toiletries as well as a consumer health, feminine hygiene, first aid, and oral care products.

Biggest Challenge: The company's main challenge is to identify and enter new markets, specifically the baby care toiletries market. Also, to achieve and maintain superiority in capabilities throughout the organization.

Gross Sales: 1994   US$74.2 million
1995   US$76.0 million
1996   US$96.3 million

Jollibee Foods Corporation

—— ☆ ——

Founding Concept: To establish a quick service restaurant that serves foods catering to the native Filipino taste

Country of Operations: Philippines

Description of Operations: Jollibee is a local hamburger fast-food chain with over 240 outlets in the Philippines, Indonesia, Brunei, Malaysia, Guam, Hong Kong, Vietnam, Bahrain, Jeddah, Kuwait, Riyadh, and Dubai.

Address: Jollibee Center Building, San Miguel Avenue, Ortigas Complex, Pasig City, Philippines
Tel: (632) 634-1111
Fax: (632) 635-8888

Date Founded and History: Jollibee evolved into a fast-food corporation in January 1978, when founder Tony Tan Caktiong decided to convert his ice cream parlor into a hamburger outlet serving high-quality yet reasonably priced food products suited to the Filipino taste. Since then, the company has realized steady growth and commands a majority share of the hamburger business. The company has established itself as the leader in the local fast-food industry and has opened stores throughout Southeast Asia and the Middle East. Soon it is expected to open outlets in the U.S.

Founder: Tony Tan Caktiong

Current Leadership: Tony Tan Caktiong, President
Regina Navarrete, VP – Marketing

Significant Events: Jollibee captured the Philippine market during its initial years of operations, and has continued to maintain that distinction. It leads its industry with a 58% share (1996), and is the only local fast-food company to be publicly listed.

Biggest Challenge: The biggest challenge facing Jollibee is maintaining its leadership in the Philippine fast-food industry while expanding its food service to international markets. To achieve this goal, the company continues to improve its technology as well as to provide customers with good food and excellent service.

New Markets or Products Being Pursued: Spurred by its success in the Philippines, Jollibee aims to penetrate foreign markets and become known as a global food service company.

Gross Sales: 1994   US$131.1 million
1995   US$168.8 million
1996   US$245.6 million

Kumpulan Barkath
☆

Founding Concept: To manufacture and distribute confectioneries, beverages, and other consumer products.

Country of Operations: Malaysia

Description of Operations: Kumpulan Barkath is involved in the manufacture and supply of beverages, confectioneries, marine products, and canned foods to West and East Malaysia, Singapore, and Brunei.

Address: Kumpulan Barkath, Standard Chartered Bank Chambers, 2 Beach Street, 3/F, 10300 Penang, Malaysia
Tel: (604) 261-9991
Fax: (604) 261-2925

Date Founded and History: Founded in 1945 by Haji Abubacker bin Mohd. Hussain, Kumpulan Barkath started off as a family sundry shop. In the mid-1950s it started to manufacture and distribute a variety of food products, including Hacks candies and Sunquick juice concentrate. It has since diversified its business and is presently involved in manufacturing, import-export distribution, property development, plantations investment, and communications. Besides Malaysia, this group of 22 companies has operations in Singapore, India, and Britain.

Founder: Haji Abubacker bin Mohd. Hussain

Current Leadership: Barkath Ali bin Hj. Abubacker, Group Chairman and Managing Director

Significant Events: Kumpulan Barkath has been awarded the International Food Quality and Export Award for its worldwide export, import, and manufacture of quality food products. It received MS ISO 9002 certification in 1997.

Biggest Challenge: Upgrading its existing confectionery lines to produce various types of confectionery apart from its existing product range.

New Markets or Products Being Pursued: The company continues to seek new markets and set up joint ventures with new partners. Kumpulan Barkath is looking towards the Middle East and Europe for its expansion plans in the foods and confectionery markets. It has received franchising offers from overseas companies to produce an international brand of confectionery for manufacture locally in Malaysia and Singapore.

Gross Sales: 1994   US$36 million
                1995   US$42.8 million
                1996   US$72.4 million

Kang Yong Electric Public Co. Ltd.

Founding Concept: To manufacture electrical household appliances.

Country of Operations: Thailand

Description of Operations: Kang Yong produces parts and assembles electric fans under the Mitsubishi trademark.

Address: 67 Moo II Bangna-tart Km. 20 Rd., Samut Prakarn 10540, Thailand
Tel: (602) 337-2429
Fax: (602) 337-2439

Date Founded and History: Established on January 12, 1964, Kang Yong's initial business was the manufacture of electric fans under the Mitsubishi trademark. The company now manufactures its own designs and develops a wide range of electrical household appliances, including refrigerators, televisions, water pumps, and rice cookers. It is a market leader in its industry in the domestic and overseas markets.

Current Leadership: Prapad Phodivorakhun, President
Precha Thiengburanathum,
Corporate Planning Department
Manager

Significant Events: The company has achieved an annual growth rate of 25%.

Biggest Challenge: Applying for ISO 9001 certification is the biggest challenge currently facing the company.

New Markets or Products Being Pursued: The company is increasing its production of washing machines and is planning to introduce new models to the market.

Gross Sales: 1994   US$85 million
1995   US$102 million
1996   US$103 million

Kimberly-Clark (Phils.), Inc.

☆

Founding Concept: To produce high-quality household, feminine, and baby care products in response to customers' needs.

Country of Operations: Philippines

Description of Operations: Kimberly-Clark Philippines is a leading manufacturer of paper and paper-related products. Its products include table tissues, feminine napkins, and disposable diapers.

Address: 2/F, Goodwill Bldg., 393 Sen Gil Puyat Ave. Makati City, Philippines

Tel: (632) 897-6651
Fax: (632) 890-9353

Date Founded and History: Kimberly-Clark Philippines started operations in January 1964, producing facial tissues, feminine napkins, and sterilized cotton. By 1966, it was manufacturing paper napkins, bathroom tissues, household paper towels, cigarette paper, and speciality fine paper. Its range of products now includes disposable baby diapers.

Current Leadership: Cornelio Peralta,
                    Chairman of the Board and President
                    Marino M. Abes, HRD Director

Significant Events: The company's initial products included feminine napkins, facial tissues, and sterilized cotton. Positive reception by the market prompted the production of other paper-related products, such as cigarette paper, disposable diapers, bathroom tissues, and paper napkins.

Biggest Challenge: The biggest challenge facing the company is product development and manufacturing, especially in baby care toiletries. The company, not having any experience in this line of production, tapped experts in this field and a reputable contract manufacturer to address the new business.

Staying ahead of the competition remains the biggest challenge to Kimberly-Clark. To respond to competition, the company strives to keep pace with new developments in product manufacturing and technology, conducts employee training programs, implements quality programs (such as TQM, 5S), periodically upgrades machinery, and reviews systems and procedures to address the company's weaknesses and strengths.

New Markets or Products Being Pursued: Investments are currently focused on existing products to improve their performance, availability, and cost.

Gross Sales: 1994   US$82.0 million
                 1995   US$98.4 million
                 1996   US$107.8 million

Malayan Banking Berhad

Country of Operations: Malaysia

Description of Operations: Malayan Banking Berhad is Malaysia's largest bank – twice the size of its nearest competitors – and offers a comprehensive range of financial products and services. Affiliates include a merchant bank, a finance company, an insurance company, a securities company, a factoring company, a discount house, a leasing company, a trustees company, and a unit trust company.

Address: 14/F Menara Maybank, Bukit Mahkamah, 100 Jalan Tun Perak, 52050 Kuala Lumpur, Malaysia
Tel: (603) 230-8833
Fax: (603) 238-1464

Current Leadership: Mohamed Basir bin Ahmad, Chairman
Amirsham A. Aziz,
Managing Director

Significant Events: Maybank was the first Malaysian bank to computerize and the first to install ATMs. It has the largest service network in the country.

Gross Sales: 1994   US633.9 million
1995   US$657.2 million

Malaysia Airlines

Founding Concept: To provide Malaysians with an efficient air transport service.

Country of Operations: Malaysia

Description of Operations: Malaysia Airlines is Malaysia's flag carrier, serving most domestic and all international flight routes originating in Malaysia.

Address: 33/F Bangunan MAS, Jalan Sultan Ismail, 50250 Kuala Lumpur, Malaysia

Tel: (603) 265-5010
Fax: (603) 263-5012
WWW: http://www.malaysiaairlines.com.my/airline

Date Founded and History: Malaysia Airlines was incorporated on April 3, 1971, and initially provided services to six international and 34 domestic destinations. Today Malaysia's national carrier operates most of the country's domestic routes and all its international services. In 1994 the government, in a controversial privatization, sold its 32% share of the airline to Tajudin Ramli, who also controls Technology Resources Industries.

Current Leadership: Tajudin Ramli, Chairman
Baharuddin Nordin,
Deputy Managing Director

Significant Events: Following Ramli's acquisition of a controlling interest in August 1994, the airline has expanded rapidly "in terms of routes, revenues, and passengers. Capacity has doubled, while staff, management, and customers have been scurrying to keep pace. The unions, accustomed to a more laid-back management style, have complained bitterly about being overworked and underpaid."[2]

Biggest Challenge: The airline is striving to be on par with the world's best. "If we are just a good Malaysian airline or a good regional airline, we would become irrelevant,"[3] according to Ramli. The race will be fierce as other airlines also gear up for world-class competition.

New Markets or Products Being Pursued: In line with its vision to be a global player in the airline industry, Malaysia Airlines is currently expanding its fleet and routes. It is also investing heavily in its cargo business.

Gross Sales: 1995   US$2.245 billion
1996   US$2.603 billion

---

[2] Shameen, Assif. "Fasten Seat Belts!" (*Asiaweek*, April 25, 1997)

[3] *Ibid.*

Manila Electric Company

⸺⸺⸺⸺⸺ ☆ ⸺⸺⸺⸺⸺

Founding Concept: To serve its customers by providing efficient, adequate, and reliable electric utility at a reasonable cost.

Country of Operations: Philippines

Description of Operations: Manila Electric Company's (Meralco) primary business is the purchase of electricity from power producers and its distribution to residential, commercial, and industrial customers in its franchise area, which includes Metro Manila and the nearby provinces. Its franchise area covers 9,328 square kilometers encompassing 15 cities and 96 municipalities. Meralco's service area, equivalent to only 3% of the country's total land area, produces about 50% of the Philippines' gross domestic product, 30% from Metro Manila alone. The company served 2.9 million customers in 1996, in a franchise inhabited by almost a quarter of the Philippine population of 70.8 million. The company is the biggest among 146 electric utility distributors throughout the country and currently ranks as the second biggest firm in gross revenues.

Address: Meralco Compound, Ortigas Avenue, Pasig City, Philippines 0300
Tel: (632) 631-5557/631-6220/631-2222
Fax: (632) 632-8501/631-5590
WWW: http://meralco.com.ph

Date Founded and History: Meralco was established in 1903 as the Manila Electric Railroad and Light Company. Its original business included the operation of Manila's streetcar or *tranvia*, aside from being a fully integrated electricity generation and distribution company. Meralco's generation business was taken over by the government in the 1970s with the declaration of martial law. Today Meralco is back to power generation through subsidiaries, joint ventures, and power purchase contracts with independent power producers or IPPs. A privately owned corporation, Meralco is the second most widely held company in the country, with roughly 88,000 shareholders worldwide.

Founder: Charles M. Swift

Current Leadership: Manuel M. Lopez, President and Chief Executive Officer

Significant Events: The company is undergoing a self-initiated, complete transformation of business processes, organization, corporate culture, information technology, telecommunications, and facilities to enhance customer focus. For its investors and shareholders, Meralco says it will remain a blue-chip company and a viable long-term investment. For employees, it intends to continue to be the best employer in the country, where opportunities for personal and professional growth "thrive." For customers, Meralco is changing to "delight" its customers.

Biggest Challenge: The biggest challenge currently being faced by the company is the growing demand for cheaper electricity, increased reliability, and good power quality, which is motivating some of its industrial customers to go into self-generation. To meet this challenge, Meralco is improving its operations to increase its overall efficiency. It has also been making representation to the legislative branch to lift compulsory cross-subsidies, which serve to subsidize the rates of residential and small power users as well as some electric cooperatives outside Meralco's franchise area. The company aims to be a world-class electric utility distributor by the year 2000 and to be among the best, if not the best, in the region.

New Markets or Products Being Pursued: Through strategic alliances and partnerships, Meralco is involved in power generation, power plant rehabilitation, business process reengineering, information technology consulting, and real estate development. It has formed a number of subsidiaries in pursuit of these new ventures. These include Computer Information Systems, Inc., Meralco Industrial Engineering Corporation, Iber-Pacific, Rockwell Land Corporation, and the Meralco Stock Transfer Office.

Gross Sales: 1994   US$1.5 billion
1995   US$1.65 billion
1996   US$2 billion

MegaLink, Inc.
—————————————— ☆ ——————————————

Founding Concept: To provide world-class shared resources and value-added services to its member institutions and clients.

Country of Operations: Philippines

Description of Operations: MegaLink was created to manage the shared ATM network facilities of its member banks. Its primary service is the switching of ATM transactions among member institutions, allowing for ease and convenience among clients of these banks. MegaLink also offers a wide range of other services, including point of sale, phone banking, debit bills payment, and shared card production.

Address: 2/F Zeta II Annex Building, 191 Salcedo St., Legaspi Village, Makati City, Philippines
Tel: (632) 892-1046
Fax: (632) 812-0606

Date Founded: September 1989

Founders: Four local banks: Far East Bank and Trust Co., Philippine National Bank, United Coconut Planters Bank, and Equitable Banking Corporation.

Current Leadership: Justo A. Ortiz,
President (Chairman and CEO, Union Bank of the Philippines)
Criselda B. Santillan,
General Manager

Significant Events: MegaLink institutionalized phone banking in the Philippines. Through PhoneLink, cardholders are able to conduct their banking business via ordinary telephones. The company also spearheaded the inter-connection with BancNet and Expressnet, two competing networks, giving MegaLink cardholders the widest access to ATMs in the country (2,700).

Biggest Challenge: The biggest challenges currently facing the company are application for ISO 9000 certification and expansion of its automated interbank back-office systems into a fully secure and operational centralized help desk and intranet facility.

New Markets or Products Being Pursued: The company is expanding its PayLink service, which already has nearly 5,000 terminals in 800 locations nationwide. It also plans to introduce home banking, expand electronic payment systems, introduce share telecommunications, and provide a centralized help desk facility.

Gross Sales: 1994   US$1.2 million
1995   US$1.3 million
1996   US$1.3 million

Modernform Group Public Company Limited

Country of Operations: Thailand

Description of Operations: Modernform imports furniture hardware, materials, and interior furnishing materials for local and retail distribution, and offers a comprehensive range of furniture products.

Address: 699 Srinakarin Road, Suan Luang, Bangkok 10250, Thailand
Tel: (662) 722-8250
Fax: (662) 722-8184

Date Founded and History: Modernform started operations in 1978. Since that time it has grown to become a furniture business group of nine companies. The company has firmly established itself in all segments of the market, offering a comprehensive range of furniture products for both commercial and residential markets.

Current Leadership: Jajjai Dhammarungruang,
President and CEO
Vichian Potajatikul, VP – Corporate
Planning and Business Development

Significant Events: A number of recent events have and will continue to play deciding roles in the coming years. Some of these important events are market liberalization, the impact of AFTA and APEC, and strategic alliances. All these translate to lower tariffs and more sales opportunities in overseas markets.

Biggest Challenge: Modernform's biggest challenge is not merely to maintain its overall market leadership but to excel in its leadership position with greater competitive distinction and management excellence.

New Markets or Products Being Pursued: The concept of "One-Stop Shopping" for all furniture requirements is a management innovation being unrolled with Modernform's newly opened showroom. This innovation will eventually result in a completely revamped retail sales distribution and logistics network.

Gross Sales: 1994   US67.8 million
1995   US$82.5 million
1996   US$84.0 million

Motorola Malaysia Sdn. Bhd.

Founding Concept: To be the leading manufacturer of semiconductors.

Country of Operations: Malaysia

Description of Operations: Motorola Malaysia is engaged in the assembly and final manufacturing of semiconductors, including microprocessors, microcontrollers, and power PCs.

Address: #2 Jalan S.S. 8/2, 47300 Petaling Jaya, Selangor Darul Ehsan, Malaysia
Tel: (603) 773-1133
Fax: (603) 773-1015
WWW: http://www.mot.com

Date Founded and History: Motorola began operations in Malaysia in 1972, with a semiconductor plant in Kuala Lumpur.

Current Leadership: Lew Jin Aun, Managing Director

Mount Elizabeth Hospital Ltd.

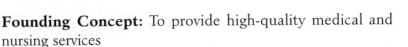

Founding Concept: To provide high-quality medical and nursing services

Country of Operations: Singapore

Description of Operations: Mount Elizabeth Hospital is a premier 505-bed private hospital with a wide range of acute and tertiary (specialist) services. It has sophisticated medical and surgical facilities, as well as subsidiaries that include a laboratory and a nursing agency.

Address: 3 Mount Elizabeth, Singapore 228510
Tel: (65) 737-2666/470-5675
Fax: (65) 731-1189/473-0081

Founders: The hospital is owned by Singapore-based Parkway Group Healthcare, which has three acute care hospitals in Singapore, two in Malaysia, three in Indonesia, and one each in India, Sri Lanka, and the U.K.

Current Leadership: Joshua Goh, General Manager

Significant Events: MEH was the first hospital in the region to receive ISO 9002 certification. It performs the largest number of cardiac surgeries and neurosurgeries in the private sector in the region.

National Steel Corporation

☆

Founding Concept: To manufacture steel products vital to Philippine industry.

Country of Operations: Philippines

Description of Operations: The National Steel Corporation is the leading manufacturer of steel products in the Philippines, with one of the biggest and most modern steel mill installations in Southeast Asia and assets in excess of US$1 billion.

Address: 377 Sen. Gil Puyat Avenue, Makati City, Philippines
Tel: (632) 897-6152
Fax: (632) 895-0280/895-0286

Date Founded and History: The National Steel Corporation was founded by the Philippine government in 1974 to address the acute shortage of steel in the country. Initially built from the ruins of financially distressed businesses, it emerged as one of the largest, most profitable corporate institutions in the country. Today it has one of the biggest and most modern steel mill installations in Southeast Asia.

Current Leadership: Tom L. Galanis, EVP and COO

Biggest Challenge: Diminishing market share as a result of increasing foreign competition is the biggest challenge facing the National Steel Corporation. In response, the company implemented a program that aims to imbibe in each employee the importance of the customer. It conducted a series of workshops and conferences on customer-orientation and held management-driven and people-driven activities to continuously improve products and services.

New Markets or Products Being Pursued: The company is investing in facilities that will produce "modern steel materials" needed in the automotive, appliance, and packaging industries. The acquisition of modern facilities, the upgrading of old ones, and continual technology transfer are geared toward the company's vision of becoming a world-class steel producer.

Neptune Orient Lines Ltd.

Founding Concept: To build up a modern mercantile marine fleet capable of competing with the best merchant shipping companies in the world.

Country of Operations: Singapore

Description of Operations: Primarily a shipping/container company, Neptune Orient Lines has adopted a new corporate identity since 1989, establishing over 62 subsidiaries, 34 associate companies, and 18 investment interests in companies locally and overseas.

Address: 456 Alexandra Road, #06-00 NOL Building, Singapore 119962
Tel: (65) 278-9000
Fax: (65) 278-4900

Date Founded and History: Founded on December 30, 1968, Neptune Orient Lines was the first initiative of the Singapore government to build up a modern mercantile marine fleet. In its early years it offered only liner service. The company has since expanded and ventured into a wide range of business activities spanning the globe. At present the company has dealings in ship management, charter service, shipping agencies, information technology, warehousing and distribution, shipyard and marine engineering, and property ownership.

Current Leadership: Lua Cheng Eng, Chairman

NTUC FairPrice Co-operative Ltd.

Founding Concept: To engage in the business of supermarket and department store retailing.

Country of Operations: Singapore

Description of Operations: NTUC FairPrice Co-operative is engaged in the business of supermarket and department store retailing, with investments in trading, real estate, warehousing, and distribution. It has 59 stores and 3,000 employees.

Address: 680 Upper Thomson Road, Singapore 787103
Tel: (65) 456-0233
Fax: (65) 458-8975
WWW: http://www.ntuc-fairprice.org.sg

Date Founded: May 1, 1983

Current Leadership: Tan Kian Chew, Deputy CEO

Biggest Challenge: The mission of FairPrice is to be the best place to shop by providing customers value for money, fresh products, and service excellence in a pleasant shopping environment as well as the best place to work by providing staff with opportunities and resources to develop their careers and rewarding them fairly for their contributions.

Gross Sales: 1996/97   US$501 million

Perusahaan Otomobil Nasional Berhad (Proton)
☆

Founding Concept: To produce affordable, high-quality cars.

Country of Operations: Malaysia

Description of Operations: Proton manufactures, assembles, and sells motor vehicles and related products. It produced its first cars in 1985, and has since marketed its products in Southeast Asia, Europe, and the U.K.

Address: Wisma HICOM, No. 2 Jalan Usahawan U1/8, Seksyen U1, 40150 Shah Alam, Selangor Darul Ehsan, Malaysia

Tel: (603) 511-1055
Fax: (603) 511-1252

Date Founded and History: Proton was established on May 23, 1983, to manufacture, assemble and sell motor vehicles and related products. In July 1985 it rolled out its first car, the Proton Saga. Since its inception, Proton has become a major player in the industry and is considered by the government to be a major strategic initiative. Until 1995 the company was controlled indirectly by the government's investment arm, Khazanah Holdings, which held a 32% interest in Hicom Holdings, Proton's parent. The government sold its stake in Hicom to then DRB magnate Yahaya Ahmad.

Current Leadership: Saleh Sulong, Chairman, DRB-Hicom Group

Significant Events: The company started showing profits after three years of operation. Since then Proton has realized consistent growth, in part as a result of indirect government subsidies. The company suffered a setback in March 1997 when Yahaya Ahmad died in a helicopter crash.

Biggest Challenge: Proton's biggest challenge is to achieve global competitiveness in terms of product quality and cost. According to Saleh Sulong, "Proton must be more competitive. We have to prepare for when the tariff protection we enjoy is no longer there. That means being price competitive, especially against models that are direct rivals. Our target is to cut costs by a third. While trimming costs, performance and reliability must not suffer. The styling of our cars must remain attractive. These are our top concerns."[4]

New Markets or Products Being Pursued: In addition to new passenger car models, Proton is currently pursuing the production of diesel-engine cars and four-wheel drive vehicles. Lackluster exports have been a concern.

---

[4] Saleh Sulong in an interview in the April 11, 1997, issue of *Asiaweek*.

Gross Sales: 1994 US$1.3 billion
1995 US$1.4 billion

Petron Corporation
———————————————— ☆ ————————————————

Founding Concept: To provide petroleum products to Philippine consumers.

Country of Operations: Philippines

Description of Operations: Petron is the leading refiner and marketer of petroleum products in the country. The company owns the largest petroleum refinery in the Philippines, with a crude distillation capacity of 165,000 barrels per stream day. It supplies a complete range of petroleum products and maintains a dominant position in the local industry, with an overall market share of 42.8% as of end June 1997.

Address: 7901 Petron Building, Makati Avenue, Makati City, Philippines
Tel: (632) 817-5395/840-3152
Fax: (632) 812-1070/815-3921
WWW: http://www.petron.com

Date Founded and History: The refinery was originally constructed by Bataan Refinery Corporation (formerly Standard Vacuum Refinery Corporation), a joint venture between Esso Standard Eastern Inc. and Mobil Oil Corporation, and commenced operations in 1960 with an initial capacity of 25,000 bpsd. Philippine National Oil Company purchased the shares of the Bataan Refinery Corporation from Esso in 1973, and from Mobil in 1983, providing the government with 100% ownership. Between 1987 and 1988, PNOC merged its refining, marketing, tires, batteries, and accessories operations into one entity, Petron Corporation.

Current Leadership: Monico V. Jacob, Chairman
Ali A. Al-Ajmi, President and CEO

Significant Events: Since the start of operations, Petron incurred a loss only in 1975, during the oil crisis. It has held its market leadership for 19 straight years, acquiring nearly 50% of the local market. On August 12, 1993, President Fidel V. Ramos approved the privatization of Petron, with the government retaining a 40% interest, a strategic partner purchasing a 40% interest, and employees and the public eligible to purchase 20% of the corporation. In 1994 the privatization program was completed, with the sale of a 40% equity block to Saudi Aramco. An additional 20% of Petron's equity was sold to employees and the public through an Initial Public Offering that attracted more than 496,000 individual investors, most investing for the first time. Privatization has given the company greater flexibility to operate in an increasingly competitive oil industry.

Biggest Challenge: In 1996 President Ramos approved the deregulation of the oil industry. This development poses, the company believes, a great challenge with the expected increase in competition. To address this challenge, the company's strategy is as follows: expansion and upgrading of refinery and marketing facilities; major re-imaging of retail outlets, with the view of reflecting its service and customer orientation; ensuring safety, efficiency, reliability, and cost-effectiveness of operations, optimization of refinery capacity, organizational restructuring to maintain a lean and efficient workforce; adoption of SAP, an enterprise-wide information technology solution to further improve business processes; and enhancement of a customer-focused culture.

New Markets or Products Being Pursued: In 1996 Petron undertook an aggressive marketing program with the launching of several new products:

- Petron was the first oil company in the Philippines to produce unleaded and 95-octane gasoline and low-sulfur diesel.
- Petron with XCS was launched in June 1996. The product uses the latest generation fully synthetic gasoline additive developed principally to achieve better engine performance and longer

service life. It is available in premium low lead and unleaded Petron gasoline at no extra cost to motorists.

■ Two household products were launched in September 1996 – the Gasulito, a more affordable midsize LPG cylinder ideal for small families; and the Gasul SVM Regulator, a new LPG cylinder regulator designed to enhance the safety and welfare of the household user.

■ The company acquired an exclusive license to distribute Pennzoil Motor Oil.

Gross Sales: 1994   US$1.6 billion
1995   US$1.56 billion
1996   US$1.87 billion

Philippine Appliance Corporation

Founding Concept: To provide world-class refrigerators

Country of Operations: Philippines

Description of Operations: Philippine Appliance Corporation (Philacor) is engaged in the manufacture and distribution of refrigerators, air conditioners, gas cooking appliances, televisions, and stereos. Its partners are White Westinghouse and General Electric Appliances.

Address: 8377 Dr. A. Santos Avenue, Paranaque, Manila, Philippines
Tel: (632) 829-4921/815-8811
Fax: (632) 828-2731/828-7465

Date Founded and History: Incorporated in August 1963, Philacor started as a small office of 13 people and produced 200 refrigerators during its first year of operation. It started to manufacture other household appliances when it was granted a technical license and brand agreement by White Westinghouse. In 1976, General Electric Appliances became its new partner. The company's present brands include GE, Hotpoint, White Westinghouse, and Winner.

Founder: Dante G. Santos

Current Leadership: Dante G. Santos, Chairman and CEO
Marsha R. Santos, Sr. Vice President,
Corplan and Services

Significant Events: Despite the highly competitive nature of the industry, Philacor's refrigerators account for a 65% share of the total market.

Biggest Challenge: Trade and tariff liberalization has opened up the market to global competition and new technology. The company is responding through the manufacture of globally competitive products with world-class features, appearance, costs, and quality. The company is investing approximately $125 million in a new technologically advanced refrigerator manufacturing facility in Calamba, Laguna.

New Markets or Products Being Pursued: Philacor is currently implementing strategies to sustain growth and maintain leadership. Some of its plans include competitive pricing, consumer financing support, and nationwide after-sales service.

Gross Sales: 1994   US$78.7 million
1995   US$111.19 million
1996   US$116.1 million

Philippine Business for Social Progress

Founding Concept: To form and organize an institution that would serve as the member business organizations' arm for corporate social responsibility.

Country of Operations: Philippines

Description of Operations: Established and funded by a group of corporations to express corporate social responsibility, the Philippine Business for Social Progress (PBSP) undertakes social and community development programs and projects in the areas of social credit, enterprise development, agrarian reform, institution building, community organizing, housing, environment, disaster relief and rehabilitation, and corporate involvement.

Address: 3/F Philippine Social Development Center, Magallanes cor. Real St. Intramuros, Manila, Philippines
Tel: (632) 527-7741
Fax: (632) 527-3743
WWW: http://www.pinsph.net/pbsp

Date Founded and History: On December 6, 1970, 50 Filipino businessmen established PBSP with the vision of improving the quality of life of the Filipino poor. In contrast to the practice of charity, the organization provided long-term assistance through projects promoting self-reliance. In its early years PBSP developed project prototypes in low-cost housing, nutrition and health, community organizing, and social credit. More than 20 years later PBSP had evolved its sustainable development strategy, the Area Resource Management Strategy, which brings together ecology management, economic development, and organization planning in long-term projects in six priority areas nationwide. As the country industrializes, PBSP has scaled up its operations to rapidly urbanizing or "high growth" areas where its traditional communities/partners are being affected. Here, PBSP will promote multisectoral partnerships between the business sector, government, donors, and NGO networks. Since its founding, PBSP has taken the lead in promoting good corporate citizenship and developed more than 1,000 partner organizations. Its membership has grown to 187 firms that provide consultancy, financial, and technical support to social development activities.

Current Leadership: Andres Soriano III, Chairman
Ma. Aurora Francisco-Tolentino,
Executive Director

Significant Events: Since its inception, PBSP has provided more than P1.2 billion for the implementation of 3,639 projects benefiting at least 1.8 million Filipino poor households. In addition, PBSP has brokered monies to projects worth P1.88 billion in the last six years (of this amount, P1.36 billion financed small- and medium-scale enterprises in the countryside, generating 30,826 full-time jobs).

Biggest Challenge: Decentralization and local democracy changed the focus of development from Metro Manila to the provinces. This prompted the organization to redesign its programs to be responsive to the demands of increased local autonomy. Market liberalization spurred PBSP to respond with programs assisting the rural poor, especially in high-growth areas. It is directing more member company involvement to the effort of encouraging communities to be more entrepreneurial and competitive, enabling them to join the mainstream in their economic development. A downward trend in donations prompted the organization to leverage its resources with the business sector, local governments, and other donors.

New Markets or Products Being Pursued: In the future, the organization aims to be the leader in harnessing business sector commitment to social development. It plans to assist member firms in exploring more innovative community relations projects, and to implement collectively high-impact development projects. To the larger business community, PBSP, through its Center for Corporate Citizenship, continues to encourage business leaders to address the critical issues of Philippine society (education, environment, local governance, and countryside development).

Gross Sales: 1994   US$5.8 million
            1995   US$3.7 million

Philippine Long Distance Telephone Company

Founding Concept: To provide telephone services.
Country of Operations: Philippines

Description of Operations: The Philippine Long Distance Telephone Company (PLDT) is the largest and most diversified telecommunications company in the Philippines, with a network of 170 central offices serving Metro Manila and 181 other cities and municipalities.

Address: Ramon Cojuangco Building, Makati Avenue, Makati City, Philippines
Tel: (632) 819-1577
Fax: (632) 815-1703
WWW: http://www.pldt.com.ph

Date Founded and History: PLDT was established on November 28, 1928, following the signing into law of a bill signed by Gov. Gen. Henry Stimson, which enfranchised the company to engage in the provision of telephone services. In two years it acquired the assets, properties, and franchises of businesses of the telephone systems then existing in the country. The succeeding years saw the company's steady growth, providing telephone connections in the provinces of Luzon and expanding rapidly into other parts of the country. Today PLDT is the largest and most diversified of more than 64 entities providing telecommunications services in the country. It now has a network of 170 central offices serving the Metro Manila area and 181 other cities and municipalities all over the Philippines, accounting for around 85% of all telephone lines in the country. Its range of services has gone beyond voice to include data as well as image and video transmission. It has also introduced a line of value-added network services, such as leased digital lines, high-speed data transmission, private networking, and high-performance packet switching services.

Current Leadership: Antonio Cojuangco,
President and CEO
Roberto Romulo,
Chairman of the Board
Enrique D. Perez,
SEVP – Chief Operating Officer

Biggest Challenge: PLDT is faced with increasing levels of competition in the industry. To address this threat, the company has developed a set of strategies aimed at delivering services at a more competitive cost, improving its service levels, optimizing its revenues from traditional and new services, obtaining new and more innovative means of financing for its expansion programs, and asserting leadership in the industry.

New Markets or Products Being Pursued: In addition to maintaining its dominant position in the provision of basic telephone and toll services, PLDT would also like to make its presence felt in other areas of the telecommunications sector, such as dedicated leased line services, switched services, and value-added services.

Gross Sales: 1994   US$779 million
1995   US$884 million
1996   US$1 billion

Procter & Gamble (Phils.), Inc.

Founding Concept: To fulfill social and environmental responsibilities in order to improve the quality of life in the communities of the company's operations.

Country of Operations: Philippines

Description of Operations: Procter & Gamble (P&G) Philippines develops, manufactures, and markets consumer products in the laundry, cleaning, food, beauty, and health care segments.

Address: 6750 Ayala Avenue Office Tower, Ayala Center, Makati City, Philippines
Tel: (632) 814-8100
Fax: (632) 818-2190
WWW: http://www.pg.com

Date Founded and History: Established in 1935, P&G

Philippines started its business with only a handful of products in laundry and edible fats and oils. The succeeding years saw the expansion of the company's product lines. At present the company deals in nine product categories: laundry and cleaning, personal cleansing, hair care, disposable diapers, catamenials, health care, snacks, cosmetics, and fragrances and skin care. Considered the market leader in most of its core businesses, P&G products have become part of the Filipino home.

Founders: Two American ex-soldiers who founded the Philippine Manufacturing Company (PMC); acquired by Procter & Gamble Co. in 1935

Current Leadership: Johnip G. Cua,
President and General Manager
Renato M. Jiao, Director – HRD

Significant Events: In its first year total sales amounted to less than US$1 million. In financial year 1996–97 sales reached US$500 million. The company is ranked among the top 20 companies in the Philippines and is larger than any of its major competitors in the country.

Biggest Challenge: P&G Philippines strives to bring world-class products to the Philippine market and make them affordable to the majority of Filipino consumers. When the company introduced a sanitary napkin brand designed with its patented sanitary weave topsheet in the country, its packaging served as a major challenge. Since the price was steep for the regular packs of 20 (standard in most countries) for the Filipino market, P&G Philippines produced packs of eight and four, and later singles, to respond to the budgetary constraints of the market.

The biggest challenge being faced by P&G Philippines is building the organizational capability to respond to the demands of the constantly changing business environment.

New Markets or Products Being Pursued: Downy Fabric Conditioner has expanded the fabric conditioner market sevenfold within months of its introduction.

Gross Sales: 1994 US$359 million
1995 US$450 million

PT. Aqua Golden Mississippi
☆

Founding Concept: To provide clean bottled water products of international standards.

Country of Operations: Indonesia

Description of Operations: Manufactures and produces bottled water products distributed throughout the country.

Address: Jalan Pulo Lentut No. 3 Kawasan Industri Pulo Gadung, Jakarta 13920, Indonesia
Tel: (6221) 460-3070
Fax: (6221) 460-9177

Date Founded: February 23, 1974

Founders: Tirto Utomo, Slamet Utomo, and Willy Sidharta

Current Leadership: Willy Sidharta, President-Director
John Abdi, Finance Director
Purnama Sidhi,
General Affairs Director
Tanty Irawati, Production Director

Significant Events: Aqua Golden Mississippi has enjoyed steady growth in terms of liters of water products produced. To date, its growth in terms of volume is 23%, and growth in terms of value is 34%.

Biggest Challenge: The company is facing rising competition due to the increasing numbers of new players entering the market. The company will benefit from a new government regulation providing for "more fair competition," according to officials.

New Markets or Products Being Pursued: The company is expanding all 11 factories in Indonesia and constructing four new facilities. It is also launching two new products, a 600 ml bottle and a 240 ml bottle.

Gross Sales: 1994   US$49 million
1995   US$66 million
1996   US$73 million

PT. Bakrie Pipe Industries

———————— ☆ ————————

Founding Concept: To produce electrical resistance welded steel pipes for the international market.

Country of Operations: Indonesia

Description of Operations: Bakrie Pipe Industries is the pioneer manufacturer and producer of electrical resistance welded steel pipes for oil and gas pipes in Indonesia.

Address: Wisma Bakrie, 1F Jalan H.R. Rasuna Aid Kav. B-1, Jakarta 12920, Indonesia
Tel: (6221) 522-5546/522-5550/527-7035
Fax: (6221) 525-0527

Date Founded: 1981

Current Leadership: Tanri Abeng, President-Commissioner
Tongam H. Loebis, President-Director

Significant Events: Bakrie Pipe Industries was the first Indonesian pipe manufacturing company to receive ISO 9002 certification as well as certification by the American Petroleum Institute (February 1991). The company has 45% of its market.

Biggest Challenge: The company is focusing on becoming an internationally competitive producer of steel pipes. It has, therefore, worked on improving its operations by introducing total quality management, in-depth worker training and involvement, and customer contact programs. However, the company benefits "from both a 20% import tariff as well as a Presidential Decree which mandates the use of domestically processed pipes, even if the price of these pipes is 15% more expensive than imported ones."

Gross Sales: 1995   US$514 million
1996   US$640 million

PT. Bank Bali

Country of Operations: Indonesia

Address: Bank Bali Tower I, Jalan Jend. Sudarman Kav. 27, Jakarta 12910, Indonesia
Tel: (6221) 523-7899
Fax: (6221) 250-0882

Date Founded: 1955

Current Leadership: Rudy Ramli, President-Commissioner

New Markets or Products Being Pursued: Bank Bali is aiming to strengthen its competitive position in the banking industry by providing comprehensive, convenient, and high-quality financial services. The bank will become more active in trade finance and financial brokerage. It also intends to move aggressively into housing loans/mortgages and passenger car financing.

PT. Blue Bird Group

Founding Concept: To provide quality transportation services.

Country of Operations: Indonesia

Description of Operations: Starting as a small taxi company with 25 taxis, the company has expanded to become the Blue Bird Group, with four main divisions – Land Transportation, Property, Industry, and Other Services. It now has 3,800 vehicles for its eight different types of services.

Address: Jalan Hos. Cokroaminoto, Jakarta Pusat, Indonesia
Tel: (6221) 798-9000/798-9111
Fax: (6221) 799-9102/798-9101/798-9102

Date Founded and History: Blue Bird began operating in May 1972 and has grown into an established transportation company. Today, Blue Bird also has interests in property, manages petrol and filling stations, and manufactures and assembles vehicle parts.

Current Leadership: Mutiara Djokosoetono, President-Director

Purnomo Prawiro, Director of Operations

Significant Events: Blue Bird was the first taxi company in Indonesia to use argometers and the first to adopt radio communications to enable customers to phone for a taxi.

Gross Sales: 1994   US$62 million

PT. Bridgestone Tire Indonesia
☆

Founding Concept: To manufacture vehicle tires and tubes.

Country of Operations: Indonesia

Description of Operations: Bridgestone Tire Indonesia is the country's leading manufacturer and distributor of tires and tubes for automobiles, trucks, and buses.

Address: 18/F Nusantara Bldg., Jalan M. H. Thamrin 59, Jakarta, Indonesia
Tel: (6221) 336-591
Fax: (6221) 331-136/336-345

Current Leadership: Atsumi Kawaguchi, President-Director

Biggest Challenge: In response to increasing competition, the company is adopting more customer-oriented strategies. For instance, "The Fleet Guidance Program" has enabled the company to establish closer business relationships with truck and bus tire users. In this program, the company's service engineers periodically visit major clients to provide technical seminars on tire maintenance.

New Markets or Products Being Pursued: Bridgestone Tire Indonesia is presently increasing its export business.

Gross Sales: 1994 US$153.0 million
1995 US$187.0 million
1996 US$203.6 million

PT. Caltex Pacific Indonesia
————————————— ☆ —————————————

Founding Concept: To engage in oil and gas exploration and the production of oil and gas products.

Country of Operations: Indonesia

Description of Operations: Caltex Pacific Indonesia explores, develops, and produces oil and gas products.

Address: Menara Thamrin Suite 2501, Jalan M. H. Thamrin Kav. 3, Jakarta 10340, Indonesia
Tel: (6221) 601-0404/380-3730
Fax: (6221) 230-2565

Date Founded and History: Chevron and Texaco Inc. jointly established Caltex Pacific Indonesia in 1936 to engage in oil exploration. In 1952 the company started refining oil. Today, it is the largest crude oil refiner in Indonesia, generating approximately 750,000 barrels of oil per day.

Current Leadership: Baihaki H. Hakim,
President and Chairman

Significant Events: The company is the largest oil producer in Indonesia, accounting for more than half the country's total oil production and more than 60% of its oil gross revenues.

Biggest Challenge: The challenges facing the company are: reserve replacements, increasing cost per barrel, and sustaining its status as a preferred investment option to shareholders. Caltex Pacific Indonesia's response to these challenges was the major restructuring of the company from a functional into a process-based strategic business unit organization. The company "is assessing the 'downstream' market ahead of anticipated deregulation which will permit access to significant opportunities. Refining, distribution, and marketing projects are envisaged to complement the activities of Caltex Pacific Indonesia."

New Markets or Products Being Pursued: The company is currently pursuing exploration of new areas offering high potential for oil and gas reserves.

Gross Sales: 1994   US$4.7 billion

PT. Charoen Pokphand Indonesia
☆

Founding Concept: To develop and provide feed products with a high protein content.

Country of Operations: Indonesia

Description of Operations: Charoen Pokphand is a leading agro-industrial company, with high-quality animal feed and poultry livestock as its major business. The company is also engaged in aquaculture and has established its own support operations.

Address: Jalan Ancol VIII No. 1 Ancol Barat Jakarta, Utara, Indonesia
Tel: (6221) 691-2501
Fax: (6221) 690-7324

Date Founded: 1972

Founders: Sumet Jiaravanon, Montri Jiaravanont, Jaran Chearavanont, and Johannes Purnama Sudarma

Current Leadership: Thong Chotirat, President-Director

Biggest Challenge: The company faces increasing competition in the business of livestock and animal feed. It is responding through good after-sales technical service and consistent quality assurance of its products.

Gross Sales: 1994   US$401 million

PT. Great Giant Pineapple Company
————————— ☆ —————————

Founding Concept: To establish a world-class food company.

Country of Operations: Indonesia

Description of Operations: Great Giant Pineapple Co. manufactures canned pineapple products (slices, chunks, tidbits, crushed), pineapple juice concentrate, and tropical fruit salad. The company is the leader in Indonesia in pineapple exports, and it has acquired an 18% share of the world canned pineapple market.

Address: 20/F Chase Plaza Tower, Jalan Jend. Sudirman Kav. 21, Jakarta 12910, Indonesia
Tel: (6221) 570-6438
Fax: (6221) 570-6443

Date Founded and History: Great Giant Pineapple Co. was established in 1979 and started producing commercially in 1985. In a span of ten years, company sales grew from US$5 million to US$150 million, making it one of the fastest growing pineapple companies in the world.

Founders: Husodo Angkosubroto and Setiawan Achmad

Current Leadership: Husodo Angkosubroto, President
Setiawan Achmad, Managing Director
Iswanto, Production Director
Sacharia Tanuwidjaja, Finance Director
Terry Bahar, Marketing Director

Significant Events: The company has achieved steady growth. It maintains a 20% average annual growth and is currently one of the world's largest pineapple companies.

Biggest Challenge: The company is faced with the challenge of maintaining its leadership in a growing market with increasing competition. It is responding by increasing efficiency in all parts of production. It plans to invest heavily in technology and computerize all parts of the operation.

New Markets or Products Being Pursued: In line with its mission to be a world leader in the pineapple industry, the company is currently focusing on new markets, such as South America and Asia, as well as the domestic market.

Gross Sales: 1994   US$57 million
1995   US$70 million
1996   US$150 million

PT. Indorama Synthetics

Founding Concept: To be the leading producer of polyester and spun yarns in Indonesia.

Country of Operations: Indonesia

Description of Operations: Indorama is Indonesia's single largest producer of synthetic textile raw materials. It has manufacturing facilities in Thailand, India, Nepal, Sri Lanka, and Indonesia.

Address: 10/F Central Plaza, Jalan Jend. Sudirman Kav. 47-48, Jakarta 12930, Indonesia
Tel: (6221) 526-1555
Fax: (6221) 526-1501/526-1508
WWW: http://www/indoekchange.com/jsx/indorama/bawah.html

Date Founded and History: Established by the textile trader M.L. Lohia, Indorama traces its beginnings to 1976 when the company was best described as a modest spinning plant. Today it is Indonesia's largest producer of synthetic textile raw materials, such as spun yarns, polyester staple fiber, filament yarns, fabric, and resins.

Founder: M.L. Lohia

Current Leadership: S.P. Lohia, Managing Director

Significant Events: Indorama is the only Indonesian producer of polyester and spun yarns with ISO 9002 certification. It is also the only producer to be exempted from the EU anti-dumping duty on imports of polyester textured yarns into Europe in 1996.

Biggest Challenge: The challenges faced by Indorama are global competition and the sourcing of raw materials. With the goal "Asian Costs European Quality" the company is developing new markets, minimizing waste and maximizing high-quality production, focusing on product innovation, investing in the latest technology, and entering into long-term arrangements with customers and suppliers.

New Markets or Products Being Pursued: Indorama is planning to invest heavily in petrochemicals production. It is also entering the China market.

Gross Sales: 1994   US$176 million
1995   US$301 million
1996   US$289 million

PT. Mustika Ratu

Founding Concept: To establish a home industry producing cosmetics and health supplements using natural ingredients.

Country of Operations: Indonesia

Description of Operations: Mustika Ratu is the local market leader in cosmetics and natural supplements (*jamu*). It produces over 500 cosmetic products and over 60 *jamus* distributed to both local and foreign markets.

Address: Mustika Ratu Center, Jalan Gatot Subroto Kav. 74-75, Jakarta 12870, Indonesia
Tel: (6221) 830-6754
Fax: (6221) 830-6760
WWW: http://www.mustika-ratu.co.id

Date Founded and History: Mustika Ratu was established in March 1978 when founder B.R.A. Mooryati Soedibyo (a descendant of the Javanese royal family) decided to commercially manufacture traditional Indonesian herbal-based health and beauty products. Known as *jamu*, these products were based on preparations used by the royal family. Since then the company has introduced different lines of makeup and cosmetic products, and it is presently considered Indonesia's leading manufacturer of natural cosmetic supplements.

Founder: B.R.A. Mooryati Soedibyo

Current Leadership: B.R.A. Mooryati Soedibyo, President-Director

Significant Events: Mustika Ratu has achieved steady growth. It has posted 30% annual sales growth.

New Markets or Products Being Pursued: The company intends to penetrate new market segments, and has launched a new line of body care products for infants and toddlers. Labeled "Ananda," the line includes such products as baby powder, baby lotion, and baby oil.

Gross Sales: 1994 US17.8 million
1995 US$19.8 million

PT. Sempati Air

Founding Concept: To provide high-quality, safe, and customer-oriented air transportation service

Country of Operations: Indonesia

Description of Operations: Sempati Air operated for 21 years as a charter carrier. It became a scheduled Indonesian airline in 1990, competing with the government's Garuda and Merpati airlines.

Address: Ground Floor, Terminal Building Halim Perdana Kusuma Airport, Jakarta, Indonesia
Tel: (6221) 550-2208/809-4407/809-1612
Fax: (6221) 809-4420
WWW: http://www.sempati.co.id/teknik

Date Founded and History: Sempati Air began operations

in 1968 as a charter carrier. In 1990 it became a scheduled airline. Its most important shareholder is the Humpuss Group, which is controlled by Hutomo Mandala Putra, better known as Tommy Suharto, the 34-year-old son of Indonesia's President Suharto.

Current Leadership: Santun Nainggolan, President-Director

Significant Events: Sempati Air led the industry in Indonesia in on-time performance and service improvement programs. Previously, other Indonesian carriers were known for their unreliable schedules and poor customer service. However, the airline has struggled financially, and undertook a restructuring that was to be completed by July 1997.

Biggest Challenge: Sempati Air's major challenge is achieving and sustaining profitable operations.

New Markets or Products Being Pursued: Sempati Air is focusing on customer retention and frequent-flying domestic business travellers. To achieve this goal, the airline prioritizes on-time departures, convenient schedules, and convenient reservation procedures.

PT. Telekomunikasi Indonesia

Founding Concept: To provide telephone services in Indonesia.

Country of Operations: Indonesia

Description of Operations: Telekomunikasi Indonesia provides domestic and international telecommunications services, including telephone, telex, telegraph, leased channels, data communications, and mobile phone services.

Address: Jalan Cisanggarung II, Bandung, West Java, Indonesia
Tel: (6222) 436-1000/452-7101/452-1510
Fax: (6222) 440-313/707-105
WWW: http://www.telkom.net.id

Date Founded and History: The company was established in 1965 when the Indonesian government decided to separate postal and telecommunications services into two state-owned companies. In 1970 Telekomunikasi Indonesia became a public company.

Current Leadership: Setianto P. Sentosa, President-Director

Biggest Challenge: There is an increasing demand for telephone services in Indonesia. The company has responded by forging joint venture agreements with other telecommunications operators. Singapore Telecom and U.S. West have recently begun operations in the company's five regional divisions.

New Markets or Products Being Pursued: Telekomunikasi Indonesia plans to deliver new multimedia services, such as videoconferencing. It intends to sustain market leadership in the fixed wire business by digitizing its network, replacing copper with fiber optic, and introducing broadband technology.

Gross Sales: 1994   US$1.93 billion

PT. Wastika Karya

Founding Concept: To establish a premier construction company.

Country of Operations: Indonesia

Description of Operations: Wastika Karya is a general contractor and developer for civil works, building and industrial construction, realty and property, material and equipment rental and trading, and mechanical and electrical works.

Address: Jalan Biru Laut X Kau, No. 18 Cawang, Jakarta 13340, Indonesia
Tel: (6221) 850-8501/850-8500
Fax: (6221) 850-8506

Date Founded and History: Wastika Karya was incorporated on March 15, 1973, to undertake a wide range of construction works. Its initial ventures consisted of waterworks, airports, and office building construction. The company has expanded its business and is presently engaged in the construction of hotels, condominiums, apartments, and factories in several Indonesian cities.

Founder: The government of Indonesia, through Government Regulation No. 40/1970

Current Leadership: Christiawan, President-Director

Gross Sales: 1994   US$210.8 million
　　　　　　1995   US$271.7 million

Renong Berhad

☆

Founding Concept: To build infrastructure projects in Malaysia.

Country of Operations: Malaysia

Description of Operations: Renong is a strategic investment holding company heading a group of 12 other publicly listed companies. The company is an integrated infrastructure conglomerate involved in construction, engineering and infrastructure, expressways and tolls, and property development.

Address: 42 Jalan Syed Putra, 50460 Kuala Lumpur, Malaysia
Tel: (603) 274-2166
Fax: (603) 274-3985/272-5724

Date Founded and History: Renong was incorporated on October 7, 1982, and became a public listed company in January 1984. It was initially involved in general construction and the manufacture of building materials.

Current Leadership: Mohd. Zakhir Siddiqy Sidek, CEO

Biggest Challenge: Expanding its business to foreign

markets is the biggest challenge being faced by the company. To meet this challenge, Renong has begun to investigate opportunities in developing countries. In India, the company is undertaking a feasibility study that aims to develop a comprehensive expressway system. It has also recently secured projects in South Africa, the Philippines, Vietnam, Uzbekistan, and Indonesia.

New Markets or Products Being Pursued: The company is currently implementing projects critical to the economic development and improvement of the quality of life in Malaysia. These projects include expressways, telecommunications, urban transportation, townships and industrial zones, oil and gas, power, and airports. It is also undertaking infrastructure projects in other countries.

Royal Sporting House

Founding Concept: To engage in the marketing, retail, and distribution of sporting goods and lifestyle products.

Country of Operations: Singapore

Description of Operations: Royal Sporting House is one of the largest distributors and retailers of sporting goods and lifestyle products in Asia. It has a network of over 200 stores in ten countries and the total will exceed 300 stores by 1998. Group sales is expected to hit S$300 million in 1997. The group's portfolio of distribution lines grew rapidly to include more than 25 international namebrands including Reebok, Mizuno, Wilson, Spalding, Taylor Made, Ellesse, Speedo, Jacoste, Niblick Mitre, Rockport, Next, Dr. Martens, Unionbay, Hot Tuna, and Reactor.

Address: 190 MacPherson Road, Wisma Gulab, Singapore 348548

Date Founded and History: The Royal Sporting House group was established by J.S. Gill in September 1977 to engage in the marketing of sporting goods and apparel. From a single enterprise located at High Street, Singapore, Royal Sporting House has expanded to include more than 25 internationally-renowned distribution lines. Many of its stores are award-winning concepts. By 1997, the company had grown to incorporate a group of more than 26 subsidiary companies in ten countries.

Current Leadership: J.S. Gill, Chairman
K.V. Gomber, CEO

Biggest Challenge: Since its inception in 1977, Royal Sporting House has grown into a regional powerhouse. Its biggest challenge is to catapult Royal Sporting House on to the global stage and to establish the group as a leading global player in the sports and lifestyle arena.

New Markets or Products Being Pursued: The group is expanding into South Korea.

Gross Sales: 1994   US$135 million
1995   US$149 million
1996   US$173 million

San Miguel Corporation

Country of Operations: Philippines

Description of Operations: San Miguel Corporation is the largest publicly listed food, beverage, and packaging company in the Philippines. Founded in 1890 as a small brewery, the company and its subsidiaries today generate about 4% of the Philippines' GNP and about 6% of government tax revenues.

Address: San Miguel Corporation, 40 San Miguel Avenue, Mandaluyong City, Philippines
Tel: (632) 632-3000
Fax: (632) 632-2878
WWW: http://www.sanmiguel.com.ph

Date Founded and History: San Miguel Corporation was

originally the product of a partnership formed in 1890 between Don Enrique Barretto y de Ycaza and Don Pedro Pablo Roxas. The company is now the Philippines' biggest private employer with over 30,000 employees. Manufacturing operations have extended to Hong Kong, China, Indonesia, Taiwan, and Guam. Its products are exported to 24 countries around the world. The company has been consistently cited as one of the most-admired multinational corporations in Asia in surveys conducted by international business publications such as the *Far Eastern Economic Review* and *Asian Business*.

Founders: Don Enrique Barretto y de Ycaza
Don Pedro Pablo Roxas

Current Leadership: Andres Soriano, III,
Chairman and CEO
Francisco Eizmendi,
President and COO
Delfin C. Gonzalez, Jr., CFO

Significant Events: SMC's flagship product, San Miguel Beer, holds about 80% of the Philippine market. It is among the world's best selling beers and among the top three brands in Asia. The company has five breweries in the Philippines, one brewery each in Hong Kong and Vietnam, and joint ventures in Indonesia, Guangdong province and Baoding in China. In recent years, the company has struggled with declining market share in Hong Kong and, increased competition in the Philippines.

Biggest Challenge: The company is facing challenges from the Asian and international breweries in its key markets, and must devise products and marketing programs to effectively meet these challenges.

New Markets or Products Being Pursued: In recent years, the company has expanded through foreign joint ventures although it also has long-standing partnerships in the Coca-Cola company and Nestle. Other joint venture partners include the New Zealand Dairy Board, Yamamura Glass,

Fuso Machine and Mold Manufacturing, Bull Corporation, and Conselbera CampoSio.

Gross Sales: 1994   US$2.35 billion
                1995   US$2.69 billion
                1996   US$2.98 billion

Sime Darby Berhad

Country of Operations: Malaysia

Description of Operations: Sime Darby is one of Asia's leading multinational conglomerates, with more than 300 companies in 22 countries worldwide.

Address: 21/F Wisma Sime Darby, Jalan Raja Laut, 50350 Kuala Lumpur, Malaysia
Tel: (603) 291-4122
Fax: (603) 298-7398
WWW: http://www.simenet.com

Date Founded and History: Sime Darby was founded in 1910 by William Middleton Sime and Henry Darby to manage 500 acres of rubber estates. It has since widened its involvement in plantations and expanded into other areas, beginning with general trading and subsequently getting into the distribution of Caterpillar equipment. Today Sime Darby has core business activities that include plantations, manufacturing, heavy equipment and motor vehicle distribution, property development, oil and gas generation, banking, and insurance services. It is presently one of Southeast Asia's leading multinationals.

Current Leadership: Nik Mohamed Yaacob,
                      Group Chief Executive

Significant Events: From a plantation-based company, Sime Darby has become Malaysia's premier corporation and the largest multinational in Southeast Asia, with an annual profit of US$300 million.

Biggest Challenge: Sime Darby's major challenge is to sustain market leadership in its businesses and to ensure continued growth and profits. To achieve this goal, the company plans to enter more joint ventures with leading global companies. The company believes this will provide a competitive edge in both technology and marketing. It is also implementing action programs that emphasize efficiency, cost and wastage reduction, and productivity. Export marketing initiatives will also be intensified.

New Markets or Products Being Pursued: Aside from stepping up its local production of consumer goods to meet increasing demand, Sime Darby plans to broaden its operations by expanding to China, Vietnam, and Australia, which the company considers growth markets for heavy equipment sales and services. It is also targeting North America, Europe, and Japan as markets for an array of products such as golf balls, aircraft tires, and gloves.

Gross Sales: 1994   US$3.2 billion
1995   US$3.68 billion
1996   US$4.22 billion

Sime UEP Properties Berhad

Founding Concept: To be the Best Malaysian Property developer.

Country of Operations: Malaysia

Description of Operations: Sime UEP is a property developer with real estate and residential property development as major activities.

Address: 3/F Wisma Tractors, No. 7 Jalan SS 16/1 Subang Jaya, 47500 Petaling Jaya, Selangor Darul Ehsan, Malaysia
Tel: (603) 766-0088/733-0088
Fax: (603) 733-2122

Current Leadership: Mohamed Hj. Said,
Managing Director

Significant Events: Sime UEP was the first Malaysian property developer to be accredited with ISO 9002 certification and the first to receive the International Real Estate Federation (FIABCI) Award, which is intended to recognize leading organizations for their achievements in the property industry.

Biggest Challenge: The biggest challenge facing the company is maintaining sales volume in spite of the continuing increase of prices in the property market. By increasing its range of products, the company plans to capture a wider market segment.

New Markets or Products Being Pursued: The company has recently ventured into commercial and industrial projects in addition to its various residential developments.

Gross Sales: 1994   US$150.6 million
            1995   US$142.6 million
            1996   US$202.2 million

Singapore Airlines Limited

Founding Concept: To engage in air transportation and related businesses.

Country of Operations: Singapore

Description of Operations: Singapore Airlines (SIA) is engaged in air transportation services to 90 cities in more than 40 countries.

Address: 25 Airline Road, Airline House, Singapore 819829
Tel: (65) 541-5032
Fax: (65) 545-6375
WWW: http://www.singaporeair.com

Date Founded and History: SIA had its beginnings in May 1947, when Malayan Airways operated its first commercial flight. The airline was renamed twice in the 1960s. At SIA's launch on October 1, 1972, its ten aircraft linked 22 cities in 18 countries.

Current Leadership: Cheong Choong Kong,
Deputy Chairman and CEO

Significant Events: From a small regional carrier, Singapore Airlines has grown to become one of the top five international carriers in the world in terms of revenue passenger kilometers.

Biggest Challenge: SIA recognizes the need to meet the challenge of rising labor costs and a strong local currency. The airline will stand by the policies that have served it well in the past, including steady fleet and network growth; product and service excellence and innovation; prudent financial management; investment in training and infrastructure; and a drive for greater operational efficiency.

New Markets or Products Being Pursued: SIA will continue with the business that it knows best – flying passengers and freight all over the world and providing aircraft engineering and airport ground handling services.

Gross Sales: 1994/95 US$4.1 billion
1995/96 US$4.37 billion
1996/97 US$4.51 billion

Singapore General Hospital
— ☆ —

Founding Concept: To provide good medical services.

Country of Operations: Singapore

Description of Operations: Singapore General Hospital (SGH) is Singapore's largest acute and tertiary hospital and national referral center, with 1,660 beds and a pool of about 500 doctors. It accounts for 32% of the total beds in the public hospital sector and 26% of the acute beds in both private and public hospitals.

Address: Outram Road, Singapore 169608
Tel: (65) 222-3322
Fax: (65) 222-1720
WWW: http://www.sgh.gov.sg

Date Founded and History: The Singapore General Hospital was established in the early 19th century, soon after Singapore was founded in 1819.

Current Leadership: Lawrence Lim, CEO

Significant Events: The restructuring of SGH was the hospital's most important event in recent years. Restructuring involved the transfer of management responsibility for the hospital from the Ministry of Health to a 100% government-owned company. This allowed for greater autonomy and flexibility of SGH's operations, helping it become more responsive to the rapid pace of change in health care services.

Biggest Challenge: As the government's flagship hospital, SGH bears the political responsibility of ensuring access, equity, affordability, and a high quality of medical services for all Singaporeans, regardless of socioeconomic status.

New Markets or Products Being Pursued: The hospital is committed to providing quality care at affordable costs to all its patients, and improvements in facilities and equipment are continuously being pursued to keep SGH up-to-date and cost effective.

Gross Sales: 1994   US$245.7 million
                        1995   US$275.3 million
                        1996   US$302.3 million

Singapore International Media

Founding Concept: To establish a modern broadcasting organization geared to meet the entertainment and information needs of Singaporeans.

Country of Operations: Singapore

Description of Operations: Singapore International Media provides radio and television programs for the Singapore audience.

Address: Caldecott Hill, Andrew Road, Singapore 299939
Tel: (65) 256-0401
Fax: (65) 253-8808
WWW: http://www.mediacity.com.sg

Date Founded and History: Singapore International Media traces its beginnings to February 1980. Through an Act of Parliament, Radio and Television Singapore was transformed into the Singapore Broadcasting Corporation (SBC) and provided with greater autonomy and flexibility in personnel, financial, and production matters. The change nurtured creativity and developed a modern broadcasting organization geared to meet the entertainment and information needs of Singaporeans. Over the years, SBC (now known as Singapore International Media) has continued to refine and improve television and radio programs, providing the Singapore audience with quality programming.

Current Leadership: Kwa Chong Seng, Chairman

Biggest Challenge: Faced with increasing competition, the company's biggest challenge is to provide quality programs and services. Thus, Singapore International Media invests heavily in recruiting and training highly skilled staff and upgrading its technology.

New Markets or Products Being Pursued: Singapore International Media plans to widen the scope of its activities by developing telecommunications and multimedia services.

Singapore Productivity and Standards Board (formerly the National Productivity Board)
☆

Founding Concept: To help Singapore face the economic challenges of the 21st century, the Singapore Productivity and Standards Board (PSB) was established in April 1996 as the national agency charged with raising productivity.

Country of Operations: Singapore

Description of Operations: PSB takes a total approach to productivity improvement by addressing the key determinants: manpower development, economic restructuring, and technical progress. The aim is to enable Singapore to make more efficient use of its labor and capital resources to generate economic growth; and through growth, to enhance competitiveness.

PSB's mission is to raise productivity to enhance competitiveness and economic growth for a better quality of life for people. Its six main thrusts are:

- productivity promotion
- manpower development
- technology application
- industry development
- standards and quality development
- incentives management

Address: PSB Building, 2 Bukit Merah Central, Singapore 159835
Tel: (65) 278-6666
Fax: (65) 278-6665/278-6667
WWW: http://www.psb.gov.sg.
E-mail: queries@psb.gov.sg.

Date Founded: April 1, 1966

Founders: PSB was formed through the merger of the National Productivity Board (NPB) and the Singapore Institute of Standards and Industrial Research (SISIR). This merger integrated the functions of the NPB and SISIR as well as the small- and medium-sized enterprise development function of the Economic Development Board.

Current Leadership: Lim Boon Heng, Chairman
Lee Suan Hiang, Chief Executive

Significant Events: Inauguration of the Productivity Campaign, The Singapore Quality Award, Awards Dinner for ISO certified organizations, The Excellent Service Award, The International Exposition of Quality Circles, The National Quality Circles Convention

Singapore Telecommunications Limited

———————————— ☆ ————————————

Founding Concept: To be a world-class telecommunications and postal group providing a comprehensive range of excellent and value-for-money services and products and the highest level of quality and reliability, while honoring our obligations to society by being an economic and social asset to Singapore.

Country of Operations: Singapore

Description of Operations: Singapore Telecommunications was established to provide telecommunications and postal services. It was rated best in Asia in terms of infrastructure by the IMEDE World Competitiveness Report (1991–94) for efficiency and reliability.

Address: Comcentre, 31 Exeter Road, Singapore 239732
Tel: (65) 838-3388
Fax: (65) 733-8255
WWW: http://www.singtel.com

Date Founded and History: Singapore Telecommunications was established on April 1, 1972, to provide telecommunications and postal services in Singapore. Today the company not only serves Singapore but is active in major cities in other parts of the world. Starting out as a public listed company, Singapore Telecommunications was listed on the Stock Exchange of Singapore in November 1993. Its exclusive license to provide mobile telecommunications services expired in March 1997. An exclusive license for "basic telecommunications services" will expire in March 2000. In assets, it is the largest company in Asia outside Japan.

Current Leadership: Koh Boon Hwee, Chairman
Lee Hsien Yang, President and CEO

Significant Events: The most significant events in the company's history were its evolution from a government statutory board to a corporate entity and its ultimate privatization in October 1993. This allowed the company to have more autonomy in decision-making and flexibility to respond to rapid changes in the highly dynamic and competitive telecommunications industry.

New Markets or Products Being Pursued: The company aims to establish viable operations in major world markets. It is continually investing internationally, expanding its market through joint marketing arrangements, and providing emerging and advanced technologies.

Gross Sales: 1994   US$2.22 billion
             1995   US$2.43 billion
             1996   US$2.77 billion
             1997   US$3.1 billion

Social Security System

Founding Concept: To establish, develop, promote, and perfect a sound and viable tax-exempt social security system suitable to the needs of the people throughout the Philippines, which would promote social justice and provide meaningful protection to members and their beneficiaries against the hazards of disability, sickness, maternity, old age, death, and other situations resulting in loss of income or financial burden.

Country of Operations: Philippines

Description of Operations: The Social Security System (SSS) provides Filipinos with social security protection such as medical and retirement insurance, disability benefits, and loans.

Address: SSS Building, East Avenue, Diliman, Quezon City, Philippines
Tel: (632) 920-6401/920-6446
Fax: (632) 921-2022

Date Founded and History: SSS was created on September 1, 1957, to provide social security protection to workers in the private sector. It addressed the financial needs of private-sector workers resulting from sickness, maternity, disability, retirement, and death. It also addressed their Medicare needs and assisted beneficiaries and their dependants in cases of employment-related injury or death.

In 1980 self-employed workers and professionals were included in its coverage. Recently other individuals, such as farmers and fishermen, household helpers, and members of the informal sector, were placed under compulsory coverage. Overseas Filipino workers and nonworking spouses are now also covered under the voluntary membership program.

SSS administers three programs: 1) social security, 2) Medicare for hospitalization benefits, and 3) employees' compensation for work-related injuries and death. It is one of the strongest, most stable, and largest financial institutions in the country, and continues to expand its services.

Founder: The Philippine government under President Elpidio Quirino, through Republic Act No. 1161

Current Leadership: Renato C. Valencia, Administrator
Horacio Templo,
Executive Vice President
Leopoldo S. Veroy,
Executive Vice President

Significant Events:

- Benefits: Has granted a total of P121.2 billion in benefits. Of this amount, P99.7 billion or 82% was paid in the last seven years.
- Member loans: Released a total of P89.4 billion. Seventy-seven percent of this amount was granted between 1990 and 1997.
- Coverage: Total membership of over 18 million employees and over 500,000 employers.
- Contributions: SSS contributions now stand at P140.9 billion.
- Investments: Total investments of P139.1 billion. Of this, P59.6 billion is invested in government securities, P53.7 billion in member loans, and P25.8 billion in private securities.
- Assets: P147.2 billion at the end of 1996

Biggest Challenge: One of the biggest challenges currently facing SSS is providing quality social security service to all Filipinos. To achieve quality service, SSS began computerization and decentralization of major processes in the early 1990s and reengineered its operations. Today it has a total of 100 on-line branches and 25 representative offices. Most of these offices have computer capabilities that allow them to replicate the full service available at the main office.

To attain universal coverage, the organization simplified its qualification requirements. Another challenge facing the organization is protecting the viability and sustainability of its fund. SSS has diversified its investments and improved collections.

New Markets or Products Being Pursued: SSS intends to expand its mandatory and optional coverage programs to other sectors to attain its target of 100% coverage. It will continue to contribute to the socioeconomic growth of the country. Special lending programs will be opened to generate more employment, encourage exports, accelerate countryside development, and develop the Filipinos' spirit of entrepreneurship.

St. Luke's Medical Center

Founding Concept: To provide state-of-the-art medical services.

Country of Operations: Philippines

Description of Operations: Started as a small medical clinic in Tondo, Manila in 1903. St. Luke's Medical Center is now one of the leading medical institutions in Manila. It is equipped with 650 beds and sophisticated state-of-the-art equipment and facilities.

Address: 279 E. Rodriguez Sr. Blvd., Quezon City, Philippines
Tel: (632) 722-6161/723-0101
Fax: (632) 521-7753/724-4227
WWW: http://www/stluke.comp.ph

Date Founded and History: Founded by Episcopalian bishop Charles Henry Brent in 1903, St. Luke's started as a small medical clinic. In August 1975 it ceased to be a church-run institution. A group of prominent business leaders, headed by Episcopalian lawyer William Quasha, took over management of the company to save it from financial crisis.

Founder: Charles Henry Brent

Current Leadership: Jose F.G. Ledesma,
Chairman and President

Biggest Challenge: The biggest challenge currently facing St. Luke's is the proliferation of independent medical centers run by entrepreneurial doctors. The hospital is meeting this challenge by continuously improving its technology, facilities, and overall service.

New Markets or Products Being Pursued: In line with its vision to be one of the world's best hospitals, St. Luke's continues to acquire the latest technology available to the medical field.

Gross Sales: 1994 US$31.98 million
1995 US$34.8 million
1996 US$43.1 million

SIRIM Berhad (formerly Standards of Industrial Research of Malaysia)

Founding Concept: To develop national capability in industrial technology.

Country of Operations: Malaysia

Description of Operations: SIRIM Berhad is a government-owned company involved in industrial research, development, and quality.

Address: No. 1, Persiaran Dató Menteri, Section 2, P.O. Box 7035, 40911 Shah Alam, Selangor Darul Ehsan, Malaysia

Tel: (603) 559-1888
Fax: (603) 550-9477
WWW: http://www.sirim.my

Date Founded and History: Standards of Industrial Research of Malaysia (SIRIM) was established in September 1975 under the Ministry of Science, Technology and Environment. The successor company, SIRIM Berhad, was formed on September 1, 1996, under the Ministry of Finance. Its principal objective is to contribute to national economic development through its involvement in quality, research, and technology development. However, it still maintains its traditional role in standardization and quality assurance testing and technology transfer activities.

Current Leadership: Mohd. Ariffin bin Hj. Aton, President and Chief Executive
Abdul Aziz bin Abdul Manan, Senior Vice President

Significant Events: The emergence of SIRIM as a government-owned corporation on September 1, 1996, marked the beginning of a new era and another milestone for the institute. SIRIM is now poised to operate as a contract research organization and to negotiate for joint ventures with local and foreign companies.

Biggest Challenge: SIRIM's main challenge is to transform itself into a self-funding government-owned corporate entity. Its becoming a corporation will give the organization the flexibility required to provide up-to-date technical support and contract research services to industries.

New Markets or Products Being Pursued: SIRIM's development in new technology areas and new facilities will focus on the areas of advanced manufacturing, advanced materials, and multimedia applications. To back up research and technologies in these areas, SIRIM is also developing state-of-the-art facilities, such as rapid prototyping, EMC, and CAD/CAM.

Starlite Holdings Limited

———————— ☆ ————————

Founding Concept: To produce paper products, including print labels and packaging materials.

Country of Operations: Hong Kong

Description of Operations: Starlite is engaged in the printing and manufacture of paper-based packaging materials, paper products, and labels, and the provision of design and color separation services for high-end quality products.

Address: 3/F Perfect Industrial Building, 31 Tai Yau Street, Sanpokong, Kowloon, Hong Kong
Tel: (852) 2726-0325
Fax: (852) 2352-3928
WWW: http://www.starlitegroup.com

Current Leadership: Lam Kwong Yu, President and CEO

Significant Events: In September 1993 Starlite became the first printing and packaging group in Asia to receive the ISO 9001 International Quality System certificate.

New Markets or Products Being Pursued: The company is currently investing in the manufacture of environment-friendly packaging products. It is now implementing pulp-molding systems that recycle wastepaper into environment-friendly packaging materials. In addition, Starlite is establishing a "one-stop packaging" concept that will provide customers with a service covering design, printing, and production of interior packaging materials. The group has also expanded its business by manufacturing and distributing licensed copyrighted Hallmark and Warner Bros. products.

Gross Sales: 1994   US$27.6 million
              1995   US$29.94 million

Sukhothai Thammathirat Open University

---- ☆ ----

Founding Concept: To provide equal access to higher education to people throughout Thailand and to make the concept of lifelong education a practical reality.

Country of Operations: Thailand

Description of Operations: Sukhothai Thammathirat Open University (STO) provides higher education through the media, including radio and television programs, and other methods that enable students to study on their own without having to enter an actual classroom.

Address: Bangpood, Pakkred Nonthaburi 11120, Thailand
Tel: (662) 503-2121
Fax: (662) 503-3556/503-3607
WWW: http://www.stou.ac.th

Date Founded and History: STO was founded on September 5, 1978, as the first distance teaching university in Thailand. From an initial three academic schools offering programs of study, there are presently ten schools representing all major study areas.

Current Leadership: Iam Chaya-Ngam, President-Senator
Nipone Sookpreedee,
VP – Development

Biggest Challenge: With more lucrative salaries being offered in the private sector, STO's biggest challenge is attracting and retaining suitable personnel. The university approaches this dilemma by providing a competitive welfare package as well as personnel development schemes ranging from in-service training courses to further education overseas.

New Markets or Products Being Pursued: STO is planning to invest in a number of new education programs that will enable the University to remain the leading distance education institution both in Thailand and in the Asia Pacific region. To achieve this goal, STO is currently offering new courses, preparing to increase its master's programs, and developing international cooperative projects with other universities.

TA Enterprises Berhad
————————— ☆ —————————

Country of Operations: Malaysia

Description of Operations: TA Enterprises is involved in stockbroking, investment holding, property investments, construction and development, and trading and manufacturing.

Address: 24/F Menara TA One, 22 Jalan P. Ramlee, 50250 Kuala Lumpur, Malaysia
Tel: (603) 232-1277
Fax: (603) 232-2369

Date Founded: March 13, 1990

Founders: Tan Kuay Pong
Zainab Binti Ahmad

Current Leadership: Tiah Thee Kian, Executive Chairman
and Managing Director

Significant Events: July 1, 1996 – launch of TA Unit Trust Management Berhad, TA Balance Fund for RM100 million; August 29, 1996 – P10 billion Joint Development Project with the Philippine National Construction Corporation; December 20, 1996 – launching of the Securities Borrowing and Leading Facility; February 28, 1997 – opening of TA Bank of the Philippines, Inc.; May 13, 1997 – RM400 million privatization of the Kuching Riverfront, Sarawak, East Malaysia; July 15, 1997 – opening of TA Bank South Africa.

TA established an Islamic Stockbroking Unit in October 1995 and Securities Borrowing and Lending in December 1996. After expanding its stockbroking operations to Hong Kong, Sri Lanka, Australia, the Philippines, Indonesia and South Africa, the TA Group is shifting its attention to other areas, such as banking and financial services to sustain growth and strengthen synergy. TA is also expanding into leasing and hire purchase services for the entrepreneurial and medium-scale business sector.

Gross Sales: 1995   US$609 million
1996   US$238 million
1997   US$373 million

Tahanang Walang Hagdanan, Inc.
☆

Founding Concept: To provide vocational and educational rehabilitation to physically disabled individuals and help them to be socially and educationally productive.

Country of Operations: Philippines

Description of Operations: Tahanang Walang Hagdanan has been providing service to the physically handicapped, out-of-school youth, and hearing impaired for 25 years and developing them into productive individuals through skills development, employment, and education. Presently the organization is heavily involved in establishing community-based rehabilitation centers.

Address: 175 Aida Street, Marick Subdivision, 1900 Cainta Rizal, Philippines
Tel: (632) 655-0055/655-0059
Fax: (632) 655-0812

Date Founded and History: Tahanang Walang Hagdanan was founded on February 21, 1973 to serve as a workshop for disabled people. It initially provided training courses for wheelchair making and needlecraft. At present, Tahanang Walang Hagdanan is a well-known nongovernment organization, managed by people with disabilities. It provides various skills and vocational training as well as employment. The center's products include wheelchairs, artificial arms and legs, crutches, canes and other mobility aids, wooden kitchenware, small furniture, and novelty items.

Founders: Ma. Paula Valeriana Baerts
                Marieke Guelkens

Current Leadership: Ma. Paula Valeriana Baerts,
                              Chairman and Founder
                              Felix M. Gonzalez, President
                              Jess H. Docot,
                              EVP and General Manager

Significant Events: The center saw a large influx of disabled citizens requiring training during its initial years. Today, these disabled citizens are contributing nearly 87% of the charity institution's annual revenues.

Biggest Challenge: The organization has difficulty securing the capital needed to purchase raw materials for its workshops. To meet this challenge, Tahanang Walang Hagdanan continues to tap foreign and local nongovernment organizations to provide funds for its projects.

New Markets or Products Being Pursued: The organization manufactures its own wheelchairs and other mobility aids (crutches, walkers, canes, artificial legs) for its handicapped workforce. It plans to provide these products to hospitals and government, nongovernment, and civic agencies concerned with the welfare of people with disabilities. It is also starting a new program to provide job opportunities for people with disabilities. To generate revenues, the organization offers computer services such as encoding, typesetting, desktop publishing, and tutorials. It has started offering packaging services as well.

Gross Sales: 1994 US$0.64 million
                 1995 US$0.76 million

Tan & Tan Developments Sdn. Bhd.

Founding Concept: To be Malaysia's leading residential and commercial developer.

Country of Operations: Malaysia

Description of Operations: Tan & Tan is one of Malaysia's leading property developers, known for its innovative lifestyle property developments.

Address: Menara Tan & Tan, 207 Jalan Tun Razak, 50400 Kuala Lumpur, Malaysia
Tel: (603) 263-1111
Fax: (603) 264-0084

Date Founded and History: Founded in 1972 by Tan Chin Nam, Tan & Tan was established to engage in the business of property development. Today it is an integrated property group involved in a wide range of property-based activities.

Founder: Tan Chin Nam

Current Leadership: Abu Talib bin Othman, Chairman
                       Tan Lei Cheng, CEO

Significant Events: Tan & Tan argues that it is the country's most versatile and innovative property developer, introducing new lifestyle concepts such as luxury condominiums, hotel apartments, corporate apartments, and luxury executive accommodations.

New Markets or Products Being Pursued: New product areas include health care and the expansion of the Micasa Hotel Apartments brand name in the Asia Pacific region.

Gross Sales: 1994   US$89.6 million
                1995   US$115 million
                1996   US$145 million

Texas Instruments (Phils.) Inc.

Founding Concept: To manufacture semiconductors and electronic products and components.

Country of Operations: Philippines

Description of Operations: Texas Instruments Philippines is one of the company's most sophisticated integrated circuit assembly-test sites. Its output serves the computer, telecommunications, aerospace, and automotive industries in Asia, Japan, the U.S., and Europe.

Address: Baguio City Export Processing Zone Authority, Baguio City, Philippines
Tel: (632) 636-0980/ (6374) 442-5681
Fax: (632) 845-0997

Date Founded and History: Texas Instruments Philippines was established in 1978 to manufacture and sell semiconductors and other electronic products and components. After a decade of operations, the company has become one of the most sophisticated integrated circuit assembly-test sites for Texas Instruments worldwide. The company continues to produce millions of world-class products.

Current Leadership: Norberto Viera, CEO

Biggest Challenge: Faced with the challenge of a growing market demand, the company continues to increase its manufacturing capacity by improving processes and space utilization, optimizing equipment utilization, implementing total productive maintenance, recruiting and training new employees, and maintaining a seven-day work week.

New Markets or Products Being Pursued: The company is currently increasing its production of application specific products to meet market demand.

Gross Sales: 1994   US$652 million

Thailand Board of Investment

Country of Operations: Thailand

Description of Operations: The Thailand Board of Investment (BOI) promotes projects that use domestic resources, strengthen Thailand's industrial and technology capability, create employment opportunities, develop basic and supporting industries, develop infrastructure, and conserve natural resources.

Address: 555 Vipavadee Rangsit Road, Catuchal, Bangkok 10900, Thailand
Tel: (662) 537-8111/537-8168
Fax: (662) 537-8177/537-8130
WWW: http://www.boi.go.th

Date Founded and History: The BOI came into existence some 30 years ago and is officially governed by the 1977 Investment Promotion Act. The Prime Minister chairs the agency. The value of applications for BOI incentives grew to more than US$20 billion by 1994.

Current Leadership: Staporn Kavitanon, Secretary General

Biggest Challenge: The biggest challenge the BOI faces is the need to continually change and adapt to the needs of the increasingly competitive global marketplaces of the 21st century.

New Markets or Products Being Pursued: The BOI continues the process of strengthening its overseas and regional offices. It is also looking for ways to communicate with present and prospective investors. Furthermore, the BOI is undergoing reengineering designed to streamline the delivery time for application review and business-related services.

The Hong Kong Electric Co. Ltd.
☆

Country of Operations: Hong Kong

Description of Operations: Hong Kong Electric generates and supplies electricity to Hong Kong, Ap Lei Chau, and Lamma Islands. It is also involved in technical consultancy and property development.

Address: The Electric Centre, 28 City Garden Road, North Point, Hong Kong

Tel: (852) 2843-3396
Fax: (852) 2869-4905
WWW: http://www.hec.com.hk

Date Founded and History: Hong Kong Electric started operations on December 1, 1890 and is one of the world's oldest power companies. Its first power station, located in Wan Chai, had an initial installed capacity of 100 kW. As Hong Kong grew, so did the company, providing the territory with its electricity needs. The company's Lamma Island Power Station (with a 2,955 MW capacity) provides efficient electrical services to Hong Kong.

Current Leadership: K. S. Tso, Managing Director

Biggest Challenge: The growing demand for energy-efficient and environment-friendly electricity demands that the company be an environmentally responsible supplier of electricity service. The company meets this challenge by deploying energy-efficient and environmentally safe technologies. Investments are continuously being made to ensure that the company's facilities and services comply with local environmental standards.

Total Units Sold (Millions of kWh):

       1994   US$8.275
       1995   US$8.380
       1996   US$8.873

The Philippine American Life Insurance Co. Inc.

Founding Concept: To provide life insurance to Filipinos.

Country of Operations: Philippines

Description of Operations: The Philippine American Life Insurance Company (Philamlife) is the largest and most diversified life insurance organization in the Philippines, with affiliates in health care systems, pre-need plans, banking, mutual funds, property management, and industrial development.

Address: Philamlife Building, United Nations Ave. Ermita, Manila, Philippines
Tel: (632) 521-6300/521-0991
Fax: (632) 521-7057

Date Founded and History: Philamlife was conceived in 1947 to raise the savings rates of Filipinos through life insurance. It mobilized savings of individual families and helped rebuild various sectors of the country. Today Philamlife is the largest and most diversified life insurance organization in the Philippines, with more than a hundred offices and over a million policyholders.

Founders: Cornelius V. Starr
Earl Caroll

Current Leadership: Jose L. Cuisia, President and CEO

Significant Events: The company has grown to become the country's largest and most diversified insurance company. It currently stands as the industry leader in the country.

Biggest Challenge: The presence of aggressive and highly competitive forces in the industry plus the entry of foreign players into the market represents the greatest threat to Philamlife. To meet this challenge, the company undertook several initiatives with the view of attaining long-term competitiveness. For example, it has recently undertaken a decentralization/regionalization program to enhance its closeness to the market; productivity and quality programs; reorganization to support its corporate strategies; and product innovation. It is also continually working at improving service and efficiency in order to achieve customer satisfaction.

New Markets or Products Being Pursued: The company plans to strengthen its presence in high growth market segments; i.e., the upscale and middle-income markets. The company aims to take advantage of technology to develop creative presentations of insurance products that will appeal to upscale clients.

Gross Sales: 1994   US$229 million
                  1995   US$256.9 million

Theme International Holdings Limited
☆

Founding Concept: To provide the latest high-quality fashion wear at reasonable prices.

Country of Operations: Hong Kong

Description of Operations: Theme International is engaged in the retailing of ladies' and men's casual and executive wear through its Theme shops located in Hong Kong and other countries in Southeast Asia.

Address: 16/F, Wyler Centre II, 200 Tai Lin Pai Road, Kwai Chung, N.T., Hong Kong
Tel: (852) 2840-8960
Fax: (852) 2841-2778
WWW: http://www.theme.com.hk

Date Founded and History: Kenneth Lai founded Theme International in 1986 to meet the demand for low-cost but high-quality ladies' wear. Since then the company has also started the manufacture and retail of men's and teens' wear. Theme's retail network consists of 150 outlets in Asia, Europe, and North America.

Current Leadership: Kenneth Lai Ngan-Long, Chairman and CEO

Significant Events: The company received ISO 9002 certification in 1995 in recognition of the company's achievement in delivering high-quality products and services. It also received the Hong Kong Productivity Council's Productivity Award in 1995. The award recognizes Hong Kong enterprises that attain competitive advantage through well-planned and well-executed productivity programs and which demonstrate outstanding and continuous productivity improvement.

In June 1997 the company sold a 20% stake to China Everbright group, an arm of China's State Council.[5]

Biggest Challenge: In order to survive increasing competition, the company believes that it is essential to have a well-trained staff that will deliver excellent customer service. As such, the company provides appropriate training and job-related courses to its staff. A good working environment and individual career path planning are also provided to improve the quality of work life and encourage personal advancement.

New Markets or Products Being Pursued: The company is currently investing in different overseas markets, with the Southeast Asian region its major focus. Theme also plans to invest heavily in the distribution of cosmetic products.

Tractors Malaysia Holdings Bhd.
— ☆ —

Founding Concept: To distribute Caterpillar heavy equipment in Malaysia.

Country of Operations: Malaysia

Description of Operations: Tractors Malaysia supplies the fast-growing demand for Caterpillar heavy equipment in Southeast Asia. It also assembles and distributes BMW, Ford, Land Rover, and Scania vehicles.

Address: P.O. Box 12465, 50778 Kuala Lumpur, Malaysia
Tel: (603) 734-6688
Fax: (603) 734-6623

Date Founded and History: Founded in 1964, Tractors Malaysia served as Sime Darby's distributor of Caterpillar heavy equipment in Singapore. In 1968 the company went public as Tractors Malaysia Berhad, with Sime Darby

---

[5] Stein, Peter. "Beijing-Controlled Business Tightens Grip on Hong Kong." (*The Asian Wall Street Journal*, August 7, 1997, p. 1)

retaining 75% of the equity. In 1972 the company moved its headquarters to Malaysia.

Current Leadership: Oh Teik Tatt, Managing Director

Significant Events: The company obtained approval in March 1966 from City and Guilds of London Institute (C&G), U.K., and the Ministry of Education to conduct two C&G professional examinations relevant to the heavy equipment and motor vehicle industries in Malaysia, making Tractors Malaysia the first private sector company in the country to receive recognition from C&G.

Biggest Challenge: Increased competition and changing expectations of customers are the biggest challenges currently facing the company. In response, Tractors Malaysia launched a five-year change program that will increase focus on customers' needs. The program is expected to make the company more efficient and competitive.

New Markets or Products Being Pursued: The company is planning to not only distribute but also manufacture some of its products.

Gross Sales: 1994   US$362.00 million
1995   US$495.68 million

Visayas Cooperative Development Center

Founding Concept: To provide an education and training center on cooperative operation and management.

Country of Operations: Philippines

Description of Operations: The Visayas Cooperative Development Center was established as the Visayas Cooperative Training Organization, with training and education as its sole service. It has since developed to include audit, consultancy, inter-cooperative trading, and financing.

Address: 1st Street, Beverly Hills, Lahug, Cebu City, Philippines

Tel: (63-32) 253-3145
Fax: (63-32) 253-3153

Date Founded and History: The Visayas Cooperative Development Center was established in 1970 to orient people on cooperative philosophy, principles, and practices. Back then, little information was available on the need for cooperatives and what the cooperative movement was intended to accomplish. In its first year the organization had only 14 cooperative members. Today, it is the most viable cooperative-owned institution in the Visayas region, with a membership of 250 cooperative societies.

Current Leadership: Edgardo Comeros, Executive Director

Biggest Challenge: The Visayas Cooperative Development Center's biggest challenge is its organizational and financial sustainability. In order to build up funds, the center tries to strengthen its mass base, collects consulting and training fees, and enters into joint ventures with other nongovernment organizations, cooperative federations, and business groups.

New Markets or Products Being Pursued: In keeping with the organization's philosophy to invest in people's needs, the center is planning to venture into cooperative housing and memorial/funeral services.

Yaohan International Holdings, Ltd.
———————————— ☆ ————————————

Founding Concept: To establish an international distribution group.

Country of Operations: Hong Kong

Description of Operations: Yaohan is a conglomerate with interests in retailing, catering, and food processing, with subsidiaries in Hong Kong, China, and Taiwan.

Address: 49-50/F, Office Tower, Convention Plaza, 1 Harbour Road, Wan Chai, Hong Kong

Tel: (852) 2968-8300/2968-8376
Fax: (852) 2968-1068/2968-1025

Date Founded: 1930

Founders: Ryohei Wada and Katsu Wada

Current Leadership: Katsu Wada, Chairman

Significant Events: Yaohan's relocation from Japan to Hong Kong in 1990 initially advanced the company's scope of operation. It marked the beginning of the company's involvement in food manufacturing and trading, property activities, and development of the "one-stop shopping" concept.

Biggest Challenge: Adverse market conditions in the retail industry in Hong Kong caused a slowdown in the business of department stores, restaurants, and specialty shops in 1995. The company sought to attract and keep customers by giving discounts, offering new products, and providing better services. Growth in China has been likewise slower than originally expected, and the company has put its development plans on hold. Yaohan Japan was placed in receivership in 1997 when it was unable to service its debt.

Gross Sales: 1994   US$305.73 million
1995   US$202.98 million

SURVEY FORMS

The Asian Management Awards

ASIA'S BEST COMPANIES

The Winners of The Asian Management Awards

ORGANIZED BY

TEAMASIA
THE EVENTS AND AWARDS MANAGERS OF ASIA

GENERAL SURVEY FORM

All information provided will be used exclusively for the purpose of reviewing corporate performance in conjunction with a publishing project focusing on the winners of The Asian Management Awards. This project is being undertaken in cooperation with Simon & Schuster (Asia).

The Asia-Pacific Management Awards is organized by The Events and Awards Managers of Asia
308 Lirio & Zodiac, Palm Village, Makati City, Philippines
Tel (632) 896-1022 to 24; 896-0862; 896-0864 Fax (632) 896-0866
E-mail: 74147.477@compuserve.com
Internet: mah@globe.com.ph
World Wide Web: http://globe.com.ph/~mah/home.hmtl

1. Please supply all financial data in U.S. dollars. For uniformity, please use the following conversion rates:

Hong Kong	HK$	7.75
Indonesia	Rp	2100.00
Malaysia	RM	2.50
Philippines	P	25.00
Singapore	S$	1.40
Thailand	Bht	25.45

2. Each winning company will be provided with a general survey form, and a category-specific survey form corresponding to The Asian Management category/ies in which your company was recognized. This form is the **general survey form**.

3. Each award category will be reviewed separately. If your company has received The Asian Management Award for more than one category, please answer all questions in each category-specific survey form.

4. Please answer each of the questions on a separate sheet. Please indicate the name of your company, the category corresponding to the survey form, and the relevant question number on the separate sheet you attach. Where boxes are provided, please indicate your answer by ticking the appropriate box provided on the questionnaire as well as indicating the appropriate response on the attached sheet.

5. If you have any questions regarding the questionnaire, please call or fax Mr. Michael Alan Hamlin, managing director, Hamlin-Iturralde Corporation; Ms. Maria Montserrat I. Hamlin, president, TeamAsia; or, Mr. Renato S. Ramos, research associate, at Tel (632) 896-1022 to 24; 896-0862; 896-0864 or Fax (632) 896-0866.

6. Please courier your accomplished survey forms (both general and category-specific), **sealed,** directly to:

   ASIA'S BEST COMPANIES
   THE WINNERS OF THE ASIAN MANAGEMENT
   AWARDS
   c/o The Events and Awards Managers of Asia
   308 Lirio & Zodiac, Palm Village
   Makati City, Philippines
   Tel (632) 896-1022 to 24; 896-0862; 896-0864
   Fax (632) 896-0866

DEADLINE FOR SUBMISSION

Please send two (2) copies of the completed survey forms and all attachments and forward these to TeamAsia by 8 October, 1995.

CERTIFICATION AND AUTHORIZATION

Please fill out the certification and authorization below (to be signed by the President, EVP, GM or CEO of the Company):

I hereby certify that to the best of my knowledge and ability, the information provided therein is a true and accurate representation of the company.

I also authorize The Events and Awards Managers of Asia to use the information provided for the sole purpose of completing its publishing project focusing on the winners of The Asian Management Awards.

Signature: _____
Name: _____
Position: _____
Tel: _____
Fax: _____

CONTACT PERSON

Please indicate the name, telephone and fax number/s of the person in your company whom we should contact for clarification, for further details or for interview/s, if needed.

Signature: _____
Name: _____
Position: _____
Tel: _____
Fax: _____

1. Please indicate below the name of your company, your company address, The Asian Management Awards category/ies in which your company was recognized, and the year/s you received the award/s.

Name of Company:_____

Address:_____

Asian Management Award/s Received	Year/s Received
_____	_____
_____	_____
_____	_____

2. Please give a short history of your company (Give particular attention to the year your company was established, the initial business interests of your company, and the growth of your company.).

3. Please estimate the total number of employees in your company both in this country and in your entire firm, including all divisions, plants, branches and subsidiaries throughout the world (Indicate the number of employees.).

_____In this country
_____In all countries

4. Please estimate the gross sales revenue of your company in this country and in all countries throughout the world, from the period three years before your company received its first Asian Management Award/s until the present year.

Year	In this country	Total in all countries
1987	_____	_____
1988	_____	_____
1989	_____	_____
1990	_____	_____
1991	_____	_____
1992	_____	_____
1993	_____	_____
1994	_____	_____
1995	_____	_____

5. Please estimate the net sales profit of your company in this country and in all countries throughout the world, from the period three years before your company received its first Asian Management Award/s until the present year.

Year	In this country	Total in all countries
1987	_____	_____
1988	_____	_____
1989	_____	_____
1990	_____	_____
1991	_____	_____
1992	_____	_____
1993	_____	_____
1994	_____	_____
1995	_____	_____

6. Please indicate below the total amount of taxes paid to the government from the period three years before you received your first Asian Management Award/s until the present year.

Year	In this country	Total in all countries
1987	_____	_____
1988	_____	_____
1989	_____	_____
1990	_____	_____
1991	_____	_____
1992	_____	_____
1993	_____	_____
1994	_____	_____
1995	_____	_____

7. Please indicate below the return on sales of your company from the period three years before you received your first Asian Management Award/s until the present year.

Year	In this country	Total in all countries
1987	_____	_____
1988	_____	_____
1989	_____	_____
1990	_____	_____
1991	_____	_____
1992	_____	_____
1993	_____	_____
1994	_____	_____
1995	_____	_____

8. Has your company received any award/s from other award-giving organizations (with relation to The Asian Management Awards category wherein you won)?
   ❏ Yes   ❏ No

   If yes, please list the name of the award/s, a brief description and the year/s when your company received them.

9. Please estimate your company's return on sales (ROS) from the period three years before your company received its first Asian Management Award/s until the present year.

Year	In this country	Total in all countries
1987	_____	_____
1988	_____	_____
1989	_____	_____
1990	_____	_____
1991	_____	_____
1992	_____	_____
1993	_____	_____
1994	_____	_____
1995	_____	_____

10. Please indicate your company's basic financial indices from the period three years before you received your first Asian Management Award/s until the present year. Add any additional information/comments which would help in analyzing the information you provide.

- Return on Stockholders Equity **(RSE)** = Before tax net income divided by total average equity
- Return on Assets **(ROA)** = Net income before interest and taxes divided by the total average assets
- Cost of Debt **(COD)** = Interest Expense divided by the total average debt
- Debt/Equity Ratio **(D/ER)** = Total average debt divided by total average equity

Year	RSE	ROA	COD	D/ER
1987	____	____	____	____
1988	____	____	____	____
1989	____	____	____	____
1990	____	____	____	____
1991	____	____	____	____
1992	____	____	____	____
1993	____	____	____	____
1994	____	____	____	____
1995	____	____	____	____

11. Does your company consult with external consultancy firms?

❑ Yes   ❑ No

If yes, what are these consultancy firms, and what reasons prompted the need for external consultation/s? Please explain, and if possible, give a brief background.

12. How does your company relate, deal with and/or engage issues affecting corporate structure like downsizing, innovating, reengineering and reorganizing? Please explain. Add additional information/attachments which you think will help explain your answer.

13. What has been the biggest challenge to your company in terms of new market opportunities? How did your company respond to meet the needs of this challenge?

14. What is currently the biggest challenge faced by your organization? What step/s is/are your company considering to meet the demands of this challenge?

15. What impacts have the following issues on the business of your organization, in general, and to your organization, in particular? (Please give particular attention to the effects pertaining initiative opportunities and challenges presented by these issues.)
- Market liberalization
- Asian Free Trade Agreement (AFTA) and Asia Pacific Economic Cooperation (APEC)?
- Cost of labor, power and real estate
- Cost of technology transfer and its role in new product development
- Indigenous technology and its role in new product development
- Strategic Alliances

16. What market/s or product/s is/are your company currently planning to invest in, if any, which would enable your organization to remain a market leader? Please give a brief background/description, providing your vision of the future.

17. Please supply a copy of your latest audited financial statement.

The Award for People Development and Management is for excellence in the strategic management and development of the people in the organization, geared towards productivity, professional development and enhancement of the quality of life..

1. This is the **category-specific survey form** for **People Development and Management**. Please answer all the questions in this form as completely as possible. For financial data, please supply your answer in U.S. dollars. For uniformity, please use the following conversion rates:

Hong Kong	HK$	7.75
Indonesia	Rp	2100.00
Malaysia	RM	2.50
Philippines	P	25.00
Singapore	S$	1.40
Thailand	Bht	25.45

2. Please provide your answers to the questions on a separate sheet. It is important that you indicate your company name, the category in which your company was recognized and the year when you received the Asian Management Award/s on each of the pages of your answer sheets.

3. If you have any questions regarding the questionnaire, please call or fax Mr. Michael Alan Hamlin, managing director, Hamlin-Iturralde Corporation, Ms. Maria Montserrat I. Hamlin, president, TeamAsia or Mr. Renato Ramos, research associate, at Tel (632) 896-1022 to 24; 896-0862; 896-0864 or Fax (632) 896-0866.

4. Please courier your accomplished category-specific survey form, attached with the general survey form, and the release and authorization form, **sealed**, directly to:

ASIA'S BEST COMPANIES:
THE WINNERS OF THE ASIAN MANAGEMENT AWARDS
c/o The Events and Awards Managers of Asia
308 Lirio & Zodiac, Palm Village
City of Makati, Philippines

INFORMATION UPDATE

1. Please indicate why your company has been awarded the People Development and Management Award. Please attach whatever supporting documents you think will support your answer.

2. Has your company received any other award/s or recognition pertaining to innovations in people development and management? Please list and give a brief description for each.

3. Please indicate below the percentage of total annual operating budget of your company spent in training and/or development of staff (excluding payroll costs) for the period from three years before you won your first Asian Management Award in this category until the present year.

	Year								
	'87	'88	'89	'90	'91	'92	'93	'94	'95
% of budget spent on training and development									

4. How much does your company spend per employee per year, in US $, for staff training and development (since three years before you won your first Asian Management Award until the present year)? Please include both formal training costs such as seminars and university courses, as well as informal training costs such as observation tours abroad, if any.

	Year								
	'87	'88	'89	'90	'91	'92	'93	'94	'95
Training expenditure per employee per year									

5. Please indicate below the percentage of the total annual budget spent in employee expenses including all expenses involving salaries, perks, medical insurance, social security, provident or other funds, bonus, etc., for the period from three years before you won your first Asian Management Award in this category until the present year.

	Year								
	'87	'88	'89	'90	'91	'92	'93	'94	'95
% of budget spent in employees' expenses									

6. What is the annual average salary and benefits, in US $, for all your employees (management and rank and file) for the period from three years before you won your first Asian Management Award in this category until the present year? Please include total value of salaries, perks, medical insurance, social security, provident or other funds, bonus, etc. divided by the total number of employees.

	Year								
	'87	'88	'89	'90	'91	'92	'93	'94	'95
Ave. annual salary and benefits for employees									

7. Did your company maintain a career development plan for all the employees for the period from three years before you won your first Asian Management Award in this category until the present year?

❏ Yes   ❏ No

8. Describe the training and professional development programs employed by your company for your workers. Indicate the measures used in determining the effectiveness of your training programs and the rate of appreciation among your employees.

9. Please indicate below the rate of employee turnover per year for the period from three years before your company received its first Asian Management Award in this category until the present year.

	Rate of Employee Turnover								
	'87	'88	'89	'90	'91	'92	'93	'94	'95
Top Management	___	___	___	___	___	___	___	___	___
Middle Management	___	___	___	___	___	___	___	___	___
Rank and File	___	___	___	___	___	___	___	___	___
Others (please specify)	___	___	___	___	___	___	___	___	___

10. Please indicate the percentage of employees who receive training, per year, for the period from three years before you first received the Asian Management Award in this category, until the present year.

	Percent of each level who receive training per year (%)								
	'87	'88	'89	'90	'91	'92	'93	'94	'95
Top Management	___	___	___	___	___	___	___	___	___
Middle Management	___	___	___	___	___	___	___	___	___
Rank and File	___	___	___	___	___	___	___	___	___
Others (please specify)	___	___	___	___	___	___	___	___	___

11. Please describe how the industry your company belongs to measures employee productivity. Please explain the measures used, as well as your company's performance levels in terms of these measures.

12. Please estimate the time devoted to employee training per year (in number of hours per year).

	Number of Hours of Training per Year								
	'87	'88	'89	'90	'91	'92	'93	'94	'95
Top Management	___	___	___	___	___	___	___	___	___
Middle Management	___	___	___	___	___	___	___	___	___
Rank and File	___	___	___	___	___	___	___	___	___
Others (please specify)	___	___	___	___	___	___	___	___	___

13. Indicate your company's return on skills (ROSK) for the period from three years before you received the Asian Management Award in this category until the present year. Use the formula given below:

$$ROSK = \frac{\text{Skills income*}}{\text{Salary + Bonuses}}$$

*Skills income is defined as revenues less expenses (including cost of capital employed; excluding personnel costs)

	Return on Skills (ROSK) per Year								
	'87	'88	'89	'90	'91	'92	'93	'94	'95
Top Management	___	___	___	___	___	___	___	___	___
Middle Management	___	___	___	___	___	___	___	___	___
Rank and File	___	___	___	___	___	___	___	___	___
Others (please specify)	___	___	___	___	___	___	___	___	___

DEADLINE FOR SUBMISSION

Please send two (2) copies of the completed survey forms and all attachments and forward these to TeamAsia by 8 October, 1995.

CERTIFICATION AND CONTACT PERSON

Please fill out the certification and authorization below (to be signed by the President, EVP, GM or CEO of the Company):

I hereby certify that to the best of my knowledge and ability, the information provided therein is a true and accurate representation of the company.

I also authorize The Events and Awards Managers of Asia to use the information provided for the sole purpose of completing its publishing project focusing on the winners of The Asian Management Awards.

Signature: _____
Name: _____
Position: _____
Tel: _____
Fax: _____

Company Name: _____
Address: _____
_____
_____

Please indicate the name, telephone and fax number/s of the person whom we should contact for clarification, for further details or for interview/s, if needed, in relation with the data supplied with this survey form.

Signature: _____
Name: _____
Position: _____
Tel: _____
Fax: _____

INFORMATION TECHNOLOGY MANAGEMENT SURVEY FORM

The Award for Information Technology Management is for the strategic use of information technology to enhance the competitive position of the Company.

1. This is the **category-specific survey form** for **Information Technology Management**. Please answer all the questions in this form as completely as possible. For financial data, please supply your answer in U.S. dollars. For uniformity, please use the following conversion rates:

Hong Kong	HK$	7.75
Indonesia	Rp	2100.00
Malaysia	RM	2.50
Philippines	P	25.00
Singapore	S$	1.40
Thailand	Bht	25.45

2. Please provide your answers to the questions on a separate sheet. It is important that you indicate your company name, the category in which your company was recognized and the year when you received the Asian Management Award/s on each of the pages of your answer sheets.

3. If you have any questions regarding the questionnaire, please call or fax Mr. Michael Alan Hamlin, managing director, Hamlin-Iturralde Corporation, Ms. Maria Montserrat I. Hamlin, president, TeamAsia or Mr. Renato Ramos, research associate, at Tel (632) 896-1022 to 24; 896-0862; 896-0864 or Fax (632) 896-0866.

4. Please courier your accomplished category-specific survey form, attached with the general survey form, and the release and authorization form, **sealed,** directly to:

ASIA'S BEST COMPANIES:
THE WINNERS OF THE ASIAN MANAGEMENT
AWARDS
c/o The Events and Awards Managers of Asia
308 Lirio & Zodiac, Palm Village
City of Makati, Philippines

INFORMATION UPDATE

1. Please indicate why your company has been awarded the Information Technology Management Award. Please attach whatever supporting documents you think will support your answer.

2. Has your company received any other award/s or recognition from other local, regional or international award-giving body in relation with excellence and innovation in Information Technology Management? If yes, please list and give a brief description for each award.

3. How much, in terms of percentage, does your company spend in information technology development for the period from three years before you received your first Asian Management Award in this category until the present year?

	Year								
	'87	'88	'89	'90	'91	'92	'93	'94	'95
Percent of Revenues	__	__	__	__	__	__	__	__	__
Percent of Total Assets	__	__	__	__	__	__	__	__	__

4. Does your company conduct employee training program/s for the use of new developments in Information Technology?

☐ Yes   ☐ No

If yes, please describe the program.

5. How much has your company allocated for the training of employees in IT, if any, for the period from three years before you first received an Asian Management Award in this category until the present year?

Year	Amount spent for IT training for employees (US$)
1987	_____
1988	_____
1989	_____
1990	_____
1991	_____
1992	_____
1993	_____
1994	_____
1995	_____

6. Do you interconnect with your subcontractors, suppliers and/or customers? Please check the appropriate box/es below:

Interconnection with:	Present	Three Years Ago (1992)	Six Years Ago (1989)
Subcontractor	&#9744;	&#9744;	&#9744;
Suppliers	&#9744;	&#9744;	&#9744;
Customers	&#9744;	&#9744;	&#9744;

If so, please describe these systems/interconnections and the nature by which they operate.

7. Which of the following levels in your company are involved in the use of IT? Please check all that apply.

- ❑ Senior Management
- ❑ Middle Management
- ❑ Supervisors
- ❑ Rank and File

8. Which of the following departments in your company are involved in the use of IT at present?

- ❑ Sales and Marketing
- ❑ EDP
- ❑ IT Section or Department
- ❑ Manufacturing or Operations
- ❑ Quality Control
- ❑ Customer Service
- ❑ Finance/Accounting
- ❑ Research
- ❑ Purchasing
- ❑ Personnel/ HRD
- ❑ Others, please specify _____

9. Please indicate below the types of hardware your company currently use. Please check all items that apply.

- ❑ Mainframe
- ❑ Mini
- ❑ Workstations
- ❑ PCs
- ❑ LAN/WAN
- ❑ Communication Modems

10. What is the level of connectivity within your organization?

11. What are your newest IT acquisitions, and why?

12. What percentage of your operations are performed on-line?

13. What multi-media devices/software (DTP, graphic scanning, etc.) do you have/use?

14. Please describe your IT efforts in enhancing customer service and in creating new products and services.

DEADLINE FOR SUBMISSION

Please send two (2) copies of the completed survey forms and all attachments and forward these to TeamAsia by 8 October, 1995.

CERTIFICATION AND CONTACT PERSON

Please fill out the certification and authorization below (to be signed by the President, EVP, GM or CEO of the Company):

I hereby certify that to the best of my knowledge and ability, the information provided therein is a true and accurate representation of the company.

I also authorize The Events and Awards Managers of Asia to use the information provided for the sole purpose of completing its publishing project focusing on the winners of The Asian Management Awards.

Signature: _____
Name: _____
Position: _____
Tel: _____
Fax: _____

Company Name: _____
Address: _____
_____
_____

Please indicate the name, telephone and fax number/s of the person whom we should contact for clarification, for further details or for interview/s, if needed, in relation with the data supplied with this survey form.

Signature: _____
Name: _____
Position: _____
Tel: _____
Fax: _____

OPERATIONS MANAGEMENT SURVEY FORM

The Award for Operations Management is for outstanding achievement in the quality and delivery of products and services through high productivity, technology innovation, and continuous improvement.

1. This is the **category-specific survey form** for **Operations Management**. Please answer all the questions in this form as completely as possible. For financial data, please supply your answer in U.S. dollars. For uniformity, please use the following conversion rates:

Hong Kong	HK$	7.75
Indonesia	Rp	2100.00
Malaysia	RM	2.50
Philippines	P	25.00
Singapore	S$	1.40
Thailand	Bht	25.45

2. Please provide your answers to the questions on a separate sheet. It is important that you indicate your company name, the category in which your company was recognized and the year when you received the Asian Management Award/s on each of the pages of your answer sheets.

3. If you have any questions regarding the questionnaire, please call or fax Mr. Michael Alan Hamlin, managing director, Hamlin-Iturralde Corporation, Ms. Maria Montserrat I. Hamlin, president, TeamAsia or Mr. Renato Ramos, research associate, at Tel (632) 896-1022 to 24; 896-0862; 896-0864 or Fax (632) 896-0866.

4. Please courier your accomplished category-specific survey form, attached with the general survey form, and the release and authorization form, **sealed,** directly to:

   ASIA'S BEST COMPANIES:
   THE WINNERS OF THE ASIAN MANAGEMENT AWARDS
   c/o The Events and Awards Managers of Asia
   308 Lirio & Zodiac, Palm Village
   City of Makati, Philippines

INFORMATION UPDATE

1. Please indicate why your company has been awarded the Operations Management Award. Please attach whatever supporting documents you think will support your answer.

2. Has your company received any award/s or recognition from other local, regional or international award-giving organizations in relation to excellence in quality and operations management? If yes, please list them and give a brief description for each award or recognition.

3. Please describe the quality indices (e.g. number of customer complaints, returns and replacements, repairs at customer sites, etc.) achieved by your company for the period from three years before you won your first Asian Management Award in this category until the present year.

Product Line	Quality Index	'87	'88	'89	'90	'91	'92	'93	'94	'95

4. Please indicate below the latest estimates of the indices mentioned above achieved by the industry as a whole, and by your closest competitor, and the accepted best company in the world, where applicable.

Product Line	Quality Index	Industry	Competitor	Best Company in the World

5. Please indicate below the product/service delivery performance indices (on-time delivery, delays, etc.) achieved by your company for the period from three years before you first won your first Asian Management Award in this category until the present year.

Product Line	Productivity Index	'87	'88	'89	'90	'91	'92	'93	'94	'95

6. Please indicate below the internal quality indices (e.g. percentage of defects during production, rejection rate, scrap rate, yield, rework rate, etc.) achieved by your company for the period from three years before you won your first Asian Management Award in this category until the present year.

Product Line	Internal Quality Index	'87	'88	'89	'90	'91	'92	'93	'94	'95

7. Please describe the most recent major innovation/s your company has undertaken to significantly improve productivity (within the last two years).

8. Please indicate the productivity indices (e.g. labor index, labor utilization, downtime due to accidents, energy consumption, etc.) achieved by your company for the period from three years before you won your first Asian Management Award in this category until the present year.

Product Line	Productivity Index	Results/Year '87	'88	'89	'90	'91	'92	'93	'94	'95

9. Please describe your company's efforts in maintaining and preserving the environment in your operations.

10. Please rate your company's use of technology in relation to your competitors. Please check one and briefly explain your answer.

   ❏ Superior
   ❏ Above Average
   ❏ About Average
   ❏ Below Average

11. Please indicate below the inventory turnaround achieved by your company in terms of cost of sales/finished goods inventory (cos/fg), cost of sales/work-in-process (cos/wip), and the cost of sales/raw materials (cos/rm) for the period from three years before you won your first Asian Management Award in this category until the present year.

Product Line Inventory	Inventory Turn-around	Results '87	'88	'89	'90	'91	'92	'93	'94	'95
_____	cos/fg									
_____	cos/wip									
_____	cos/rm									

Product Line Inventory	Inventory Turn-around	Results '87	'88	'89	'90	'91	'92	'93	'94	'95
_____	cos/fg									
_____	cos/wip									
_____	cos/rm									

Product Line Inventory	Inventory Turn-around	Results '87	'88	'89	'90	'91	'92	'93	'94	'95
_____	cos/fg									
_____	cos/wip									
_____	cos/rm									

DEADLINE FOR SUBMISSION

Please send two (2) copies of the completed survey forms and all attachments and forward these to TeamAsia by 8 October, 1995.

CERTIFICATION AND CONTACT PERSON

Please fill out the certification and authorization below (to be signed by the President, EVP, GM or CEO of the Company):

I hereby certify that to the best of my knowledge and ability, the information provided therein is a true and accurate representation of the company.

I also authorize The Events and Awards Managers of Asia to use the information provided for the sole purpose of completing its publishing project focusing on the winners of The Asian Management Awards.

Signature: _____
Name: _____
Position: _____
Tel: _____
Fax: _____

Company Name: _____
Address: _____
_____
_____

Please indicate the name, telephone and fax number/s of the person whom we should contact for clarification, for further details or for interview/s, if needed, in relation with the data supplied with this survey form.

Signature: _____
Name: _____
Position: _____
Tel: _____
Fax: _____

FINANCIAL MANAGEMENT SURVEY FORM	The Award for Financial Management is for oustanding management of the company's assets, liability and equities, in keeping with the owner's best long term interests.

1. This is the **category-specific survey form** for **Financial Management**. Please answer all the questions in this form as completely as possible. For financial data, please supply your answer in U.S. dollars. For uniformity, please use the following conversion rates:

Hong Kong	HK$	7.75
Indonesia	Rp	2100.00
Malaysia	RM	2.50
Philippines	P	25.00
Singapore	S$	1.40
Thailand	Bht	25.45

2. Please provide your answers to the questions on a separate sheet. It is important that you indicate your company name, the category in which your company was recognized and the year when you received the Asian Management Award/s on each of the pages of your answer sheets.

3. If you have any questions regarding the questionnaire, please call or fax Mr. Michael Alan Hamlin, managing director, Hamlin-Iturralde Corporation, Ms. Maria Montserrat I. Hamlin, president, TeamAsia or Mr. Renato Ramos, research associate, at Tel (632) 896-1022 to 24; 896-0862; 896-0864 or Fax (632) 896-0866.

4. Please courier your accomplished category-specific survey form, together with the general survey form, and the release and authorization form, **sealed,** directly to:

ASIA'S BEST COMPANIES:
THE WINNERS OF THE ASIAN MANAGEMENT AWARDS
c/o The Events and Awards Managers of Asia
308 Lirio & Zodiac, Palm Village
City of Makati, Philippines

INFORMATION UPDATE

1. Please indicate why your company has been awarded the Financial Management Award. Please attach whatever supporting documents you think will support your answer.

2. Is your company publicly listed?
   ☐ Yes   ☐ No
   If yes, please indicate when and where your company was originally listed, as well as subsequent listings, if any.

3. If your company is publicly listed, please supply the data requested below pertaining to your company's market indicators. Supply the data for the period from three years before you won your first Asian Management Award in this category until the present year.

   Please provide the following six indicators, as defined, using year-end figures.

   - **Earnings per share** = Net profit divided by average number of shares outstanding
   - **Price earnings ratio** = Average market price per share divided by earnings per share
   - **Average market price per share** = Total value traded for the year divided by the number of shares outstanding
   - **Book value per share** = Average stockholder's equity divided by the number of shares outstanding
   - **Ratio of market share to book value** = Market price per share of stock divided by book value per share
   - **Dividend yield** = Annual cash dividend per share divided by market price share

	Year								
	'87	'88	'89	'90	'91	'92	'93	'94	'95
Earnings per share	__	__	__	__	__	__	__	__	__
Price earnings ratio	__	__	__	__	__	__	__	__	__
Average market price per share	__	__	__	__	__	__	__	__	__
Book value per share	__	__	__	__	__	__	__	__	__
Ratio of market share to book value	__	__	__	__	__	__	__	__	__
Dividend yield	__	__	__	__	__	__	__	__	__

4. Please describe the most recent major innovations your company has undertaken in the field of financial management such as:
   a. Public and private placements
   b. Actions undertaken with respect to achieving the company's Optimal Capital Structure.

5. Please provide a listing of financial institutions your company has transacted business with over the past 10 years on a year-by-year basis.

6. Has your company received other award/s or recognition locally, regionally or internationally in relation to innovations in financial management? Please list, if any, and provide a brief description for each.

7. If your company is publicly listed, please indicate the market value performance of the company's stock over the last 10 years.

8. Please indicate the number of new stockholders who invested in your company over the last 10 years, on a year-by-year basis. Please provide the actual number and the percent increase in total investors annually.

9. Please indicate below your company's EPS (earnings per share) performance and EPS growth rate over the past 10 years, and relate this to the country's growth in terms of GNP (gross national product) over the same 10-year period.

10. Please indicate below your company's DPS (Dividend per share) performance and DPS growth rate over the past 10 years, and relate this to the country's growth in terms of GNP (gross national product) over the same 10-year period.

11. Please indicate your company's Net Income After Tax (NIAT)/ Assets during the last 10 years, on a year-by-year basis.

12. Please indicate your company's Net Income After Tax (NIAT)/ Equity during the last 10 years, on a year-by-year basis.

DEADLINE FOR SUBMISSION

Please send two (2) copies of the completed survey forms and all attachments and forward these to TeamAsia by 8 October, 1995.

CERTIFICATION AND CONTACT PERSON

Please fill out the certification and authorization below (to be signed by the President, EVP, GM or CEO of the Company):

I hereby certify that to the best of my knowledge and ability, the information provided therein is a true and accurate representation of the company.

I also authorize The Events and Awards Managers of Asia to use the information provided for the sole purpose of completing its publishing project focusing on the winners of The Asian Management Awards.

Signature: _____

Name: _____

Position: _____

Tel: _____

Fax: _____

Company Name: _____

Address: _____
_____
_____

Please indicate the name, telephone and fax number/s of the person whom we should contact for clarification, for further details or for interview/s, if needed, in relation with the data supplied with this survey form.

Signature: _____

Name: _____

Position: _____

Tel: _____

Fax: _____

MARKETING MANAGEMENT SURVEY FORM

The Award for Marketing Management is for outstanding and successful innovation in the use of the elements of marketing leading to customer satisfaction.

1. This is the **category-specific survey form** for **Marketing Management**. Please answer all the questions in this form as completely as possible. For financial data, please supply your answer in U.S. dollars. For uniformity, please use the following conversion rates:

Hong Kong	HK$	7.75
Indonesia	Rp	2100.00
Malaysia	RM	2.50
Philippines	P	25.00
Singapore	S$	1.40
Thailand	Bht	25.45

2. Please provide your answers to the questions on a separate sheet. It is important that you indicate your company name, the category in which your company was recognized and the year when you received the Asian Management Award/s on each of the pages of your answer sheets.

3. If you have any questions regarding the questionnaire, please call or fax Mr. Michael Alan Hamlin, managing director, Hamlin-Iturralde Corporation, Ms. Maria Montserrat I. Hamlin, president, TeamAsia or Mr. Renato Ramos, research associate, at Tel (632) 896-1022 to 24; 896-0862; 896-0864 or Fax (632) 896-0866.

4. Please courier your accomplished category-specific survey form, attached with the general survey form, and the release and authorization form, **sealed**, directly to:

ASIA'S BEST COMPANIES:
THE WINNERS OF THE ASIAN MANAGEMENT
AWARDS
c/o The Events and Awards Managers of Asia
308 Lirio & Zodiac, Palm Village
City of Makati, Philippines

INFORMATION UPDATE

1. Please indicate why your company has been awarded the Marketing Management Award. Please attach whatever supporting documents you think will support your answer.

2. Has your company been awarded any local, regional or international award/s or recognition of any kind for innovation in marketing? If yes, please describe briefly.

3. Please list below the estimates of your company's market performance, for the period from three years before you won your first Asian Management Award in this category until the present year.

Year	Total Sales/ Total Marketing Expenses	Total Sales/ Total Number of Marketing Staff	Total Sales/ Total Advertising and Promotion Expenses
1987			
1988			
1989			
1990			
1991			
1992			
1993			
1994			
1995			

4. Please indicate your company's overall market share based on sales volume for the period from three years before you won your first Asian Management Award in this category until the present year.

Year	Market Share (in %)
1987	
1988	
1989	
1990	
1991	
1992	
1993	
1994	
1995	

Is the above data your estimate or from industry sources?
☐ An estimate   ☐ From industry sources

5. Please estimate the market share (based on sales volume) of each of your main product lines. Please supply the data for the period from three years before you won your first Asian Management Award in this category until the present year.

Main Product Line	Market Share (Percentage)								
	'87	'88	'89	'90	'91	'92	'93	'94	'95
(i)									
(ii)									
(iii)									
(iv)									

6. What is the total sales volume of your company by major product lines for the period from three years before you won your first Asian Management Award in this category until the present year?

Product
Line   Market Share (Percentage)
(Specify)   '87   '88   '89   '90   '91   '92   '93   '94   '95

a. _____   ___   ___   ___   ___   ___   ___   ___   ___   ___
b. _____   ___   ___   ___   ___   ___   ___   ___   ___   ___
c. _____   ___   ___   ___   ___   ___   ___   ___   ___   ___
d. _____   ___   ___   ___   ___   ___   ___   ___   ___   ___
e. _____   ___   ___   ___   ___   ___   ___   ___   ___   ___
f. (others)   ___   ___   ___   ___   ___   ___   ___   ___   ___
Total
company
sales
volume   ___   ___   ___   ___   ___   ___   ___   ___   ___

7. Please estimate the following, describing how your company has fared in sales volume in relation to your major competitors for the period from three years before you won your first Asian Management Award in this category until the present year.

	Total Industry Sales	Top Three Competitors (Indicate)		
Year		A	B	C
1987	_____	_____	_____	_____
1988	_____	_____	_____	_____
1989	_____	_____	_____	_____
1990	_____	_____	_____	_____
1991	_____	_____	_____	_____
1992	_____	_____	_____	_____
1993	_____	_____	_____	_____
1994	_____	_____	_____	_____
1995	_____	_____	_____	_____

Is the data above your estimates or data available from trade/industry sources? Please explain the source/s of your estimates, if any.

❑ Own Estimate   ❑ From Industry Sources

DEADLINE FOR SUBMISSION

Please send two (2) copies of the completed survey forms and all attachments and forward these to TeamAsia by 8 October, 1995.

CERTIFICATION AND CONTACT PERSON

Please fill out the certification and authorization below (to be signed by the President, EVP, GM or CEO of the Company):

I hereby certify that to the best of my knowledge and ability, the information provided therein is a true and accurate representation of the company.

I also authorize The Events and Awards Managers of Asia to use the information provided for the sole purpose of completing its publishing project focusing on the winners of The Asian Management Awards.

Signature: _____
Name: _____
Position: _____
Tel: _____
Fax: _____

Company Name: _____
Address: _____
_____
_____

Please indicate the name, telephone and fax number/s of the person whom we should contact for clarification, for further details or for interview/s, if needed, in relation with the data supplied with this survey form.

Signature: _____
Name: _____
Position: _____
Tel: _____
Fax: _____

GENERAL MANAGEMENT SURVEY FORM

The Award for General Management is for success in strategically positioning the company within the industry and transforming it into an outstanding company.

1. This is the **category-specific survey form** for **General Management**. Please answer all the questions in this form as completely as possible. For financial data, please supply your answer in U.S. dollars. For uniformity, please use the following conversion rates:

Hong Kong	HK$	7.75
Indonesia	Rp	2100.00
Malaysia	RM	2.50
Philippines	P	25.00
Singapore	S$	1.40
Thailand	Bht	25.45

2. Please provide your answers to the questions on a separate sheet. It is important that you indicate your company name, the category in which your company was recognized and the year when you received the Asian Management Award/s on each of the pages of your answer sheets.

3. If you have any questions regarding the questionnaire, please call or fax Mr. Michael Alan Hamlin, managing director, Hamlin-Iturralde Corporation, Ms. Maria Montserrat I. Hamlin, president, TeamAsia or Mr. Renato Ramos, research associate, at Tel (632) 896-1022 to 24; 896-0862; 896-0864 or Fax (632) 896-0866.

4. Please courier your accomplished category-specific survey form, attached with the general survey form, and the release and authorization form, **sealed**, directly to:

ASIA'S BEST COMPANIES:
THE WINNERS OF THE ASIAN MANAGEMENT AWARDS
c/o The Events and Awards Managers of Asia
308 Lirio & Zodiac, Palm Village
City of Makati, Philippines

INFORMATION UPDATE

1. What initiatives have you undertaken in the past three years that strengthened your company's position in the industry?

2. Please indicate the gross revenues, net profits and total assets of the industry in which your company operates. If industry data is not available, please provide your own estimate. (For financial institutions, please use equivalent indices.) Please provide this information for the period from three years before you received your first Asian Management Award in this category until the present year.

Year	Total Industry Revenues	Total Industry Net Profits	Total Industry Assets
1987			
1988			
1989			
1990			
1991			
1992			
1993			
1994			
1995			

Is the data provided above from industry sources or based on your own estimates?

❑ Industry sources ❑ Own Estimates

3. Please indicate below the gross revenues, net profits and total assets of each of the major market segments or niches in your industry. Please identify niche A, B, and C in the space provided. Please provide the data for the period from three years before you first received your first Asian Management Award in this category until the present year.

a. Major Niche A _____

Year	Total Industry Revenues	Total Industry Net Profits	Total Industry Assets
1987			
1988			
1989			
1990			
1991			
1992			
1993			
1994			
1995			

b. Major Niche B _____

Year	Total Industry Revenues	Total Industry Net Profits	Total Industry Assets
1987			
1988			
1989			
1990			
1991			
1992			
1993			
1994			
1995			

c. Major Niche C _____

Year	Total Industry Revenues	Total Industry Net Profits	Total Industry Assets
1987			
1988			
1989			
1990			
1991			
1992			
1993			
1994			
1995			

Is the data provided above from industry sources or based on your own estimates?

❑ Industry sources ❑ Own Estimates

4. Please indicate why your company has been awarded The General Management Award. Please attach whatever supporting documents you think will support your answer.

5. Who are your major competitors? Please give the names of these companies.

6. What are the product/market opportunities your company has exploited and/or seek to exploit?

7. Please indicate your target/market niche, and your company's share of the target market/market niche.

8. What are the important features that customers in these markets or market niches look for in the products or services that you offer?

9. Please provide below the results achieved by your company and your main competitors in the following areas (For financial institutions, please use the equivalent index.).

a. Your Company

Year	Sales/ Gross Revenues	Net Profits	Return on Sales	A	Share of Market Niche B	C	D
1987	____	____	____	__	__	__	__
1988	____	____	____	__	__	__	__
1989	____	____	____	__	__	__	__
1990	____	____	____	__	__	__	__
1991	____	____	____	__	__	__	__
1992	____	____	____	__	__	__	__
1993	____	____	____	__	__	__	__
1994	____	____	____	__	__	__	__
1995	____	____	____	__	__	__	__

b. Direct Competitor A _____

Year	Sales/ Gross Revenues	Net Profits	Return on Sales	A	Share of Market Niche B	C	D
1987	____	____	____	__	__	__	__
1988	____	____	____	__	__	__	__
1989	____	____	____	__	__	__	__
1990	____	____	____	__	__	__	__
1991	____	____	____	__	__	__	__
1992	____	____	____	__	__	__	__
1993	____	____	____	__	__	__	__
1994	____	____	____	__	__	__	__
1995	____	____	____	__	__	__	__

c. Direct Competitor B _____

Year	Sales/ Gross Revenues	Net Profits	Return on Sales	A	Share of Market Niche B	C	D
1987	____	____	____	__	__	__	__
1988	____	____	____	__	__	__	__
1989	____	____	____	__	__	__	__
1990	____	____	____	__	__	__	__
1991	____	____	____	__	__	__	__
1992	____	____	____	__	__	__	__
1993	____	____	____	__	__	__	__
1994	____	____	____	__	__	__	__
1995	____	____	____	__	__	__	__

10. To what extent does your organization practise any of the following management technologies? Please check all that apply.

Management Technology and Practice	A lot	Somewhat	Rarely	Not at all
● Working closely with suppliers	____	____	____	____
● Just-in-time principles	____	____	____	____
● Parallel processing	____	____	____	____
● Quick setup routines	____	____	____	____
● Kanban/visible control devices	____	____	____	____
● Reduction of cycle time	____	____	____	____
● Reengineering	____	____	____	____
● 5/S	____	____	____	____
● Quality	____	____	____	____

DEADLINE FOR SUBMISSION

Please send two (2) copies of the completed survey forms and all attachments and forward these to TeamAsia by 8 October, 1995.

CERTIFICATION AND CONTACT PERSON

Please fill out the certification and authorization below (to be signed by the President, EVP, GM or CEO of the Company):

I hereby certify that to the best of my knowledge and ability, the information provided therein is a true and accurate representation of the company.

I also authorize The Events and Awards Managers of Asia to use the information provided for the sole purpose of completing its publishing project focusing on the winners of The Asian Management Awards.

Signature: _____
Name: _____
Position: _____
Tel: _____
Fax: _____

Company Name: _____
Address: _____
_____
_____

Please indicate the name, telephone and fax number/s of the person whom we should contact for clarification, for further details or for interview/s, if needed, in relation with the data supplied with this survey form.

Signature: _____
Name: _____
Position: _____
Tel: _____
Fax: _____

DEVELOPMENT MANAGEMENT SURVEY FORM

The Award for Development Management is for creating substantial and measurable positive impact on its target beneficiaries through innovative, sustainable and effective management. This award is given to a not-for-profit organization, foundation, or public sector organization which has its main objective the improvement of the quality of life of its people.

1. This is the **category-specific survey form** for **Development Management**. Please answer all the questions in this form as completely as possible. For financial data, please supply your answer in U.S. dollars. For uniformity, please use the following conversion rates:

Hong Kong	HK$	7.75
Indonesia	Rp	2100.00
Malaysia	RM	2.50
Philippines	P	25.00
Singapore	S$	1.40
Thailand	Bht	25.45

2. Please provide your answers to the questions on a separate sheet. It is important that you indicate your company name, the category in which your company was recognized and the year when you received the Asian Management Award/s on each of the pages of your answer sheets.

3. If you have any questions regarding the questionnaire, please call or fax Mr. Michael Alan Hamlin, managing director, Hamlin-Iturralde Corporation, Ms. Maria Montserrat I. Hamlin, president, TeamAsia or Mr. Renato Ramos, research associate, at Tel (632) 896-1022 to 24; 896-0862; 896-0864 or Fax (632) 896-0866.

4. Please courier your accomplished category-specific survey form, attached with the general survey form, and the release and authorization form, **sealed,** directly to:

ASIA'S BEST COMPANIES:
THE WINNERS OF THE ASIAN MANAGEMENT AWARDS
c/o The Events and Awards Managers of Asia
308 Lirio & Zodiac, Palm Village
City of Makati, Philippines

INFORMATION UPDATE

1. Please indicate why your company has been awarded the Development Management Award. Please attach whatever supporting documents you think will support your answer.

2. Has your company received other award/s or recognition from other local, regional or international award-giving bodies in relation to efforts in Development Management? If yes, please list them and give a brief description of each award.

3. How substantial were the effects of the benefits directly received by your target groups? Please quantify if possible. Where quantification is not possible, please specify verifiable indicators of successful impact.

4. How much did your organization spend to deliver the development-oriented services (in US$) annually for the past three years?

5. What additional measures has your organization taken to ensure the continuing delivery of development-oriented services?

6. Has your target group demonstrated the ability to act on its own as a result of your organization's services? Please elaborate.

7. Have you set goals to reach groups other than your present target groups/ recipients?
   ❑ Yes   ❑ No
   If yes, please specify which groups and provide a brief background for each additional group/s you have included as your target audience.

8. How does your organization plan and implement development-oriented programs and projects?

DEADLINE FOR SUBMISSION

Please send two (2) copies of the completed survey forms and all attachments and forward these to TeamAsia by 8 October, 1995.

CERTIFICATION AND CONTACT PERSON

Please fill out the certification and authorization below (to be signed by the President, EVP, GM or CEO of the Company):

I hereby certify that to the best of my knowledge and ability, the information provided therein is a true and accurate representation of the company.

I also authorize The Events and Awards Managers of Asia to use the said provided information for the sole purpose of completing its publishing project focusing on the winners of The Asian Management Awards.

Signature: _____
Name: _____
Position: _____
Tel: _____
Fax: _____

Company Name: _____
Address: _____
_____
_____

Please indicate the name, telephone and fax number/s of the person whom we should contact for clarification, for further details or for interview/s, if needed, in relation with the data supplied with this survey form.

Signature: _____
Name: _____
Position: _____
Tel: _____
Fax: _____

INDEX

317

Shape and Shape Theory

Shape and Shape Theory

D. G. KENDALL
Churchill College, University of Cambridge, UK

D. BARDEN
Girton College, University of Cambridge, UK

T. K. CARNE
King's College, University of Cambridge, UK

H. LE
University of Nottingham, UK

JOHN WILEY & SONS, LTD
Chichester • New York • Weinheim • Brisbane • Singapore • Toronto

Other Wiley Editorial Offices

John Wiley & Sons, Inc., 605 Third Avenue,
New York, NY 10158-0012, USA

Wiley-VCH Verlag GmbH, Pappelallee 3,
D-69469 Weinheim, Germany

Jacaranda Wiley Ltd, 33 Park Road, Milton,
Queensland 4064, Australia

John Wiley & Sons (Asia) Pte Ltd, 2 Clementi Loop #02-01,
Jin Xing Distripark, Singapore 129809

John Wiley & Sons (Canada) Ltd, 22 Worcester Road,
Rexdale, Ontario, M9W 1L1, Canada

Library of Congress Cataloging-in-Publication Data

Shape and shape theory / D.G. Kendall ... [et al.].
        p.   cm.—(Wiley series in probability and statistics)
    Includes bibliographical references and index.
    ISBN 0-471-96823-4 (alk. paper)
    1. Shape theory (Topology)—Statistical methods   I. Kendall, D.G. (David George),
1918- . II. Series.
    QA612. 7. S48   1999   99-12433
    514′ .24—dc21   CIP

British Library Cataloguing in Publication Data

A catalogue record for this book is available from the British Library

ISBN 0-471-96823-4

Typeset in 10/12pt Times by Laser Words, Madras, India
Printed and bound in Great Britain by Antony Rowe Ltd, Chippenham, Wiltshire
This book is printed on acid-free paper responsibly manufactured from sustainable forestry
in which at least two trees are planted for each one used for paper production.

Contents

Preface

Everyone knows what is meant by 'shape'. However, it is not a trivial matter to define shape in a manner that is susceptible to mathematical and statistical analysis and it is only over the last two or three decades that appropriate definitions have been developed and studied. In this book we assume that the shape of an object is essentially captured by the shape of a finite subset of its points and, for the latter, we carry out much of the fundamental analysis that is likely to lie at the heart of further progress. Although this may seem a severe restriction, there is no theoretical limit to the number of points we consider and it has the significant advantage that the dimensions of the resulting shape spaces are always finite and only increase linearly with the number of points.

One of the central problems in shape theory is that it is not possible to represent the full range of possible shapes of an object in standard Euclidean coordinates without destroying our intuitive feel for the quantitative differences between them. Consequently, classical statistical methods are not always adequate or, at least, not clearly appropriate for the statistical analysis of shape and it is necessary to adapt them to work on unfamiliar spaces. We therefore need to describe the topological and geometric properties of these new spaces in some detail, as result of which this book is multidisciplinary. However, we have tried to make it accessible to as wide a range of readers as possible by giving, for each topic, more detail than the specialist in that subject might require. Where possible, we do this within the body of the text itself, with just a few of the more technical topological concepts and results reserved for the appendix.

We start with an introductory survey of the spaces in which we shall represent shapes and describe some of their more important properties and then, in Chapter 2, we investigate their global topological structure. The next three chapters lead up to a full calculation of the homology and cohomology groups of shape spaces. In the first of these we define homology theory and show how it is calculated in the special context that is adequate for our purposes because, although they are unfamiliar, shape spaces are still elementary. In Chapter 4 we examine the necessary chain complex for these computations that arises naturally from the topological structure of the spaces, and make some initial general deductions about their homology groups. Then, in Chapter 5, after giving a range of low-dimensional illustrative examples, we calculate all the groups explicitly and also derive some intriguing relationships between them.

In Chapters 6 and 7 we study the more subtle and more localised geometric properties of the spaces. Although there is only one topology, the natural quotient topology, that one can put on shape space, there is more than one metric. Here we discuss the Riemannian metric that arises from the theory of submersions, to which we shall relate any other metrics that we use. Once again, the elementary way in which shape spaces are produced enables us to prove most of the results that we require from that theory directly in our context, with little reference to the general case. In Chapter 6 we examine the geodesics, the analogues of straight lines in Euclidean space, between two shapes and find simple expressions for the distance between those shapes, as well as the distance from a shape to certain subsets of practical significance. In Chapter 7, after introducing a little more differential geometry, we are able to obtain explicit expressions for the main geometric invariants of the spaces. In particular, we are able to measure the precise extent to which they are curved. This is vital, for example, when assessing the extent to which a local linear approximation to shape space is valid. Since the curvature can be arbitrarily large, that is certainly not always the case.

In the next two chapters we turn to the probabilistic and statistical topics that were the prime motivation for the introduction of shape spaces. In Chapter 8 we investigate the distributions that arise on shape space from various standard distributions on the points that determine those shapes. We describe them generally by referring to the volume measure on shape space obtained in Chapter 7. As the initial distributions become more general, the range of shape spaces on which we give explicit formulae for the induced distributions tends to become more restricted. However, in principle, our results are quite general. Moreover, although, as was the case for the homology groups, the formulae can become quite intricate, they are still elementary and susceptible to computation. We illustrate this claim by obtaining, in the final sections of this chapter, an explicit description of the density function for the shape of a random triangle whose vertices are uniformly independently distributed in a given convex planar polygon.

In classical statistics the mean is well-defined and simple to compute. However, problems can arise both in defining a 'mean' shape in theory and also in calculating it in practice. It turns out that various 'obvious' approaches do not necessarily lead to the same results or even, in each case, to a unique result. In Chapter 9 we discuss some of the relations between different possible definitions and also identify circumstances, fortunately fairly general, in which the results we would like to take for granted are actually true.

In Chapter 10 we address the problem of visualising the first, that is, lowest dimensional, shape space that is not already familiar. That is the five-dimensional space of shapes of tetrahedra in 3-space. Although this is topologically a sphere, it is by no means a standard one, as it has a singular subset in the neighbourhood of which the curvature becomes arbitrarily large. The visualisation uses a carefully selected family of 24 two-dimensional sections that, rather surprisingly, do allow us to follow what is going on in the space. We illustrate this by describing some typical geodesics, some sample paths for a diffusion and a comparison of two distributions on the space.

We conclude by putting our work into a broader setting where similar studies may be carried out. In particular, this enables us to look at some shape spaces related to those that have been the subject of the rest of this book. The first applications still concern finite sets of points in Euclidean space but here we study their size-and-shape, for which size is no longer quotiented out, and also an alternative metric, one having negative curvature, on the non-degenerate part of the shape space. In the final sections we consider the shapes of finite sets of points in the other standard spaces of constant curvature, the sphere and hyperbolic space, as well as some connections with the classical theory of elliptic functions.

We are, of course, indebted to all who have worked on shape theory, whether or not it lies in the area that we specifically address. Much of the material presented is previously unpublished work given in local seminars or work produced explicitly for this book, and we are grateful to all our colleagues, but especially to Marge Batchelor, for many helpful discussions over the years of gestation of this project. Thanks are also due to our publishers, particularly to Helen Ramsey for her constant encouragement and patience over our ever-receding deadlines.

CHAPTER 1

Shapes and Shape Spaces

1.1 ORIGINS

There have been at least three distinct origins of what we call *shape theory*. The first approach seems to have been that of Kendall (1977) who was, at that time, concerned with 'shape' in archaeology and astronomy, but it soon became clear that the subject could profitably be studied from a more general standpoint. At about the same time Bookstein (1978a,b) began to study shape-theoretic problems in the particular context of zoology. A third early contributor was Ziezold (1977). In this present book the theory will be developed largely along the lines initiated by Kendall in his 1977 paper, but much new material will be presented.

In a typical case the calculations will be concerned with sets of, say, k labelled points in a Euclidean space $\mathbb{R}^m$, where $k \geqslant 2$. Normally, the centroid of the k points will serve as an origin, and the scale will be such that the sum of the squared distances of the points from that origin will be equal to unity. The basic object just described will be called the *pre-shape*, and any two configurations of k labelled points will be regarded as having the same shape *if either of their pre-shapes can be transformed into the other by a rotation about the shared centroid*. The resulting assemblage of all possible shapes will be called the *shape space* and will be denoted by Σ_m^k. Accordingly, the *shape* is defined as the *pre-shape modulo rotations*. These definitions and the related constructions provide the basis for the present book. It should be observed that the k constituent labelled points determine the shape. At a later stage we shall define 'size-and-shape' in a similar way by omitting the 'unit-sum-of-squares' standardisation.

While we do not wish to go deeply into the details of Bookstein's parallel work, it is appropriate here to stress the fact that for us *the labelled points are basic and determine the object being studied*. In Bookstein's work, however, the 'marker points' are selected from a usually two-dimensional or three-dimensional continuum. Thus, if the object in question is a planar representation of a human hand with fingers out-stretched, then the markers could be the tips of the fingers, the common roots of each pair of adjacent fingers and a few more points on the planar outline of the hand reaching down, say, as far as the wrist. Already in this simple case it is clear that the choice of markers is far from being a simple matter even in the two-dimensional case, and it would be still more difficult if the complete three-dimensional surface were to be the object being studied. To take a still more difficult example, consider the problem of coding the shape of a potato!

A further difference between the two approaches arises at the next stage. Bookstein is concerned to represent real objects, often biological ones, and the markers are chosen sufficiently well spaced to identify those objects. Thus, he is not interested in configurations in which the markers all lie in a lower-dimensional subspace or two or more of them coincide. This contrasts with Kendall's spaces, which contain the shapes of all possible configurations except those for which all the points coincide. This provides a context in which it is possible to measure the statistical significance of apparent collinearities or other degeneracies in archaeological or astronomical data.

Bookstein's work includes many delicate and important studies concerning the continuous deformation of *biological* shapes, this being a topic first studied by Thompson [1917] (1942). It is appropriate here to associate Thompson's work with that of Bower (1930) who studied 'size and form' in plants. A copy of Bower's book was given by him to Kendall, and it was this event that led many years later to the formulation of shape-theoretic studies in a general mathematical context.

1.2   SOME PRELIMINARY OBSERVATIONS

Consider the shape of a configuration of $k \geqslant 2$ labelled and not totally coincident points $x_1^*, x_2^*, \ldots, x_k^*$ in a Euclidean space having $m \geqslant 1$ Euclidean dimensions. How is the *shape* of such a configuration to be represented?

Since we are not interested in the location of the k-ad, we may start by uniformly translating its component points x_j^* in $\mathbb{R}^m$ in such a way that their centroid, x_c^*, is moved to the origin of the coordinates. The 'size' of this k-ad is, of course, important as an aspect of 'size-and-shape', but as far as shape alone is concerned it is of no interest, so we normally shrink or expand the size of the centred k-ad about the new origin so as to make the natural quadratic measure of 'size'

$$\sqrt{||x_1^* - x_c^*||^2 + \cdots + ||x_k^* - x_c^*||^2}$$

equal to unity. This convention makes sense because we have deliberately excluded the maximally degenerate case in which all the points x_j^* coincide.

To take the most trivial example, the only such sized-and-centred configurations when $k = 2$ and $m = 1$ are the labelled point-pairs:

$$\left(-\frac{1}{\sqrt{2}}, \frac{1}{\sqrt{2}}\right) \text{ and } \left(\frac{1}{\sqrt{2}}, -\frac{1}{\sqrt{2}}\right)$$

in $\mathbb{R}^2$, so we see that Σ_1^2 consists of just two shapes, and that it can be identified with the two-point unit sphere $\{-1, 1\}$ of dimension zero.

A straightforward generalisation of this argument, which we shall give in more detail later, tells us that shape space Σ_1^k consists of all standardised k-ads of the form:

$$\left\{ (x_1, x_2, \ldots, x_k) : \sum_{i=1}^{k} x_i = 0, \sum_{i=1}^{k} x_i^2 = 1 \right\}$$

for $k \geqslant 2$. Thus, shape space Σ_1^k is a unit-radius $(k-2)$-sphere $\mathbf{S}^{k-2}(1)$ for all $k \geqslant 2$.

But now suppose that $m \geqslant 2$ and $k \geqslant 2$, and let us move the centroid of the k-ad to the origin and standardise the size as before. If we write $\widetilde{X}^*$ for the sized-and-centred $m \times k$ coordinate matrix with components

$$(\tilde{x}_{ij}^* : 1 \leqslant i \leqslant m, 1 \leqslant j \leqslant k),$$

then the k individual columns of the matrix can be thought of as column m-vectors specifying the positions of the k points $x_j^* - x_c^*$ in $\mathbb{R}^m$ where, as above, x_c^* is the centroid of the k-ad and $1 \leqslant j \leqslant k$. Then, from the shape-theoretic point of view, we will never wish to distinguish between $\widetilde{X}^*$ and $T\widetilde{X}^*$ where T is in $\mathbf{SO}(m)$. This is because it is a basic feature of our work that rotations acting on the left of $\widetilde{X}^*$ are to be regarded as irrelevant. We therefore call the sized-and-centred configuration described by $\widetilde{X}^*$ the *pre-shape*, and we define the *shape itself* to be $\widetilde{X}^*$ viewed modulo the rotations in $\mathbf{SO}(m)$ acting from the left.

It is easily checked that the complete set of all such pre-shapes is a unit sphere of dimension $m(k-1) - 1$, and we call this $\mathcal{S}_m^k$. That is the *pre-shape space*, and the corresponding shape space Σ_m^k is $\mathcal{S}_m^k$ modulo $\mathbf{SO}(m)$ with the rotations acting from the left. Provided that $k \geqslant m + 1$, the dimension of Σ_m^k is

$$d_m^k = m(k-1) - \tfrac{1}{2}m(m-1) - 1.$$

In this formula the first term on the right follows from the fact that, while there are m rows and k columns in the matrix $\widetilde{X}^*$, k is here reduced to $k-1$ because we want to have the centroid of the k points at the origin of the coordinates. The second term on the right arises because we must quotient out the effect of rotations of $\mathbf{SO}(m)$ acting from the left, while the final term, -1, takes account of the fact that we wish to ignore scale effects. In particular, we note that $d_1^k = k - 2$ agrees with our earlier calculations. When $k \leqslant m$, a configuration of k labelled points in $\mathbb{R}^m$ lies in a $(k-1)$-dimensional subspace and so its shape lies in Σ_{k-1}^k. However, now the extra dimensions give us room to rotate the configuration onto its mirror image. This means that the pre-shape is quotiented out by $\mathbf{O}(k-1)$ rather than $\mathbf{SO}(k-1)$ to obtain the shape. Thus, for $k \leqslant m$, Σ_m^k is a 'halved' version of Σ_{k-1}^k, this being the result of identifying the shapes of configurations of k labelled points in $(k-1)$-space that are mirror images of each other. In particular, when $k \leqslant m$, Σ_m^k is 'over-dimensioned' in the sense that $d_m^k > \dim(\Sigma_m^k) = d_{k-1}^k$.

Note that, while the construction of the pre-shape is entirely elementary, the quotient operation that yields the shape itself is very far from being so, save in a few trivial cases. When $m = 1$ the shape is identical with the pre-shape $\tilde{X}^*$ because there are no non-trivial rotations T in $\mathbf{SO}(1)$, but the corresponding situation when m is equal to two or more can be quite complicated. To illustrate the non-triviality of shape spaces in general it suffices to remark that when $k \geqslant 2$ the shape of k labelled points in the plane will turn out to be a point in the classical complex projective space $\mathbf{CP}^{k-2}(4)$, where the '4' is the appropriate value for the curvature parameter. This is its name as a classical object, but as a shape space we call it Σ_2^k. In particular, Σ_2^3 is $\mathbf{CP}^1(4)$. This, in more familiar terms, is the 2-sphere $\mathbf{S}^2(\frac{1}{2})$ of radius one-half. More details about this will be given later in Section 1.3.

Before discussing general shape spaces Σ_m^k we introduce two important diagrams shown in Tables 1.1 and 1.2. These will be useful in reminding the reader of 'what goes where' and we here mention some of their most important features.

Obviously, it is desirable that in the diagrams we should be able to recognise those shape spaces that are over-dimensioned, that is, those for which $k \leqslant m$. In Table 1.1 the over-dimensioned shape spaces are emphasised by the use of lower case σ instead of upper case Σ, which will be used elsewhere. Here, the entry at (k, m) in the table is the name of the shape space associated with k labelled points in m dimensions.

The accompanying Table 1.2 follows the same pattern, but now the entry in position (k, m) is *the dimension of the corresponding shape space*, and a bold font is used to indicate *the region $k \geqslant m + 1$ in which shape spaces are not over-dimensioned*. For example, Σ_3^4 in Table 1.1 is the shape space for four labelled points in three dimensions and, from the corresponding entry in Table 1.2, we see that this is a five-dimensional shape space—actually we shall find that it is a *topological 5-sphere* that possesses singularities.

As already mentioned, the spaces listed in the first column, where $m = 1$, are all unit spheres, while the second column also has familiar entries: Σ_2^k for each choice of k is the classical complex projective space with a complex dimension $k - 2$ and a real dimension $2k - 4$.

A striking feature of Table 1.1 is that the main diagonal consists entirely of, mainly only topological, spheres. We already know that Σ_1^2 is the two-point, zero-dimensional, metric sphere of radius unity. We shall see later that Σ_2^3 is a metric 2-sphere of radius one-half, while the further entries on the main diagonal hold the *topological* spheres of the dimensions 5, 9, 14, ..., etc. indicated by the corresponding entries on the main diagonal in Table 1.2, where the mth entry is

$$d_m^{m+1} = \tfrac{1}{2}m^2 + \tfrac{1}{2}m - 1.$$

Table 1.1 The array of shape spaces (the σ-entries are 'over-dimensioned')

k\m	1	2	3	4	5	6	7	8	9	10
2	Σ_1^2	σ_2^2	σ_3^2	σ_4^2	σ_5^2	σ_6^2	σ_7^2	σ_8^2	σ_9^2	σ_{10}^2
3	Σ_1^3	Σ_2^3	σ_3^3	σ_4^3	σ_5^3	σ_6^3	σ_7^3	σ_8^3	σ_9^3	σ_{10}^3
4	Σ_1^4	Σ_2^4	Σ_3^4	σ_4^4	σ_5^4	σ_6^4	σ_7^4	σ_8^4	σ_9^4	σ_{10}^4
5	Σ_1^5	Σ_2^5	Σ_3^5	Σ_4^5	σ_5^5	σ_6^5	σ_7^5	σ_8^5	σ_9^5	σ_{10}^5
6	Σ_1^6	Σ_2^6	Σ_3^6	Σ_4^6	Σ_5^6	σ_6^6	σ_7^6	σ_8^6	σ_9^6	σ_{10}^6
7	Σ_1^7	Σ_2^7	Σ_3^7	Σ_4^7	Σ_5^7	Σ_6^7	σ_7^7	σ_8^7	σ_9^7	σ_{10}^7
8	Σ_1^8	Σ_2^8	Σ_3^8	Σ_4^8	Σ_5^8	Σ_6^8	Σ_7^8	σ_8^8	σ_9^8	σ_{10}^8
9	Σ_1^9	Σ_2^9	Σ_3^9	Σ_4^9	Σ_5^9	Σ_6^9	Σ_7^9	Σ_8^9	σ_9^9	σ_{10}^9
10	Σ_1^{10}	Σ_2^{10}	Σ_3^{10}	Σ_4^{10}	Σ_5^{10}	Σ_6^{10}	Σ_7^{10}	Σ_8^{10}	Σ_9^{10}	σ_{10}^{10}
11	Σ_1^{11}	Σ_2^{11}	Σ_3^{11}	Σ_4^{11}	Σ_5^{11}	Σ_6^{11}	Σ_7^{11}	Σ_8^{11}	Σ_9^{11}	Σ_{10}^{11}
12	Σ_1^{12}	Σ_2^{12}	Σ_3^{12}	Σ_4^{12}	Σ_5^{12}	Σ_6^{12}	Σ_7^{12}	Σ_8^{12}	Σ_9^{12}	Σ_{10}^{12}
13	Σ_1^{13}	Σ_2^{13}	Σ_3^{13}	Σ_4^{13}	Σ_5^{13}	Σ_6^{13}	Σ_7^{13}	Υ_8^{13}	Σ_9^{13}	Σ_{10}^{13}
14	Σ_1^{14}	Σ_2^{14}	Σ_3^{14}	Σ_4^{14}	Σ_5^{14}	Σ_6^{14}	Σ_7^{14}	Σ_8^{14}	Σ_9^{14}	Σ_{10}^{14}
15	Σ_1^{15}	Σ_2^{15}	Σ_3^{15}	Σ_4^{15}	Σ_5^{15}	Σ_6^{15}	Σ_7^{15}	Σ_8^{15}	Σ_9^{15}	Σ_{10}^{15}
16	Σ_1^{16}	Σ_2^{16}	Σ_3^{16}	Σ_4^{16}	Σ_5^{16}	Σ_6^{16}	Σ_7^{16}	Σ_8^{16}	Σ_9^{16}	Σ_{10}^{16}
17	Σ_1^{17}	Σ_2^{17}	Σ_3^{17}	Σ_4^{17}	Σ_5^{17}	Σ_6^{17}	Σ_7^{17}	Σ_8^{17}	Σ_9^{17}	Σ_{10}^{17}
18	Σ_1^{18}	Σ_2^{18}	Σ_3^{18}	Σ_4^{18}	Σ_5^{18}	Σ_6^{18}	Σ_7^{18}	Σ_8^{18}	Σ_9^{18}	Σ_{10}^{18}
19	Σ_1^{19}	Σ_2^{19}	Σ_3^{19}	Σ_4^{19}	Σ_5^{19}	Σ_6^{19}	Σ_7^{19}	Σ_8^{19}	Σ_9^{19}	Σ_{10}^{19}
20	Σ_1^{20}	Σ_2^{20}	Σ_3^{20}	Σ_4^{20}	Σ_5^{20}	Σ_6^{20}	Σ_7^{20}	Σ_8^{20}	Σ_9^{20}	Σ_{10}^{20}

This fact was first observed by Casson (1977, private communication), and it plays an important role in many later contexts. Casson's proof of this theorem will be given at the end of this chapter and alternative proofs will be given elsewhere in this book. We shall also show, in Chapter 6, that none of these spheres is a *metric* sphere except for the first two.

Another important feature arises from the fact that in the kth row of Table 1.1 the spaces beyond the main diagonal are those Σ_m^k for which $k \leqslant m$ so, as we have seen, they are all *identical* to halved versions of Σ_{k-1}^k, which is the corresponding diagonal entry. In fact, a simple modification of Casson's proof would show that they are all topological balls, and we shall give an alternative proof in Chapter 2. To take the simplest example, the row labelled $k = 2$ starts with a two-point, zero-dimensional space, its two points being separated by two units, and this two-point space is followed on the right by an infinite part-row of one-point spaces. Similarly, the row $k = 3$ begins with a one-dimensional circle of radius one, followed by a 2-sphere of radius one-half, this in its turn being followed by an infinite part-row of metric hemispheres having the same dimension and radius.

Table 1.2 Shape space dimensions

k\m	1	2	3	4	5	6	7	8	9	10
2	0	0	0	0	0	0	0	0	0	0
3	1	2	2	2	2	2	2	2	2	2
4	2	4	5	5	5	5	5	5	5	5
5	3	6	8	9	9	9	9	9	9	9
6	4	8	11	13	14	14	14	14	14	14
7	5	10	14	17	19	20	20	20	20	20
8	6	12	17	21	24	26	27	27	27	27
9	7	14	20	25	29	32	34	35	35	35
10	8	16	23	29	34	38	41	43	44	44
11	9	18	26	33	39	44	48	51	53	54
12	10	20	29	37	44	50	55	59	62	64
13	11	22	32	41	49	56	62	67	71	74
14	12	24	35	45	54	62	69	75	80	84
15	13	26	38	49	59	68	76	83	89	94
16	14	28	41	53	64	74	83	91	98	104
17	15	30	44	57	69	80	90	99	107	114
18	16	32	47	61	74	86	97	107	116	124
19	17	34	50	65	79	92	104	115	125	134
20	18	36	53	69	84	98	111	123	134	144

However, when $k = 4$ the row starts off with a unit metric 2-sphere, followed by a four-dimensional complex projective space of complex curvature 4, and then by a five-dimensional *topological* sphere, this last space having singularities. That space lies on the diagonal and is followed on its right by an infinite sequence of *identical topological hemispheres*, or, equivalently, topological balls, which are precisely 'halves' of the 5-sphere on the diagonal. The situation is highlighted in Table 1.1 by the use of upper-case and lower-case sigmas.

After inspecting Table 1.1 the reader will notice that we have still to describe the shape spaces Σ_m^k in the infinite triangular region determined by the inequalities $m \geqslant 3$ and $k \geqslant m + 2$, that is, those that lie to the right of the column $m = 2$ and to the left of the spheres on the diagonal of the array. These particular shape spaces are truly peculiar in that they appear not to have occurred in any earlier contexts. They have not yet been determined up to homeomorphism, but in due course we will present the integral homology for each one and describe its global geodesic geometry as well as the Riemannian metric and associated curvature tensors.

Since they have different dimensions, *no two* of the 'diagonal' shape spaces are the same, but to the left of the diagonal the dimension alone is not sufficient to distinguish between them. For example, Σ_7^9 and Σ_5^{10} each have dimension 34. In later chapters we will make use of a 'topological recurrence' that provides useful structural information about all of them and, in principle, leads to a complete characterisation of the whole family of shape spaces. It will be shown, in particular, that the shape spaces in the infinite triangular region mentioned above possess the following interesting properties:

  (i) no one of these is a sphere, and indeed no one is even a homotopy sphere or a manifold,

 (ii) all of these spaces have torsion in homology,

(iii) no two of them share the same homology, even at the $\mathbb{Z}_2$-level.

These facts were first established by making use of the exact sequences for shape space homology that we introduce in Chapter 5 and that results from the above-mentioned topological recurrence. Note, in particular, an important consequence implied by (iii): *the shape spaces located in the infinite triangular region of Table 1.1 are all topologically distinct from one another.* They are also distinct from those in the first two columns so that apart from Σ_1^4 and Σ_2^3, which are different sized copies of the 2-sphere, all shape spaces with $k \geqslant m$ are topologically distinct.

1.3 A MATRIX REPRESENTATION FOR THE SHAPE OF A k-ad

Let us consider a labelled set of k points in $\mathbb{R}^m$, where $k \geqslant 2$, whose coordinates $x_1^*, x_2^*, \ldots, x_k^*$ we shall write as the columns of the matrix X^*. We recall that degeneracies are allowed except that we insist that the points are not totally coincident, and that the *shape* of the k-ad is what is left when all effects attributable to translation, rotation and dilatation have been quotiented out.

We now orthogonally transform the k-ad X^* as follows:

$$x_0 = \sqrt{k}x_c^* = \frac{1}{\sqrt{k}}(x_1^* + x_2^* + \cdots + x_k^*)$$

and

$$\tilde{x}_j = \frac{1}{\sqrt{j+j^2}}\{jx_{j+1}^* - (x_1^* + x_2^* + \cdots + x_j^*)\}$$

for $1 \leqslant j \leqslant k-1$. We can see that the matrix $(\sqrt{k}x_c^* \; \tilde{x}_1 \; \cdots \; \tilde{x}_{k-1})$ representing the new k-ad is obtained from X^* by multiplying on the right by a special $k \times k$ matrix Q_k. The second equation also shows that, for each $j > 0$, $\tilde{x}_j$ is a scalar multiple of

$$x_{j+1}^* - \frac{x_1^* + \cdots + x_j^*}{j},$$

and a striking feature of this construction is the progressive re-centring of x_{j+1}^* relative to its predecessors $x_1^*, \ldots, x_j^*$. This follows from the form of Q_k and it provides the main justification for its use. As an example we present the matrix

Q_k in the particular case $k = 6$ as follows:

$$
\begin{pmatrix}
\frac{1}{\sqrt{6}} & -\frac{1}{\sqrt{2}} & -\frac{1}{\sqrt{6}} & -\frac{1}{\sqrt{12}} & -\frac{1}{\sqrt{20}} & -\frac{1}{\sqrt{30}} \\[6pt]
\frac{1}{\sqrt{6}} & \frac{1}{\sqrt{2}} & -\frac{1}{\sqrt{6}} & -\frac{1}{\sqrt{12}} & -\frac{1}{\sqrt{20}} & -\frac{1}{\sqrt{30}} \\[6pt]
\frac{1}{\sqrt{6}} & 0 & \frac{2}{\sqrt{6}} & -\frac{1}{\sqrt{12}} & -\frac{1}{\sqrt{20}} & -\frac{1}{\sqrt{30}} \\[6pt]
\frac{1}{\sqrt{6}} & 0 & 0 & \frac{3}{\sqrt{12}} & -\frac{1}{\sqrt{20}} & -\frac{1}{\sqrt{30}} \\[6pt]
\frac{1}{\sqrt{6}} & 0 & 0 & 0 & \frac{4}{\sqrt{20}} & -\frac{1}{\sqrt{30}} \\[6pt]
\frac{1}{\sqrt{6}} & 0 & 0 & 0 & 0 & \frac{5}{\sqrt{30}}
\end{pmatrix}.
$$

It should be noted that

(i)   in each column of the array the squares of the entries sum to unity,
(ii) each column is orthogonal to all of the other columns,
(iii) the integers, the square roots of which appear in the denominators in the second and later positions in row one, are as follows:

$$
2 = 1 \times 2, \quad 6 = 2 \times 3, \quad 12 = 3 \times 4,
$$
$$
20 = 4 \times 5, \quad 30 = 5 \times 6, \quad \dots
$$

these entries being repeated in the rows below in the same horizontal locations until just before the main diagonal is reached.

In fact, these properties suffice to specify the matrix Q_k in the general case up to the sign of each column. For our particular choice it turns out that Q_k is a rotation. Indeed, the fact that it is orthogonal is immediate from properties (i) and (ii) above. However, it remains for us to show that Q_k has determinant $+1$ rather than -1. In order to do this we start by adding to the top row of the matrix the sum of all the subsequent rows. This yields a new top row consisting of $\sqrt{k}$ followed by zeros. It follows that the value of the determinant is

$$
\sqrt{k} \times 1 \times 2 \times 3 \times \cdots \times (k-1)
$$

divided by

$$
\{(1 \times 2) \times (2 \times 3) \times (3 \times 4) \times \cdots \times ((k-1) \times k)\}^{1/2},
$$

which reduces to $+1$ as required.

For most purposes it is convenient to shift the configuration so that its centroid is moved to the origin of coordinates after which the matrix X^* will have all its row sums equal to zero. If we now examine the product

$$
(x_1^* \ x_2^* \ \cdots \ x_k^*)Q_k
$$

we find that it has the form

$$(0\ \tilde{\boldsymbol{x}}_1\ \tilde{\boldsymbol{x}}_2\ \cdots\ \tilde{\boldsymbol{x}}_{k-1})$$

because the first column of Q_k is 'constant' and each row-sum of the matrix

$$\boldsymbol{x}_1^* + \boldsymbol{x}_2^* + \cdots + \boldsymbol{x}_k^*$$

is equal to zero. We also note that our normalisation for size, dividing by

$$\{||\boldsymbol{x}_1^* - \boldsymbol{x}_c^*||^2 + \cdots + ||\boldsymbol{x}_k^* - \boldsymbol{x}_c^*||^2\}^{1/2},$$

now corresponds to dividing by $\left\{\sum_{i=1}^{k}||\boldsymbol{x}_i^*||^2\right\}^{1/2}$ and, since Q_k is orthogonal,

to dividing by $\left\{\sum_{i=1}^{k-1}||\tilde{\boldsymbol{x}}_i||^2\right\}^{1/2}$.

The result of this normalisation will be a matrix

$$(0\ \boldsymbol{x}_1\ \boldsymbol{x}_2\ \cdots\ \boldsymbol{x}_{k-1})$$

and, if we throw away the zero first column, we can represent the pre-shape by

$$X = (\boldsymbol{x}_1\ \boldsymbol{x}_2\ \cdots\ \boldsymbol{x}_{k-1}),$$

and then the shape itself is represented by this $m \times (k-1)$ array modulo $\mathbf{SO}(m)$ acting on the left. We also note that, if we identify the space of $m \times (k-1)$ real matrices with Euclidean ($m \times (k-1)$)-space, our normalisation implies that this pre-shape will lie on the unit ($m(k-1)-1$)-sphere in that space.

Thus, the shape is to be identified with the equivalence class or 'orbit' associated with the left action of $\mathbf{SO}(m)$ on the pre-shape, and we shall be free to represent each such class by any one of its members. In particular, we can if we wish transform the pre-shape matrix

$$X = (\boldsymbol{x}_1\ \boldsymbol{x}_2\ \cdots\ \boldsymbol{x}_{k-1})$$

by using one of the rotations in $\mathbf{SO}(m)$ to perform various 'left-hand' tidying-up operations. Thus, we can exploit these procedures to yield

(i) an upper semi-diagonal matrix that has a strictly positive sign for the first non-zero entry in each of the first $m-1$ rows, all the entries in the last row being 0 or $\pm$, as in

$$\begin{pmatrix} 0 & + & \pm & \pm & \pm & \pm & \pm & \pm & \pm & \pm & \pm \\ 0 & 0 & 0 & + & \pm & \pm & \pm & \pm & \pm & \pm & \pm \\ 0 & 0 & 0 & 0 & \pm & \pm & \pm & \pm & \pm & \pm & \pm \end{pmatrix},$$

or

(ii) an upper semi-diagonal matrix with a strictly positive sign for the first non-zero entry in each of the first $j \leqslant m-2$ rows, with 'zero' rows below this, as in the further example with $j=2$:

$$\begin{pmatrix} 0 & 0 & + & \pm & \pm & \pm & \pm & \pm & \pm & \pm & \pm & \pm \\ 0 & 0 & 0 & + & \pm & \pm & \pm & \pm & \pm & \pm & \pm & \pm \\ 0 & 0 & 0 & 0 & 0 & 0 & 0 & 0 & 0 & 0 & 0 & 0 \\ 0 & 0 & 0 & 0 & 0 & 0 & 0 & 0 & 0 & 0 & 0 & 0 \\ 0 & 0 & 0 & 0 & 0 & 0 & 0 & 0 & 0 & 0 & 0 & 0 \end{pmatrix}.$$

Such 'tidying-up' operations involving an $(m \times m)$-rotation on the left will often be useful. Of course, on replacing each $\pm$ by the actual numerical entry we get a tidied-up version of the original data. In fact, when we come to perform our mathematical computations on these matrices it will sometimes be more convenient to have all the potentially non-zero elements at the beginning of each row.

Another presentation of the pre-shape $X = (x_1 \ x_2 \ \cdots \ x_{k-1})$ is based on a 'pseudo-singular values decomposition' of X. This allows us to present the pre-shape in the three-factor form

$$U(\Lambda \ 0)V.$$

Here, U is an element of $\mathbf{SO}(m)$, V is an element of $\mathbf{SO}(k-1)$ and Λ is the $m \times m$ diagonal matrix

$$\text{diag}\{\lambda_1, \lambda_2, \ldots, \lambda_m\}$$

with

$$\lambda_1 \geqslant \lambda_2 \geqslant \cdots \geqslant \lambda_{m-1} \geqslant |\lambda_m|.$$

In this formula the sum of the squares of the λ's is equal to unity, and $\lambda_m \geqslant 0$ unless $k = m + 1$.

We can re-write this decomposition in either of the forms

$$U(\Lambda D \ 0) \ \text{diag}\{D^{-1}, 0\}V,$$

or, equivalently,

$$U D(\Lambda \ 0) \ \text{diag}\{D^{-1}, 0\}V,$$

where D is any diagonal $(m \times m)$-matrix of the form

$$\text{diag}\{\pm 1, \pm 1, \ldots, \pm 1\}$$

with an even number of minus signs.

Accordingly, UD is a left-rotation and can be dismissed when we are only interested in the shape, so that in that case we are left with

$$(\Lambda D^{-1} \ 0)V.$$

These transformations will be useful later.

1.4 'ELEMENTARY' SHAPE SPACES Σ_1^k AND Σ_2^k

We have already claimed that

$$\Sigma_1^k = \mathbf{S}^{k-2}(1),$$

and that

$$\Sigma_2^k = \mathbf{CP}^{k-2}(4),$$

and in this section we provide the evidence for these assertions. We begin with Σ_1^k.

When $k = 2$ we start with a non-degenerate point-pair (x_1^*, x_2^*), and we carry out our standard reduction using Q_2 to yield the singleton

$$\tilde{x}_1 = \tfrac{1}{2}(x_2^* - x_1^*).$$

Because, with our conventions, x_1^* and x_2^* must be distinct when $k = 2$, it is clear that we can divide out the size $|x_2^* - x_1^*|/\sqrt{2}$ to get $+1$ when $x_2^* > x_1^*$, and -1 when $x_2^* < x_1^*$. Accordingly, we find that $\Sigma_1^2 = \{-1, 1\}$, and this is $\mathbf{S}^0(1)$ as already noted. Of course, quotienting on the left by $\mathbf{SO}(1)$ is here irrelevant because $\mathbf{SO}(1)$ is the trivial group.

Next, suppose that $k = 3$. We then find, using Q_3, that

$$\tilde{x}_1 = \tfrac{1}{\sqrt{2}}(x_2^* - x_1^*) \quad \text{and} \quad \tilde{x}_2 = \tfrac{1}{\sqrt{6}}\{2x_3^* - (x_1^* + x_2^*)\},$$

and after dividing by the size s, where

$$s = \sqrt{\tilde{x}_1^2 + \tilde{x}_2^2},$$

the components $x_1 = \tilde{x}_1/s$ and $x_2 = \tilde{x}_2/s$ of the shape will satisfy the equation

$$x_1^2 + x_2^2 = 1,$$

so that

$$\Sigma_1^3 = \mathbf{S}^1(1).$$

This argument extends to general k, and it tells us that $\Sigma_1^k = \mathbf{S}^{k-2}(1)$, confirming our claim for these spaces.

We turn next to the identification of the shape spaces Σ_2^k. Here, we consider a not totally coincident k-ad of points

$$x_1^*, x_2^*, \ldots, x_k^*$$

in two dimensions. Assuming that these are the coordinates after we have moved the centroid to the origin and normalised the size, we construct the pre-shape in the form

$$x_j = \frac{1}{\sqrt{j + j^2}}\{jx_{j+1}^* - (x_1^* + x_2^* + \cdots + x_j^*)\}, \qquad j = 1, 2, \ldots, k - 1,$$

following the specification of Q_k. For $m = 2$ it is, of course, natural to think of each x_j as a complex number, z_j, so we can think of the $2 \times (k-1)$ matrix X as identified with the ordered set of complex numbers $z = (z_1, z_2, \ldots, z_{k-1})$. To get the shape from this pre-shape we still have to quotient out the action of $\mathbf{SO}(2)$ acting on the left, which is just scalar multiplication of $z = (z_1, z_2, \ldots, z_{k-1})$ by the group $\{e^{i\alpha} : \alpha \in [0, 2\pi)\}$ of complex numbers of unit modulus. The resulting quotient space is known as the complex projective space $\mathbf{CP}^{k-2}(4)$, where the '4' is the value of the complex curvature constant that is determined by our unit-size convention.

Since we have excluded the totally coincident k-ad, not all the z_j will be zero. Then, if $z_j \neq 0$ for some particular j, the ordered set of complex numbers

$$(z_1/z_j, z_2/z_j, \ldots, z_{j-1}/z_j, 1, z_{j+1}/z_j, \ldots, z_{k-1}/z_j)$$

is invariant under the above action of $\mathbf{SO}(2)$. Ignoring the redundant entry '1', this provides us with a local coordinate system, which we shall employ from time to time, on all the shape space except for the points where $z_j = 0$. These excluded points, in fact, form a subspace isometric with $\mathbf{CP}^{k-3}(4)$. We have thus confirmed the identification of Σ_2^k in the column for $m = 2$ in Table 1.1. Note, in particular, that $\Sigma_2^2 = \mathbf{CP}^0(4)$, this being a one-point space.

A particular identification already referred to is

$$\Sigma_2^3 = \mathbf{CP}^1(4) = \mathbf{S}^2(\tfrac{1}{2}).$$

Now the metric identification of $\mathbf{CP}^1(4)$ with $\mathbf{S}^2(\tfrac{1}{2})$ is a classical theorem, but for the sake of completeness we will set out the details below. We shall make frequent use of this both as it stands and also in a flat, but not isometric, version obtained by stereographic projection from a point of the sphere $\mathbf{S}^2(\tfrac{1}{2})$ onto the tangent plane at the antipodal or some other point.

Before entering into a more detailed study of Σ_2^k, it will be helpful to note a few common features of the general shape spaces Σ_m^k. For every k and m, Σ_m^k is $\mathcal{S}_m^k$ modulo $\mathbf{SO}(m)$, where $\mathcal{S}_m^k$ denotes the *pre-shape* unit sphere $\mathbf{S}^{m(k-1)-1}(1)$ and the rotations T in $\mathbf{SO}(m)$ act from the left on the matrices X that are the points of $\mathcal{S}_m^k$. We write

$$\pi : \mathcal{S}_m^k \longrightarrow \Sigma_m^k; \quad X \mapsto \pi(X)$$

for the quotient mapping. Although, in some papers, the shape is denoted by $[X]$ rather than $\pi(X)$, we shall use the latter notation throughout this book. It is natural to choose the customary metric topology on $\mathcal{S}_m^k$ and the corresponding quotient topology on Σ_m^k for which the open sets are the images of the $\mathbf{SO}(m)$-saturated open sets in $\mathcal{S}_m^k$. Then, the mapping π is continuous. It follows that, with this topology, shape space Σ_m^k is *compact* and that it is *connected* whenever $\mathcal{S}_m^k$ is connected, that is, whenever (k, m) is not $(2, 1)$.

Equivalently, we can say that the open sets in Σ_m^k are those determined by the quotient metric ρ defined by the fundamental formula

$$\rho(\pi(X), \pi(Y)) = \min_{T \in \mathbf{SO}(m)} d(X, TY), \tag{1.1}$$

in which each of X and Y is a pre-shape and, when $m \geqslant 2$,

$$d(X, Y) = 2 \arcsin \left(\tfrac{1}{2} \| X - Y \| \right),$$

which is equal to

$$\arccos \operatorname{tr}(YX^t) \tag{1.2}$$

and so is, in fact, *the great-circle metric on the unit sphere* $\mathcal{S}_m^k$. This d-metric on $\mathcal{S}_m^k$ is topologically equivalent to the norm-metric or 'chordal metric' inherited from $\mathbb{R}^{m(k-1)}$.

When (1.1) and (1.2) are combined we see that for $m \geqslant 2$ *the distance ρ between two shapes $\pi(X)$ and $\pi(Y)$ is given by*

$$\rho(\pi(X), \pi(Y)) = \min_{T \in \mathbf{SO}(m)} \arccos \operatorname{tr}(TYX^t), \tag{1.3}$$

where we always have $0 \leqslant \rho \leqslant \pi$. *This important result underlies the whole discussion of the metric geometry of shape spaces for all values of $m \geqslant 2$.*

We now return to the special, but particularly interesting, case Σ_2^3 and, as before, we take x_1^*, x_2^* and x_3^* to be the labelled vertices of a not totally degenerate triangle in $\mathbb{R}^2$. We then have a number of different ways to represent the shapes of such triangles. If for the moment we leave on one side the special case when x_1^* and x_2^* coincide, then the triangle (x_1^*, x_2^*, x_3^*) with O as the mid-point of $x_1^* x_2^*$ can be arranged to have the vector $O x_2^*$ horizontal and of unit length without altering the shape situation. In this way, all except the excluded shape are represented uniquely by the resulting position of x_3^* in the plane.

Alternatively, we may reduce the specification to $(\tilde{x}_1, \tilde{x}_2) \in \mathbb{R}^2 \times \mathbb{R}^2$ or $(z_1, z_2) \in \mathbb{C}^2$ in the manner already explained. Then, as explained above, because of the freedom to rotate and rescale the data we can specify the shape either by

   (i) $(1, \zeta)$ where $\zeta = z_2 / z_1$ and $z_1 \neq 0$,

or by

   (ii) $(\zeta, 1)$ where $\zeta = z_1 / z_2$ and $z_2 \neq 0$.

It may be checked that the coordinate ζ in (i) is $x_3^* / \sqrt{3}$ when x_3^* is obtained as in the previous paragraph. Alternatively, if we normalise $O x_2^*$ to have length $1/\sqrt{3}$ in the previous paragraph, then the resulting x_3^* will have coordinate precisely ζ.

When a more symmetrical parameterisation of the shapes in Σ_2^3 is required, then it is convenient to use

$$\frac{(z_1, z_2)}{\sqrt{|z_1|^2 + |z_2|^2}}$$

for the pre-shape, and similarly for points in Σ_2^k with general k.

When $k = 3$ and $z_1 \neq 0$ another useful coding of the shape is

$$\frac{1}{\sqrt{1 + r^2}} \begin{pmatrix} 1 & r \cos\theta \\ 0 & r \sin\theta \end{pmatrix} = \frac{(1, \zeta)}{\sqrt{1 + |\zeta|^2}},$$

where $r = |z_2/z_1|$. That version is often convenient for calculation and it leads to informative pictorial representations. When $z_1 = 0$, that is, when x_1^* coincides with x_2^*, we can find out what happens by letting r tend to infinity. There the coded shape reduces to

$$\begin{pmatrix} 0 & \cos\theta \\ 0 & \sin\theta \end{pmatrix},$$

or, equivalently,

$$(0, \ e^{i\theta}),$$

and this, modulo $\mathbf{SO}(2)$ acting on the left, is the shape point $(0, 1)$ in complex coordinates, which is the only shape excluded from the coordinate representation (i) above.

Whichever of the above representations of the shapes is chosen, however, we must not lose sight of the fact that *the shape really is the ratio z_2/z_1*, and similar remarks apply when working with shape spaces Σ_2^k for general k.

Now suppose that we are interested in *two* shapes, these being identified, say, as

$$\zeta_1 = r_1 e^{i\theta_1}$$

and

$$\zeta_2 = r_2 e^{i\theta_2},$$

where r_1 and r_2 are real, non-negative and finite. To find the shape-theoretic distance $\rho(\zeta_1, \zeta_2)$ between these two shapes we calculate the trace of the triple matrix-product

$$\begin{pmatrix} \cos\alpha & \sin\alpha \\ -\sin\alpha & \cos\alpha \end{pmatrix} \begin{pmatrix} 1 & r_1\cos\theta_1 \\ 0 & r_1\sin\theta_1 \end{pmatrix} \begin{pmatrix} 1 & 0 \\ r_2\cos\theta_2 & r_2\sin\theta_2 \end{pmatrix}$$

divided by $\sqrt{(1 + r_1^2)(1 + r_2^2)}$, which reduces to

$$\frac{\{1 + r_1 r_2 \cos(\theta_1 - \theta_2)\}\cos\alpha + r_1 r_2 \sin(\theta_1 - \theta_2)\sin\alpha}{\sqrt{(1 + r_1^2)(1 + r_2^2)}}.$$

We now need the maximum value of this ratio for $0 \leqslant \alpha < 2\pi$: namely,

$$\sqrt{\frac{1 + r_1^2 r_2^2 + 2r_1 r_2 \cos(\theta_2 - \theta_1)}{(1 + r_1^2)(1 + r_2^2)}}.$$

The value of the inter-shape distance $\rho(\zeta_1, \zeta_2)$ is then the arc-cosine of the above expression.

This formula for the shape-distance, which is necessarily always finite, simplifies if we introduce super-abundant shape variables $(\tilde{a}, \tilde{b}, \tilde{c})$ that are related to the variables (r, θ) by the formulae

$$\tilde{a} = \frac{r \cos \theta}{1 + r^2},$$

$$\tilde{b} = \frac{r \sin \theta}{1 + r^2},$$

$$\tilde{c} = \frac{r^2 - 1}{2(1 + r^2)},$$

for then it will be seen that the new shape coordinates $(\tilde{a}, \tilde{b}, \tilde{c})$ satisfy the equation

$$\tilde{a}^2 + \tilde{b}^2 + \tilde{c}^2 = \tfrac{1}{4}.$$

Thus, $(\tilde{a}, \tilde{b}, \tilde{c})$ *is a point on the sphere* $\mathbf{S}^2(\tfrac{1}{2})$. Moreover, this one-to-one corre-spondence between the points of that sphere and the shapes in Σ_2^3 is an *isometric correspondence*, since

$$2 \cos^2 \rho(\zeta_1, \zeta_2) - 1 = \cos 2\rho(\zeta_1, \zeta_2) = 4 \langle (\tilde{a}_1, \tilde{b}_1, \tilde{c}_2), (\tilde{a}_2, \tilde{b}_2, \tilde{c}_2) \rangle.$$

Accordingly, we see that *the shape space* Σ_2^3 *is indeed the sphere* $\mathbf{S}^2(\tfrac{1}{2})$, with the point $(0, 0, \tfrac{1}{2})$ replacing the compactification point at infinity. This takes care of the otherwise excluded point $(0, 0, \tfrac{1}{2})$ on the sphere.

To visualise how the various triangular shapes lie upon this sphere we note first that $\mathbf{SO}(3)$ acts naturally on it as a group of isometries. In particular, there is the group of six isometries induced by the permutations of the labels for the vertices of the original triangles. The result of this is that $\mathbf{S}^2(\tfrac{1}{2})$ is split into six equivalent lunes with their common 'upper' and 'lower' vertices corresponding to the two possible shapes of equilateral triangles. Then, for each unlabelled triangle, the six shapes obtained by labelling the vertices will occur at corresponding points in the six lunes. Thus, if we are only interested in the shapes of unlabelled triangles, these may be specified in just one of these lunes. In addition, the mapping of each triangle to its reflection induces an isometry ι_2 of the shape space, which, in the above representation, corresponds to mapping the 'upper' half of each lune onto its 'lower' half. As a result, up to labelling and reflection, all possible shapes may be represented in such a half-lune. If we now project this lune onto a right circular cylinder that touches $\mathbf{S}^2(\tfrac{1}{2})$ along a great circle and then open out that cylinder onto a plane, then we obtain, for a suitable choice of cylinder, the outline in Figure 1.1 on which a selection of shapes are indicated at their representative points on the projection. It is important to note that although this projection is not isometric it *is* measure-preserving and the metric distortions are reasonably controlled. In this diagram the shapes of degenerate triangles, that is, those in which the three vertices are collinear, lie along the base curve and the shape of the regular, equilateral triangles at the upper vertex is maximally remote from them. The shapes of isosceles triangles appear along the other two

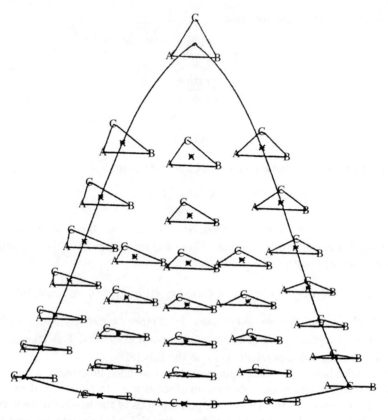

Figure 1.1 Reproduced with permission from D.G. Kendall, The statistics of shape, in V. Barnett (ed), *Interpreting Multivariate Date*. Copyright John Wiley & Sons Ltd

boundary arcs with those whose third angle is less than $\pi/3$ on the left-hand arc and the third angle progressively increasing to π as they move down the right-hand arc.

To compute the metric on the shape space sphere $\mathbf{S}^2(\frac{1}{2})$ in terms of the coordinate ζ in (i) above we look first at the way in which stereographic projection links the points on the shape sphere to the points in the compactified plane. We start by translating the above sphere of radius one-half upwards along the $\tilde{c}$-axis so that it sits on the plane spanned by $O\tilde{a}$ and $O\tilde{b}$ with the point of contact at the origin O and $O\tilde{c}$ passing through the centre of the sphere. We label the new coordinates a, b, c, so that the equation of the translated sphere is $a^2 + b^2 + c^2 = c$. The point N at the top of the sphere with coordinate $(0, 0, 1)$ corresponds to the shape of those triangles that have their first two vertices coincident, and the point of contact $(0, 0, 0)$ between the sphere and the plane corresponds to the shape of those triangles whose third vertex lies midway between the first two. If $(x, y, 0)$ is an arbitrary point of the supporting plane and if (a, b, c), where $c \neq 1$, is the other point of the sphere collinear with $(0, 0, 1)$ and $(x, y, 0)$, then we shall have

$$x = \frac{a}{1 - c} \quad \text{and} \quad y = \frac{b}{1 - c}.$$

These formulae will reflect the fact that $(x, y, 0)$ in the plane and (a, b, c) on the sphere are images of one another under an inversion with pole at $N = (0, 0, 1)$ and radius of inversion equal to unity. Since

$$\frac{a}{1 - c} = r \cos \theta \quad \text{and} \quad \frac{b}{1 - c} = r \sin \theta,$$

we see the shape coordinate ζ in (i) above is just $x + iy$. These arguments also show that in this planar representation the shapes of degenerate triangles correspond to the points with $y = 0$ and the points $\zeta = \pm i$ are the shapes of the cyclically and the anticyclically labelled equilateral triangles.

Now let $P = (a_1, b_1, c_1)$ and $Q = (a_2, b_2, c_2)$ be two points on the sphere and let $p = (x_1, y_1, 0)$ and $q = (x_2, y_2, 0)$ be their projections in the plane, so that N, P, p are collinear and N, Q, q are also collinear. From the geometry of the inversion process we shall have

$$|NP| \cdot |Np| = |NQ| \cdot |Nq| = 1,$$

so that

$$\frac{|NP|}{|NQ|} = \frac{|Nq|}{|Np|},$$

and thus NPQ and Nqp are similar triangles.

It follows from this that

$$\frac{|PQ|}{|pq|} = \frac{|NP|}{|Nq|} = \frac{|NP| \cdot |Np|}{|Nq| \cdot |Np|} = \frac{1}{|Np| \cdot |Nq|}$$

and

$$|PQ| = \frac{|pq|}{|Np| \cdot |Nq|},$$

so that the chordal distance from P to Q is equal to

$$\frac{|\zeta_2 - \zeta_1|}{\sqrt{(1 + |\zeta_1|^2)(1 + |\zeta_2|^2)}}$$

and the corresponding arc-distance on the sphere is then the arc-sine of this last expression.

1.5   THE FUBINI–STUDY METRIC ON Σ_2^k

As Σ_2^2 is a one-point space and, as Σ_2^3 has already been considered, we shall here be concerned with the spaces Σ_2^k for $k \geqslant 4$. As before, we write $z =$

$(z_1, \ldots, z_{k-1}) \in \mathbb{C}^{k-1}$ and w similarly for the result of our standard normalisation under translation of two k-ads in $\mathbb{R}^2$. We begin by noting two relevant symmetries. The first of these is $\mathbf{O}(2)/\mathbf{SO}(2)$ acting on the left. There is just one non-trivial element here and we can take it to be the conjugation that sends z to $\bar{z} = (\bar{z}_1, \ldots, \bar{z}_{k-1})$. In matrix terms this is the operator that switches all the algebraic signs in the second row of the $2 \times (k-1)$ matrix. The other symmetry is $\mathbf{U}(k-1)/\mathbf{U}(1)$ acting on the right. This includes the operators that permute the columns of the matrix. These symmetries preserve the pre-shape sphere and commute with the left action of $\mathbf{SO}(2)$ and hence induce isometries of the shape space. This means, in particular, that the shape space is homogeneous and so, for any given shape, we can always find an isometry that takes that shape into any standard shape that simplifies our calculations.

We now show that Σ_2^k is isometric with the complex projective space $\mathbf{CP}^{k-2}(4)$. We do this by calculating the Riemannian metric and taking into account the global implications of the symmetries noted above.

As a start we consider $\cos \rho(\pi(z), \pi(w))$. This is equal to

$$\max_{\alpha \in [0, 2\pi)} \; \mathrm{tr} \left\{ \frac{e^{i\alpha}(z_1, \ldots, z_{k-1})(w_1, \ldots, w_{k-1})^t}{\sqrt{\sum_{j=1}^{k-1} |z_j|^2 \sum_{j=1}^{k-1} |w_j|^2}} \right\}.$$

In more detail this is

$$\max_{\alpha \in [0, 2\pi)} \; \mathrm{tr} \left\{ \begin{pmatrix} \cos \alpha & \sin \alpha \\ -\sin \alpha & \cos \alpha \end{pmatrix} \begin{pmatrix} x_1 & x_2 & \cdots & x_{k-1} \\ y_1 & y_2 & \cdots & y_{k-1} \end{pmatrix} \begin{pmatrix} u_1 & u_2 & \cdots & u_{k-1} \\ v_1 & v_2 & \cdots & v_{k-1} \end{pmatrix}^t \right\}$$

divided by

$$\left\{ \sum_{j=1}^{k-1} |z_j|^2 \sum_{j=1}^{k-1} |w_j|^2 \right\}^{1/2},$$

where we have written $x_j + iy_j$ for z_j and $u_j + iv_j$ for w_j. This reduces to

$$\max_{\alpha \in [0, 2\pi)} \; \mathrm{tr} \begin{pmatrix} \cos \alpha \sum_{j=1}^{k-1} x_j u_j + \sin \alpha \sum_{j=1}^{k-1} y_j u_j & \cos \alpha \sum_{j=1}^{k-1} x_j v_j + \sin \alpha \sum_{j=1}^{k-1} y_j v_j \\ -\sin \alpha \sum_{j=1}^{k-1} x_j u_j + \cos \alpha \sum_{j=1}^{k-1} y_j u_j & -\sin \alpha \sum_{j=1}^{k-1} x_j v_j + \cos \alpha \sum_{j=1}^{k-1} y_j v_j \end{pmatrix}$$

$$= \max_{\alpha \in [0, 2\pi)} \left\{ \cos \alpha \sum_{j=1}^{k-1} (x_j u_j + y_j v_j) + \sin \alpha \sum_{j=1}^{k-1} (y_j u_j - x_j v_j) \right\} \qquad (1.4)$$

divided by

$$\left\{ \sum_{j=1}^{k-1} |z_j|^2 \sum_{j=1}^{k-1} |w_j|^2 \right\}^{1/2}.$$

We now carry out the maximisation for (1.4) and so obtain

$$\left\{ \left(\sum_{j=1}^{k-1} (x_j u_j + y_j v_j) \right)^2 + \left(\sum_{j=1}^{k-1} (y_j u_j - x_j v_j) \right)^2 \right\}^{1/2},$$

and accordingly we have

$$\cos \rho(\pi(z), \pi(w)) = \frac{\left| \sum_{j=1}^{k-1} z_j \overline{w}_j \right|}{\sqrt{\sum_{j=1}^{k-1} |z_j|^2 \sum_{j=1}^{k-1} |w_j|^2}}.$$

This gives us the distance ρ in Σ_2^k between the shapes $\pi(z)$ and $\pi(w)$.

It is now a simple matter to calculate the Riemannian metric for Σ_2^k. First, we write $w_j = z_j + \varepsilon_j$. Then, in an obvious notation, we find that up to quadratic terms in the ε_j the value of $\sin^2 \rho(\pi(z), \pi(w))$ is

$$\frac{\sum_{j=1}^{k-1} |z_j|^2 \sum_{j=1}^{k-1} |\varepsilon_j|^2 - \left| \sum_{j=1}^{k-1} \overline{z}_j \varepsilon_j \right|^2}{\left(\sum_{j=1}^{k-1} |z_j|^2 \right)^2}.$$

Using the fact that, for small ρ, $\sin \rho \simeq \rho$, this gives

$$d\rho^2 = \frac{\sum_{j=1}^{k-1} |z_j|^2 \sum_{j=1}^{k-1} |dz_j|^2 - \left| \sum_{j=1}^{k-1} \overline{z}_j dz_j \right|^2}{\left(\sum_{j=1}^{k-1} |z_j|^2 \right)^2}.$$

Then, using the isometries that permute the coordinates z_j, we may assume $z_1 \neq 0$. Then, a standard calculation transforms this expression in terms of the z-coordinates into the following in terms of the shape space coordinates $\zeta_j = z_{j+1}/z_1$, $j = 1, \ldots, k-2$:

$$d\rho^2 = \frac{\left\{ 1 + \sum_{j=1}^{k-2} |\zeta_j|^2 \right\} \sum_{j=1}^{k-2} |d\zeta_j|^2 - \left| \sum_{j=1}^{k-2} \overline{\zeta}_j d\zeta_j \right|^2}{\left\{ 1 + \sum_{j=1}^{k-2} |\zeta_j|^2 \right\}^2}.$$

This is exactly the classical Fubini–Study metric for the complex projective space $\mathbf{CP}^{k-2}(4)$ and so Σ_2^k can be identified with that classical space for all values of k.

The value '4' for the curvature constant is not surprising when we recall that Σ_2^3, which we know to be $\mathbf{S}^2(\frac{1}{2})$, is a sphere of curvature 4.

1.6   THE PROOF OF CASSON'S THEOREM

We now present an expanded version of Casson's proof of the 'spherical' character of the shape spaces Σ_m^{m+1}.

Theorem 1.1. *Shape space Σ_m^{m+1} is homeomorphic with a sphere of dimension d_m^{m+1}.*

Proof.   Let $\mathcal{X}$ denote the space of all non-zero $m \times m$ real matrices A, $\mathcal{X}_+$ the non-linear subspace consisting of those for which $\det(A)$ is non-negative, $\mathcal{X}_-$ the subspace of those for which $\det(A)$ is non-positive and $\mathcal{X}_0$ the subspace of those for which $\det(A)$ is zero. Let us also write $\mathcal{Y}$ for the $m(m+1)/2$-dimensional linear subspace of $\mathbb{R}^{m^2}$ corresponding to symmetric matrices, $\mathcal{Y}_+$ for its non-linear subspace of non-zero positive semi-definite symmetric matrices and $\mathcal{Y}_0$ for the subspace of singular matrices in $\mathcal{Y}_+$. We also recall that the dimension d_m^{m+1} of Σ_m^{m+1} is $(m-1)(m+2)/2$, which is one less than the dimension of $\mathcal{Y}$. In all cases we give our spaces the topology they inherit as subsets of $\mathbb{R}^{m^2}$ with the standard Euclidean metric. For any $m \times m$ matrix A, the matrix $A^t A$ is symmetric and positive semi-definite and so has a unique square root, $f(A)$, in $\mathcal{Y}_+$, which varies continuously with A, so that we obtain a continuous map

$$f : \mathcal{X} \longrightarrow \mathcal{Y}_+.$$

Since, for any $T \in \mathbf{O}(m)$, $(TA)^t TA = A^t A$, this map sends all the points of each $\mathbf{O}(m)$-orbit in $\mathcal{X}$ to the same point of $\mathcal{Y}_+$. Conversely, since for $A \in \mathcal{X}$ there exists $T \in \mathbf{O}(m)$ such that TA is positive semi-definite and then $TA = f(TA) = f(A)$, two matrices with the same image under f must lie in the same $\mathbf{O}(m)$-orbit in $\mathcal{X}$. However, we are interested in the $\mathbf{SO}(m)$-orbits and, if A is non-singular, then its $\mathbf{O}(m)$-orbit splits into two $\mathbf{SO}(m)$-orbits, one in $\mathcal{X}_+$ and one in $\mathcal{X}_-$. Whereas, if A is singular, then $A = TA$ where T is the reflection in any hyperplane containing the column space of A, and it follows that the orbits of A under left multiplication by $\mathbf{O}(m)$ and $\mathbf{SO}(m)$ coincide. Each of the maps $f_\pm = f|\mathcal{X}_\pm$ is clearly surjective since $f_+(A) = A$ and $f_-(TA) = A$ for any $A \in \mathcal{Y}_+$ and any $T \in \mathbf{O}(m) \setminus \mathbf{SO}(m)$. Hence, they induce bijections

$$\overline{f}_\pm : \mathcal{X}_\pm / \mathbf{SO}(m) \longrightarrow \mathcal{Y}_+$$

between the spaces of $\mathbf{SO}(m)$ orbits in $\mathcal{X}_\pm$ and the points of $\mathcal{Y}_+$. Moreover, with respect to the quotient topology on $\mathcal{X}_\pm / \mathbf{SO}(m)$, the induced maps $\overline{f}_\pm$ are continuous.

It remains to quotient by the action of the group of dilations, that is, the multiplicative group of positive reals acting by scalar multiplication. This commutes with the action of $\mathbf{SO}(m)$ and also with the map f, and hence it commutes with the induced maps $f_\pm$ and $\overline{f}_\pm$. Thus, we have further induced maps between the corresponding quotient spaces, which maps are again continuous and clearly bijective:

$$\tilde{f}_\pm : \mathcal{X}_\pm/\text{similarities} \longrightarrow \mathcal{Y}_+/\text{dilations}.$$

We note that these maps agree on the common subspace $\mathcal{X}_0/\text{similarities}$, mapping it onto $\mathcal{Y}_0/\text{dilations}$.

We shall show below that there is a continuous bijective mapping from $\mathcal{Y}_+/\text{dilations}$ onto the upper or 'northern' hemisphere $\mathcal{H}_+$ of the standard d_m^{m+1}-dimensional unit sphere $\mathbf{S}^{d_m^{m+1}}$ taking $\mathcal{Y}_0/\text{dilations}$ onto the 'equatorial' ($d_m^{m+1} - 1$)-sphere. Composing this map with $\tilde{f}_+$ and $\tilde{f}_-$, respectively, and, in the latter case, further composing with the 'vertical' projection of the upper hemisphere $\mathcal{H}_+$ onto the lower hemisphere $\mathcal{H}_-$, we obtain continuous bijective maps

$$g_\pm : \mathcal{X}_\pm/\text{similarities} \longrightarrow \mathcal{H}_\pm,$$

which agree on the common subspace $\mathcal{X}_0/\text{similarities}$, mapping it onto the equator $\mathcal{H}_0$. Taken together these maps give us a continuous bijection:

$$g : \mathcal{X}/\text{similarities} \longrightarrow \mathbf{S}^{d_m^{m+1}}.$$

However, $\mathcal{X}/\text{similarities}$, being the continuous image of the compact pre-shape sphere $\mathcal{X}/\text{dilations}$, is itself compact and the sphere $\mathbf{S}^{d_m^{m+1}}$ is Hausdorff so the continuous bijection g is, in fact, a homeomorphism.

To complete the proof of Casson's theorem it remains to construct the continuous bijection of $\mathcal{Y}_+/\text{dilations}$ onto the d_m^{m+1}-dimensional hemisphere $\mathcal{H}_+$, taking $\mathcal{Y}_0/\text{dilations}$ onto the equator $\mathcal{H}_0$. Now $\mathcal{Y}_+$ is a convex subset of the linear subspace $\mathcal{Y}$ of $\mathbb{R}^{m^2}$ and it contains an open neighbourhood in $\mathcal{Y}$ of the identity matrix I. For any positive definite matrix A let e_i be an eigenvector of norm one with eigenvalue λ_i. Then

$$e_i^t\{(1-\lambda)I + \lambda A\}e_i = 1 - \lambda + \lambda\lambda_i,$$

which is positive if $\lambda(1 - \lambda_i) < 1$. Since A has an orthonormal basis of eigenvectors, it follows that, if $\mu = \mu(A)$ is its least eigenvalue, then, provided $\mu < 1$, the segment

$$\{(1 - \lambda)I + \lambda A : 0 \leqslant \lambda \leqslant 1/(1 - \mu)\},$$

which ends at the singular matrix

$$\frac{1}{1 - \mu}(A - \mu I),$$

is the complete intersection with $\mathcal{Y}_+$ of the ray from I through A.

If $\mu \geqslant 1$, then the entire semi-infinite ray from I through A lies in $\mathcal{Y}_+$. However, it is clear that for every non-singular matrix A in $\mathcal{Y}_+$ there is a real $\lambda > 0$ such that λA, in the same *dilation class* as A, has its least eigenvalue less than one and so lies on such a finite segment from I to a singular positive semi-definite matrix. Conversely, the segment from I to any singular matrix A in $\mathcal{Y}_0$ lies entirely in $\mathcal{Y}_+$, with only A itself lying in $\mathcal{Y}_0$. More precisely, let $\mathcal{N}$ be the $(d_m^{m+1} - 1)$-dimensional sphere in $\mathcal{Y}$ centred on $\frac{1}{2}I$, of radius ε and lying in the hyperplane through $\frac{1}{2}I$ perpendicular to $\frac{1}{2}I$. We may choose $\varepsilon > 0$ sufficiently small that for every $A \in \mathcal{N}$ all the eigenvalues of A lie between 0 and 1. Thus, A lies in $\mathcal{Y}_+$ and only a finite closed segment of the ray from I through A lies in $\mathcal{Y}_+$. Note that the length of these finite segments, being determined as above by the least eigenvalue, is a continuous function of the choice of A in $\mathcal{N}$. Moreover, every dilation class in $\mathcal{Y}_+$ is represented uniquely on such a segment from I through $\mathcal{N}$, since the points of any segment from I are dilation-equivalent to those of one through $\mathcal{N}$, except for that through O, the zero matrix. However, except for O itself, which we are excluding, these are all represented by the matrix I.

Thus, if we map the 'north pole' of $\mathcal{H}_+$ onto the matrix I and the 'longitudinal' arcs from the pole to $\mathcal{H}_0$ onto the segments of $\mathcal{Y}_+$ from I through $\mathcal{N}$, then we have a continuous bijective map of $\mathcal{H}_+$ onto $\mathcal{Y}_+/$dilations which, as $\mathcal{H}_+$ is compact and the cone on $\mathcal{N}$ representing $\mathcal{Y}_+/$dilations is Hausdorff, is in fact a homeomorphism. Its inverse is the map we require.   ∎

CHAPTER 2

The Global Structure of Shape Spaces

In the next sequence of chapters, Chapters 2–5, we turn to the global description of shape spaces so far as we are able to achieve it. We shall mainly consider the shape spaces introduced in Chapter 1, which are at once those for which most is known as well as those that are involved in the most applications. However, in discussing them, the spaces that arise from identifying a shape with its reflection are also involved. In fact, these latter spaces are simple quotients of the former ones and, particularly when computing homology groups, we shall find it convenient to work with both types of shape space at the same time.

2.1   THE PROBLEM

Recall that shape space Σ_m^k is the quotient of the unit pre-shape sphere $\mathcal{S}_m^k$ in $\mathbb{R}^{m(k-1)}$ by the appropriate left action of $\mathbf{SO}(m)$. The sphere $\mathcal{S}_m^k$ has a standard metric in which the distance is measured along great circular arcs and, since $\mathbf{SO}(m)$ is compact and so are its orbits in $\mathcal{S}_m^k$, Σ_m^k has the natural induced Hopf metric, which we denote by ρ, for which the distance between two shapes is the minimum distance between any two corresponding pre-shapes. In Chapter 1 we showed that the spaces Σ_1^k were isometric with the unit spheres $\mathbf{S}^{k-2}(1)$ and the spaces Σ_2^k were isometric with the complex projective spaces $\mathbf{CP}^{k-2}(4)$, where '4' is the complex sectional curvature. These are the only shape spaces that we can identify with other metric spaces that have already been sufficiently well studied in their own right to be able to be regarded as 'familiar'.

Rather than metric equivalence we could ask only for *topological equivalence*, that is, identification via a homeomorphism, which is a continuous bijection with a continuous inverse. Then, we may add the 'diagonal' spaces Σ_m^{m+1} to our list of known spaces since, by Casson's theorem, these are all homeomorphic to spheres. Similarly, although they are of limited practical interest, we may also add the spaces that lie above the diagonal in Table 1.1, since these are all topological hemispheres.

However, that does not get us much further since most familiar spaces are manifolds, that is, they have a dimension n such that every point has a neighbourhood homeomorphic to an open subset of $\mathbb{R}^n$, whereas, as was mentioned in Chapter 1 and will be proved below, none of the shape spaces other than those explicitly mentioned above is homeomorphic to a manifold. Topologists have certainly studied many spaces that are not manifolds. However, these are spaces with very particular properties, constructed explicitly for special purposes, and, to the best of our knowledge, no one has ever studied any of the remaining unidentified shape spaces in any other context. Thus, we must somehow render them more familiar ourselves.

2.2 WHEN IS A SPACE FAMILIAR

There are perhaps two aspects of familiarity shared by the above identifications. First, we have identified shape space with a space having a much simpler description. This is certainly true of the spheres and hemispheres, but it is also true of the complex projective spaces if we think of them as the spaces of complex lines in the next higher dimension complex space. This is something we are very unlikely to be able to achieve for the remaining spaces. There are just not enough simply described spaces to hand. Indeed, there is a sense in which our spaces are already as simple as they could be and, having arisen in the natural way we have described, should be regarded as elementary spaces themselves. Each is the orbit space of a sphere under a very important, 'diagonal', subgroup of its isometries. However, another aspect of familiarity is the feeling of 'having been here before': the standard spaces arise so frequently and in so many different situations that we already have a good deal of information about their nature and behaviour. This *is* something we may achieve for shape spaces, except that, since they have not been studied before, we must build up our own databank of 'previous experiences'.

What then are the properties we should endeavour to elucidate here? As we shall be studying the fine local Riemannian structure of the spaces in Chapter 7, it will be helpful first to look at the coarser global topological structure, that is, to identify the spaces up to homeomorphism. In fact, we shall not strictly achieve that aim, but we shall work towards it from two complementary directions. First, we shall describe how the spaces are built up out of standard elementary building blocks, although this description will not be fully detailed in the sense of giving full instructions for anyone to follow in building a copy of the space. Instead, we find global topological invariants that will allow the builder to check whether he has assembled the pieces correctly. If the invariants are wrong, he knows that he has not assembled the space he intended. The converse, unfortunately, is not true. For example, the simplest global invariant is the dimension, and the correct set of building blocks, however assembled, will always have the correct dimension. To complete this classification program we would need to find sufficient such invariants and, to prove that we had done so, we would need to show that they could only all be correct if the entire construction were correct.

2.3 CW COMPLEXES

The building blocks we shall use will be topological cells and the building regulations we shall observe are those for CW complexes which are described below. The main global invariants we compute will be the homology groups; however, we shall first undertake a preliminary assembly of the cells into larger groups of cells that render these computations more transparent and, at the same time, give some additional insight into the structure of our spaces.

We should look first, then, at the structure and basic properties of CW complexes that were introduced by Whitehead precisely in order to describe efficiently, and deal effectively with, the topological properties of spaces such as ours that were not quite, but almost, as well behaved as manifolds.

By a closed cell of dimension d, or *closed d-cell*, we mean any homeomorphic image of the closed unit ball $\mathbf{B}^d$ in $\mathbb{R}^d$. Its interior, homeomorphic with the open unit ball, is called an *open d-cell*. Then, a CW complex is a space that may be constructed inductively by 'attaching closed cells' of increasing dimensions, so that it is the disjoint union of the corresponding open cells. The union of the cells of dimension less than, or equal to, n is called the *n-skeleton* of the complex and the idea is to prove results about CW complexes by induction over its skeleta. For this to work in general, certain additional conditions have to be observed that account for the adjective 'CW'. They are, however, automatically satisfied if the complex has only finitely many cells and, since that will be our case, we only need give the following simplified formal definition.

A given Hausdorff topological space $\mathcal{P}$ is a finite CW complex, or *finite cell complex*, if it may be expressed as the disjoint union of open cells $\{e_\omega : \omega \in \Omega\}$ in such a way that for each $\omega \in \Omega$ there is a continuous map $h_\omega : \mathbf{B}^{d_\omega} \to \mathcal{P}$, which restricts to a homeomorphism of the interior of $\mathbf{B}^{d_\omega}$ with e_ω and such that $h_\omega(\mathbf{S}^{d_\omega - 1})$ is contained in the union of the cells of lower dimension. More precisely, a cell complex is a particular choice of such data and provides a *cellular decomposition* of $\mathcal{P}$.

Cells may be further decomposed and re-combined so that a cell complex has uncountably many possible decompositions. Among those for shape spaces we shall choose ones that have the additional special property that each $h_\omega(\mathbf{S}^{d_\omega - 1})$ *is* the union of a set of cells of lower dimension. Moreover, for each cell $e_{\omega'}$ in $h_\omega(\mathbf{S}^{d_\omega - 1})$, its inverse image $h_\omega^{-1}(e_{\omega'})$ will be a finite disjoint union of, in fact, one or two $d_{\omega'}$-cells in $\mathbf{S}^{d_\omega - 1}$, each mapped homeomorphically into the shape space by h_ω. This decomposition is derived from the following decomposition of unit spheres, which we shall apply to the pre-shape spheres.

2.4 A CELLULAR DECOMPOSITION OF THE UNIT SPHERE

Turning our attention to $\mathbf{S}^d$ in $\mathbb{R}^{d+1}$, let e_i denote the unit vector in the positive direction along the ith coordinate axis. Then we take zero-cells, or vertices, at each of the points $\pm e_i$ in $\mathbf{S}^d$. Next, if ε_i take the values ± 1, then for each pair $(\varepsilon_i e_i, \varepsilon_j e_j)$ there is a unique 1-cell in $\mathbf{S}^d$ having these two zero-cells for its boundary: namely, the appropriate part of the unit circle in the (x_i, x_j)-plane. Thus, if $\varepsilon_i = -1, \varepsilon_j = +1$, this 1-cell, which we shall denote by the pair $(-e_i, +e_j)$ of vertices that determine it, is the part of that circle for which $x_i < 0 < x_j$. Similarly, for any set of vectors $(\varepsilon_{i_1} e_{i_1}, \ldots, \varepsilon_{i_{n+1}} e_{i_{n+1}})$, where each $\varepsilon_i = \pm 1$ and the i_j are all distinct, there is a unique n-cell on the sphere having precisely those $n + 1$ zero-cells on its boundary. It is easily checked that the closure of each of these n-cells is indeed the homeomorphic image of a closed ball by, for example, projecting onto the obvious coordinate space of dimension n, and that the other conditions for a cellular decomposition are satisfied.

For example, Figure 2.1 indicates the decomposition of the upper hemisphere of $\mathbf{S}^2$ in $\mathbb{R}^3$. It has five zero-cells, four in the (x_1, x_2)-plane and one, $+e_3$, above it. Four 1-cells lie in the plane of the diagram and four others lie above it. There are then four 2-cells that also lie above the plane. The lower hemisphere has one more vertex, $-e_3$, together with four more 1-cells and four 2-cells, none of which are indicated. All the cells of a given dimension are, in fact, isometric with each other.

We shall refer to the cells in the above decomposition of a sphere as *basic cells*. Note that the basic cell $(\varepsilon_{i_1} e_{i_1}, \ldots, \varepsilon_{i_{n+1}} e_{i_{n+1}})$ is determined as the set of points on the sphere for which $x_{i_j} > 0$ if $\varepsilon_{i_j} = +1$, $x_{i_j} < 0$ if $\varepsilon_{i_j} = -1$ and $x_{i_j} = 0$ otherwise. We shall require cells that are unions of these basic cells, and which, to distinguish them, we shall refer to as *elementary cells*. They are determined similarly but with some, usually most, of the non-zero coordinates unrestricted. Thus, if x_i is such a coordinate, then the corresponding elementary cell will have both vertices e_i and $-e_i$ on its boundary. We shall indicate this by letting

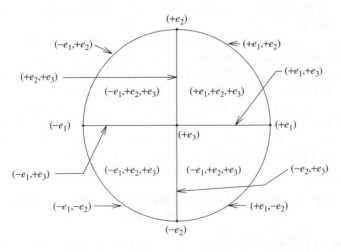

Figure 2.1   Cells of the upper hemisphere in $\mathbb{R}^3$

$\varepsilon_i = *$. Thus, the elementary 1-cell $(*e_1, +e_2)$ is the union of the basic cells $(+e_1, +e_2)$ and $(-e_1, +e_2)$, together with their common vertex $+e_2$, forming the upper open semi-circle in the (x_1, x_2)-plane. Similarly, $(-e_1, *e_2, +e_3)$ is the union of the basic cells $(-e_1, +e_2, +e_3)$ and $(-e_1, -e_2, +e_3)$, together with the common boundary 1-cell $(-e_1, +e_3)$. The elementary cell $(*e_1, *e_2, +e_3)$ is the entire open upper hemisphere comprising the vertex e_3, the four upper 1-cells and the four upper 2-cells. Thus, the symbols for the basic cells in an elementary cell are formed from the symbol for the elementary cell by allowing the '$*$'s independently to take the values $+1$ or -1 or the corresponding vertices to be omitted. Note that, if all the ε_i in the symbol $(\varepsilon_{i_1} e_{i_1}, \ldots, \varepsilon_{i_{n+1}} e_{i_{n+1}})$ are '$*$'s, then it represents the n-sphere in the relevant $(n+1)$-subspace. However, if at least one ε_i is ± 1, then it determines an elementary n-cell lying on that sphere.

2.5   THE CELLULAR DECOMPOSITION OF SHAPE SPACES

We now study the cellular decomposition of shape spaces that was already implicit in our discussion of the matrix representations of shapes in Chapter 1. We shall first use it directly to gain some insight into the global topological structure of shape spaces. Then, in the following chapters, Chapters 3–5, we shall obtain from it a chain complex with which to compute the homology and cohomology of the spaces.

We recall that, using the row operations that are achieved by left multiplication by suitable elements of $\mathbf{SO}(m)$, from any $m \times (k-1)$ pre-shape matrix X we can obtain a matrix $\mathrm{can}(X)$ that is in canonical form and has the same shape as X. Rather than the form that we discussed in Chapter 1, we shall now choose the canonical form that is 'reversed echelon': that is, the last non-zero entry in each row occurs before that in the preceding one, and for which, except possibly in the last row, the last non-zero entry in each row is strictly positive. It is easy to see that such a canonical choice always exists and is unique. We then define the *pattern* $\mathrm{patt}(X)$ of the pre-shape X to be the symbolic matrix, such as

$$\begin{pmatrix} * & * & * & * & * & + & 0 \\ * & * & * & + & 0 & 0 & 0 \\ * & + & 0 & 0 & 0 & 0 & 0 \\ \pm & 0 & 0 & 0 & 0 & 0 & 0 \end{pmatrix},$$

which is obtained from $\mathrm{can}(X)$ by replacing the final positive entry in each row except the last by '$+$' followed by the appropriate number of zeros, the final non-zero entry in the last row, if it exists, by '$\pm$' followed by zeros and all other entries by '$*$'. Note that this allows for the possibility that the final row or rows in a pattern matrix consist entirely of zeros. However, all preceding rows must still end in '$+$' rather than '$\pm$'. In other words, recalling that we are writing π for the quotient map of the pre-shape sphere onto shape space and $\pi(X)$ for the shape of X, what we have done is to select, from among the entire

$\mathbf{SO}(m)$-orbit $\pi^{-1}(\pi(X))$ of pre-shapes on the pre-shape sphere that have the same shape as X, the unique one can(X) that has our chosen canonical form and that then determines patt(X). Clearly, then, both can(X) and patt(X) are functions of the shape $\pi(X)$.

Conversely, any pre-shape Y in canonical form $Y = \text{can}(Y)$, which shares the same pattern as X, can be found from patt(X) by replacing '+' by a strictly positive number, replacing $\pm$ by a strictly positive or strictly negative number and replacing '∗' by a positive, negative or zero number with the additional requirement, in order for the resulting matrix to lie on the pre-shape sphere, that the sum of the squares of all these entries be equal to unity. The set of all such pre-shapes Y sharing a common pattern $J = \text{patt}(X)$ forms one or, if the pattern has a final '$\pm$' entry, two of the elementary spherical cells σ_J on the pre-shape sphere that we described above. Note, however, that not all elementary cells correspond to patterns. For the moment, the ambiguity as to whether σ_J denotes one or two cells will not matter. However, we shall have to be more precise when we wish to compute the homology groups.

Since each shape has a unique canonical pre-shape, each of these spherical cells is mapped injectively into shape space by the quotient map π, no two distinct cells having a common image point and the union of the images of all the cells being determined by the various patterns covering the entire shape space. On the other hand, since each point of an elementary cell corresponding to an allowable pattern represents an entire $\mathbf{SO}(m)$-orbit, such a cell σ_J must have a codimension in the pre-shape sphere at least equal to the dimension of $\mathbf{SO}(m)$, so that we are making a very restricted selection from the full set of elementary cells available on the pre-shape sphere.

Since $\mathbf{SO}(m)$ acts as a group of homeomorphisms on the pre-shape sphere, π is an open mapping and so the bijection, which is the restriction of π to each relevant elementary cell σ_J, is, in fact, a homeomorphism. We refer to the images $c_J = \pi(\sigma_J)$ as cells in shape space.

The dimension of the cell σ_J is one less than the number of non-zero entries in the pattern J, which differs, of course, from the number at certain of its points. If we examine the cells in the boundary of σ_J in the pre-shape sphere, we find that they are either cells $\sigma_{J'}$ corresponding to other patterns J' with $\dim(\sigma_{J'}) = \dim(\sigma_J) - 1$; or they are cells that correspond in a similar manner to $\overline{J'}$, which is a pattern J' with one of its '+' entries replaced by a '−'; or they correspond to a symbolic matrix L that fails to be a pattern because two of its rows are of equal length. The first of these types obviously maps to a lower dimensional cell or cells in shape space. We can deal with the second type by pre-multiplying by the diagonal matrix in $\mathbf{SO}(m)$, all of whose diagonal entries are $+1$ except for the ith and the last, which are -1, where the '−' in $\overline{J'}$ is in the ith row. This simultaneously reduces all the pre-shapes in that cell to the canonical forms that belong to $\sigma_{J'}$, so that $\pi(\sigma_{\overline{J'}}) = c_{J'}$ is again a lower dimensional cell in shape space. Similarly, if we reduce the pre-shapes that correspond to L to canonical form, then we find that their images comprise a union of cells of lower dimension.

Note that, when determining the cells in the boundary of σ_J and replacing an entry '+', or '±', in the pattern by '0' to reveal a final '∗', although what we get is an elementary cell on the pre-shape sphere, it is not one that corresponds to a pattern. It is the union of two such cells, corresponding to the patterns in which the new '∗' is replaced by '+' and '−', respectively, together with others that are obtained by replacing the new '∗' by '0' and repeating the procedure and, if necessary, reducing to canonical form again. Nevertheless, it is clear that, at the end of the day, we shall have expressed the boundary of $c_J = \pi(\sigma_J)$ as a union of cells of lower dimension.

Finally, we note that, since shape space has a metric compatible with its topology, it is certainly Hausdorff, and so we have established all the requirements to express shape space as a finite cell complex.

2.6 INCLUSIONS AND ISOMETRIES

This cellular decomposition of shape spaces already reveals or confirms some of their important properties. We note, in particular, that, if we map $\mathcal{S}_m^k$ into $\mathcal{S}_m^{k+1}$ by appending a column of zeros on the right-hand side, this commutes with the left action of $\mathbf{SO}(m)$ and so induces a map of Σ_m^k into Σ_m^{k+1} with each cell of the former mapping bijectively onto a similarly named cell of the latter. Thus, we may think of Σ_m^k as being embedded in Σ_m^{k+1}, and so forming a 'tower' of spaces as k varies in a manner analogous to that of the well-known special case of the projective spaces Σ_2^k.

On the other hand, the mapping of Σ_m^k to Σ_{m+1}^k, induced by appending a *row* of zeros at the bottom of each pre-shape matrix, behaves slightly differently. Each cell of Σ_m^k maps bijectively to a similarly named cell in Σ_{m+1}^k with all the image cells being distinct, except that the two cells in Σ_m^k determined by a pattern with final entry '±' in the final row both map to the single cell in Σ_{m+1}^k corresponding to the pattern in which that '±' is replaced by '+' before appending the row of zeros. This reflects the fact that on shape space Σ_m^k we have the isometric involution ι_m, which arises as follows. Let T be any element of $\mathbf{O}(m)\backslash\mathbf{SO}(m)$. Then, left multiplication by T is an isometry of the pre-shape sphere, which, since $\mathbf{SO}(m)$ is a normal subgroup of $\mathbf{O}(m)$, maps each $\mathbf{SO}(m)$-orbit onto another such orbit. That is, it induces an isometry of Σ_m^k onto itself. Moreover, this isometry is independent of the choice of T and is an involution. We shall denote it by ι_m. If we use the element $\mathrm{diag}\{1, \ldots, 1, -1\}$ to induce ι_m, since this leaves fixed all the cells determined by patterns with zero last row and interchanges the two cells determined by each of the remaining patterns, whose final entry is '±', we see that the image of Σ_m^k in Σ_{m+1}^k, under the mapping induced by appending a row of zeros at the bottom of each pre-shape matrix, is precisely Σ_m^k/ι_m. Its inverse image in $\mathcal{S}_{m+1}^k$ is the set of matrices of rank at most m. Similarly, the image of Σ_{m-n}^k in Σ_{m+1}^k, induced by appending $n+1$ rows of zeros, where $n > 0$, is isometric with the quotient $\Sigma^k_{m-n}/\iota_{m-n}$, which is the image of the set of matrices of rank at most $m - n$ in $\mathcal{S}^k_{m+1}$. As a special case, we note that the image of Σ^{m+1}_m in Σ^{m+1}_{m+1} is Σ^{m+1}_m/ι_m but, as there are no cells in the decomposition of Σ^{m+1}_{m+1} that are not images of those in Σ^{m+1}_m, this is the entire image. Thus, $\Sigma^{m+1}_{m+1} \cong \Sigma^{m+1}_m/\iota_m$.

These quotients are, of course, shape spaces in their own right. They are the spaces of shapes of configurations for which, in addition to translation, re-scaling and rotation, we identify each configuration with any of its reflections. In the case of Σ^k_1/ι_1 we can identify the quotient explicitly. Since the group $\mathbf{SO}(1)$ is trivial, Σ^k_1 is identical with its pre-shape sphere $\mathbf{S}^{k-2} = \{(x_1, \ldots, x_{k-1}) : \sum^{k-1}_{i=1} x_i^2 = 1\}$ and ι_1 changes the sign of all the coordinates simultaneously. In other words, ι_1 is the antipodal map of the sphere and the resulting quotient is well-known to be the real projective space $\mathbf{RP}^{k-2}$. At the other extreme, ι_m acting on Σ^{m+1}_m can be represented by an involution that changes the sign of only one coordinate. Although this evidence falls well short of a proof, it is certainly consistent with the quotient of the action of ι_m on the topological sphere Σ^{m+1}_m, that is, Σ^{m+1}_{m+1}, being a topological ball.

We shall be meeting the involution ι_m again. For example, in order to compute homology, we shall need to define orientations of the cells and just how ι_m affects those orientations will be important for the homology calculations.

There is another significant difference between the above two types of inclusion. As for the two-dimensional case described in Chapter 1, multiplication on the right of the pre-shape sphere by an element T of $\mathbf{O}(k-1)$ is an isometry that commutes with the left action of $\mathbf{SO}(m)$ and so induces a mapping T_* of Σ^k_m onto itself, which is, therefore, an isometry with respect to the induced metric ρ. Then, since T acts as column operations, or, equally, since it preserves rank, its induced action T_* on Σ^k_{m+1} must restrict to an isometry of each subspace $\Sigma^k_{m-n}/\iota_{m-n}$ onto itself. On the other hand, if $X = U(\Lambda \quad 0)V$ is a pseudo-singular values decomposition of $X \in \mathcal{S}^k_m$, where $k > m + 1$, and T is V^{-1} composed with the permutation that reverses the order of the first m columns, then $T_*(\pi(X))$ lies in Σ^{m+1}_m and further isometries, induced by swapping the mth column for the $(n-1)$st, will take it into Σ^n_m for any n such that $m + 1 \leqslant n \leqslant k$. Thus, the subspaces Σ^n_m in Σ^k_m are not geometrically determined in the way that the subspaces $\Sigma^k_{m-n}/\iota_{m-n}$ are. We therefore refer to the latter sequence of subspaces as a *stratification* of Σ^k_m. We shall meet this again when we study the Riemannian structure of shape spaces.

2.7 SIMPLE CONNECTIVITY AND HIGHER HOMOTOPY GROUPS

A space is said to be simply-connected if every loop, by which we mean the continuous image of a circle, in it may be shrunk to a point. More precisely, we say that two continuous maps f and g between topological spaces $\mathcal{P}$ and $\mathcal{Q}$ are *homotopic* if there is a continuous map $h : \mathcal{P} \times [0, 1] \to \mathcal{Q}$ such that $h|_{\mathcal{P} \times \{0\}} = f$

and $h|_{\mathcal{P}\times\{1\}} = g$. Such a map h is called a *homotopy* between the maps f and g. Then, a space is simply-connected if every loop in it is homotopic to a constant loop. We can now deduce quite easily that all shape spaces, except for the circle Σ_1^3, are simply-connected. It is a typical theorem for CW complexes that, if to a simply-connected CW complex we attach further cells of dimension greater than one, then it remains simply-connected, since any segment of a loop that lies in such a cell can be deformed by a homotopy to avoid the centre and then moved, radially, off the interior of the cell altogether. A similar argument shows that, in any case, a loop in a CW complex is homotopic to one that lies in the 1-skeleton. Thus, it suffices for simple connectivity that the 2-skeleton contains a simply-connected subcomplex that contains the 1-skeleton.

Since the dimension of the cell, or cells, that a pattern represents is one less than the number of its non-zero entries, our cell decomposition of shape spaces Σ_m^k, where m is at least two, has only one zero-cell: namely, that which corresponds to the pattern with the single non-zero entry '+' in the top left-hand corner. Similarly, there is just one 1-cell, corresponding to the pattern with the entries $(* +)$ in the first row and zeros everywhere else. Then, if m and k are each at least three, there is also the 2-cell represented by the pattern whose only non-zero entries are

$$\begin{pmatrix} * & + \\ + & 0 \end{pmatrix}$$

in the top left-hand corner. These three cells form the entire cell decomposition of Σ_3^3, which, by Casson's theorem, we know to be homeomorphic with a 2-ball and so simply-connected. Hence, every Σ_m^k with $m \geqslant 3$ and $k \geqslant 3$ must be simply-connected: it is formed from this ball in its 2-skeleton by adding further cells of dimension at least two. In fact, the only further two-dimensional cell, for $k \geqslant 4$, is that represented by the pattern whose only non-zero entries are $(* * +)$ in the first row.

In fact, we already have sufficiently detailed information on the structure of shape spaces to prove the above special case of Casson's theorem directly, and so to give an elementary self-contained proof of simple connectivity. If we consider the points on the pre-shape sphere whose non-zero coordinates are

$$\begin{pmatrix} a & b \\ c & 0 \end{pmatrix}$$

in the top left-hand corner, where $b \geqslant 0$, $c \geqslant 0$ and $a^2 + b^2 + c^2 = 1$, then the zero-cell is the image of the point where $a = 1$ and so $b = c = 0$; the 1-cell is the image of the cell comprising the points where $b > 0$ and $c = 0$; and the 2-cell is the image of the cell comprising the points where $b > 0$ and $c > 0$. This 2-cell on the pre-shape sphere is the quarter-sphere lying in the quadrant $b > 0$, $c > 0$. The part of its boundary given by $c = 0$ maps bijectively onto the 1-cell in shape space. However, for any point with $b = 0$, the corresponding canonical matrix is

$$\begin{pmatrix} 1 & 0 \\ 0 & 0 \end{pmatrix}.$$

Thus, all these points map to the unique zero-cell in shape space. It follows that the image, with the quotient topology, is a closed ball with a closed circular arc on its boundary collapsed to a point. This is easily seen to be still homeomorphic with the ball, showing that $\Sigma_3^3 \cong \mathbf{B}^2$.

Since the image of Σ_2^3 in Σ_3^3 is homeomorphic with the quotient of Σ_2^3 by the involution ι_2, which interchanges the two top dimensional open cells and fixes the rest of the space, it follows that the space Σ_2^3, which is also the 2-skeleton of Σ_2^k for all $k > 2$, may be constructed from Σ_3^3 by attaching the additional 2-cell determined by the pattern

$$\begin{pmatrix} * & + \\ - & 0 \end{pmatrix}.$$

Thus, Σ_2^3 is the image of the set of points on the pre-shape sphere with coordinates

$$\begin{pmatrix} a & b \\ c & 0 \end{pmatrix},$$

where $b \geqslant 0$ and both a and c are unrestricted except that $a^2 + b^2 + c^2 = 1$. In this case, we have a hemisphere in the pre-shape sphere with its entire boundary identified with a single point in shape space, confirming the homeomorphism $\Sigma_2^3 \cong \mathbf{S}^2$.

There are similar elementary proofs, directly from the cell decompositions, of the homeomorphisms $\Sigma_1^k \cong \mathbf{S}^{k-2}$. However, we should note that our current methods have lost the metric precision of those of Chapter 1, where we first met Σ_1^k and Σ_2^k. On the other hand, we shall be able to extend these methods to obtain an alternative proof of Casson's theorem, which, except for the first two cases, we shall show in Chapter 6 is certainly not a metric result.

Simple connectivity has a natural generalisation that arises as follows. The nth homotopy group of a topological space $\mathcal{P}$, usually taken to be connected, is defined to be the set of homotopy classes of maps of $\mathbf{S}^n$ into $\mathcal{P}$ fixing some chosen base point. Thus, simple connectivity implies the vanishing of the first homotopy group and, for a connected space, is equivalent to it. Then, a space that is connected and in which the first n homotopy groups vanish is called n-connected. As far as shape spaces are concerned, we shall be showing that, for $k > m$, Σ_m^k is $(d_m^{m+1} - 1)$-connected, where we recall that d_m^{m+1} is our notation for the dimension of Σ_m^{m+1}. That is, we show that Σ_m^k has the same connectivity as that which we already know for Σ_m^{m+1} by Casson's theorem. We shall first give a geometric proof of this, analogous to the above direct proof of simple connectivity. However, in later chapters we shall compute the homology groups of our spaces and, for a connected and simply-connected CW complex $\mathcal{P}$, the first non-zero homology group is isomorphic with the first non-zero homotopy group. Thus, granted that the spaces are simply-connected, $(d_m^{m+1} - 1)$-connectivity would also follow from the vanishing of all the homology groups in degrees less than d_m^{m+1}. The essence of our homology computations is to identify which cells in the above decomposition actually affect the homology, and these are indeed all of dimension at least d_m^{m+1}.

2.8   THE MAPPING CONE DECOMPOSITION

For many purposes the decomposition of shape space into cells is too fine. As just mentioned, even when using it to compute homology groups we shall find it convenient to concentrate just on those cells that are essential to express the homology and to discard a large subcomplex that makes no contribution to it. We have already described the much coarser stratification of Σ_m^k and also its tower of subspaces Σ_m^l, both of which have their uses. The former we shall find is closely related to the Riemannian structure that we are able to put on shape spaces, stratum by stratum. The latter is more closely tied in with the topological structure and we shall now examine it in more detail. There is, in fact, a simple topological recipe for building shape space Σ_m^k, starting from its subspace Σ_m^{k-1}, without going back to the individual cells. The additional part can be constructed from Σ_{m-1}^{k-1} using only a $(k-3)$-sphere in addition to two standard topological constructs, and it is glued on using the quotient map from $\mathcal{S}_m^{k-1}$ to Σ_m^{k-1}. The first of these constructs that we require is the *join*, $\mathcal{P} * \mathcal{Q}$, of two topological spaces $\mathcal{P}$ and $\mathcal{Q}$. This is the quotient space of $\mathcal{P} \times [0, 1] \times \mathcal{Q}$ under the equivalence relation: $(p, 0, q) \equiv (p, 0, q')$ and $(p, 1, q) \equiv (p', 1, q)$ for all p, p' in $\mathcal{P}$ and q, q' in $\mathcal{Q}$. In the special case that $\mathcal{Q}$ is two points, for example the zero-sphere, we obtain the *suspension of* $\mathcal{P}$, $S(\mathcal{P}) = \mathbf{S}^0 * \mathcal{P}$. For example, $S(\mathbf{S}^0) = \mathbf{S}^1$, $S(\mathbf{S}^{m-1}) = \mathbf{S}^m$ and, more generally, since the operation $*$ is both associative and commutative, we see that $\mathcal{P} * \mathbf{S}^{n-1}$ is the nth iterated suspension $S^n(\mathcal{P})$ of $\mathcal{P}$. In particular, if $\mathcal{P}$ is a d-dimensional ball, then $\mathcal{P} * \mathbf{S}^{n-1}$ is a $(d+n)$-dimensional ball.

When $\mathcal{Q}$ is a single point the join $\mathcal{P} * \mathcal{Q}$ is called the *cone* on $\mathcal{P}$, denoted by $C(\mathcal{P})$, in which we may identify $\mathcal{P}$ with the copy $\mathcal{P} \times \{0\}$. The complement $C(\mathcal{P})\backslash\mathcal{P}$ is the *open cone* $C_0(\mathcal{P})$. The other topological construct that we need is a variant of this cone, the so-called *mapping cone*, denoted by $C_f(\mathcal{P}, \mathcal{Q})$, associated with a continuous map $f : \mathcal{P} \to \mathcal{Q}$. It is the quotient space of $(P \times [0, 1]) \bigcup \mathcal{Q}$ under the equivalence relation: $(p, 1) \equiv (p', 1)$ and $(p, 0) \equiv f(p)$ for all p, p' in $\mathcal{P}$. Equivalently, $C_f(\mathcal{P}, \mathcal{Q})$ is $C(\mathcal{P})\bigcup_f \mathcal{Q}$, where each point in the base, $\mathcal{P} \times \{0\}$, of the cone is identified with its image under f. It is important to observe that this equivalence relation never identifies two separate points of $\mathcal{Q}$, although it does identify each set $f^{-1}(q)$ in $\mathcal{P}$ to the single point q in $\mathcal{Q}$. Thus, the mapping cone contains a subspace homeomorphic with $\mathcal{Q}$, which we shall usually identify with $\mathcal{Q}$ itself.

We can now show how to express Σ_m^k as a mapping cone. Since two other shape spaces will be involved we shall write π_m^k, instead of simply π, for the quotient map from S_m^k to Σ_m^k. If $X = \text{can}(X)$ is any canonical pre-shape matrix with pattern J having a full first row, we can decompose X in block form as

$$\begin{pmatrix} aU & b \\ cW & 0 \end{pmatrix},$$

where a, b and c are non-negative real numbers such that $a^2 + b^2 + c^2 = 1$, the row matrix U is such that $U^t \in \mathbf{S}^{k-3}$ and W is a canonical pre-shape in S_{m-1}^{k-1} with pattern J' derived from J by removing the first row and last column. However, as J and X vary, J' will run through all possible patterns, and thus W through all possible canonical pre-shapes, in S_{m-1}^{k-1}. Thus, fixing $b \neq 0$, 1 and allowing the other variables to take all possible values, the image that we get in Σ_m^k is a copy of $\mathbf{S}^{k-3} * \Sigma_{m-1}^{k-1}$. The quotient map π_m^k is injective on the entire set for which $b \neq 0$, 1 and so its image, together with the image of the point for which $b = 1$, forms the open cone $C_0(\mathbf{S}^{k-3} * \Sigma_{m-1}^{k-1})$. The base of the cone is the image of points for which $b = 0$, where π_m^k ceases to be injective. Thus, we have established the following result.

Theorem 2.1. *If $m \geqslant 2$ and $k \geqslant 3$, shape space Σ_m^k is homeomorphic with the mapping cone*

$$C_{f_m^k}\left(\mathbf{S}^{k-3} * \Sigma_{m-1}^{k-1}, \Sigma_m^{k-1}\right) = C\left(\mathbf{S}^{k-3} * \Sigma_{m-1}^{k-1}\right) \bigcup_{f_m^k} \Sigma_m^{k-1},$$

where $f_m^k \circ (\text{id} * \pi_{m-1}^{k-1})$ is the restriction of π_m^{k-1} to the subset of all the

$$\begin{pmatrix} aU \\ cW \end{pmatrix}$$

embedded in S_m^{k-1} and where the inclusion of the base space Σ_m^{k-1} in the mapping cone is the natural inclusion of Σ_m^{k-1} in Σ_m^k.

Of course, the weak link in this result is the map f_m^k, which it will generally be very difficult to describe explicitly. Thus, any applications of it will tend to be those that only require the existence of such a continuous map. However, we shall illustrate the theorem, and also provide the start of our inductive topological proof of Casson's theorem, by looking at the special case

$$\Sigma_4^4 \cong C\left(\mathbf{S}^1 * \Sigma_3^3\right) \bigcup_{f_4^4} \Sigma_4^3,$$

where it is possible to identify f_4^4 explicitly. We observe first that Σ_4^3 is homeomorphic with Σ_3^3, which we have already shown to be homeomorphic with a 2-ball $\mathbf{B}^2$.

Then, the decomposition of Σ_4^4 contains the three cells of Σ_3^3, determined by

$$(+), \quad (* \quad +) \quad \text{and} \quad \begin{pmatrix} * & + \\ + & 0 \end{pmatrix},$$

together with the four other cells determined by

$$(* \quad * \quad +), \quad \begin{pmatrix} * & * & + \\ + & 0 & 0 \end{pmatrix}, \quad \begin{pmatrix} * & * & + \\ * & + & 0 \end{pmatrix} \quad \text{and} \quad \begin{pmatrix} * & * & + \\ * & + & 0 \\ + & 0 & 0 \end{pmatrix},$$

which have dimensions 2, 3, 4 and 5, respectively. We note that the last three of these patterns may be formed by placing the first above each of those for the three cells of Σ_3^3. We write

$$\begin{pmatrix} au & av & b \\ cw & cx & 0 \\ cy & 0 & 0 \end{pmatrix}$$

for a general point on the pre-shape sphere that has such a pattern, where all the letters represent real numbers with a, b, c, x and y non-negative subject to the relations $a^2 + b^2 + c^2 = 1$, $u^2 + v^2 = 1$ and $w^2 + x^2 + y^2 = 1$. Then, we see that the set of points for which each of a, b and c is fixed and neither of a or c is zero is homeomorphic with the product of the circle parameterised by the variables u and v and the quarter-sphere determined by the variables w, x and y, of which the former is mapped injectively into Σ_4^4 and the latter is collapsed onto a 2-ball in exactly the same way as the cells that produced Σ_3^3. When $a = 1$ we just get a copy of the circle and when $c = 1$ we get the 2-ball. Thus, for a fixed choice of $b \neq 1$ still, as a and c vary subject to $a^2 + c^2 = 1 - b^2$, we get a copy of the join $\mathbf{S}^1 * \mathbf{B}^2$. This is easily seen to be homeomorphic with a 4-ball $\mathbf{B}^4$: at least $\mathbf{S}^1 * \mathbf{B}^1 \cong \mathbf{B}^3$ can be visualised in $\mathbb{R}^3$ and the case we want is analogous in $\mathbb{R}^4$.

When $b = 1$ we get a single point that, as in the theorem, forms the vertex of the open cone $C_0(\mathbf{B}^4)$, which is the image in Σ_4^4 of all the points except those for which $c = 0$. When we include these last points the result is the full cone $C(\mathbf{B}^4)$ with its base $\mathbf{B}^4$ collapsed onto $\mathbf{B}^2 \cong \Sigma_3^3$ by the map f_4^4, which it remains to identify.

We recall that f_4^4 describes the way in which the points

$$\begin{pmatrix} au & av & 0 \\ cw & cx & 0 \\ cy & 0 & 0 \\ 0 & 0 & 0 \end{pmatrix}$$

collapse onto Σ_3^3 under the left action of $\mathbf{SO}(4)$. Similarly to the case for the boundary component '$b = 0$' in Σ_3^3, where a semi-circle collapsed onto a single point on the boundary of Σ_3^3, here a hemispherical ball collapses onto a single point. This can be seen directly for the points

$$\begin{pmatrix} a & 0 & 0 \\ cw & 0 & 0 \\ cy & 0 & 0 \\ 0 & 0 & 0 \end{pmatrix}$$

which collapse onto the vertex $(+)$. For the remaining points we think of the left action of $\mathbf{SO}(4)$ rotating the non-zero column vectors of the above matrix until the second vector lies along the first axis and then rotating in the space orthogonal to this axis until the first vector has only its first two coordinates non-zero. In each case, the resulting direction along the axis may be positive or negative, since we may rotate in the plane spanned by this and the, so far unused, fourth dimension to change the sign to the required positive value. It follows that the matrices of the above form that project to a given one in Σ_3^3 are obtained by rotating the standard one through an angular interval of size π in two orthogonal directions. Hence, they form a two-dimensional hemispherical cell as required.

It follows from this description of the collapsing map f_4^4 of the base of $C(\mathbf{B}^4)$ onto the 2-ball Σ_3^3 that the quotient space Σ_4^4 is still homeomorphic with $\mathbf{B}^5 = C(\mathbf{B}^4)$. We could now show that $\Sigma_3^3 \cong \mathbf{S}^5$ in a similar manner to that in which we showed $\Sigma_2^3 \cong \mathbf{S}^2$ and continue to give similar direct proofs of the higher dimensional cases of Casson's theorem. However, the necessary visualisation is already getting tricky and, in the next section, we shall instead employ more powerful topological techniques.

2.9   HOMOTOPY TYPE AND CASSON'S THEOREM

A weaker classification than the topological one is that of homotopy type. As a basic reference for the results that we shall need to quote here and in later sections see Spanier (1966). Two spaces $\mathcal{P}$ and $\mathcal{Q}$ are said to have the same *homotopy type* if there are continuous maps $f : \mathcal{P} \to \mathcal{Q}$ and $g : \mathcal{Q} \to \mathcal{P}$ such that the composition $f \circ g$ is homotopic to the identity map of $\mathcal{Q}$ and $g \circ f$ is homotopic to the identity map of $\mathcal{P}$. Then, each of the maps f and g is called a homotopy equivalence. Obviously, homeomorphic spaces have the same homotopy type but the converse is far from true. However, spaces of the same homotopy type do have the same homotopy groups and a necesssary and sufficient condition for the map $f : \mathcal{P} \to \mathcal{Q}$ to be a homotopy equivalence is that it induces isomorphisms of all homotopy groups. We can now recover Casson's theorem in two stages.

Theorem 2.2. *Shape space Σ_m^{m+1} has the same homotopy type as a sphere of dimension d_m^{m+1} and Σ_{m+n}^{m+1}, for $n \geqslant 1$, has the same homotopy type as a ball of dimension d_m^{m+1}.*

Proof. We work by induction from the cases $m = 1$ and $m = 2$ using either the metric results given in Chapter 1 or, for a purely topological proof, those that we proved or, for $m = 1$, indicated above. We also use the homeomorphisms $\Sigma^{m+1}_{m+n} \cong \Sigma^{m+1}_{m+1}$, for $n \geqslant 1$.

The previous theorem gives us homeomorphisms

$$\Sigma^{m+1}_m \cong C_{f^{m+1}_m} \left(\mathbf{S}^{m-2} * \Sigma^m_{m-1}, \Sigma^m_m \right)$$

$$\Sigma^{m+1}_{m+1} \cong C_{f^{m+1}_{m+1}} \left(\mathbf{S}^{m-2} * \Sigma^m_m, \Sigma^m_{m+1} \right),$$

where in each case the relevant map has its image in a shape space, Σ^m_m or Σ^m_{m+1}, which we are assuming by induction to have the homotopy type of a ball and so also that of a point. In that case, our mapping cones have the same homotopy type as the corresponding suspensions $S(\mathbf{S}^{m-2} * \Sigma^m_{m-1})$ and $S(\mathbf{S}^{m-2} * \Sigma^m_m)$. Then, given a homotopy equivalence between a sphere of dimension d^m_{m-1} and Σ^m_{m-1}, it is a straightforward matter, at least for a topologist, to construct one between a sphere of dimension $d^m_{m-1} + m - 1$ and $\mathbf{S}^{m-2} * \Sigma^m_{m-1}$ and hence between a sphere of dimension $d^{m+1}_m = d^m_{m-1} + m$ and Σ^{m+1}_m.

Similarly, since the suspension of a ball is again a ball, we obtain the required homotopy equivalence between a d^{m+1}_m-dimensional ball and Σ^{m+1}_{m+1}. ∎

We may develop this theorem in two ways. First, we show that the initial sequence of homotopy groups that vanish for Σ^{m+1}_m, that is, all those up to, but not including, its dimension, remain zero on inclusion in Σ^k_m for $k > m + 1$. Of course, for the spheres $\Sigma^k_1 \cong \mathbf{S}^{k-2}$ much more is true since $\mathbf{S}^{k-2}$ is $(k-3)$-connected. However, in general, this result is the best possible.

Theorem 2.3. Σ^k_m is $(d^{m+1}_m - 1)$-connected for all $k \geqslant m \geqslant 2$.

Proof. This follows immediately from the previous theorem for $k = m$ and $k = m + 1$, since the relevant homotopy groups of the ball and sphere vanish. We complete the proof by induction on m and then on k.

Since, by induction on m or from our knowledge of Σ^k_1 when $m = 2$, the cone $C(\mathbf{S}^{m+k-3} * \Sigma^{m+k-1}_{m-1})$ is at least

$$1 + (m + k - 3) + d^m_{m-1} - 1 \geqslant m + d^m_{m-1} - 1 = d^{m+1}_m - 1$$

connected if $k \geqslant 2$, the homeomorphism

$$\Sigma^{m+k}_m \cong C \left(\mathbf{S}^{m+k-3} * \Sigma^{m+k-1}_{m-1} \right) \bigcup_{f^{m+k}_m} \Sigma^{m+k-1}_m$$

shows us that the image of any map of a d-sphere into Σ^{m+k}_m, for $d < d^{m+1}_m$, may be slid by a homotopy into the base Σ^{m+k-1}_m of the mapping cone. Since, by induction on k, this base is already known to be $(d_m^{m+1} - 1)$-connected, we may then further contract the image to a point. ∎

This theorem, of course, includes a proof that the shape spaces in this range are simply-connected, though our earlier proof, by showing that the 2-skeleton is a ball, may be more satisfying. Similarly, we shall show later that that part of the algebraic analogue of the cellular decomposition that carries all the homology has no 'algebraic cells' in the dimensions below d_m^{m+1}. Since the first non-zero homotopy and homology groups coincide, this gives us a direct explanation of the result in the theorem. We shall also establish there that the theorem is the best possible. The top dimensional homotopy group in Σ_m^{m+1} remains non-zero on inclusion in Σ_m^{m+k}, although for odd m it then has order two rather than infinite order.

Our second extension of Theorem 2.2 is to go from homotopy type to homeomorphism, in other words, to give a topological proof of Casson's theorem. To achieve this we shall use a result of Newman (1966), which states that, if a topological manifold of dimension at least five is homotopy equivalent to a sphere, then it is homeomorphic to that sphere, with an analogous result for balls. First, we recall Casson's theorem (Theorem 1.1), which we restate in full.

Theorem 2.4. *Shape space Σ_m^{m+1} is homeomorphic with a sphere of dimension d_m^{m+1} and Σ_{m+n}^{m+1} is homeomorphic with a ball of dimension d_m^{m+1} for all $n \geq 1$.*

Proof. We take the cases $m = 1$ and $m = 2$ as known. Then, in view of Newman's theorem, Theorem 2.2 and the fact that $d_m^{m+1} \geq 5$ for $m \geq 3$, it suffices now to show that shape space Σ_m^{m+1} is a topological manifold. That is, we must show every point has a neighbourhood homeomorphic with a ball and, again, we may assume by induction that we already know this for smaller m. Then, the open cone $C_0(\mathbf{S}^{m-2} * \Sigma_{m-1}^m)$ in Σ_m^{m+1} is an open ball of dimension $1 + (m - 1) + d_{m-1}^m = d_m^{m+1}$. So, certainly all the points of this open cone have the required ball neighbourhood. However, for any pre-shape matrix with a given shape, we can permute its rows, preserving the shape, to ensure that the first row has a non-zero entry and then permute its columns, corresponding to an isometry of shape space, to ensure that the final entry in the first row is non-zero. The resulting shape then lies in the above open cone and its ball neighbourhood is carried back by the inverse of the isometry to a neighbourhood of the given shape.

Similarly, assuming that Σ_m^m is known to be homeomorphic to a ball, since then $C_0(\mathbf{S}^{m-2} * \Sigma_m^m)$ is a cone on a ball, we find that Σ_{m+1}^{m+1} is a manifold with boundary: each point has a neighbourhood homeomorphic with that of a point either in the interior or on the boundary of the standard ball. Then, for the relative version of Newman's theorem, we need either to know that boundary is simply-connected and of dimension at least five or to know already that it is a sphere. For Σ_4^4, when the dimension of the boundary is four, we have shown above that this boundary is a sphere, and in higher dimensions simple connectivity follows from the fact that the boundary is composed of the cone on a sphere together with a ball, the base ball of the mapping cone, with identifications on the latter induced by a map into another ball of lower dimension.

Thus, Σ_{m+1}^{m+1}, which we recall is Σ_m^{m+1}/ι_m, is indeed a ball of dimension d_m^{m+1}. Then, so too is Σ_{m+n}^{m+1} for $n > 1$ since that is also isometric with Σ_m^{m+1}/ι_m. ∎

Since all shape spaces we have looked at in detail so far are topological manifolds, it is natural to enquire whether there are any other such manifolds among shape spaces. However, the answer is *no*, there are no more. One proof again follows from the mapping cone decomposition of shape spaces. For Σ_m^k to be a topological manifold and also to be homeomorphic with the mapping cone $C_{f_m^k}(\mathbf{S}^{k-3} * \Sigma_{m-1}^{k-1}, \Sigma_m^{k-1})$, the space Σ_{m-1}^{k-1} would have at least to have its homology identical to that of a sphere. We defer the proof of this statement until we are also able to show that the relevant shape spaces do not have the homology of a sphere. By that time we shall be able to give an alternative proof that the other shape spaces are not topological manifolds since their homology groups do not satisfy the 'duality' relations that the homology groups of a manifold would have to satisfy.

CHAPTER 3

Computing the Homology of Cell Complexes

In this chapter we introduce homology groups and make some initial deductions about them for shape spaces. We first show how these groups are defined and calculated for a finite cell complex, restricting the technicalities of orientations and the computation of boundaries to the special case of spherical cells, which is all that we shall require in the context of shape spaces. In particular, we emphasise the use of reduced homology to simplify theorems and proofs, especially those of an inductive nature.

In Section 3.6 we give sufficient topological definitions to be able to state, without proof, the Eilenberg–Steenrod axioms that the homology groups satisfy and that suffice to determine them. These axioms enable us to derive, from the mapping cone decomposition of the previous chapter, a 'long exact sequence' involving the homology groups of three closely related shape spaces. Such exact sequences are a standard tool of topologists and do indeed enable us to draw some initial inferences about the homology groups of shape spaces without actually calculating them. However, we conclude the chapter with a warning that we still have more to do to distinguish between various shape spaces. For example, the obvious topological invariant, dimension, which in our case is also the highest degree in which the homology is non-zero, is far weaker than might appear from Table 1.2: there are arbitrarily large sets of shape spaces for which all members of a set have the same dimension.

3.1 THE ORIENTATION OF CERTAIN SPACES

For most of our homological calculations it will be necessary for our cells to be oriented, and for the cells on their boundary to be oriented 'coherently'. Since the cells in the decomposition of shape space that we described in Chapter 2 are all homeomorphic images, under the quotient map, of cells on the pre-shape sphere, it will be sufficient to discuss orientations in that context. For, as we shall see, a homeomorphism of an oriented cell onto another cell determines an orientation of the latter.

We recall that the particular cells on the sphere that we use are unions of contiguous sets of the cells into which the sphere is divided by the coordinate hyperplanes. In fact, our cells are obtained by restricting certain of the coordinates to be zero, others to be positive, possibly one to be negative and making no restriction on the remaining coordinates. We shall give an account of the orientation of such cells, based on that in Hilton and Wylie (1960, p. 278).

The natural home of an orientation is in Euclidean space, where, particularly in low dimensions, it may be viewed from a number of different points of view. In $\mathbb{R}^1$ an orientation is simply a choice of direction, usually indicated by an arrow. In $\mathbb{R}^2$ it is a direction of rotation of the plane, often indicated by a circular arc with an arrow at one end. In $\mathbb{R}^3$ an orientation is most commonly interpreted as a choice of 'handed-ness' for the axes, the usual choice of a 'positive' orientation being that which aligns the positive x-, y- and z-axes in the directions of the thumb, fore finger and middle finger, respectively, of the right hand. This last is the approach that generalises most readily. In $\mathbb{R}^n$ we may define an orientation to be a permutation class, even or odd, of orderings of the axes. Thus, in $\mathbb{R}^4$, the sequence x_2, x_1, x_4, x_3 is a member of the positive orientation, the even permutations of the natural ordering.

To orient more general spaces we first note that an orthogonal transformation either preserves the orientation classes or interchanges them, depending on whether its determinant is $+1$ or -1, respectively. Thus, we may declare a linear isomorphism to be 'orientation preserving' if its determinant is positive and 'orientation reversing' otherwise. In effect, this just extends each orientation class of axes to include those obtainable from any particular member by a linear isomorphism of positive determinant. Finally, at least for our purposes, we may define a diffeomorphism, that is, a differentiable homeomorphism with a differentiable inverse, between connected open subsets of $\mathbb{R}^n$ to be *orientation preserving* if its Jacobian matrix is orientation preserving, and *orientation reversing* otherwise. Note that this quality cannot vary on a connected set. Now, an orientation of a space $\mathcal{P}$ diffeomorphic with a connected open subset $\mathbf{U}$ of $\mathbb{R}^n$ is a class of diffeomorphisms $\{f_\omega : \omega \in \Omega\}$ of $\mathcal{P}$ onto $\mathbf{U}$ such that, for any two members f_ω, $f_{\omega'}$ of the class, the composition $f_{\omega'} \circ (f_\omega)^{-1}$ is an orientation-preserving diffeomorphism of $\mathbf{U}$ onto itself. Such an orientation is, of course, determined by any particular diffeomorphism in the class.

3.2   THE ORIENTATION OF SPHERICAL CELLS

As described above, the cells in which we are interested lie on the sphere, within the intersection of certain of the coordinate hyperplanes and delineated by others. We need to define a standard orientation for such cells with which to compare those orientations that occur in the course of our calculations. We recall that for $\mathbf{S}^d$ in $\mathbb{R}^{d+1}$, writing e_i for the unit vector along the ith coordinate axis, a basic cell, that is, one whose boundary contains at most one member from each pair $(+e_i, -e_i)$, is uniquely determined by a set of vectors $(\varepsilon_{i_1} e_{i_1}, \ldots, \varepsilon_{i_{n+1}} e_{i_{n+1}})$, where each $\varepsilon_i = \pm 1$ and the i_j are all distinct. In describing these cells, the order in which we wrote the vertices in the symbol did not matter. However, now we need to insist that, when there is an even number of the ε_{i_j} equal to -1, we write the vertices in the symbol in their natural order, or an even permutation of this order, following the order of the axes along which they lie, irrespective of whether that is in the positive or negative direction. If there is an odd number of the ε_{i_j} equal to -1, then we take an odd permutation of this natural ordering. We shall next show how to use an ordering of the vertices of a spherical cell to determine an orientation of the cell itself. This will then give us a standard orientation for our particular spherical cells.

In $\mathbb{R}^n$ we have the standard linear cell or *n-simplex*, which is determined as the convex linear hull of the origin and the positive unit coordinate vectors and has a natural orientation as an open subset of $\mathbb{R}^n$. We may also take its vertices in the order of the origin followed by the unit vectors in their natural order. A diffeomorphism of a basic n-cell on the sphere with this standard n-simplex, and hence an orientation of that n-cell, is then determined as follows. First, we project the cell radially onto the simplex determined by the vertices that define it. This is a diffeomorphism on the open cell and extends to a homeomorphism on the closed cell, which is also given by radial projection. We then map this simplex linearly onto the standard n-simplex, choosing a linear map that preserves the chosen orderings of their two sets of vertices. The ordering of the vertices of the cell is only determined up to an even permutation, but a linear map inducing an even permutation of the vertices of the standard simplex is orientation preserving. Thus, the orientation of the n-cell determined by the composite of these two diffeomorphisms is well-defined. In this way, the basic 1-cells and 2-cells in the upper hemisphere receive the orientations that are indicated in Figure 3.1 in the usual manner for one-dimensional and two-dimensional cells.

We note that the standard orientations of the basic cells of, say, $(*e_2, +e_3)$ are compatible with an orientation of the full elementary cell. This means that homeomorphisms determining the orientation of the basic cells can be chosen to fit together to provide a homeomorphism of the entire elementary cell with an open subset of Euclidean space. It is not difficult to see that this is true in general, so it makes sense to define the standard orientation of an elementary cell as that which restricts to the standard orientation of each of its component basic cells, and we may think of a standardly oriented elementary cell as the union of its standardly oriented basic cells.

3.3 THE BOUNDARY OF AN ORIENTED CELL

In Figure 3.1 there is an obvious way in which the orientation of a 2-cell induces an orientation of each of the 1-cells on its boundary. We also note, for example, that the standard orientations of the two basic cells that comprise the elementary

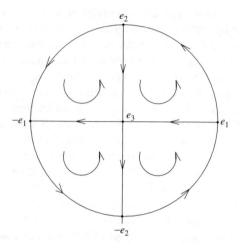

Figure 3.1 Standard orientations of the cells of the upper hemisphere in $\mathbb{R}^3$

cell $(+e_1, *e_2, +e_3)$ induce opposite orientations on the common boundary cell $(+e_1, +e_3)$. This reflects the fact, just mentioned, that the elementary cell has an orientation compatible with the standard orientations of its basic cells.

These phenomena are completely general and, in order to describe them, as well as to proceed to the computation of the boundary formula in the chain complex for shape spaces, it will be convenient to introduce an alternative notation for our oriented cells. Instead of changing the order of the vertices in a symbol for a basic cell, we always write them in the natural order but, when there is an odd number of the ε_i equal to -1, we precede the entire symbol by a minus sign so that, in this representation, the total number of minus signs appearing is always even. In other words, a change of orientation is indicated by formal multiplicaiton by -1. Thus, the four 2-cells that we would previously have denoted by $(+e_1, +e_2, +e_3)$, $(-e_1, +e_3, +e_2)$, $(-e_1, -e_2, +e_3)$ and $(+e_1, +e_3, -e_2)$ would now be denoted by $(+e_1, +e_2, +e_3)$, $-(-e_1, +e_2, +e_3)$, $(-e_1, -e_2, +e_3)$ and $-(+e_1, -e_2, +e_3)$, respectively.

Then, to extend to cells of arbitrary dimension the definition of an induced orientation of the boundary cells, we apply, first for basic cells, the following rule.

If the $(n + 1)$-cell is determined by the sequence of vertices $(\varepsilon_{i_1} e_{i_1}, \ldots, \varepsilon_{i_{n+1}} e_{i_{n+1}})$, then a boundary n-cell is determined by the same sequence with just one vertex, say the jth vertex $\varepsilon_{i_j} e_{i_j}$, omitted. Then, the orientation chosen as the induced orientation of that boundary cell is $(-1)^{j-1}$ times the standard one determined by the remaining sequence of vertices.

This is equivalent to requiring that the vertex to be deleted first be moved to the front of the sequence, with each transposition that is necessary reversing the orientation, before it is removed. If we write ∂ for the operation of taking the union of the oriented n-cells in the boundary of an oriented $(n + 1)$-cell, then we have, for example, in the notation introduced above:

$$\partial(-(+e_1, -e_2, +e_3)) = -(+e_1, -e_2)\bigcup(+e_1, +e_3)\bigcup-(-e_2, +e_3).$$

Here, each of the cells in the boundary of the standardly oriented basic cell again has the standard orientation, because the total number of minus signs involved in each term on the right-hand side is even. However, if we consider

$$\partial(+e_1, +e_2, +e_3) = (+e_1, +e_2)\bigcup-(+e_1, +e_3)\bigcup(+e_2, +e_3),$$

then the second of these boundary cells, having only one minus sign in its symbol, has the opposite of the standard orientation chosen for it.

Note, however, that we have given each of the contiguous cells $(+e_1, +e_2, +e_3)$ and $-(+e_1, -e_2, +e_3)$ their standard orientation, so their union is the standardly oriented elementary cell $(+e_1, *e_2, +e_3)$. On the other hand, the union of their oriented boundaries is just the set of cells in the boundary of the elementary cell, each with its standard orientation, provided we agree to extend our formalism to allow the cancellation of the two occurrences of $(+e_1, +e_3)$ that appear with opposite signs. Once again, this phenomenon is quite general and enables us to define the oriented boundary of an oriented elementary cell as the union, with appropriate cancellations, of the boundaries of the oriented basic cells that comprise it.

3.4   THE CHAIN COMPLEX, HOMOLOGY AND COHOMOLOGY GROUPS

Given an oriented cell complex $\mathcal{P}$, that is, a cell complex in which every cell has a chosen orientation, we may, for each natural number n up to the dimension of the complex, consider the free abelian group $C_n(\mathcal{P}; \mathbb{Z})$ with one generator for each oriented n-cell. This is called the *nth chain group of* $\mathcal{P}$ or, more precisely, the *nth chain group of* $\mathcal{P}$ *with integer coefficients*. Then, for example, writing the same symbol for the generator of $C_n(\mathbf{S}^d; \mathbb{Z})$ as for the cell to which it corresponds, we may rewrite the above equation for the boundary of a 2-cell as

$$\partial(+e_1, +e_2, +e_3) = (+e_1, +e_2) - (+e_1, +e_3) + (+e_2, +e_3),$$

where the image is now regarded as an element of $C_1(\mathbf{S}^d; \mathbb{Z})$. In general, the boundary map extends to a homomorphism

$$\partial : C_n(\mathcal{P}; \mathbb{Z}) \longrightarrow C_{n-1}(\mathcal{P}; \mathbb{Z}),$$

which has the property that $\partial^2 = 0$, which may easily be checked for the examples given above. Such a sequence of groups and homomorphisms satisfying $\partial^2 = 0$ is called a *chain complex*; elements in the kernel of ∂ are referred to as *cycles* and elements in the image as *boundaries*. It follows that boundaries are always cycles, but the converse is false and the *nth homology group, with integer coefficients*, of $\mathcal{P}$ is defined to be the quotient

$$H_n(\mathcal{P}; \mathbb{Z}) = \frac{\ker(\partial : C_n(\mathcal{P}; \mathbb{Z}) \longrightarrow C_{n-1}(\mathcal{P}; \mathbb{Z}))}{\text{image}(\partial : C_{n+1}(\mathcal{P}; \mathbb{Z}) \longrightarrow C_n(\mathcal{P}; \mathbb{Z}))},$$

of cycles modulo boundaries. The suffix n here is called the *degree* of the homology group, or of its elements. For a cycle c the homology class, the equivalence class modulo boundaries that it determines is usually denoted $[c]$. It is also standard notation to write $C_*(\mathcal{P}; \mathbb{Z})$ for the direct sum of all the indicated chain groups and $H_*(\mathcal{P}; \mathbb{Z})$ for the direct sum of the corresponding homology groups.

Similarly, we may define the homology groups of any chain complex (D_*, ∂) where D_* is the direct sum of abelian groups D_n and ∂ is a sequence of homomorphisms $\partial_n : D_n \to D_{n-1}$ such that $\partial_n \circ \partial_{n+1} = 0$ for all n. When (D_*, ∂) does not arise, as above, from a specific topological context, the homology group $\ker(\partial_n)/\text{image}(\partial_{n+1})$ would be denoted by $H_n(D_*, \partial)$, or just by $H_n(D_*)$. For example, when computing the homology of shape space, we shall look for a subcomplex D_* of its chain complex whose homology is the same as that of the space.

To obtain homology groups with coefficients in the abelian group $\mathbb{G}$ we form the chain group $C_n(\mathcal{P}; \mathbb{G})$, which is a direct sum of copies of $\mathbb{G}$ with one summand for each oriented n-cell, where we denote by ge_i the element of the chain group that is the element g of $\mathbb{G}$ in the copy that corresponds to the cell e_i. We then define the boundary operator $\partial_{\mathbb{G}}$ just as before with $-(ge_i)$ being interpreted as $(-g)e_i$, where $-g$ is the inverse of g in the additively notated group $\mathbb{G}$. As before, $\partial_{\mathbb{G}}^2 = 0$ so that we have a chain complex $(C_*(\mathcal{P}; \mathbb{G}), \partial_{\mathbb{G}})$ and we define its homology groups to be the homology groups, $H_n(\mathcal{P}; \mathbb{G})$, of $\mathcal{P}$ with coefficients in $\mathbb{G}$.

To define *cohomology* groups we work with the *cochain complex* derived from the chain complex as follows. The *nth cochain group* $C^n(\mathcal{P}; \mathbb{G})$ is the group of homomorphisms from $C_n(\mathcal{P}; \mathbb{G})$ to $\mathbb{G}$ and the *coboundary* homomorphism $\delta_{\mathbb{G}}$ is that from $C^n(\mathcal{P}; \mathbb{G})$ to $C^{n+1}(\mathcal{P}; \mathbb{G})$ induced by $\partial_{\mathbb{G}}$. Then, $\partial_{\mathbb{G}}^2 = 0$ implies $\delta_{\mathbb{G}}^2 = 0$ and, although $\delta_{\mathbb{G}}$ raises rather than lowers degree, we can still define the *nth cohomology group, with coefficients in* $\mathbb{G}$, of $\mathcal{P}$ to be

$$H^n(\mathcal{P}; \mathbb{G}) = \frac{\ker(\delta_{\mathbb{G}} : C^n(\mathcal{P}; \mathbb{G}) \longrightarrow C^{n+1}(\mathcal{P}; \mathbb{G}))}{\text{image}(\delta_{\mathbb{G}} : C^{n-1}(\mathcal{P}; \mathbb{G}) \longrightarrow C^n(\mathcal{P}; \mathbb{G}))}.$$

In fact, there are 'Universal Coefficient Theorems' (see the Appendix) that spell out how to compute the homology or cohomology of a space, starting from its homology with integer coefficients and we could proceed in that way. However, in this book we shall mainly be concerned with the integers $\mathbb{Z}$, the group $\mathbb{Z}_2$ of two elements or the rationals $\mathbb{Q}$ as coefficients, and the chain complex from which we compute the integral homology is so simple that it is just as easy to compute those other homology and cohomology groups directly.

3.5   REDUCED HOMOLOGY

For a connected complex $\mathcal{P}$ we always have $H_0(\mathcal{P}; \mathbb{G}) \cong \mathbb{G}$, which we see as follows. First, observe that the 1-skeleton $\mathcal{P}^{(1)}$ of $\mathcal{P}$, the union of its zero-cells and 1-cells, must be connected. If σ_1 is an oriented 1-cell with bounding zero-cells σ_0 and σ_0' and with σ_1 oriented from σ_0 to σ_0', then, for the corresponding generators of $C_1(\mathcal{P}; \mathbb{G})$ and $C_0(\mathcal{P}; \mathbb{G})$, we have $\partial c_1 = c_0 - c_0'$. It follows that for *any* two generators c_0 and c_0' of $C_0(\mathcal{P}; \mathbb{G})$ we may find a chain $c_1 = \sum_i \varepsilon_i c_1^i$ in $C_1(\mathcal{P}; \mathbb{G})$ such that $\partial c_1 = c_0 - c_0'$. Hence, all zero-cells determine the same homology class $[c_0]$, which therefore generates $H_0(\mathcal{P}; \mathbb{G})$. When $\mathcal{P}$ has r components, then, similarly, $H_0(\mathcal{P}; \mathbb{G})$ will be the direct sum of r copies of $\mathbb{G}$, one for each component. *Reduced homology*, which we denote by $\tilde{H}_*(\mathcal{P}; \mathbb{G})$, is just ordinary homology with one summand $\mathbb{G}$ removed from $H_0(\mathcal{P}; \mathbb{G})$ and we shall be working with reduced homology since that tends to simplify many statements and proofs. Since the cell complex that we shall use for shape spaces has a unique zero-cell, we shall obtain the reduced homology by simply omitting the corresponding generator from the chain complex.

3.6   THE HOMOLOGY EXACT SEQUENCE FOR SHAPE SPACES

Most of our discussion and calculations will concern integer coefficients and, when the cofficients are unspecified in any reference to homology or cohomology, or the corresponding chain or cochain groups, they are to be understood to be the integers.

Even before we settle down to compute the homology and cohomology groups of shape spaces, we can obtain some information from standard results in homology theory. For that we shall need to recall the Eilenberg–Steenrod axioms that are satisfied by any homology theory, including, of course, that which we have just defined, the so-called *cellular homology*. First, if $\mathcal{P}_0$ is a subspace of $\mathcal{P}$ we need to define the *relative homology group* $H_n(\mathcal{P}, \mathcal{P}_0)$. In the case of the cellular homology, $\mathcal{P}_0$ will need to be a cellular subcomplex and then $H_n(\mathcal{P}, \mathcal{P}_0)$ is defined using the chain complex $C_*(\mathcal{P}, \mathcal{P}_0)$, where each $C_n(\mathcal{P}, \mathcal{P}_0)$ is the subgroup of $C_n(\mathcal{P})$ in which the coefficient of every generator corresponding to a cell in $\mathcal{P}_0$ is zero and, on taking the boundary map, all such generators are similarly ignored. We check that this does form a chain complex and then the $H_n(\mathcal{P}, \mathcal{P}_0)$ are the corresponding homology groups. Note that we recover $H_n(\mathcal{P})$ by taking $\mathcal{P}_0 = \emptyset$. When we need to make the distinction, we refer to the groups $H_n(\mathcal{P})$ as *absolute* homology groups. The linear combination of generators that we ignored on taking the boundary map in the chain complex forms an $(n-1)$-chain in $C_{n-1}(\mathcal{P}_0)$, which is, in fact, a cycle and may be shown to induce a homomorphism, also denoted by ∂, from $H_n(\mathcal{P}, \mathcal{P}_0)$ to $H_{n-1}(\mathcal{P}_0)$.

If $\mathcal{P}_0$ is a subspace of $\mathcal{P}$ and $\mathcal{Q}_0$ is a subspace of $\mathcal{Q}$ and if f and g are continuous maps from $\mathcal{P}$ to $\mathcal{Q}$ each mapping $\mathcal{P}_0$ into $\mathcal{Q}_0$, then f is called a *relative mapping of the pair* $(\mathcal{P}, \mathcal{P}_0)$ *into the pair* $(\mathcal{Q}, \mathcal{Q}_0)$ and a homotopy from f to g is called a *relative homotopy of the pair* $(\mathcal{P}, \mathcal{P}_0)$ *into the pair* $(\mathcal{Q}, \mathcal{Q}_0)$ if, at every stage, it is a relative mapping: that is, it also maps $\mathcal{P}_0$ into $\mathcal{Q}_0$. We may now state the axioms.

(i)   *Functoriality.* Each map $f : (\mathcal{P}, \mathcal{P}_0) \to (\mathcal{Q}, \mathcal{Q}_0)$ of pairs induces a homomorphism $f_* : H_n(\mathcal{P}, \mathcal{P}_0) \to H_n(\mathcal{Q}, \mathcal{Q}_0)$ such that

$$(\mathrm{id})_* = \mathrm{id}$$
$$(f \circ g)_* = f_* \circ g_*.$$

(ii) *Homotopy.* If the maps f and g of the pair $(\mathcal{P}, \mathcal{P}_0)$ into the pair $(\mathcal{Q}, \mathcal{Q}_0)$ are relatively homotopic, then $f_* = g_*$.

(iii) *Exactness.* If $\mathcal{P}_0$ is a cellular subcomplex of the cellular complex $\mathcal{P}$, then there is an exact sequence of groups and group homomorphisms

$$\cdots \longrightarrow H_n(\mathcal{P}_0) \longrightarrow H_n(\mathcal{P}) \longrightarrow H_n(\mathcal{P}, \mathcal{P}_0)$$
$$\longrightarrow H_{n-1}(\mathcal{P}_0) \longrightarrow \cdots.$$

To say that the sequence is exact means that the image, necessarily a subgroup, of each homomorphism is the kernel of the next. If $\mathcal{P}_0 \neq \emptyset$ it is also valid when the groups $H_n(\mathcal{P}_0)$ and $H_n(\mathcal{P})$ are replaced by the corresponding reduced homology groups. In either case, it ends with $H_0(\mathcal{P}, \mathcal{P}_0) \to 0$.

(iv) *Excision.* If $\mathcal{P}_1$ is an open subset whose closure is a subcomplex of $\mathcal{P}$ contained in the interior of the subcomplex $\mathcal{P}_0$, then $H_n(\mathcal{P}, \mathcal{P}_0) \cong H_n(\mathcal{P} \backslash \mathcal{P}_1, \mathcal{P}_0 \backslash \mathcal{P}_1)$.

(v)   *Dimension.* The reduced homology of a point is zero in every degree.

The homology theory is, in fact, completely determined by these axioms. An immediate consequence of axioms (i) and (ii) is that homotopically equivalent pairs or spaces have isomorphic homology groups. This, together with axiom (v), implies that any contractible space, that is, any space that is homotopically equivalent to a point, also has all its reduced homology groups zero. The axioms also imply that $\tilde{H}_n(\mathcal{P}) \cong H_n(\mathcal{P}, p)$ for any point p in $\mathcal{P}$ or, more generally, for p any contractible subcomplex of $\mathcal{P}$.

From the exact sequence (iii) and the mapping cone decomposition given in Theorem 2.1, we obtain the following exact sequence for shape spaces.

Theorem 3.1. *For $m \geq 2$ and $k \geq 2$ we have the long exact sequence*

$$\cdots \longrightarrow \tilde{H}_n\left(\Sigma_m^k\right) \xrightarrow{\imath_*} \tilde{H}_n\left(\Sigma_m^{k+1}\right) \xrightarrow{J_*} \tilde{H}_{n-k}\left(\Sigma_{m-1}^k\right)$$

$$\xrightarrow{d_*} \tilde{H}_{n-1}\left(\Sigma_m^k\right) \longrightarrow \cdots.$$

Proof. We represent Σ_m^k and Σ_m^{k-1} indirectly using the mapping cone decomposition of Σ_m^k. We write $\mathbf{C}_{[s,t]}$ for the part of the mapping cone that is the image, under the quotient mapping, of $(\mathbf{S}^{k-3} * \Sigma_{m-1}^{k-1}) \times [s,t]$ if $s > 0$, or of $((\mathbf{S}^{k-3} * \Sigma_{m-1}^{k-1}) \times [s,t]) \bigcup \Sigma_m^{k-1}$ if $s = 0$, and pick b with $0 < b < 1$. Then, by Theorem 2.1, the mapping cone $\mathbf{C}_{[0,1]}$ is homeomorphic with, and so has the same homology groups as, Σ_m^k. On $\mathbf{C}_{[0,b]}$ there is a homotopy, fixing $\mathbf{C}_{[0,0]} = \Sigma_m^{k-1}$, from the identity to the obvious projection, along the $[0,1]$ factor, of $\mathbf{C}_{[0,b]}$ onto $\mathbf{C}_{[0,0]}$. This, called a deformation retraction, implies that $\mathbf{C}_{[0,b]}$ and Σ_m^{k-1} are homotopically equivalent and so have the same homology and reduced homology groups. Then, taking the exact sequence (iii) with $\mathcal{P} = \mathbf{C}_{[0,1]}$ and $\mathcal{P}_0 = \mathbf{C}_{[0,b]}$, we have

$$\cdots \longrightarrow \tilde{H}_n(\mathbf{C}_{[0,b]}) \longrightarrow \tilde{H}_n(\mathbf{C}_{[0,1]}) \longrightarrow H_n(\mathbf{C}_{[0,1]}, \mathbf{C}_{[0,b]})$$

$$\longrightarrow \tilde{H}_{n-1}(\mathbf{C}_{[0,b]}) \longrightarrow \cdots$$

in which the absolute groups are already as required by the theorem.

To re-interpret the relative group in the sequence we choose a with $0 < a < b$ and use the excision axiom to conclude that

$$H_n(\mathbf{C}_{[0,1]}, \mathbf{C}_{[0,b]}) \cong H_n(\mathbf{C}_{[a,1]}, \mathbf{C}_{[a,b]}).$$

We next observe that the deformation retraction of $\mathbf{C}_{[a,b]}$ onto $\mathbf{C}_{[a,a]}$ extends to a relative homotopy equivalence between the pairs $(\mathbf{C}_{[a,1]}, \mathbf{C}_{[a,b]})$ and $(\mathbf{C}_{[a,1]}, \mathbf{C}_{[a,a]})$ so that

$$H_n(\mathbf{C}_{[a,1]}, \mathbf{C}_{[a,b]}) \cong H_n(\mathbf{C}_{[a,1]}, \mathbf{C}_{[a,a]}).$$

Then, the exact sequence for the pair $(\mathbf{C}_{[a,1]}, \mathbf{C}_{[a,a]})$, in which $\tilde{H}_n(\mathbf{C}_{[a,1]}) = 0$ for all n since the cone $\mathbf{C}_{[a,1]}$ is contractible, shows that

$$H_n(\mathbf{C}_{[a,1]}, \mathbf{C}_{[a,a]}) \cong \tilde{H}_{n-1}(\mathbf{C}_{[a,a]}) \equiv \tilde{H}_{n-1}\left(\mathbf{S}^{k-3} * \Sigma_{m-1}^{k-1}\right).$$

This last group may be re-interpreted using the fact that for any space $\mathcal{P}$ the suspension $S(\mathcal{P}) = \mathbf{S}^0 * \mathcal{P}$ is, in fact, the mapping cone of the mapping of $\mathcal{P}$ to a single point. Then, writing $S_{[0,1]}$ for the suspension of Σ_{m-1}^{k-1} and $S_{[s,t]}$ for that part of the suspension that is the image, under the quotient mapping, of $\Sigma_{m-1}^{k-1} \times [s,t]$, we have the following sequence of isomorphisms, similar to those that we have just used, where again we take $0 < a < b < 1$.

$$\tilde{H}_n(S(\Sigma_{m-1}^{k-1})) \equiv \tilde{H}_n(S_{[0,1]}) \cong H_n(S_{[0,1]}, S_{[0,0]}) \cong H_n(S_{[0,1]}, S_{[0,b]})$$

$$\cong H_n(S_{[a,1]}, S_{[a,b]}) \cong H_n(S_{[a,1]}, S_{[a,a]})$$

$$\cong \tilde{H}_{n-1}(S_{[a,a]}) \equiv \tilde{H}_{n-1}\left(\Sigma_{m-1}^{k-1}\right).$$

Here, the five non-identity isomorphisms follow respectively from the fact that $S_{[0,0]}$ is a single point; from the homotopy axiom together with the fact that there is a deformation retraction of $S_{[0,b]}$ onto $S_{[0,0]}$; from the excision axiom; from the homotopy axiom again; and from the homology exact sequence together with the fact that $S_{[a,1]}$ is contractible. Iterating this result we see that

$$\tilde{H}_{n-1}(\mathbf{S}^{k-3} * \Sigma_{m-1}^{k-1}) \cong \tilde{H}_{n-k+1}(\Sigma_{m-1}^{k-1})$$

so that from our original sequence we obtain the one stated in the theorem. ■

Stating the theorem in terms of reduced homology groups has the advantage that, as in the above proof, we do not have to keep treating the case $n = 0$ as special. It has no real disadvantage since, for $n > 0$, the reduced and usual homology groups are identical anyway.

3.7 APPLICATIONS OF THE EXACT SEQUENCE

When $k < m$, since by Theorem 2.4 all three spaces are topological balls, the entire sequence is a trivially exact sequence of zeros. Similarly, when $k = m$, the space Σ_m^m is a ball and the other two spaces are topological spheres, Σ_m^{m+1} of dimension $d_m^{m+1} = (m-1)(m+2)/2$ and Σ_{m-1}^m of dimension $d_m^{m-1} - m$, and the only non-trivial part of the long exact sequence is the suspension isomorphism between their respective unique non-zero reduced homology groups.

When $k > m$, however, we do get new information. Since Σ_{m-1}^k is d-connected, where $d = d_{m-1}^m - 1 = d_m^{m+1} - m - 1$, we have $\tilde{H}_n(\Sigma_m^k) \cong \tilde{H}_n(\Sigma_m^{k+1})$ for all n such that $n - k + 1 \leqslant d$, that is, for all $n \leqslant d_m^{m+1} + k - m - 2$. Since Σ_m^k and Σ_m^{k+1} are known to be $(d_m^{m+1} - 1)$-connected, this means that the first $k - m - 1$ of their homology groups that we do not yet know are isomorphic, with the isomorphism induced by the natural inclusion of Σ_m^k in Σ_m^{k+1}. Note that this just fails to tell us whether, for $n = d_m^{m+1}$, $\tilde{H}_n(\Sigma_m^{m+2})$ is isomorphic with the group $\mathbb{Z} = \tilde{H}_n(\Sigma_m^{m+1})$. However, it is always a homomorphic image of it and the sequence

$$\tilde{H}_{d_{m-1}^m}\left(\Sigma_{m-1}^{m+1}\right) \longrightarrow \tilde{H}_{d_m^{m+1}}\left(\Sigma_m^{m+1}\right) = \mathbb{Z} \longrightarrow \tilde{H}_{d_m^{m+1}}\left(\Sigma_m^{m+2}\right)$$

$$\longrightarrow \tilde{H}_{d_{m-1}^m - 1}\left(\Sigma_{m-1}^{m+1}\right) = 0$$

tells us that, if for any m the group $\tilde{H}_{d_m^{m+1}}(\Sigma_m^{m+2})$ is finite, then, for the next m, the corresponding group is $\mathbb{Z}$. In fact, we shall find that for m odd $\tilde{H}_{d_m^{m+1}}(\Sigma_m^{m+k}) \cong \mathbb{Z}_2$ for $k \geqslant 2$ and so for m even $\tilde{H}_{d_m^{m+1}}(\Sigma_m^{m+k}) \cong \mathbb{Z}$ for $k \geqslant 1$.

At the other end of the sequence we find that, since Σ_m^k has no cells in dimensions greater than d_m^k and hence certainly no homology in those degrees, there is an isomorphism between $\tilde{H}_n(\Sigma_m^{k+1})$ and $\tilde{H}_{n-k}(\Sigma_{m-1}^k)$ for $n > d_m^k$. Since $d_m^{k+1} - d_m^k = m$ and $d_m^{k+1} - d_{m-1}^k = k$, this means that the 'top' m potentially non-zero homology groups of Σ_m^{k+1}, ranging up to the dimension of the space, are isomorphic with the kth suspension of those of Σ_{m-1}^k. In particular, iterating the isomorphism between the groups in the top degree we find that

$$H_{d_m^{k+1}}\left(\Sigma_m^{k+1}\right) \cong H_{d_1^{k-m+2}}\left(\Sigma_1^{k-m+2}\right) \cong \mathbb{Z}.$$

In the intermediate degrees it is less obvious how the homology groups of Σ_m^k combine with the suspended homology groups of Σ_{m-1}^k to form those of Σ_m^{k+1}. Nevertheless, it is possible to gain sufficient knowledge of the boundary homomorphism in the chain complex to identify the cycles that generate the homology groups, and also sufficient insight into the homomorphisms

$$\tilde{H}_{n-k}(\Sigma_{m-1}^k) \to \tilde{H}_{n-1}(\Sigma_m^k)$$

to be able to use the exact sequence as a basis for an inductive computation of all the homology groups starting from the known special cases. Indeed, this is how most of the homology computations were first carried out. The information needed for this approach, however, falls little short of complete knowledge of the boundary homomorphism and, in the next chapter, we shall indeed compute it explicitly. We shall then be able to see how to choose a new basis in the chain complex, adapted to that homology, so that all the generators and relators appear in the basis. The full integral homology can then be read off immediately and the homology groups with other coefficients can be deduced using the Universal Coefficient Theorem or again read off directly, since the re-based chain complex is particularly simple.

However, the exact sequence will still be of value when discussing and interpreting our results. To do so we shall require the following identification of the cellular maps that induce the homomorphisms in the exact sequence and which, since they are inherently plausible and no longer required for the calculation, we state without detailed proof. The homomorphism $i_* : \tilde{H}_n(\Sigma_m^k) \to \tilde{H}_n(\Sigma_m^{k+1})$ is induced by the natural inclusion i of Σ_m^k in Σ_m^{k+1} and so, at cellular level, is induced by mapping the cell in Σ_m^k determined by a pattern J to the cell in Σ_m^{k+1} determined by the same pattern. The main component of the homomorphism $j_* : \tilde{H}_n(\Sigma_m^{k+1}) \to \tilde{H}_{n-k}(\Sigma_{m-1}^k)$ is the 'de-suspension', which is the inverse of the suspension isomorphism. This is achieved at cellular level by mapping the cell corresponding to a pattern J to the cell corresponding to the pattern J', which is derived from J by removing its first row and last column. However, the homomorphism j_* also factors through the relative group

$H_n(\Sigma_m^{k+1}, \Sigma_m^k)$ and so is zero on all cells, or generators, which correspond to patterns without a full first row of $k - 1$ '*'s and a '+'. This also ensures that the decrease in degree is indeed k as stated in the theorem. Finally, the homomorphism $d_* : \tilde{H}_{n-k}(\Sigma_{m-1}^k) \to \tilde{H}_{n-1}(\Sigma_m^k)$ is essentially suspension followed by the boundary homomorphism of the homology exact sequence. It is induced by first mapping the cell corresponding to a pattern J' to that corresponding to the pattern J formed from J' by adding a column of zeros at the right and then adding a full first row, of the new length, at the top. We then take the boundary components of this cell that lie in Σ_m^k.

3.8 TOPOLOGICAL INVARIANTS THAT DISTINGUISH BETWEEN SHAPE SPACES

In the next two chapters, when we calculate the full homology groups of shape spaces, we shall see that, provided we exclude the contractible spaces, Σ_m^k with $k \leqslant m$, for which all homotopy invariants must vanish, any two different shape spaces have very different sets of homology groups and so cannot be homeomorphic. The limited topological information we already have is not quite sufficient to characterise the shape spaces among themselves, although the dimension $d_m^{m+1} + (k - m - 1)m$ of Σ_m^k is determined by the degree of its top non-zero homology group, which, as we have seen, is isomorphic with $\mathbb{Z}$. To complete the characterisation we would need, for example, the fact referred to above, but not yet proved, that the first non-zero homology group of Σ_m^k is in degree d_m^{m+1} for all $k > m$. This would determine m and then k could be deduced from the above expression for the dimension.

The fact that dimension alone will not suffice is clear from Table 1.2. Even if we make restrictions such as $m > 2$ or $k > m + 2$, some dimensions occur more than once. Thus, the first set of three spaces of the same dimension lying in the triangle $m \geqslant 3$, $k \geqslant m + 2$ corresponds to

$$d_3^{12} = d_4^{10} = d_5^9 = 29,$$

and the next is

$$d_3^{16} = d_4^{13} = d_7^{10} = 41.$$

The first set of four such spaces is

$$d_3^{23} = d_6^{14} = d_7^{13} = d_9^{12} = 62.$$

Even if we allow a space on the 'main diagonal', there is no earlier set of three. However, there is then the earlier set of four:

$$d_3^{17} = d_5^{12} = d_6^{11} = d_9^{10} = 44.$$

In fact, the repetition of dimensions is about as bad as it could be and we may show the following.

Proposition 3.1. *For each natural number r there are infinitely many sets of r shape spaces such that all the members of each set share a common dimension. There are also arbitrarily large integers that are not the dimension of any shape space Σ_m^k with $k > m > 1$.*

Proof. Since Σ_m^k has dimension $d_m^k = mk - 1 - m(m+1)/2$, we may easily check that, if m is an odd multiple of n, then $d_m^k = d_n^l$ for some integer l. Thus, multiplying m by a sequence of $r - 1$, similar or distinct, odd integers to obtain m', every one of the spaces $\Sigma_{m'}^k$ for $k > m'$ will lie in a set of r spaces with the same dimension as one of the Σ_m^k's.

On the other hand, the dimensions of Σ_m^k, for various k, are congruent modulo m to $d_m^{m+1} = m(m+1)/2 - 1$, which is congruent to

$$\begin{cases} -1 \bmod m & \text{if } m \text{ is odd,} \\ (m/2 - 1) \bmod m & \text{if } m \text{ is even.} \end{cases}$$

Suppose then that Σ_m^k had dimension $2^n - 1$. If m were odd, then this would require $2^n \equiv 0 \bmod m$; while if m were even, then it would require $2^n \equiv m/2 \bmod m$, which again leads to a contradiction. ∎

It is clear from the examples above that there are other ways of producing sets of spaces of the same dimension as that used in the proof. Similarly, there are other sequences of dimensions that are not realisable under appropriate restrictions on m and k.

CHAPTER 4

A Chain Complex for Shape Spaces

We are now in a position to make our initial computations of the homology of shape spaces. We shall find it convenient throughout this chapter to work with the spaces Σ_m^k/ι_m of unoriented shapes at the same time as the spaces Σ_m^k. We start by labelling the generators or basis elements in the chain complexes determined by our cell decomposition of shape spaces and then give an explicit formula for the boundary map in terms of these generators.

This enables us in Section 4.4 to identify a maximal sub-chain-complex that is generated by a subset of the basis elements and makes no contribution to the homology. After a simple change of basis, leaving this subset fixed, the remaining basis elements generate a direct complement to the first subcomplex. This complement we call the essential chain complex since it determines the homology of the shape space and no smaller sub-chain-complex could do so.

In Section 4.5 we make a slight modification to the basis of the essential complex as a result of which each new basis element carries either a generator or a necessary relation for the homology of shape space. The changes of basis in this and the preceding section are sufficiently modest that these generators and relations can be associated with particular patterns for the cells in the original decomposition of shape spaces.

Although this does not yet give us a closed form for the homology groups, it does allow us to compute any particular group and also to prove general results, such as the connectivity of the spaces and the fact that they are not topological manifolds. We are also able to identify the non-zero reduced homology group of lowest degree and in the final section we calculate the homology of the space of 'shapes of infinite sequences of points' in $\mathbb{R}^m$, formed by taking the direct limit of the spaces Σ_m^k with respect to the natural inclusions $\Sigma_m^k \hookrightarrow \Sigma_m^{k+1}$.

4.1   THE CHAIN COMPLEX

To compute the boundary map in the chain complex, and hence the homology and cohomology of shape spaces using the cellular decomposition obtained in the previous chapters, we shall introduce some terminology that we shall use throughout this and the next chapters.

We note that a pre-shape pattern is determined by the lengths of the rows of non-zero symbols. These form a sequence of integers $J = (j_1, \ldots, j_m)$, which are strictly decreasing until they reach zero. It will be convenient also to refer to this sequence as a pattern, referring to the pattern matrix or pattern sequence when we need to clarify the distinction.

We shall need to distinguish the two cases

(i) $k > j_1 > j_2 > \cdots > j_m > 0$, or

(ii) $k > j_1 > j_2 > \cdots > j_n = 0 = j_{n+1} = \cdots = j_m$ for some $n \leqslant m$.

Denote by $\mathcal{J}_1 = \mathcal{J}_1\binom{k}{m}$ the set of pattern sequences of type (i) and similarly define $\mathcal{J}_2$ and write $\mathcal{J}\binom{k}{m} = \mathcal{J}_1\binom{k}{m} \cup \mathcal{J}_2\binom{k}{m}$. For $J \in \mathcal{J}_1$ there are two elementary cells on the pre-shape sphere $\mathcal{S}_m^k$, which we denote by σ_J when the final entry in the last row is restricted to be positive, and by $\overline{\sigma_J}$ when the final entry in the last row is restricted to be negative. For $J \in \mathcal{J}_2$ there is a unique elementary cell in $\mathcal{S}_m^k$, which we denote by σ_J. The cell σ_J or, when relevant, $\overline{\sigma_J}$ corresponding to J has dimension $|J| = \left(\sum_{i=1}^m j_i\right) - 1$.

These cells are oriented as elementary spherical cells in the manner described in Chapter 3, with the coordinates on the pre-shape sphere taken in the order in which they appear, row by row, in the representative matrices. Recall that the orientation of an elementary spherical cell is compatible with that of each component basic cell and that that is determined by its sequence of vertices, which are positive or negative unit vectors along various coordinate axes. The standard orientation is then that determined by the natural order of the axes or its opposite according to whether an even or odd number of negative unit vectors is involved. We denote the images of these cells in Σ_m^k with their induced orientations by c_J and $\overline{c_J}$, respectively.

For homology computations with integer coefficients, recall that we require the chain complex $C_*(\Sigma_m^k)$, where $C_n(\Sigma_m^k)$ is the free abelian group, or $\mathbb{Z}$-module, with one generator, or basis element, corresponding to each of the above oriented cells of dimension n in Σ_m^k. We shall give each of these generators the same name as the cell to which it corresponds. Thus, $C_n(\Sigma_m^k)$ has two generators c_J and $\overline{c_J}$ for each $J \in \mathcal{J}_1\binom{k}{m}$ and one generator c_J for each $J \in \mathcal{J}_2\binom{k}{m}$, where, in each case, $|J| = n$. Note however that, as explained above, since we are only concerned with reduced homology we shall throughout adopt the following convention.

We exclude the shape with pattern sequence $(1, 0, \ldots, 0)$ from all the sets $\mathcal{J}$ and the corresponding generator $c_{(1,0,\ldots,0)}$ from $C_0(\Sigma_m^k)$, so that we have $C_0(\Sigma_m^k) = 0$.

In addition, since all our spaces are connected and so have reduced homology zero in degree zero and since otherwise the reduced and standard homology groups are the same, we shall henceforth use H instead of $\widetilde{H}$ to denote them.

4.2 THE SPACE OF UNORIENTED SHAPES

Recall that the shape space Σ_m^k is the space of *oriented* shapes, obtained as the quotient of the pre-shape sphere by the left action of $\mathbf{SO}(m)$, and that, if instead we quotient out by $\mathbf{O}(m)$, we get the space of unoriented shapes, which is the quotient of Σ_m^k by the isometric involution ι_m. If, as in Chapter 2, we use the element $\text{diag}\{1, \ldots, 1, -1\}$ to induce ι_m, then it is clear that, for $J \in \mathcal{J}_1$, the basic cell of σ_J that is determined by positive unit vectors along each relevant coordinate axis is mapped isometrically onto a basic spherical cell of $\overline{\sigma_J}$ with j_m negative unit vectors, since each of the final j_m coordinate axes is reversed. Since the order of the axes is preserved the image has $(-1)^{j_m}$ times the standard orientation. It is also clear that each cell σ_J for J in $\mathcal{J}_2$ is fixed by ι_m. Thus, in $C_*(\Sigma_m^k)$ the involution ι_m induces the isomorphism, which we denote by $(\iota_m)_*$, which maps c_J to $(-1)^{j_m}\overline{c_J}$ for $J \in \mathcal{J}_1$ and fixes c_J for $J \in \mathcal{J}_2$.

It follows that the space of unoriented shapes Σ_m^k/ι_m has a cell decomposition with just one cell for each pattern sequence J in $\mathcal{J}\binom{k}{m}$ with no longer any distinction between $\mathcal{J}_1$ and $\mathcal{J}_2$. We also see that our cell decomposition fits in nicely with the stratification of shape spaces described in Section 2.6, since $\bigcup_{J \in \mathcal{J}_1} c_J$ forms the topmost stratum of Σ_m^k and $\bigcup_{J \in \mathcal{J}_2} c_J$ is a subcomplex, which is a finite cell decomposition for the subspace $\Sigma_{m-1}^k/\iota_{m-1}$ formed by the union of all the lower strata.

4.3 THE BOUNDARY MAP IN THE CHAIN COMPLEX

For each $J \in \mathcal{J}$ and each i such that $1 \leqslant i \leqslant m$, define

$$\partial_i J = \begin{cases} (j_1, \ldots, j_{m-1}, j_m - 1) & \text{when } i = m \text{ and } J \in \mathcal{J}_1, \\ (j_1, \ldots, j_{i-1}, j_i - 1, j_{i+1}, \ldots, j_m) & \text{when } i < m \text{ and} \\ & \qquad \text{either } j_i = 1 \text{ or } j_i > j_{i+1} + 1, \\ \emptyset & \text{otherwise.} \end{cases}$$

Note that $\partial_i J$ is non-empty if and only if the sequence formed by lowering the ith entry in the pattern sequence J by one, and leaving all the other elements of J unchanged, is still a member of $\mathcal{J}$. It will be convenient to let $c_\emptyset = 0$. Then, we have the following result on which all our computations of homology and cohomology groups will be based.

Theorem 4.1. *The boundary map for the chain complex* $C_*(\Sigma_m^k)$ *is given by*

$$\partial c_J = \sum_{i=1}^{m-1} (-1)^{j_1 + \cdots + j_i - 1} \{ c_{\partial_i J} - (-1)^{j_i + j_m} (1 - \delta_{j_i 1}) \overline{c_{\partial_i J}} \}$$

$$+ (-1)^{|J|} \{ c_{\partial_m J} + (1 - \delta_{j_m 1}) \overline{c_{\partial_m J}} \}$$

and, when $J \in \mathcal{J}_1$,

$$\partial \overline{c_J} = \sum_{i=1}^{m-1} (-1)^{j_1 + \cdots + j_i - 1} \{ \overline{c_{\partial_i J}} - (-1)^{j_i + j_m} c_{\partial_i J} \}$$

$$- (-1)^{|J|} \{ c_{\partial_m J} + (1 - \delta_{j_m 1}) \overline{c_{\partial_m J}} \},$$

where δ_{ij} *is* 1 *if* $i = j$ *and* 0 *if* $i \neq j$.

Proof. Since the elementary cells in $\mathcal{S}_m^k$ corresponding to the chosen patterns are mapped homeomorphically and disjointly into Σ_m^k and since the latter is the result of quotienting out the action of $\mathbf{SO}(m)$ on the former, it follows that the boundary map for $C_*(\Sigma_m^k)$ may be computed in $C_*(\mathcal{S}_m^k)$ modulo the action of $\mathbf{SO}(m)$. That is, when taking the boundary of an elementary cell corresponding to a pattern, we must use the action of $\mathbf{SO}(m)$ to identify each elementary cell in the boundary with one that corresponds to a pattern.

We note first that for $i = m$ and for each $i < m$ with either $j_i = 1$ or with $j_i > j_{i+1} + 1$ the elementary cell $\sigma_{\partial_i J}$ appears on the boundary of σ_J and that $\overline{\sigma_{\partial_i J}}$ also occurs there if $i = m$ and $j_m > 1$ or if $i < m$ and $j_i > j_{i+1} + 1$. Moreover, since σ_J is open, so that its boundary is closure$(\sigma_J) \backslash \sigma_J$, these are the only cells of next lower dimension appearing on the boundary. Note that the factor $(1 - \delta_{j_i 1})$ is equal to 1 if $j_i > 1$ and, although it is also equal to 1 if $j_i = 0$, we then have $\partial_i J = \emptyset$ and so $\overline{c_{\partial_i J}} = 0$. Hence, the boundary formulae for the chain complex given in the theorem are correct up to the various signs and it remains to check that their orientations are as stated.

We may determine the orientations of the elementary cells appearing in the boundary of an elementary cell by considering those for representative basic cells. So, for $J \in \mathcal{J}_1$, we take that determined by positive unit vectors along each coordinate axis corresponding to an '$*$' or '$+$' in the pattern determined by J, together with the positive unit vector along the axis corresponding to the final $\pm$ entry when dealing with σ_J and the negative unit vector for $\overline{\sigma_J}$. In the latter case we must take an odd permutation of the natural order of the vectors since just one of them is negative. The coefficient of $\sigma_{\partial_i J}$ in $\partial \sigma_J$ is then determined by the fact that the unit vector corresponding to the final '$+$' in the ith row has to be moved past $j_1 + \cdots + j_i - 1$ previous unit vectors before being deleted to obtain a similar correctly oriented basic cell of the corresponding elementary boundary cell. When $j_i > 1$ we also have to consider the boundary cell determined by the negative unit vector along the axis corresponding to the final '$*$' entry in the ith row of the pattern. When $i = m$ this is just $\overline{\sigma_{\partial_m J}}$ since we took the unit vectors in an odd permutation of their natural order as required for $\overline{\sigma_{\partial_m J}}$. On the other hand, when $i < m$ it is not the chosen form for a basic cell in any of the elementary cells corresponding to a pattern. However, after multiplying on the left, as we may, by the diagonal matrix all of whose diagonal entries are $+1$ except for the ith and the mth which are -1, we do obtain a basic cell that belongs to $\overline{\sigma_{\partial_i J}}$ but with $(-1)^{j_i + j_m + 1}$ times its standard orientation since the unit vectors that span it are in an odd permutation of their natural order and $j_i - 2 + j_m$ of them are negative.

This completes the computation for $\partial \sigma_J$ and hence for ∂c_J. That for $\partial \overline{c_J}$ is similar with the differences accounted for by the facts that for $J \in \mathcal{J}_1$ and $i < m$ we must have $j_i > 1$ and that ∂_m removes the vertex that is a negative unit vector.   ∎

It is clear from this theorem that the sum of basis elements $c_J + \overline{c_J}$ will play a special role, so we shall denote it by c_J^*. Then, our homology computations will be based on the following special cases of the theorem.

Corollary 4.1. *The boundary maps have the following properties:*

(i)   *in* $C_*(\Sigma_m^k)$, *for J such that $j_m \geqslant 1$,*

$$\partial c_J^* = 2\Sigma_{i=1, \, j_i \not\equiv j_m (mod 2)}^{m-1} (-1)^{j_1 + \cdots + j_i - 1} c_{\partial_i J}^*,$$

(ii)   *in* $C_*(\Sigma_m^k / \iota_m)$, *for any J,*

$$\partial c_J = \Sigma_{i=1}^{m} (-1)^{j_1 + \cdots + j_i - 1} (1 - (-1)^{j_i} (1 - \delta_{j_i 1})) c_{\partial_i J},$$

(iii)   *in* $C_*(\Sigma_m^k / \iota_m)$, *for J such that $j_m > 1$,*

$$\partial c_J = 2\Sigma_{i=1, \, j_i \equiv 1 (mod 2)}^{m} (-1)^{j_1 + \cdots + j_i - 1} c_{\partial_i J}.$$

Proof.   The first statement holds since the last summands in ∂c_J and $\partial \overline{c_J}$, respectively, cancel, as do those for which $i < m$ and $j_i + j_m$ is even; the second statement follows immediately from the theorem and the facts that, in the chain complex, $\overline{c_{\partial_i J}} = (-1)^{j_m} c_{\partial_i J}$ for $i < m$ and $\overline{c_{\partial_m J}} = -(-1)^{j_m} c_{\partial_m J}$ and the third statement is an immediate consequence of the second since, if $j_m > 1$, no j_i can equal one.   ∎

4.4   DECOMPOSING THE CHAIN COMPLEX

It will be convenient now to write $C_n \binom{k}{m}$ ambiguously for the chain modules $C_n(\Sigma_m^k; \mathbb{Z})$ or $C_n(\Sigma_m^k / \iota_m; \mathbb{Z})$. We shall also write $C_* \binom{k}{m}$ for the corresponding chain complexes and $H_n \binom{k}{m}$ for the corresponding reduced homology groups.

As a subcomplex of Σ_m^k, Σ_m^{k-1} comprises just those cells c_J corresponding to J for which $j_1 < k - 1$. The subcomplex Σ_m^{k-1} / ι_m of Σ_m^k / ι_m is characterised similarly. Hence, in each case, the corresponding chain complex $C_* \binom{k-1}{m}$ is a sub-chain-complex of $C_*\binom{k}{m}$: that is, the boundary ∂ maps $C_*\binom{k-1}{m}$ into itself. Let K_n be the submodule generated by $\{c_J | j_1 = k - 1, |J| = n\}$, so that

$$C_n\binom{k}{m} = C_n\binom{k-1}{m} \oplus K_n.$$

If $K_* = \oplus_n K_n$ were also a subcomplex, then the homology of $C_*\binom{k}{m}$ that is, that of the relevant shape space, would be the direct sum, in each degree, of that of $C_*\binom{k-1}{m}$ with that of K_*. However, K_* is not, in general, a subcomplex, although it is very close to being one since, for each relevant J, just zero, one or two components of ∂c_J lie in $C_n\binom{k-1}{m}$: namely, those corresponding to $\partial_1 J$. Indeed, K_* *is* a subcomplex of $C_*(\Sigma_m^k / \iota_m; \mathbb{Z})$ when k is even.

Our aim will be to decompose our chain complexes as direct sums of subcomplexes in a manner that is valid for all k and m and that facilitates the computation of homology and the inductive checking of related hypotheses. Thus, we propose first to find decompositions, $C_n\binom{k}{m} \cong D_n \oplus E_n$, for each n and both cases, such that $D_* = \oplus_n D_n$ and $E_* = \oplus_n E_n$ are *both* subcomplexes and hence, as above, $H_n\binom{k}{m}$ will be the direct sum $H_n(D_*) \oplus H_n(E_*)$. Moreover, in this decomposition $H_*(D_*)$ will be zero and D_* will be maximal for this property, so that E_*, which we shall refer to as the *essential chain complex*, will carry all the homology $H_*\binom{k}{m}$ and do so as efficiently as possible. We shall thereafter work directly with the essential complexes.

To this end, we introduce some additional notation. We shall refer to each $c_{\partial_i J}$ or $\overline{c_{\partial_i J}}$ where $\partial_i J \neq \emptyset$ and, for the latter, $j_i > 1$ as a *component of the boundary* of c_J, saying, for example, that it is non-zero when it has a non-zero coefficient as a summand of ∂c_J. In view of the difference in behaviour when the last non-zero term of the pattern sequence J is one, we subdivide the sets $\mathcal{J}_1$ and $\mathcal{J}_2$ of patterns so that $\mathcal{J}_1 = \mathcal{J}_1^1 \bigcup \mathcal{J}_1^2$ and $\mathcal{J}_2 = \mathcal{J}_2^1 \bigcup \mathcal{J}_2^2$, where

$$\mathcal{J}_1^1 = \{J : j_m = 1\}, \qquad \mathcal{J}_1^2 = \{J : j_m > 1\},$$
$$\mathcal{J}_2^1 = \{J : j_n = 1 \text{ for some } n < m\}$$

and

$$\mathcal{J}_2^2 = \{J : j_n > 1, j_{n+1} = 0 \text{ for some } n < m\}.$$

We shall also need to subdivide $\mathcal{J}_1$ as $\mathcal{J}_1^\nu \bigcup \mathcal{J}_1^\mu$, where

$$\mathcal{J}_1^\nu = \{J : j_{m-1} = j_m + 1 > 1\} \quad \text{and} \quad \mathcal{J}_1^\mu = \{J : j_{m-1} > j_m + 1 > 1\}.$$

For $J \in \mathcal{J}_1^\mu$, define $sJ = (j_1, \ldots, j_{m-1}, j_m + 1)$ and, for $J \in \mathcal{J}_2^2$ with j_n, $n \leqslant m$, the first zero term, define $sJ = (j_1, \ldots, j_{n-1}, 1, 0, \ldots, 0)$. Then, for these J, sJ is always a pattern and, since the pattern sequence $J = (1, 0, \ldots, 0)$ has been excluded, s induces a bijection between $\mathcal{J}_2^2$ and $\mathcal{J}_2^1 \bigcup \mathcal{J}_1^1$ and between $\mathcal{J}_1^\mu$ and $\mathcal{J}_1^2$

being, in each case, the inverse to the operation of taking $\partial_i J$ for the maximum i for which this is non-empty. We also note that the coefficient of the component c_J in ∂c_{sJ} is ± 1 in both cases for $J \in \mathcal{J}_2^2$, and in the case of Σ_m^k this is also true for $J \in \mathcal{J}_1^\mu$. We may now describe the first decompositions as follows. For Σ_m^k we let $D_*(\Sigma_m^k)$ be the submodule spanned by

$$\left\{\partial c_{sJ} : J \in \mathcal{J}_1^\mu \bigcup \mathcal{J}_2^2\right\} \bigcup \left\{c_J : J \in \mathcal{J}_1 \bigcup \mathcal{J}_2^1\right\},$$

and $E_*(\Sigma_m^k)$ be the submodule spanned by

$$\{c_J^* : J \in \mathcal{J}_1^\nu\};$$

for Σ_m^k/ι_m we let $D_*(\Sigma_m^k/\iota_m)$ be the submodule spanned by

$$\left\{c_J : J \in \mathcal{J}_1^1 \bigcup \mathcal{J}_2\right\},$$

and $E_*(\Sigma_m^k/\iota_m)$ be the submodule spanned by

$$\{c_J : J \in \mathcal{J}_1^2\}.$$

Lemma 4.1. *In each case,* $C_n\binom{k}{m} = D_n \oplus E_n$, $D_* = \oplus_n D_n$ *and* $E_* = \oplus_n E_n$ *are subcomplexes and* $H_*(D_*, \partial) = 0$.

Proof. Each $C_n\binom{k}{m}$ comes equipped with a natural basis: the one used to define it. Our method of proof will be to change that basis until the results we require are self-evident. The changes we shall use will be a sequence of elementary changes where an elementary change of basis leaves all but one basis element alone and either changes the sign of that one or adds to it one of the other basis elements. It is clear that such a change does indeed produce a new basis.

Taking the case Σ_m^k first, we replace the natural basis of $C_*(\Sigma_m^k)$ by that required for $D_* \oplus E_*$ by first replacing c_J by ∂c_{sJ} for all $J \in \mathcal{J}_2^2$. It is possible to replace c_J by ∂c_{sJ} by a sequence of elementary changes since, as noted above, for $J \in \mathcal{J}_2^2$, c_J occurs with coefficient ± 1 in ∂c_{sJ}. All the sequences of changes for the various J may be carried out independently since the other components of ∂c_{sJ} are all in $\mathcal{J}_2^1 \bigcup \mathcal{J}_2^1$, and so are left unchanged by all moves of each sequence.

We then perform elementary changes to replace $\overline{c_J}$ by ∂c_{sJ} for $J \in \mathcal{J}_1^\mu$. Again, the required moves are possible since $\overline{c_J}$ has coefficient ± 1 as a component of ∂c_{sJ} when J is in $\mathcal{J}_1^\mu$ and, although the moves are not independent, they may be carried out in increasing order of j_m since the boundary components of ∂c_{sJ} other than c_J and $\overline{c_J}$ all have j_m increased by one. Finally, we make the obvious elementary changes to replace $\overline{c_J}$ by c_J^* for $J \in \mathcal{J}_1^\nu$. It is now clear that $C_n(\Sigma_m^k) = D_n \oplus E_n$ since D_n and E_n are spanned by complementary unions of the new basis elements of $C_n(\Sigma_m^k)$. Since

$$\left\{c_J : J \in \mathcal{J}_1 \bigcup \mathcal{J}_2^1\right\} \equiv \left\{c_{sJ} : J \in \mathcal{J}_1^\mu \bigcup \mathcal{J}_2^2\right\},$$

D_* is generated by pairs of generators, with one member of each pair being the boundary of the other, which shows both that D_* is a subcomplex and that it has trivial homology. That E_* is a subcomplex follows from the boundary formulae since, for $J \in \mathcal{J}_1^v$, $\partial_{m-1} J = \emptyset$ and, by part (i) of Corollary 4.1, the component $c_{\partial_m J}^*$ of ∂c_J^* is zero, and so all the non-zero components of ∂c_J^* also have their patterns in $\mathcal{J}_1^v$.

Turning now to the case Σ_m^k / ι_m, it is already clear that $C_n(\Sigma_m^k / \iota_m) = D_n \oplus E_n$ since D_n and E_n are spanned by complementary unions of the natural basis elements. It remains to show that D_* has trivial homology. To achieve that we change the basis of D_* by a sequence of elementary moves to obtain the new basis comprising

$$\left\{ \partial c_{sJ} : J \in \mathcal{J}_2^2 \right\} \bigcup \left\{ c_J : J \in \mathcal{J}_1^1 \bigcup \mathcal{J}_2^1 \right\}.$$

As before, these changes are possible since, for $J \in \mathcal{J}_2^2$, c_J occurs with coefficient ± 1 in ∂c_{sJ} and they may be carried out independently since all the other components are in $\mathcal{J}_1^1 \bigcup \mathcal{J}_2^1$ and so are left unchanged. Once again, these new basis elements for D_* are paired under ∂ so that D_* has trivial homology. ∎

As a result of this lemma, the picture is considerably simplified. We now know that the homology of Σ_m^k is determined by a complex with one basis element in degree n for each pattern J with $|J| = n$ and $j_{m-1} - 1 = j_m > 0$, rather than the much larger complex we started with. For Σ_m^k / ι_m the relevant patterns are those with $|J| = n$ and $j_m > 1$. In the next section we shall perform changes of bases to render the homology calculations transparent. Once again, these changes will be sufficiently simple that we can still describe the homology generators in terms of the patterns that originally determined the cells in our decomposition of shape space.

4.5 HOMOLOGY AND COHOMOLOGY OF THE SPACES

We recall that homology refers to *reduced* homology and that coefficients, when unspecified, will be the integers. The new bases mentioned above for the spaces of oriented and unoriented shapes are rather different, so we shall deal with them separately and it also makes sense to consider integer coefficients first since then, as we shall see, the other cases are obvious.

To describe the generators for $H_*(\Sigma_m^k)$ we need to examine the extent to which the behaviour, $j_{m-1} - 1 = j_m > 0$, of the last two members of each pattern determining a basis element of $E_*(\Sigma_m^k)$ is repeated throughout the pattern. Thus, we pair the entries of a pattern J from the right-hand end and call a pair *nice* if it is of the form $(n + 1, n)$. When m is odd we dub the left-hand singleton an honorary pair and call it *nice* if it is equal to $k - 1$, the maximum that it could be. We further call a pair *even*, respectively, *odd*, if its right-hand, or only, member is congruent to j_m modulo 2, respectively, not congruent to j_m modulo 2. Then, each basis element of the essential complex corresponds to a pattern of one and only one of the following types:

(i) all pairs are nice and even,
(ii) the first pair from the right that is not both nice and even is odd,
(iii) the first pair from the right that is not both nice and even is even.

Note that the pair in (ii) that is the first to fail to be both nice and even may or may not be nice, whereas that in (iii) cannot be nice.

Theorem 4.2. *The basis elements in the essential complex for Σ_m^k corresponding to patterns of type* (i), *defined as above, carry the generators of infinite cyclic direct summands in both the homology and cohomology with integer coefficients. There is a direct summand in homology isomorphic with $\mathbb{Z}_2$ for each pattern of type* (iii) *and a similar summand in cohomology for each pattern of type* (ii).

It follows that, when m is odd, generators of infinite summands can occur only in the complement of $E_*(\Sigma_m^{k-1})$ in $E_*(\Sigma_m^k)$. For then, to be nice, the first entry in the pattern sequence must equal $k - 1$, which is precisely the criterion for the corresponding cell to lie in Σ_m^k and not in Σ_m^{k-1}.

Proof. Patterns J of type (i) correspond to infinite summands because each corresponding basis element has zero boundary by part (i) of Corollary 4.1. For the first member of a nice pair can never give rise to a non-empty boundary component and $\partial_i J$ is also empty when the right-hand member, or for m odd the initial singleton, j_i is congruent to j_m modulo 2. For such an element c_J^* to be involved in a boundary $\partial c_{J'}^*$ it would have to correspond to $\partial_i J'$ where j_i is the first member of a pair, or the initial singleton when m is odd, in J. However, in the former case, since j_{i+1} is even, that is, of the same parity as j_m, j_{i+1} is odd and the corresponding entry j'_{i+1} in J' would be even again and so give rise to no boundary component. For m odd the initial singleton must be nice, that is, equal to $k - 1$, so the J' for which it would be $\partial_1 J'$ does not exist in Σ_m^k. It does exist in Σ_m^{k+1} but there J no longer has type (i). Thus, the basis element c_J^* corresponding to a pattern J of type (i) is a cycle and it is not involved in any boundaries at all. So neither it itself, nor any multiple of it, can possibly be a boundary, which means that it generates a direct summand isomorphic with the integers $\mathbb{Z}$.

There is a one-to-one correspondence between the sets of basis elements of the remaining two types in which the corresponding patterns are identical, except that the right-hand member of the first pair from the right that is not both nice and even is odd in the type (ii) pattern and one less in the corresponding pattern of type (iii). Thus, each basis element determined by a pattern of type (iii) occurs with coefficient ± 2 in the boundary of the element determined by the corresponding pattern of type (ii). Since all boundary coefficients are ± 2, we may make a change of basis replacing each element of type (iii) by half the boundary of the corresponding element of type (ii). To see that it is possible to carry out all these basis changes, note that the maximal right-hand block of nice and even pairs of an element is shared by all its boundary components, since a nice and even pair contributes nothing to the boundary and an additional even pair cannot be created in the components corresponding to the first pair that is either non-nice or odd or both. Then, among such basis elements, sharing a common right-hand block of nice and even pairs, we may carry out the changes of basis in increasing order of the right-hand member of the next pair.

The stated results now follow since, for the cohomology, the dual of the map

$$\mathbb{Z} \xrightarrow{\;2\;} \mathbb{Z}$$

is the same map in the reverse direction.   ∎

Turning to spaces of unoriented shapes, the essential complex for Σ_m^k/ι_m is now spanned by $\{c_J : J \in \mathcal{J}_1^2\}$, the cells corresponding to patterns in which $j_m > 1$. This gives a somewhat larger set of patterns than that for Σ_m^k, although it does not include the latter set. However, examination of parts (i) and (iii) of Corollary 4.1 shows that the boundary formulae differ only in that, for Σ_m^k/ι_m, $c_{\partial_i J}$ occurs with coefficient ± 2 in the boundary of c_J whenever j_i is odd, whereas, for Σ_m^k, it required j_i to have opposite parity to j_m. In addition, $c_{\partial_m J}$ may occur as a boundary component of c_J in Σ_m^k/ι_m.

It follows that if, for Σ_m^k/ι_m, we now define a pair in a pattern J to be *even*, respectively, *odd*, if its right-hand, or only, member is even, respectively, odd, then the three types of pattern we identified for Σ_m^k will, with this modified definition, serve the same function for Σ_m^k/ι_m. Thus, we have the following analogous result to Theorem 4.2.

Theorem 4.3. *The basis elements in the essential complex for Σ_m^k/ι_m corresponding to patterns of type* (i)*, with the previous definition modified as above, carry the generators of infinite cyclic direct summands in both the homology and cohomology with integer coefficients. There is a direct summand in homology isomorphic with $\mathbb{Z}_2$ for each pattern of type* (iii) *and a similar summand in cohomology for each pattern of type* (ii)*.*

Having computed the homology with integer coefficients, a topologist would usually use the Universal Coefficient Theorems to deduce the homology and cohomology groups for other coefficients. However, as advertised, the essential complexes are so simple that it is just as easy to compute these groups directly. For example, when the coefficients are $\mathbb{Z}_2$, the boundary map $\mathbb{Z} \xrightarrow{2} \mathbb{Z}$ from generators of type (ii) to those of type (iii) is zero in each case and so every basis element of the essential complex, for either type of shape space, is a cycle and there are no boundaries. Thus, each generator of the essential complex carries the generator of a summand $\mathbb{Z}_2$ for both the homology and cohomology.

When the coefficients are a field of characteristic other than two, such as the rationals $\mathbb{Q}$, the boundary map from generators of type (ii) to those of type (iii) is an isomorphism. So neither type of generator of the essential complex contributes to the homology, or cohomology, with such coefficients and it follows, for example, that the rational homology and cohomology has a summand $\mathbb{Q}$ for each pattern of type (i), but none for the other patterns. Thus, we have established the following theorem.

Theorem 4.4. $H_*(\Sigma_m^k; \mathbb{Z}_2)$ *and* $H_*(\Sigma_m^k/\iota_m; \mathbb{Z}_2)$ *each have one generator of a direct summand in the appropriate dimension for each of the patterns of the relevant types* (i), (ii) *and* (iii).

$H_*(\Sigma_m^k; \mathbb{Q})$ *and* $H_*(\Sigma_m^k/\iota_m; \mathbb{Q})$ *each have one generator of a direct summand in the appropriate dimension for each of the patterns of the relevant type* (i).

4.6 CONNECTIVITY OF SHAPE SPACES

Before computing the homology groups of shape spaces in detail, we close this chapter by making some specific observations that follow directly from these theorems. For example, the fact that the essential complexes carry all the reduced homology and yet have no cells in low dimensions confirms our previous result that the shape spaces are highly connected.

In fact, we may now compute their first non-zero homology groups and so complete the characterisation of shape spaces among themselves as indicated at the beginning of Section 3.8. Thus, the constraints on the cells that carry generators of the homology of Σ_m^{m+n} are such that the one of lowest dimension corresponds to the pattern $(m, m-1, \ldots, 2, 1)$. That cell occurs in all the spaces Σ_m^{m+n}, irrespective of $n > 0$, and it has the same dimension $m(m+1)/2 - 1 = d_m^{m+1}$ as Σ_m^{m+1}. For the latter space it is the only cell of the essential complex and so necessarily determines an infinite cyclic summand of the homology. Indeed, it is of type (i) and this remains true in Σ_m^{m+n} when $n > 1$, provided m is even. On the other hand, when m is odd, the first, singleton, entry in the pattern ceases to be nice so the pattern is now of type (iii) and it determines a summand of order two in the homology.

Similar considerations apply in Σ_m^{m+n}/ι_m, except that the constraints on members of the essential complex mean that the lowest dimensional cell corresponds to the pattern $(m+1, m, \ldots, 3, 2)$ and so has dimension $d_m^{m+1} + m$. Once again, this is of type (i), unless m is odd and $n > 2$ when it becomes type (iii).

Since the shape spaces are simply-connected and so the homotopy and homology groups agree up to and including the first no-zero one, we have established the following extension of our earlier theorem.

Theorem 4.5. *All the spaces* Σ_m^{m+n}, *for* $n \geqslant 1$, *are* $(d_m^{m+1} - 1)$-*connected with*

$$H_{d_m^{m+1}}\left(\Sigma_m^{m+n}\right) = \begin{cases} \mathbb{Z} & \text{if } m \text{ is even or } n = 1, \\ \mathbb{Z}_2 & \text{if } m \text{ is odd and } n > 1. \end{cases}$$

Similarly, all the spaces Σ_m^{m+n}/ι_m, *for* $n \geqslant 1$, *are* $(d_m^{m+1} + m - 1)$-*connected with*

$$H_{d_m^{m+1}+m}\left(\Sigma_m^{m+n}/\iota_m\right) = \begin{cases} \mathbb{Z} & \text{if } n = 2 \text{ or } m \text{ is even and } n > 2, \\ \mathbb{Z}_2 & \text{if } m \text{ is odd and } n > 2. \end{cases}$$

Of course, since, by Casson's theorem, Σ_m^{m+1} is a sphere of dimension d_m^{m+1} and Σ_m^{m+1}/ι_m is a ball of the same dimension, we already knew that these particular spaces would have the homology stated in this theorem. We could similarly have shown that Σ_m^{m+2}/ι_m is homeomorphic to a sphere of dimension $d_m^{m+1} + m$, thereby explaining its homology groups.

We are also now in a position to prove that none of the shape spaces are topological manifolds other than those we already know explicitly to be so. We use the following result from topological 'folklore' for which we shall include a proof since, despite being so well-known, it is not easy to locate a proof in the literature. We recall that a map is called *proper* if the inverse image of every compact set is itself compact.

Lemma 4.2. *Let* $\mathcal{P}$ *and* $\mathcal{Q}$ *be compact topological spaces and* f *be an embedding of* $\mathcal{P} \times [0\ 2]$ *in* $\mathcal{Q} \times [0\ 2]$ *such that* $f(\mathcal{P} \times \{1/2\}) \subseteq \mathcal{Q} \times (0, 1)$, $f(\mathcal{P} \times \{3/2\}) \subseteq \mathcal{Q} \times (1, 2)$ *and* $\mathcal{Q} \times \{1\} \subseteq f(\mathcal{P} \times [1/2, 3/2])$. *Then* $\mathcal{P} \times \mathbb{R}$ *is properly homeomorphic with* $\mathcal{Q} \times \mathbb{R}$.

Proof. Such a homeomorphism will be proper if for all n the projection of the inverse image of $\mathcal{Q} \times [-n, n]$ onto $\mathbb{R}$ is bounded. Consider the closure $\mathcal{K}$ of the component of $\mathcal{Q} \times [0, 2] \backslash f(\mathcal{P} \times [1/2, 3/2])$ that contains $\mathcal{Q} \times \{0\}$, and the closures $\mathcal{K}'$, $\mathcal{K}''$ of the components of $f(\mathcal{P} \times [1/2, 3/2]) \backslash \mathcal{Q} \times \{1\}$ that contain $f(\mathcal{P} \times \{1/2\})$ and $f(\mathcal{P} \times \{3/2\})$, respectively. The proof rests on the facts that $\mathcal{K} \bigcup \mathcal{K}'$ is equal to $\mathcal{Q} \times [0, 1]$ and that $\mathcal{K}' \bigcup \mathcal{K}''$ is homeomorphic with $\mathcal{P} \times [0, 1]$, together with the existence of a homeomorphism h of $\mathcal{K}$ onto $\mathcal{K}''$, which restricts to the natural identification of the 'lower' boundary $\mathcal{Q} \times \{0\}$ of $\mathcal{K}$ with that $\mathcal{Q} \times \{1\}$ of $\mathcal{K}''$, and which, on the 'upper' boundary, restricts to the natural identification of $f(\mathcal{P} \times \{1/2\})$ with $f(\mathcal{P} \times \{3/2\})$.

The required homeomorphism of $\mathcal{P} \times \mathbb{R}$ onto $\mathcal{Q} \times \mathbb{R}$ then follows by the so-called 'Mazur trick'. We regard $\mathcal{Q} \times \mathbb{R}$ as $\bigcup_{n \in \mathbb{Z}} \mathcal{Q} \times [n, n + 1]$, where the two copies of $\mathcal{Q} \times \{n\}$ are identified naturally, and write $\mathcal{Q} \times [n, n + 1] = \mathcal{K}_n \bigcup \mathcal{K}'_n$, where $\mathcal{K}_n \cong \mathcal{K}$ and $\mathcal{K}'_n \cong \mathcal{K}'$ for each n. Then, we may describe a homeomorphism g_n of $\mathcal{P} \times [n - 1/2, n + 1/2]$ onto $\mathcal{K}'_{n-1} \bigcup \mathcal{K}_n$ as the composition of a sequence of homeomorphisms: first identify $\mathcal{P} \times [n - 1/2, n + 1/2]$ naturally with $\mathcal{P} \times [1/2, 3/2]$; then map by f onto $\mathcal{K}' \bigcup \mathcal{K}''$; then identify $\mathcal{K}'$ with $\mathcal{K}'_0$ and map $\mathcal{K}''$ onto $\mathcal{K}_1$ by the inverse of h followed by the natural identification of $\mathcal{K}$ with $\mathcal{K}_1$; finally translate $\mathcal{K}'_0 \bigcup \mathcal{K}_1$ onto $\mathcal{K}'_{n-1} \bigcup \mathcal{K}_n$. Two things need to be checked. Firstly, since the maps of $\mathcal{K}'$ and $\mathcal{K}''$ onto $\mathcal{K}'_0$ and $\mathcal{K}_1$, respectively, on their common boundary $\mathcal{Q} \times \{1\}$ are both the identity, that stage of the composition is indeed well-defined and a homeomorphism. Secondly, because of our choice of h between the 'upper' boundaries,

$$g_n|_{\mathcal{P} \times \{n+1/2\}} = g_{n+1}|_{\mathcal{P} \times \{n+1/2\}}$$

and so the homeomorphisms g_n, $n \in \mathbb{Z}$, fit together to form a homeomorphism, which by the nature of this construction is necessarily proper, between $\mathcal{P} \times \mathbb{R}$ and $\mathcal{Q} \times \mathbb{R}$.

It remains to construct the homeomorphism h. We do this in two stages by means of the product structures on $\mathcal{P} \times [0, 2]$ and $\mathcal{Q} \times [0, 2]$, respectively. First, a homeomorphism of $\mathcal{P} \times [0, 2]$ onto itself, fixing the boundaries and mapping $\mathcal{P} \times \{1/2\}$ onto $\mathcal{P} \times \{3/2\}$, which could, for example, be induced by a suitable increasing function of the factor $[0, 2]$ onto itself, will induce a homeomorphism of $\mathcal{Q} \times [0, 2]$ onto itself, fixing the boundaries and taking $f(\mathcal{P} \times \{1/2\})$ onto $f(\mathcal{P} \times \{3/2\})$. Then, by compactness, we can find $\varepsilon > 0$ such that $\mathcal{Q} \times [1, 1 + \varepsilon] \subseteq \mathcal{K}''$ and we can produce a homeomorphism of $\mathcal{Q} \times [0, 2]$ onto $\mathcal{Q} \times [1, 2]$, fixed on $\mathcal{Q} \times [1 + \varepsilon, 2]$, extending the natural identification of the 'lower' boundaries. The composition of the two homeomorphisms, when restricted to $\mathcal{K}$, is the required homeomorphism h.   ∎

Corollary 4.2. *If $\mathcal{P}$ and $\mathcal{Q}$ are compact spaces and the open cone $C_0(\mathcal{P})$ embeds in the open cone $C_0(\mathcal{Q})$, respecting the cone points, then $\mathcal{P} \times \mathbb{R} \cong \mathcal{Q} \times \mathbb{R}$ and $C_0(\mathcal{P}) \cong C_0(\mathcal{Q})$, respecting cone points.*

Proof. The hypotheses of Lemma 4.2 are easily achieved, using compactness of $\mathcal{P}$ and $\mathcal{Q}$. The resulting proper homeomorphism of $\mathcal{P} \times \mathbb{R}$ onto $\mathcal{Q} \times \mathbb{R}$ induces the required homeomorphism between the open cones since these are the one-point compactifications at one end of each space.   ∎

In fact, the only information we use from this corollary is that $\mathcal{P}$ and $\mathcal{Q}$ must be homotopically equivalent and so have the same homology groups.

Theorem 4.6. *No shape space Σ_m^k, with $m > 2$ and $k > m + 1$, is a topological manifold.*

Proof. This uses the fact that in a topological manifold every point must have a neighbourhood that is a topological ball, which we can also think of as a cone on a sphere with the given point at its vertex. However, we already know from the mapping cone decomposition that there are points in Σ_m^k that are at the vertex of a neighbourhood homeomorphic with the cone $C(\mathbf{S}^{k-3} * \Sigma_{m-1}^{k-1})$. We can obviously shrink one of these neighbourhoods, fixing the vertex until it lies in the interior of the other as required by Corollary 4.2. This then implies that $\mathbf{S}^{k-3} * \Sigma_{m-1}^{k-1}$ has the same homology as a sphere of dimension $d_m^k - 1$. However, provided $k > m + 1$ and $m \geqslant 3$, Theorem 4.5 shows that Σ_{m-1}^{k-1} has non-zero homology groups that are not shared by a sphere of the same dimension. Hence neither does its $(k - 3)$-fold suspension since for any suspension $S^l(\mathcal{P})$ of a space $\mathcal{P}$ the homology group $H_n(S^l(\mathcal{P}))$ is isomorphic with $H_{n-l}(\mathcal{P})$.   ∎

4.7 LIMITS OF SHAPE SPACES

A further direct consequence of our basic homology theorems concerns the limit of the shape spaces for fixed m and varying k, which may be thought of as the space of shapes of infinite sequences of points in $\mathbb{R}^m$ and arises as follows.

Since Σ_m^k is a subspace of Σ_m^{k+1} for each k we may define the limit

$$\Sigma_m^\infty = \lim_{\rightarrow} \Sigma_m^k$$

to be the union of the $\Sigma_m^k, k = m + 1, m + 2, \ldots$, with the topology determined by requiring a set in Σ_m^∞ to be open if and only if its intersection with every Σ_m^k is open. There is a corresponding inclusion of the essential complex $E_*(\Sigma_m^k)$ in $E_*(\Sigma_m^{k+1})$ and the lowest dimensional cell of the latter that does not appear in the former corresponds to the pattern $(k, m - 1, m - 2, \ldots, 1)$ and so has dimension $d_m^{m+1} + k - m$. In addition, the cells of $E_*(\Sigma_m^k)$ determine cells of the same type in $E_*(\Sigma_m^{k+1})$, except that when m is odd cells corresponding to patterns of type (i) in which $j_1 = k - 1$ become type (iii) in $E_*(\Sigma_m^{k+1})$.

We may define $\Sigma_m^\infty / \iota_m = \lim_{\rightarrow} \Sigma_m^k / \iota_m$ and its topology similarly. Alternatively, we could observe that the involution ι_m has the same effect on a cell to whichever space it is regarded as belonging. Hence, it is well-defined on Σ_m^∞ and consequently the notation we have used for the limit is not misleading. Similar remarks apply to the homology of unoriented shape spaces, with the identical proviso for change of pattern type. Thus, we have shown the following result.

Theorem 4.7. $H_n(\Sigma_m^\infty) \cong H_n(\Sigma_m^k)$ *for* $k \geqslant n - d_m^{m+1} + m$, *when* m *is even, and for* $k > n - d_m^{m+1} + m$, *when* m *is odd.*

Similarly, $H_n(\Sigma_m^\infty / \iota_m) \cong H_n(\Sigma_m^k / \iota_m)$ *for* $k \geqslant n - d_m^{m+1} + 2m$, *when* m *is even, and for* $k > n - d_m^{m+1} + 2m$, *when* m *is odd.*

When $m = 2$ the shape space Σ_m^∞ is well-known to topologists as $\mathbf{CP}^\infty$, infinite dimensional complex projective space, and plays a fundamental role in both algebraic and geometric topology.

CHAPTER 5

The Homology Groups of Shape Spaces

In this chapter we obtain closed formulae for homology, and hence also cohomology, groups of shape spaces. However, these are not particularly transparent or easy to use so, before giving the general results, we shall illustrate the computations in spaces of shapes of configurations in two, three and four dimensions that have a sufficiently small number of vertices. These examples are varied enough to display the different types of behaviour that occur in general and to check our formulae. The results are displayed in a sequence of tables. Note that in each table the value of m, the dimension of the space in which the shapes lie, is fixed, while the value of k, the number of points defining the shape, increases along the horizontal axis, contrary to the arrangement in Tables 1.1 and 1.2. Then, the dimensions of the cells or, equivalently, the degrees of the corresponding generators of the chain complex, or of the resulting homology groups, increase down the vertical axis and remain constant along each row. A generator of a chain complex is indicated just by the pattern that determines it. Where, as will now frequently be the case, all the members of the pattern sequence J are known explicitly we shall write it more concisely without intervening commas or enclosing brackets. Thus, $J = (4, 3, 2, 1)$ would now be written $J = 4321$. This also applies when J is used as a suffix to name a cell or generator.

In Section 5.7 we study a number of ways in which the essential complexes may be decomposed as a direct sum of subcomplexes. This leads to recurrence relations among the various homology groups, which could, in theory at least, allow an inductive computation of all the groups. For the spaces Σ_m^k / ι_m this could be self-contained but any inductive calculation of the homology of the spaces Σ_m^k seems to require prior knowledge of that for the spaces of unoriented shapes.

In Section 5.8 we give the explicit formulae for the homology groups. Since the generators were identified in the previous chapter, all that remains is to count those generators. In addition to binomial coefficients, this counting will require the partition function, which we call $P(i; j; l)$, which is the number of partitions of a set of size i into j parts each of which may be empty but has at most l elements. Some of the formulae are rather too intricate to give directly in terms of these functions, but our results do allow an explicit formula to be obtained for any particular homology group or family of such groups. In the final section we show that the notable feature, akin to duality, that appears in our first examples does indeed hold in general.

5.1 SPACES OF SHAPES IN 2-SPACE

Table 5.1 shows the essential complexes for spaces of oriented shapes in 2-space, where the letters A,B,C,... represent the numbers 10,11,12,.... The cumulative nature of the essential complexes as k increases is clear. Each complex is a subcomplex of its right-hand neighbour and, once a cell occurs in Σ_2^k, it also appears in Σ_2^n for all $n > k$. In all subsequent diagrams we shall use this feature to simplify the picture, by displaying each cell only once: in the complex in which it first appears. The corresponding version of this diagram would just be a single diagonal of entries, comprising the leftmost one in each non-empty row.

In these complexes all the cells are of type (i) and hence carry generators of infinite cyclic summands of the homology. In this case, granted that the only essential cells are the ones displayed, it is already obvious that all boundary maps

Table 5.1   The essential complexes for spaces of shapes in 2-space

deg	Σ_2^3	Σ_2^4	Σ_2^5	Σ_2^6	Σ_2^7	Σ_2^8	Σ_2^9	Σ_2^{10}	Σ_2^{11}	Σ_2^{12}	Σ_2^{13}	Σ_2^{14}	Σ_2^{15}	Σ_2^{16}
2	21	21	21	21	21	21	21	21	21	21	21	21	21	21
3														
4		32	32	32	32	32	32	32	32	32	32	32	32	32
5														
6			43	43	43	43	43	43	43	43	43	43	43	43
7														
8				54	54	54	54	54	54	54	54	54	54	54
9														
10					65	65	65	65	65	65	65	65	65	65
11														
12						76	76	76	76	76	76	76	76	76
13														
14							87	87	87	87	87	87	87	87
15														
16								98	98	98	98	98	98	98
17														
18									A9	A9	A9	A9	A9	A9
19														
20										BA	BA	BA	BA	BA
21														
22											CB	CB	CB	CB
23														
24												DC	DC	DC
25														
26													ED	ED
27														
28														FE

must be zero since, for the only cells that appear, there is never any essential cell in the next lower dimension. We recover the well-known homology groups of the complex projective spaces: $\mathbb{Z}$ in each even dimension up to the real dimension of the space, which for $\Sigma_2^k \cong \mathbf{CP}^{k-2}$ is $2k - 4$.

5.2 SPACES OF SHAPES IN 3-SPACE

In Table 5.2 we show the essential complexes for spaces of shapes in 3-space. In this and all subsequent diagrams the complexes are cumulative: each space is a subcomplex of its right-hand neighbour, and we have adopted the convention of displaying each generator only once: in the complex in which it first appears. Thus, the essential complex for Σ_3^k for $k \geqslant 10$ has three generators in degree eleven: c_{543}^*, c_{732}^* and c_{921}^*. Of these the first always has type (iii) and the second type (ii). However c_{921}^* is of type (i) in Σ_3^{10} but becomes type (iii) on inclusion in Σ_3^k for $k > 10$. Thus, we find that $H_{11}(\Sigma_3^{10}) = \mathbb{Z}_2 \oplus \mathbb{Z}$ and $H_{11}(\Sigma_3^k) = \mathbb{Z}_2 \oplus \mathbb{Z}_2$ for $k > 10$.

Each arrow in the diagram indicates, at its tail, a cell with non-zero boundary and, at its head, a cell that appears in that boundary with coefficient ± 2. In these complexes there is only one such cell in each non-zero boundary. Hence, there is no need to re-base the essential complex in order to read off the homology.

In Table 5.3 we show the resulting homology groups of these shape spaces. This diagram is also mainly cumulative in that each summand $\mathbb{Z}_2$ also exists, in the same degree, in each shape space to the right of its first occurrence. However, there are also generators of infinite cyclic summands, indicated by ∞, which do not persist but on inclusion in the next largest space generate the summand $\mathbb{Z}_2$ noted there. This is the case, for example, in $H_{11}(\Sigma_3^{10})$ and $H_{11}(\Sigma_3^{11})$ calculated above.

Similarly, we see that $H_*(\Sigma_3^{2+2n})$ and $H_*(\Sigma_3^{3+2n})$ each have n summands equal to $\mathbb{Z}$, all of which become $\mathbb{Z}_2$ on inclusion in $H_*(\Sigma_3^{3+2n})$ and $H_*(\Sigma_3^{4+2n})$, respectively. This shows, in particular, that $H_*(\Sigma_3^k)$ is never a direct summand of $H_*(\Sigma_3^{k+1})$ and, hence, that the homology exact sequence of Chapter 3 does not break up into a set of short exact sequences as we might have hoped. We note also that, as we showed directly from the homology exact sequence, each shape space has its non-zero homology group of highest degree isomorphic to $\mathbb{Z}$ and its degree is the same as the dimension of the space itself.

In Table 5.4 we display the cohomology groups of the spaces of shapes in 3-space. These results may be obtained, as indicated in the theorems, by reversing the arrows in the essential complex. Alternatively, they follow directly from the homology computations, using the Universal Coefficient Theorem.

As before, each entry $\mathbb{Z}_2$ in the diagram exists not only at its location but also, in the same degree, in every space to the right of that in which it appears, while the entries '∞' are only relevant to the locations in which they appear. However, unlike the case for the homology, the summand represented by '∞' corresponds

Table 5.2   The essential complexes for spaces of shapes in 3-space

deg	Σ_3^4	Σ_3^5	Σ_3^6	Σ_3^7	Σ_3^8	Σ_3^9	Σ_3^{10}	Σ_3^{11}	Σ_3^{12}	Σ_3^{13}	Σ_3^{14}	Σ_3^{15}	Σ_3^{16}
5	321												
6		421											
7			521										
8		432		621									
9			532		721								
10				632		821							
11			543		732		921						
12				643		832		A21					
13					743		932		B21				
14				654		843		A32		C21			
15					754		943		B32		D21		
16						854		A43		C32		E21	
17					765		954		B43		D32		F21
18						865		A54		C43		E32	
19							965		B54		D43		F32
20						876		A65		C54		E43	
21							976		B65		D54		F43
22								A76		C65		E54	
23							987		B76		D65		F54
24								A87		C76		E65	
25									B87		D76		F65
26								A98		C87		E76	
27									B98		D87		F76
28										C98		E87	
29									BA9		D98		F87
30										CA9		E98	
31											DA9		F98
32										CBA		EA9	
33											DBA		FA9
34												EBA	
35											DCB		FBA
36												ECB	
37													FCB
38												EDC	
39													FDC
40													
41													FED

to a summand $\mathbb{Z}_2$ in the next higher degree cohomology group of the next space in the sequence.

5.3   SPACES OF SHAPES IN 4-SPACE

The essential complexes for these spaces are indicated in Table 5.5. As before, each arrow goes from a cell to one of its non-zero boundary components and every such boundary component is indicated. However, now there are cells with more

Table 5.3 The homology groups of spaces of shapes in 3-space

deg	Σ_3^4	Σ_3^5	Σ_3^6	Σ_3^7	Σ_3^8	Σ_3^9	Σ_3^{10}	Σ_3^{11}	Σ_3^{12}	Σ_3^{13}	Σ_3^{14}	Σ_3^{15}	Σ_3^{16}	Σ_3^{17}
5	∞	$\mathbb{Z}_2$												
6														
7			∞	$\mathbb{Z}_2$										
8		∞	$\mathbb{Z}_2$											
9				∞	$\mathbb{Z}_2$									
10			∞	$\mathbb{Z}_2$										
11		∞	$\mathbb{Z}_2$			∞	$\mathbb{Z}_2$							
12					∞	$\mathbb{Z}_2$								
13				∞	$\mathbb{Z}_2$				∞	$\mathbb{Z}_2$				
14			∞	$\mathbb{Z}_2$				∞	$\mathbb{Z}_2$					
15							∞	$\mathbb{Z}_2$			∞	$\mathbb{Z}_2$		
16						∞	$\mathbb{Z}_2$			∞	$\mathbb{Z}_2$			
17				∞	$\mathbb{Z}_2$				∞	$\mathbb{Z}_2$			∞	$\mathbb{Z}_2$
18								∞	$\mathbb{Z}_2$			∞	$\mathbb{Z}_2$	
19							∞	$\mathbb{Z}_2$			∞	$\mathbb{Z}_2$		
20						∞	$\mathbb{Z}_2$			∞	$\mathbb{Z}_2$			∞
21									∞	$\mathbb{Z}_2$			∞	$\mathbb{Z}_2$
22								∞	$\mathbb{Z}_2$			∞	$\mathbb{Z}_2$	
23							∞	$\mathbb{Z}_2$			∞	$\mathbb{Z}_2$		
24										∞	$\mathbb{Z}_2$			∞
25									∞	$\mathbb{Z}_2$			∞	$\mathbb{Z}_2$
26								∞	$\mathbb{Z}_2$			∞	$\mathbb{Z}_2$	
27											∞	$\mathbb{Z}_2$		
28										∞	$\mathbb{Z}_2$			∞
29									∞	$\mathbb{Z}_2$			∞	$\mathbb{Z}_2$
30												∞	$\mathbb{Z}_2$	
31											∞	$\mathbb{Z}_2$		
32										∞	$\mathbb{Z}_2$			∞
33													∞	$\mathbb{Z}_2$
34												∞	$\mathbb{Z}_2$	
35											∞	$\mathbb{Z}_2$		
36														∞
37													∞	$\mathbb{Z}_2$
38												∞	$\mathbb{Z}_2$	
39														
40														∞
41													∞	$\mathbb{Z}_2$

than one non-zero boundary component. For example, c_{7532}^*, which first appears in Σ_4^8, has boundary $2c_{6532}^* - 2c_{7432}^*$. All boundary coefficients are ± 2 and the sign does not affect the calculation, so the diagram contains all the information we need to read off the homology of the spaces. However, the structure is clearer if we first carry out the change of basis used in the proof of Theorem 4.2. This we do in the next table, Table 5.6, where we show the same essential complexes for spaces of shapes in 4-space but with the new choice of basis. The symbols that are not overlined represent the same basis elements as before; however, $\overline{J}$ indicates

Table 5.4 The cohomology groups of spaces of shapes in 3-space

deg	Σ_3^4	Σ_3^5	Σ_3^6	Σ_3^7	Σ_3^8	Σ_3^9	Σ_3^{10}	Σ_3^{11}	Σ_3^{12}	Σ_3^{13}	Σ_3^{14}	Σ_3^{15}	Σ_3^{16}	Σ_3^{17}
5	∞													
6		$\mathbb{Z}_2$												
7			∞											
8		∞		$\mathbb{Z}_2$										
9			$\mathbb{Z}_2$		∞									
10				∞		$\mathbb{Z}_2$								
11			∞		$\mathbb{Z}_2$		∞							
12				$\mathbb{Z}_2$		∞		$\mathbb{Z}_2$						
13					∞		$\mathbb{Z}_2$		∞					
14				∞		$\mathbb{Z}_2$		∞		$\mathbb{Z}_2$				
15					$\mathbb{Z}_2$		∞		$\mathbb{Z}_2$		∞			
16						∞		$\mathbb{Z}_2$		∞		$\mathbb{Z}_2$		
17					∞		$\mathbb{Z}_2$		∞		$\mathbb{Z}_2$		∞	
18						$\mathbb{Z}_2$		∞		$\mathbb{Z}_2$		∞		$\mathbb{Z}_2$
19							∞		$\mathbb{Z}_2$		∞		$\mathbb{Z}_2$	
20						∞		$\mathbb{Z}_2$		∞		$\mathbb{Z}_2$		∞
21							$\mathbb{Z}_2$		∞		$\mathbb{Z}_2$		∞	
22								∞		$\mathbb{Z}_2$		∞		$\mathbb{Z}_2$
23							∞		$\mathbb{Z}_2$		∞		$\mathbb{Z}_2$	
24								$\mathbb{Z}_2$		∞		$\mathbb{Z}_2$		∞
25									∞		$\mathbb{Z}_2$		∞	
26								∞		$\mathbb{Z}_2$		∞		$\mathbb{Z}_2$
27									$\mathbb{Z}_2$		∞		$\mathbb{Z}_2$	
28										∞		$\mathbb{Z}_2$		∞
29									∞		$\mathbb{Z}_2$		∞	
30										$\mathbb{Z}_2$		∞		$\mathbb{Z}_2$
31											∞		$\mathbb{Z}_2$	
32										∞		$\mathbb{Z}_2$		∞
33											$\mathbb{Z}_2$		∞	
34												∞		$\mathbb{Z}_2$
35											∞		$\mathbb{Z}_2$	
36												$\mathbb{Z}_2$		∞
37													∞	
38												∞		$\mathbb{Z}_2$
39													$\mathbb{Z}_2$	
40														∞
41													∞	

a new basis element to replace the basis element c_j^* previously represented by J. For such J, $2c_j^*$ is one component of the boundary of a cell $c_{j'}^*$, which fact is indicated by an arrow from the symbol J' to the symbol J in Table 5.5. Then, the symbol $\overline{J}$ in Table 5.6 represents half of the full boundary of $c_{j'}^*$, which, for some symbol J'', is $c_j^* \pm c_{j''}^*$ since all boundary components have coefficient ± 2 and in all cases here there are just two of them. Thus, the entry $\overline{7432}$ represents the sum $c_{6532}^* - c_{7432}^*$, twice which is the boundary of c_{7532}^* and which replaces the old basis element c_{7432}^*. The element c_{6532}^* remains in the new basis.

Table 5.5 The essential complexes for spaces of shapes in 4-space

deg	Σ_4^5	Σ_4^6	Σ_4^7	Σ_4^8	Σ_4^9	Σ_4^{10}	Σ_4^{11}
9	4321						
10		5321					
11		5421	6321				
12			6421	7321			
13		5432	6521	7421	8321		
14			6432	7521	8421	9321	
15			6532	7432 7621	8521	9421	A321
16				7532	8621 8432	9521	A421
17			6543	7632	8721 8532	9432 9621	A521
18				7543	8632	9532 9721	A621 A432
19				7643	8543 8732	9632 9821	A721 A532
20					8643	9732 9543	A821 A632
21				7654	8743	9832 9643	A543 A921 A732
22					8654	9743	A643 A832
23					8754	9654 9843	A743 A932
24						9754	A843 A654
25					8765	9854	A943 A754
26						9765	A854
27						9865	A765 A954
28							A865
29						9876	A965
30							A876
31							A976
32							
33							A987

Table 5.6 The re-based essential complexes for spaces of shapes in 4-space

deg	Σ_4^5	Σ_4^6	Σ_4^7	Σ_4^8	Σ_4^9	Σ_4^{10}	Σ_4^{11}
9	4321						
10		5321 ↑					
11		5421	$\overline{6321}$ ↑				
12			6421	7321 ↑			
13	5432		6521	7421	$\overline{8321}$ ↑		
14			6432 ↑	7521 ↑	8421	9321 ↑	
15			6532	$\overline{7432}$ ↑ 7621	$\overline{8521}$ ↑	9421	$\overline{A321}$
16				7532	8621 8432 ↑	9521 ↑	A421
17			6543	7632	8721 8532	$\overline{9432}$ ↑ 9621	$\overline{A521}$ ↑
18				7543 ↑	8632 ↑	9532 9721 ↑	A621 A432 ↑
19				7643	$\overline{8543}$ ↑ 8732	$\overline{9632}$ ↑ 9821	$\overline{A721}$ ↑ A532
20					8643	9732 9543 ↑	A821 A632 ↑
21				7654	8743	9832 9643	$\overline{A543}$ ↑ A921 A732 ↑
22					8654 ↑	9743 ↑	A643 A832 ↑
23					8754	$\overline{9654}$ ↑ 9843	$\overline{A743}$ ↑ A932
24						9754	A843 A654 ↑
25					8765	9854	A943 A754 ↑
26						9765 ↑	A854 ↑
27						9865	$\overline{A765}$ ↑ A954
28							A865
29						9876	A965
30							A876 ↑
31							A976
32							
33							A987

This choice ensures that all the boundary maps with respect to the new basis are either zero or map to twice another new basis element. The proof that the new elements do form a basis follows from the facts that each new element is the sum of an old one, together with, plus or minus, one from a previous space in the sequence, and that we can always take the sum or difference of two existing basis elements to replace one of them in a new basis. For example, in $E_*(\Sigma_4^9)$ we can form $\overline{8543}$, then $\overline{8521}$ and $\overline{8321}$, then move on to $\overline{7432}$ and finally $\overline{6321}$. Working thus in decreasing degree of the homology and then decreasing value of k we ensure that we never change an old basis element that we may need later to add to another to form a new basis element.

More generally for larger m, when there may be more than one component of the boundary that does not appear in a previous space of the sequence, we take as 'foundation' for the new basis element that component of the boundary that is determined by the largest symbol with respect to their natural ordering. Then, since all components $c_{J'}^*$ of ∂c_J^* have $J' < J$, forming c_J^* in decreasing order of J will not lead us into any trouble.

Moreover, because of the choices of new basis elements that we have made, all the revised boundary maps in Table 5.6 are vertical, so this choice of bases makes it clear that $E_*(\Sigma_4^k)$ is a direct summand, *qua* chain complex, of $E_*(\Sigma_4^{k+1})$. In particular, the type of the generator does not change on inclusion in the next larger shape space. This phenomenon also occurs for all other even values of m, although never for odd values as we have already seen for the case $m = 3$. The reason is that the boundary formula ensures that, for m even and any J with leading entry k, the boundary ∂c_J^* will have at least one component $c_{J'}^*$ for which the leading entry of J' is also k, whereas for m odd there will always be J, corresponding to a basis element of the essential complex, for which this is not the case.

The homology groups of spaces of shapes in 4-space are shown in Table 5.7. It includes most of those for the next five spaces whose chain complexes are not displayed in Tables 5.5 and 5.6. As usual, the diagram is cumulative. In this case, the infinite cyclic groups also persist in the next space, so are denoted by $\mathbb{Z}$, rather than ∞, to signify this fact. For example,

$$H_{17}(\Sigma_4^{13}) = \mathbb{Z} \oplus \mathbb{Z} \oplus \mathbb{Z} \oplus \mathbb{Z}_2 \oplus \mathbb{Z}_2 \oplus \mathbb{Z}_2.$$

The last three spaces also have non-zero groups in degree greater than 41, which are not shown in the table.

Corresponding to the direct sum decomposition of the essential complexes, we see that the homology $H_*(\Sigma_4^k)$ is a direct summand of $H_*(\Sigma_4^{k+1})$. It follows that the exact homology sequence of Chapter 3 must split (see the Appendix) and that the complementary summand must be isomorphic with $H_*(\Sigma_4^k)$ suspended k times. This fact is visible in the table. For example, that part of $H_*(\Sigma_4^9)$ that is not the image of $H_*(\Sigma_4^8)$ lies in the column under the symbol Σ_4^9. From Table 5.3 we see that this is identical with the homology of Σ_3^8, except that all the degrees have been increased by eight. This suspension isomorphism onto the complementary summand is perhaps even clearer at the level of the essential complex where it is

Table 5.7 The homology groups of spaces of shapes in 4-space

deg	Σ_4^5	Σ_4^6	Σ_4^7	Σ_4^8	Σ_4^9	Σ_4^{10}	Σ_4^{11}	Σ_4^{12}	Σ_4^{13}	Σ_4^{14}	Σ_4^{15}	Σ_4^{16}
9	$\mathbb{Z}$											
10		$\mathbb{Z}_2$										
11			$\mathbb{Z}_2$									
12				$\mathbb{Z}_2$								
13		$\mathbb{Z}$	$\mathbb{Z}$		$\mathbb{Z}_2$							
14			$\mathbb{Z}_2$	$\mathbb{Z}_2$		$\mathbb{Z}_2$						
15				$\mathbb{Z}_2$	$\mathbb{Z}_2$		$\mathbb{Z}_2$					
16					$\mathbb{Z}_2$	$\mathbb{Z}_2$		$\mathbb{Z}_2$				
17			$\mathbb{Z}$	$\mathbb{Z}$	$\mathbb{Z}$	$\mathbb{Z}_2$	$\mathbb{Z}_2$		$\mathbb{Z}_2$			
18				$\mathbb{Z}_2$	$\mathbb{Z}_2$	$\mathbb{Z}_2$	$\mathbb{Z}_2$	$\mathbb{Z}_2$		$\mathbb{Z}_2$		
19					$\mathbb{Z}_2$	$\mathbb{Z}_2$	$\mathbb{Z}_2$	$\mathbb{Z}_2$	$\mathbb{Z}_2$		$\mathbb{Z}_2$	
20						$\mathbb{Z}_2$	$\mathbb{Z}_2$	$\mathbb{Z}_2$	$\mathbb{Z}_2$	$\mathbb{Z}_2$		$\mathbb{Z}_2$
21				$\mathbb{Z}$	$\mathbb{Z}$	$\mathbb{Z}$	$\mathbb{Z} \oplus \mathbb{Z}_2$	$\mathbb{Z}_2$	$\mathbb{Z}_2$	$\mathbb{Z}_2$	$\mathbb{Z}_2$	
22					$\mathbb{Z}_2$	$\mathbb{Z}_2$	$\mathbb{Z}_2$	$\mathbb{Z}_2 \oplus \mathbb{Z}_2$	$\mathbb{Z}_2$	$\mathbb{Z}_2$	$\mathbb{Z}_2$	$\mathbb{Z}_2$
23						$\mathbb{Z}_2$	$\mathbb{Z}_2$	$\mathbb{Z}_2$	$\mathbb{Z}_2 \oplus \mathbb{Z}_2$	$\mathbb{Z}_2$	$\mathbb{Z}_2$	$\mathbb{Z}_2$
24							$\mathbb{Z}_2$	$\mathbb{Z}_2$	$\mathbb{Z}_2$	$\mathbb{Z}_2 \oplus \mathbb{Z}_2$	$\mathbb{Z}_2$	$\mathbb{Z}_2$
25					$\mathbb{Z}$	$\mathbb{Z}$	$\mathbb{Z}$	$\mathbb{Z} \oplus \mathbb{Z}_2$	$\mathbb{Z} \oplus \mathbb{Z}_2$	$\mathbb{Z}_2$	$\mathbb{Z}_2 \oplus \mathbb{Z}_2$	$\mathbb{Z}_2$
26						$\mathbb{Z}_2$	$\mathbb{Z}_2$	$\mathbb{Z}_2$	$\mathbb{Z}_2 \oplus \mathbb{Z}_2$	$\mathbb{Z}_2 \oplus \mathbb{Z}_2$	$\mathbb{Z}_2$	$\mathbb{Z}_2 \oplus \mathbb{Z}_2$
27							$\mathbb{Z}_2$	$\mathbb{Z}_2$	$\mathbb{Z}_2$	$\mathbb{Z}_2 \oplus \mathbb{Z}_2$	$\mathbb{Z}_2 \oplus \mathbb{Z}_2$	$\mathbb{Z}_2$
28								$\mathbb{Z}_2$	$\mathbb{Z}_2$	$\mathbb{Z}_2$	$\mathbb{Z}_2 \oplus \mathbb{Z}_2$	$\mathbb{Z}_2 \oplus \mathbb{Z}_2$
29						$\mathbb{Z}$	$\mathbb{Z}$	$\mathbb{Z}$	$\mathbb{Z} \oplus \mathbb{Z}_2$	$\mathbb{Z} \oplus \mathbb{Z}_2$	$\mathbb{Z} \oplus \mathbb{Z}_2$	$\mathbb{Z} \oplus \mathbb{Z}_2$
30							$\mathbb{Z}_2$	$\mathbb{Z}_2$	$\mathbb{Z}_2$	$\mathbb{Z}_2 \oplus \mathbb{Z}_2$	$\mathbb{Z}_2 \oplus \mathbb{Z}_2$	$\mathbb{Z}_2 \oplus \mathbb{Z}_2$
31								$\mathbb{Z}_2$	$\mathbb{Z}_2$	$\mathbb{Z}_2$	$\mathbb{Z}_2 \oplus \mathbb{Z}_2$	$\mathbb{Z}_2 \oplus \mathbb{Z}_2$
32									$\mathbb{Z}_2$	$\mathbb{Z}_2$	$\mathbb{Z}_2$	$\mathbb{Z}_2 \oplus \mathbb{Z}_2$
33							$\mathbb{Z}$	$\mathbb{Z}$	$\mathbb{Z}$	$\mathbb{Z} \oplus \mathbb{Z}_2$	$\mathbb{Z} \oplus \mathbb{Z}_2$	$\mathbb{Z} \oplus \mathbb{Z}_2$
34								$\mathbb{Z}_2$	$\mathbb{Z}_2$	$\mathbb{Z}_2$	$\mathbb{Z}_2 \oplus \mathbb{Z}_2$	$\mathbb{Z}_2 \oplus \mathbb{Z}_2$
35									$\mathbb{Z}_2$	$\mathbb{Z}_2$	$\mathbb{Z}_2$	$\mathbb{Z}_2 \oplus \mathbb{Z}_2$
36										$\mathbb{Z}_2$	$\mathbb{Z}_2$	$\mathbb{Z}_2$
37								$\mathbb{Z}$	$\mathbb{Z}$	$\mathbb{Z}$	$\mathbb{Z} \oplus \mathbb{Z}_2$	$\mathbb{Z} \oplus \mathbb{Z}_2$
38									$\mathbb{Z}_2$	$\mathbb{Z}_2$	$\mathbb{Z}_2$	$\mathbb{Z}_2 \oplus \mathbb{Z}_2$
39										$\mathbb{Z}_2$	$\mathbb{Z}_2$	$\mathbb{Z}_2$
40											$\mathbb{Z}_2$	$\mathbb{Z}_2$
41									$\mathbb{Z}$	$\mathbb{Z}$	$\mathbb{Z}$	$\mathbb{Z} \oplus \mathbb{Z}_2$

achieved by prefixing a symbol that represents an essential cell in Σ_3^8 by an '8' to produce the symbol for the corresponding cell in Σ_4^9. However, in appropriate cases, the new symbol is an overlined one, whereas that in Σ_3^8 would not have been.

The cohomology groups differ from the homology groups only in that each summand isomorphic with $\mathbb{Z}_2$ appears in the next higher degree precisely as was the case for the cohomology of the spaces Σ_3^k, and so we have not shown them.

5.4 SPACES OF UNORIENTED SHAPES IN 2-SPACE

The essential complexes for spaces of unoriented shapes in 2-space are shown in Table 5.8. Unlike the oriented case, the shapes of configurations in 2-space already produce cells with more than one non-zero boundary component.

Table 5.8 The essential complexes for spaces of unoriented shapes in 2-space

deg	Σ_2^4/ι_2	Σ_2^5/ι_2	Σ_2^6/ι_2	Σ_2^7/ι_2	Σ_2^8/ι_2	Σ_2^9/ι_2	Σ_2^{10}/ι_2	Σ_2^{11}/ι_2	Σ_2^{12}/ι_2	Σ_2^{13}/ι_2	Σ_2^{14}/ι_2	Σ_2^{15}/ι_2	Σ_2^{16}/ι_2
4	32												
5		42											
6		43	52										
7			53	62									
8			54	63	72								
9				64	73	82							
10				65	74	83	92						
11					75	84	93	A2					
12					76	85	94	A3	B2				
13						86	95	A4	B3	C2			
14						87	96	A5	B4	C3	D2		
15							97	A6	B5	C4	D3	E2	
16							98	A7	B6	C5	D4	E3	F2
17								A8	B7	C6	D5	E4	F3
18								A9	B8	C7	D6	E5	F4
19									B9	C8	D7	E6	F5
20									BA	C9	D8	E7	F6
21										CA	D9	E8	F7
22										CB	DA	E9	F8
23											DB	EA	F9
24											DC	EB	FA
25												EC	FB
26												ED	FC
27													FD
28													FE

However, as in Σ_4^k, the change of basis will remove the diagonal components since, for each cell in $E_*(\Sigma_2^k/\iota_2)\backslash E_*(\Sigma_2^{k-1}/\iota_2)$ with more than one boundary component, at least one of those components is also in $E_*(\Sigma_2^k/\iota_2)\backslash E_*(\Sigma_2^{k-1}/\iota_2)$ and so as before we can choose the new basis elements so that all the non-zero boundary maps become vertical. These re-based essential complexes for spaces of unoriented shapes in 2-space are shown in Table 5.9. As before, the new basis elements, where different from the old, are indicated by an overline. The fact that no 'diagonal' boundaries are now required means that the essential complex $E_*(\Sigma_2^k/\iota_2)$ is a direct summand of $E_*(\Sigma_2^{k+1}/\iota_2)$ and so the corresponding homology group $H_*(\Sigma_2^k/\iota_2)$ will be a direct summand of $H_*(\Sigma_2^{k+1}/\iota_2)$. This feature will occur in $H_*(\Sigma_m^k/\iota_m)$ for all even m and all k.

Table 5.10 shows the resulting homology groups of spaces of unoriented shapes in 2-space. As usual, the diagram is cumulative. The zeros indicate homology groups that are zero and whose degree is equal to the dimension of the space: a phenomenon that did not occur for spaces of oriented shapes. Note also that here again the infinite cyclic groups are indicated by $\mathbb{Z}$ since they do persist as infinite groups in the next space.

Since the cohomology is similar, with each $\mathbb{Z}_2$ appearing in the next higher degree, the spaces with top homology group zero have top cohomology group, that is, that in the dimension of the shape space itself, equal to $\mathbb{Z}_2$, whereas the other spaces, as was the case for all spaces of oriented shapes, have their top cohomology group equal to $\mathbb{Z}$.

5.5   SPACES OF UNORIENTED SHAPES IN 3-SPACE

We move straight to the re-based essential complexes for spaces of unoriented shapes in 3-space, which are shown in Table 5.11. As before, the overlined basis elements represent generators c_J that have been replaced by $(1/2)\partial c_{sJ}$. Here, for $J = (j_1, j_2, j_3)$, sJ will be $(j_1, j_2, j_3 + 1)$ so that such replacements can only occur when $j_2 > j_3 + 1$. Thus, the generator at the head of an arrow is half the boundary of that at the tail. All the revised boundaries are vertical. Note, however, that the change of basis does not remove all the 'diagonal' boundaries. Thus, $E_*(\Sigma_3^{2n-1}/\iota_3)$ cannot be a direct summand of $E_*(\Sigma_3^{2n}/\iota_3)$ since the homology is not a direct summand. On the other hand, $E_*(\Sigma_3^{2n}/\iota_3)$ is a direct summand of $E_*(\Sigma_3^{2n+1}/\iota_3)$.

The homology of these spaces of unoriented shapes is displayed in Table 5.12. As above, the summands $\mathbb{Z}_2$ persist in each space to the right and '∞' represents an infinite cyclic summand $\mathbb{Z}$, which, on inclusion in the next space, becomes the group, or one of the groups, $\mathbb{Z}_2$ indicated there. Thus, $H_{18}(\Sigma_3^{12}/\iota_3)$ is a direct sum of six copies of $\mathbb{Z}_2$. In general, $H_*(\Sigma_3^{3+2n}/\iota_3)$ has n summands equal to $\mathbb{Z}$, all of which become $\mathbb{Z}_2$ on inclusion in $H_*(\Sigma_3^{4+2n}/\iota_3)$, so that $H_*(\Sigma_3^{3+2n}/\iota_3)$ cannot be a direct summand of $H_*(\Sigma_3^{4+2n}/\iota_3)$. Similarly, for all odd m, $H_*(\Sigma_m^{m+2n}/\iota_m)$ will not be a direct summand of $H_*(\Sigma_m^{m+2n+1}/\iota_m)$. On the other hand, we can see

Table 5.9   The re-based essential complexes for spaces of unoriented shapes in 2-space

deg	Σ_2^4/ι_2	Σ_2^5/ι_2	Σ_2^6/ι_2	Σ_2^7/ι_2	Σ_2^8/ι_2	Σ_2^9/ι_2	Σ_2^{10}/ι_2	Σ_2^{11}/ι_2	Σ_2^{12}/ι_2	Σ_2^{13}/ι_2	Σ_2^{14}/ι_2	Σ_2^{15}/ι_2	Σ_2^{16}/ι_2
4	32												
5		42											
6		43	$\overline{52}$										
7			53	62									
8			54	63	$\overline{72}$								
9				64	73	82							
10				65	$\overline{74}$	83	$\overline{92}$						
11					75	84	93	A2					
12					76	85	$\overline{94}$	A3	$\overline{B2}$				
13						86	95	A4	B3	C2			
14						87	$\overline{96}$	A5	B4	C3	$\overline{D2}$		
15							97	A6	B5	C4	D3	E2	
16							98	A7	$\overline{B6}$	C5	$\overline{D4}$	E3	$\overline{F2}$
17								A8	B7	C6	D5	E4	F3
18								A9	$\overline{B8}$	C7	$\overline{D6}$	E5	$\overline{F4}$
19									B9	C8	D7	E6	F5
20									BA	C9	$\overline{D8}$	E7	$\overline{F6}$
21										CA	D9	E8	F7
22										CB	$\overline{DA}$	E9	$\overline{F8}$
23											DB	EA	F9
24											DC	EB	$\overline{FA}$
25												EC	FB
26												ED	$\overline{FC}$
27													FD
28													FE

Table 5.10 The homology of spaces of unoriented shapes in 2-space

deg	Σ_2^4/ι_2	Σ_2^5/ι_2	Σ_2^6/ι_2	Σ_2^7/ι_2	Σ_2^8/ι_2	Σ_2^9/ι_2	Σ_2^{10}/ι_2	Σ_2^{11}/ι_2	Σ_2^{12}/ι_2	Σ_2^{13}/ι_2	Σ_2^{14}/ι_2	Σ_2^{15}/ι_2	Σ_2^{16}/ι_2
4	$\mathbb{Z}$												
5		$\mathbb{Z}_2$											
6		0	$\mathbb{Z}_2$										
7				$\mathbb{Z}_2$									
8			$\mathbb{Z}$		$\mathbb{Z}_2$								
9				$\mathbb{Z}_2$		$\mathbb{Z}_2$							
10				0	$\mathbb{Z}_2$		$\mathbb{Z}_2$						
11						$\mathbb{Z}_2$		$\mathbb{Z}_2$					
12					$\mathbb{Z}$		$\mathbb{Z}_2$		$\mathbb{Z}_2$				
13						$\mathbb{Z}_2$		$\mathbb{Z}_2$		$\mathbb{Z}_2$			
14						0	$\mathbb{Z}_2$		$\mathbb{Z}_2$		$\mathbb{Z}_2$		
15								$\mathbb{Z}_2$		$\mathbb{Z}_2$		$\mathbb{Z}_2$	
16							$\mathbb{Z}$		$\mathbb{Z}_2$		$\mathbb{Z}_2$		$\mathbb{Z}_2$
17								$\mathbb{Z}_2$		$\mathbb{Z}_2$		$\mathbb{Z}_2$	
18								0	$\mathbb{Z}_2$		$\mathbb{Z}_2$		$\mathbb{Z}_2$
19										$\mathbb{Z}_2$		$\mathbb{Z}_2$	
20									$\mathbb{Z}$		$\mathbb{Z}_2$		$\mathbb{Z}_2$
21										$\mathbb{Z}_2$		$\mathbb{Z}_2$	
22										0	$\mathbb{Z}_2$		$\mathbb{Z}_2$
23												$\mathbb{Z}_2$	
24											$\mathbb{Z}$		$\mathbb{Z}_2$
25												$\mathbb{Z}_2$	
26												0	$\mathbb{Z}_2$
27													
28													$\mathbb{Z}$

that each homology group $H_*(\Sigma_3^{2+2n}/\iota_3)$ *is* a direct summand of $H_*(\Sigma_3^{3+2n}/\iota_3)$ since all summands of the former are $\mathbb{Z}_2$, which map to isomorphic summands of the latter.

There is a homology exact sequence for the homology groups of spaces of unoriented shapes analogous to, and easily derived from, that for spaces of oriented shapes and we see here that, once again, the complementary homology groups are the 2*n*th suspension of those of $H_*(\Sigma_2^{2+2n}/\iota_2)$. Note, however, that the suspension of an element of infinite order in $H_*(\Sigma_2^{2+2n}/\iota_2)$ does not persist with infinite order in $H_*(\Sigma_3^{4+2n}/\iota_3)$, although the original element did so persist into $H_*(\Sigma_2^{3+2n}/\iota_2)$. This, in fact, is precisely what prevents $H_*(\Sigma_3^{3+2n}/\iota_3)$ being a direct summand of $H_*(\Sigma_3^{4+2n}/\iota_3)$. Similar results hold for all odd m.

As before, the zeros indicate 'missing' groups in degree equal to the dimension of the space and the corresponding cohomology groups are all equal to $\mathbb{Z}_2$.

5.6 SPACES OF UNORIENTED SHAPES IN 4-SPACE

For our final examples we calculate the homology of spaces of unoriented shapes in 4-space. Again, we start from the re-based essential complexes, which

Table 5.11   The re-based essential complexes for spaces of unoriented shapes in 3-space

deg	Σ_3^5/ι_3	Σ_3^6/ι_3	Σ_3^7/ι_3	Σ_3^8/ι_3	Σ_3^9/ι_3	Σ_3^{10}/ι_3	Σ_3^{11}/ι_3
8	432						
9		532					
10		542	632				
11		543	642	732			
12			643 $\overline{652}$	$\overline{742}$	832		
13			653	$\overline{752}$ 743	842	932	
14			654	753 762	843 $\overline{852}$	$\overline{942}$	A32
15				754 763	862 853	$\overline{952}$ 943	A42
16				764	863 $\overline{872}$ 854	953 $\overline{962}$	A43 $\overline{A52}$
17				765	864 873	954 963 $\overline{972}$	A62 A53
18					865 $\overline{874}$	964 982 973	A63 A54 $\overline{A72}$
19					875	965 983 $\overline{974}$	A64 A82 A73
20					876	984 975	A65 A83 $\overline{A92}$ $\overline{A74}$
21						976 985	A84 A93 A75
22						986	A76 A85 $\overline{A94}$
23						987	A86 A95
24							A87 $\overline{A96}$
25							A97
26							A98

are displayed, for spaces up to and including Σ_4^{10}/ι_4, in Table 5.13. The resulting homology groups are in Table 5.14, as well as those for Σ_4^{11}/ι_4 for whose essential complex there was insufficient space in Table 5.13: it has six cells in each of the dimensions twenty-four to twenty-seven. In this case, as for Σ_2^k/ι_2, all the boundary maps are vertical in the re-based essential complex and so each $H_n(\Sigma_4^k/\iota_4)$ is a direct summand of $H_n(\Sigma_4^{k+1}/\iota_4)$. The complementary summand is equal to $H_{n-k}(\Sigma_3^k/\iota_3)$. This can easily be seen from Tables 5.12 and 5.14. The

Table 5.12 The homology of spaces of unoriented shapes in 3-space

deg	Σ_3^5/ι_3	Σ_3^6/ι_3	Σ_3^7/ι_3	Σ_3^8/ι_3	Σ_3^9/ι_3	Σ_3^{10}/ι_3	Σ_3^{11}/ι_3	Σ_3^{12}/ι_3
8	∞	$\mathbb{Z}_2$						
9								
10		$\mathbb{Z}_2$	∞	$\mathbb{Z}_2$				
11		0	$\mathbb{Z}_2$					
12		$\mathbb{Z}_2$		$\mathbb{Z}_2$	∞	$\mathbb{Z}_2$		
13				$\mathbb{Z}_2$	$\mathbb{Z}_2$			
14			∞	$\mathbb{Z}_2 \oplus \mathbb{Z}_2$	$\mathbb{Z}_2$	$\mathbb{Z}_2$	∞	$\mathbb{Z}_2$
15					$\mathbb{Z}_2$	$\mathbb{Z}_2$	$\mathbb{Z}_2$	
16				$\mathbb{Z}_2$	∞ $\oplus \mathbb{Z}_2$	$\mathbb{Z}_2 \oplus \mathbb{Z}_2$	$\mathbb{Z}_2$	$\mathbb{Z}_2$
17				0	$\mathbb{Z}_2$	$\mathbb{Z}_2$	$\mathbb{Z}_2$	$\mathbb{Z}_2$
18					$\mathbb{Z}_2$	$\mathbb{Z}_2 \oplus \mathbb{Z}_2$	∞ $\oplus \mathbb{Z}_2$	$\mathbb{Z}_2 \oplus \mathbb{Z}_2$
19					$\mathbb{Z}_2$	$\mathbb{Z}_2 \oplus \mathbb{Z}_2$	$\mathbb{Z}_2$	
20					∞	$\mathbb{Z}_2 \oplus \mathbb{Z}_2$	$\mathbb{Z}_2 \oplus \mathbb{Z}_2$	$\mathbb{Z}_2 \oplus \mathbb{Z}_2$
21							$\mathbb{Z}_2$	$\mathbb{Z}_2 \oplus \mathbb{Z}_2$
22						$\mathbb{Z}_2$	∞ $\oplus \mathbb{Z}_2$	$\mathbb{Z}_2 \oplus \mathbb{Z}_2 \oplus \mathbb{Z}_2$
23						0	$\mathbb{Z}_2$	$\mathbb{Z}_2$
24							$\mathbb{Z}_2$	$\mathbb{Z}_2 \oplus \mathbb{Z}_2$
25								$\mathbb{Z}_2$
26							∞	$\mathbb{Z}_2 \oplus \mathbb{Z}_2$
27								
28								$\mathbb{Z}_2$
29								0

reason is clear from a comparison of Tables 5.11 and 5.13. For example, the list of additional generators in the essential complex for Σ_4^{10}/ι_4, which were not already in the essential complex for Σ_4^9/ι_4, are in bijective correspondence with the entire set of generators in the essential complex for Σ_3^9/ι_3, the correspondence being achieved by preceding the pattern for a generator in Σ_3^9/ι_3 by a '9' to obtain the pattern for the corresponding generator in Σ_4^{10}/ι_4. This correspondence respects boundary maps and, since those resulting in Σ_4^{10}/ι_4 are vertical, the stated isomorphism of homology groups follows. This is a special case of the first theorem in the next section.

5.7 DECOMPOSING THE ESSENTIAL COMPLEXES

In this section we continue our analysis of the chain complexes for shape spaces by further decomposing the essential subcomplexes in ways that lead to relationships between the homology groups of two or more different spaces. First, we

Table 5.13 The re-based essential complexes for spaces of unoriented shapes in 4-space

deg	Σ_4^6/ι_4	Σ_4^7/ι_4	Σ_4^8/ι_4	Σ_4^9/ι_4	Σ_4^{10}/ι_4
13	5432				
14		6432			
15		6532	$\overline{7432}$		
16		6542	7532	8432	
17		6543	$\overline{7542}$ 7632	8532	$\overline{9432}$
18			7543 7642	8542 8632	9532
19			$\overline{7652}$ 7643	8543 8732 8642	$\overline{9542}$ $\overline{9632}$
20			7653	$\overline{8652}$ $\overline{8742}$ 8643	9543 9732 $\overline{9642}$
21			7654	8653 8743 $\overline{8752}$	9652 9742 9832 9643
22				8654 8762 8753	9653 9743 $\overline{9752}$ 9842
23				8754 8763	$\overline{9654}$ $\overline{9762}$ $\overline{9852}$ 9753 9843
24				8764	9754 9763 9853 9862
25				8765	$\overline{9764}$ $\overline{9872}$ 9854 9863
26					9765 9873 9864
27					$\overline{9874}$ 9865
28					9875
29					9876

look at the isomorphisms, which are the result of the splitting, in special cases, of the homology exact sequence for shape spaces:

$$H_{n-k+1}\binom{k}{m-1} \xrightarrow{\; d_* \;} H_n\binom{k}{m} \xrightarrow{\; \imath_* \;} H_n\binom{k+1}{m}$$

$$\xrightarrow{\; \jmath_* \;} H_{n-k}\binom{k}{m-1} \xrightarrow{\; d_* \;} \cdots .$$

In fact, the sequence splits in nearly all cases: there are just two circumstances, m odd for Σ_m^k and m and k both odd for Σ_m^k/ι_m, when it does not split and

Table 5.14 The homology of spaces of unoriented shapes in 4-space

deg	Σ_4^6/ι_4	Σ_4^7/ι_4	Σ_4^8/ι_4	Σ_4^9/ι_4	Σ_4^{10}/ι_4	Σ_4^{11}/ι_4
13	$\mathbb{Z}$					
14		$\mathbb{Z}_2$				
15			$\mathbb{Z}_2$			
16		$\mathbb{Z}_2$		$\mathbb{Z}_2$		
17			$\mathbb{Z}\oplus\mathbb{Z}_2$		$\mathbb{Z}_2$	
18			$\mathbb{Z}_2$	$\mathbb{Z}_2\oplus\mathbb{Z}_2$		$\mathbb{Z}_2$
19			$\mathbb{Z}_2$	$\mathbb{Z}_2$	$\mathbb{Z}_2\oplus\mathbb{Z}_2$	
20				$\mathbb{Z}_2\oplus\mathbb{Z}_2$	$\mathbb{Z}_2$	$\mathbb{Z}_2\oplus\mathbb{Z}_2$
21			$\mathbb{Z}$	$\mathbb{Z}_2$	$\mathbb{Z}\oplus\mathbb{Z}_2\oplus\mathbb{Z}_2$	$\mathbb{Z}_2$
22				$\mathbb{Z}_2\oplus\mathbb{Z}_2$	$\mathbb{Z}_2\oplus\mathbb{Z}_2$	$\mathbb{Z}_2\oplus\mathbb{Z}_2\oplus\mathbb{Z}_2$
23					$\mathbb{Z}_2\oplus\mathbb{Z}_2\oplus\mathbb{Z}_2$	$\mathbb{Z}_2\oplus\mathbb{Z}_2$
24				$\mathbb{Z}_2$	$\mathbb{Z}_2$	$\mathbb{Z}_2\oplus\mathbb{Z}_2\oplus\mathbb{Z}_2\oplus\mathbb{Z}_2$
25					$\mathbb{Z}\oplus\mathbb{Z}_2\oplus\mathbb{Z}_2$	$\mathbb{Z}_2\oplus\mathbb{Z}_2$
26					$\mathbb{Z}_2$	$\mathbb{Z}_2\oplus\mathbb{Z}_2\oplus\mathbb{Z}_2\oplus\mathbb{Z}_2$
27					$\mathbb{Z}_2$	$\mathbb{Z}_2\oplus\mathbb{Z}_2$
28						$\mathbb{Z}_2\oplus\mathbb{Z}_2\oplus\mathbb{Z}_2$
29					$\mathbb{Z}$	$\mathbb{Z}_2$
30						$\mathbb{Z}_2\oplus\mathbb{Z}_2$
31						
32						$\mathbb{Z}_2$

so prevents the homology groups being particularly simple to compute. It also splits in all cases when we take the homology with $\mathbb{Z}_2$-coefficients. The results for integral homology are illustrated in the special cases we discussed in the previous sections, from which it is also clear that they are the best possible. To write them uniformly for all n we take the reduced homology groups in negative degrees to be zero.

Theorem 5.1. *For all $m \geqslant 1$, k and $n \geqslant 0$ there is an isomorphism of reduced homology groups*

$$H_n \binom{k+1}{2m} \cong H_n \binom{k}{2m} \oplus H_{n-k} \binom{k}{2m-1}.$$

Proof. The inclusions $\imath : \Sigma_m^k \hookrightarrow \Sigma_m^{k+1}$ and $\imath : \Sigma_m^k/\iota_m \hookrightarrow \Sigma_m^{k+1}/\iota_m$ induce homomorphisms

$$\imath_* : E_n \binom{k}{m} \longrightarrow E_n \binom{k+1}{m},$$

which provide an isomorphism of the essential complex $E_*\binom{k}{m}$ onto a direct summand of $E_*\binom{k+1}{m}$. This follows from the bases of the essential complexes that we used above to elicit the homology and cohomology generators, since each of the new basis elements that does not lie in $E_n\binom{k}{m}$ has no boundary component in $E_{n-1}\binom{k}{m}$. For, in both cases, the elements of type (i) have no boundary, and the correspondence between those of types (ii) and (iii) preserves the first entry in the pattern and only $\partial_1 J$ can produce components in $E_{n-1}\binom{k}{m}$. Thus, those basis elements not in the image of the complex $E_*\binom{k}{m}$ form a sub-chain-complex that is a direct complement of it in $E_*\binom{k+1}{m}$.

However, the homomorphism $\imath_*$ induces, in each case, the similarly labelled homomorphism that occurs in the exact homology sequence. Then, since $\imath_*$ injects, each d_* is zero and we have the short exact sequence:

$$0 \longrightarrow H_n\binom{k}{m} \xrightarrow{\imath_*} H_n\binom{k+1}{m} \xrightarrow{J_*} H_{n-k}\binom{k}{m-1} \longrightarrow 0$$

for each value of n. This shows that the homology of the direct complement to $E_*\binom{k}{m}$ is the same as $H_{*-k}\binom{k}{m-1}$, and we have the result. ∎

The above result only has content, of course, if $k \geqslant 2m$ for the case of Σ_m^k and $k \geqslant 2m + 1$ for Σ_m^k/ι_m. Similarly, we have the following results, which again have content only for the analogous values of k.

Theorem 5.2. *For all $m \geqslant 2$, k and $n \geqslant 0$ there are isomorphisms of reduced homology groups*

(i) $H_n(\Sigma_m^{2k+1}/\iota_m) \cong H_n(\Sigma_m^{2k}/\iota_m) \oplus H_{n-k}(\Sigma_{m-1}^{2k}/\iota_{m-1})$,

(ii) $H_n\binom{k+1}{m};\mathbb{Z}_2 \cong H_n\binom{k}{m};\mathbb{Z}_2 \oplus H_{n-k}\binom{k}{m-1};\mathbb{Z}_2$.

Proof. In the case of Σ_m^{2k+1}/ι_m, the $c_{\partial_1 J}$ component of the boundary is zero and, as explained in the proof of Theorem 5.1, that is the only possible obstruction to the direct sum decomposition.

In all cases, the boundary components have coefficients ± 2 so, in the chain complex for computing $\mathbb{Z}_2$-homology where all coefficients are evaluated in $\mathbb{Z}_2$, all the boundary maps are zero for either type of space. Thus, once again, the complex $E_*\binom{k}{m}$ maps to a direct summand of $E_*\binom{k+1}{m}$ and the rest of the proof is as before. ∎

Note that, since the isomorphisms in Theorem 5.1 and part (i) of this theorem are valid for all n, the Universal Coefficient Theorems ensure that the isomorphisms hold for reduced homology groups with any coefficients. So, part (ii) of this theorem is really only filling in the cases for $\mathbb{Z}_2$-coefficients that those theorems omitted. There is no similar extension for homology with coefficients in $\mathbb{Q}$, since the summands there are generated by elements of type (i), which, in the excluded cases, are precisely those that prevent the direct sum decomposition by changing their nature on inclusion in the next space.

Historically, the above isomorphisms were expected since they arose from the known homology exact sequence and were involved in the initial computation of the homology groups. We note that, except for homology with coefficients in $\mathbb{Z}_2$, they just fail to give a simple inductive computation of all the groups, starting from the known ones. In the next two theorems we give isomorphisms that only became apparent to us on studying the special cases that we computed in the first sections of this chapter. The topological identities, if any, that underlie them are, as yet, unclear. However, these isomorphisms do have the advantage of allowing an inductive computation of all the homology groups. Thus, starting from the known homology of the real projective spaces Σ_1^k / ι_1 and the inductive computation of the homology of the spaces Σ_2^k / ι_2 in the special case of Theorem 5.4, Corollary 5.3 gives the inductive computation of the homology of Σ_m^k / ι_m for all $m > 2$. Then, this information, together with the known homology of the spheres Σ_1^k and the complex projective spaces Σ_2^k, enables the inductive calculation of the homology of Σ_m^k for $m > 2$.

The first result involves spaces of both oriented and unoriented shapes.

Theorem 5.3. *For all $m \geqslant 3$, k and $n \geqslant 0$*

$$H_n\left(\Sigma_m^{k+1}\right) \cong H_{n-m}\left(\Sigma_m^k\right) \oplus H_{n-m-1}\left(\Sigma_{m-2}^k / \iota_{m-2}\right).$$

Proof. This results from a decomposition of the essential complex, $E_* = F_* \oplus G_*$, where F_* is generated by the basis elements corresponding to those pattern sequences J, in $\mathcal{J}_1^v$, whose last two entries are '21', and G_* is generated by the remaining basis elements. That these are subcomplexes follows easily from the boundary formulae.

Then, each basis element $c_J \in E_n(\Sigma_m^{k+1})$ of G_* corresponds to a basis element $c_{J'} \in E_{n-m}(\Sigma_m^k)$, where J' is the pattern sequence $(j_1 - 1, \ldots, j_m - 1)$. Moreover, this correspondence respects boundaries since the ith boundary component is determined by the parity of $j_i - j_m$, which is unchanged. Thus, it is a chain isomorphism and hence induces an isomorphism of homology groups.

Similarly, for $J = (j_1, \ldots, j_{m-2}, 2, 1)$ the basis element $c_J \in E_n(\Sigma_m^{k+1})$ of F_* corresponds to a basis element $c_{J'} \in E_{n-m-1}(\Sigma_{m-2}^k / \iota_{m-2})$, where J' is the pattern sequence $(j_1 - 1, \ldots, j_{m-2} - 1)$. Again, this correspondence respects boundaries since the ith boundary component in Σ_m^{k+1} is non-zero if and only if $j_i - j_m$ is odd, while that in $\Sigma_{m-2}^k / \iota_{m-2}$ is non-zero if and only if j_i is odd. So, again, the correspondence induces an isomorphism of homology groups.   ∎

A fairly obvious modification of this theorem holds for $m = 2$. However, since these homology groups are already known we shall not spell it out.

Corollary 5.1. *For each $m \geqslant 3$, $l \geqslant 1$ and $n \geqslant 0$ the homology group $H_n(\Sigma_m^{m+l})$ may be expressed as the direct sum*

$$H_{n-m-1}\left(\Sigma_{m-2}^{m+l-1}/\iota_{m-2}\right) \oplus H_{n-2m-1}\left(\Sigma_{m-2}^{m+l-2}/\iota_{m-2}\right) \oplus \cdots$$
$$\cdots \oplus H_{n-lm-1}\left(\Sigma_{m-2}^{m}/\iota_{m-2}\right).$$

Proof. Since Σ_m^{m+1}/ι_m is contractible, the decomposition of Theorem 5.3 when iterated gives the direct sum decomposition stated, where each summand corresponds to a particular choice of the last, necessarily nice, pair of elements of the patterns. ∎

Corollary 5.2. *For $n > d_m^{k+1} - 2(k - m)$ we have*

$$H_n\left(\Sigma_m^{k+1}\right) \cong H_{n-m}\left(\Sigma_m^k\right).$$

Proof. Recalling our notation d_m^k for the dimension of Σ_m^k and so also of Σ_m^k/ι_m, this isomorphism follows from Theorem 5.3 when $n - m - 1 > d_{m-2}^k$. However, the facts that $d_m^{m+1} = d_{m-2}^{m-1} + 2m - 1$, $d_m^{k+1} = d_m^{m+1} + (k - m)m$ and $d_{m-2}^k = d_{m-2}^{m-1} + (k - m + 1)(m - 2)$ imply that $d_{m-2}^k + m + 1 = d_m^{k+1} - 2(k - m)$. ∎

In other words, the suspension isomorphism holds in the top $2(k - m)$ degrees. This is obviously the best possible whenever $H_{d_{m-2}^k}(\Sigma_{m-2}^k/\iota_{m-2}) \neq 0$, for example, for $m = 4$ and k even or $m = 5$ and k odd. In fact, the general necessary and sufficient condition is that m and k have the same parity, for it is then, and only then, that the generator of the essential complex for $\Sigma_{m-2}^k/\iota_{m-2}$ of highest degree, that corresponding to the pattern sequence $(k - 1, k - 2, \ldots, k - m + 2)$, is of type (i). When m and k have opposite parity this top group is zero, but then the group in the next lower degree is non-zero, so that the suspension isomorphism holds in just the one extra degree.

Our next result gives an isomorphism that allows an inductive calculation of the homology of spaces of unoriented shapes.

Theorem 5.4. *For $m \geqslant 3$ and $n \geqslant 0$ the reduced homology group $H_n(\Sigma_m^{k+1}/\iota_m)$ is isomorphic with*

$$H_{n-2m}\left(\Sigma_m^{k-1}/\iota_m\right) \oplus H_{n-2m}\left(\Sigma_{m-1}^{k-1}/\iota_{m-1}; \mathbb{Z}_2\right) \oplus H_{n-2m-1}\left(\Sigma_{m-2}^{k-1}/\iota_{m-2}\right).$$

When $m = 2$ we have $H_4(\Sigma_2^{k+1}/\iota_2) \cong \mathbb{Z}$ and, for $n > 4$,

$$H_n\left(\Sigma_2^{k+1}/\iota_2\right) = H_{n-4}\left(\Sigma_2^{k-1}/\iota_2\right) \oplus H_{n-4}\left(\Sigma_1^{k-1}/\iota_1; \mathbb{Z}_2\right).$$

Proof. This results from a decomposition of the essential complex, $E_* = F_* \oplus G_* \oplus K_*$, where F_* is generated by the basis elements corresponding to pattern sequences J in $\mathcal{J}_1^2$ with $j_m \geq 4$, then G_* is generated by the basis elements corresponding to pattern sequences J with $j_m = 2$ or 3 and $j_{m-1} > 3$, and K_* is generated by the remaining basis elements corresponding to pattern sequences J with $j_{m-1} = 3$ and $j_m = 2$. Again, these are subcomplexes, and the stated homology groups are evident for F_* from the correspondence

$$(j_1, \ldots, j_m) \longleftrightarrow (j_1 - 2, \ldots, j_m - 2)$$

and for K_* from the correspondence

$$(j_1, \ldots, j_{m-2}, 3, 2) \longleftrightarrow (j_1 - 2, \ldots, j_{m-2} - 2).$$

In the case of G_*, for each pattern sequence J with $j_{m-1} \geq 4$ there is one pattern in G_* with $j_m = 3$ and one with $j_m = 2$, the latter being replaced, in the change of basis, by half the boundary of the former. It follows that we get a $\mathbb{Z}_2$-summand for each pattern sequence $(j_1 - 2, \ldots, j_{m-1} - 2)$: that is, for each pattern in the essential complex of $\Sigma_{m-1}^{k-1}/\iota_{m-1}$. Hence, the stated result.

When $m = 2$ the subcomplex K_* has just the single generator, of degree four, corresponding to the pattern '32'. This gives the stated homology group in degree four. The other subcomplexes may be interpreted as before. ∎

Again, we may iterate this formula to express the homology in terms of that of spaces of unoriented shapes in $\mathbb{R}^{m-1}$ and $\mathbb{R}^{m-2}$.

Corollary 5.3. *For* $m \geq 3$, $l \geq 2$ *and* $n \geq 0$ *the reduced homology group* $H_n(\Sigma_m^{m+l}/\iota_m)$ *is isomorphic with the direct sum*

$$H_{n-2m}\left(\Sigma_{m-1}^{m+l-2}/\iota_{m-1}; \mathbb{Z}_2\right) \oplus H_{n-2m-1}\left(\Sigma_{m-2}^{m+l-2}/\iota_{m-2}\right)$$

$$\oplus H_{n-4m}\left(\Sigma_{m-1}^{m+l-4}/\iota_{m-1}; \mathbb{Z}_2\right) \oplus H_{n-4m-1}\left(\Sigma_{m-2}^{m+l-4}/\iota_{m-2}\right)$$

$$\oplus \cdots \oplus \cdots$$

$$\oplus \begin{cases} H_{n-lm+m}\left(\Sigma_{m-1}^{m+1}/\iota_{m-1}; \mathbb{Z}_2\right) \oplus H_{n-lm+m-1}\left(\Sigma_{m-2}^{m+1}/\iota_{m-2}\right) & \text{if } l \text{ is odd,} \\ H_{n-lm}\left(\Sigma_{m-2}^{m}/\iota_{m-2}\right) & \text{if } l \text{ is even.} \end{cases}$$

The corresponding full decomposition of the essential complex is not quite as simple as in the case of spaces of oriented shapes. For example, for the re-based essential complex of Σ_3^9/ι_3, those generators whose patterns end in '32' form the subcomplex that gives the homology of Σ_1^7/ι_1, but with all degrees increased by seven; those whose patterns end in '54' form the subcomplex that gives the homology of Σ_1^5/ι_1 with degrees increased by 13; and the generator with pattern '876' gives the homology of Σ_1^3/ι_1, which is just $\mathbb{Z}$ in degree one, with that degree increased by 19. Of the remaining generators, those pairs whose patterns are identical, except that one ends in '2' and the other in '3', generate the homology of Σ_2^7/ι_2 with coefficients in $\mathbb{Z}_2$ but with degrees increased by six, and the three similar pairs of generators with patterns ending in '4' or '5' produce $H_*(\Sigma_2^5/\iota_2; \mathbb{Z}_2)$ with degrees increased by 12.

5.8   CLOSED FORMULAE FOR THE HOMOLOGY GROUPS

Having obtained some feeling for the general nature of the results, as well as various relationships between them, we now give closed formulae for the various homology groups. To state our results we shall require, in addition to the common combinatorial functions, the function $P(i; j; l)$ that is the number of partitions of a set of size i into j parts each of which may be empty but has at most l elements. Note that this implies that $P(0; j; l) = 1$. For consistency we take $P(i; j; l) = 0$ when i is not a non-negative integer. Each of our groups is a direct sum of a number of summands isomorphic with $\mathbb{Z}$ and a number of summands isomorphic with $\mathbb{Z}_2$. We shall call these numbers of summands the $\mathbb{Z}$-rank and the $\mathbb{Z}_2$-rank, respectively, although the latter terminology is not standard. In addition to computing these ranks for the homology groups in each degree we shall give the, rather simpler, 'total ranks': that is, the total number of such summands in the homology groups of all degrees, for each space. We look first at homology with coefficients in $\mathbb{Z}_2$.

Theorem 5.5. *The homology $H_*(\Sigma_m^k; \mathbb{Z}_2)$ has total $\mathbb{Z}_2$-rank*

$$\binom{k-2}{m-1}.$$

The $\mathbb{Z}_2$-rank of $H_n(\Sigma_m^k; \mathbb{Z}_2)$ is

$$P\left(n - \frac{(m+2)(m-1)}{2}; k-1-m; m\right)$$
$$- P\left(n - \frac{(m+4)(m-1)}{2}; k-2-m; m\right).$$

Proof.   Theorem 4.4 shows that the total number of $\mathbb{Z}_2$-summands in all degrees is equal to the number of generators of the essential complex. In other words, we need to find the number of patterns for which the final pair is nice: $j_{m-1} - 1 = j_m > 0$. These are determined by the $m - 1$ numbers $j_1 > j_2 > \cdots > j_{m-1}$ where $j_1 \leqslant k - 1$ and $j_{m-1} \geqslant 2$. Thus, there are

$$\binom{k-2}{m-1}$$

of them.

To count the number of these generators in each degree we note that all such patterns contain the top left-hand triangle of $m(m+1)/2$ non-zero symbolic entries, accounting for degree $m(m+1)/2 - 1 = (m+2)(m-1)/2$. To correspond to a generator of degree n the remaining $n - (m+2)(m-1)/2$ non-zero entries must be arranged in initial segments of weakly decreasing length along successive counter-diagonals. Ignoring the requirement that in the resulting pattern the last pair be nice there are

$$P\left(n - \frac{(m+2)(m-1)}{2}; k-1-m; m\right)$$

ways of achieving this. Those whose last pair is not nice can be seen to be precisely those for which at least one part has size $m - 1$. The number of these is

$$P\left(n - \frac{(m+4)(m-1)}{2}; k-2-m; m\right).$$

■

Looking now at spaces of unoriented shapes we again have a relatively straightforward computation for the homology with $\mathbb{Z}_2$-coefficients. The only constraint now on the pattern for a generator of the essential complex is that its final entry j_m be greater than or equal to two. There are thus $k - 2$ possibilities from which the m distinct row lengths j_i may be chosen, giving a total $\mathbb{Z}_2$-rank of

$$\binom{k-2}{m}.$$

Then, of the $n + 1$ non-zero entries in the pattern for a cell of dimension n, a total of $m(m+1)/2 + m$ must lie in the upper right-hand triangle and the first counter-diagonal adjacent to it. The remaining non-zero entries must be placed along the remaining $k - 2 - m$ counter-diagonals of length at most m. Thus, we have the following result.

Theorem 5.6. The $\mathbb{Z}_2$-rank of $H_*(\Sigma_m^k/\iota_m; \mathbb{Z}_2)$ is

$$\binom{k-2}{m}$$

with

$$P\left(n + 1 - \frac{m(m+3)}{2}; k - 2 - m; m\right)$$

summands in $H_n(\Sigma_m^k/\iota_m; \mathbb{Z}_2)$ *for each n.*

Turning to the integral homology, the corresponding formulae are somewhat more complicated, especially those counting the $\mathbb{Z}_2$-summands. For the number of $\mathbb{Z}$-summands we have the following, in which [a] denotes the integer part of a.

Theorem 5.7. *The homology* $H_*(\Sigma_m^k; \mathbb{Z})$ *has total $\mathbb{Z}$-rank*

$$\binom{[\frac{k-1}{2}]}{\frac{m}{2}} + \binom{[\frac{k-2}{2}]}{\frac{m}{2}}$$

if m is even and

$$\binom{[\frac{k-2}{2}]}{\frac{m-1}{2}}$$

when m is odd. The $\mathbb{Z}$-rank of $H_n(\Sigma_m^k; \mathbb{Z})$ *is*

$$P\left(\frac{2n - (m+2)(m-1)}{8}; \left[\frac{k-1-m}{2}\right]; \frac{m}{2}\right)$$
$$+ P\left(\frac{2(n-m) - (m+2)(m-1)}{8}; \left[\frac{k-2-m}{2}\right]; \frac{m}{2}\right)$$

when m is even and, when m is odd, it is

$$P\left(\frac{2n - (m+2)(m-1) - 2(k-1-m)}{8}; \frac{k-1-m}{2}; \frac{m-1}{2}\right)$$

if k is even and

$$P\left(\frac{2n - (m+2)(m-1) - 2(k-2)}{8}; \frac{k-2-m}{2}; \frac{m-1}{2}\right)$$

if k is odd.

Proof. *The total number of summands isomorphic with $\mathbb{Z}$ is the number of generators of type (i): that is, those in whose patterns all pairs are nice and even. We consider the cases m even and m odd, separately. When m is even the allowable patterns are determined by the lengths: that is, the number of non-zero entries with which they start, of the even rows, each being at least two shorter than its predecessor and all differences being even. There are*

$$\binom{[\frac{k-1}{2}]}{\frac{m}{2}}$$

in which j_m is congruent to $k - 1$ and

$$\left(\begin{array}{c} \left[\frac{k-2}{2}\right] \\ \frac{m}{2} \end{array} \right)$$

in which j_m is congruent to $k - 2$.

When m is odd the first row must be full, and so of length $k - 1$, and the final row must have the same parity. This allows

$$\left(\begin{array}{c} \left[\frac{k-2}{2}\right] \\ \frac{m-1}{2} \end{array} \right)$$

choices.

To identify the degrees in which these summands lie we note that again the contribution $(m + 2)(m - 1)/2$ to the degree is accounted for automatically by the top left-hand triangle of the pattern. This time, however, the remaining $n - (m + 2)(m - 1)/2$ non-zero entries have to be arranged in pairs of initial segments of equal even length along the counter-diagonals with the lengths of successive pairs weakly decreasing. This means, if there are to be any such generators, that $n - (m + 2)(m - 1)/2$ must be a multiple of four and there are then, for m even,

$$P\left(\frac{2n - (m + 2)(m - 1)}{8}; \left[\frac{k - 1 - m}{2}\right]; \frac{m}{2} \right)$$
$$+ P\left(\frac{2(n - m) - (m + 2)(m - 1)}{8}; \left[\frac{k - 2 - m}{2}\right]; \frac{m}{2} \right)$$

generators of $\mathbb{Z}$-summands in this degree, the first of these partition functions counting the relevant patterns with j_m odd and the second counting those with j_m even. This expression remains valid for all n on account of our convention that $P(i; j; l)$ is zero when i is not a non-negative integer. When m is odd the number of such generators is

$$P\left(\frac{2n - (m + 2)(m - 1) - 2(k - 1 - m)}{8}; \frac{k - 1 - m}{2}; \frac{m - 1}{2} \right)$$

if k is even and

$$P\left(\frac{n - (m + 2)(m - 1) - (k - 2)}{4}; \frac{k - 2 - m}{2}; \frac{m - 1}{2} \right)$$

if k is odd, since the first row must be full and the remaining $m - 1$ rows are chosen as before.   ■

Thus, for the case m = 4, the total $\mathbb{Z}$-ranks are

$$1+0, 1+1, 3+1, 3+3, 6+3,$$

for k = 5, 6, 7, 8, 9 and so on, where, for example, the nine infinite summands in $H_*(\Sigma_4^9; \mathbb{Z})$ are distributed with

$$P\left(\frac{n-9}{4}; 2; 2\right) + P\left(\frac{n-13}{4}; 1; 2\right)$$

in degree n, giving us totals of 1, 2, 3, 2, 1 summands in degrees 9, 13, 17, 21 and 25, respectively. These details may be checked against the data in Table 5.7. For m = 3 we have $\mathbb{Z}$-ranks 1, 1, 2, 2, etc. for k = 4, 5, 6, 7 with the distribution of summands determined by the partition function

$$P\left(\frac{n-k-1}{4}; \frac{k}{2} - 2; 1\right)$$

for k even and

$$P\left(\frac{n-k-3}{4}; \frac{k-1}{2} - 2; 1\right)$$

for k odd. In this case, since all non-empty subsets in the partition are singletons, the partition, if it exists, is unique. Thus, we get an infinite cyclic summand in $H_n(\Sigma_3^k; \mathbb{Z})$ if and only if $n - k - 1 = 4l$ with $0 \leqslant l \leqslant k/2 - 2$ for k even and if and only if $n - k - 3 = 4l$ with $0 \leqslant l \leqslant (k-1)/2 - 2$ for k odd. This is evident in Table 5.3, since the infinite cyclic summands there do not persist on inclusion in the next spaces to the right.

We look next at the $\mathbb{Z}_2$-rank of the homology with integer coefficients, by which we recall we mean the number of summands isomorphic with $\mathbb{Z}_2$. The total $\mathbb{Z}_2$-rank is easily found since the essential complex has the minimum number of generators consistent with the $\mathbb{Z}$-homology, which is also the same as the $\mathbb{Z}_2$-rank of $H_*(\Sigma_m^k; \mathbb{Z}_2)$. Of these generators, a known number are required for the $\mathbb{Z}$-summands, one generator for each summand, and, of the rest, two are required for each $\mathbb{Z}_2$-summand. The computation of the $\mathbb{Z}_2$-rank of $H_n(\Sigma_m^k; \mathbb{Z})$ requires a little more effort. To describe it as concisely as possible we shall use the $\mathbb{Z}_2$-rank of $H_n(\Sigma_m^k; \mathbb{Z}_2)$, which was computed in Theorem 5.6, and the $\mathbb{Z}$-rank of $H_n(\Sigma_m^k; \mathbb{Z})$, which was computed in Theorem 5.7. The closed expressions found there can, of course, be substituted in the formulae given here to convert them into fully explicit, if somewhat unwieldy, expressions.

Theorem 5.8. *The total $\mathbb{Z}_2$-rank of $H_*(\Sigma_m^k; \mathbb{Z})$ is*

$$\binom{k-2}{m-1} - \binom{\left[\frac{k-1}{2}\right]}{\frac{m}{2}} - \binom{\left[\frac{k-2}{2}\right]}{\frac{m}{2}}$$

if m is even and

$$\binom{k-2}{m-1} - \binom{\left[\frac{k-2}{2}\right]}{\frac{m-1}{2}}$$

if m is odd. The $\mathbb{Z}_2$-rank of $H_n(\Sigma_m^k; \mathbb{Z})$ is

$$\sum_{r=0}^{[(m-2)/2]} \sum_{l} \sum_{n_1+n_2+(m-2r-1)l=n-1} \operatorname{rank}_{\mathbb{Z}_2} \left(H_{n_1} \left(\Sigma_{m-2r-1}^{k-l} / \iota_{m-2r-1}; \mathbb{Z}_2 \right) \right)$$

$$\times \quad \operatorname{rank}_{\mathbb{Z}} \left(H_{n_2} \left(\Sigma_{2r+1}^l; \mathbb{Z} \right) \right).$$

Proof. *As indicated before the statement of the theorem, the total $\mathbb{Z}_2$-rank of $H_*(\Sigma_m^k; \mathbb{Z})$ is*

$$\tfrac{1}{2} \left\{ \operatorname{rank}_{\mathbb{Z}_2} \left(H_* \left(\Sigma_m^k; \mathbb{Z}_2 \right) \right) - \operatorname{rank}_{\mathbb{Z}} \left(H_* \left(\Sigma_m^k; \mathbb{Z} \right) \right) \right\}$$

so the stated result follows from Theorems 5.5 and 5.7.

To calculate how many of these summands lie in each homology group we recall that the $\mathbb{Z}_2$-generators are of type (iii). These are those whose pattern is such that the first pair of entries, counting from the right, which are not both even and nice, are even, and so not nice. Since, for $H_*(\Sigma_m^k; \mathbb{Z})$, a pair is even if its right-hand member has the same parity as the last entry in the pattern, the type (iii) generators are those for which the pattern $J = (j_1, j_2, \ldots, j_{m-1}, j_m)$ ends with a number of pairs $j_{m-2i-1} = j_{m-2i} + 1$, $i = 1, \ldots, r$ with $j_{m-2i} \equiv j_m$ (mod 2) and $j_{m-2r-2} \equiv j_m$ (mod 2) but $j_{m-2r-3} > j_{m-2r-2} + 1$ and j_h arbitrary, subject to the monotonic decreasing rule, for $h \leqslant m - 2r - 4$.

We look at the block decomposition of such a pattern determined by the first $l = j_{m-2r-2}$ columns and by the last $2r + 1$ rows, those that form the nice even pairs, together with the right-hand, or only, member of the first even, but not nice, pair. The top left-hand block of this decomposition is full, that is, all its entries are non-zero, and the bottom right-hand block is empty, that is, all its entries are zero. In the top right-hand block is a pattern in which the last row has length at least two since $j_{m-2r-3} \geqslant j_{m-2r-2} + 2 = l + 2$. Since there is no other restriction, it determines a $\mathbb{Z}_2$-summand of $H_{n_1}(\Sigma_{m-2r-1}^{k-l} / \iota_{m-2r-1}; \mathbb{Z}_2)$, where $n_1 + 1$ is the total number of non-zero entries in that block. Similarly, we can interpret the lower left-hand block as representing a generator of a $\mathbb{Z}$-summand of $H_{n_2}(\Sigma_{2r+1}^l; \mathbb{Z})$. The fact that $2r + 1$ is odd here guarantees that, for each such generator, j_m and the right-hand member of each intervening nice pair have the same parity as $l = j_{m-2r-2}$.

The constraints on r in the above block decomposition are that r may be zero but $2r$ must be less than or equal to $m - 2$ to allow for a non-nice even pair.

This is clear when m is even, but also holds for m odd since, if then $2r = m - 1$, the bottom left-hand block would be the entire non-zero part of the pattern and would represent a generator of a $\mathbb{Z}$-summand.

A lower bound $2r$ for l is necessary to ensure that a type (i) pattern will fit in the lower left-hand block and an upper bound $2r + k - m$ is necessary to allow a pattern representing a generator of the relevant homology group to fit in the top right-hand block. However, these bounds need not be mentioned explicitly in the statement of the theorem since they will be automatically enforced by the appropriate values of $\text{rank}_{\mathbb{Z}_2}(H_{n_1}(\Sigma^{k-l}_{m-2r-1}/\iota_{m-2r-1}; \mathbb{Z}_2))$ or $\text{rank}_{\mathbb{Z}}(H_{n_2}(\Sigma^l_{2r+1}; \mathbb{Z}))$ being zero for the given choice of r and l.

For the constraints on n_1 and n_2 we note that there will be $n_1 + 1$ non-zero entries in the top right-hand block and $n_2 + 1$ in the lower left-hand block. If the result is to be a generator of degree n, then there will be $n + 1$ together. Since the top left-hand block has all of its $(m - 2r - 1)l$ entries non-zero, we get

$$n_1 + 1 + n_2 + 1 + (m - 2r - 1)l = n + 1,$$

as given in the theorem. With s and l already chosen, we must also restrict n_1 to be at least the dimension of $\Sigma^{m-2r}_{m-2r-1}/\iota_{m-2r-1}$ and n_2 to be at least that of Σ^{2r+2}_{2r+1}, otherwise we shall be counting patterns that do not fit properly into the appropriate blocks. However, once again, this is automatically accounted for by the fact that such patterns do not represent homology generators, so that these constraints also do not need to be explicitly mentioned. ∎

Since the 'triangular region' in Tables 1.1 and 1.2 is specified by $k > m + 1$ and $m > 2$, for any space Σ^k_m in that region we have $k - 2 > m - 1 > 1$. Then we can easily check that Theorem 5.8 confirms our assertion that the homology groups of such spaces always have torsion, necessarily of order two. In fact, we could use Theorem 4.2 to identify such a generator: when m is odd the generator corresponding to the pattern $(m + 1, m - 1, \ldots, 3, 2, 1)$ has a boundary twice that corresponding to $(m, m - 1, \ldots, 3, 2, 1)$ and both lie in Σ^k_m for $k \geqslant m + 2$; when m is even we similarly have generators corresponding to

$$(m + 1, m, m - 2, \ldots, 2, 1) \text{ and } (m + 1, m - 1, m - 2, \ldots, 2, 1).$$

As was the case for oriented shape spaces, the integral homology of unoriented shape spaces is rather more complicated than that with $\mathbb{Z}_2$-coefficients. Although again the total $\mathbb{Z}$-rank and $\mathbb{Z}_2$-rank have simple expressions, we find, as before, that the ranks, especially the $\mathbb{Z}_2$-rank, of the homology group in a particular degree are given by more complex formulae. Once again, the results depend on the parity of m and, when m is odd, also on that of k. We deal first with the $\mathbb{Z}$-ranks.

Theorem 5.9. *The total $\mathbb{Z}$-rank of $H_*(\Sigma_m^k/\iota_m; \mathbb{Z})$ is*

$$\binom{\left[\frac{k-2}{2}\right]}{\frac{m}{2}}$$

when m is even, with

$$P\left(\frac{2(n+1) - m(m+3)}{8}; \left[\frac{k-2-m}{2}\right]; \frac{m}{2}\right)$$

summands in $H_n(\Sigma_m^k/\iota_m; \mathbb{Z})$. When m is odd the total $\mathbb{Z}$-rank is zero unless k is also odd. Then it is

$$\binom{\frac{k-3}{2}}{\frac{m-1}{2}}$$

with

$$P\left(\frac{2(n+3) - m(m+1) - 2k}{8}; \frac{k-2-m}{2}; \frac{m-1}{2}\right)$$

summands in degree n.

Proof. We recall from Theorem 4.3, and the definitions that preceded it, that the generator of an infinite summand of $H_*(\Sigma_m^k/\iota_m; \mathbb{Z})$ has pattern $J = (j_1, \ldots, j_m)$ of row lengths in which j_m is even and all pairs (j_{m-2i-1}, j_{m-2i}) are nice: that is, $j_{m-2i-1} = j_{m-2i} + 1$, with all right-hand members j_{m-2i} even. When m is even that specifies the patterns J that determine infinite cyclic summands. When m is odd the unpaired first entry j_1 must be even and also equal to $k - 1$, so k must be odd.

When m is even such a pattern is determined by the $m/2$ entries $j_2, j_4, \ldots, j_m$, which may take any decreasing sequence of even values in the range $[2, k - 2]$. There are thus

$$\binom{\left[\frac{k-2}{2}\right]}{\frac{m}{2}}$$

such patterns.

We can count those of a given degree n as before: of the $n + 1$ non-zero entries in the pattern matrix, a total of $m + m(m+1)/2$ are accounted for in the top left-hand triangle, together with the first counter-diagonal; the remainder are then shared among pairs of counter-diagonals of equal length, with the pair lengths being weakly decreasing. As in the case of oriented shape spaces, this requires the degree n to be such that the number of these remaining entries is divisible by four and then the number of patterns in such a degree is given by the stated partition function.

When m is odd we need k to be odd also so that the first row with $k-1$ non-zero entries has even length. The remainder of the pattern is then determined exactly as it would be for $m-1$ and $k-1$. This gives the stated results on allowing for the shift in degree caused by the entries in the first row. ∎

We turn finally to the $\mathbb{Z}_2$-rank of the groups $H_n(\Sigma_m^k/\iota_m; \mathbb{Z})$. Once again, the total $\mathbb{Z}_2$-rank of all the homology groups of a particular such space is easily found as half of the difference of the total number of generators, which is the same as the total $\mathbb{Z}_2$-rank of $H_*(\Sigma_m^k/\iota_m; \mathbb{Z}_2)$, and those required for each $\mathbb{Z}$-summand. The expression for the $\mathbb{Z}_2$-rank of $H_n(\Sigma_m^k/\iota_m; \mathbb{Z})$ is, as before, rather less elegant and more conveniently expressed in terms of other previously computed ranks.

Theorem 5.10. *The total $\mathbb{Z}_2$-rank of $H_*(\Sigma_m^k/\iota_m; \mathbb{Z})$ is*

$$\frac{1}{2}\left\{\binom{k-2}{m} - \binom{\left[\frac{k-2}{2}\right]}{\frac{m}{2}}\right\}$$

for m even,

$$\frac{1}{2}\binom{k-2}{m}$$

for m odd and k even and

$$\frac{1}{2}\left\{\binom{k-2}{m} - \binom{\frac{k-3}{2}}{\frac{m-1}{2}}\right\}$$

for m and k both odd. The $\mathbb{Z}_2$-rank of $H_n(\Sigma_m^k/\iota_m; \mathbb{Z})$ is

$$\sum_{r=0}^{[(m-2)/2]} \sum_{l} \sum_{n_1+n_2+(m-2r-1)l=n-1} \mathrm{rank}_{\mathbb{Z}_2}\left(H_{n_1}\left(\Sigma_{m-2r-1}^{k-l}/\iota_{m-2r-1}; \mathbb{Z}_2\right)\right)$$

$$\times \mathrm{rank}_{\mathbb{Z}}\left(H_{n_2}\left(\Sigma_{2r+1}^{l}/\iota_{2r+1}; \mathbb{Z}\right)\right).$$

Proof. The total number of summands of $H_*(\Sigma_m^k/\iota_m; \mathbb{Z})$ isomorphic with $\mathbb{Z}_2$ is, as for oriented shape spaces, just

$$\frac{1}{2}\left\{\mathrm{rank}_{\mathbb{Z}_2}\left(H_*\left(\Sigma_m^k/\iota_m; \mathbb{Z}_2\right)\right) - \mathrm{rank}_{\mathbb{Z}}\left(H_*\left(\Sigma_m^k/\iota_m; \mathbb{Z}\right)\right)\right\}.$$

By Theorems 5.6 and 5.8 that gives the stated expressions.

Since the characterisation of a type (iii) pattern that determines a $\mathbb{Z}_2$-summand of $H_*(\Sigma^k_m/\iota_m; \mathbb{Z})$ is the same as for $H_*(\Sigma^k_m; \mathbb{Z})$, except for the more restricted meaning of a pair being even, the calculation of the $\mathbb{Z}_2$-rank of $H_n(\Sigma^k_m/\iota_m; \mathbb{Z})$ follows from a similar block decomposition of the appropriate pattern matrices to that used in the proof of Theorem 5.8. The only difference is that the lower left-hand block here necessarily determines a generator of a $\mathbb{Z}$-summand in the integral homology of a space of unoriented shapes. We omit the details. ∎

5.9 DUALITY IN SHAPE SPACES

There may be observed in the tables of homology and cohomology groups of shape spaces de facto isomorphisms that are similar to those induced in manifolds by intersection, for infinite summands, and linking for finite summands, except for a shift in the degrees involved. In this section we show that these isomorphisms can be explained, at least at the chain level, in the essential chain complexes, and hence also at the cellular level. In particular, we shall establish that these isomorphisms are valid for all appropriate shape spaces, not just the ones in which they were observed.

5.9.1 Spaces of Unoriented Shapes

The most complete example of such 'duality' occurs in the homology of spaces of unoriented shapes with $\mathbb{Z}_2$-coefficients. Recall that this has one $\mathbb{Z}_2$-summand for each generator of the essential complex and that the dimension of Σ^{k+1}_m or Σ^{k+1}_m/ι_m is $d^{k+1}_m = d^{m+1}_m + (k-m)m$, where $d^{m+1}_m = (m^2 + m)/2 - 1$. Then, in the essential complex for Σ^{k+1}_m/ι_m, the unique generator of the lowest degree $d^{m+1}_m + m$ is mirrored by a unique generator in the top degree $d^{m+1}_m + (k-m)m$ and for each r, $0 < r \leqslant (k-m)m/2$, there are as many generators of degree $d^{m+1}_m + m + r$ as there are of degree $d^{m+1}_m + (k-m)m - r$ (cf. Tables 5.8, 5.11 and 5.13). This is explicable as follows.

Given a pattern $J = (j_1, \ldots, j_m)$, determining a generator in Σ^{k+1}_m/ι_m, we may define a 'dual' pattern, and corresponding generator, by

$$\tilde{J} = (k+2-j_m, \ldots, k+2-j_1).$$

This duality restricts to an involution between the generators of the essential complex, since the necessary and sufficient condition for J to determine a generator of the essential complex for Σ^{k+1}_m/ι_m is that $k+1 > j_1 > \ldots > j_m > 1$ and this is satisfied for $\tilde{J}$ if and only if it is satisfied for J. In the first instance, this induces a corresponding duality in homology and cohomology with $\mathbb{Z}_2$-coefficients since, in this case, every generator of the essential complex determines a generator of the homology.

Recall, however, that, having paired the entries of a pattern J from the right-hand end, we called a pair *nice* if it were of the form $(n+1, n)$ and, when there remains a left-hand singleton, we called it nice if it were equal to $k-1$. Then, for Σ^{k+1}_m/ι_m we further called a pair even or odd according to the parity of its right-hand, or only, member. Then, the generator corresponding to J carries an infinite cyclic summand if all pairs are nice and even; it carries a $\mathbb{Z}_2$-summand in homology if the first pair from the right that is not both nice and even is even; and it carries a $\mathbb{Z}_2$-summand in cohomology if the first pair that is not both nice and even is odd.

For this 'suspended intersection' type of duality to preserve the set of generators of infinite cyclic summands it needs, and needs only, to preserve both niceness and parity of the pairs of integers j_{m-2i}, j_{m-2i-1} in the sequence J. Clearly, niceness of *all* pairs is preserved if and only if m is even and, since the right-hand member of the corresponding pair in $\tilde{J}$ is $k + 2 - j_{m-2i}$, which is congruent to $k + 1 + j_{m-2i-1}$ modulo 2, the 'parity' of the pair is preserved if and only if $k + 1$ is even. Scanning Tables 5.10, 5.12 and 5.14 and remembering that they are cumulative, we see that these are indeed the only cases where the duality exists: when m is even the infinite cyclic summands in the homology of Σ_m^{2l+1}/ι_m are isomorphic with those in Σ_m^{2l}/ι_m, so cannot satisfy the appropriate duality; when m is odd there is either no infinite cyclic summand, when $k + 1$ is even, or those that occur, when $k + 1$ is odd, do not fit the above intersection-duality pattern.

For a generator of an element of infinite order all pairs of integers in the sequence J had to be nice and even and, provided m is even, in the above duality the preservation of nice pairs was clear by symmetry. However, for elements of order two we have made an asymmetric choice. When a generator in the essential complex has several boundary components, we have chosen one particular component to represent the entire boundary in such a way that the rightmost pair that is not both nice and even determines the character of the corresponding basis element: that is, whether it carries a generator for the homology or whether its boundary carries twice such a generator. On dualising, as above, for m even when at least the pairs are preserved, this translates to a different choice of new basis for the essential complex such that it is now the leftmost pair that is not both nice and even, which determines the character of the corresponding basis element. So, for the duality between elements of order two we shall work in the essential complex with its original basis, the elements corresponding to the generators determined by a sequence J in $\mathcal{J}_1^2$, that is, a sequence with $j_m > 1$. For such a basis element c_J^* part (iii) of Corollary 4.1 tells us that the basis element $c_{\partial_i J}$ appears, with coefficient ± 2, in the boundary of c_J if and only if j_i is odd and, in order that $c_{\partial_i J}$ be non-zero, $j_i > j_{i+1} + 1$. Recall that $\partial_i J$ differs from J only in that j_i is replaced by $j_i - 1$. However, then the corresponding entries in $\widetilde{\partial_i J}$ and $\tilde{J}$ are $k + 2 - j_i + 1$ and $k + 2 - j_i$, respectively, and, when $k + 1$ is odd, the former has the same parity as j_i. We also note that, since $j_{i-1} > j_i$, the entry $k + 2 - j_{i-1}$, which follows $k + 2 - j_i + 1$ in $\widetilde{\partial_i J}$, differs from it by at least two. These facts ensure that, whenever $\partial_i J$ determines a basis element that has coefficient ± 2 in the boundary of the basis element determined by J, the same is true of the element determined by $\tilde{J}$ in the boundary of that determined by $\widetilde{\partial_i J}$. However, that is precisely the relationship between a homomorphism from one free abelian group to another and the dual homomorphism between the dual groups, which gives rise to the usual duality isomorphisms in manifolds (see the Appendix). It follows that, except for the shift in the degrees of the groups between which it occurs, we have similar isomorphisms here.

Combining the above results, since when m is odd and $k + 1$ even there are no infinite summands, we have established that for all m, when $k + 1$ is even, the full homology groups of Σ_m^{k+1}/ι_m satisfy all the duality isomorphisms that would be exhibited by the homology groups of the $(d_m^{m+1} + m)$th suspension of a manifold of dimension $m(k - m - 1)$. Once again, this is clearly visible in the homology of spaces of unoriented shapes in 2-space, 3-space and 4-space (cf. Tables 5.10, 5.12 and 5.14, respectively). In the case of even dimensional spaces this involves summands of both finite and infinite orders, although in the case of odd dimensional spaces the relevant shape spaces only have torsion groups on their homology.

5.9.2 Spaces of Oriented Shapes

In the case of spaces of oriented shapes the observed duality is restricted to the infinite summands and its precise form depends on the parity of m and, if m is odd, also on the parity of k. When $m = 2$ the spaces *are* manifolds, so there is perfect duality. Then, for all even m there is a suspended form of the intersection duality between the free quotients of the homology groups. In particular, there is a suspended form of Hodge Duality for the real cohomology of these spaces. However, duality fails dismally on the torsion subgroups: there is no linking duality.

That the intersection duality holds for all even m follows from the bijection between $J = (j_1, \ldots, j_m)$ and $\tilde{J} = (k + 1 - j_m, \ldots, k + 1 - j_1)$. Recall that a generator of an infinite cyclic summand in the homology corresponds to a pattern J in which all pairs are nice and even: that is, $j_{2i} = j_{2i-1} + 1$ for $i = 1, 2, \ldots, m/2$ and $j_{2i} \equiv j_{2n} (\mathrm{mod}\ 2)$ for all i and n. Then, since j_1 and j_m have opposite parities, both properties are preserved under the duality. Thus, this induces a bijection between infinite summands, as required. In this case, if the pattern J determines a generator of degree $d_m^{m+1} + l = j_1 + \ldots + j_m - 1$, then the dual determines a generator of degree

$$km + m - (j_1 + \ldots + j_m) - 1 = m(k - m) + m^2 + m - d_m^{m+1} - l - 2$$
$$= d_m^{m+1} + m(k - m) - l = \dim\left(\Sigma_m^{k+1}\right) - l.$$

Since d_m^{m+1} and $\dim(\Sigma_m^{k+1})$ are the extreme degrees in which infinite summands occur, this is indeed a complete duality, suspended d_m^{m+1} times, between all such summands.

When m is odd (cf. Tables 5.2 and 5.3) there is again an 'intersection' duality between the free summands, or, more naturally, the free quotients, but now the amount by which the degree is suspended depends on the parity of k. This arises from the fact that to be 'nice' the first singleton must be equal to k and remain so under the duality. Then, the right-hand member of each succeeding pair must have the same parity as k. So, when $k + 1$ is even, the correspondence between $(k, j_2, \ldots, j_m)$ and $(k, k - j_m, \ldots, k - j_2)$ has the required properties: since k is odd, j_2 is even and so $k - j_2$ is again odd as required. If the former has degree $(d_m^{m+1} + k - m) + l = k + j_2 + \ldots + j_m - 1$, then the dual has degree

$$mk - (j_2 + \cdots + j_m) - 1 = d_m^{m+1} + m(k - m) - l = \dim\left(\Sigma_m^{k+1}\right) - l.$$

So, since the least degree in which an infinite summand occurs is $d_m^{m+1} + k - m$, as the sequences $(k, j_2, \ldots, j_m)$ run through all the sequences J that determine generators of infinite summands, so too will their duals.

When $k + 1$ is odd, in order for the right-hand members of the pairs in the dual sequence to have the same parity as k, the correspondence must be between $(k, j_2, \ldots, j_m)$ and $(k, k + 1 - j_m, \ldots, k + 1 - j_2)$. This does indeed give rise to a duality, suspended $d_m^{m+1} + k - 1$ times, which involves all the infinite summands.

It is difficult to imagine that the phenomena we have described in this section do not have an underlying topological explanation. For example, that all the spaces Σ_m^{2l}/ι_m should have homology groups consistent with their being suspensions of manifolds seems unlikely to be fortuitous. However, any explanation would need to be quite subtle in view of the limited extent to which this is true in the other cases. In the case of the spaces Σ_m^k, we wonder what it can mean for the rational cohomology to be the suspension of that of a manifold when the integral cohomology is not.

CHAPTER 6

Geodesics in Shape Spaces

In studying the topology of shape spaces we discovered the extent to which shape spaces differ 'globally' from familiar Euclidean spaces. By saying that, for example, a certain homology group is a global and not a local invariant we mean that, although we may, and did, identify cells that determine it, those cells are not unique and may be moved around the space. For instance, any circle $\mathbf{S}^1 \times \{x\}$ in the torus $\mathbf{S}^1 \times \mathbf{S}^1$ carries the same generator of the first homology group.

We now begin the study of the geometric structure of shape spaces, which provides some measure of the *local* differences between shape spaces and more familiar standard spaces. The full range of geometric properties is determined by a Riemannian metric, which is already a fairly sophisticated concept, and our account will require further technical ideas. However, in this chapter we shall concentrate on results that may be expressed in terms of geodesics and we shall give the necessary formal definitions only in the context of shape spaces where they are usually much simpler and more transparent than in the general case. Indeed, shape spaces provide an excellent domain in which to illustrate these basic geometric structures, being as elementary and straightforward to compute as the usual examples but much less trivial.

A geodesic, then, is the analogue in a curved space of a straight line in flat Euclidean space. On a sphere the geodesics are arcs of great circles. The projection

$$\pi : \mathcal{S}_m^k \longrightarrow \Sigma_m^k$$

of the pre-shape sphere onto shape space is such that certain geodesics on the pre-shape sphere, the 'horizontal' ones, project isometrically onto geodesics on the shape space. This, elaborated in Section 6.2, gives us a firm grasp of the geodesics in shape space and enables us to achieve the following results.

In Section 6.3 we revisit the stratification of shape space that we first described in Chapter 2. The successive strata fit together so smoothly that it is possible to extend the definition of shape space geodesics from Section 6.2, which was, in fact, only between two points of the upper two strata, to join arbitrary pairs of points in shape space. As for antipodal points on the sphere, there may be many geodesics between two given points of shape space. In Sections 6.5 and 6.6 we find the full set of geodesics of minimal length between any two shapes and also examine when that set has more than one element.

Starting from a fixed shape point, as we move out along each geodesic we arrive at a point immediately beyond which it fails to be minimal. The locus of such points along various geodesics from the fixed point is called its cut locus. It plays an important role in stochastic analysis and in Section 6.7 we identify it for each shape point.

An important application of these shape spaces is in the evaluation of the statistical significance of degeneracies and in Section 6.8 we compute the nearest degenerate shape to a given one and the distance between these two shapes, the degree of degeneracy being measured by the stratum in which it lies. As for the distance between shapes, the expressions that arise lend themselves well to computation.

6.1 THE ACTION OF SO(m) ON THE PRE-SHAPE SPHERE

We recall from Chapter 1 that our standard procedure for representing by a matrix the shape of a configuration of k labelled points, which are not all identical, in $\mathbb{R}^m$ is via the sized-and-centred $m \times (k-1)$ pre-shape matrix $X \in \mathcal{M}(m, k-1)$, where $\mathcal{M}(m, k-1)$ denotes the space of $m \times (k-1)$ real-valued matrices. Because of its size-normalisation, X is a point on the unit pre-shape sphere $\mathcal{S}_m^k = \mathbf{S}^{m(k-1)-1}$. The space Σ_m^k is then the quotient space of $\mathcal{S}_m^k$ by $\mathbf{SO}(m)$ and, if it is given the quotient topology, the quotient map π is both continuous and, since $\mathbf{SO}(m)$ acts as a group of homeomorphisms, also open.

For any given X in the pre-shape sphere the subset

$$\pi^{-1}(\pi(X)) = \{TX : T \in \mathbf{SO}(m)\},$$

which is the orbit of X under the action of $\mathbf{SO}(m)$, is also referred to as the *fibre* of π over $\pi(X)$. This fibre, which we think of as lying vertically above $\pi(X)$, consists of all the pre-shapes that have the same shape as X. For each pre-shape X, an important subgroup of $\mathbf{SO}(m)$ is the *isotropy subgroup of* $\mathbf{SO}$ (m) *at* X or, as it is also known, the *stabiliser* of X, which is $\mathcal{I}_X = \{T \in \mathbf{SO}(m) : TX = X\}$. The isotropy subgroup at each point in the orbit of X is conjugate in $\mathbf{SO}(m)$ to $\mathcal{I}_X$ and hence is isomorphic with it. Moreover, $\pi^{-1}(\pi(X))$ is homeomorphic with the quotient space $\mathbf{SO}(m)/\mathcal{I}_X$ and, to identify this quotient, we assume that X has rank j and, without loss of generality, also that its representing matrix has its last $m - j$ rows zero. Then $TX = X$ implies that T lies in the subgroup, isomorphic with $\mathbf{SO}(m - j)$, which fixes the subspace spanned by the first j rows. Therefore, the fibre of π above $\pi(X)$ is homeomorphic with $\mathbf{SO}(m)$, if $j \geqslant m - 1$, and with the Stiefel manifold $\mathbf{V}_{m,j} = \mathbf{SO}(m)/\mathbf{SO}(m - j)$ of orthonormal j frames in $\mathbb{R}^m$, if $j < m - 1$. We may also observe at this point that, since these fibres are compact, Σ_m^k is Hausdorff.

Let $\mathcal{D}_j$ denote the subset of $\mathcal{S}_m^k$ comprising all pre-shapes whose representing matrices have rank less than or equal to j, so that $\pi(\mathcal{D}_j)$ consists of the shapes of those configurations of k labelled points for which there is a j-dimensional affine hyperplane in $\mathbb{R}^m$ that contains all k points.

Before proceeding further we recall from Chapter 1 that it is sufficient to consider the case $k \geqslant m + 1$ and we shall indeed make that assumption for the remainder of this chapter, since otherwise we would need continually to make exceptions and special statements for the other cases. However, we shall, in due course, return to the case $k \leqslant m$ to flesh out the reasons that it is already covered by the general case.

Under the above assumption that $k \geqslant m + 1$, $\mathcal{D}_{m-2}$ is the subset of $\mathcal{S}_m^k$ of points at which the isotropy subgroup is non-trivial. Outside $\mathcal{D}_{m-2}$ the action of $\mathbf{SO}(m)$ is free, that is, no element except the identity has any fixed points, and basic theorems from differential geometry tell us that the corresponding part of the shape space inherits a differential structure, compatible with its topology, from that on the sphere. We therefore refer to $\pi(\mathcal{D}_{m-2})$ as the *singularity set* and its complement as the *non-singular part* of shape space. Since all matrices in the pre-shape sphere have rank at least one, the singular part of Σ_2^k is empty. However, for all $m > 2$, the singularity set is non-empty and is an important feature of shape space.

Since $\mathbf{SO}(m)$ acts as isometries of the sphere, the non-singular part of shape space also inherits a unique Riemannian metric that is compatible with its differential structure and with respect to which the quotient map π is particularly well-behaved. It is, in fact, an example of a Riemannian submersion, a concept introduced and studied by O'Neill (1966, 1967). However, it is sufficiently elementary that, rather than quote the general theorems, we are able to give a direct proof of all the properties we require, and also to make a modest extension of the general results in our context.

6.2   VIEWING THE INDUCED RIEMANNIAN METRIC THROUGH HORIZONTAL GEODESICS

A Riemannian metric on a differential manifold is a smooth choice of inner product on its various tangent spaces. In the case of the pre-shape sphere, thought of as naturally embedded as the unit sphere in $\mathbb{R}^{m(k-1)}$, this is just the usual inner product between vectors in a Euclidean space. In particular, if X is the 'position vector' of a point on the sphere, then the tangent vectors to the sphere at that point correspond to the vectors orthogonal to X. Thus, in our notation, with the coordinates arranged in an $m \times (k - 1)$ matrix, the tangent space $T_X(\mathcal{S}_m^k)$ to the pre-shape sphere at X is the subspace

$$\{Z \in \mathcal{M}(m, k - 1) : \operatorname{tr}(XZ^t) = 0\}$$

of $\mathcal{M}(m, k - 1) \cong \mathbb{R}^{m(k-1)}$, which is, as usual for the latter, thought of as being 'parallel translated' to act at X.

A Riemannian metric on a manifold enables us to define geodesics, the curves that may be characterised as taking the shortest path between any two sufficiently close points upon them. We shall conversely start by defining the geodesics and use them to define and explore the Riemannian structure of shape spaces. In Euclidean space geodesics are, of course, segments of straight lines and on a sphere, arcs of great circles. For a point X on the pre-shape sphere and any other point Z orthogonal to it, there is the geodesic

$$\Gamma_Z(s) = X \cos s + Z \sin s, \quad 0 \leqslant s \leqslant \pi, \tag{6.1}$$

joining them. The parameter s here is so chosen that, when it is positive, it is the distance travelled along Γ_Z from $\Gamma_Z(0) = X$ to $\Gamma_Z(s)$ and so, when $0 < s \leqslant \pi$, it is the *geodesic distance*, the length of the shortest great circular arc, between X and $\Gamma_Z(s)$. Any geodesic has, for each direction, a unique such *path-length parameterisation* and we shall always assume that is the parameterisation chosen. Since the tangent vector to the geodesic (6.1) at X is

$$\left. \frac{d\Gamma_Z(s)}{ds} \right|_{s=0} = Z,$$

we see that there is a natural bijection between directed geodesics through X and tangent vectors of unit length at X. The map

$$T_X(\mathcal{S}_m^k) \longrightarrow \mathcal{S}_m^k; \quad Z \mapsto \Gamma_{Z/\|Z\|}(\|Z\|)$$

is known as the *exponential map*. We note that it restricts to a diffeomorphism of $\{Z \in T_X(\mathcal{S}_m^k) : \|Z\| < \pi\}$ onto the whole of the sphere, except for the point antipodal to X.

When $\mathbf{SO}(m)$ is similarly regarded as a Riemannian submanifold of $\mathbb{R}^{m^2}$, the exponential map at the identity is

$$\hat{\Gamma}_A(s) = \exp(sA),$$

where

$$\exp(sA) = I + sA + \frac{s^2}{2!}A^2 + \cdots$$

is the obvious series of powers of $m \times m$ matrices, which converges for all s and A. This is indeed the origin of the term 'exponential' map for a general manifold and it is easily checked at least that, for suitable matrices A, $\hat{\Gamma}_A$ is a curve in $\mathbf{SO}(m)$ starting at I so that its tangent vector at $s = 0$,

$$\left. \frac{d\hat{\Gamma}_A(s)}{ds} \right|_{s=0} = A,$$

is tangent to $\mathbf{SO}(m)$ at the identity. For

$$\exp(sA) \in \mathbf{SO}(m) \iff \exp(sA)\exp(sA)^t = I$$
$$\iff \exp(s(A + A^t)) = I \iff A + A^t = 0.$$

Thus, any such skew-symmetric matrix A represents a vector tangent to $\mathbf{SO}(m)$ at I and, since the space of $m \times m$ skew-symmetric matrices has the same dimension, $m(m-1)/2$, as $\mathbf{SO}(m)$, it is the entire tangent space to $\mathbf{SO}(m)$ at I.

Since the geodesic $\exp(sA)$ lies in $\mathbf{SO}(m)$ whenever $A^t = -A$, it follows that $\hat{\gamma}_A(s) = \exp(sA)X$ lies in the fibre, or orbit, through X. We refer to the subspace of tangent vectors

$$\left. \frac{d\hat{\gamma}_A(s)}{ds} \right|_{s=0} = AX$$

to such curves at X as the *vertical* tangent subspace at X, and to its orthogonal complement in $\mathcal{T}_X(\mathcal{S}_m^k)$ as the *horizontal* tangent subspace of $\mathcal{T}_X(\mathcal{S}_m^k)$. Thus, the vertical subspace at X is given by

$$\mathcal{V}_X = \{AX : A^t = -A\}.$$

When $\pi(X)$ is a non-singular point, that is, $X \notin \mathcal{D}_{m-2}$, this vertical subspace is isomorphic with the tangent space to $\mathbf{SO}(m)$ at I. However, at a singular point the vectors A that are tangent to the isotropy subgroup give rise to the zero tangent vector AX since the corresponding curves initially remain stationary at X. Thus, at points X of $\mathcal{D}_j \setminus \mathcal{D}_{j-1}$, $\mathcal{V}_X$, specified as above, is indeed isomorphic to the tangent space to $\mathbf{V}_{m,j}$ at the frame corresponding to the first j rows of I. It follows that the horizontal subspace at X is

$$\mathcal{H}_X = \{Z \in \mathcal{M}(m, k-1) : \mathrm{tr}(XZ^t) = 0 \quad \text{and} \quad \mathrm{tr}(AXZ^t) = 0 \quad \forall A \text{ s.t. } A^t = -A\}$$
$$= \{Z \in \mathcal{M}(m, k-1) : \mathrm{tr}(XZ^t) = 0 \quad \text{and} \quad XZ^t = ZX^t\}.$$

Again, the specification is independent of the rank of X. When X has rank less than $m-1$, so that $\dim(\mathcal{V}_X) < \dim(\mathbf{SO}(m))$, then the space of matrices Z that are tangent to $\mathcal{S}_m^k$ and such that $XZ^t = ZX^t$ is correspondingly larger.

We are now in a position to make two crucial observations.

Proposition 6.1. (i) *If a geodesic in $\mathcal{S}_m^k$ starts out in a horizontal direction, then its tangent vectors remain horizontal throughout its length.*

(ii) *If $\Gamma_Z(s)$ is the distance-parameterised geodesic through X with initial direction Z, then, for any T in $\mathbf{SO}(m)$, $T\Gamma_Z(s)$ is the distance-parameterised geodesic $\Gamma_{TZ}(s)$ through TX with initial tangent vector TZ. Moreover, $\Gamma_Z(s)$ is horizontal if and only if $T\Gamma_Z(s)$ is horizontal.*

Proof.   (i) The geodesic $\Gamma_Z(s)$ is horizontal at $s = 0$ if and only if $XZ^t = ZX^t$. Then, for all s,

$$\Gamma_Z(s)\left(\frac{\mathrm{d}\Gamma_Z(s)}{\mathrm{d}s}\right)^t = (X\cos s + Z\sin s)(-X^t\sin s + Z^t\cos s)$$

$$= (-X\sin s + Z\cos s)(X^t\cos s + Z^t\sin s) = \frac{\mathrm{d}\Gamma_Z(s)}{\mathrm{d}s}\Gamma_Z(s)^t.$$

That is, each tangent vector $\frac{\mathrm{d}\Gamma_Z}{\mathrm{d}s}(s)$ is horizontal at $\Gamma_Z(s)$.

(ii) That $T\Gamma_Z(s) = TX\cos s + TZ\sin s$ is a distance-parameterised geodesic through TX follows from Equation (6.1) since $\mathrm{tr}\{TX(TZ)^t\} = \mathrm{tr}(TXZ^tT^t) = \mathrm{tr}(XZ^t) = 0$. Then, $\Gamma_Z(s)$ is horizontal if and only if $XZ^t = ZX^t$ and so if and only if

$$TX(TZ)^t = TXZ^tT^t = TZX^tT^t = TZ(TX)^t,$$

which is if and only if $T\Gamma_Z(s)$ is horizontal.   ∎

It follows that $\exp|_{\mathcal{H}_X}$ maps the subset of vectors of length less than π onto a submanifold $\mathbb{H}_X$ of $\mathcal{S}_m^k$ all of whose tangent vectors at X are horizontal. Now, if X lies outside $\mathcal{D}_{m-2}$, then so do all sufficiently close points and, since the tangent spaces to the fibre and to the $\mathbb{H}_X$ at X are orthogonal, there is a neighbourhood $\mathcal{U}_X$ of X in $\mathbb{H}_X$ such that, for all Y in $\mathcal{U}_X$, the tangent spaces to the fibre and to $\mathbb{H}_X$ at Y remain transverse. Thus, the fibre at Y meets $\mathcal{U}_X$ only at Y and we have established the following picture. Given X outside $\mathcal{D}_{m-2}$, through each point TX of the fibre at X there is a submanifold $\mathcal{U}_{TX}$, traced out by local horizontal geodesics through TX, such that

(i) the submanifolds $\mathcal{U}_{T_1X}$ and $\mathcal{U}_{T_2X}$ are disjoint if $T_1 \neq T_2$,

(ii) each submanifold $\mathcal{U}_{TX}$ is mapped by the quotient map bijectively, and hence homeomorphically with respect to the quotient topology, onto a neighbourhood of $\pi(X)$ in Σ_m^k,

(iii) the action of each $S \in \mathbf{SO}(m)$ restricts to a diffeomorphism of $\mathcal{U}_{TX}$ onto $\mathcal{U}_{STX}$ that also preserves the Riemannian metric, that is, it maps geodesics to geodesics of the same length and its derivative maps horizontal tangent vectors at TX to horizontal tangent vectors of the same length at STX.

It follows, first, that we may use $\mathcal{U}_X$ and $\pi|_{\mathcal{U}_X}$ to determine a differential structure on the non-singular part of shape space $\Sigma_m^k \setminus \pi(\mathcal{D}_{m-2})$, since for any other choice $(\mathcal{U}_{TX}, \pi|_{\mathcal{U}_{TX}})$ the composition $(\pi|_{\mathcal{U}_{TX}})^{-1} \circ (\pi|_{\mathcal{U}_X})$ is just the diffeomorphism $T|_{\mathcal{U}_X}$. We may also define a Riemannian structure there by defining the inner product of two tangent vectors at $\pi(X)$ to be the inner product of the corresponding horizontal vectors at X. Again, by (iii) above, it does not matter at which point in the fibre $\pi^{-1}(\pi(X))$ we do this. This Riemannian metric on the non-singular part of shape space will be investigated in more detail in Chapter 7.

The way we have defined the induced metric means, of course, that the projection π maps the horizontal subspace of the tangent space to the pre-shape sphere at X *isometrically* onto the tangent space to the shape space at $\pi(X)$, making it a so-called *Riemannian submersion*. It is usual to deduce from this that geodesics that start out in a horizontal direction remain horizontal and that they are mapped isometrically onto geodesics in the quotient manifold. However, in our case, we have already proved the former property and used it to derive the Riemannian submersion itself, and the definition ensures that horizontal geodesics are mapped onto curves of the same length. That they are also geodesics follows from the fact that *any* curve in shape space may be lifted to one of the same length in $\mathcal{S}_m^k$ whose tangents are everywhere horizontal.

If, instead of $\mathbf{SO}(m)$, we consider the action of $\mathbf{O}(m)$ on the pre-shape sphere, similar considerations to the above apply outside $\mathcal{D}_{m-1}$, which is the set of points with non-trivial isotropy subgroup in $\mathbf{O}(m)$. However, as $\mathbf{O}(m) = \mathbf{SO}(m) \bigcup \mathbf{SO}(m)T$, where T is any matrix in $\mathbf{O}(m)$ of determinant -1, each $\mathbf{O}(m)$-orbit may break up into two $\mathbf{SO}(m)$-orbits and $\mathcal{S}_m^k/\mathbf{O}(m) = \Sigma_m^k/\iota_m$, where ι_m maps each shape to the shape of the reflected configuration. Since ι_m is induced by multiplication by any $T \in \mathbf{O}(m)$ of determinant -1 on the pre-shape sphere, which is an isometry mapping fibres to fibres and hence horizontal subspaces to horizontal subspaces, this confirms that ι_m is an isometric involution of Σ_m^k and so induces a metric on the quotient space Σ_m^k/ι_m of unoriented shapes. The $\mathbf{O}(m)$ and $\mathbf{SO}(m)$ orbits of X coincide if and only if X lies in $\mathcal{D}_{m-1}$, since there we may find $T \in \mathbf{SO}(m)$ such that $\pi(TX)$ is the reflection of $\pi(X)$ and this is, of course, impossible if X has rank m. Hence ι_m leaves fixed all points of $\pi(\mathcal{D}_{m-1})$ but no others.

6.3   THE SINGULAR POINTS AND THE NESTING PRINCIPLE

To understand the singular part of shape space we observe first that each $\mathcal{D}_j$, $1 \leqslant j \leqslant m - 1$, is a submanifold of $\mathcal{S}_m^k$. The following elementary proof of this fact is due to Milnor. Without loss of generality, we may write any matrix $X \in \mathcal{S}_m^k$ of rank j in block form as

$$\begin{pmatrix} A & B \\ C & D \end{pmatrix},$$

where A is $j \times j$ and non-singular. Then, left multiplication by

$$\begin{pmatrix} I & 0 \\ -CA^{-1} & I \end{pmatrix}$$

shows that the rank of X is j if and only if $D = CA^{-1}B$. So the map

$$\begin{pmatrix} A_1 & B_1 \\ C_1 & D_1 \end{pmatrix} \mapsto \begin{pmatrix} A_1 & B_1 \\ C_1 & C_1 A_1^{-1} B_1 + D_1 \end{pmatrix}$$

is a diffeomorphism of a neighbourhood

$$\left\{ \begin{pmatrix} A_1 & B_1 \\ C_1 & D_1 \end{pmatrix} : \|A_1 - A\| < \varepsilon, \|B_1 - B\| < \varepsilon, \|C_1 - C\| < \varepsilon, \|D_1\| < \varepsilon \right\}$$

of

$$\begin{pmatrix} A & B \\ C & 0 \end{pmatrix}$$

onto a neighbourhood of X in $\mathcal{M}(m, k - 1)$, taking matrices with $D_1 = 0$ onto matrices of rank j. This is precisely the form of *chart* that is needed to show that the latter matrices form a submanifold of dimension

$$m(k - 1) - (m - j)(k - 1 - j) = j(k - 1 + m - j).$$

Since $\text{rank}(X) = \text{rank}(\lambda X)$ for $\lambda \neq 0$, it follows that $\mathcal{S}_m^k$ meets this submanifold transversely in a submanifold $\mathcal{D}_j$ of one lower dimension.

We also have a natural embedding $\mathcal{E}$ of the pre-shape sphere $\mathcal{S}_j^k$ in $\mathcal{S}_m^k$: that is, a diffeomorphism with a submanifold $\mathcal{E}\mathcal{S}_j^k$, mapping a matrix $X_1 \in \mathcal{S}_j^k$ to the same matrix extended by $m - j$ rows of zeros,

$$X = \begin{pmatrix} X_1 \\ 0 \end{pmatrix} \in \mathcal{E}S_m^k.$$

Then, $\mathcal{E}S_j^k$ is clearly the submanifold of $\mathcal{D}_j$ given in the above chart by $C_1 = D_1 = 0$.

We now consider the action of $\mathbf{SO}(m)$ on these submanifolds. The whole of $\mathbf{SO}(m)$ maps $\mathcal{D}_j$ into itself and, since each $\mathbf{SO}(m)$ orbit in $\mathcal{D}_j$ contains points of $\mathcal{E}S_j^k$, it follows that $\pi(\mathcal{D}_j) = \pi(\mathcal{E}S_j^k)$. However, the subgroup mapping $\mathcal{E}S_j^k$ into itself is isomorphic with $\mathbf{O}(j)$ and acts precisely as it does on $\mathcal{S}_j^k$ itself, and so $\pi(\mathcal{E}S_j^k)$ is isometric with Σ_j^k / ι_j. Thus, the nested sequence of submanifolds

$$\mathcal{D}_m \supset \mathcal{D}_{m-1} \supset \cdots \supset \mathcal{D}_j \supset \cdots \supset \mathcal{D}_1$$

gives rise to the nested sequence of subspaces in Σ_m^k, or stratification,

$$\Sigma_m^k \supset \Sigma_{m-1}^k / \iota_{m-1} \supset \cdots \supset \Sigma_j^k / \iota_j \supset \cdots \supset \Sigma_1^k / \iota_1,$$

which we first met in Chapter 2. Each *stratum*, the difference between two consecutive subspaces $(\Sigma_j^k / \iota_j) \setminus (\Sigma_{j-1}^k / \iota_{j-1})$, has a differential and Riemannian structure induced on it in the same manner as for $\Sigma_m^k \setminus \pi(\mathcal{D}_{m-2})$, with the restriction of the projection π to $\mathcal{D}_j \setminus \mathcal{D}_{j-1}$ being a Riemannian submersion.

This is a convenient point to look at the special case $k \leqslant m$ that we have been excluding. Since the pre-shape matrices are $m \times (k - 1)$ and $k < m + 1$, we now have $\mathcal{S}_m^k = \mathcal{D}_{k-1}$ and $\Sigma_m^k = \pi(\mathcal{D}_{k-1}) = \pi(\mathcal{E}S_{k-1}^k)$, which, as above, is isometric with $\Sigma_{k-1}^k / \iota_{k-1}$. Thus, the special case is indeed covered by knowledge of the Σ_{k-1}^k, which lie on the diagonal in Table 1.1, and of the isometric involutions ι_{k-1}.

Returning to the general case $k \geqslant m + 1$, we have already seen that the first two strata together form a non-singular manifold and, in fact, the second stratum $(\Sigma_{m-1}^k / \iota_{m-1}) \setminus (\Sigma_{m-2}^k / \iota_{m-2})$ is a submanifold of this since $\mathbf{SO}(m)$ acts freely on the invariant submanifold $\mathcal{D}_{m-1} \setminus \mathcal{D}_{m-2}$ of $\mathcal{S}_m^k$. This is the only case where adjacent strata combine in this way. Nevertheless, consecutive strata are embedded in each other in a regular manner, which, like the metric structure itself, is best explored through the geodesics.

Proposition 6.2. *All geodesics through points of $\mathcal{D}_j$ that start out in horizontal directions tangent to $\mathcal{D}_j$ remain in $\mathcal{D}_j$. Those that start out in directions tangent to $\mathcal{D}_j \setminus \mathcal{D}_{j-1}$ will only meet the submanifolds $\mathcal{D}_i$ for $i < j$ in isolated points.*

Proof. The horizontal subspace at

$$X = \begin{pmatrix} X_1 \\ 0 \end{pmatrix}$$

for the action of the subgroup, isomorphic with $\mathbf{O}(j)$, mapping $\mathcal{E}S_j^k$ into itself is

$$\left\{ \begin{pmatrix} Z_1 \\ 0 \end{pmatrix} : \text{tr}(X_1 Z_1^t) = 0 \quad \text{and} \quad X_1 Z_1^t = Z_1 X_1^t \right\}.$$

Since $\pi(\mathcal{D}_j) = \pi(\mathcal{E}S_j^k)$, this must also be the full horizontal subspace at X for the action of $\mathbf{SO}(m)$ on $\mathcal{D}_j$. It follows that a horizontal direction Z tangent to $\mathcal{D}_j$ at $X \in \mathcal{E}S_j^k$ is, in fact, a horizontal vector

$$Z = \begin{pmatrix} Z_1 \\ 0 \end{pmatrix}$$

tangent to $\mathcal{E}S_j^k$. Thus, the horizontal geodesic Γ_Z through X is the image $\mathcal{E}\Gamma_{Z_1}$ in $\mathcal{E}S_j^k$ of the horizontal geodesic Γ_{Z_1} through X_1 in $\mathcal{S}_j^k$. In particular, Γ_Z remains in $\mathcal{D}_j$. However, the general point of $\mathcal{D}_j$ is TX for some $T \in \mathbf{SO}(m)$ and some $X \in \mathcal{E}S_j^k$, and a horizontal direction tangent to $\mathcal{D}_j$ at TX is TZ for some Z, which is horizontal and tangent to $\mathcal{E}S_j^k$ at X. Then, the corresponding geodesic Γ_{TZ} at TX is $T\Gamma_Z$ by Proposition 6.1, and this lies in $\mathcal{D}_j$ since Γ_Z does. As horizontal geodesics are reversible, if TZ is tangent to $\mathcal{D}_j \setminus \mathcal{D}_{j-1}$ and Γ_{TZ} meets $\mathcal{D}_i$ with $i < j$, then it must do so transversely and hence in isolated points, since if it were tangent to $\mathcal{D}_i$ it would have to remain in it and hence be tangent to $\mathcal{D}_i$ throughout its length and, in particular, at TX.   ∎

Note that, if $j < m$, there will always be horizontal geodesics meeting $\mathcal{D}_j$ transversely, since the fibre through X in $\mathcal{D}_j$ is the full fibre through X in $\mathcal{S}_m^k$, and so the horizontal subspace at X for the action of $\mathbf{SO}(m)$ on $\mathcal{S}_m^k$ must have a further direct summand: namely, the orthogonal complement to the subspace tangent to $\mathcal{D}_j$.

Now, horizontality is definable everywhere in $\mathcal{S}_m^k$ and a geodesic in each stratum is the image of a horizontal geodesic. Thus, we may extend the usual definition of a geodesic in a Riemannian manifold to shape spaces as follows.

Definition 6.1. A geodesic in Σ_m^k is the image of any horizontal geodesic in $\mathcal{S}_m^k$.

This concept of a geodesic is well defined by Proposition 6.1, and it applies whether or not the image remains in a single stratum. It is a geodesic in the usual sense, except at isolated points where it meets lower strata, and even there it is locally a limit of geodesics in an obvious manner. This definition makes each subspace Σ_j^k / ι_j totally geodesic in each higher one in the usual sense that a geodesic in one subspace is still a geodesic when it is regarded as a subset of a larger one. In particular, $(\Sigma_{m-1}^k \setminus \pi(\mathcal{D}_{m-2})) / \iota_{m-1}$ is a totally geodesic submanifold of $\Sigma_m^k \setminus \pi(\mathcal{D}_{m-2})$.

6.4   THE DISTANCE BETWEEN SHAPES

A Riemannian metric on a manifold determines a distance function that is the minimum length of the geodesics between two points and this definition extends naturally to the whole of shape space using our extended definition of geodesics. Since a geodesic between two shapes $\pi(X)$ and $\pi(Y)$ is the image of a horizontal geodesic Γ from X to some point TY in the fibre over $\pi(Y)$ and since Γ meets the fibres through X and TY orthogonally at those points, it follows that the induced distance between any two shapes $\pi(X)$ and $\pi(Y)$ is given by

$$\rho(\pi(X), \pi(Y)) = \min_{T \in \mathbf{SO}(m)} d(X, TY) = \arccos \max_{T \in \mathbf{SO}(m)} \operatorname{tr}(TYX^t), \qquad (6.2)$$

where d is the shortest great circular arc distance on the pre-shape sphere. This is precisely the formula (1.3) already given in Chapter 1.

Another commonly used distance $\hat{\rho}$ on the shape space, sometimes called the *procrustean distance*, is the one induced from the chordal distance $\hat{d}$ on the pre-shape sphere. Here, $\hat{d}$ is the distance measured directly in the Euclidean space in which the pre-shape sphere lies, so that

$$\hat{d}(X, Y) = ||X - Y||$$

and

$$\hat{\rho}(\pi(X), \pi(Y)) = \min_{T \in \mathbf{SO}(m)} ||X - TY||.$$

Although the distance $\hat{\rho}$ does not give the Riemannian metric on the shape space, these two induced distances ρ and $\hat{\rho}$ are topologically equivalent and there is even a simple functional relation between them. This relation is obtained by noting that

$$\hat{d}(X, Y)^2 = \operatorname{tr}\{(X - Y)(X - Y)^t\} = 2 - 2\operatorname{tr}(XY^t),$$

which leads to

$$\hat{\rho}(\pi(X), \pi(Y))^2 = \min_{T \in \mathbf{SO}(m)} \operatorname{tr}\{(X - TY)(X - TY)^t\}$$

$$= 2\{1 - \cos(\rho(\pi(X), \pi(Y)))\}. \qquad (6.3)$$

To simplify the expression on the right-hand side of (6.2) we shall use pseudo-singular values decompositions of the $m \times m$ square matrix YX^t. We recall, from Chapter 1, that this is the expression $YX^t = U \Lambda V$, where U and V are in $\mathbf{SO}(m)$ and $\Lambda = \operatorname{diag}\{\lambda_1, \ldots, \lambda_m\}$ with the diagonal elements λ_i satisfying $\lambda_1 \geqslant \cdots \geqslant \lambda_{m-1} \geqslant |\lambda_m|$ and $\operatorname{sign}(\lambda_m) = \operatorname{sign}(\det(YX^t))$. Then, the λ_i are called the *pseudo-singular values* of YX^t, or of XY^t. Two points should be emphasised.

Firstly, we should distinguish the above from the analogous, more familiar, *singular values decomposition* for which the matrices U and V may be chosen in $\mathbf{O}(m)$ rather than $\mathbf{SO}(m)$. Consequently, for uniqueness, we require $\lambda_m \geqslant 0$ and we now call the λ_i *singular values*. We note that, for both singular and pseudo-singular values, their squares are the eigenvalues of XY^tYX^t, the rows of V are unit length eigenvectors of XY^tYX^t and the columns of U are unit length eigenvectors of YX^tXY^t, these rows and columns being arranged in the same order as the corresponding eigenvalues λ_i^2. Thus, although the matrices U and V are not unique, *the diagonal matrix Λ is uniquely determined by XY^tYX^t and*, for the pseudo-singular values decomposition, *the sign of* $\det(YX^t)$. The matrix Λ also remains unaltered if X and Y are each pre-multiplied by, perhaps different, rotations in $\mathbf{SO}(m)$, so it depends only on the pair of shapes $\pi(X)$ and $\pi(Y)$. We also note that, if we denote by $\overline{Y}$ the matrix obtained from Y by changing the signs of the entries of the last row so that $\pi(\overline{Y})$ is the reflection $\iota_m(\pi(Y))$ of the shape $\pi(Y)$, then YX^t and $\overline{Y}X^t$ have the same pseudo-singular values save that the last one has a different sign if it is not zero.

Secondly, it should be noted that we use the pseudo-singular values of the square matrix YX^t to compute the distance between the shapes $\pi(X)$ and $\pi(Y)$ and later we shall use the full decomposition to describe the geodesics between these shapes. Whereas, psuedo-singular values decompositions of the $m \times (k-1)$ matrix X as $U(\Lambda \quad 0)V$, introduced in Chapter 1, will be used in Section 6.8 to investigate the projections onto lower strata and also in Lemma 7.2 to obtain local coordinates on shape space in the neighbourhood of the shape $\pi(X)$. In general, there is not a simple relationship between the pseudo-singular values decomposition of YX^t and those of the individual pre-shapes X and Y themselves.

A pseudo-singular values decomposition of YX^t gives rise to an alternative decomposition

$$YX^t = RQ, \quad \text{where} \quad R \equiv UV \quad \text{and} \quad Q \equiv V^t\Lambda V.$$

Then, R is in $\mathbf{SO}(m)$ and Q is symmetric and, since $Q = V^t\Lambda V$ is a pseudo-singular values decomposition, its pseudo-singular values coincide with its eigenvalues. Again by analogy with the classical case, we refer to such a decomposition as a *pseudo-polar decomposition.*

If at least one of X and Y is in $\mathcal{D}_{m-1}$, then we have $\lambda_m = 0$, so Q is positive semi-definite and we have a polar decomposition. In particular, when $k = m + 1$, the corresponding pre-shapes are square matrices and hence $\lambda_m = 0$ if and only if at least one of $\pi(X)$ and $\pi(Y)$ is in $\pi(\mathcal{D}_{m-1})$. However, if $k > m$ and neither of X and Y is in $\mathcal{D}_{m-1}$, then Q is *not* necessarily positive semi-definite.

Now,

$$\max_{T\in\mathbf{SO}(m)} \text{tr}(TYX^t) = \max_{T\in\mathbf{SO}(m)} \text{tr}(VTU\Lambda) = \sum_{i=1}^{m} \lambda_i \geqslant 0,$$

the supremum being attained when $VTU = I$ (cf. Kendall, 1984), that is, when $T = (UV)^t$, and hence we have

$$\rho(\pi(X), \pi(Y)) = \arccos \sum_{i=1}^{m} \lambda_i. \tag{6.4}$$

Thus, it is clear that the calculation required to find the Riemannian distance between any two shapes is elementary and simple to program.

If, throughout the above, we replace $\mathbf{SO}(m)$ by $\mathbf{O}(m)$ and pseudo-singular values by singular values, we obtain analogous results for Σ_m^k/ι_m. In particular, the distance has the same expression (6.4), except that the summands λ_i are now the singular values. Thus, we see that the distance between $\pi(X)$ and $\pi(Y)$ in Σ_m^k/ι_m is the minimum of the distances $\rho(\pi(X), \pi(Y))$ and $\rho(\pi(X), \pi(\overline{Y}))$ in Σ_m^k.

Since $0 \leqslant \sum_{i=1}^m \lambda_i \leqslant 1$, we deduce that the diameter of shape space is bounded above by $\pi/2$, and we shall call shapes that are $\pi/2$ apart *maximally remote*. For $m = 2$, the existence of maximally remote pairs $\pi(X)$ and $\pi(Y)$ is equivalent to the condition that the pseudo-singular values of YX^t satisfy $\lambda_1 = -\lambda_2$, so that such pairs always exist. When $m \geqslant 3$, $\sum_{i=1}^m \lambda_i = 0$ is equivalent to $\Lambda = 0$: that is, to $YX^t = 0$. Note that this statement is false when $m = 2$. However, if X lies in $\mathcal{D}_{m-1}$, we can always find a non-zero Y such that $YX^t = 0$, and again $\pi(X)$ and $\pi(Y)$ will be maximally remote. Hence, *maximally remote pairs $\pi(X)$ and $\pi(Y)$ exist in all cases*, and the diameter of shape space *is $\pi/2$*.

More generally, $YX^t = 0$ means that the row space of Y is orthogonal to the row space of X, which means that if $\rho(\pi(X), \pi(Y)) = \pi/2$ we must have

$$\text{rank}(X) + \text{rank}(Y) \leqslant k - 1.$$

Then, as each of $\text{rank}(X)$ and $\text{rank}(Y)$ is not less than one, we obtain the following result.

Theorem 6.1. (i) *If $k = m + 1 > 3$ and $\pi(X)$ and $\pi(Y)$ are maximally remote, then both $\pi(X)$ and $\pi(Y)$ must lie in $\pi(\mathcal{D}_{m-1})$.*

(ii) *If $m + 1 < k \leqslant 2m$ and $\pi(X)$ and $\pi(Y)$ are maximally remote, then at least one of $\pi(X)$ and $\pi(Y)$ must lie in $\pi(\mathcal{D}_{m-1})$.*

(iii) *If $k > 2m$, then there exist maximally remote $\pi(X)$ and $\pi(Y)$ with neither of $\pi(X)$ and $\pi(Y)$ in $\pi(\mathcal{D}_{m-1})$.*

6.5 THE SET OF GEODESICS BETWEEN TWO SHAPES

To study the geodesics in shape space between any two given shapes we define $\mathcal{R}(X, Y)$ to be the set of all $R \in \mathbf{SO}(m)$ such that $Q = R^t YX^t$ is symmetric and its pseudo-singular values coincide with its eigenvalues. That is, $\mathcal{R}(X, Y)$ is the set of all rotations R that can occur in a pseudo-polar decomposition of YX^t. Then,

$$\mathcal{R}(Y, X) = \{R^t : R \in \mathcal{R}(X, Y)\}$$

and, if $T_1, T_2 \in \mathbf{SO}(m)$, there are natural bijections between $\mathcal{R}(T_1X, Y)$, $\mathcal{R}(X, T_2Y)$ and $\mathcal{R}(X, Y)$ since

$$\mathcal{R}(T_1X, Y) = \mathcal{R}(X, Y)T_1^t \equiv \{RT_1^t : R \in \mathcal{R}(X, Y)\} \text{ and } \mathcal{R}(X, T_2Y) = T_2\mathcal{R}(X, Y).$$

In the case that $m = 2$, if we use $(k - 1)$-dimensional complex vectors, instead of $2 \times (k - 1)$ matrices, to represent the pre-shapes and identify $SO(2)$ with S^1, then the corresponding YX^t will be a complex number, and $e^{i\theta} = R \in SO(2)$ is in $\mathcal{R}(X, Y)$ if and only if the complex number corresponding to R^tYX^t is, in fact, real and equal to the norm of the complex number corresponding to YX^t.

Proposition 6.3. *Let $R \in SO(m)$. Then $R \in \mathcal{R}(X, Y)$ if and only if R^tYX^t is symmetric and $\rho(\pi(X), \pi(Y)) = d(X, R^tY)$.*

Proof.   Suppose that $R \in SO(m)$ and that R^tYX^t is symmetric with eigenvalues $\tilde{\lambda}_i$. Then, $\{\tilde{\lambda}_i^2 : 1 \leqslant i \leqslant m\}$ is the set of eigenvalues of XY^tYX^t. Since the pseudo-singular values of R^tYX^t are the same as those λ_i of YX^t, we have, after relabelling to make $\{\tilde{\lambda}_i^2 : 1 \leqslant i \leqslant m\}$ non-increasing, that each $\tilde{\lambda}_i$ is $\pm|\lambda_i|$. However, $d(X, R^tY) = \arccos \sum_{i=1}^m \tilde{\lambda}_i$. So, $d(X, R^tY) = \rho(\pi(X), \pi(Y))$ if and only if $\sum_{i=1}^m \tilde{\lambda}_i = \sum_{i=1}^m \lambda_i$, and it easily follows that this holds if and only if $\tilde{\lambda}_i = \lambda_i$ for all $1 \leqslant i \leqslant m$. So, the equivalence between the two statements is established.   ∎

It follows from Proposition 6.3 that the point R^tY for $R \in \mathcal{R}(X, Y)$ is a point on the fibre above $\pi(Y)$ whose great circular distance from X is the minimum possible for all points on the fibre above $\pi(Y)$, which implies that the great circle through X and R^tY on the pre-shape sphere is orthogonal to the fibre above $\pi(Y)$. However, such a point R^tY on the fibre *will not always be unique*. This lack of uniqueness is associated with (i) the fact that U and V can be varied independently in the decomposition $YX^t = U\Lambda V$ when $\mathrm{rank}(YX^t) \leqslant m - 2$, and (ii) the non-uniqueness of Q in the pseudo-polar decomposition $YX^t = RQ$ when $\lambda_m = -\lambda_{m-1} < 0$. The claim that these features create a situation in which $R \in \mathcal{R}(X, Y)$ fails to be unique will be confirmed later. We first use the set $\mathcal{R}(X, Y)$ to characterise the horizontal lifts of minimal geodesics between $\pi(X)$ and $\pi(Y)$ as follows.

Theorem 6.2. *If $\rho(\pi(X), \pi(Y)) = s_0$ with $0 < s_0 \leqslant \pi/2$, then a curve in the pre-shape sphere is a horizontal lift starting at X of a minimal geodesic from $\pi(X)$ to $\pi(Y)$ if and only if it can be expressed in the form*

$$\gamma_R(s) = \frac{1}{\sin s_0} \left\{ X \sin(s_0 - s) + R^tY \sin s \right\}, \quad 0 \leqslant s \leqslant s_0,$$

with $R \in \mathcal{R}(X, Y)$.

Proof.   For $R \in \mathcal{R}(X, Y)$ we know that R^tYX^t is symmetric with trace $\sum_{i=1}^m \lambda_i$ and that $\rho(\pi(X), \pi(Y))$ is $s_0 = \arccos(\mathrm{tr}(R^tYX^t))$, where $0 < s_0 \leqslant \pi/2$ assuming $\pi(X) \neq \pi(Y)$. Choosing $Z \in T_X(\mathcal{S}_m^k)$ to be

$$Z = \frac{1}{\sin s_0} \{R^tY - X \cos s_0\},$$

we have $\mathrm{tr}(XZ^t) = 0$ and $XZ^t = ZX^t$ so that Z determines a horizontal great circle through X of which the restriction to $[0, s_0]$ is γ_R. Then, $\pi \circ \gamma_R$ is minimal since its length is s_0, the distance between $\pi(X)$ and $\pi(Y)$.

Conversely, all minimal geodesics in Σ_m^k arise in this way. For suppose a minimal geodesic from $\pi(X)$ to $\pi(Y)$ lifts to a horizontal great circular arc γ starting at X. Then, γ will be some Γ_Z as in (6.1) for $s \in [0, s_0]$, where $s_0 = \rho(\pi(X), \pi(Y))$. However, $\gamma(s_0) = R^t Y$ and by Proposition 6.3, since $d(\gamma(0), \gamma(s_0)) = s_0$, we must have $R \in \mathcal{R}(X, Y)$. Whence $Z = (R^t Y - X \cos s_0)/\sin s_0$ as required. ∎

Thus,

$$\mathcal{G}(\pi(X), \pi(Y)) = \{\pi \circ \gamma_R([0, s_0]) : R \in \mathcal{R}(X, Y)\}$$

gives all possible minimal geodesics between $\pi(X)$ and $\pi(Y)$ in Σ_m^k. Note, however, that $\mathcal{G}(\pi(X), \pi(Y))$ is not necessarily in one-to-one correspondence with $\mathcal{R}(X, Y)$. In other words, there may exist $R_1 \neq R_2 \in \mathcal{R}(X, Y)$ such that the corresponding curves $\gamma(s)$ give the same great circular arcs in the pre-shape sphere. Nevertheless, the curves $\gamma(s)$ corresponding to two different R in $\mathcal{R}(X, Y)$ either coincide for all s such that $0 < s < s_0$ or never meet for any such s. The relation between $\mathcal{G}(\pi(X), \pi(Y))$ and $\mathcal{R}(X, Y)$ will be investigated later.

The following result follows immediately from Theorem 6.2, together with Proposition 6.3.

Corollary 6.1. *If $\gamma([0, s_0])$ is a horizontal lift starting at X of a minimal geodesic from $\pi(X)$ to $\pi(Y)$, then $\pi \circ \gamma([0, s])$ remains a minimal geodesic for $s > s_0$ if and only if the eigenvalues of $\gamma(s)X^t$ are the same as its pseudo-singular values.*

In Section 6.3 we showed that geodesics meet the lower strata of Σ_m^k in isolated points. For minimal geodesics we can say more, using their identification in Theorem 6.2.

Theorem 6.3. *A minimal geodesic between $\pi(X)$ and $\pi(Y)$ in Σ_m^k lies entirely in a single stratum except possibly for its end points being in lower strata and, if $\rho(\pi(X), \pi(Y)) > \rho(\pi(X), \iota_m(\pi(Y)))$, at most one point of $\pi(\mathcal{D}_{m-1} \setminus \mathcal{D}_{m-2})$.*

Proof. We observe that XX^t is symmetric, positive semi-definite and has the same rank as X and that, when $\lambda_m \geqslant 0$ and $R \in \mathcal{R}(X, Y)$, $R^t Y X^t$ is also positive semi-definite. Thus, if v is a non-zero eigenvector corresponding to a non-zero eigenvalue of XX^t, we have

$$v^t \gamma_R(s) X^t v \geqslant \frac{\sin(s_0 - s)}{\sin s_0} v^t XX^t v > 0,$$

provided $0 < s < s_0$. So, for such s, $\mathrm{rank}(\gamma_R(s)) \geqslant \mathrm{rank}(\gamma_R(s)X^t) \geqslant \mathrm{rank}(XX^t) = \mathrm{rank}(X)$. It follows that, if $\lambda_m \geqslant 0$, $\mathrm{rank}(\gamma_R(s)) \geqslant \max\{\mathrm{rank}(X), \mathrm{rank}(Y)\}$. When $\lambda_m < 0$, which can only occur if $\mathrm{rank}(X) = \mathrm{rank}(Y) = m$ and is equivalent to the condition $\rho(\pi(X), \pi(Y)) > \rho(\pi(X), \iota_m(\pi(Y)))$ stated in the theorem, XX^t is positive definite and there is a subspace of dimension $m - 1$ on which $R^t Y X^t$ is positive definite. Then, a similar argument to the above shows that γ_R can only meet $\mathcal{D}_{m-1}$, and we already know from Proposition 6.2 that it can only do so in isolated points. However, if $\gamma_R(s_1)$ and $\gamma_R(s_2)$ were in $\mathcal{D}_{m-1}$, where $0 < s_1 < s_2 < s_0$, then $\pi \circ \gamma_R |_{[0,s_2]}$ would be a minimal geodesic between a point $\pi(X)$ not in $\pi(\mathcal{D}_{m-1})$ and a point $\pi(\gamma_R(s_2))$ in $\pi(\mathcal{D}_{m-1})$ that meets $\pi(\mathcal{D}_{m-1})$ again at $\pi(\gamma_R(s_1))$, contrary to what we have just proved.

Suppose that the tangent vector

$$\frac{\mathrm{d}\gamma_R(s)}{\mathrm{d}s}\bigg|_{s=0}$$

to the curve γ_R at $s = 0$ is tangent to $\mathcal{D}_j$ and not to $\mathcal{D}_{j-1}$. Then, $j \geqslant \mathrm{rank}(X)$ and, by Proposition 6.2, $\gamma_R([0, s_0])$ lies in $\mathcal{D}_j$ and only meets the lower strata in isolated points. Hence, there must be points $X' = \gamma_R(s')$ in $\mathcal{D}_j \setminus \mathcal{D}_{j-1}$ arbitrarily close to X. Since the restriction of a minimal geodesic is necessarily still a minimal geodesic, the above result shows that $\gamma_R(s) \in \mathcal{D}_j \setminus \mathcal{D}_{j-1}$ for $0 < s < s_0$, except possibly when $j = m$.

When $j = m = \max\{\mathrm{rank}(X), \mathrm{rank}(Y)\}$ the results stated in the theorem are already established. If $j = m > \max\{\mathrm{rank}(X), \mathrm{rank}(Y)\}$, we can find points X' arbitrarily close to X and Y' arbitrarily close to Y, and lying between X and Y along γ_R, with X' and Y' of rank m. If γ_R meets $\mathcal{D}_{m-1}$, then, by the above, we must have $\rho(\pi(X'), \pi(Y')) > \rho(\pi(X'), \iota_m(\pi(Y')))$ for such X' and Y' sufficiently close to X and Y, respectively. However, ι_m is an isometry, $\iota_m(\pi(Y)) = \pi(Y)$ and both $\pi(X')$ and $\pi(Y')$ lie along a minimal geodesic from $\pi(X)$ to $\pi(Y)$, so this would imply that

$$
\begin{aligned}
\rho(\pi(X), \pi(Y)) &\leqslant \rho(\pi(X), \pi(X')) + \rho(\pi(X'), \iota_m(\pi(Y'))) + \rho(\iota_m(\pi(Y')), \pi(Y)) \\
&= \rho(\pi(X), \pi(X')) + \rho(\pi(X'), \iota_m(\pi(Y'))) + \rho(\pi(Y'), \pi(Y)) \\
&< \rho(\pi(X), \pi(X')) + \rho(\pi(X'), \pi(Y')) + \rho(\pi(Y'), \pi(Y)) \\
&= \rho(\pi(X), \pi(Y)),
\end{aligned}
$$

which is impossible. So, in this case, $\gamma_R(s) \in \mathcal{D}_m \setminus \mathcal{D}_{m-1}$ for $0 < s < s_0$ and the proof of the theorem is complete.   ∎

Note that, when $k = m + 1$, if $\rho(\pi(X), \pi(Y)) > \rho(\pi(X), \pi(\iota_m(Y)))$, then γ_R must meet $\mathcal{D}_{m-1}$ at least once, and hence precisely once. For, if v is an eigenvector of $R^t Y X^t$ with eigenvalue $\lambda_m < 0$ and if $v^t X X^t v = \alpha v^t v$, where $\alpha > 0$, then $v^t \gamma_R(s) X^t v = 0$ when

$$\tan s = \frac{\tan s_0}{1 - (\lambda_m/\alpha) \sec s_0}$$

and so $0 < s < s_0$. Thus, $\gamma_R(s)X^t$ is singular at this point and so $\gamma_R(s)$ must be singular since X^t is a non-singular square matrix.

On the other hand, the following shows that, when $k > m + 1$ and $\rho(\pi(X), \pi(Y)) > \rho(\pi(X), \pi(\iota_m(Y)))$, the geodesic may avoid $\pi(\mathcal{D}_{m-1})$ altogether. Let

$$X = \begin{pmatrix} \frac{1}{\sqrt{2}} & 0 & 0 \\ 0 & \frac{1}{\sqrt{2}} & 0 \end{pmatrix} \quad \text{and} \quad Y = \begin{pmatrix} \frac{1}{\sqrt{2}} & 0 & 0 \\ 0 & -\frac{1}{2} & \frac{1}{2} \end{pmatrix}.$$

Then, $YX^t = \text{diag}\{1/2, -1/(2\sqrt{2})\}$ so that $\lambda_2 < 0$ and we are in the exceptional case. However, we also have $\mathcal{R}(X, Y) = \{I\}$ and the horizontal lift starting at X of the unique minimal geodesic between $\pi(X)$ and $\pi(Y)$ is

$$\gamma(s) = \frac{1}{\sin s_0}\{X \sin(s_0 - s) + Y \sin s\}$$

$$= \frac{1}{\sin s_0} \begin{pmatrix} \frac{1}{\sqrt{2}}\{\sin(s_0 - s) + \sin s\} & 0 & 0 \\ 0 & \frac{1}{\sqrt{2}}\sin(s_0 - s) - \frac{1}{2}\sin s & \frac{1}{2}\sin s \end{pmatrix}$$

for $0 \leqslant s \leqslant s_0$, where s_0 in $[0, \pi/2]$ is determined by $\cos s_0 = 1/2 - 1/(2\sqrt{2})$. It is clear that the rank of $\gamma(s)$ for all $s \in [0, s_0]$ is two, so that $\pi(\gamma([0, s_0]))$ avoids $\pi(\mathcal{D}_1)$.

We shall also see in the next section that when $\max\{\text{rank}(X), \text{rank}(Y)\} = j < m$ it may be possible for a minimal geodesic from $\pi(X)$ to $\pi(Y)$ to lie in a higher stratum than $(\Sigma_j^k/\iota_j) \setminus (\Sigma_{j-1}^k/\iota_{j-1})$. Indeed, we shall be able to identify precisely when this does occur.

6.6   THE NON-UNIQUENESS OF MINIMAL GEODESICS

Recall that the shape space Σ_2^3 of three labelled points in the plane is $S^2(\frac{1}{2})$, a 2-sphere with radius one-half. Thus, for any point $\pi(X) \in \Sigma_2^3$, the set $\mathcal{G}(\pi(X), \pi(Y))$ of all minimal geodesics joining $\pi(X)$ and the antipodal point $\pi(Y)$ at a distance $\pi/2$ from it can be identified with $S^1(\frac{1}{2})$, which we could take to be the equator associated with $\pi(X)$. This phenomenon of the non-uniqueness of minimal geodesics between two shapes is associated with the fact that $\mathcal{R}(X, Y)$ may contain more than one element, as we pointed out earlier. For then Theorem 6.2 indicates that, from any point on the fibre above $\pi(X)$, we may be able to find more than one minimal horizontal great circular path to the fibre above $\pi(Y)$, each being of length s_0. Correspondingly, in shape space, although distinct members of $\mathcal{R}(X, Y)$ do not necessarily give rise to distinct geodesics, there may then be more than one minimal geodesic of length s_0 from $\pi(X)$ to $\pi(Y)$. The following example illustrates that this situation can occur in Σ_3^4. Although this is a topological sphere, it is not a metric one, as we shall see in Section 6.8. Thus, the non-uniqueness of geodesics between two shapes is no longer as obvious as it was in the metric sphere Σ_2^3. Let us take

$$X = \begin{pmatrix} \frac{1}{\sqrt{2}} & 0 & 0 \\ 0 & \frac{1}{\sqrt{2}} & 0 \\ 0 & 0 & 0 \end{pmatrix} \quad \text{and} \quad Y = \begin{pmatrix} 0 & 0 & 1 \\ 0 & 0 & 0 \\ 0 & 0 & 0 \end{pmatrix},$$

so that $\text{rank}(X) = 2$ and $\text{rank}(Y) = 1$. Since $YX^t = 0$, $\mathcal{R}(X, Y) = \mathbf{SO}(3)$ so that the choice of R is unrestricted. Thus, the horizontal geodesics are

$$\gamma(s) = \begin{pmatrix} \frac{1}{\sqrt{2}} \cos s & 0 & a \sin s \\ 0 & \frac{1}{\sqrt{2}} \cos s & b \sin s \\ 0 & 0 & c \sin s \end{pmatrix},$$

where the only restriction is that $a^2 + b^2 + c^2 = 1$. This two-parameter family of horizontal geodesics in the pre-shape sphere does map to a two-parameter family of minimal geodesics from $\pi(X)$ to $\pi(Y)$ since

$$\gamma(s)^t \gamma(s) = \begin{pmatrix} \frac{1}{2}\cos^2 s & 0 & \frac{1}{\sqrt{2}} a \sin s \cos s \\ 0 & \frac{1}{2}\cos^2 s & \frac{1}{\sqrt{2}} b \sin s \cos s \\ \frac{1}{\sqrt{2}} a \sin s \cos s & \frac{1}{\sqrt{2}} b \sin s \cos s & \sin^2 s \end{pmatrix},$$

which shows that the shape $\pi(\gamma(s))$ depends on a and b for $0 < s < s_0 = \pi/2$. We note also that, except when $c = 0$, that is, when $a^2 + b^2 = 1$, these minimal geodesics lie in the top stratum, despite their endpoints being in lower strata.

In this section we shall determine the size of the set $\mathcal{G}(\pi(X), \pi(Y))$ of minimal geodesics between two arbitrary points of shape space, using our extended definition of geodesics. We first examine the lack of uniqueness of $R \in \mathcal{R}(X, Y)$.

Lemma 6.1. (i) *When* $\text{rank}(YX^t) = m$, *then* $R \in \mathcal{R}(X, Y)$ *is unique unless* $\lambda_{m-1} + \lambda_m = 0$, *in which case the set* $\mathcal{R}(X, Y)$ *is in one-to-one correspondence with* $\mathbf{RP}^{l-1}$, *where l is the multiplicity of the eigenvalue λ_m^2 of XY^tYX^t.*
(ii) *When* $\text{rank}(YX^t) \leqslant m - 1$, *the set* $\mathcal{R}(X, Y)$ *is in one-to-one correspondence with* $\mathbf{SO}(m - l)$, *where $l = \text{rank}(YX^t)$.*

Thus, $R \in \mathcal{R}(X, Y)$ is unique if and only if $\lambda_{m-1} + \lambda_m > 0$.

Proof. We examine first the indeterminacy in the factor Q in the pseudo-polar decomposition $YX^t = RQ$, where, for some pseudo-singular values decomposition $YX^t = U\Lambda V$, we have $Q = V^t \Lambda V$. Then, if $\lambda_m \geqslant 0$, Q is the unique non-negative square root of $Q^2 = V^t \Lambda^2 V = XY^tYX^t$ and so is uniquely determined by X and Y.
If $\lambda_m < 0$, let v_m be the final row of V, which means that it is an eigenvector of XY^tYX^t with eigenvalue λ_m^2. Then, $Q^* = Q - 2\lambda_m v_m^t v_m$ is the unique positive

square root of XY^tYX^t since $Q^* = V^t\bar{\Lambda}V$, where $\bar{\Lambda}$ is Λ with the final diagonal entry λ_m replaced by $-\lambda_m > 0$. Thus, Q is determined by v_m, which may be any unit vector in the l-dimensional eigenspace in $\mathbb{R}^m$ associated with the eigenvalue λ_m^2 of Q^2. However, the sign of v_m is irrelevant, so the resolution of the indeterminacy in Q is equivalent to choosing a point in the real projective space $\mathbf{RP}^{l-1}$.

Now, if $\lambda_m \neq 0$, then YX^t is non-singular and there is a one-to-one correspondence between the R's and the Q's that occur in the pseudo-polar decomposition $YX^t = RQ$ since then $Q = R^{-1}YX^t$ is non-singular and $R = YX^tQ^{-1}$. Hence, the indeterminacy of R coincides with that of Q.

Finally, if $\lambda_m = 0$, the factor Q, as we have seen, is unique, say, $Q = V_0^t\Lambda V_0$. Suppose then that R_1 and R_2 are any two possible elements of $\mathcal{R}(X, Y)$. Then, $R_1^{-1}R_2Q = Q$, so that

$$V_0R_1^{-1}R_2V_0^t\Lambda = \Lambda.$$

This implies that $V_0R_1^{-1}R_2V_0^t = \mathrm{diag}\{I_l, T\}$ with $T \in \mathbf{SO}(m-l)$ and thus, if $R_0 = U_0V_0$ is any element of $\mathcal{R}(X, Y)$, the others are given by $R = U_0\,\mathrm{diag}\{I_l, T\}V_0$, where T is an arbitrary element of $\mathbf{SO}(m-l)$. ∎

We next use our knowledge of $\mathcal{R}(X, Y)$ to identify $\mathcal{G}(\pi(X), \pi(Y))$.

Theorem 6.4. (i) *When* $\mathrm{rank}(YX^t) = m$, $\mathcal{G}(\pi(X), \pi(Y))$ *consists of a single geodesic save in the special case when* $\lambda_{m-1} + \lambda_m = 0$, *and then it is in one-to-one correspondence with* $\mathbf{RP}^{l-1}$, *where* $l \geqslant 2$ *is the multiplicity of the eigenvalue* λ_m^2 *of* XY^tYX^t.

(ii) *When* $\mathrm{rank}(YX^t) < m$, $\mathcal{G}(\pi(X), \pi(Y))$ *is in one-to-one correspondence with the Stiefel manifold* $\mathbf{V}_{m-l,r_0-l}$, *where* $r_0 = \min\{\mathrm{rank}(X), \mathrm{rank}(Y)\} \geqslant 1$ *and* $l = \mathrm{rank}(YX^t)$.

Proof. Two, path-length parameterised, geodesics from $\pi(X)$ to $\pi(Y)$ coincide if and only if they have the same tangent vector at $\pi(X)$. However, the quotient map π is a Riemannian submersion and so maps the horizontal tangent space at X isomorphically onto the tangent space at $\pi(X)$. So, if γ_R and $\gamma_{\tilde{R}}$ are the horizontal lifts starting at X of the two minimal geodesics, the two geodesics in shape space coincide if and only if

$$\left.\frac{\mathrm{d}\gamma_R(s)}{\mathrm{d}s}\right|_{s=0} = \left.\frac{\mathrm{d}\gamma_{\tilde{R}}(s)}{\mathrm{d}s}\right|_{s=0}:$$

that is, if and only if $R^tY = \tilde{R}^tY$.

In case (i), $\mathrm{rank}(YX^t) = m$ implies that $\mathrm{rank}(Y) = m$ and so the minimal geodesics coincide if and only if $R = \tilde{R}$. Thus, the result follows from Lemma 6.1(i).

In case (ii), without loss of generality, we assume that $\mathrm{rank}(Y) = r_0$ and we may choose Y within its orbit to lie in $\mathcal{ES}_{r_0}^k$. Then, the last $m - r_0$ rows of YX^t must also vanish and so the matrix $U \in \mathbf{SO}(m)$ in the pseudo-singular values decomposition $U \Lambda V$ of YX^t may be chosen to have the form $U = \mathrm{diag}\{U_1, I_{m-r_0}\}$, where $U_1 \in \mathbf{SO}(r_0)$. We know from the proof of Lemma 6.1(ii) that each element of $\mathcal{R}(X, Y)$ can be uniquely written in the form $\widetilde{R} = U \mathrm{diag}\{I_l, T\}V$, for $T \in \mathbf{SO}(m - l)$, and that each T generates an element of $\mathcal{R}(X, Y)$ in this way. Then, if $R = UV$,

$$R^t Y = \widetilde{R}^t Y \iff U^t Y = \mathrm{diag}\{I_l, T^t\}U^t Y$$

$$\iff T = \mathrm{diag}\{I_{r_0-l}, T_2\},$$

that is, if and only if $T \in \mathbf{SO}(m - l)$ has the above form with $T_2 \in \mathbf{SO}(m - r_0)$. This completes the proof. ∎

The following corollary follows from Theorem 6.4.

Corollary 6.2. *There is a unique minimal geodesic joining $\pi(X)$ and $\pi(Y)$ if and only if either $\lambda_{m-1} + \lambda_m > 0$ or $\mathrm{rank}(YX^t) = \min\{\mathrm{rank}(X), \mathrm{rank}(Y)\} < m$.*

Note, in particular, that there is a unique minimal geodesic between $\pi(X)$ and $\pi(Y)$ when $\mathrm{rank}(YX^t) = \mathrm{rank}(Y) < \mathrm{rank}(X)$. For example, $\pi(X)$ could be a non-singular point and $\pi(Y)$ a singular point. When $k = m + 1$ and $\mathrm{rank}(X) = m$ we always have $\mathrm{rank}(YX^t) = \mathrm{rank}(Y)$. So, then $\mathrm{rank}(Y) < m$ is sufficient for the minimal geodesic between $\pi(X)$ and $\pi(Y)$ to be unique.

In Theorem 6.3 we allowed for the possibility that a minimal geodesic may move into a higher stratum than that in which it starts and, at the beginning of this section, we gave an example of such behaviour in Σ_3^4. We are now in a position to say precisely when it can occur.

Corollary 6.3. *If $\max\{\mathrm{rank}(X), \mathrm{rank}(Y)\} = r_1 < m$, then there are minimal geodesics between $\pi(X)$ and $\pi(Y)$ that do not lie in $\pi(\mathcal{D}_{r_1})$ if and only if there is more than one minimal geodesic between them.*

Proof. Without loss of generality we may assume that $l = \mathrm{rank}(YX^t) \leqslant r_0 = \mathrm{rank}(Y) \leqslant r_1 = \mathrm{rank}(X)$. We may also choose

$$X = \begin{pmatrix} X_1 \\ 0 \end{pmatrix}$$

to lie in $\mathcal{E}S_{r_1}^k$ and

$$Y = \begin{pmatrix} Y_1 \\ 0 \end{pmatrix}$$

to lie in $\mathcal{E}S_{r_0}^k$. Thus, if $U_1 (\Lambda_1 \ 0) V_1$ is a singular values decomposition of $Y_1 X_1^t$ and if

$$U = \mathrm{diag}\{\det(U_1)U_1, I_{m-r_0}\} \quad \text{and} \quad V = \mathrm{diag}\{\det(V_1)V_1, I_{m-r_1}\},$$

then UV will be in $\mathcal{R}(X, Y)$. So R is in $\mathcal{R}(X, Y)$ if and only if it can be expressed as $R = U \operatorname{diag}\{I_l, T\}V$ with $T \in \mathbf{SO}(m - l)$. However, the whole of the corresponding γ_R lies in $\mathcal{ES}_{r_1}^k$ if and only if the last $m - r_1$ rows of $R^t Y$ are all zero: that is, if and only if $T = \operatorname{diag}\{T_1, T_2\}$, where $T_1 \in \mathbf{O}(r_0 - l)$, $T_2 \in \mathbf{O}(m - r_0)$ and $\det(T_1)\det(T_2) = 1$. Thus, there are minimal geodesics between $\pi(X)$ and $\pi(Y)$ that do not lie in $\pi(\mathcal{D}_{r_1})$ if and only if $r_0 > l$: that is, if and only if $\operatorname{rank}(Y) > \operatorname{rank}(YX^t)$. By Corollary 6.2 this last condition holds if and only if there is more than one minimal geodesic between $\pi(X)$ and $\pi(Y)$. ∎

6.7 THE CUT LOCUS IN SHAPE SPACES

We are now ready to determine the cut locus associated with *any* point $\pi(X)$ in Σ_m^k. Here, by the *cut locus* $\mathcal{C}(\pi(X))$ of $\pi(X)$, we mean the locus of *cut points* $\pi(Y)$, one on each geodesic through $\pi(X)$, beyond which that geodesic ceases to be minimal. That is, for each point $\pi(Z)$ beyond $\pi(Y)$ along the geodesic, there is at least one alternative and shorter geodesic back to $\pi(X)$ that will not pass through $\pi(Y)$. This is a standard definition of the cut locus for a manifold. However, since we have extended the definition of geodesics into the singular part of shape space, this automatically extends the definition of the cut locus also. In a manifold the cut locus is characterised, outside a set of codimension two, as the set of points to which there is more than one minimal geodesic. Similarly, in shape space we shall see that, apart from the singularity set, there is an *equivalence* between non-extensibility and the existence of a multiplicity of minimal geodesics from $\pi(X)$ to $\pi(Y)$. The precise situation is reminiscent of that on a sphere, and this is no accident: it can be traced back to the fact that the pre-shape space is a sphere and the restriction of the quotient map to each stratum is a Riemannian submersion.

We first note a rather surprising lemma that ties together the geometry and the algebra and leads in Theorem 6.5 to a neat characterisation of the cut locus. We shall denote by $\mathcal{C}_0(\pi(X))$ the set $\{\pi(Y) : |\mathcal{G}(\pi(X), \pi(Y))| > 1\}$ of shapes to which there is more than one minimal geodesic from $\pi(X)$.

Lemma 6.2. *When* $\operatorname{rank}(X) = m$

$$\mathcal{C}_0(\pi(X)) \bigcup \pi(\mathcal{D}_{m-2}) = \{\pi(Y) : \lambda_m + \lambda_{m-1} = 0\},$$

and when $\operatorname{rank}(X) < m$

$$\mathcal{C}_0(\pi(X)) \bigcup \pi(\mathcal{D}_{l-1}) = \{\pi(Y) : \operatorname{rank}(YX^t) < \operatorname{rank}(X)\},$$

where $l = \operatorname{rank}(X)$.

Proof. Since $\lambda_{m-1} \geqslant 0$, $\lambda_m + \lambda_{m-1} = 0$ is equivalent to $\lambda_m = -\lambda_{m-1} \leqslant 0$. From Theorem 6.4 we see that, when $\operatorname{rank}(X) = m$, $\mathcal{C}_0(\pi(X))$ is the union of $\{\pi(Y) : \lambda_m = -\lambda_{m-1} < 0\}$ with

$$\{\pi(Y) : \operatorname{rank}(YX^t) < \operatorname{rank}(Y) < m\} \bigcup \{\pi(Y) : \operatorname{rank}(YX^t) + 1 < \operatorname{rank}(Y) = m\},$$

from which the stated result follows since $\lambda_m = -\lambda_{m-1} = 0$ is equivalent to rank$(YX^t) \leqslant m - 2$. Similarly, when rank$(X) < m$ and so rank$(YX^t) < m$, the identity follows from

$$C_0(\pi(X)) = \{\pi(Y) : \text{rank}(YX^t) < \min\{\text{rank}(X), \text{rank}(Y)\}\}. \qquad \blacksquare$$

We now employ Lemma 6.2 to give a complete characterisation of the cut locus of an arbitrary shape $\pi(X)$.

Theorem 6.5. *If* rank$(X) = m$, *the cut locus* $C(\pi(X))$ *of* $\pi(X)$ *is the union of the singularity set* $\pi(\mathcal{D}_{m-2})$ *of* Σ_m^k *with the set* $C_0(\pi(X))$ *and, if* $l = \text{rank}(X) < m$, *it is the union of the subspace* $\pi(\mathcal{D}_{l-1})$ *of* Σ_m^k *with the set* $C_0(\pi(X))$.

Proof. By Lemma 6.2 it is sufficient to prove that

$$C(\pi(X)) = \begin{cases} \{\pi(Y) : \lambda_m + \lambda_{m-1} = 0\} & \text{if rank}(X) = m, \\ \{\pi(Y) : \text{rank}(YX^t) < \text{rank}(X)\} & \text{if rank}(X) < m. \end{cases}$$

Note that, for any $R \in \mathcal{R}(X, Y)$,

$$\gamma_R(s_0 + \varepsilon)X^t = \frac{1}{\sin s_0}\{-XX^t \sin \varepsilon + R^t YX^t \sin(s_0 + \varepsilon)\},$$

so that it is a symmetric matrix. Let $\tilde{\lambda}_1(s) \geqslant \tilde{\lambda}_2(s) \geqslant \cdots \geqslant \tilde{\lambda}_m(s)$ be the eigenvalues of $\gamma_R(s)X^t$ for $s \geqslant s_0$, so that $\tilde{\lambda}_i(s_0) = \lambda_i$. Since $\gamma_R([0, \pi/2])$ is horizontal everywhere, $\pi(Y) \notin C(\pi(X))$ if and only if there is an $\varepsilon > 0$ such that $s_0 + \varepsilon$ is the distance between $\pi(X)$ and $\pi(\gamma_R(s_0 + \varepsilon))$. That occurs if and only if there is an $\varepsilon > 0$ such that the eigenvalues $\tilde{\lambda}_i(s_0 + \varepsilon)$ coincide with the pseudo-singular values of $\gamma_R(s_0 + \varepsilon)X^t$: that is, if and only if $\tilde{\lambda}_{m-1}(s_0 + \varepsilon) \geqslant |\tilde{\lambda}_m(s_0 + \varepsilon)|$. Since $\tilde{\lambda}_{m-1}(s_0 + \varepsilon) \geqslant \tilde{\lambda}_m(s_0 + \varepsilon)$, $\pi(Y)$ contributes to the cut locus precisely when there exists $\varepsilon_0 > 0$ such that, for $0 < \varepsilon < \varepsilon_0$, we have $\tilde{\lambda}_{m-1}(s_0 + \varepsilon) + \tilde{\lambda}_m(s_0 + \varepsilon) < 0$.

(i) The case that rank$(X) = m$. The eigenvalues of $\gamma_R(s)X^t$ can be expressed as

$$\tilde{\lambda}_i(s) = \max_{BB^t = I_{m-i}} \min_{Bv=0} \frac{v^t \gamma_R(s)X^t v}{v^t v},$$

where B is an $(m - i) \times m$ matrix (cf. Magnus and Heudecker, 1988). If we write $\alpha > 0$ for the smallest eigenvalue of XX^t, then for $v \neq 0$ we have $0 < \alpha v^t v \leqslant v^t XX^t v$. Hence, for any $v \neq 0$ and $\varepsilon = s - s_0 > 0$,

$$v^t \gamma_R(s)X^t v \leqslant \frac{\sin s}{\sin s_0} v^t R^t YX^t v - \frac{\sin \varepsilon}{\sin s_0}\alpha v^t v,$$

from which it follows that

$$\tilde{\lambda}_i(s) < \frac{\sin s}{\sin s_0}\lambda_i, \quad 1 \leqslant i \leqslant m.$$

When $\lambda_{m-1} + \lambda_m > 0$, then for small enough $\varepsilon > 0$ we have, by continuity, that $\tilde{\lambda}_{m-1}(s_0 + \varepsilon) + \tilde{\lambda}_m(s_0 + \varepsilon) > 0$. Therefore, $\gamma_R([0, s_0 + \varepsilon])$ is still a horizontal lift of a minimal geodesic and $\pi(Y) \notin C(\pi(X))$.

When $\lambda_{m-1} = -\lambda_m > 0$, however, for any small enough $\varepsilon > 0$, although $\gamma_R(s_0 + \varepsilon)X^t$ still has $m - 1$ positive eigenvalues

$$\tilde{\lambda}_1(s_0 + \varepsilon) \geqslant \cdots \geqslant \tilde{\lambda}_{m-1}(s_0 + \varepsilon) > 0,$$

we have

$$\tilde{\lambda}_m(s_0 + \varepsilon) < a\,\tilde{\lambda}_m = -a\,\tilde{\lambda}_{m-1} < -\tilde{\lambda}_{m-1}(s_0 + \varepsilon) < 0,$$

where $a = \sin(s_0 + \varepsilon)/\sin s_0$, so that $\pi(Y) \in C(\pi(X))$.

Finally, when $\lambda_{m-1} = -\lambda_m = 0$, $\tilde{\lambda}_m(s_0 + \varepsilon) \leq \tilde{\lambda}_{m-1}(s_0 + \varepsilon) < 0$ for any small enough $\varepsilon > 0$, and hence again $\pi(Y)$ will lie in the cut locus of $\pi(X)$.

(ii) *The case that* rank$(X) < m$. If rank$(YX^t) = $ rank(X), then XX^t and YX^t, and so also R^tYX^t, have the same null space of dimension at least one since it is always true that $\ker(YX^t) \supset \ker(X^t) = \ker(XX^t)$. So, for $\varepsilon > 0$ small enough,

$$v^t\gamma_R(s_0 + \varepsilon)X^tv \begin{cases} > 0 & \text{if } v \text{ is an eigenvector of } \lambda_i \text{ for } 1 \leqslant i \leqslant \text{rank}(X), \\ = 0 & \text{if } v \text{ is an eigenvector of } \lambda_i \text{ for rank}(X) < i \leqslant m. \end{cases}$$

It follows that $\gamma_R(s_0 + \varepsilon)X^t$ has rank(X) positive eigenvalues and $m - $ rank$(X) > 0$ zero eigenvalues, which therefore agree with its pseudo-singular values, so that $\gamma_R([0, s_0 + \varepsilon])$ is a horizontal lift of a minimal geodesic.

If rank$(YX^t) < $ rank(X), however, there is a non-zero $v_1 \in \ker(XX^t) \subseteq \ker(R^tYX^t)$ and there is also a non-zero $v_2 \in \ker(R^tYX^t) \setminus \ker(XX^t)$ such that $v_2^t XX^t v_2 > 0$. Hence, $\gamma_R(s_0 + \varepsilon)X^t$ will have one negative eigenvalue and one zero eigenvalue for any $\varepsilon > 0$. Thus, its pseudo-singular values cannot equal these eigenvalues and therefore $\pi(Y)$ is in the cut locus of $\pi(X)$. ∎

When $m = 2$, $\pi(\mathcal{D}_{m-2}) = \emptyset$ and so $C(\pi(X)) = C_0(\pi(X))$. This is not suprising if we notice that the spaces $\Sigma_2^k = \mathbf{CP}^{k-2}(4)$ are complete Riemannian manifolds for all $k > 2$.

If $\rho(\pi(X), \pi(Y)) = \pi/2$, that is, $\pi(X)$ and $\pi(Y)$ are a maximally remote pair, then if $m = 2$ we must have the two pseudo-singular values of YX^t satisfying $\lambda_1 = -\lambda_2$ and if $m > 2$ we must have $YX^t = 0$, so that $\pi(Y) \in C(\pi(X))$ in either case. Hence, when $m = 2$, the cut locus of $\pi(X)$ consists precisely of all shapes that are most remote from it. However, this is no longer the case when $m > 2$: then the cut locus of $\pi(X)$ contains more shapes than just those that are most remote from it.

In a manifold the relationship of one point lying in the cut locus of another is symmetric. For our extended definition in shape space this is no longer the case: it is possible for a minimal geodesic to remain minimal when extended beyond one end point but not when extended beyond the other. However, that is not possible when there is more than one minimal geodesic between the two points: a symmetric relationship, which, as in manifolds, ensures that each point is in the cut locus of the other. The situation for shape space is described in the following corollary, which follows from Theorem 6.5 and Corollary 6.2.

Corollary 6.4. *If* rank$(X) \geqslant$ rank(Y), *then* $\pi(X) \in C(\pi(Y))$ *implies that* $\pi(Y) \in C(\pi(X))$. *However, the converse implication holds if and only if there is more than one minimal geodesic between* $\pi(X)$ *and* $\pi(Y)$.

In particular, we see that, if $\pi(X)$ and $\pi(Y)$ are in the same stratum or one each in the two uppermost strata, then $\pi(X) \in C(\pi(Y))$ if and only if $\pi(Y) \in C(\pi(X))$, which is if and only if there exists more than one minimal geodesic between them.

6.8   THE DISTANCES AND PROJECTIONS TO LOWER STRATA

In this section we calculate the distance from a given shape $\pi(X)$ to the various strata $\pi(\mathcal{D}_j \setminus \mathcal{D}_{j-1})$, $1 \leqslant j \leqslant m - 1$, and find the nearest points to the shape on these strata. The most interesting and important case in applications will be when $j = m - 1$ since $\pi(\mathcal{D}_1)$ in Σ_2^k is the collinearity set of shapes of k labelled points in $\mathbb{R}^2$ and $\pi(\mathcal{D}_{m-1})$ in Σ_m^k is its generalisation to $\mathbb{R}^m$.

Once again, these basic properties turn out to have simple expressions involving pseudo-singular values, except that now, as mentioned above, it is the pseudo-singular values of X itself that we need. Since we shall need to allow the $m \times (k - 1)$ matrix X to vary, we shall, for this section, write its pseudo-singular values decomposition as

$$X = U_X (\Lambda_X \quad 0) V_X,$$

where we recall that $U_X \in \mathbf{SO}(m)$, $V_X \in \mathbf{SO}(k - 1)$ and Λ_X is the diagonal matrix with diagonal entries the pseudo-singular values $\lambda_i(X)$ of X. Note that the zero $m \times (k - m - 1)$ matrix that borders Λ_X is only required if $k > m + 1$ and in this case we may, and do, insist that $\lambda_m(X) \geqslant 0$. We note first that, since rank$(X) =$ rank(Λ_X), $\pi(X)$ is in $\pi(\mathcal{D}_j)$ if and only if $\lambda_{j+1}(X) = \cdots = \lambda_m(X) = 0$, and it lies in the jth stratum if and only if in addition $\lambda_j(X) \neq 0$.

Lemma 6.3. *Suppose that* X *and* Y *are two* $m \times (k - 1)$ *matrices such that* $\lambda_m(X)\lambda_m(Y) \geqslant 0$. *Then,* $\max\{\mathrm{tr}(TYSX^t) : T \in \mathbf{SO}(m), S \in \mathbf{SO}(k - 1)\}$ *is attained for some* $T_0 \in \mathbf{SO}(m)$, $S_0 \in \mathbf{SO}(k - 1)$, *and this maximal value is equal to* $\sum_{i=1}^m \lambda_i(X)\lambda_i(Y)$.

Proof.   On the one hand, (cf. Ben-Israel and Greville, 1974)

$$\max_{\substack{T \in \mathbf{SO}(m) \\ S \in \mathbf{SO}(k-1)}} \mathrm{tr}(TYSX^t) \leqslant \max_{\substack{T \in \mathbf{O}(m) \\ S \in \mathbf{O}(k-1)}} \mathrm{tr}(YSX^tT) \leqslant \sum_{i=1}^m \lambda_i(X)\lambda_i(Y),$$

and, on the other, if $U_X (\Lambda_X \quad 0) V_X$ and $U_Y (\Lambda_Y \quad 0) V_Y$ give pseudo-singular values decompositions of X and Y, respectively, then, for $T_0 = U_X U_Y^t \in \mathbf{SO}(m)$ and $S_0 = V_Y^t V_X \in \mathbf{SO}(k - 1)$, $\mathrm{tr}(T_0 Y S_0 X^t) = \sum_{i=1}^m \lambda_i(X)\lambda_i(Y)$.   ∎

Now, denote by $s_j(\pi(X))$ the distance $\rho(\pi(X), \pi(\mathcal{D}_j))$ from $\pi(X) \in \Sigma_m^k$ to the closed set $\pi(\mathcal{D}_j)$ and by $\pi(X^{(j)})$ any point at which a geodesic of length $s_j(\pi(X))$ from $\pi(X)$ hits $\pi(\mathcal{D}_j)$, necessarily doing so perpendicularly. We emphasise that the $\pi(X^{(j)})$ are not necessarily unique, but in any case it is natural to regard them as the projections of $\pi(X)$ onto $\pi(\mathcal{D}_j)$.

Theorem 6.6. (i) *If* $U_X (\Lambda_X \quad 0) V_X$ *is a pseudo-singular values decomposition of X, then*

$$\cos^2(s_j(\pi(X))) = \sum_{i=1}^{j} \lambda_i(X)^2, \quad 1 \leqslant j \leqslant m - 1,$$

and we may take $X^{(j)} = (\Lambda_X^{(j)} \quad 0) V_X$, *where* $\Lambda_X^{(j)} = \mathrm{diag}\{\lambda_1^{(j)}, \ldots, \lambda_m^{(j)}\}$ *and*

$$\lambda_i^{(j)} = \lambda_i(X) \left(\sum_{r=1}^{j} \lambda_r(X)^2 \right)^{-1/2}, \quad 1 \leqslant i \leqslant j, \quad and \quad \lambda_i^{(j)} = 0, \quad j+1 \leqslant i \leqslant m.$$

Moreover, if $X \notin \mathcal{D}_{j-1}$, *then any choice for* $\pi(X^{(j)})$ *lies in the stratum* $\pi(\mathcal{D}_j \setminus \mathcal{D}_{j-1})$.

(ii) *If* $\lambda_1(X) > \cdots > \lambda_{j+1}(X)$, *then both* $\pi(X^{(j)})$ *and the corresponding geodesic will be unique.*

Proof. (i) For Y in $\mathcal{D}_j$ let λ_i, $1 \leqslant i \leqslant m$, be the pseudo-singular values of YX^t. Then,

$$\cos(\rho(\pi(X), \pi(Y))) = \sum_{i=1}^{m} \lambda_i = \max_{T \in \mathbf{SO}(m)} \mathrm{tr}(TYX^t)$$

$$\leqslant \max_{\substack{T \in \mathbf{SO}(m) \\ S \in \mathbf{SO}(k-1)}} \mathrm{tr}(TYSX^t) = \sum_{i=1}^{j} \lambda_i(X)\lambda_i(Y),$$

by Lemma 6.3, since $\lambda_i(Y) = 0$ for $i > j$. Moreover, the last maximum is achieved if we choose, as we may, V_Y to be equal to V_X. If we next vary the $\{\lambda_i(Y)\}$ subject to the condition $\sum_{i=1}^{j} \lambda_i(Y)^2 = 1$, then, for given $\{\lambda_i(X)\}$, the maximum of the function $\sum_{i=1}^{j} \lambda_i(X)\lambda_i(Y)$ is the square root of $\sum_{i=1}^{j} \lambda_i(X)^2$, which is achieved when $\lambda_i(Y)$ is equal to the $\lambda_i^{(j)}$ stated for $1 \leqslant i \leqslant j$. Thus, the given choice of $X^{(j)}$ is valid and, if $\lambda_j(X) \neq 0$, any choice of $X^{(j)}$ will have its jth pseudo-singular value $\lambda_j^{(j)} \neq 0$ and so $\pi(X^{(j)})$ will not lie in $\pi(\mathcal{D}_{j-1})$.

(ii) If $\pi(\hat{Y})$ is one of the nearest points in $\pi(\mathcal{D}_j)$ to $\pi(X)$, then the above argument shows that the diagonal matrix of the pseudo-singular values of $\hat{Y}$ must be $\Lambda_X^{(j)}$, and

$$\max_{T \in \mathbf{SO}(m)} \mathrm{tr}(T X \hat{Y}^t) = \sum_{i=1}^{j} \lambda_i(X) \lambda_i^{(j)}$$

$$= \max_{T, S \in \mathbf{SO}(k-1)} \mathrm{tr}\left\{ T \begin{pmatrix} \Lambda_X & 0 \\ 0 & 0 \end{pmatrix} S \begin{pmatrix} \Lambda_X^{(j)} & 0 \\ 0 & 0 \end{pmatrix} \right\}.$$

Write

$$A = \begin{pmatrix} \Lambda_X & 0 \\ 0 & 0 \end{pmatrix} \quad \text{and} \quad B = S_0 \begin{pmatrix} \Lambda_X^{(j)} & 0 \\ 0 & 0 \end{pmatrix} T_0$$

with T_0, S_0 chosen in $\mathbf{SO}(k-1)$ such that $\mathrm{tr}(AB) = \sum_{i=1}^{j} \lambda_i(X) \lambda_i^{(j)}$. Since $\lambda_1(X) > \cdots > \lambda_j(X) > \lambda_{j+1}(X)$, the first j rows of V_X are uniquely determined up to signs and S_0 must have the form $V_X V_{\hat{Y}}^t \, \mathrm{diag}\{I_j, \tilde{S}_0\}$ where the submatrix $\tilde{S}_0$ is in $\mathbf{SO}(k-1-j)$. On the other hand, $\mathrm{tr}(AB) \geqslant \mathrm{tr}(TAB)$ and $\mathrm{tr}(BA) \geqslant \mathrm{tr}(TBA)$ for all $T \in \mathbf{SO}(k-1)$. This implies (cf. von Neumann, 1937) that AB and BA are both symmetric so that there is an $S_1 \in \mathbf{SO}(k-1)$ such that AS_1 and $S_1^t B$ are both symmetric and, hence, $AB = S_1^t BAS_1$. Now, the fact that A is a diagonal matrix with the first j diagonal entries distinct, from each other and from the remaining entries, means that S_1 must take the form $\mathrm{diag}\{I_j, \hat{S}_1\}$. It then follows that the first j basis vectors, each generating one-dimensional eigenspaces of A, are also eigenvectors for B. Hence

$$B = \begin{pmatrix} \xi_1 & & & & \\ & \xi_2 & & & \\ & & \ddots & & \\ & & & \xi_j & \\ & & & & \hat{B} \end{pmatrix}.$$

However, since $B^t B$ only has eigenvalues zero or $(\lambda_i^{(j)})^2$, $1 \leqslant i \leqslant j$, each ξ_r must be $\pm \lambda_{i_r}^{(j)}$ or zero. Then, the fact that $\lambda_1(X) > \cdots > \lambda_j(X) > 0$ implies that $\xi_i = \lambda_i^{(j)}$ for $1 \leqslant i \leqslant j$. It follows that S_0 has the form $\mathrm{diag}\{I_j, \hat{S}_0\}$: that is, the first j rows of $V_{\hat{Y}}$ and V_X are identical. Since the last $m-j$ pseudo-singular values of $\hat{Y}$ are all zero, we have $\pi(\hat{Y}) = \pi((\Lambda_X^{(j)} \quad 0) V_X)$: that is, $\pi(X^{(j)})$ is unique. The uniqueness of the geodesic between $\pi(X)$ and $\pi(X^{(j)})$ follows from Corollary 6.2. ∎

Thus, the diagonal matrix Λ_X supplies us with information on the position of $\pi(X)$ relative to the various strata in Σ_m^k, and the geometric meaning of the eigenvalues $\lambda_i(X)^2$ of $X^t X$ is now obvious:

$$\lambda_i(X)^2 = \cos^2\{s_i(\pi(X))\} - \cos^2\{s_{i-1}(\pi(X))\}.$$

In particular, the smallest eigenvalue $\lambda_m(X)^2$ is the square of the sine of the distance from $\pi(X)$ to $\pi(\mathcal{D}_{m-1})$ and, for $\pi(X) \in \pi(\mathcal{D}_j)$, $\lambda_j(X)^2$ is the square of the sine of the distance between $\pi(X)$ and $\pi(\mathcal{D}_{j-1})$. It is interesting to compare this with the expression we obtained in Section 6.4 for the distance between any two shapes $\pi(X)$ and $\pi(Y)$. That involve the pseudo-singular values of $Y^t X$, whereas here we have expressed the distance between $\pi(X)$ and $\pi(\mathcal{D}_j)$ in terms of the squares of the pseudo-singular values of X, which in this case are the eigenvalues of $X^t X$. It is also worth noting that

$$\rho(\pi(X), \iota_m(\pi(X))) = 2s_{m-1}(\pi(X)) = 2s_{m-1}(\iota_m(\pi(X)))$$

since the first term is $\arccos(1 - 2\lambda_m(X)^2)$. This implies that any shortest geodesic from $\pi(X)$ to $\pi(\mathcal{D}_{m-1})$ extends to pass through $\iota_m(\pi(X))$.

From Theorem 6.6 we can deduce the following properties of $s_j(\pi(X))$ and $\pi(X^{(j)})$.

Corollary 6.5. (i) *For* $\pi(X) \in \Sigma_m^k$,

$$s_{m-1}(\pi(X)) \leqslant s_{m-2}(\pi(X)) \leqslant \cdots \leqslant s_1(\pi(X)),$$

and, if $\pi(X) \notin \pi(\mathcal{D}_j)$, *then*

$$s_j(\pi(X)) < s_{j-1}(\pi(X)) \leqslant \cdots \leqslant s_1(\pi(X)).$$

(ii) *For* $1 \leqslant j_1 < j_2 \leqslant m - 1$,

$$\cos\{s_{j_1}(\pi(X))\} = \cos\{s_{j_1}(\pi(X^{(j_2)}))\}\,\cos\{s_{j_2}(\pi(X))\},$$

and

$$\pi(X^{(j_1)}) = \pi((X^{(j_2)})^{(j_1)}).$$

Proof. Each of (i) and the second result of (ii) is obvious, and the first result of (ii) follows from

$$\cos^2\left(s_{j_1}(\pi(X^{(j_2)}))\right) = \cos^2\left(\rho(\pi(X^{(j_2)}), \pi(\mathcal{D}_{j_1}))\right)$$

$$= \frac{\displaystyle\sum_{i=1}^{j_1} \lambda_i(X)^2}{\displaystyle\sum_{i=1}^{j_2} \lambda_i(X)^2}, \quad 1 \leqslant j_1 < j_2 \leqslant m - 1.$$

∎

The second statement in (ii) says that, for any $1 \leqslant j_1 < j_2 \leqslant m - 1$, the projection of $\pi(X)$ onto $\pi(\mathcal{D}_{j_1})$ is the composite of the projection of $\pi(X)$ onto $\pi(\mathcal{D}_{j_2})$ with that of $\pi(\mathcal{D}_{j_2})$ onto $\pi(\mathcal{D}_{j_1})$. Also, when $s_{j_1}(\pi(X))$ is small enough, it follows from (ii) that whenever $1 \leqslant j_1 < j_2 \leqslant m - 1$ we shall have

$$s_{j_1}(\pi(X))^2 \approx s_{j_2}(\pi(X))^2 + s_{j_1}(\pi(X^{(j_2)}))^2.$$

Corollary 6.6. *The maximum possible value of the distance of shapes from* $\pi(\mathcal{D}_j)$ *is*

$$\arccos \sqrt{\frac{j}{m}},$$

and the shapes $\pi(X)$ *that are maximally remote from* $\pi(\mathcal{D}_{m-1})$ *have the pseudo-singular values* $\lambda_1(X) = \cdots = |\lambda_m(X)| = 1/\sqrt{m}$ *and are also maximally remote from* $\pi(\mathcal{D}_j)$, *for* $1 \leqslant j \leqslant m - 2$.

This corollary allows us to take a more detailed look at the special case $k = m + 1$. First, we recall that, by Casson's theorem, Σ_m^{m+1} is homeomorphic with a sphere. If we take $X^+ = \frac{1}{\sqrt{m}}I_m$ and $X^- = \frac{1}{\sqrt{m}}\,\mathrm{diag}\{1, \ldots, 1, -1\}$, then $\pi(X^+)$ and $\pi(X^-)$ are both maximally remote from $\pi(\mathcal{D}_j)$ for all j, $1 \leqslant j \leqslant m - 1$, and behave very like antipodal poles of the sphere, with $\pi(\mathcal{D}_{m-1})$ as the corresponding 'equator'. Thus, for any point $\pi(Y)$ in $\pi(\mathcal{D}_j)$ the distances $\rho(\pi(X^+), \pi(Y))$ and $\rho(\pi(X^-), \pi(Y))$ are both equal to $\arccos\left\{\frac{1}{\sqrt{m}}\sum_{i=1}^{j}\lambda_i(Y)\right\}$ since $\lambda_{j+1}(Y) = \cdots = \lambda_m(Y) = 0$ and the pseudo-singular values of $Y(X^{\pm})^t$ are the $\{\lambda_i(Y)/\sqrt{m} : 1 \leqslant i \leqslant m\}$. In particular, if Y_0 is any matrix with pseudo-singular values $\lambda_1(Y_0) = 1$ and $\lambda_2(Y_0) = \cdots = \lambda_m(Y_0) = 0$, then the geodesic distance between $\pi(X^{\pm})$ and $\pi(Y_0)$ is $\arccos(1/\sqrt{m})$, which is the greatest distance between $\pi(X^{\pm})$ and points of $\pi(\mathcal{D}_j)$ for any j, $1 \leqslant j \leqslant m - 1$. When $m = 2$, all points of $\pi(\mathcal{D}_1)$ are of the form $\pi(Y_0)$ so that the distances from $\pi(X^{\pm})$ to all points of $\pi(\mathcal{D}_1)$ are the same. However, for $m \geqslant 3$ this is no longer the case and, as m increases, the distance of $\pi(X^{\pm})$ from $\pi(\mathcal{D}_j)$ decreases to zero and the longest distance to its points, the distance to $\pi(Y_0)$, increases to $\pi/2$. These observations may be expanded to give an alternative proof of Casson's theorem and, at the same time, to show that Σ_m^{m+1} is not *isometric* with a sphere (cf. Le, 1991). However, since we have already given more than one proof of Casson's theorem, we shall now assume it and deduce the latter result.

Theorem 6.7. Σ_m^{m+1} *is not isometric with* $\mathbf{S}^{d_m^{m+1}}$ *if* $m \geqslant 3$.

Proof. Suppose it were possible to find an isometry $f : \Sigma_m^{m+1} \longrightarrow \mathbf{S}^{d_m^{m+1}}$ of the shape space with a standard sphere in $\mathbb{R}^{d_m^{m+1}+1}$. Then, the fact that $\pi(X^+)$ and $\pi(X^-)$ are equi-distant from all points of $\pi(\mathcal{D}_{m-1})$ means that $f(\pi(\mathcal{D}_{m-1}))$ would have to be contained in a totally geodesic sphere $\mathcal{S}$ of codimension one. However, the isometry ι_m interchanges $\pi(X^+)$ and $\pi(X^-)$ and, when $\pi(Y)$ is not in $\pi(\mathcal{D}_{m-1})$, we have $\lambda_m(Y) \neq 0$ so that

$$\rho(\pi(X^-), \pi(Y)) = \rho(\pi(X^+), \iota_m(\pi(Y)))$$

$$= \arccos\left(\frac{1}{\sqrt{m}}\sum_{i=1}^{m-1}\lambda_i(Y) - \frac{1}{\sqrt{m}}\lambda_m(Y)\right)$$

$$\neq \rho(\pi(X^+), \pi(Y)).$$

Thus, $\pi(Y)$ cannot map into $\mathcal{S}$ and, as f is bijective, we must have $f(\pi(\mathcal{D}_{m-1})) = \mathcal{S}$. However, then it would not be possible for each of $f(\pi(X^+))$ and $f(\pi(X^-))$ to be maximally remote from $f(\pi(\mathcal{D}_{m-1}))$ and, at the same time, for there to be points $f(\pi(Y_1))$ and $f(\pi(Y_2))$ in $f(\pi(\mathcal{D}_{m-1}))$ at different distances from $f(\pi(X^+))$, which would be required, when $m \geqslant 3$, if f were an isometry. ∎

In Σ_m^{m+1} the configurations whose shapes are maximally remote from $\pi(\mathcal{D}_{m-1})$ are characterised by their pre-shapes X satisfying $X^t X = \frac{1}{m}I$. Geometrically, such a configuration is a regular simplex. This result has already been seen for the case $m = 2$ in Figure 1.1. To prove it in general we write $\bar{r}$ for the circumradius and $\bar{x}_0^*$ for the circumcentre of the simplex with vertices x_i^*. Then, $x_i^* = \bar{x}_0^* + \bar{r}\bar{x}_i^*$, where $\bar{x}_i^* \in S^{m-1}$ and the ith coordinate of the corresponding pre-shape is

$$x_i = c' \frac{i\bar{x}_{i+1}^* - (\bar{x}_1^* + \ldots + \bar{x}_i^*)}{\sqrt{i(i+1)}},$$

where c' is a scaling constant. Using the increasing sequence of submatrices of X^tX formed by the first j rows and columns, $1 \leqslant j \leqslant m$, we may show by induction that $X^tX = \frac{1}{m}I$ if and only if $\langle \bar{x}_i^*, \bar{x}_j^* \rangle$ is constant for all $i \neq j$. If we rotate the configuration so that $\bar{x}_1^* = (1, 0, \ldots, 0)$, then, for $1 < i \leqslant m+1$, we must have the first coordinate of $\bar{x}_i^*$ equal to the common inner product c so that, for those i, we may write $\bar{x}_i^* = (c, \sqrt{1-c^2}\bar{x}_i')$, where $\bar{x}_i' \in S^{m-2}$. We then have, for $i > 1$, $j > 1$ and $i \neq j$,

$$c = \langle \bar{x}_i^*, \bar{x}_j^* \rangle = c^2 + (1-c^2)\langle \bar{x}_i', \bar{x}_j' \rangle, \tag{6.5}$$

which implies that the $\langle \bar{x}_i', \bar{x}_j' \rangle$ are all equal to $c/(1+c)$ since the other solution $c = 1$ of (6.5) corresponds to the totally degenerate configuration. When $m = 2$ the points $\bar{x}_1'$ and $\bar{x}_2'$ of S^0 must be ± 1 and then the constant c appearing in (6.5) must be $-1/2$. We may then use the non-trivial solution of (6.5) to show by induction that, for all m, $\langle \bar{x}_i^*, \bar{x}_j^* \rangle = -1/m$ for all $1 \leqslant i \neq j \leqslant m+1$. This is equivalent to the original configuration X^* being a regular simplex.

As a further application of the results in this section, we calculate the x-coordinate of the orthogonal projection of a shape onto the collinearity set $\pi(\mathcal{D}_1)$ in the planar representation of the punctured version of Σ_2^3 (cf. Chapter 1). The planar representation of Σ_2^3 to which we refer is obtained by translating, rotating and scaling a labelled triangle in the plane to move its first vertex to $(-1/\sqrt{3}, 0)$ and its second vertex to $(1/\sqrt{3}, 0)$. We then use the coordinate (x, y) of the third vertex of this resultant triangle as the coordinate of the shape of the original triangle. Clearly, the collinearity set is then represented by the x-axis. A pre-shape for the shape (x, y) is

$$X = \frac{1}{\sqrt{1+x^2+y^2}} \begin{pmatrix} 1 & x \\ 0 & y \end{pmatrix}$$

and a pre-shape for its projection onto the collinearity set is determined by a unit eigenvector (a, b) corresponding to the larger eigenvalue λ_1^2 of X^tX. However, the eigenvalues of X^tX are

$$\lambda^2 = \frac{1}{2}\left\{1 \pm \sqrt{1 - \left(\frac{2y}{1+x^2+y^2}\right)^2}\right\},$$

so we obtain

$$a = -\frac{x}{\sqrt{(1 - \tilde{\lambda}_1^2)^2 + x^2}} \quad \text{and} \quad b = \frac{1 - \tilde{\lambda}_1^2}{\sqrt{(1 - \tilde{\lambda}_1^2)^2 + x^2}},$$

where $\tilde{\lambda}_1^2 = \lambda_1^2(1 + x^2 + y^2)$. The planar representation of the projection is thus given, when $x \neq 0$, by $(b/a, 0)$ so that its x-coordinate is

$$-\frac{1 - x^2 - y^2 - \sqrt{(1 + x^2 + y^2)^2 - 4y^2}}{2x}$$
$$= \frac{2x}{1 - x^2 - y^2 + \sqrt{(1 + x^2 + y^2)^2 - 4y^2}}.$$

This is different from the x-coordinate of the given shape unless $y = 0$, which was to be expected since we know that the geometry of the planar representation of Σ_2^3 differs from the standard Euclidean geometry of $\mathbb{R}^2$.

CHAPTER 7

The Riemannian Structure of Shape Spaces

In Chapter 6 we introduced the Riemannian metric and made an initial qualitative study of it through its geodesics. We now turn to the problem of quantifying those aspects of the metric that are necessary for statistical purposes. In particular, we shall compute the volume element, in terms of which it is natural to describe probability measures on shape space, and the Laplace–Beltrami operator, which is the infinitesimal generator of Brownian motion. In the final section we calculate various standard measures of the curvature of shape space. These quantify the extent to which it is feasible, as is often convenient, to ignore the Riemannian structure and treat shape coordinates as if they were standard Euclidean coordinates. It is an important feature of these results that the geometric invariants are all expressed in terms of the pseudo-singular values of the pre-shape matrices that we use to represent the configurations that determine particular shapes, and that these pseudo-singular values are easily computed in practice.

Since, when $k \leqslant m$, Σ_m^k is isometric with the quotient of Σ_{k-1}^k by the involution ι_{k-1} and since the geometric quantities with which we are concerned are all local in nature, it follows that we may, as usual, restrict our attention to the case $k \geqslant m + 1$ throughout this chapter.

7.1   THE RIEMANNIAN METRIC

We recall from Chapter 6 that a Riemannian metric is a choice of inner product on each tangent space, which varies smoothly as we move around the manifold. In that chapter we represented the tangent space to $\mathcal{S}_m^k$ at X as the set of matrices Z such that $\operatorname{tr}(XZ^t) = 0$. That is, Z is orthogonal to X with respect to the standard inner product on the Euclidean space $\mathbb{R}^{m(k-1)}$ in which $\mathcal{S}_m^k$ lies. More precisely, the entries of Z are the coordinates of a tangent vector $\underline{\zeta}$ with respect to the standard basis $\left\{ \frac{\partial}{\partial x_{ij}} : 1 \leqslant i \leqslant m, 1 \leqslant j \leqslant k - 1 \right\}$ of the tangent space to $\mathbb{R}^{m(k-1)}$

at X. Accordingly, we shall refer to Z as the *standard coordinate matrix* of ζ. Since we shall need to change basis from time to time in this chapter it will be necessary to make this distinction between a tangent vector itself and its matrix of coordinates with respect to a particular basis.

As explained in Chapter 6, in the non-singular part $\Sigma_m^k \backslash \pi(\mathcal{D}_{m-2})$ of shape space, the Riemannian structure at a shape $\pi(X)$ is directly inherited from that of the horizontal subspace of the tangent space to the pre-shape sphere $\mathcal{S}_m^k$ at any pre-shape X in the fibre above $\pi(X)$. To specify that metric we shall require a more precise analysis of the horizontal subspaces above non-singular points of shape space. Recall that we are writing $\mathcal{M}(n, p)$ for the space of all $n \times p$ real-valued matrices and we shall write E_{ij} for the matrix whose (i, j)th entry is one and all of whose other entries are zero, where the relevant choice of n and p will be determined by the context. We further define matrix spaces

$$\mathcal{W}_0 = \{(w_{ij}) \in \mathcal{M}(m, m) : w_{ij} = 0 \text{ if } i \neq j\},$$
$$\mathcal{W}_1 = \{(w_{ij}) \in \mathcal{M}(m, m) : w_{ij} = w_{ji} \text{ and } w_{ii} = 0\}$$

and

$$\mathcal{W}_2 = \mathcal{M}(m, k - 1 - m).$$

We may now use these spaces of matrices to identify the horizontal subspace at X as follows.

Lemma 7.1. *Suppose that the pre-shape matrix X has a pseudo-singular values decomposition $U(\Lambda\ 0)V$ and let $\mathcal{H}_X$ be the space of standard coordinate matrices of horizontal vectors at X. Then, if $\mathrm{rank}(X) \geqslant m - 1$, $\mathcal{H}_X$ is the subspace*

$$\left\{ U\{\Lambda\ (W_1\quad 0) + (W_0\quad W_2)\} V : W_i \in \mathcal{W}_i, 0 \leqslant i \leqslant 2; \sum_{i=1}^{m} \lambda_i w_{ii} = 0 \right\} \quad (7.1)$$

of $\mathcal{M}(m, k - 1)$, where the w_{ii} are the diagonal elements of W_0.

Proof. If $Z = U\{\Lambda\ (W_1\quad 0) + (W_0\quad W_2)\} V$, then $Z \in \mathcal{M}(m, k - 1)$,

$$\mathrm{tr}(XZ^t) = \mathrm{tr}(\Lambda W_0) = \sum_{i=1}^{m} \lambda_i w_{ii} = 0$$

and

$$XZ^t = U\{\Lambda W_1 \Lambda + \Lambda W_0\} U^t = U\{\Lambda W_1 \Lambda + W_0 \Lambda\} U^t = ZX^t.$$

Hence, $\mathcal{H}_X$ contains the subspace specified in (7.1). However, since $\lambda_1 \geqslant \cdots \geqslant \lambda_{m-1} > 0$, Λ multiplies each of the first $m - 1$ rows of $W_1 \in \mathcal{W}_1$ by a non-zero multiple and so acts as a monomorphism of $\mathcal{W}_1$ into $\mathcal{M}(m, m)$. Thus, the dimension of the subspace (7.1) is

$$\dim(\mathcal{W}_0) + \dim(\mathcal{W}_1) + \dim(\mathcal{W}_2) - 1 = m + \tfrac{1}{2}m(m - 1) + m(k - 1 - m) - 1,$$

which is the dimension of $\mathcal{H}_X$. It follows that $\mathcal{H}_X$ is specified by (7.1) as required. ∎

This description of $\mathcal{H}_X$ gives rise to a simple choice of basis vectors involving the components of a pseudo-singular values decomposition $U(\Lambda \quad 0)V$ of X, with respect to which we may calculate the Riemannian metric on shape space. This basis is the set of horizontal tangent vectors $\underline{\zeta}_{ij}$ whose standard coordinate matrices Z_{ij} in $\mathcal{H}_X$ are given by

$$Z_{ij} = U W_{ij} V, \tag{7.2}$$

where

$$
\begin{aligned}
W_{ii} &= E_{ii} - \frac{\lambda_i}{\lambda_1} E_{11}, && 1 < i \leqslant m, \\
W_{ij} &= \Lambda \{ E_{ij} + E_{ji} \}, && 1 \leqslant i < j \leqslant m, \\
W_{ij} &= E_{ij}, && 1 \leqslant i \leqslant m < j \leqslant k - 1.
\end{aligned}
$$

Theorem 7.1. *Suppose that X has a pseudo-singular values decomposition $U(\Lambda \quad 0)V$. If $\operatorname{rank}(X) \geqslant m - 1$, the tangent space to $\Sigma_m^k \setminus \pi(\mathcal{D}_{m-2})$ at $\pi(X)$ has a basis*

$$\{ \pi_*(\underline{\zeta}_{ii}) : 1 < i \leqslant m \} \bigcup \{ \pi_*(\underline{\zeta}_{ij}) : 1 \leqslant i \leqslant m, i < j \leqslant k - 1 \} \tag{7.3}$$

such that the inner product is given by

$$
\langle \pi_*(\underline{\zeta}_{i_1 j_1}), \pi_*(\underline{\zeta}_{i_2 j_2}) \rangle =
\begin{cases}
1 + \dfrac{\lambda_{i_1}^2}{\lambda_1^2} & \text{if } 1 < i_1 = i_2 = j_1 = j_2 \leqslant m, \\[2mm]
\dfrac{\lambda_{i_1} \lambda_{i_2}}{\lambda_1^2} & \text{if } 1 < i_1 = j_1 \neq i_2 = j_2 \leqslant m, \\[2mm]
\lambda_{i_1}^2 + \lambda_{j_1}^2 & \text{if } 1 \leqslant i_1 = i_2 < j_1 = j_2 \leqslant m, \\[1mm]
1 & \text{if } 1 \leqslant i_1 = i_2 \leqslant m < j_1 = j_2 \leqslant k - 1, \\[1mm]
0 & \text{otherwise,}
\end{cases}
$$

where π_* is the derivative at X of the projection π of $\mathcal{S}_m^k$ onto Σ_m^k.

Proof. By Lemma 7.1, the matrices Z_{ij} given by (7.2) form a basis of $\mathcal{H}_X$. Hence, the images $\pi_*(\underline{\zeta}_{ij})$ in $T_{\pi(X)}(\Sigma_m^k \setminus \pi(\mathcal{D}_{m-2}))$ of the corresponding vectors form a basis of that tangent space and, since π_* is an isometry when restricted to $\mathcal{H}_X$, the inner products of the vectors $\pi_*(\underline{\zeta}_{ij})$ are the same as those of $\underline{\zeta}_{ij}$. It is thus sufficient to compute the inner products of the Z_{ij} to obtain the required result. However,

$$\langle Z_{i_1 j_1}, Z_{i_2 j_2} \rangle = \operatorname{tr}\left(Z_{i_1 j_1} Z_{i_2 j_2}^t \right) = \operatorname{tr}\left(W_{i_1 j_1} W_{i_2 j_2}^t \right)$$

and since, for example, $\operatorname{tr}\left(E_{i_1 j_1} E_{i_2 j_2}^t \right) = \delta_{i_1 i_2} \delta_{j_1 j_2}$, where $\delta_{ij} = 1$ if $i = j$ and 0 if $i \neq j$, the stated results follow. ∎

7.2 THE METRIC RE-EXPRESSED THROUGH NATURAL LOCAL VECTOR FIELDS

In the previous section we found, for each pre-shape outside $\mathcal{D}_{m-2}$, a set of independent horizontal tangent vectors $\underline{\zeta}_{ij}$ that span the horizontal subspace, so that their images under π_* form a basis for the tangent space to shape space at the corresponding shape. Note, however, that, although the matrices Z_{ij} given by (7.2) are defined in terms of globally defined vectors $W_{ij} \in \mathcal{M}(m, k-1)$, the Z_{ij} themselves are only defined locally, since the way in which they are expressed depends on a particular choice of pseudo-singular values decomposition of X, which is a local phenomenon. The nature of this involvement of the pseudo-singular values decomposition in these fields, varying as X varies, may also make general computations difficult. For example, it is not always easy to find the expression for the Poisson bracket between two corresponding tangent vectors. Hence, it will be convenient to turn to the study of another family of local vector fields that arise naturally via a pseudo-singular values decomposition $X = U (\Lambda \quad 0) V$ of a *fixed* $m \times (k-1)$ matrix X.

We note that, since $\mathrm{tr}(X^t X) = \mathrm{tr}(\Lambda^2)$, X lies on the pre-shape sphere $\mathcal{S}_m^k$ if and only if the point $(\lambda_1, \ldots, \lambda_m)$ determined by Λ lies on the unit sphere $\mathbf{S}^{m-1}$ in $\mathbb{R}^m$. When $k > m+1$, the presence of the $m \times (k-m-1)$ block of zeros in a pseudo-singular values decomposition means that the last $k-m-1$ rows of V are not involved in the determination of X, so that we are really concerned with the Stiefel manifold $\mathbf{V}_{k-1,m}$ of orthonormal m frames $[V]$ in $\mathbb{R}^{k-1}$. When $k = m+1$ and there is no such block of zeros, we may still use the same notation since $\mathbf{V}_{m,m}$ is $\mathbf{SO}(m)$ itself. In all cases, since $\Lambda D = D\Lambda$ for any diagonal matrix D, such factors may be transferred from the Stiefel manifold component on the right into $\mathbf{SO}(m)$ on the left. However, we are able to describe open subsets $\mathbf{S}_0^{m-1}$ of $\mathbf{S}^{m-1}$ and $\mathbb{F}_{[V]}$ of $\mathbf{V}_{k-1,m}$ such that the product $\mathbf{SO}(m) \times \mathbf{S}_0^{m-1} \times \mathbb{F}_{[V]}$ is mapped diffeomorphically onto a neighbourhood of X in the pre-shape sphere, and hence $\mathbf{S}_0^{m-1} \times \mathbb{F}_{[V]}$ is mapped diffeomorphically onto a neighbourhood of $\pi(X)$ in shape space. The union of these neighbourhoods will be an open, dense subset of shape space, and the local embeddings enable us to transfer naturally defined vector fields on $\mathbf{SO}(m)$, $\mathbf{S}_0^{m-1}$ and $\mathbb{F}_{[V]}$ into local vector fields on the image neighbourhoods.

To describe the required vector fields on $\mathbf{SO}(m)$ we recall that, when it is embedded in the space of $m \times m$ real-valued matrices that is identified with $\mathbb{R}^{m^2}$ with coordinates x_{ij}, the tangent space to $\mathbf{SO}(m)$ at the identity I is the set of vectors whose standard coordinates form $m \times m$ skew-symmetric matrices. Thus, if we denote the standard basis of the tangent space to $\mathbb{R}^{m^2}$ formally by ∂X, where $(\partial X)_{ij} = \frac{\partial}{\partial x_{ij}}$, and by ∂X_U when we wish to specify the point U of $\mathbb{R}^{m^2}$ at which we are taking that basis, then the tangent vector itself that a skew-symmetric matrix A determines at the identity is the linear combination $\mathrm{tr}(A \, \partial X_I^t) = \mathrm{tr}(A^t \, \partial X_I)$. Left multiplication by an element U of $\mathbf{SO}(m)$ is a linear transformation of the matrix space sending $\mathbf{SO}(m)$ onto itself and mapping ∂X_I to $U^t \partial X_U$. Then, by linearity, the tangent vector $\text{tr}(A \, \partial X_I^t)$ maps to $\text{tr}\{A(U^t \partial X_U)^t\} = \text{tr}(UA \partial X_U^t)$, which is necessarily tangent to $\mathbf{SO}(m)$ at U. It follows that the space of standard coordinate matrices of the tangent vectors to $\mathbf{SO}(m)$ at U is $\{UA : A^t = -A\}$. If S_{ij} is the $m \times m$ skew-symmetric matrix $E_{ij} - E_{ji}$, then $\{S_{ij} : 1 \leqslant i < j \leqslant m\}$ are the standard coordinate matrices for a basis of $\mathcal{T}_I(\mathbf{SO}(m))$ and so $\{US_{ij} : 1 \leqslant i < j \leqslant m\}$ are those for a basis $\{\eta_{ij}(U) : 1 \leqslant i < j \leqslant m\}$ of $\mathcal{T}_U(\mathbf{SO}(m))$. These basis vectors are double those that lie above the diagonal in the skew-symmetric matrix $U^t \partial X_U$ of tangent vectors at U. However, since $\text{tr}(UA \, \partial X_U^t) = \text{tr}\{A(U^t \partial X_U)^t\}$, it will frequently be convenient to use the full matrix $U^t \partial X_U$, so that we may regard the skew-symmetric matrix A as the matrix of coordinates with respect to this 'basis' of our tangent space at U. Without this convention we should need to take double the entries appearing above the diagonal in A as our coordinates with respect to the true basis. Since left multiplication by U_1 sends ∂X_{U_0} to $U_1^t \partial X_{U_1 U_0}$ and so $U_0^t \partial X_{U_0}$ to $U_0^t U_1^t \partial X_{U_1 U_0} = (U_1 U_0)^t \partial X_{U_1 U_0}$, these vectors form global left-invariant fields on $\mathbf{SO}(m)$.

To describe the subsets of $\mathbf{V}_{k-1,m}$ that we require we embed the product $\mathbf{SO}(m) \times \mathbf{SO}(k - 1 - m)$ in $\mathbf{SO}(k - 1)$ in the usual manner by mapping (T_1, T_2) to $\text{diag}\{T_1, T_2\}$, so that we may represent $\mathbf{V}_{k-1,m}$, the Stiefel manifold of orthonormal m-frames in $\mathbb{R}^{k-1}$, as the quotient of $\mathbf{SO}(k - 1)$ by the subgroup $\{I_m\} \times \mathbf{SO}(k - 1 - m)$ acting on the left. Since that subgroup leaves the first m rows of $V \in \mathbf{SO}(k - 1)$ unchanged, the frame $[V]$ is that determined by the first m rows of V. Hence, we shall also use $[V]$ to denote the corresponding $m \times (k - 1)$ submatrix of V.

The Stiefel manifold component of the pseudo-singular values decomposition is not mapped injectively into shape space. We have to consider instead its quotient by the subgroup $\mathbf{D}$ of diagonal matrices in $\mathbf{SO}(m)$, where $D = \text{diag}\{d_1, \ldots, d_m\}$ is in $\mathbf{D}$ if and only if each $d_i = \pm 1$ and, since $\det(D) = 1$, the number of minus signs is even. However, since $\mathbf{D}$ is a finite group of isometries and $\mathbf{V}_{k-1,m}$ is a metric space, if $[V]$ is any point of $\mathbf{V}_{k-1,m}$ and $D_i([V])$, $1 \leqslant i \leqslant i_0$, are its images under the elements of $\mathbf{D}$ and if we choose a set of disjoint balls $\mathcal{B}_i$ with each $\mathcal{B}_i$ containing $D_i([V])$, then the intersection

$$\mathbb{F}_{[V]} = \bigcap_{i=1}^{i_0} D_i^{-1}(\mathcal{B}_i)$$

is an open set in $\mathbf{V}_{k-1,m}$ containing $[V]$ on which the restriction of the quotient map *is* injective. For each given $[V]$, we assume such a choice made.

To define the vector fields on $\mathbf{V}_{k-1,m}$, or, more precisely, on each $\mathbb{F}_{[V]}$, which we shall use, we note first that, similar to the above left-invariant fields on $\mathbf{SO}(m)$, there is a matrix $\partial X_V V^t$ of right-invariant vector fields on $\mathbf{SO}(k - 1)$. The fields above the diagonal in this matrix provide a basis $\{\xi_{ij}(V) : 1 \leqslant i < j \leqslant k - 1\}$ of $\mathcal{T}_V(\mathbf{SO}(k - 1))$, whose standard coordinate matrices are $\{S_{ij}V : 1 \leqslant i < j \leqslant k - 1\}$, where the S_{ij} are now the analogous $(k - 1) \times (k - 1)$ matrices to those similarly named above. Since $\text{tr}\{\xi_{i_1 j_1}(V)\xi_{i_2 j_2}(V)^t\} = 2\delta_{i_1 i_2}\delta_{j_1 j_2}$ when $i_1 < j_1$ and $i_2 < j_2$, these basis vectors are all orthogonal to each other and each has norm $\sqrt{2}$.

Since the elements of the group $\{I_m\} \times \mathbf{SO}(k-1-m)$ act as isometries of $\mathbf{SO}(k-1)$, it follows, in the same manner as was explained in Chapter 6 for the non-singular part of shape space, that $\mathbf{V}_{k-1,m}$ inherits a Riemannian metric with respect to which the projection $\pi_0 : V \mapsto [V]$ of $\mathbf{SO}(k-1)$ onto $\mathbf{V}_{k-1,m}$ is a Riemannian submersion. The fibre $\pi_0^{-1}(\pi_0(V))$ of π_0 above $[V]$ is given by $(\{I_m\} \times \mathbf{SO}(k-1-m))V$, so the vertical tangent subspace at V is given, with respect to the basis $\{\xi_{ij}(V) : 1 \leqslant i < j \leqslant k-1\}$, by the set of $(k-1) \times (k-1)$ coordinate matrices $\{\mathrm{diag}\{0_m, A\} : A^t = -A\}$. Thus, if we partition our matrix of vector fields on $\mathbf{SO}(k-1)$ in the obvious way as

$$\partial X_V V^t = \Xi(V) = \begin{pmatrix} \Xi_1(V) & \Xi_2(V) \\ -\Xi_2(V)^t & \Xi_3(V) \end{pmatrix},$$

then the vertical tangent space at V is spanned by the elements above the diagonal in $\Xi_3(V)$. Since the vector fields of $\Xi(V)$ are everywhere orthogonal and the horizontal subspace is the orthogonal direct complement to the vertical subspace, the elements of $\Xi_2(V)$ together with those above the diagonal in $\Xi_1(V)$ will form a basis of the horizontal subspace and so be mapped isometrically onto a basis of the tangent space to $\mathbf{V}_{k-1,m}$ at $[V]$. Using our 'doubled basis' convention, the coordinate matrix with respect to the $\Xi(V)$ of a horizontal vector on $\mathbf{SO}(k-1)$ will therefore be a skew-symmetric matrix of the form

$$\widetilde{B} = \begin{pmatrix} B_1 & B_2 \\ -B_2^t & 0 \end{pmatrix}.$$

Finally, we define the open subset

$$\mathbf{S}_0^{m-1} = \begin{cases} \{(x_1, \ldots, x_m) \in \mathbf{S}^{m-1} : x_1 > \cdots > x_{m-1} > |x_m| > 0\} & \text{if } k = m+1, \\ \{(x_1, \ldots, x_m) \in \mathbf{S}^{m-1} : x_1 \cdots > x_{m-1} > x_m > 0\} & \text{if } k > m+1 \end{cases}$$

of $\mathbf{S}^{m-1}$ and the corresponding open subset

$$\mathcal{X}_m^k = \begin{cases} \{X \in \mathcal{S}_m^k : \lambda_1 > \cdots > \lambda_{m-1} > |\lambda_m| > 0\} & \text{if } k = m+1, \\ \{X \in \mathcal{S}_m^k : \lambda_1 > \cdots > \lambda_{m-1} > \lambda_m > 0\} & \text{if } k > m+1 \end{cases}$$

of the pre-shape sphere, into which we shall be mapping. Note that, as open subsets of their respective spaces, $\mathcal{X}_m^k$ and $\mathbf{S}_0^{m-1}$ both inherit natural differential structures and also that $\pi(\mathcal{X}_m^k)$ is an open and *dense* submanifold of the non-singular part of Σ_m^k. We are now ready to state the lemma that will enable us to transfer our vector fields onto shape space.

Lemma 7.2. *For any $X \in \mathcal{X}_m^k$ with a pseudo-singular values decomposition $U(\Lambda \ 0)V$, the map $\Phi_{[V]}$ from $\mathbf{SO}(m) \times \mathbf{S}_0^{m-1} \times \mathbb{F}_{[V]}$ to $\mathcal{X}_m^k$ defined by*

$$(S, (x_1, \ldots, x_m), [T]) \mapsto S\,(\mathrm{diag}\{x_1, \ldots, x_m\} \ \ 0)\,T$$

is a diffeomorphism onto an open subset of $\mathcal{X}_m^k$ containing X. It induces a diffeomorphism $\overline{\Phi}_{[V]}$ of $\mathbf{S}_0^{m-1} \times \mathbb{F}_{[V]}$ onto an open neighbourhood of $\pi(X)$.

Proof. Since

$$S(\,\mathrm{diag}\{x_1, \ldots, x_m\} \quad 0\,)\,\mathrm{diag}\{I_m, \hat{T}\}T = S(\,\mathrm{diag}\{x_1, \cdots, x_m\} \quad 0\,)\,T$$

for any $\hat{T}$ in $\mathbf{SO}(k-1-m)$, it follows that $\Phi_{[V]}$ is well-defined. It is clearly continuous, and its image is open and contains X.

For a general element $Y = S(\,\mathrm{diag}\{x_1, \ldots, x_m\} \quad 0\,)\,T$ in $\mathcal{X}_m^k$, the diagonal entries x_i are uniquely determined, since they are the pseudo-singular values of Y, S is determined up to a right diagonal factor $D \in \mathbf{D}$ and the first m rows of T are determined up to a same left diagonal factor D. Hence, if

$$S_1(\,\mathrm{diag}\{x_1, \ldots, x_m\} \quad 0\,)\,T_1 = S_2(\,\mathrm{diag}\{x_1, \ldots, x_m\} \quad 0\,)\,T_2 \in \mathcal{X}_m^k,$$

then we have $S_2 = S_1 D$ and $\mathrm{diag}\{D, I_{k-1-m}\}T_2 = \mathrm{diag}\{I_m, \hat{T}\}T_1$ for some $\hat{T}$ in $\mathbf{SO}(k-1-m)$. However, if we know further that $[T_1]$ and $[T_2]$ are both in $\mathbb{F}_{[V]}$, then $D = I$ so that $S_1 = S_2$ and $[T_1] = [T_2]$. This implies that $\Phi_{[V]}$ is injective. It now suffices, by the Inverse Function Theorem, to show that the derivative $(\Phi_{[V]})_*$ is an isomorphism at each point of the domain.

Since $\mathcal{X}_m^k$ has the same dimension as the domain of $\Phi_{[V]}$, to prove that $(\Phi_{[V]})_*$ is an isomorphism it is enough to show that the entire tangent space to $\mathcal{S}_m^k$ at X lies in its image. For that purpose we shall realise elements of $\mathcal{T}_X(\mathcal{S}_m^k)$ as the tangent vectors at X to curves $\widetilde{\Gamma}(s)$ in $\mathcal{X}_m^k$ starting at X and lying in the image of $\Phi_{[V]}$. So, for any skew-symmetric matrix A determining a vector in $\mathcal{T}_U(\mathbf{SO}(m))$, any diagonal matrix D with $\mathrm{tr}(\Lambda D) = 0$ determining a vector in $\mathcal{T}_\Lambda(\mathbf{S}^{m-1})$, and any skew-symmetric matrix

$$\widetilde{B} = \begin{pmatrix} B_1 & B_2 \\ -B_2^t & 0 \end{pmatrix}$$

determining a horizontal tangent vector in $\mathcal{T}_V(\mathbf{SO}(k-1))$, we consider the curve $\widetilde{\Gamma}(s)$ on $\mathcal{S}_m^k$ given by

$$\widetilde{\Gamma}(s) = U e^{sA}(\,\cos s\,\Lambda + \sin s\,D \quad 0\,)\,e^{s\widetilde{B}}V. \tag{7.4}$$

Since $\widetilde{B}$ is horizontal with respect to the projection of $\mathbf{SO}(k-1)$ onto $\mathbf{V}_{k-1,m}$, the path $e^{s\widetilde{B}}V$ is the horizontal lift of the path $[e^{s\widetilde{B}}V] = \pi_0(e^{s\widetilde{B}}V)$ in $\mathbf{V}_{k-1,m}$. Thus, $\widetilde{\Gamma}(s)$ is the composition of $\Phi_{[V]}$ with a path in $\mathbf{SO}(m) \times \mathbf{S}_0^{m-1} \times \mathbb{F}_{[V]}$ and so its derivative at $s = 0$ is a tangent vector in the image of $(\Phi_{[V]})_*$. However, that derivative has a standard coordinate matrix

$$\left.\frac{\mathrm{d}\widetilde{\Gamma}(s)}{\mathrm{d}s}\right|_{s=0} = UA(\,\Lambda \quad 0\,)V + U(\,D \quad 0\,)V + U\Lambda BV,$$

where $B = (\,B_1 \quad B_2\,)$, the first m rows of $\widetilde{B}$. Since $\lambda_m \neq 0$ and so Λ^{-1} exists, we may re-write this coordinate matrix as $U\Lambda WV$, where

$$W = (\,\Lambda^{-1}A\Lambda + \Lambda^{-1}D + B_1 \quad B_2\,). \tag{7.5}$$

On the other hand, the standard coordinate matrix Z of an arbitrary tangent vector to $\mathcal{S}_m^k$ at X may also be expressed in the form $Z = U\Lambda WV$ by taking $W = \Lambda^{-1}U'ZV'$. If we then separate out the diagonal part of W by writing $W = (W_0 + W_1 \quad W_2)$, where $W_0 \in \mathcal{W}_0$, $W_2 \in \mathcal{W}_2$ and W_1 is $m \times m$ with all its diagonal entries zero, we have

$$\operatorname{tr}(XZ') = \operatorname{tr}\{U\,(\Lambda \quad 0)\,VV'W'\Lambda U'\} = \operatorname{tr}\{(\Lambda^2 \quad 0)\,W'\} = \operatorname{tr}(\Lambda^2 W_0),$$

so that the condition for Z to represent a tangent vector at X becomes $\operatorname{tr}(\Lambda^2 W_0) = 0$.

We now claim that, as A, B_1, B_2 and D vary, the resulting matrix W given by (7.5) ranges over the subset of $\mathcal{M}(m, k-1)$ satisfying this tangency condition. For, if we define $D = \Lambda W_0$, we have $\operatorname{tr}(\Lambda D) = 0$ as specified for (7.4) and an arbitrary choice of W_2 is obviously realised by the same choice of B_2. Finally, for any $m \times m$ matrix $W_1 = (w_{ij})$ with $w_{ii} = 0$, $1 \leqslant i \leqslant m$, we define the skew-symmetric matrices $A = (a_{ij})$ and $B_1 = (b_{ij})$ by

$$a_{ij} = \frac{\lambda_i \lambda_j}{\lambda_j^2 - \lambda_i^2}\{w_{ij} + w_{ji}\} \quad \text{and} \quad b_{ij} = \frac{\lambda_i^2 w_{ij} + \lambda_j^2 w_{ji}}{\lambda_i^2 - \lambda_j^2}.$$

Then, $W_1 = \Lambda^{-1}A\Lambda + B_1$, so that all choices of W_1 can be realised by the appropriate choice of A and B_1 in (7.5).

Since the dimension of the subspace of $\mathcal{M}(m, k-1)$ comprising those W for which $\operatorname{tr}(\Lambda^2 W_0) = 0$ has the same dimension as $T_X(\mathcal{S}_m^k)$, this completes the proof that $(\Phi_{[V]})_*$ is surjective and hence an isomorphism, and so completes the proof of the lemma. ∎

For Lemma 7.2 it was sufficient to observe that, regarding the diagonal entries in Λ as standard coordinates $(x_1, \ldots, x_m)$ in $\mathbb{R}^m$, a second diagonal matrix D such that $\operatorname{tr}(\Lambda D) = 0$ would define a tangent vector to $\mathbf{S}_0^{m-1}$ at Λ in the usual way. However, for our next result we need to identify a specific basis of $T_\Lambda(\mathbf{S}^{m-1})$ for $\Lambda \in \mathbf{S}_0^{m-1}$. To that end we change to the coordinates

$$y_1 = \left\{\sum_{i=1}^m x_i^2\right\}^{1/2} \quad \text{and} \quad y_i = \frac{x_i}{\left\{\sum_{i=1}^m x_i^2\right\}^{1/2}}, \quad 1 < i \leqslant m.$$

From the inverse transformation

$$x_1 = y_1\left\{1 - \sum_{i=2}^m y_i^2\right\}^{1/2} \quad \text{and} \quad x_i = y_1 y_i, \quad 1 < i \leqslant m,$$

we find

$$\frac{1}{y_1}\frac{\partial}{\partial y_i} = \frac{\partial}{\partial x_i} - \frac{x_i}{x_1}\frac{\partial}{\partial x_1}, \quad 1 < i \leqslant m, \tag{7.6}$$

which, since the corresponding integral curves with $y_1 = 1$ lie on $\mathbf{S}^{m-1}$, we may take as a basis for $T_\Lambda(\mathbf{S}^{m-1})$. As we shall only use the coordinates λ_i when they are the diagonal entries of $\Lambda \in \mathbf{S}_0^{m-1}$, it will be convenient to denote these tangent vectors $\frac{\partial}{\partial y_i}$ at Λ by $\frac{\partial}{\partial \lambda_i}$.

We may, of course, identify the tangent space to the product $\mathbf{SO}(m) \times \mathbf{S}_0^{m-1} \times \mathbb{F}_{[V]}$ with the direct sum of the three tangent spaces and then Lemma 7.2 implies that, for any $X = U(\Lambda \quad 0)V$ in $\mathcal{X}_m^k$, the images under $(\Phi_{[V]})_*$ of the tangent vectors

$$\{\eta_{ij}(U) : 1 \leqslant i < j \leqslant m\} \bigcup \left\{ \frac{\partial}{\partial \lambda_i} : 1 < i \leqslant m \right\}$$

$$\bigcup \{(\pi_0)_*(\xi_{ij}(V)) : 1 \leqslant i \leqslant m, i < j \leqslant k - 1\}$$

form a basis of $T_X(\mathcal{S}_m^k)$. Henceforth, we shall follow the usual convention and omit explicit mention of $(\Phi_{[V]})_*$ and $(\pi_0)_*$ when the context makes it clear which particular vectors are involved. We now look at the relation between this basis and the basis

$$\{\underline{\zeta}_{ii} : 1 < i \leqslant m\} \bigcup \{\underline{\zeta}_{ij} : 1 \leqslant i \leqslant m, i < j \leqslant k - 1\}$$

of the horizontal subspace at X, whose standard coordinate matrices are the corresponding Z_{ii} and Z_{ij} given by (7.2).

Lemma 7.3. *For X in $\mathcal{X}_m^k$,*

$$\underline{\zeta}_{ii} = \frac{\partial}{\partial \lambda_i}, \quad 1 < i \leqslant m,$$

$$\underline{\zeta}_{ij} = \frac{\lambda_i^2 + \lambda_j^2}{\lambda_i^2 - \lambda_j^2} \left\{ \xi_{ij} - 2\frac{\lambda_i \lambda_j}{\lambda_i^2 + \lambda_j^2} \eta_{ij} \right\}, \quad 1 \leqslant i < j \leqslant m,$$

$$\underline{\zeta}_{ij} = \frac{1}{\lambda_i}\xi_{ij}, \quad 1 \leqslant i \leqslant m < j \leqslant k - 1.$$

Proof. We note first that Equation (7.6) implies that the diagonal matrix D in (7.5) corresponding to $\frac{\partial}{\partial \lambda_i}$ for $1 < i \leqslant m$ has diagonal coordinates

$$d_j = \delta_{ij} - \frac{\lambda_i}{\lambda_1}\delta_{1j}, \quad 1 \leqslant j \leqslant m.$$

Hence, the standard coordinate matrix of the vector $\frac{\partial}{\partial \lambda_i}$ will be the matrix Z_{ii} in (7.2), so that $\frac{\partial}{\partial \lambda_i} = \underline{\zeta}_{ii}$ as stated.

To determine the $\underline{\zeta}_{ij}$ for $1 \leqslant i < j \leqslant m$ we need to consider the special case $D = 0$ and $B_2 = 0$ of (7.4) and (7.5). Recall that A and B_1 are both skew-symmetric and, via the fields $\eta_{ij}(U)$ and $\xi_{ij}(V)$, determine tangent vectors in $\mathcal{T}_U(\mathbf{SO}(m))$ and $\mathcal{T}_V(\mathbf{SO}(k-1))$, respectively. For simplicity, we write $\Lambda^{-1}A\Lambda + B_1 = C = (c_{ij})$ and write c_{ij}^h and c_{ij}^v for the components of the matrices C_h and C_v, respectively, where $U\Lambda\,(C_h \quad 0)\,V$ and $U\Lambda\,(C_v \quad 0)\,V$ are the standard coordinate matrices of the horizontal and vertical components of the tangent vector with the standard coordinate matrix $U\Lambda\,(C \quad 0)\,V$. Clearly, any vertical vectors at X correspond to those in $\mathcal{T}_U(\mathbf{SO}(m))$, so the vertical subspace at X is $\mathcal{V}_X = \{UA\,(\Lambda \quad 0)\,V : A^t = -A\}$, which, since $UA = (UAU^t)U$ and UAU^t is also skew-symmetric, does agree with the expression for the vertical subspace used in Chapter 6. Moreover, since for any X in $\mathcal{X}_m^k$ we have $\lambda_m \neq 0$, so that Λ is invertible, this may be further rewritten as

$$\mathcal{V}_X = \{U\Lambda\,(\widetilde{A} \quad 0)\,V : \widetilde{A}^t = -\Lambda^2\widetilde{A}\Lambda^{-2}\}.$$

Thus, we have $\lambda_i^2 c_{ij}^v = -\lambda_j^2 c_{ji}^v$ and, since $c_{ij}^h = c_{ji}^h$ from Lemma 7.1, we deduce that

$$c_{ij}^h = \frac{\lambda_i^2 c_{ij} + \lambda_j^2 c_{ji}}{\lambda_i^2 + \lambda_j^2} \quad \text{and} \quad c_{ij}^v = \frac{\lambda_j^2}{\lambda_i^2 + \lambda_j^2}\left\{c_{ij} - c_{ji}\right\}.$$

Since ξ_{ij} corresponds to the case in which $A = 0$ and B_1 is the basic skew-symmetric matrix S_{ij} defined above, the standard coordinate matrix of the horizontal component of ξ_{ij}, its projection onto the horizontal subspace at X, is that which corresponds to

$$\frac{\lambda_i^2 - \lambda_j^2}{\lambda_i^2 + \lambda_j^2}\{E_{ij} + E_{ji}\}.$$

Since the corresponding c_{ij}^v is $2\lambda_j^2/(\lambda_i^2 + \lambda_j^2)S_{ij}$, the standard coordinate matrix of its vertical component is that corresponding to

$$A = 2\frac{\lambda_i\lambda_j}{\lambda_i^2 + \lambda_j^2}S_{ij}.$$

Thus,

$$\xi_{ij} = \frac{\lambda_i^2 - \lambda_j^2}{\lambda_i^2 + \lambda_j^2}\underline{\zeta}_{ij} + 2\frac{\lambda_i\lambda_j}{\lambda_i^2 + \lambda_j^2}\eta_{ij},$$

so that the $\underline{\zeta}_{ij}$, $1 \leqslant i < j \leqslant m$, are as stated.

Finally, we note that, since for $1 \leqslant i \leqslant m < j \leqslant k - 1$ we may re-write Z_{ij} in (7.2) as $U\Lambda\{\Lambda^{-1}E_{ij}\}V$ and since the vector field ξ_{ij} has integral curve $\widetilde{\Gamma}(s)$ at X, given by (7.4), corresponding to $A = 0$, $D = 0$ and $B = E_{ij}$, it follows that for $1 \leqslant i \leqslant m < j \leqslant k - 1$ the matrix Z_{ij} gives the standard coordinates of ξ_{ij}/λ_i.   ■

Since the ζ_{ij} are horizontal and the η_{ij} are vertical, Lemma 7.3 tells us that the tangent vectors $\frac{\partial}{\partial\lambda_i}$ for $1 < i \leqslant m$ and ξ_{ij} for $1 \leqslant i \leqslant m < j \leqslant k-1$ are horizontal and so are mapped isometrically onto their images in the tangent space to shape space at $\pi(X)$. However, for $1 \leqslant i < j \leqslant m$, it is the horizontal component $\overline{\xi}_{ij}$ of ξ_{ij} that is mapped isometrically onto its image. This component is

$$\overline{\xi}_{ij} = \frac{\lambda_i^2 - \lambda_j^2}{\lambda_i^2 + \lambda_j^2}\zeta_{ij} = \xi_{ij} - 2\frac{\lambda_i\lambda_j}{\lambda_i^2 + \lambda_j^2}\eta_{ij}, \qquad (7.7)$$

whose standard coordinate matrix is

$$\frac{\lambda_i^2 - \lambda_j^2}{\lambda_i^2 + \lambda_j^2}Z_{ij}.$$

Since, for X in $\mathcal{X}_m^k$, λ_i and λ_j are never zero, it follows that ξ_{ij} is never horizontal for i and j in the latter range. However, λ_i and λ_j are unequal for X in $\mathcal{X}_m^k$ and so the ξ_{ij} are also not vertical. Then, since their horizontal components together with the vectors $\frac{\partial}{\partial\lambda_i}$, $1 < i \leqslant m$, and ξ_{ij}, $1 \leqslant i \leqslant m < j \leqslant k-1$, form a basis of the horizontal subspace at X, the image vectors

$$\left\{\pi_*\left(\frac{\partial}{\partial\lambda_i}\right) : 1 < i \leqslant m\right\}\bigcup\left\{\pi_*\left(\xi_{ij}(V)\right) : 1 \leqslant i \leqslant m, i < j \leqslant k-1\right\} \quad (7.8)$$

form a basis of $\mathcal{T}_{\pi(X)}(\pi(\mathcal{X}_m^k))$.

We should note two points about this choice of basis. Firstly, it is not available outside $\pi(\mathcal{X}_m^k)$, since for X in the remainder of $\mathcal{S}_m^k\backslash\mathcal{D}_{m-2}$ there could, for example, be indices i and j such that $\lambda_i = \lambda_j$ and then ξ_{ij} will be vertical at X and hence $\pi_*(\xi_{ij})$ will be zero. Nevertheless, it will often be possible to use this basis to obtain results on $\pi(\mathcal{X}_m^k)$, which can then be seen by continuity to hold throughout the non-singular part of shape space. Secondly, although the vectors $\pi_*(\xi_{ij})$ for $1 \leqslant i < j \leqslant m$ remain orthogonal to those in the rest of the basis and to each other, their norms differ from those of ξ_{ij} since their inner products $\langle\pi_*(\xi_{i_1j_1}), \pi_*(\xi_{i_2j_2})\rangle$ are equal to $\langle\overline{\xi}_{i_1j_1}, \overline{\xi}_{i_2j_2}\rangle$, which, from the proof of Theorem 7.1, we see are given by

$$\langle\overline{\xi}_{i_1j_1}, \overline{\xi}_{i_2j_2}\rangle = \frac{\left(\lambda_{i_1}^2 - \lambda_{j_1}^2\right)^2}{\lambda_{i_1}^2 + \lambda_{j_1}^2}\delta_{i_1i_2}\delta_{j_1j_2}, \quad 1 \leqslant i_1 < j_1 \leqslant m \text{ and } 1 \leqslant i_2 < j_2 \leqslant m.$$

Lemma 7.2 also provides a diffeomorphism $\overline{\Phi}_{[V]}$ of $\mathbf{S}_0^{m-1} \times \mathbb{F}_{[V]}$ onto a neighbourhood of $\pi(X)$, and the image under $(\overline{\Phi}_{[V]})_*$ of the natural vector fields $\left\{\frac{\partial}{\partial\lambda_i} : 1 < i \leqslant m\right\}$ and $\{\xi_{ij} : 1 \leqslant i \leqslant m, i < j \leqslant k-1\}$ on $\mathbf{S}_0^{m-1} \times \mathbb{F}_{[V]}$ gives us another basis of $\mathcal{T}_{\pi(X)}(\pi(\mathcal{X}_m^k))$, which, with our previous convention of omitting explicit reference to the relevant linear map, we could and shall denote by the same symbols. Since $\pi_* \circ (\Phi_{[V]})_*$ restricted to $T_\Lambda(\mathbf{S}_0^{m-1}) \oplus T_{[V]}(\mathbb{F}_{[V]})$ is just $(\overline{\Phi}_{[V]})_*$, these are precisely the vectors $\pi_* \left(\frac{\partial}{\partial \lambda_i} \right)$ and $\pi_*(\xi_{ij}(V))$ in (7.8). This will cause no confusion as far as the $\frac{\partial}{\partial \lambda_i}$, $1 < i \leqslant m$, or the ξ_{ij}, $1 \leqslant i \leqslant m < j \leqslant k - 1$, are concerned. However, for the remaining ξ_{ij}, their inner products will depend on whether they represent tangent vectors on $\mathcal{X}_m^k$ or on $\pi(\mathcal{X}_m^k)$. Re-interpreting the basis (7.8) in this way, that is, writing

$$\left\{ \frac{\partial}{\partial \lambda_i} : 1 < i \leqslant m \right\} \bigcup \{ \xi_{ij} : 1 \leqslant i \leqslant m, \ i < j \leqslant k - 1 \} \qquad (7.9)$$

for that basis of $T_{\pi(X)}(\pi(\mathcal{X}_m^k))$, Lemma 7.3 and the above remarks imply that we have the following relation between our two bases of the tangent space to shape space at $\pi(X)$.

Corollary 7.1. *For* $\pi(X)$ *in* $\pi(\mathcal{X}_m^k)$,

$$\pi_*(\underline{\zeta}_{ii}) = \frac{\partial}{\partial \lambda_i}, \quad 1 < i \leqslant m,$$

$$\pi_*(\underline{\zeta}_{ij}) = \frac{\lambda_i^2 + \lambda_j^2}{\lambda_i^2 - \lambda_j^2} \xi_{ij}, \quad 1 \leqslant i < j \leqslant m,$$

$$\pi_*(\underline{\zeta}_{ij}) = \frac{1}{\lambda_i} \xi_{ij}, \quad 1 \leqslant i \leqslant m < j \leqslant k - 1.$$

It follows that the dual 1-forms of $\pi_*(\underline{\zeta}_{ij})$ are $\mathrm{d}\lambda_i$ for $1 < i = j \leqslant m$, $\frac{\lambda_i^2 - \lambda_j^2}{\lambda_i^2 + \lambda_j^2} \phi_{ij}$ for $1 \leqslant i < j \leqslant m$ and $\lambda_i \phi_{ij}$ for $1 \leqslant i \leqslant m < j \leqslant k - 1$, where ϕ_{ij} are the dual 1-forms of ξ_{ij} on $\mathbf{SO}(k - 1)$. Since the Riemannian metric on a Riemannian manifold with local coordinates x_i may be expressed in terms of those coordinates as $\mathrm{d}s^2 = \sum g_{ij} \mathrm{d}x_i \mathrm{d}x_j$, where $g_{ij} = \left\langle \frac{\partial}{\partial x_i}, \frac{\partial}{\partial x_j} \right\rangle$, the next theorem follows from Theorem 7.1.

Theorem 7.2. *On* $\pi(\mathcal{X}_m^k)$, *the Riemannian metric can be expressed as*

$$\mathrm{d}\rho^2 = \sum_{i=2}^{m} \mathrm{d}\lambda_i^2 + \left(\sum_{i=2}^{m} \frac{\lambda_i}{\lambda_1} \mathrm{d}\lambda_i \right)^2$$

$$+ \sum_{1 \leqslant i < j \leqslant m} \frac{(\lambda_i^2 - \lambda_j^2)^2}{\lambda_i^2 + \lambda_j^2} \phi_{ij}^2 + \sum_{i=1}^{m} \sum_{j=m+1}^{k-1} \lambda_i^2 \phi_{ij}^2. \qquad (7.10)$$

Note that, if we choose $j < m$ and put $\lambda_i \equiv 0$, and hence $\mathrm{d}\lambda_i = 0$, for $i > j$ in expression (7.10) for the metric on $\pi(\mathcal{X}_m^k)$, we then obtain *exactly* the corresponding expression for the Riemannian metric on $\pi(\mathcal{X}_j^k)$. This throws further light on the stratification of shape space that we described in Section 6.3. What it means for the lower stratum to be isometric with Σ_j^k/ι_j and so locally isometric with Σ_j^k is that, as we approach that stratum by letting $\lambda_i \to 0$ for $i > j$, so the metric of Σ_m^k approaches that of Σ_j^k.

The $(m-1) \times (m-1)$ matrix of the inner products $g_{ij} = \left\langle \frac{\partial}{\partial\lambda_{i+1}}, \frac{\partial}{\partial\lambda_{j+1}} \right\rangle$ is, by (7.10),

$$
g = (g_{ij}) = \frac{1}{\lambda_1^2}
\begin{pmatrix}
\lambda_1^2 + \lambda_2^2 & \lambda_2\lambda_3 & \cdots & \lambda_2\lambda_m \\
\lambda_2\lambda_3 & \lambda_1^2 + \lambda_3^2 & \cdots & \lambda_3\lambda_m \\
\vdots & \vdots & \ddots & \vdots \\
\lambda_2\lambda_m & \lambda_3\lambda_m & \cdots & \lambda_1^2 + \lambda_m^2
\end{pmatrix},
\tag{7.11}
$$

so the vectors $\left\{ \frac{\partial}{\partial\lambda_i} : 1 < i \leqslant m \right\}$ do not form part of an orthogonal basis of $T_{\pi(X)}(\Sigma_m^k \backslash \pi(\mathcal{D}_{m-2}))$ at $\pi(X)$ in $\pi(\mathcal{X}_m^k)$. Nevertheless, because of the simple relation between the bases (7.9) and (7.3), we shall be using formula (7.10) to obtain the geometric invariants of shape space. First, we use it to find the Laplace–Beltrami operator, which will enable us to study Brownian motion, on shape space. For that we require the determinant of g in (7.11), which is equal to $1/\lambda_1^2$, and the inverse of g, which gives the corresponding inner products $g^{ij} = \langle d\lambda_{i+1}, d\lambda_{j+1} \rangle$ and is equal to

$$
(g^{ij}) =
\begin{pmatrix}
1 - \lambda_2^2 & -\lambda_2\lambda_3 & \cdots & -\lambda_2\lambda_m \\
-\lambda_2\lambda_3 & 1 - \lambda_3^2 & \cdots & -\lambda_3\lambda_m \\
\vdots & \vdots & \ddots & \vdots \\
-\lambda_2\lambda_m & -\lambda_3\lambda_m & \cdots & 1 - \lambda_m^2
\end{pmatrix}.
$$

The Laplace–Beltrami operator on a Riemannian manifold may be given locally in one of two ways. For an orthonormal basis of vector fields v_i it may be expressed as

$$
\sum_i \left\{ v_i^2 - \nabla_{v_i} v_i \right\},
$$

where ∇ is the Levi–Cività connection determined by the metric. Alternatively, for local coordinates x_i, it is

$$
\sum_{i,j} (\det(g))^{-1/2} \frac{\partial}{\partial x_i} \left(g^{ij} (\det(g))^{1/2} \frac{\partial}{\partial x_j} \right).
$$

Since the subspace spanned by $\left\{ \frac{\partial}{\partial\lambda_i} : 1 < i \leqslant m \right\}$ is orthogonal to that spanned by $\{\xi_{ij} : 1 \leqslant i \leqslant m, \, i < j \leqslant k-1\}$, we may combine these two approaches to obtain the following result.

Corollary 7.2. *On* $\pi(\mathcal{X}_m^k)$, *the Laplace–Beltrami operator can be expressed as*

$$
\sum_{i=2}^{m} \frac{\partial^2}{\partial \lambda_i^2} - \sum_{i,j=2}^{m} \lambda_i \lambda_j \frac{\partial^2}{\partial \lambda_i \partial \lambda_j} - (m-1) \sum_{i=2}^{m} \lambda_i \frac{\partial}{\partial \lambda_i}
$$

$$
+ \sum_{1 \leqslant i < j \leqslant m} \frac{\lambda_i^2 + \lambda_j^2}{(\lambda_i^2 - \lambda_j^2)^2} \{ \xi_{ij}\xi_{ij} - \nabla_{\xi_{ij}}\xi_{ij} \} + \sum_{i=1}^{m} \frac{1}{\lambda_i^2} \sum_{j=m+1}^{k-1} \{ \xi_{ij}\xi_{ij} - \nabla_{\xi_{ij}}\xi_{ij} \}.
$$

Similarly, the volume element on a Riemannian manifold may be given either as the product of the forms dual to an orthonormal basis of vector fields or, for local coordinates x_i, as $(\det(g))^{1/2}$ times the product of forms dx_i. Thus, we may compute the volume element, which we shall use to describe probability measures on shape space.

Corollary 7.3. *The volume element of* $\Sigma_m^k \backslash \pi(\mathcal{D}_{m-2})$ *on* $\pi(\mathcal{X}_m^k)$ *is*

$$
\frac{1}{\lambda_1} \prod_{i=1}^{m} |\lambda_i|^{k-1-m} \prod_{1 \leqslant i < j \leqslant m} \frac{|\lambda_i^2 - \lambda_j^2|}{\sqrt{\lambda_i^2 + \lambda_j^2}} \prod_{i=2}^{m} d\lambda_i \prod_{i=1}^{m} \prod_{j=i+1}^{k-1} \phi_{ij}.
$$

Note that the product $\prod_{i=1}^{m} \prod_{j=i+1}^{k-1} \phi_{ij}$ depends only on $[V]$ and is invariant relative to the transformations $[V] \mapsto T[V]$ for T in $\mathbf{SO}(m)$ and $[V] \mapsto [V]T$ for T in $\mathbf{SO}(k-1)$. Hence, $\prod_{i=1}^{m} \prod_{j=i+1}^{k-1} \phi_{ij}$ defines a constant multiple of the usual invariant measure on $\mathbf{V}_{k-1,m}$ (cf. Muirhead, 1982).

We may also find the volume element and hence the volume of the fibre on the pre-shape sphere above any non-singular point of shape space.

Corollary 7.4. *If* $\pi(X)$ *is a non-singular point of shape space, then the volume of the fibre* $\pi^{-1}(\pi(X))$ *is*

$$
c_m^k \prod_{1 \leqslant i < j \leqslant m} \sqrt{\lambda_i^2 + \lambda_j^2}
$$

for some positive constant c_m^k.

Proof. Since

$$
\langle \eta_{i_1 j_1}, \eta_{i_2 j_2} \rangle = \delta_{i_1 i_2} \delta_{j_1 j_2} \left\{ \lambda_{i_1}^2 + \lambda_{j_1}^2 \right\}, \tag{7.12}
$$

it follows that the volume element of the fibre $\pi^{-1}(\pi(X))$ for any $\pi(X)$ in $\pi(\mathcal{X}_m^k)$ is

$$
\prod_{1 \leqslant i < j \leqslant m} \sqrt{\lambda_i^2 + \lambda_j^2} \prod_{1 \leqslant i < j \leqslant m} \psi_{ij},
$$

where the ψ_{ij} are the dual 1-forms of η_{ij} on $\mathbf{SO}(m)$, and so the expression for the volume of the fibre holds for $\pi(X)$ in $\pi(\mathcal{X}_m^k)$. Then, by continuity, it is also true for any non-singular point. ∎

Note that when $m = 2$ we have $\lambda_1^2 + \lambda_2^2 = 1$, so that in this case the fibre has constant volume everywhere.

Although we shall find it convenient to work with the non-orthogonal tangent vectors on $\mathbf{S}_0^{m-1}$, it is possible, if necessary, to obtain an orthogonal basis by using the customary stereographic coordinates u_i on the unit sphere. These are given by the formulae

$$\hat{\lambda}_i = \frac{\lambda_{i+1}}{1 + \lambda_1}, \quad 1 \leqslant i \leqslant m - 1, \tag{7.13}$$

which, on substitution into (7.10), lead to the following result.

Corollary 7.5. On $\pi(\mathcal{X}_m^k)$, the Riemannian metric can also be expressed as

$$d\rho^2 = (1 + \lambda_1)^2 \sum_{i=1}^{m-1} d\hat{\lambda}_i^2 + \sum_{1 \leqslant i < j \leqslant m} \frac{(\lambda_i^2 - \lambda_j^2)^2}{\lambda_i^2 + \lambda_j^2} \phi_{ij}^2 + \sum_{i=1}^{m} \sum_{j=m+1}^{k-1} \lambda_i^2 \phi_{ij}^2.$$

A useful observation is that (7.13) can be replaced by

$$\hat{\lambda}_i = \frac{\lambda_i}{1 + \lambda_l}, \ i < l, \quad \text{and} \quad \hat{\lambda}_i = \frac{\lambda_{i+1}}{1 + \lambda_l}, \quad l \leqslant i \leqslant m - 1,$$

when convenient. Then, (7.13) is the case $l = 1$, and in the general case the metric can be expressed as in Corollary 7.5, but with the factor $(1 + \lambda_1)^2$ replaced by $(1 + \lambda_l)^2$.

7.3   THE RIEMANNIAN CURVATURE TENSOR

The curvature of a two-dimensional surface is intimately bound up with its shape, measuring whether, and to what extent, it is convex, concave, saddle-shaped or, if it is none of these, flat. This information will, of course, vary from point to point on the surface. It is an intrinsic property of the surface that does not depend on how it may be embedded isometrically in any Euclidean space or higher dimensional manifold. For that higher dimensional manifold itself, the situation is more complex but still well-structured. For each two linearly independent tangent vectors at a point there is an invariant, the *sectional curvature*, with the remarkable property that, for any surface embedded in the manifold with its tangent space spanned by those two vectors, its curvature at that point will be equal to this sectional curvature. This apparent plethora of information was encapsulated by Riemann in a single tensor having four, rather than just two, arguments. The full set of sectional curvatures determine, and are determined by, this Riemannian curvature tensor, which in turn determines other standard measures of curvature, such as the Ricci and scalar curvatures.

Rather than working directly from the definition of shape space itself, we shall employ a famous theorem of O'Neill that expresses how the curvature changes when passing from the 'top' space to the 'bottom' space of a Riemannian submersion. In particular, *the sectional curvatures never decrease.* In our case the 'top' space is the pre-shape sphere of radius one. So, as the measure of scalar curvature is normalised so that a unit sphere in any Euclidean space has all its sectional curvatures equal to unity, it follows that *all* the sectional curvatures of each shape space are greater than, or equal to, unity. We shall also find that some of the sectional curvatures, and so also the scalar curvature of shape space, tend to infinity as we approach a singularity.

To state O'Neill's theorem (cf. O'Neill, 1966) we consider vector fields v_i, $1 \leqslant i \leqslant 4$, on $\Sigma_m^k \setminus \pi(\mathcal{D}_{m-2})$ and their horizontal lifts $\tilde{v}_i$ on $\mathcal{S}_m^k$. Thus, the $\tilde{v}_i$ are horizontal and $\pi_*(\tilde{v}_i) = v_i$. Then O'Neill's theorem tells us that the Riemannian curvature tensors $R_{\mathcal{S}_m^k}$ and $R_{\Sigma_m^k}$ on the pre-shape sphere and on shape space, respectively, are related by

$$
\begin{aligned}
R_{\Sigma_m^k}&(v_1, v_2, v_3, v_4)\\
&= R_{\mathcal{S}_m^k}(\tilde{v}_1, \tilde{v}_2, \tilde{v}_3, \tilde{v}_4) + \tfrac{1}{2}\langle [\tilde{v}_1, \tilde{v}_2]^{\mathrm{v}}, [\tilde{v}_3, \tilde{v}_4]^{\mathrm{v}} \rangle\\
&\quad - \tfrac{1}{4}\langle [\tilde{v}_2, \tilde{v}_3]^{\mathrm{v}}, [\tilde{v}_1, \tilde{v}_4]^{\mathrm{v}} \rangle - \tfrac{1}{4}\langle [\tilde{v}_3, \tilde{v}_1]^{\mathrm{v}}, [\tilde{v}_2, \tilde{v}_4]^{\mathrm{v}} \rangle,
\end{aligned}
\tag{7.14}
$$

where v^{v} denotes the vertical component of the vector v and $[\tilde{v}_1, \tilde{v}_2]$ denotes the bracket of the vector fields $\tilde{v}_1$ and $\tilde{v}_2$ that acts on a smooth function f as

$$
[\tilde{v}_1, \tilde{v}_2]f = \tilde{v}_1 \tilde{v}_2 f - \tilde{v}_2 \tilde{v}_1 f.
$$

However, since $\mathcal{S}_m^k$ has all its sectional curvatures everywhere equal to unity, we also know that

$$
R_{\mathcal{S}_m^k}(\tilde{v}_1, \tilde{v}_2, \tilde{v}_3, \tilde{v}_4) = \langle \tilde{v}_3, \tilde{v}_1 \rangle \langle \tilde{v}_2, \tilde{v}_4 \rangle - \langle \tilde{v}_3, \tilde{v}_2 \rangle \langle \tilde{v}_1, \tilde{v}_4 \rangle.
$$

Recall that the vectors in (7.9) form a basis of the tangent space to $\pi(\mathcal{X}_m^k)$ at $\pi(X)$ and that the horizontal lifts of these vectors are those of the same name for $\left\{ \frac{\partial}{\partial \lambda_i} : 1 < i \leqslant m \right\}$ and for $\{ \xi_{ij} : 1 \leqslant i \leqslant m < j \leqslant k - 1 \}$, while, for the remaining vectors, they are the horizontal components $\overline{\xi}_{ij}$ in (7.7). For simplicity, we shall denote all the horizontal lifts, ξ_{ij} or $\overline{\xi}_{ij}$, by $\tilde{\xi}_{ij}$.

Since $[\tilde{v}_1, \tilde{v}_2] = -[\tilde{v}_2, \tilde{v}_1]$ and $\left[\frac{\partial}{\partial \lambda_i}, \frac{\partial}{\partial \lambda_j} \right] = 0$, the non-zero brackets of the pairs of horizontal vector fields from our chosen basis are determined by

$$\left[\frac{\partial}{\partial \lambda_l}, \tilde{\xi}_{ij}\right] = -2\frac{\partial}{\partial \lambda_l}\left\{\frac{\lambda_i \lambda_j}{\lambda_i^2 + \lambda_j^2}\right\}\eta_{ij}, \quad 1 < l \leqslant m \text{ and } 1 \leqslant i < j \leqslant m,$$

$$[\tilde{\xi}_{i_1 j_1}, \tilde{\xi}_{i_2 j_2}] = [\xi_{i_1 j_1}, \xi_{i_2 j_2}] + 4\frac{\lambda_{i_1}\lambda_{j_1}}{\lambda_{j_1}^2 + \lambda_{j_1}^2}\frac{\lambda_{i_2}\lambda_{j_2}}{\lambda_{i_2}^2 + \lambda_{j_2}^2}[\eta_{i_1 j_1}, \eta_{i_2 j_2}],$$

$$1 \leqslant i_1 < j_1 \leqslant m \text{ and } 1 \leqslant i_2 < j_2 \leqslant m,$$

$$[\tilde{\xi}_{i_1 j_1}, \tilde{\xi}_{i_2 j_2}] = [\xi_{i_1 j_1}, \xi_{i_2 j_2}], \qquad 1 \leqslant i_1, i_2 \leqslant m, \quad i_1 < j_1 \leqslant k-1,$$

$$i_2 < j_2 \leqslant k-1 \text{ and } \max\{j_1, j_2\} > m.$$

Using the fact that $[\eta_{ij}, \eta_{ls}] = -[\eta_{ij}, \eta_{sl}]$ as $\eta_{ls} = -\eta_{sl}$, direct computation shows that

$$[\eta_{i_1 j_1}, \eta_{i_2 j_2}] = -\left\{\delta_{i_1 j_2}\eta_{i_2 j_1} + \delta_{i_2 j_1}\eta_{j_2 i_1} + \delta_{i_1 i_2}\eta_{j_1 j_2} + \delta_{j_1 j_2}\eta_{i_1 i_2}\right\},$$

$$[\xi_{i_1 j_1}, \xi_{i_2 j_2}] = \delta_{i_1 j_2}\xi_{i_2 j_1} + \delta_{i_2 j_1}\xi_{j_2 i_1} + \delta_{i_1 i_2}\xi_{j_1 j_2} + \delta_{j_1 j_2}\xi_{i_1 i_2}$$

and that for $1 < l \leqslant m$ and $1 \leqslant i < j \leqslant m$

$$\frac{\partial}{\partial \lambda_l}\left\{\frac{\lambda_i \lambda_j}{\lambda_i^2 + \lambda_j^2}\right\} = \begin{cases} \dfrac{1}{\lambda_1}\dfrac{\lambda_1^2 - \lambda_j^2}{\lambda_1^2 + \lambda_j^2} & \text{if } i = 1 \text{ and } l = j, \\[2ex] \dfrac{\lambda_j \lambda_l}{\lambda_1}\dfrac{\lambda_1^2 - \lambda_j^2}{(\lambda_1^2 + \lambda_j^2)^2} & \text{if } i = 1 \text{ and } l \neq j, \\[2ex] \lambda_j\dfrac{\lambda_j^2 - \lambda_i^2}{(\lambda_i^2 + \lambda_j^2)^2} & \text{if } 1 < i \text{ and } l = i, \\[2ex] \lambda_i\dfrac{\lambda_i^2 - \lambda_j^2}{(\lambda_i^2 + \lambda_j^2)^2} & \text{if } 1 < i \text{ and } l = j, \\[2ex] 0 & \text{otherwise.} \end{cases}$$

Thus, the non-zero vertical components of the brackets of the pairs of horizontal vector fields from the basis are determined by

$$\left[\frac{\partial}{\partial \lambda_l}, \tilde{\xi}_{ij}\right]^{\mathrm{v}} = 2\begin{cases} \dfrac{1}{\lambda_1}\dfrac{\lambda_j^2 - \lambda_1^2}{\lambda_1^2 + \lambda_j^2}\eta_{ij} & \text{if } i = 1 \text{ and } 1 < l = j \leqslant m, \\[2ex] \dfrac{\lambda_j \lambda_l}{\lambda_1}\dfrac{\lambda_j^2 - \lambda_1^2}{(\lambda_1^2 + \lambda_j^2)^2}\eta_{ij} & \text{if } i = 1 \text{ and } 1 < l \neq j \leqslant m, \\[2ex] \lambda_j\dfrac{\lambda_i^2 - \lambda_j^2}{(\lambda_i^2 + \lambda_j^2)^2}\eta_{ij} & \text{if } 1 < i \leqslant m \text{ and } l = i < j \leqslant m, \\[2ex] \lambda_i\dfrac{\lambda_j^2 - \lambda_i^2}{(\lambda_i^2 + \lambda_j^2)^2}\eta_{ij} & \text{if } 1 < i \leqslant m \text{ and } i < l = j \leqslant m, \\[2ex] 0 & \text{otherwise,} \end{cases}$$

$$[\tilde{\xi}_{ij_1}, \tilde{\xi}_{ij_2}]^{\mathrm{v}} = -[\tilde{\xi}_{ij_1}, \tilde{\xi}_{j_2i}]^{\mathrm{v}}$$

$$= \left\{ -4\frac{\lambda_i \lambda_{j_1}}{\lambda_i^2 + \lambda_{j_1}^2} \frac{\lambda_i \lambda_{j_2}}{\lambda_i^2 + \lambda_{j_2}^2} + 2\frac{\lambda_{j_1} \lambda_{j_2}}{\lambda_{j_1}^2 + \lambda_{j_2}^2} \right\} \eta_{j_1 j_2},$$

$$1 \leqslant i < j_1 \leqslant m \text{ and } 1 \leqslant i \neq j_2 \leqslant m,$$

$$[\tilde{\xi}_{i_1 j}, \tilde{\xi}_{i_2 j}]^{\mathrm{v}} = -[\tilde{\xi}_{i_1 j}, \tilde{\xi}_{j i_2}]^{\mathrm{v}}$$

$$= \left\{ -4\frac{\lambda_{i_1} \lambda_j}{\lambda_{i_1}^2 + \lambda_j^2} \frac{\lambda_{i_2} \lambda_j}{\lambda_{i_2}^2 + \lambda_j^2} + 2\frac{\lambda_{i_1} \lambda_{i_2}}{\lambda_{i_1}^2 + \lambda_{i_2}^2} \right\} \eta_{i_1 i_2},$$

$$1 \leqslant i_1 < j \leqslant m \text{ and } 1 \leqslant i_2 \neq j \leqslant m,$$

$$[\tilde{\xi}_{i_1 j}, \tilde{\xi}_{i_2 j}]^{\mathrm{v}} = 2\frac{\lambda_{i_1} \lambda_{i_2}}{\lambda_{i_1}^2 + \lambda_{i_2}^2} \eta_{i_1 i_2}, \quad 1 \leqslant i_1, i_2 \leqslant m < j \leqslant k - 1. \tag{7.15}$$

Formulae (7.14) and (7.15), together with Theorem 7.2, allow us to compute the Riemannian curvature tensor on $\pi(\mathcal{X}_m^k)$ in terms of the above choice of basis vectors. If we then re-interpret this in terms of the alternative basis of the image of the horizontal fields $\underline{\zeta}_{ij}$, using the relations given in Lemma 7.3 and the fact that the curvature tensor is linear in all four arguments, we obtain expressions for the curvature on $\pi(\mathcal{X}_m^k)$, which, by continuity, remain valid throughout $\Sigma_m^k \backslash \pi(\mathcal{D}_{m-2})$ since, unlike the $\tilde{\xi}_{ij}$, the $\underline{\zeta}_{ij}$ form a basis of the horizontal subspace throughout $\mathcal{S}_m^k \backslash \mathcal{D}_{m-2}$. In what follows we compute the sectional curvatures and the Ricci curvature tensor, recalling that the former determine the Riemannian curvature tensor completely.

Theorem 7.3. *All the sectional curvatures K of $\Sigma_m^k \backslash \pi(\mathcal{D}_{m-2})$ associated with the distinct pairs of vectors from the basis (7.3) are unity save for*

$$K\left(\pi_*(\underline{\zeta}_{ll}), \pi_*(\underline{\zeta}_{ij})\right) = 1$$

$$+ \begin{cases} \dfrac{3}{\lambda_1^2 + \lambda_l^2} & \text{if } i = 1 \text{ and } 1 < l = j \leqslant m, \\[3mm] \dfrac{3\lambda_j^2 \lambda_l^2}{(\lambda_1^2 + \lambda_j^2)^2 (\lambda_1^2 + \lambda_l^2)} & \text{if } i = 1 \text{ and } 1 < l \neq j \leqslant m, \\[3mm] \dfrac{3\lambda_1^2 (\lambda_i^2 + \lambda_j^2 - \lambda_l^2)}{(\lambda_i^2 + \lambda_j^2)^2 (\lambda_1^2 + \lambda_l^2)} & \text{if } 1 < i < j \leqslant m \text{ and } l = i, j, \end{cases}$$

$$K\left(\pi_*(\underline{\zeta}_{i_1 j}), \pi_*(\underline{\zeta}_{j i_2})\right) = K\left(\pi_*(\underline{\zeta}_{i_1 j}), \pi_*(\underline{\zeta}_{i_2 j})\right)$$

$$= 1 + 3\frac{\lambda_{i_1}^2 \lambda_{i_2}^2}{(\lambda_{i_1}^2 + \lambda_j^2)(\lambda_{i_2}^2 + \lambda_j^2)(\lambda_{i_1}^2 + \lambda_{i_2}^2)},$$

$$1 \leqslant i_1 < j \leqslant m \text{ and } 1 \leqslant i_2 \neq i_1, j \leqslant m,$$

$$K\left(\pi_*(\underline{\zeta}_{ij_1}), \pi_*(\underline{\zeta}_{ij_2})\right) = K\left(\pi_*(\underline{\zeta}_{ij_1}), \pi_*(\underline{\zeta}_{j_2i})\right)$$

$$= 1 + 3\frac{\lambda_{j_1}^2 \lambda_{j_2}^2}{(\lambda_i^2 + \lambda_{j_1}^2)(\lambda_i^2 + \lambda_{j_2}^2)(\lambda_{j_1}^2 + \lambda_{j_2}^2)},$$

$$1 \leqslant i < j_1 \leqslant m \text{ and } 1 \leqslant j_2 \neq i, \ j_1 \leqslant m,$$

$$K\left(\pi_*(\underline{\zeta}_{i_1 j}), \pi_*(\underline{\zeta}_{i_2 j})\right) = 1 + \frac{3}{\lambda_{i_1}^2 + \lambda_{i_2}^2}, \quad 1 \leqslant i_1 \neq i_2 \leqslant m < j \leqslant k-1,$$

where we always assume that $l < s$ for $\underline{\zeta}_{ls}$ when it is not specified.

Proof. By definition, the sectional curvature of the tangent 2-plane spanned by vectors v_1 and v_2 is

$$K(v_1, v_2) = \frac{R_{\Sigma_m^k}(v_1, v_2, v_1, v_2)}{||v_1||^2 ||v_2||^2 - \langle v_1, v_2 \rangle^2},$$

which by (7.14) simplifies to

$$1 + \frac{3}{4} \frac{||[\tilde{v}_1, \tilde{v}_2]^v||^2}{||v_1||^2 ||v_2||^2 - \langle v_1, v_2 \rangle^2}.$$

Now, the sectional curvature $K(v_1, v_2)$ is independent of the basis chosen for the plane spanned by v_1 and v_2. Hence, we may compute $K(\pi_*(\underline{\zeta}_{i_1 j_1}), \pi_*(\underline{\zeta}_{i_2 j_2}))$ by replacing the $\pi_*(\underline{\zeta}_{ij})$ by the corresponding members of the basis (7.9), given by Corollary 7.1. For those, the results stated in the theorem follow from (7.15) and the equality (7.12). Thus, the theorem is true on $\pi(\mathcal{X}_m^k)$ and so on $\Sigma_m^k \setminus \pi(\mathcal{D}_{m-2})$ by continuity. ∎

Note that the summand '1' in each of the formulae in Theorem 7.3 represents the contribution from the top space, the pre-shape sphere, while the remaining non-negative term represents the effect of the submersion.

In the case of the Ricci curvature tensor we obtain the following result, where we recall that we write d_m^k for the dimension $mk - m(m+1)/2 - 1$ of Σ_m^k.

Theorem 7.4. *The components* $\mathrm{Ric}(\pi_*(\underline{\zeta}_{i_1 j_1}), \pi_*(\underline{\zeta}_{i_2 j_2}))$ *of the Ricci curvature tensor on* $\Sigma_m^k \setminus \pi(\mathcal{D}_{m-2})$, *associated with the vector fields in (7.3), are all zero except for the following:*

$\mathrm{Ric}(\pi_*(\underline{\zeta}_{ii}), \pi_*(\underline{\zeta}_{ii}))$ *for* $1 < i \leqslant m$ *is given by*

$$3\left\{2\frac{\lambda_i^2}{(\lambda_i^2 + \lambda_1^2)^2} + \sum_{l \neq i}\frac{\lambda_l^2}{(\lambda_l^2 + \lambda_i^2)^2} + \frac{\lambda_i^2}{\lambda_1^2}\sum_{l=2}^{m}\frac{\lambda_l^2}{(\lambda_l^2 + \lambda_i^2)^2}\right\} + (d_m^k - 1)\left\{1 + \frac{\lambda_i^2}{\lambda_1^2}\right\},$$

$\mathrm{Ric}(\pi_*(\underline{\zeta}_{ii}), \pi_*(\underline{\zeta}_{jj}))$ for $1 < i \neq j \leqslant m$ is given by

$$3\lambda_i\lambda_j \left\{ \frac{1}{(\lambda_i^2 + \lambda_1^2)^2} + \frac{1}{(\lambda_j^2 + \lambda_1^2)^2} + \frac{1}{(\lambda_i^2 + \lambda_j^2)^2} + \frac{1}{\lambda_1^2} \sum_{l=2}^{m} \frac{\lambda_l^2}{(\lambda_l^2 + \lambda_1^2)^2} + \frac{d_m^k - 1}{3\lambda_1^2} \right\},$$

$\mathrm{Ric}(\pi_*(\underline{\zeta}_{ij}), \pi_*(\underline{\zeta}_{ij}))$ for $1 \leqslant i < j \leqslant m$ is given by

$$\left\{ \lambda_i^2 + \lambda_j^2 \right\} \left\{ d_m^k - 1 + 3 \sum_{l=1}^{m} \frac{\lambda_l^2}{(\lambda_i^2 + \lambda_l^2)(\lambda_j^2 + \lambda_l^2)} \right\},$$

$\mathrm{Ric}(\pi_*(\underline{\zeta}_{ij}), \pi_*(\underline{\zeta}_{ij}))$ for $1 \leqslant i \leqslant m < j \leqslant k - 1$ is given by

$$d_m^k - 1 + 3 \sum_{l \neq i} \frac{1}{\lambda_i^2 + \lambda_l^2}.$$

Proof. The Ricci curvature tensor Ric is defined, at each point $\pi(X)$ of $\Sigma_m^k \backslash \pi(\mathcal{D}_{m-2})$, to be the symmetric $(0, 2)$-tensor given by

$$\mathrm{Ric}(v_1, v_2) = \sum_{ij} g_e^{ij} R_{\Sigma_m^k}(v_1, e_i, v_2, e_j),$$

where the e_i are d_m^k independent vectors on $\mathcal{T}_{\pi(X)}(\Sigma_m^k \backslash \pi(\mathcal{D}_{m-2}))$ and (g_e^{ij}) is the inverse matrix to the matrix of inner products $(\langle e_i, e_j \rangle)$. On $\pi(\mathcal{X}_m^k)$ we choose $\{e_i\}$ to be the basis (7.9). Then, the above formula becomes

$$\mathrm{Ric}(v_1, v_2) = \sum_{i,j=1}^{m-1} g^{ij} R_{\Sigma_m^k}\left(v_1, \frac{\partial}{\partial \lambda_{i+1}}, v_2, \frac{\partial}{\partial \lambda_{j+1}}\right)$$

$$+ \sum_{1 \leqslant i < j \leqslant m} \frac{\lambda_i^2 + \lambda_j^2}{(\lambda_i^2 - \lambda_j^2)^2} R_{\Sigma_m^k}(v_1, \xi_{ij}, v_2, \xi_{ij})$$

$$+ \sum_{1 \leqslant i \leqslant m < j \leqslant k-1} \frac{1}{\lambda_i^2} R_{\Sigma_m^k}(v_1, \xi_{ij}, v_2, \xi_{ij}),$$

where $g^{ij} = \langle \mathrm{d}\lambda_{i+1}, \mathrm{d}\lambda_{j+1} \rangle$. Now, replacing v_1 and v_2 by various members of our basis, we find, using (7.14), that the non-zero components of the Ricci curvature tensor on $\pi(\mathcal{X}_m^k)$ associated with this basis are

$$\mathrm{Ric}\left(\frac{\partial}{\partial \lambda_i}, \frac{\partial}{\partial \lambda_j}\right) = (d_m^k - 1)\left\langle \frac{\partial}{\partial \lambda_i}, \frac{\partial}{\partial \lambda_j} \right\rangle$$

$$+ \frac{3}{4} \sum_{1 \leqslant l < s \leqslant m} \|\xi_{ls}\|^{-2} \left\langle \left[\frac{\partial}{\partial \lambda_i}, \xi_{ls}\right]^v, \left[\frac{\partial}{\partial \lambda_j}, \xi_{ls}\right]^v \right\rangle, \quad 1 < i, j \leqslant m,$$

$$\text{Ric}(\xi_{ij}, \xi_{ij}) = (d_m^k - 1)\|\xi_{ij}\|^2 + \frac{3}{4} \sum_{1 < l,s \leqslant m} g^{l-1,s-1} \left\langle \left[\xi_{ij}, \frac{\partial}{\partial \lambda_l}\right]^{\vee}, \left[\xi_{ij}, \frac{\partial}{\partial \lambda_s}\right]^{\vee} \right\rangle$$

$$+ \frac{3}{4} \sum_{1 \leqslant l < s \leqslant m} \|\xi_{ls}\|^{-2} \langle [\xi_{ij}, \xi_{ls}]^{\vee}, [\xi_{ij}, \xi_{ls}]^{\vee} \rangle, \quad 1 \leqslant i < j \leqslant m,$$

$$\text{Ric}(\xi_{ij}, \xi_{ij}) = (d_m^k - 1)\|\xi_{ij}\|^2 + \frac{3}{4} \sum_{1 \leqslant l \leqslant m < s \leqslant k-1} \|\xi_{ls}\|^{-2}$$

$$\times \langle [\xi_{ij}, \xi_{ls}]^{\vee}, [\xi_{ij}, \xi_{ls}]^{\vee} \rangle, \quad 1 \leqslant i \leqslant m < j \leqslant k - 1.$$

However, the linearity of the Ricci curvature tensor with respect to each of its variables implies that on $\pi(\mathcal{X}_m^k)$ the non-zero components of the Ricci curvature tensor associated with $\pi_*(\underline{\zeta}_{ij})$ are given by

$$\text{Ric}(\pi_*(\underline{\zeta}_{ii}), \pi(\underline{\zeta}_{jj})) = \text{Ric}\left(\frac{\partial}{\partial \lambda_i}, \frac{\partial}{\partial \lambda_j}\right), \quad 1 < i, j \leqslant m,$$

$$\text{Ric}(\pi_*(\underline{\zeta}_{ij}), \pi_*(\underline{\zeta}_{ij})) = \text{Ric}(\xi_{ij}, \xi_{ij}) \frac{(\lambda_i^2 + \lambda_j^2)^2}{(\lambda_i^2 - \lambda_j^2)^2}, \quad 1 \leqslant i < j \leqslant m,$$

$$\text{Ric}(\pi_*(\underline{\zeta}_{ij}), \pi_*(\underline{\zeta}_{ij})) = \frac{1}{\lambda_i^2} \text{Ric}(\xi_{ij}, \xi_{ij}), \quad 1 \leqslant i \leqslant m < j \leqslant k - 1.$$

Then, the stated result is true on $\pi(\mathcal{X}_m^k)$ by Equations (7.15) and (7.12). We obtain the theorem by continuity. $\blacksquare$

Corollary 7.6. *The scalar curvature* Scal *of* $\Sigma_m^k \backslash \pi(\mathcal{D}_{m-2})$ *at* $\pi(X)$ *is*

$$\text{Scal}(\pi(X)) = d_m^k(d_m^k - 1)$$

$$+ 3 \sum_{1 \leqslant i < j \leqslant m} \left\{ \frac{2k - 2m - 1}{\lambda_i^2 + \lambda_j^2} + \sum_{l=1}^{m} \frac{\lambda_l^2}{(\lambda_i^2 + \lambda_l^2)(\lambda_j^2 + \lambda_l^2)} \right\}. \quad (7.16)$$

Proof. That the scalar curvature is given by (7.16) follows immediately from the fact that the scalar curvature is the metric contraction of the Ricci curvature tensor, that is, it is equal to

$$\sum_{1 < i,j \leqslant m} g^{i-1,j-1} \text{Ric}(\pi_*(\underline{\zeta}_{ii}), \pi_*(\underline{\zeta}_{jj}))$$

$$+ \sum_{1 \leqslant i \leqslant m, i < j \leqslant k-1} \|\pi_*(\underline{\zeta}_{ij})\|^{-2} \text{Ric}(\pi_*(\underline{\zeta}_{ij}), \pi_*(\underline{\zeta}_{ij})),$$

where $g^{ij} = \langle d\lambda_{i+1}, d\lambda_{j+1} \rangle$. Thus, the result follows from Theorem 7.4 after some computation. $\blacksquare$

The scalar curvature is equal to the sum of the sectional curvatures associated with distinct pairs of vectors from an orthogonal basis. Thus, $\mathrm{Scal}(\pi(X))/d_m^k(d_m^k - 1)$ is a measure of the 'average' sectional curvature at $\pi(X)$. In the simplest case, when $m = 3$ and $k = 4$, we have

$$\text{average sectional curvature at } \pi(X) = 1 + \frac{3}{10} \frac{1 + 2(\lambda_2^2\lambda_3^2 + \lambda_3^2\lambda_1^2 + \lambda_1^2\lambda_2^2)}{(\lambda_2^2 + \lambda_3^2)(\lambda_3^2 + \lambda_1^2)(\lambda_1^2 + \lambda_2^2)}.$$

The explicit expressions for the sectional, Ricci and scalar curvatures that we have obtained above confirm our claim, at the beginning of this section, that the scalar curvature and certain of the sectional and Ricci curvatures tend to infinity as we approach a singularity. However, we may now be more precise. Since the pseudo-singular values satisfy $\lambda_1 \geqslant \cdots \geqslant \lambda_{m-1} \geqslant |\lambda_m|$, the dominant term in the scalar curvature, and in the components of the Ricci and sectional curvature tensors that tend to infinity fastest, is a multiple of $\{\lambda_{m-1}^2 + \lambda_m^2\}^{-1}$. However, as we saw in Chapter 6,

$$\lambda_{m-1}^2 + \lambda_m^2 = \sin^2(\rho(\pi(X), \pi(\mathcal{D}_{m-2}))),$$

where ρ is the Riemannian distance on Σ_m^k. Thus, we see that scalar curvature, certain sectional curvatures and certain components of the Ricci curvature tensor all tend to infinity as $O\left(\rho(\pi(X), \pi(\mathcal{D}_{m-2}))^{-2}\right)$ as $\pi(X)$ approaches the singularity set $\pi(\mathcal{D}_{m-2})$. The remaining sectional curvatures and components of the Ricci curvature tensor either remain bounded or tend to infinity more slowly than this.

CHAPTER 8

Induced Shape-Measures

Having described the topological and geometric properties of shape spaces, we now turn our attention to probabilistic topics that arise in the study of shape and naturally involve the structure of shape spaces. In this chapter we shall discuss probability measures on shape spaces induced by various types of distribution of the vertices that determine the shape.

We shall follow our usual notation for pre-shape and shape coordinates. Thus, if $X^* = (x_1^* \cdots x_k^*) \in \mathcal{M}(m, k) \cong \mathbb{R}^{mk}$ represents a configuration in $\mathbb{R}^m$ with k labelled vertices, then we first remove the effects of translation via our standard orthogonal projection $Q_k \in \mathbf{SO}(k)$ such that $X^* Q_k = (\sqrt{k} x_c^* \ \widetilde{X})$, where x_c^* is the centroid of the x_i^*. We then remove the effect of scaling by dividing $\widetilde{X}$ by $\{\operatorname{tr}(\widetilde{X}^t \widetilde{X})\}^{1/2}$ to obtain the pre-shape X. Since the composite map from $\mathbb{R}^{mk}$ onto the shape space Σ_m^k, with the quotient topology, is continuous, it is measurable with respect to the corresponding Borel σ-fields. Thus, if $x_1^*, \ldots, x_k^*$ in $\mathbb{R}^m$ are k *labelled* random variables such that

$$P(x_1^* = \cdots = x_k^*) = 0,$$

then the shape of the configuration with labelled random vertices $x_1^*, \ldots, x_k^*$ will be a random variable in Σ_m^k and distributed there according to the measure induced by the joint distribution of $(x_1^*, \cdots, x_k^*)$.

Suppose now that μ is a joint distribution of $(x_1^*, \cdots, x_k^*)$ that satisfies the above condition. To obtain the induced measure $[\mu]$ on Σ_m^k, we write f for any bounded measurable function from Σ_m^k to $\mathbb{R}$. Then, $[\mu]$ can be uniquely determined, up to a set of measure zero, by

$$\int_{\Sigma_m^k} f(\pi(X)) \, d[\mu](\pi(X)) = \int_{\mathbb{R}^{mk}} f(\pi(X)) \, d\mu(x_1^*, \ldots, x_k^*).$$

Hence, we have that

$$d[\mu](\pi(X)) = \int_{\mathbf{SO}(m)} \int_{\mathbb{R}^+} \int_{\mathbb{R}^m} d\mu(x_1^*, \ldots, x_k^*),$$

where the integration over $\mathbb{R}^m$ is related to the procedure for quotienting out translations and that over $\mathbb{R}^+$ is related to the procedure for normalising the scale.

However, in general, these integrations are not easy to carry out. For different μ we usually need to apply different methods to quotient out these transformations or to use different coordinates on Σ_m^k to perform the integrations, in which case the resulting expression for $[\mu]$ will depend on that choice of coordinates, although, of course, the different expressions are always equivalent.

8.1   GEOMETRIC PRELIMINARIES

As in Chapter 7, we write $U(\Lambda\ 0)V$ for a pseudo-singular values decomposition of X, and $[V]$ for the projection of $V \in \mathbf{SO}(k-1)$ onto $\mathbf{V}_{k-1,m}$ that is represented by the first m rows of V, so that $\pi(X)$ has local coordinates $(\Lambda, [V])$ when the λ_i are all different. We also write (ϕ_{ij}) for the matrix $V\,dX_V^t$ of the 1-forms dual to the right-invariant vector fields $V\partial X_V^t$ on $\mathbf{SO}(k-1)$.

We recall that, when $m = 2$, we have the alternative represention of configurations of k labelled vertices in $\mathbb{R}^2$ by k-dimensional row vectors $z^* = (z_1^*, \ldots, z_k^*)$ in $\mathbb{C}^k$, instead of by $2 \times k$ real matrices. Then, after the standard real-orthogonal transformation to quotient out translations, we obtain a $(k-1)$-dimensional row vector $z = (z_1, \ldots, z_{k-1})$ in $\mathbb{C}^{k-1}$. As usual, we denote the shape of z^* by $\pi(z)$. If we write

$$z_1 = r_0 e^{i\theta_0} \quad \text{and} \quad z_{j+1} = r_0 r_j e^{i(\theta_0+\theta_j)}, \quad 1 \leqslant j \leqslant k-2,$$

then, on the subset of $\mathbb{C}^{k-1}$ determined by $z_1 \neq 0$, r_0 can be used to represent the scale factor of the labelled configuration in $\mathbb{R}^2$ and θ_0 to measure its rotation from a standard position with z_1 along the positive real axis. Thus, $\zeta = (\zeta_1, \ldots, \zeta_{k-2})$, where $\zeta_j = r_j e^{i\theta_j}$, provides a coordinate system on the corresponding subset of Σ_2^k, whose complement has volume measure zero.

When $m = 2$ and $k = 3$ and when the first two vertices z_1^* and z_2^* of a labelled triangle are distinct, the shape coordinate $\zeta = z_2/z_1 = x + iy$ is given by

$$\zeta = \frac{2z_3^* - (z_1^* + z_2^*)}{\sqrt{3}(z_2^* - z_1^*)}. \tag{8.1}$$

This planar parameterisation of Σ_2^3 also allows us to give a simple description of the isometry ϖ induced by a permutation, $(1, 2, 3) \mapsto (\varpi(1), \varpi(2), \varpi(3))$, of the labels or, equivalently, by a simultaneous re-ordering of the vertices of the triangles. In terms of the coordinate ζ, ϖ is obviously given by

$$\zeta \mapsto \varpi(\zeta) = \frac{2z_{i_3}^* - (z_{i_1}^* + z_{i_2}^*)}{\sqrt{3}(z_{i_2}^* - z_{i_1}^*)}. \tag{8.2}$$

In particular, if τ is induced by the transposition that interchanges the first two labels and fixes the third, then

$$\tau(\zeta) = -\zeta. \tag{8.3}$$

Since the cyclic permutation of the labels permutes the shapes of the three degenerate triangles with two coincident vertices, whose coordinates are ∞, $1/\sqrt{3}$ and $-1/\sqrt{3}$, respectively, we see that the induced isometry ς is given by the Möbius transformation

$$\varsigma(\zeta) = \frac{\zeta - \sqrt{3}}{\sqrt{3}\zeta + 1}. \tag{8.4}$$

The full group of six permutations of the vertex labels induces an isomorphic group Ω of isometries, generated by ς and τ in the usual way.

Returning to the general case, we write $dv_{\mathbf{M}}$ for the volume measure of a Riemannian manifold $\mathbf{M}$. Then Corollary 7.3 gives us an explicit local expression for $dv_{\Sigma_m^k}$ that is valid away from a set of measure zero. Since the projection π from $\mathcal{S}_m^k$ to Σ_m^k is, away from the singularities, a Riemannian submersion, we have, on $\mathcal{S}_m^k \setminus \mathcal{D}_{m-2}$,

$$dv_{\mathcal{S}_m^k}(X) = dv_{\Sigma_m^k}(\pi(X)) \, dv_{\pi^{-1}(\pi(X))}(X).$$

Hence, Corollary 7.4 implies that, at $X \in \mathcal{S}_m^k \setminus \mathcal{D}_{m-2}$,

$$\int_{\mathbf{SO}(m)} dv_{\mathcal{S}_m^k}(X) = \left\{ \int_{\mathbf{SO}(m)} dv_{\pi^{-1}(\pi(X))}(TX) \right\} dv_{\Sigma_m^k}(\pi(X))$$

$$= \left\{ \prod_{1 \leqslant i < j \leqslant m} \sqrt{\lambda_i^2 + \lambda_j^2} \right\} dv_{\Sigma_m^k}(\pi(X)). \tag{8.5}$$

We shall denote by $d\omega_m^k$ the uniform measure on Σ_m^k, which, on the non-singular part, is the induced volume measure $dv_{\Sigma_m^k}$ normalised so that the total volume is unity. Thus, $d\omega_m^k$ is invariant with respect to any isometric transformations on Σ_m^k and we shall normally consider Radon–Nikodým derivatives of induced shape-measures with respect to $d\omega_m^k$. However, in the case $m = 2$ and $k = 3$, if we are using the planar representation of the punctured version of Σ_2^3, we shall also consider Radon–Nikodým derivatives with respect to $d\zeta = dx\,dy$. This is a natural generalisation of the Euclidean case, but $d\zeta$ is not a constant multiple of the volume measure in the plane induced by $dv_{\Sigma_2^3}$, nor is it invariant under isometries with respect to the metric on the plane induced from the Riemannian metric on Σ_2^3. The precise relation between $d\omega_2^3$ and $d\zeta$ will be discussed in the next section.

Finally, we note that, in the case that a random shape on Σ_m^k is generated by k unlabelled iid random variables on $\mathbb{R}^m$, the corresponding shape-measure is $k!$ times the shape-measure induced by the same k labelled iid random variables on $\mathbb{R}^m$, since each unlabelled k-ad determines $k!$ shapes of labelled vertices. However, if we choose with equal probability $1/k!$ a label for each set of k unlabelled points in $\mathbb{R}^m$, then the two corresponding shape-measures would be the same.

8.2   THE SHAPE-MEASURE ON Σ_m^k INDUCED BY k LABELLED iid ISOTROPIC GAUSSIAN DISTRIBUTIONS ON $\mathbb{R}^m$

Theorem 8.1. *The Radon–Nikodým derivative at $\pi(X)$, with respect to $d\omega_m^k$, of the shape-measure on Σ_m^k induced by k labelled iid isotropic Gaussian distributions on $\mathbb{R}^m$ is, up to a normalising constant,*

$$\prod_{1\leqslant i<j\leqslant m} \sqrt{\lambda_i^2 + \lambda_j^2}.$$

Proof.   If $x_1^*, \ldots, x_k^*$ are k labelled iid Gaussian $\mathcal{N}(\mu^*, \sigma^2 I_m)$ random variables in $\mathbb{R}^m$, then since

$$\mathrm{tr}\{(X^*)^t X^*\} = \mathrm{tr}\{(X^* Q_k)^t X^* Q_k\} = \|x_c^*\|^2 + \mathrm{tr}(\widetilde{X}^t \widetilde{X}),$$

the $k-1$ columns $\tilde{x}_i$ of $\widetilde{X}$ are $k-1$ iid Gaussian $\mathcal{N}(0, \sigma^2 I_m)$ random variables. However, with respect to the measure $d\tilde{x}_1 \cdots d\tilde{x}_{k-1} = s^{m(k-1)-1} \, ds \, dv_{\mathcal{S}_m^k}$, the density of the joint distribution of $\widetilde{X}$ is a function of the squared size $s^2 = s(X^*)^2 = \mathrm{tr}(\widetilde{X}^t \widetilde{X})$, and so the induced measure of X on $\mathcal{S}_m^k$ is the normalised volume measure of $\mathcal{S}_m^k$. Thus, the result follows from (8.5).   ∎

The set of squares of the pseudo-singular values of X is invariant under the group $\mathbf{O}(k-1)$ acting on the right of X, and hence the shape-measure on Σ_m^k, given by Theorem 8.1, induced by k labelled iid Gaussian distributions on $\mathbb{R}^m$ is invariant under the group of isometries induced by $\mathbf{O}(k-1)$ acting on the right of elements of $\mathcal{S}_m^k$.

Since $\sum_{i=1}^m \lambda_i^2 = 1$, we have the following corollary.

Corollary 8.1. *The shape-measure on Σ_m^k induced by k labelled iid isotropic Gaussian distributions on $\mathbb{R}^m$ coincides with its uniform measure if and only if $m = 2$.*

This corollary suggests a method for obtaining an expression for the uniform measure on Σ_2^k, using the complex representation of configurations on $\mathbb{R}^2$. The real-orthogonality of our standard transformation from z^* to z implies that the components z_j of z are iid $\mathcal{N}(0, I_2)$ random variables when the components z_j^* of z^* are iid $\mathcal{N}(\mu^*, I_2)$ random variables. Thus, on the set $z_1 \neq 0$, the joint distribution of z_j can be expressed in terms of $z_1 = r_0 e^{i\theta_0}$ and $\zeta_j = z_{j+1}/z_1 = r_j e^{i\theta_j}$ as

$$\pi^{-(k-2)} \exp\left\{ -\frac{1}{2} r_0^2 \left(1 + \sum_{j=1}^{k-2} r_j^2 \right) \right\} \left\{ \frac{1}{2} r_0^2 \right\}^{k-2} \, d\left(\frac{1}{2} r_0^2 \right) d\left(\frac{\theta_0}{2\pi} \right) \prod_{j=1}^{k-2} d\zeta_j.$$

By integrating out z_1 we obtain, in terms of the coordinates $\zeta = (\zeta_1, \ldots, \zeta_{k-2})$, the expression for the uniform measure on the subset of Σ_2^k determined by $z_1 \neq 0$:

$$d\omega_2^k = \frac{(k-2)!}{\pi^{k-2}} \left\{ 1 + \sum_{j=1}^{k-2} |\zeta_j|^2 \right\}^{-(k-1)} \prod_{j=1}^{k-2} d\zeta_j. \tag{8.6}$$

In particular, on the subset of Σ_2^3 determined by $z_1 \neq 0$,

$$\pi(1 + |\zeta|^2)^2 \, d\omega_2^3 = d\zeta, \tag{8.7}$$

where $\zeta = z_2/z_1$ as before.

The next two theorems involve the set $\pi(\mathcal{D}_{m-1})$ of shapes lying in hyperplanes, which, when $m = 2$, is the collinearity set. They are concerned with the induced joint distribution of $s_{m-1}(\pi(X)) = \rho(\pi(X), \pi(\mathcal{D}_{m-1}))$, the Riemannian distance from the shape point $\pi(X)$ to $\pi(\mathcal{D}_{m-1})$, and with $\pi(X^{(m-1)})$, the projection of $\pi(X)$ onto $\pi(\mathcal{D}_{m-1})$. We shall consider the case when $\pi(X) \in \Sigma_m^k$ is generated by k labelled iid isotropic Gaussian points. This is less artificial than might at first be supposed, certainly when $m = 2$, since we get the same measure on Σ_2^k whether we use that Gaussian model or, alternatively, use the normalised Riemannian volume element to give a measure over Σ_2^k.

Theorem 8.2. *If $\pi(X) \in \Sigma_2^k$ is generated by k labelled iid isotropic Gaussian random variables in $\mathbb{R}^2$, then*

   (i) $\sin^{k-2}(2s_1(\pi(X)))$ *is uniformly distributed in* $[0, 1]$,
  (ii) *its projection on the collinearity set is uniformly distributed there,*
 (iii) *its distance to, and its projection on, the collinearity set are independent.*

Proof. It follows from Corollary 7.3 that the volume measure $dv_{\Sigma_2^k}$ of Σ_2^k can be expressed via a pseudo-singular values decomposition of X as

$$dv_{\Sigma_2^k} = \frac{1}{\lambda_1} \prod_{i=1}^{2} |\lambda_i|^{k-3} \{\lambda_1^2 - \lambda_2^2\} \, d\lambda_2 \prod_{j=1}^{2} \prod_{l=j+1}^{k-1} \phi_{jl}.$$

By Corollary 8.1, up to a normalising constant, this is also the shape-measure on Σ_2^k induced by k labelled iid isotropic Gaussian random variables in $\mathbb{R}^2$. However, $\prod_{j=2}^{k-1} \phi_{1j}$ gives the volume measure of $\Sigma_1^k = S^{k-2}$ and the collinearity set of Σ_2^k is isometric with the quotient of Σ_1^k by the reflection. Thus, the local expression of the uniform measure on the collinearity set of Σ_2^k only differs from $dv_{\Sigma_1^k}$ by a constant.

Using the expression for the projection of $\pi(X)$ on the collinearity set in terms of a pseudo-singular values decomposition of X obtained in Theorem 6.6, we see that the induced joint probability measure of the distance of $\pi(X)$ from the collinearity set and its projection onto it can be obtained by integrating out

$\prod_{j=3}^{k-1} \phi_{2j}$ in the above expression for $d\nu_{\Sigma_2^k}$. Thus, this joint probability measure is given, up to a normalising constant, by

$$\frac{1}{\lambda_1} \prod_{i=1}^{2} |\lambda_i|^{k-3} \{\lambda_1^2 - \lambda_2^2\} \, d\lambda_2 \, d\nu_{\Sigma_1^k}.$$

It follows that the distance of $\pi(X)$ from the collinearity set and its projection onto it are independent; that, since, by Theorem 6.6, $s_1(\pi(X)) = \arcsin(|\lambda_2|)$, the distribution of $s_1(\pi(X))$ is given by

$$\frac{1}{\lambda_1} \prod_{i=1}^{2} |\lambda_i|^{k-3} \{\lambda_1^2 - \lambda_2^2\} \, d\lambda_2 = \frac{1}{2^{k-3}} \sin^{k-3}(2s_1) \cos(2s_1) \, ds_1$$

up to the constant $\{2^{k-2}(k-1)\}^{-1}$; and that the distribution of the projection is $d\nu_{\Sigma_1^k}$ up to another constant. ∎

We now return to the case of general dimension m. Recall that $\prod_{i=1}^{m} \prod_{j=i+1}^{k-1} \phi_{ij}$ defines an invariant measure on $\mathbf{V}_{k-1,m}$.

Theorem 8.3. *If $\pi(X) \in \Sigma_m^k$ for $m > 2$ is generated by k labelled iid isotropic Gaussian random variables, then, up to some constant, the induced joint Radon–Nikodým derivative, with respect to the product measure $ds_{m-1} \times d\omega_{m-1}^k$, of the distance $s_{m-1}(\pi(X))$ of $\pi(X)$ from $\pi(\mathcal{D}_{m-1})$ and its projection $\pi(X^{(m-1)})$ onto it is*

$$\prod_{1 \leqslant i < j \leqslant m-1} \sqrt{(\lambda_i^{(m-1)})^2 + (\lambda_j^{(m-1)})^2} \prod_{l_1=1}^{m-1} \frac{1}{\lambda_{l_1}^{(m-1)}}$$

$$\times \prod_{l_2=1}^{m-1} \{(\lambda_{l_2}^{(m-1)})^2 - \tan^2(s_{m-1})\} \sin^{k-1-m}(s_{m-1}) \cos^{k(m-1)-1}(s_{m-1}),$$

where, as before, the $\lambda_i^{(m-1)}$ are the first $m-1$ pseudo-singular values of $X^{(m-1)}$.

Proof. The expression for $d\nu_{\Sigma_m^k}$, given in Corollary 7.3, and the result of Theorem 8.1 imply that the shape-measure on Σ_m^k induced by k labelled independent $\mathcal{N}(0, I_m)$ points can be expressed locally as

$$\frac{\tilde{c}_m^k}{\lambda_1} \prod_{i=1}^{m} |\lambda_i|^{k-1-m} \prod_{1 \leqslant j_1 < j_2 \leqslant m} (\lambda_{j_1}^2 - \lambda_{j_2}^2) \prod_{l=2}^{m} d\lambda_l \prod_{n_1=1}^{m} \prod_{n_2=n_1+1}^{k-1} \phi_{n_1 n_2},$$

where $\tilde{c}_m^k$ is a constant.

Now $\pi(\mathcal{D}_{m-1})$ is isometric with $\Sigma_{m-1}^k / \iota_{m-1}$, where ι_{m-1} denotes our usual isometric involution on Σ_{m-1}^k. So, away from the singularity set of Σ_m^k, the local expression for the volume element of $\pi(\mathcal{D}_{m-1})$ differs from $dv_{\Sigma_{m-1}^k}$ only by a constant. In particular, $\pi(\mathcal{D}_{m-1})$ is locally diffeomorphic to the product of $\mathbf{S}^{m-2}$, the space where the pseudo-singular values of $X^{(m-1)}$ lie, with $\mathbf{V}_{k-1,m-1}$, the space where the frame determined by the first $m-1$ rows of the matrix V occurring in a pseudo-singular values decomposition of $X^{(m-1)}$ lies. Also

$$\mathbf{V}_{k-1,m} \mapsto \mathbf{V}_{k-1,m-1}$$

is a $(k-1-m)$-sphere bundle, so that, locally, the form $\prod_{i=1}^{m}\prod_{j=i+1}^{k-1}\phi_{ij}$ on $\mathbf{V}_{k-1,m}$ can be regarded as the product of the form $\prod_{i=1}^{m-1}\prod_{j=i+1}^{k-1}\phi_{ij}$ on $\mathbf{V}_{k-1,m-1}$ and the form $\prod_{j=m+1}^{k-1}\phi_{mj}$ on $\mathbf{S}^{k-1-m}$. Hence, it follows from Theorem 6.6 that the induced joint probability measure of $s_{m-1}(\pi(X))$ and $\pi(X^{(m-1)})$ is

$$\frac{\hat{c}_m^k}{\lambda_1}\prod_{i=1}^{m}|\lambda_i|^{k-1-m}\prod_{1\leqslant j_1<j_2\leqslant m}(\lambda_{j_1}^2-\lambda_{j_2}^2)\prod_{l=2}^{m-1}d\lambda_l\prod_{n_1=1}^{m-1}\prod_{n_2=n_1+1}^{k-1}\phi_{n_1 n_2},$$

where $\hat{c}_m^k$ is another constant. On substituting in this formula the expression for $s_{m-1}(\pi(X))$ and the coordinates of $\pi(X^{(m-1)})$ given in that theorem, the induced joint probability measure becomes

$$\frac{\hat{c}_m^k}{\lambda_1^{(m-1)}}\prod_{i=1}^{m-1}\{\lambda_i^{(m-1)}\}^{k-1-m}\prod_{1\leqslant j_1<j_2\leqslant m-1}\{(\lambda_{j_1}^{(m-1)})^2-(\lambda_{j_2}^{(m-1)})^2\}$$

$$\times\prod_{l_1=1}^{m-1}\{(\lambda_{l_1}^{(m-1)})^2-\tan^2(s_{m-1})\}\sin^{k-1-m}(s_{m-1})\cos^{k(m-1)-1}(s_{m-1})$$

$$\times ds_{m-1}\prod_{l_2=2}^{m-1}d\lambda_{l_2}^{(m-1)}\prod_{n_1=1}^{m-1}\prod_{n_2=n_1+1}^{k-1}\phi_{n_1 n_2}.$$

On the other hand, this expression divided by that in the statement of the theorem is $ds_{m-1}\times d\omega_{m-1}^k$ up to a constant since the latter is given by the formula of Corollary 7.3 with m replaced by $m-1$. Hence, the theorem is established. ∎

Theorem 8.3 shows that, for $m>2$, $s_{m-1}(\pi(X))$ and $\pi(X^{(m-1)})$ are no longer independent and also that the shape-measure of $\pi(X^{(m-1)})$ is no longer uniform on $\pi(\mathcal{D}_{m-1})$. The independence breaks down because the factors

$$\prod_{i=1}^{m-1}\{(\lambda_i^{(m-1)})^2-\tan^2(s_{m-1})\}$$

of the induced joint Radon–Nikodým derivative involve both components in a non-trivial manner. However, when $m=2$, the single factor $(\lambda_1^{(1)})^2-\tan^2(s_1)$ that occurs reduces to $1-\tan^2(s_1)$ and so this only involves the first component.

By integrating the expression for the induced joint Radon–Nikodým derivative in Theorem 8.3 with respect to s_{m-1}, we can find the induced Radon–Nikodým derivative for $\pi(X^{(m-1)})$. Hence, we know the conditional distribution of $s_{m-1}(\pi(X))$ given $\pi(X^{(m-1)})$. This distribution is smooth as a function of $\pi(X^{(m-1)})$, so that, even if we only know the position of the foot of the geodesic perpendicular roughly, this enables us to get a good approximation to the conditional law of s_{m-1}. This amounts to treating the position of the foot of the perpendicular as an ancillary statistic and assessing the degree of degeneracy, the length of the perpendicular, in the light of that.

8.3   SHAPE-MEASURES ON Σ_m^{m+1} OF POISSON–DELAUNAY TILES

If we have a countably infinite discrete set of distinct points in $\mathbb{R}^m$ such that (a) no $m + 1$ points lie on an $(m - 1)$-dimensional hyperplane and (b) no $m + 2$ points lie on an $(m - 1)$-dimensional sphere, then we can construct the Delaunay tessellation of such a set of points as follows. We look at each subset of $m + 1$ points in this set in turn. Then, we draw the simplex determined by these $m + 1$ points if and only if their circumsphere contains no point of the set in its interior. This yields a Delaunay tile, and such tiles will be non-overlapping and will yield a complete tessellation of $\mathbb{R}^m$.

A homogeneous Poisson point process is characterised by the following two fundamental properties:

(i)   the number of points of the process in a bounded Borel set **U** has a Poisson distribution with mean equal to the volume of **U** multiplied by a constant $\hat{\kappa}$, where the constant $\hat{\kappa}$ is called the intensity of the process,

(ii) the numbers of points of the process in n disjoint Borel sets form n independent random variables.

From these two properties we can deduce that a realisation of an m-dimensional homogeneous Poisson point process satisfies the conditions in the previous paragraph with probability one and so we may apply the above construction to obtain the Delaunay tessellation of a realisation of an m-dimensional homogeneous Poisson point process of intensity $\hat{\kappa}$ and study the shapes of the tiles of its simplexes. We shall refer to this tessellation as a Poisson–Delaunay tessellation of intensity $\hat{\kappa}$.

To describe the shape-measure of tiles in a Poisson–Delaunay tessellation we need an ancillary shape variable. Since the condition (a) above is satisfied with probability one, we may, as at the end of Section 6.8, use the circumradius $\bar{r}$ of a simplex and its circumcentre $\bar{x}_0^*$ to write its vertices x_i^* as $x_i^* = \bar{x}_0^* + \bar{r}x_i^*$, where $\bar{x}_i^* \in S^{m-1}$. If $\bar{x}_c^*$ is the centroid of $\bar{x}_1^*, \ldots, \bar{x}_{m+1}^*$, then the shape variable ϱ that we require is given by

$$\varrho = \sqrt{(m + 1)(1 - \|\bar{x}_c^*\|^2)} = \left\{ m - \frac{1}{m + 1} \sum_{1 \leqslant i \neq j \leqslant m+1} \langle \bar{x}_i^*, \bar{x}_j^* \rangle \right\}^{1/2}. \qquad (8.8)$$

Note that, if $s = s(X^*)$ is the standard measurement that we are using of the size of a simplex, so that $s^2 = s(X^*)^2 = \sum_{j=1}^k ||x_j^* - x_c^*||^2 = \mathrm{tr}(\widetilde{X}^t\widetilde{X})$, then ϱ is equal to $\bar{r}/s$.

We may now describe the shape-measure of tiles in a Poisson–Delaunay tessellation in terms of the basic shape-measure we obtained in Theorem 8.1.

Theorem 8.4. *The Radon–Nikodým derivative at $\pi(X)$, with respect to the shape-measure induced by $m + 1$ labelled iid isotropic Gaussian distributions on $\mathbb{R}^m$, of the shape-measure of tiles of a Poisson–Delaunay tessellation of intensity $\hat{\kappa}$ on $\mathbb{R}^m$ is $c_m\varrho^{m^2}$, where c_m is a constant depending only on m.*

Proof. If $x_1^*, \ldots, x_{m+1}^*$ are $m + 1$ Poisson points of intensity $\hat{\kappa}$ on $\mathbb{R}^m$, we have, for any fixed $m + 1$ distinct points x_{i0}^* in $\mathbb{R}^m$ and incremental vectors Δx_i^*,

$$P[x_i^* \in [x_{i0}^*, x_{i0}^* + \Delta x_i^*), \quad 1 \leqslant i \leqslant m + 1]$$

$$= \hat{\kappa}^{m+1} \prod_{i=1}^{m+1} \exp\{-\hat{\kappa}|\Delta x_i^*|\}|\Delta x_i^*|$$

$$\approx \hat{\kappa}^{m+1} \prod_{i=1}^{m+1} |\Delta x_i^*|$$

as $\max\{|\Delta x_i^*| : 1 \leqslant i \leqslant m + 1\} \to 0$, where $|\Delta x_i^*|$ here denotes the product of the absolute values of the components of the vector Δx_i^*. Let

$$\hat{x}_i = x_{i+1}^* - x_1^*, \quad 1 \leqslant i \leqslant m.$$

Then, the Palm distribution of homogeneous Poisson point processes implies (cf. Stoyan et al., 1987) that, for any fixed m distinct points $\hat{x}_{i0}$ in $\mathbb{R}^m$,

$$P[\hat{x}_i \in [\hat{x}_{i0}, \hat{x}_{i0} + \Delta\hat{x}_i), \quad 1 \leqslant i \leqslant m \mid x_1^*] \approx \hat{\kappa}^m \prod_{i=1}^m |\Delta\hat{x}_i|.$$

However, the number of Poisson points that are contained in the circumsphere of these $m + 1$ points has a Poisson distribution with intensity $\hat{\kappa}\tilde{c}_m\bar{r}^m$, where $\tilde{c}_m$ is the volume of the unit ball $\mathbf{B}^m$ in $\mathbb{R}^m$. Thus, we have

$$P[\hat{x}_i \in [\hat{x}_{i0}, \hat{x}_{i0} + \Delta\hat{x}_i), \quad 1 \leqslant i \leqslant m, \text{ and the circumsphere of } x_1^*, \ldots, x_{m+1}^*$$

$$\text{contains no other Poisson points} \mid x_1^*]$$

$$\approx \hat{\kappa}^m \exp\{-\hat{\kappa}\tilde{c}_m\bar{r}^m\} \prod_{i=1}^m |\Delta\hat{x}_i|.$$

Since

$$\prod_{i=1}^{m+1} dx_i^* = dx_1^* \prod_{i=1}^m d\hat{x}_i = dx_1^* \prod_{i=1}^m d\tilde{x}_i,$$

the Radon–Nikodým derivative, with respect to the measure $\prod_{i=1}^{m} d\hat{x}_i = \prod_{i=1}^{m} d\tilde{x}_i$, of the above probability is

$$\hat{\kappa}^m \exp\{-\hat{\kappa}\tilde{c}_m \bar{r}^m\} = \hat{\kappa}^m \exp\{-\hat{\kappa}\tilde{c}_m \varrho^{-m} s^m\}. \tag{8.9}$$

Now, $(\tilde{x}_1, \ldots, \tilde{x}_m) = s(X^*) \cdot (x_1, \ldots, x_m)$, where $(x_1, \ldots, x_m) \in \mathcal{S}_m^{m+1}$, and so, to quotient out the scaling effects, we integrate the measure corresponding to (8.9) with respect to $s(X^*)$ to get

$$\hat{\kappa}^m \left\{ \int_0^\infty \exp\{-\hat{\kappa}\tilde{c}_m \varrho^{-m} s^m\} s^{m^2-1} ds \right\} dv_{\mathcal{S}_m^{m+1}}$$
$$= \frac{(m-1)!}{m} \{\tilde{c}_m\}^{-m} \varrho^{m^2} dv_{\mathcal{S}_m^{m+1}}. \tag{8.10}$$

The result of the theorem follows by comparing this with the distribution on $\mathcal{S}_m^{m+1}$ induced by $m+1$ labelled iid isotropic Gaussian distributions on $\mathbb{R}^m$, which, as we showed in the proof of Theorem 8.1, is $dv_{\mathcal{S}_m^{m+1}}$ up to a normalising constant. ∎

When $m = 2$, we have

$$\varrho^2 = 2 - \tfrac{2}{3}\{\cos 2\vartheta_1 + \cos 2\vartheta_2 + \cos 2\vartheta_3\}$$
$$= \tfrac{4}{3}\{\sin^2 \vartheta_1 + \sin^2 \vartheta_2 + \sin^2 \vartheta_3\}, \tag{8.11}$$

where the ϑ_i are the three interior angles of the triangle. Then, since the induced shape-measure of three labelled iid isotropic Gaussian distributions on $\mathbb{R}^2$ is the uniform measure on Σ_2^3, we see that, up to a constant, the square of the expression (8.11) is, in fact, the Radon–Nikodým derivative, with respect to $d\omega_2^3$, of the shape-measure of tiles of a Poisson–Delaunay tessellation on $\mathbb{R}^2$. On the other hand, if, on the subset determined by $z_1 \neq 0$, we use our usual notation $\zeta = z_2/z_1 = re^{i\theta}$, then, after some elementary calculation, we find that

$$\{\sin^2 \vartheta_1 + \sin^2 \vartheta_2 + \sin^2 \vartheta_3\}^2$$
$$= r^4 \sin^4 \theta \frac{\{|z_1^* - z_2^*|^2 + |z_2^* - z_3^*|^2 + |z_3^* - z_1^*|^2\}^2}{|z_2^* - z_3^*|^4 |z_3^* - z_1^*|^4}$$
$$= 2\sqrt{3} r \sin \theta \sin \vartheta_1 \sin \vartheta_2 \sin \vartheta_3 \frac{(1+r^2)^2}{|z_1^* - z_3^*|^2 |z_2^* - z_3^*|^2}$$

and

$$d\vartheta_1 d\vartheta_2 = 6\sqrt{3} \frac{\cos^2 \vartheta_1 \cos^2 \vartheta_2}{(1 - 3r^2 \cos^2 \theta)^2} r \sin \theta \, d\zeta$$
$$= \frac{2}{\sqrt{3}} \frac{r \sin \theta}{|z_1^* - z_3^*|^2 |z_2^* - z_3^*|^2} d\zeta.$$

Since $d\omega_2^3 = dv_{\Sigma_2^3}/(2\pi^2)$ and $\tilde{c}_2 = \pi$, Theorem 8.4, together with (8.7), (8.10) and (8.11), gives an alternative expression for the shape-measure of tiles of a

Poisson–Delaunay tessellation on $\mathbb{R}^2$ as

$$\frac{8}{3\pi} \sin \vartheta_1 \sin \vartheta_2 \sin \vartheta_3 d\vartheta_1 d\vartheta_2,$$

which is precisely the formula that Miles (1970) first derived.

As explained in Chapter 1, the shape space Σ_2^3 can be divided into twelve isometric regions such that, when labelling and sensing are of minor importance, as they are in the present context, any one of them will suffice for illustrative purposes. Having chosen a representative region, it may then be represented on a 'bell-diagram' in a way that preserves the uniform measure, as in Figure 1.1. In Figure 8.1 we illustrate in that manner the shape points resulting from a simulation of 5000 Poisson–Delaunay triangles. Similarly, we illustrate, in Figure 8.2, the contours for the Radon–Nikodým derivative of the shape measure of Poisson–Delaunay triangles with respect to the uniform measure that we obtained above.

Since ϱ is a decreasing function of $||\bar{x}_c^*||$, as shown in (8.8), the Radon–Nikodým derivative of Theorem 8.4 is a decreasing function of $||\bar{x}_c^*||$ that tends to zero when $||\bar{x}_c^*||$ tends to one. However, $||\bar{x}_c^*|| = 1$ would require all the $\bar{x}_i^*$ to be coincident on the sphere, which corresponds to the totally degenerate shape, and so this minimum cannot be achieved. This need not alarm us since we have only defined the Radon–Nikodým derivative on the, non-compact, complement of $\pi(\mathcal{D}_{m-1})$. On the other hand, the maximum is achieved at the points most remote from $\pi(\mathcal{D}_{m-1})$. This follows from the fact that $\varrho \leqslant (m+1)^{1/2}$ with equality if and only if $\bar{x}_c^* = 0$. However, it has been shown, at the end of

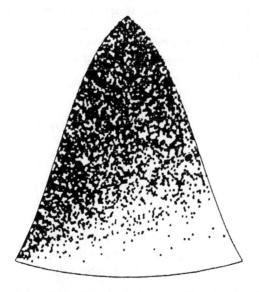

Figure 8.1 Reproduced with permission from D.G. Kendall, The shape of Poisson–Delaunay triangles, in M.C. Demetrescu and M. Losifescu (eds), *Studies in Probability and Related Topics*, pp 321–330. Nagard, Montreal, 1983

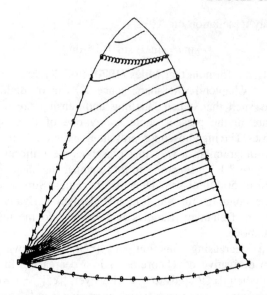

Figure 8.2 Reproduced with permission from D.G. Kendall, The shape of Poisson–Delaunay triangles, in M.C. Demetrescu and M. Losifescu (eds), *Studies in Probability and Related Topics*, pp 321–330. Nagard, Montreal, 1983

Section 6.8, that $\pi(X) \in \Sigma_m^{m+1}$ is maximally remote from $\pi(\mathcal{D}_{m-1})$ if and only if the corresponding simplex X^* is regular, and this implies that $\overline{x}_c^* = 0$.

When $m = 2$, maximal remoteness is also necessary for $\overline{x}_c^* = 0$. However, when $m > 2$, this is not true. For example, for $m = 3$, the $\overline{x}_c^*$ corresponding to each of the following two configurations is zero, but the shape of the first one is in $\pi(\mathcal{D}_{m-1})$ and that of the second one, although not in $\pi(\mathcal{D}_{m-1})$, is not maximally remote from $\pi(\mathcal{D}_{m-1})$:

$$(\overline{x}_1^* \ \cdots \ \overline{x}_4^*) = \begin{pmatrix} 1 & 0 & -1 & 0 \\ 0 & 1 & 0 & -1 \\ 0 & 0 & 0 & 0 \end{pmatrix}$$

and

$$(\overline{x}_1^* \ \cdots \ \overline{x}_4^*) = \begin{pmatrix} 1 & 0 & -\frac{1}{2} & -\frac{1}{2} \\ 0 & 1 & -\frac{1}{2} & -\frac{1}{2} \\ 0 & 0 & \frac{1}{\sqrt{2}} & -\frac{1}{\sqrt{2}} \end{pmatrix}.$$

8.4   SHAPE-MEASURES ON Σ_2^k INDUCED BY k LABELLED iid NON-ISOTROPIC GAUSSIAN DISTRIBUTIONS ON $\mathbb{R}^2$

For the remainder of this chapter we shall restrict ourselves to the case that $m = 2$ and use the complex representation of configurations that we discussed in Section 8.1.

Theorem 8.5. *The Radon–Nikodým derivative at $\pi(z)$, with respect to $d\omega_2^k$, of the shape-measure on Σ_2^k induced by k labelled iid bivariate Gaussian distributions on $\mathbb{R}^2$ with principal component variances $\sigma^2 > 1$ and $1/\sigma^2$ is given by*

$$\left\{ \frac{2f_\sigma(\pi(z))}{\sigma + \sigma^{-1}} \right\}^{k-1} P_{k-2}(f_\sigma(\pi(z))), \tag{8.12}$$

where

$$f_\sigma(\pi(z)) = (\sigma^2 + 1)\{4\sigma^2 + (\sigma^2 - 1)^2 \sin^2(2s_1(\pi(z)))\}^{-1/2} \geqslant 1, \tag{8.13}$$

$s_1(\pi(z))$ is the distance from $\pi(z)$ to $\pi(\mathcal{D}_1)$ and $P_n(x)$ is the Legendre polynomial for which the Laplace 'second' integral representation is

$$P_n(x) = \frac{1}{\pi} \int_0^\pi \{x + \sqrt{x^2 - 1} \cos \alpha\}^{-(n+1)} \, d\alpha.$$

Proof. Because of the real-orthogonality of our standard transformation from z^* to z, it follows, along similar lines to the proof of Theorem 8.1, that the components z_j of z are iid $\mathcal{N}(0, C)$ random variables, where C is the covariance matrix of z_j^*. The covariance matrix C can be expressed as $C = T^t \text{diag}\{\sigma^2, \sigma^{-2}\}T$ for some $T \in \mathbf{SO}(2)$. Thus, Tz_j are iid $\mathcal{N}(0, \text{diag}\{\sigma^2, \sigma^{-2}\})$ random variables. Since $Tz = (Tz_1, \ldots, Tz_{k-1})$ has the same shape as z, we may without loss of generality assume that the covariance matrix of z_j itself has the form $\text{diag}\{\sigma^2, \sigma^{-2}\}$. Then, on the set $z_1 \neq 0$, the joint distribution of z_j can be written in terms of z_1 and ζ_j as

$$\pi^{-(k-2)} \exp \left\{ -\frac{1}{2}r_0^2 \left(g_1(\sigma, \theta_0, 0) + \sum_{j=1}^{k-2} r_j^2 g_1(\sigma, \theta_0, \theta_j) \right) \right\}$$

$$\times \left\{ \frac{1}{2}r_0^2 \right\}^{k-2} d\left(\frac{1}{2}r_0^2 \right) d\left(\frac{\theta_0}{2\pi} \right) \prod_{j=1}^{k-2} d\zeta_j,$$

where

$$g_1(\sigma, a, b) = \sigma \sin^2(a + b) + \sigma^{-1} \cos^2(a + b).$$

The complement of the set determined by $z_1 \neq 0$ has Lebesgue measure zero on $\mathbb{C}^{k-1}$ and so, by integrating out the redundant coordinates r_0 and θ_0 from the above, we see that the induced shape-measure is

$$\frac{(k-2)!}{\pi^{k-2}} g_2(\sigma, \zeta) \prod_{j=1}^{k-2} d\zeta_j,$$

where

$$g_2(\sigma, \zeta) = \frac{1}{2\pi} \int_0^{2\pi} \{h_1(\sigma, \zeta) \cos^2 \alpha + 2h_2(\sigma, \zeta) \sin \alpha \cos \alpha$$
$$+ h_1(\sigma^{-1}, \zeta) \sin^2 \alpha\}^{-(k-1)} \, d\alpha$$

and

$$h_1(\sigma, \zeta) = \frac{1}{2} \left\{ (\sigma + \sigma^{-1}) \left(1 + \sum_{j=1}^{k-2} |\zeta_j|^2 \right) - (\sigma - \sigma^{-1}) \, \Re \left(1 + \sum_{j=1}^{k-2} \zeta_j^2 \right) \right\},$$

$$h_2(\sigma, \zeta) = \frac{1}{2} (\sigma - \sigma^{-1}) \, \Im \left(1 + \sum_{j=1}^{k-2} \zeta_j^2 \right).$$

Since

$$h_1(\sigma, \zeta) + h_1(\sigma^{-1}, \zeta) = (\sigma + \sigma^{-1}) \left(1 + \sum_{j=1}^{k-2} |\zeta_j|^2 \right),$$

$$h_1(\sigma^{-1}, \zeta) - h_1(\sigma, \zeta) = (\sigma - \sigma^{-1}) \, \Re \left(1 + \sum_{j=1}^{k-2} \zeta_j^2 \right),$$

we have

$$\frac{h_1(\sigma, \zeta) + h_1(\sigma^{-1}, \zeta)}{2\sqrt{h_1(\sigma, \zeta)h_1(\sigma^{-1}, \zeta) - h_2(\sigma, \zeta)^2}}$$

$$= \left\{ 1 - \left(\frac{\sigma - \sigma^{-1}}{\sigma + \sigma^{-1}} \right)^2 \left(\left| 1 + \sum_{j=1}^{k-2} \zeta_j^2 \right| \right)^2 \left(1 + \sum_{j=1}^{k-2} |\zeta_j|^2 \right)^{-2} \right\}^{-1/2}$$

$$= f_\sigma(\zeta)$$

and we can write

$$h_1(\sigma, \zeta) \cos^2 \alpha + 2h_2(\sigma, \zeta) \sin \alpha \cos \alpha + h_1(\sigma^{-1}, \zeta) \sin^2 \alpha$$
$$= \tfrac{1}{2} \{h_1(\sigma, \zeta) + h_1(\sigma^{-1}, \zeta)\} + \tfrac{1}{2} \{h_1(\sigma, \zeta) - h_1(\sigma^{-1}, \zeta)\} \cos 2\alpha$$
$$+ h_2(\sigma, \zeta) \sin 2\alpha$$
$$= h_3(\sigma, \zeta) \left\{ f_\sigma(\zeta) + \sqrt{f_\sigma(\zeta)^2 - 1} \cos(2\alpha + \alpha_\sigma) \right\},$$

where

$$h_3(\sigma, \zeta) = \sqrt{h_1(\sigma, \zeta)h_1(\sigma^{-1}, \zeta) - h_2(\sigma, \zeta)^2}$$

and $\alpha_\sigma \in [0, \pi/2]$ is such that

$$\sin \alpha_\sigma = \frac{2h_2(\sigma, \zeta)}{\sqrt{(h_1(\sigma, \zeta) - h_1(\sigma^{-1}, \zeta))^2 + 4h_2(\sigma, \zeta)^2}}.$$

It follows that

$$g_2(\sigma, \zeta) = h_3(\sigma, \zeta)^{-(k-1)} P_{k-2}(f_\sigma(\zeta)).$$

Finally, since

$$\frac{h_3(\sigma, \zeta)}{h_3(1, \zeta)} = \frac{\sigma + \sigma^{-1}}{2 f_\sigma(\zeta)},$$

Equation (8.6) gives the stated result. ∎

The Legendre polynomial $P_n(x)$ is an increasing function of $x \geqslant 1$ and so the Radon–Nikodým derivative (8.12) in Theorem 8.5 achieves its minimum when $f_\sigma(\pi(z)) = 1$. When $\sigma > 1$, Equation (8.13) implies that $f_\sigma(\pi(z)) = 1$ if and only if $s_1(\pi(z)) = \pi/4$: that is, if and only if $\pi(z)$ is maximally distant from the collinearity set. To identify this set we write λ_1 and λ_2 with $\lambda_1 \geqslant |\lambda_2|$ for the two pseudo-singular values of the real-valued $2 \times (k-1)$ matrix corresponding to the pre-shape $z/\|z\|$. Then, we have

$$\lambda_1^2 \lambda_2^2 = \frac{\sum_{j=1}^{k-1} x_j^2 \sum_{j=1}^{k-1} y_j^2 - \left(\sum_{j=1}^{k-1} x_j y_j\right)^2}{\left(\sum_{j=1}^{k-1} |z_j|^2\right)^2},$$

where the x_j and y_j are the real and imaginary parts of z_j. From the last equation it follows that

$$\left\{\left|\sum_{j=1}^{k-1} z_j^2\right|\right\}^2 = \{1 - 4\lambda_1^2 \lambda_2^2\} \left\{\sum_{j=1}^{k-1} |z_j|^2\right\}^2.$$

Then, since $\lambda_1^2 + \lambda_2^2 = 1$ and $|\lambda_2| = \sin(s_1(\pi(z)))$, the set consisting of all shapes maximally distant from the collinearity set is characterised by $\sum_{j=1}^{k-1} z_j^2 = 0$, and so, on this set, the Radon–Nikodým derivative (8.12) has the minimal value

$$\left\{\frac{2}{\sigma + \sigma^{-1}}\right\}^{k-1}.$$

Similarly, since $\sigma > 1$, the maximal value of $f_\sigma(\pi(z))$ is $(\sigma + \sigma^{-1})/2$, which is achieved when $s_1(\pi(z)) = 0$: that is, when $\pi(z)$ is in the collinearity set. Thus, the Radon–Nikodým derivative has its maximal value $P_{k-2}((\sigma + \sigma^{-1})/2)$ on the collinearity set. Since the function given by (8.12) is C^∞ everywhere on Σ_2^k, it is asymptotically equal to $P_{k-2}((\sigma + \sigma^{-1})/2)$ on any small neighbourhood of the collinearity set. Thus, this value gives the factor by which a degree of ellipticity σ increases the chance of an approximate multiple alignment.

Since it depends on the shape only via its Riemannian distance to the collinearity set, the Radon–Nikodým derivative (8.12) is invariant under the group of isometries induced by $\mathbf{SO}\,(k-1)$ acting on the right of the elements of S_m^k and the next result follows from Theorems 8.2 and 8.5.

Corollary 8.2. *If $\pi(z) \in \Sigma_2^k$ is generated by k labelled iid non-isotropic Gaussian random variables with principal component variances $\sigma^2 > 1$ and $1/\sigma^2$, then the Riemannian distance $s_1(\pi(z))$ of $\pi(z)$ to the collinearity set and the projection of $\pi(z)$ into it are independent and $\hat{s}(\pi(z)) = \sin(2s_1(\pi(z))) \in [0,1]$ has distribution*

$$(k-2)\{2\sigma\}^{k-1}\hat{s}^{k-3}\left\{4\sigma^2 + (\sigma^2-1)^2\hat{s}^2\right\}^{-\frac{k-1}{2}}$$
$$\times\, P_{k-2}((\sigma^2+1)\{4\sigma^2 + (\sigma^2-1)^2\hat{s}^2\}^{-1/2})\,\mathrm{d}\hat{s}.$$

When $k = 3$, $P_{k-2}(x) = x$ and so the distribution of $\hat{s}(\pi(z))$ given in the corollary becomes

$$\frac{4\sigma^2(\sigma^2+1)}{(4\sigma^2 + (\sigma^2-1)^2\hat{s}^2)^{3/2}}\,\mathrm{d}\hat{s}.$$

Thus, we have

$$\mathrm{P}[\hat{s}(\pi(z)) \leqslant s] = \frac{(\sigma^2+1)s}{\sqrt{4\sigma^2 + (\sigma^2-1)^2 s^2}}, \quad 0 \leqslant s \leqslant 1,$$

and $\mathrm{E}[\hat{s}(\pi(z))] = 2\sigma/(\sigma+1)^2$.

8.5 SHAPE-MEASURES ON Σ_2^K INDUCED BY COMPLEX NORMAL DISTRIBUTIONS

Let C^* be a positive definite $k \times k$ complex-valued Hermitian matrix. That is, if $C^* = C_1^* + iC_2^*$, where C_1^* and C_2^* are real, then C_1^* is positive-definite symmetric and C_2^* is skew-symmetric. Then, we say that $(z_1^*, \ldots, z_k^*) \in \mathbb{C}^k$, where $z_j^* = x_j^* + iy_j^*$, is a complex normal $\mathcal{CN}((z_{01}^*, \ldots, z_{0k}^*), C^*)$ random variable if $(x_1^*, \ldots, x_k^*, y_1^*, \ldots, y_k^*)$ is multivariate normal with a covariance matrix of the form

$$\widetilde{C}^* = \frac{1}{2}\begin{pmatrix} C_1^* & C_2^* \\ -C_2^* & C_1^* \end{pmatrix}.$$

The assumption that C^* is positive-definite Hermitian implies that it can be decomposed as

$$C^* = \overline{U}^t D U,$$

where U is a unitary $k \times k$ matrix and D is diagonal with all its diagonal elements positive. Thus, $\det(C^*) = \sqrt{(\det(\widetilde{C}^*))} > 0$.

Following similar arguments to those at the beginning of the proof of Theorem 8.5, we can see, after some calculation, that the assumption that the joint distribution of $(z_1^*, \ldots, z_k^*)$ is a complex normal distribution $\mathcal{CN}((z_{01}^*, \ldots, z_{0k}^*), C^*)$ implies that the joint distribution of $(z_1, \ldots, z_{k-1})$ is still a complex normal distribution, say, $z = (z_1, \ldots, z_{k-1}) \sim \mathcal{CN}(z_0, C)$. We introduce the C-based metric ρ_C on Σ_2^k defined by

$$\cos^2 \rho_C(\pi(z), \pi(w)) = \frac{\bar{z}C^{-1}w^t \bar{w}C^{-1}z^t}{\bar{z}C^{-1}z^t \bar{w}C^{-1}w^t},$$

and write $\kappa_C^2 = \bar{z}_0 C^{-1} z_0^t$ as the C-based squared size of the configuration determined by the means. We note that ρ_C is invariant under scalar multiplication of C, but that κ_C is not. Clearly, ρ_I is identical with the induced Riemannian metric on Σ_2^k and κ_I^2 is the squared size of the configuration determined by the means.

Theorem 8.6. *The Radon–Nikodým derivative at $\pi(z)$, with respect to $d\omega_2^k$, on Σ_2^k of the shape-measure induced by $\mathcal{CN}(z_0^*, C^*)$ is*

$$\frac{1}{\det(C)} \frac{\{\bar{z}z^t\}^{k-1}}{\{\bar{z}C^{-1}z^t\}^{k-1}} \exp\left\{ -\frac{1}{2}\kappa_C^2 \left(1 - \cos^2 \rho_C(\pi(z_0), \pi(z))\right) \right\}$$

$$\times {}_1F_1\left(2 - k; 1; -\frac{\kappa_C^2}{2} \cos^2 \rho_C(\pi(z_0), \pi(z))\right), \qquad (8.14)$$

where ${}_1F_1$ is Kummer's confluent hypergeometric function defined by

$$_1F_1(a; b; x) = \sum_{j=0}^{\infty} \frac{\Gamma(a+j)}{\Gamma(a)} \frac{\Gamma(b)}{\Gamma(b+j)} \frac{x^j}{j!}$$

and $\Gamma(n)$ denotes the Gamma-function.

Proof. The joint distribution of $(z_1, \ldots, z_{k-1})$ is

$$\frac{1}{(2\pi)^{k-1}\det(C)} \exp\left\{ -\frac{1}{2}(\bar{z} - \bar{z}_0)C^{-1}(z - z_0)^t \right\} \prod_{j=1}^{k-1} dz_j$$

$$= \frac{1}{(2\pi)^{k-1}\det(C)} \exp\left\{ -\frac{1}{2} \left(|z_1|^2 (1, \bar{\zeta})C^{-1}(1, \zeta)^t - z_1 \bar{z}_0 C^{-1}(1, \zeta)^t \right. \right.$$

$$\left. \left. - \bar{z}_1(1, \bar{\zeta})C^{-1}z_0^t + \bar{z}_0 C^{-1}z_0^t \right) \right\} |z_1|^{2(k-2)} dz_1 \prod_{j=1}^{k-2} d\zeta_j,$$

where $(\zeta_1, \ldots, \zeta_{k-2})$ are our usual coordinates on the subset of shape space determined by $z_1 \neq 0$, and so the induced shape-measure is the product of

$$\int_{\mathbb{C}} \exp\left\{ -\frac{1}{2} \left(|z_1|^2 (1, \bar{\zeta})C^{-1}(1, \zeta)^t - z_1 \bar{z}_0 C^{-1}(1, \zeta)^t - \bar{z}_1(1, \bar{\zeta})C^{-1}z_0^t \right) \right\}$$

$$\times |z_1|^{2(k-2)} dz_1, \qquad (8.15)$$

with

$$\frac{1}{(2\pi)^{k-1}\det(C)} \exp\left\{-\frac{1}{2}\overline{z}_0 C^{-1} z_0^t\right\} \prod_{j=1}^{k-2} d\zeta_j.$$

Write $a = (1, \overline{\zeta})C^{-1}(1, \zeta)^t > 0$ and $b = (1, \overline{\zeta})C^{-1} z_0^t \in \mathbb{C}$. Then, we can rewrite (8.15) as

$$\int_{\mathbb{C}} \exp\left\{-\frac{1}{2}\left(a|z_1|^2 - \overline{b}z_1 - b\overline{z}_1\right)\right\} |z_1|^{2(k-2)} dz_1$$

$$= \exp\left\{\frac{|b|^2}{2a}\right\} \int_{\mathbb{C}} \exp\left\{-\frac{a}{2}|z_1|^2\right\} \left|z_1 + \frac{b}{a}\right|^{2(k-2)} dz_1$$

$$= \frac{1}{2} \exp\left\{\frac{|b|^2}{2a}\right\} \int_0^\infty \int_0^{2\pi} \exp\left\{-\frac{a}{2}r_0^2\right\} \left|z_1 + \frac{b}{a}\right|^{2(k-2)} dr_0^2 d\theta_0. \qquad (8.16)$$

However,

$$\left|z_1 + \frac{b}{a}\right|^{2(k-2)} = \left(z_1 + \frac{b}{a}\right)^{k-2}\left(\overline{z}_1 + \frac{\overline{b}}{a}\right)^{k-2}$$

$$= \sum_{j=0}^{k-2}\binom{k-2}{j} z_1^j \left(\frac{b}{a}\right)^{k-2-j} \sum_{j=0}^{k-2}\binom{k-2}{j} \overline{z}_1^j \left(\frac{\overline{b}}{a}\right)^{k-2-j}$$

and, for any $n \neq 0$,

$$\int_0^{2\pi} e^{in\theta_0} d\theta_0 = 0.$$

Hence, (8.16) is equal to

$$\pi \exp\left\{\frac{|b|^2}{2a}\right\} \sum_{j=0}^{k-2}\binom{k-2}{j}^2 \left|\frac{b}{a}\right|^{2(k-2-j)} \int_0^\infty \exp\left\{-\frac{a}{2}r_0^2\right\} r_0^{2j} dr_0^2$$

$$= \pi \exp\left\{\frac{|b|^2}{2a}\right\} \sum_{j=0}^{k-2}\binom{k-2}{j}^2 \left|\frac{b}{a}\right|^{2(k-2-j)} j! \left\{\frac{a}{2}\right\}^{-(j+1)}$$

$$= 2^{k-1}\pi \frac{(k-2)!}{a^{k-1}} \exp\left\{\frac{|b|^2}{2a}\right\} \sum_{j=0}^{k-2} \frac{(k-2)!}{\{(k-2-j)!\}^2 j!} \left\{\frac{|b|^2}{2a}\right\}^{k-2-j}.$$

Finally, since

$$\frac{|b|^2}{a} = \kappa_C^2 \cos^2 \rho_C(\pi(z_0), \pi(z)),$$

we deduce that the shape-measure induced by $\mathcal{CN}(z_0^*, C^*)$ is

$$\frac{(k-2)!}{\pi^{k-2}}\frac{1}{\det(C)}\frac{1}{a^{k-1}}\exp\left\{-\frac{1}{2}\kappa_C^2(1-\cos^2\rho_C(\pi(z_0),\pi(z)))\right\}$$

$$\times\sum_{j=0}^{k-2}\frac{(k-2)!}{\{j!\}^2}\frac{1}{(k-2-j)!}\left\{\frac{\kappa_C^2}{2}\cos^2\rho_C(\pi(z_0),\pi(z))\right\}^j\prod_{l=1}^{k-2}d\zeta_l$$

$$=\frac{(k-2)!}{\pi^{k-2}}\frac{1}{\det(C)}\frac{1}{a^{k-1}}\exp\left\{-\frac{1}{2}\kappa_C^2(1-\cos^2\rho_C(\pi(z_0),\pi(z)))\right\}$$

$$\times\sum_{j=0}^{k-2}(-1)^j\frac{\Gamma(j+2-k)}{\Gamma(2-k)}\frac{\Gamma(1)}{\Gamma(j+1)}\frac{1}{j!}\left\{\frac{\kappa_C^2}{2}\cos^2\rho_C(\pi(z_0),\pi(z))\right\}^j\prod_{l=1}^{k-2}d\zeta_l$$

$$=\frac{(k-2)!}{\pi^{k-2}}\frac{1}{\det(C)}\frac{1}{a^{k-1}}\exp\left\{-\frac{1}{2}\kappa_C^2(1-\cos^2\rho_C(\pi(z_0),\pi(z)))\right\}$$

$$\times {}_1F_1\left(2-k;1;-\frac{\kappa_C^2}{2}\cos^2\rho_C(\pi(z_0),\pi(z))\right)\prod_{l=1}^{k-2}d\zeta_l.$$

The stated result then follows from the expression for the uniform measure $d\omega_2^k$ given by (8.6). ∎

When all the z_{0j}^* are identical, the z_{0j} are all zero and so $\kappa_C = 0$. In this case, the shape of the means z_{0j}^* is not defined and the Radon–Nikodým derivative (8.14) simplifies to

$$\frac{1}{\det(C)}\frac{\{\bar{z}z^t\}^{k-1}}{\{\bar{z}C^{-1}z^t\}^{k-1}}.$$

When $C = \operatorname{diag}\{\sigma_1^2,\ldots,\sigma_{k-1}^2\}$, then the z_i^* are independent, each having isotropic Gaussian $\mathcal{N}(z_{0j}^*, \sigma_j^2 I_2)$ distribution and $\bar{z}C^{-1}w^t = \sum_{j=1}^{k-1}\sigma_j^{-2}\bar{z}_j w_j$. Thus, the Radon-Nikodým derivative (8.14) can be simplified accordingly. If, in addition, all the z_{0j}^* are identical, then (8.14) becomes

$$\prod_{i=1}^{k-1}\sigma_i^{-2}\left\{\frac{\sum_{i=1}^{k-1}|z_i|^2}{\sum_{i=1}^{k-1}\sigma_i^{-2}|z_i|^2}\right\}^{k-1}.$$

When $C = \sigma^2 I$ and the z_{0j}^* are not all identical, then $\kappa_C^2 = \{\bar{z}_0 z_0^t\}/\sigma^2$ and, as already noted, ρ_C coincides with the Riemannian metric ρ induced on Σ_2^k from the standard metric on $\mathcal{S}_2^k$. It follows that the Radon-Nikodým derivative (8.14) becomes

$$\exp\left\{-\frac{\bar{z}_0 z_0^t}{2\sigma^2}(1-\cos^2\rho(\pi(z_0),\pi(z)))\right\}\times$$

$$\times \;_1F_1\left(2-k;1;-\frac{\bar{z}_0 z_0^t}{2\sigma^2}\cos^2\rho(\pi(z_0),\pi(z))\right).$$

This expression was first obtained by Mardia and Dryden (1989a) using a different method.

8.6   THE SHAPE-MEASURE ON Σ_2^3 INDUCED BY THREE LABELLED iid UNIFORM DISTRIBUTIONS IN A COMPACT CONVEX SET

The method that we shall use to obtain such measures is distantly related to what is sometimes called 'Crofton's boundary formula'. In the general case, this gives a 2-fold integral for the Radon–Nikodým derivative of the induced shape-measure with respect to the uniform measure on Σ_2^3. The method also extends naturally to the case when the number of vertices of the configuration is more than three, but we shall not discuss that here.

To describe our result we let $\partial\mathbf{K}$ denote the boundary and $|\mathbf{K}|$ the area of a compact convex subset $\mathbf{K}$ of $\mathbb{R}^2$ with non-empty interior and we let o be any fixed point in $\mathbf{K}\backslash\partial\mathbf{K}$. Then, if (z_1^*, z_2^*, z_3^*) are three labelled iid uniform random variables in $\mathbf{K}$, we let ϑ_i be the interior angle of the triangle (z_1^*, z_2^*, z_3^*) at z_i^* and (r_{oi}, θ_{oi}) be the polar coordinates, with respect to o, of the projection from o of the ith vertex onto $\partial\mathbf{K}$. When the ith vertex is already on $\partial\mathbf{K}$, then, of course, (r_{oi}, θ_{oi}) are its polar coordinates. Similarly, given that the ith vertex is on $\partial\mathbf{K}$, we let (r_{ij}, θ_{ij}) be the polar coordinates, with respect to the ith vertex, of the projection from that vertex onto $\partial\mathbf{K}$ of the jth vertex.

Theorem 8.7. *The Radon–Nikodým derivative $m_\mathbf{K}$ at $\pi(z)$, with respect to $d\omega_2^3$, of the induced shape-measure on Σ_2^3 of three labelled iid uniform random variables (z_1^*, z_2^*, z_3^*) in a compact convex set $\mathbf{K}$ in $\mathbb{R}^2$ can be expressed as*

$$m_\mathbf{K}(\pi(z)) = \frac{\pi}{432|\mathbf{K}|^3}\left\{\sum_{i=1}^{2}\sin^2\vartheta_i\right\}^2$$

$$\times \sum_{i_1=1}^{3}\sum_{i_2\neq i_1}\frac{1}{\sin^4\vartheta_{i_3}}\int_{\partial\mathbf{K}}\left\{\int_{\partial\mathbf{K}}1_\mathbf{K}(z_{i_3}^*(\pi(z)))\,r_{i_1 i_2}^4\,d\theta_{i_1 i_2}\right\}r_{oi_1}^2\,d\theta_{oi_1}. \tag{8.17}$$

Proof.   Our proof proceeds by rescaling and translating a random triangle to successively project two of its vertices onto $\partial\mathbf{K}$ in such a way that the relevant conditional distributions may be calculated. Since we are working modulo translations and scaling, we may without loss of generality suppose that the origin is inside $\mathbf{K}$, that o is at the origin and that $|\mathbf{K}| = 1$.

First, $\hat{r} = \max\{|z_j^*|/r_{oj} : 1 \leqslant j \leqslant 3\}$ takes values in the interval $(0, 1]$ and, if $\tilde{z}_j^* = z_j^*/\hat{r}$, the labelled triangle $(\tilde{z}_1^*, \tilde{z}_2^*, \tilde{z}_3^*)$ has the same shape as that of (z_1^*, z_2^*, z_3^*)

and lies in **K** with at least one vertex on $\partial\mathbf{K}$. Moreover, the probability of the vertex that lies on $\partial\mathbf{K}$ being the i_1th one is $1/3$ and, given that the i_1th vertex lies on $\partial\mathbf{K}$, the $\tilde{z}_j^*$, $j \neq i_1$, are two iid uniform random variables in **K**. Thus, we have

$$\prod_{i=1}^{3} 1_{\mathbf{K}}(z_i^*)\mathrm{d}z_i^* = \frac{1}{3}\sum_{i_1=1}^{3} 1_{\partial\mathbf{K}}(\tilde{z}_{i_1}^*)r_{oi_1}^2\,\mathrm{d}\theta_{oi_1}\hat{r}^5\mathrm{d}\hat{r}\prod_{j\neq i_1} 1_{\mathbf{K}}(\tilde{z}_j^*)\,\mathrm{d}\tilde{z}_j^*.$$

Since $\hat{r}$ is a scale factor, we may integrate it out so that each summand of the right-hand side of the above equation becomes

$$\frac{1}{18}r_{oi_1}^2\,\mathrm{d}\theta_{oi_1}\prod_{j\neq i_1} 1_{\mathbf{K}}(\tilde{z}_j^*)\,\mathrm{d}\tilde{z}_j^*,$$

where the point $(r_{oi_1}, \theta_{oi_1})$ on $\partial\mathbf{K}$ is now the location of the vertex $\tilde{z}_{i_1}^*$ of the labelled triangle $(\tilde{z}_1^*, \tilde{z}_2^*, \tilde{z}_3^*)$.

Our second projection is from the vertex $\tilde{z}_{i_1}^*$, which is now known to lie on $\partial\mathbf{K}$. If $\hat{r}_{i_1} = \max\{|\tilde{z}_{i_1}^* - \tilde{z}_j^*|/r_{i_1j}, j \neq i_1\}$, $\hat{z}_{i_1}^* = \tilde{z}_{i_1}^*$ and $\hat{z}_j^* = \tilde{z}_j^*/\hat{r}_{i_1}$ for $j \neq i_1$, then, as before, the labelled triangle $(\hat{z}_1^*, \hat{z}_2^*, \hat{z}_3^*)$ has the same shape as that of (z_1^*, z_2^*, z_3^*) and it also lies in **K** with at least two vertices on $\partial\mathbf{K}$. The probability that it is the i_2th vertex, in addition to the i_1th vertex, that lies on $\partial\mathbf{K}$ is $\frac{1}{2}$ and, given that the i_2th vertex is on $\partial\mathbf{K}$, the remaining vertex is uniformly distributed in **K**. Hence

$$\prod_{j\neq i_1} 1_{\mathbf{K}}(\tilde{z}_j^*)\,\mathrm{d}\tilde{z}_j^* = \frac{1}{2}\sum_{\substack{i_2,i_3\neq i_1\\ i_2\neq i_3}} r_{i_1i_2}^2\,\mathrm{d}\theta_{i_1i_2}\hat{r}_{i_1}^3\,\mathrm{d}\hat{r}_{i_1}\,1_{\mathbf{K}}(\hat{z}_{i_3}^*)\,\mathrm{d}\hat{z}_{i_3}^*.$$

Again, the scale factor $\hat{r}_{i_1}$ may be integrated out, so that each summand of the right-hand side of the above becomes

$$\tfrac{1}{8}r_{i_1i_2}^2\,\mathrm{d}\theta_{i_1i_2}1_{\mathbf{K}}(\hat{z}_{i_3}^*)\,\mathrm{d}\hat{z}_{i_3}^*.$$

Therefore, after two such succesive changes of scaling, the joint distribution

$$\prod_{i=1}^{3} 1_{\mathbf{K}}(z_i^*)\,\mathrm{d}z_i^*$$

of (z_1^*, z_2^*, z_3^*) reduces to the joint distribution

$$\frac{1}{144}\sum r_{oi_1}^2\,\mathrm{d}\theta_{oi_1}r_{i_1i_2}^2\,\mathrm{d}\theta_{i_1i_2}1_{\mathbf{K}}(\hat{z}_{i_3}^*)\,\mathrm{d}\hat{z}_{i_3}^*$$

of $(\hat{z}_1^*, \hat{z}_2^*, \hat{z}_3^*)$, where the sum, ranging over all permutations of the labels, runs through all possible choices of two ordered vertices on $\partial\mathbf{K}$ and the third one in **K**.

Now, for given, and almost surely distinct, $\hat{z}_{i_1}^*$ and $\hat{z}_{i_2}^*$ on $\partial\mathbf{K}$ there will be a one-to-one correspondence between $\hat{z}_{i_3}^*$ and the shape of the labelled triangle

(z_1^*, z_2^*, z_3^*). Since Σ_2^3 is a homogeneous space and the transformation ϖ on Σ_2^3 induced by the relabelling mapping $(1, 2, 3) \mapsto (\varpi(1), \varpi(2), \varpi(3))$ is an isometry, the uniform measure on Σ_2^3 is invariant with respect to such a transformation. Thus, by (8.2) and (8.7), for fixed $\hat{z}_{i_1}^*$ and $\hat{z}_{i_2}^*$, we have

$$
\begin{aligned}
\mathrm{d}\hat{z}_{i_3}^* &= \tfrac{3}{4}|\hat{z}_{i_2}^* - \hat{z}_{i_1}^*|^2 \, \mathrm{d}(\varpi(\zeta)) \\
&= \tfrac{3\pi}{4}|\hat{z}_{i_2}^* - \hat{z}_{i_1}^*|^2 \{1 + |\varpi(\zeta)|^2\}^2 \, \mathrm{d}\omega_2^3 \\
&= \tfrac{3\pi}{4} r_{i_1 i_2}^2 \{1 + |\varpi(\zeta)|^2\}^2 \, \mathrm{d}\omega_2^3.
\end{aligned}
\tag{8.18}
$$

Finally, the expression for the shape-measure on Σ_2^3 as stated in the theorem follows from

$$
\begin{aligned}
1 + |\varpi(\zeta)|^2 &= 1 + \frac{|\hat{z}_{i_3}^* - \hat{z}_{i_1}^*|^2 + |\hat{z}_{i_3}^* - \hat{z}_{i_2}^*|^2 + 2\Re\langle \hat{z}_{i_3}^* - \hat{z}_{i_1}^*, \hat{z}_{i_3}^* - \hat{z}_{i_2}^* \rangle}{3|\hat{z}_{i_2}^* - \hat{z}_{i_1}^*|^2} \\
&= \frac{2}{3} \frac{|\hat{z}_{i_2}^* - \hat{z}_{i_1}^*|^2 + |\hat{z}_{i_3}^* - \hat{z}_{i_2}^*|^2 + |\hat{z}_{i_1}^* - \hat{z}_{i_3}^*|^2}{|\hat{z}_{i_2}^* - \hat{z}_{i_1}^*|^2} \\
&= \frac{2}{3} \frac{\sin^2 \vartheta_1 + \sin^2 \vartheta_2 + \sin^2 \vartheta_3}{\sin^2 \vartheta_{i_3}}.
\end{aligned}
\tag{8.19}
$$

■

It is clear from the proof of Theorem 8.7, in particular, from (8.18) and (8.19), that the Radon–Nikodým derivative $\tilde{m}_{\mathbf{K}}$, with respect to $\mathrm{d}\zeta$, of the shape-measure associated with (8.17) at ζ can be expressed as

$$
\begin{aligned}
\tilde{m}_{\mathbf{K}}(\zeta) = \frac{1}{192|\mathbf{K}|^3} \sum_{\varpi \in \Omega} \left| \frac{\mathrm{d}(\varpi(\zeta))}{\mathrm{d}\zeta} \right|^2 \\
\times \int_{\partial \mathbf{K}} \left\{ \int_{\partial \mathbf{K}} 1_{\mathbf{K}}(z_3^*(\varpi(\zeta))) \, r_{12}^4 \, \mathrm{d}\theta_{12} \right\} r_{o1}^2 \, \mathrm{d}\theta_{o1}
\end{aligned}
\tag{8.20}
$$

where, by (8.3) and (8.4), we have

$$
\left| \frac{\mathrm{d}(\tau(\zeta))}{\mathrm{d}\zeta} \right|^2 = 1,
$$

$$
\left| \frac{\mathrm{d}(\varsigma(\zeta))}{\mathrm{d}\zeta} \right|^2 = \left| \frac{2}{1 + \sqrt{3}\zeta} \right|^4,
$$

$$
\left| \frac{\mathrm{d}(\varsigma^2(\zeta))}{\mathrm{d}\zeta} \right|^2 = \left| \frac{2}{1 - \sqrt{3}\zeta} \right|^4.
$$

This Radon–Nikodým derivative has exactly the same singularities as the corresponding Radon–Nikodým derivative with respect to $\mathrm{d}\omega_2^3$.

When $\pi(z)$ is in the collinearity set and is not any one of the three special shape points corresponding to triangles with two of their three vertices coincident, the factor $1_{\mathbf{K}}(z_{i_3}^*(\pi(z)))$ in (8.17) kills four of the six terms. The complement of the three special shape points in the collinearity set has three components and the terms to be killed depend on which of these components contains $\pi(z)$. However, the remaining two double integrals over $\partial\mathbf{K}$ are independent of the position of $\pi(z)$ within that component, so that, by (8.19), (8.17) is proportional to

$$\left\{ \frac{|z_1^* - z_2^*|^2 + |z_2^* - z_3^*|^2 + |z_3^* - z_1^*|^2}{\max\{|z_1^* - z_2^*|^2, |z_2^* - z_3^*|^2, |z_3^* - z_1^*|^2\}} \right\}^2 .$$

It is easy to verify from this formula that the first derivative of $m_{\mathbf{K}}$ in (8.17) is discontinuous as $\pi(\mathbf{z})$, travelling along the collinearity set, passes through any one of the three special shape points. This implies, by the comments in the previous paragraph, that the first derivative of $\tilde{m}_{\mathbf{K}}$ given by (8.20) is discontinuous at the two special points $\mp 1/\sqrt{3}$ on the x-axis since the special shape point corresponding to $z_1^* = z_2^*$ has been mapped to ∞. The expression (8.20) also makes it clear that the value of $\tilde{m}_{\mathbf{K}}$ is a constant in the interval $(-1/\sqrt{3}, 1/\sqrt{3})$ of x-axis. This result was first obtained by Small (1982).

To close this section we show that the double integral in (8.17) is amenable to computation by evaluating the formula for the case when $\mathbf{K}$ is a disc.

Theorem 8.8. *The Radon–Nikodým derivative, with respect to $d\omega_2^3$, of the shape-measure on Σ_2^3 induced by three labelled iid uniform distributions in a disc is given by*

$$\frac{1}{216\pi} \left\{ \sum_{i=1}^{3} \sin^2 \vartheta_i \right\}^2 \sum_{i=1}^{3} \frac{12\vartheta_i - 8\sin(2\vartheta_i) + \sin(4\vartheta_i)}{\sin^4 \vartheta_i} .$$

Proof. When $\mathbf{K}$ is a circular disc, it is convenient to take the fixed point o in $\mathbf{K}$ at its centre and its radius to be unity. Then, the fact that $z_{i_1}^*$ is assumed to be uniformly distributed inside $\mathbf{K}$ implies that its projection $(r_{oi_1}, \theta_{oi_1})$ onto $\partial\mathbf{K}$ is uniformly distributed there. In addition, if we write $\tilde{\theta}_{i_1 i_2}$ for the angle between the directed line from $z_{i_1}^*$ to $z_{i_2}^*$ and a directed tangent at $z_{i_1}^*$ when both $z_{i_1}^*$ and $z_{i_2}^*$ are on $\partial\mathbf{K}$, we have $\theta_{i_1 i_2} = \pi/2 + \tilde{\theta}_{i_1 i_2}$ and $r_{i_1 i_2} = 2\sin\tilde{\theta}_{i_1 i_2}$, which is independent of the position of $z_{i_1}^*$ on $\partial\mathbf{K}$. We also have $r_{oi_1} = 1$, since it is the radius of the disk, and so

$$\int_{\partial\mathbf{K}} r_{oi_1}^2 \, d\theta_{oi_1} \int_{\partial\mathbf{K}} 1_{\mathbf{K}}(z_{i_3}^*) \, r_{i_1 i_2}^4 \, d\theta_{i_1 i_2} = 2\pi \int_{z_{i_3}^* \in \mathbf{K}} (2\sin\tilde{\theta}_{i_1 i_2})^4 \, d\tilde{\theta}_{i_1 i_2} .$$

The condition $z_{i_3}^* \in \mathbf{K}$ is equivalent to requiring that

$$0 \leqslant \tilde{\theta}_{i_1 i_2} \leqslant \vartheta_{i_3} \quad \text{or} \quad \pi - \vartheta_{i_3} \leqslant \tilde{\theta}_{i_1 i_2} \leqslant \pi,$$

so that the above integral is equal to

$$64\pi \int_0^{\vartheta_{i_3}} \sin^4 \tilde{\theta} \, d\tilde{\theta} = 2\pi \{12\vartheta_{i_3} - 8\sin(2\vartheta_{i_3}) + \sin(4\vartheta_{i_3})\}.$$

Thus, we have the result.   ∎

The contours for the Radon–Nikodým derivative of the shape-measure obtained in Theorem 8.8 are illustrated in Figure 8.3 on a projection of the sphere $\mathbf{S}^2(\frac{1}{2}) = \Sigma_2^3$ onto a central plane chosen, so that the central horizontal line is the visible part of the collinearity set with the midpoint being the shape of the degenerate isosceles triangle having its third vertex at the midpoint of the line joining the other two. There are three major local maxima at the shapes of triangles with two coincident points; two minor local maxima at the equilateral shapes; three local minima at the three degenerate triangles with one vertex at the point mid-way between the other two; and six saddle points at a special isosceles shape and its images under permutations of the vertices.

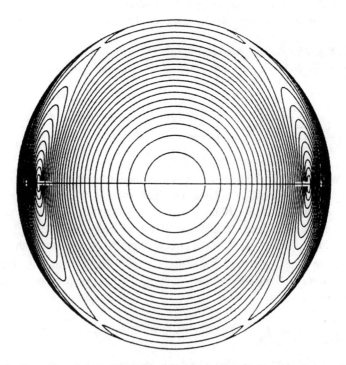

Figure 8.3 Reproduced from D.G. Kendall, Exact distribution for shapes of random trangles in convex sets, *Advances in Applied Probability* **17** (1985) 308–29, by permission of the Applied Probability Trust

8.7 THE SHAPE-MEASURE ON Σ_2^3 INDUCED BY THREE LABELLED iid UNIFORM DISTRIBUTIONS IN A CONVEX POLYGON. I: THE SINGULAR TESSELLATION

In the previous section we observed, for the first time, discontinuities appearing in the derivatives of the Radon–Nikodým derivatives of shape-measures. Those that we noted were on the collinearity set. However, they could appear anywhere and, in this and the next sections, we study a class of shape-measures whose Radon–Nikodým derivatives have singularities along the edges of an appropriate tessellation of the planar representation of the punctured version of Σ_2^3.

The shape-measures concerned are a special case of those of the previous section. In addition to the notation we used there, we now suppose that $\mathbf{K}$ is a convex polygon with n edges $e_1, \ldots, e_n$ ordered in the counter-clockwise direction of $\partial \mathbf{K}$ and, for general integer suffixes, we make the convention that i_1 and i_2 determine the same edge when $i_1 \equiv i_2$ modulo n. Since the induced shape-measure depends only on the shape of $\mathbf{K}$ itself, we set up Cartesian coordinates (u, v) in the plane of $\mathbf{K}$, which we shall use throughout, by taking the positive u-axis to start at the midpoint of e_1 and then to run along its second half in the counter-clockwise direction of $\partial \mathbf{K}$, so that $\mathbf{K}$ lies in the upper half of the (u, v)-plane. It will also be convenient to have the associated complex coordinate $w = u + iv$ and to write p_i for the complex coordinate of the vertex common to the edges e_{i-1} and e_i of $\mathbf{K}$. Then, $w_i = p_{i+1} - p_i$ is the complex representation of the edge e_i with modulus a_i equal to the length of e_i and argument β_i equal to the angle that e_i, oriented in the counter-clockwise sense, makes with the u-axis. We also write c_i for the length of the perpendicular from the fixed point o in $\mathbf{K}$ to e_i, denote the affine line that contains e_i by $\mathbf{L}_i$ and denote by p_{ij} the point of intersection of $\mathbf{L}_i$ with $\mathbf{L}_j$.

We first observe that each of the six terms of $\tilde{m}_{\mathbf{K}}$ in (8.20) has a further decomposition into terms of the form

$$\frac{1}{192|\mathbf{K}|^3} \left| \frac{d(\varpi(\zeta))}{d\zeta} \right|^2 \int_{e_i} \left\{ \int_{e_j} 1_{\mathbf{K}}(z_3^*(\varpi(\zeta))) r_{12}^4 \, d\theta_{12} \right\} r_{01}^2 \, d\theta_{01}. \qquad (8.21)$$

The arguments in the proof of Theorem 8.7 show that only the $n(n-1)$ of these terms for which the two vertices z_1^* and z_2^* of the triangle (z_1^*, z_2^*, z_3^*) that lie on $\partial \mathbf{K}$ are on different edges, will be non-zero.

For each term (8.21) associated with (i, j), where $i \neq j$, we replace the polar coordinates (r_{01}, θ_{01}) at the fixed point o in $\mathbf{K}$ by Cartesian coordinates (u_1, v_1) at o with a positive v_1-axis parallel to the direction of e_i and replace the polar coordinates (r_{12}, θ_{12}) at z_1^* by Cartesian coordinates (u_2, v_2) at z_1^* with a positive v_2-axis in the direction of e_j. Then, u_1 is equal to the constant c_i, u_2 gives the length of the perpendicular from $z_1^* \in e_i$ onto e_j and (8.21) takes the form

$$\frac{c_i}{192|\mathbf{K}|^3} \left| \frac{\mathrm{d}(\varpi(\zeta))}{\mathrm{d}\zeta} \right|^2 \int_{e_i} \left\{ \int_{e_j} r_{12}^2 1_\mathbf{K}(z_3^*(\varpi(\zeta))) \, u_2 \, \mathrm{d}v_2 \right\} \mathrm{d}v_1. \tag{8.22}$$

Now, the point z_1^* along the oriented edge e_i may be represented by the complex coordinate $p_i + sw_i$ and z_2^* along e_j by $p_j + tw_j$, where s and t lie in the real interval $[0, 1]$. Then, the term (8.22) can be rewritten as

$$\chi_{ij}(\varpi(\zeta)) = \frac{c_i a_i a_j}{192|\mathbf{K}|^3} \left| \frac{\mathrm{d}(\varpi(\zeta))}{\mathrm{d}\zeta} \right|^2 \int \int_{\mathbf{K}^+(i, j, \varpi(\zeta))} f(s, t) \, g(s) \, \mathrm{d}s \, \mathrm{d}t, \tag{8.23}$$

where $f(s, t)$ is a quadratic polynomial giving the square of the distance from $z_1^* \in e_i$ to $z_2^* \in e_j$, $g(s)$ is a linear polymonial giving the length of the perpendicular from z_1^* to e_j and $\mathbf{K}^+(i, j, \varpi(\zeta))$ is the subset of the unit square in the (s, t)-plane associated with the requirement that $z_3^*(\varpi(\zeta))$ lie in $\mathbf{K}$.

For any given convex polygon $\mathbf{K}$, the set $\mathbf{K}^+(i, j, \varpi(\zeta))$ will play a central role in our description of the singularities of $\tilde{m}_\mathbf{K}(\zeta)$ in (8.20) as $\zeta = x + iy$ varies in $\mathbb{C} = \mathbb{R}^2$. The reason for its importance is that a necessary condition for ζ to be a singularity of $\tilde{m}_\mathbf{K}(\zeta)$ is that at least one of its summands in (8.20), and so one of the summands (8.23), should have a singularity at ζ. However, the Jacobian factor $\left| \frac{\mathrm{d}(\varpi(\zeta))}{\mathrm{d}\zeta} \right|^2$ in $\chi_{ij}(\varpi(\zeta))$ is a real analytic function of (x, y) away from the special shape points $\mp 1/\sqrt{3}$, the integrand is a real analytic function of (s, t) and we shall show that $\mathbf{K}^+(i, j, \varpi(\zeta))$ is the intersection with the unit square of a, possibly degenerate, polygon whose edges vary smoothly with (x, y). Hence, it will follow that *the contribution $\chi_{ij}(\varpi(\zeta))$ to $\tilde{m}_\mathbf{K}$ is singular at ζ if and only if the same can be said of the (s, t)-coordinates of the vertices of $\mathbf{K}^+(i, j, \varpi(\zeta))$.*

To understand how such singularities can occur, we choose $\zeta \in \mathbb{C}$ and i, j such that $1 \leqslant i \neq j \leqslant n$, and examine the nature of the set $\mathbf{K}^+(i, j, \zeta)$ and, in particular, how it varies with ζ. If we take the vertices z_1^* at $p_i + sw_i$ and z_2^* at $p_j + tw_j$, the triangle (z_1^*, z_2^*, z_3^*) with shape ζ will have its third vertex

$$z_3^* = \tfrac{1}{2} \left\{ (z_1^* + z_2^*) + \sqrt{3}\zeta(z_2^* - z_1^*) \right\}$$

at the point $\varphi_{ij}(\zeta)(s, t)$ given by

$$\varphi_{ij}(\zeta)(s, t) = \tfrac{1}{2}\{sw_i(1 - \sqrt{3}\zeta) + tw_j(1 + \sqrt{3}\zeta) \\ + p_i(1 - \sqrt{3}\zeta) + p_j(1 + \sqrt{3}\zeta)\}. \tag{8.24}$$

Clearly, in terms of real coordinates, $\varphi_{ij}(\zeta)$ is an affine transformation from the (s, t)-plane to the (u, v)-plane in which $\mathbf{K}$ lies, and the inverse image

$$\mathbf{K}_0^+(i, j, \zeta) = (\varphi_{ij}(\zeta))^{-1}(\mathbf{K})$$

of $\mathbf{K}$ under $\varphi_{ij}(\zeta)$ is the set of those (s, t)-values for which triangles (z_1^*, z_2^*, z_3^*) of shape ζ, with vertices z_1^* at $p_i + sw_i$ and z_2^* at $p_j + tw_j$, have their third vertex in **K**. Being affine, $\varphi_{ij}(\zeta)$ is defined for all s and t. However, we require z_1^* and z_2^* to lie on the chosen edges of **K**, not on their prolongations $\mathbf{L}_i$ and $\mathbf{L}_j$, so we have

$$\mathbf{K}^+(i, j, \zeta) = \mathbf{K}_0^+(i, j, \zeta) \cap [0, 1]^2.$$

The set $\mathbf{K}_0^+(i, j, \zeta)$ is a compact convex polygon in the (s, t)-plane with non-empty interior, provided the affine transformation $\varphi_{ij}(\zeta)$ is non-singular. However, $\varphi_{ij}(\zeta)$ is singular if and only if the quotient

$$\frac{(1 + \sqrt{3}\zeta)\, w_j}{(1 - \sqrt{3}\zeta)\, w_i}$$

is real or infinite, which, since a complex number is real if and only if its argument is an integral multiple of π, is if and only if either ζ is at one of the special shape points $\mp 1/\sqrt{3}$ or

$$\arg \frac{\zeta - 1/\sqrt{3}}{\zeta + 1/\sqrt{3}} = \arg \frac{w_j}{w_i} + l\pi,$$

where l is an integer. Since we already know that the special shape points $\mp 1/\sqrt{3}$ are singularities of $\tilde{m}_\mathbf{K}$, we shall not consider them further. The alternative condition corresponds to the angle subtended at ζ by the real segment $[-1/\sqrt{3}, 1/\sqrt{3}]$, that is, the angle at the third vertex z_3^* of a triangle (z_1^*, z_2^*, z_3^*) of shape ζ, differing by a multiple of π from the difference $\beta_j - \beta_i$ between the arguments of w_j and w_i. Taking e_i after e_j in the cyclic order around $\partial\mathbf{K}$, we choose the arguments of w_i and w_j such that $\beta_i > \beta_j$ and $0 < \beta_i - \beta_j < 2\pi$. Since $\beta_i \neq \beta_j$, the following cases arise.

(i) *The case that* $0 < \beta_i - \beta_j < \pi$. Then, $\pi + \beta_j - \beta_i$ is the angle subtended at p_{ij} by the initial points p_i and p_j of e_i and e_j, respectively, or, equally, by z_1^* and z_2^*, which lie on these edges (cf. Figure 8.4(a)). Since **K** is convex and the points at which this angle is subtended by z_1^* and z_2^* lie on the arc of the circle through z_1^*, z_2^* and p_{ij} on which p_{ij} lies between z_1^* and z_2^*, we see that, if a triangle of shape ζ has its third angle equal to $\pi + \beta_j - \beta_i$, then, for $\mathbf{K}_0^+(i, j, \zeta)$ to be non-empty, we must have $j = i - 1$ and so $p_{ij} = p_i$. We must also have $z_3^* = p_{ij}$ (cf. Figure 8.4(b)). In that case, $\mathbf{K}^+(i, j, \zeta)$ will be the linear segment joining the vertex $(0, 1)$ of the unit square with a point on one of its opposite sides, and the image of $\varphi_{i,i-1}(\zeta)$ will be an affine line meeting **K** only at p_i (cf. Figure 8.4(c)).

(ii) *The case that* $\beta_i - \beta_j = \pi$. Now, the set $\mathbf{K}^+(i, j, \zeta)$ is non-empty, and then it is the whole of $[0, 1]^2$, if and only if $\zeta \in (-1/\sqrt{3}, 1/\sqrt{3})$, as illustrated in Figure 8.5(a). In the latter case, since $\mathbf{K}^+(i, j, \zeta)$ has a non-empty interior and the image of $\varphi_{ij}(\zeta)$ is an affine line, that line must meet **K** in an affine segment. Then, $\mathbf{K}_0^+(i, j, \zeta)$ will be a strip in the (s, t)-plane and, for each ζ in the given range, it will strictly contain the unit square. It is also clear that the intersection

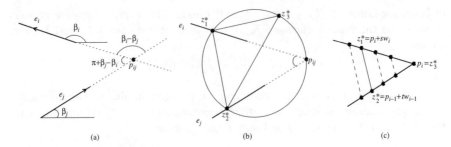

Figure 8.4 (a) All angles are measured anti-clockwise; (b) z_3^* is in **K** if and only if $j = i - 1$ and $z_3^* = p_{ij}$; (c) all triangles shown have the same shape; $s \to 0$ if and only if $t \to 1$

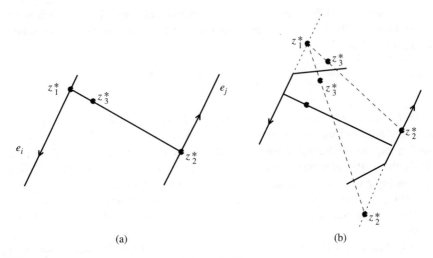

(a)   (b)

Figure 8.5 $s << 0$ requires $t << 0$ for z_3^* in **K**

of $\mathbf{K}_0^+(i, j, \zeta)$ with the second and fourth quadrants in the (s, t)-plane must be bounded (cf. Figure 8.5(b)).

(iii) *The case that $\pi < \beta_i - \beta_j < 2\pi$.* Then, the angle subtended at p_{ij} by z_1^* and z_2^* is $3\pi + \beta_j - \beta_i$, and similar results to those in the first case apply, except that now we require $i = n + j - 1$ (cf. Figures 8.6(a) and 8.6(b)).

In either of the above general cases, (i) or (iii), with the edges e_i and e_j no longer necessarily contiguous, let q_{ij} be any point concyclic with z_1^*, z_2^* and p_{ij} such that each of z_1^* and z_2^* lies between p_{ij} and q_{ij}. Then, the angle subtended at q_{ij} by z_1^* and z_2^* is $2\pi + \beta_j - \beta_i$ in each case (cf. Figures 8.7 and 8.8). Thus, if ζ is the shape of the triangle (z_1^*, z_2^*, z_3^*) with $z_3^* = q_{ij}$, then $\varphi_{ij}(\zeta)$ will be singular. Its image must be the affine line joining p_{ij} and q_{ij} since there are appropriate triangles of shape ζ arbitrarily close to the former point, so that $\mathbf{K}_0^+(i, j, \zeta)$ will be a strip in the (s, t)-plane that meets, but now need not contain, the unit square.

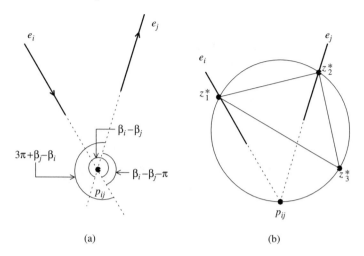

Figure 8.6 z_3^* is in **K** if and only if $i = j + n - 1$ and $z_3^* = p_{ij}$

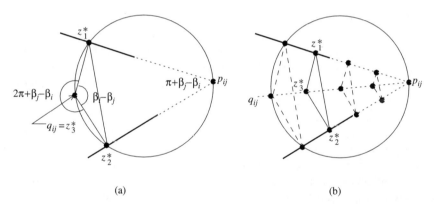

Figure 8.7   In (b) all the dashed triangles have the same shape as (z_1^*, z_2^*, z_3^*)

We now examine the boundary of $\mathbf{K}_0^+(i, j, \zeta)$. The convex polygon **K** is bounded by the n affine lines

$$\mathbf{L}_i = \{p_i + uw_i : u \in \mathbb{R}\}, \quad i = 1, \ldots, n,$$

and $\varphi_{ij}(\zeta)(s, t)$ lies on $\mathbf{L}_l$ if and only if $\{\varphi_{ij}(\zeta)(s, t) - p_l\}/w_l$ is real. That is, if and only if

$$u_{il}(\zeta)\, s + v_{jl}(\zeta)\, t + w_{ijl}(\zeta) = 0, \tag{8.25}$$

where

$$u_{il}(\zeta) = \Im\left(\frac{w_i(1 - \sqrt{3}\zeta)}{2w_l}\right), \quad v_{jl}(\zeta) = \Im\left(\frac{w_j(1 + \sqrt{3}\zeta)}{2w_l}\right)$$

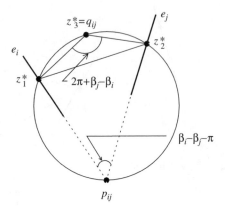

Figure 8.8

and

$$w_{ijl}(\zeta) = \Im\left(\frac{p_i(1 - \sqrt{3}\zeta) + p_j(1 + \sqrt{3}\zeta) - 2p_l}{2w_l}\right).$$

This is a line in the (s, t)-plane unless $u_{il}(\zeta) = 0 = v_{jl}(\zeta)$, and it is then empty unless $w_{ijl}(\zeta)$ is also zero, in which case it is the entire (s, t)-plane. However, the last case can only occur if $\varphi_{ij}(\zeta)$ is singular and $\varphi_{ij}(\zeta)(\mathbb{R}^2) = \mathbf{L}_l$, and the above analysis of the singular $\varphi_{ij}(\zeta)$ shows that this cannot occur.

Thus, in all cases, the inverse image $\varphi_{ij}(\zeta)^{-1}(\mathbf{L}_l)$ is either empty or an affine line whose coordinates are smooth, indeed linear, functions of ζ and it follows that $\mathbf{K}_0^+(i, j, \varpi(\zeta))$ varies smoothly with ζ. Hence, the domain of integration $\mathbf{K}^+(i, j, \varpi(\zeta))$ of $\chi_{ij}(\varpi(\zeta))$ will also be a smooth function of ζ at ζ_0, except that a continuous but non-smooth variation of the domain may be caused by a vertex of $\mathbf{K}_0^+(i, j, \varpi(\zeta_0))$ on an edge of $[0, 1]^2$ or a vertex of $[0, 1]^2$ on an edge of $\mathbf{K}_0^+(i, j, \varpi(\zeta_0))$, moving off in different directions as ζ varies and so giving rise to differently shaped domains $\mathbf{K}^+(i, j, \varpi(\zeta))$. It is also conceivable, when $\varphi_{ij}(\varpi(\zeta_0))$ is singular and so $\mathbf{K}_0^+(i, j, \varpi(\zeta_0))$ is a line or a strip, that there are points ζ arbitrarily close to ζ_0 with $\mathbf{K}_0^+(i, j, \varpi(\zeta))$ having a vertex on $[0, 1]^2$, which again could give rise to a singularity of $\chi_{ij}(\varpi(\zeta))$ at ζ_0. However, then all the non-empty inverse images of the bounding lines $\mathbf{L}_l$ are parallel since the image $\varphi_{ij}(\varpi(\zeta))(\mathbb{R}^2)$ cannot coincide with any of them. They are also distinct unless $\varphi_{ij}(\varpi(\zeta))(\mathbb{R}^2)$ meets a vertex of $\mathbf{K}$, which, since then two of them coincide, corresponds to case (i) or (iii) above when $\mathbf{K}_0^+(i, j, \varpi(\zeta_0))$ is a line meeting a vertex of $[0, 1]^2$. Otherwise, when all the inverse images of $\mathbf{L}_l$ are parallel and distinct, for ζ sufficiently close to ζ_0 the vertices of $\mathbf{K}_0^+(i, j, \varpi(\zeta))$ will be far away from the origin and certainly not on the boundary of $[0, 1]^2$. Thus, we are led to the following definition.

Definition 8.1. $\mathbf{K}_0^+(i, j, \zeta)$ is said to be in general position with respect to $[0, 1]^2$, when both of the following conditions hold:

(i) no vertex of $[0, 1]^2$ lies on an edge of $\mathbf{K}_0^+(i, j, \varpi(\zeta))$,
(ii) no vertex of $\mathbf{K}_0^+(i, j, \varpi(\zeta))$ lies on an edge of $[0, 1]^2$.

We show next that general position is equivalent to non-singularity of the corresponding contribution to $\tilde{m}_{\mathbf{K}}$.

Lemma 8.1. *The integral* $\chi_{ij}(\varpi(\zeta))$ *is non-singular at* ζ_0 *if and only if* $\mathbf{K}_0^+(i, j, \varpi(\zeta_0))$ *is in general position with respect to* $[0, 1]^2$.

Proof. The discussion motivating the definition has already shown that general position is a sufficient condition for $\chi_{ij}(\varpi(\zeta))$ to be non-singular at ζ_0 when $\mathbf{K}^+(i, j, \varpi(\zeta_0))$ is non-empty. However, if $\mathbf{K}_0^+(i, j, \varpi(\zeta))$ is in general position because it fails to meet $[0, 1]^2$, then, by continuity, this remains the case on some neighbourhood of ζ and so no singularity can be introduced.

To establish the converse, that $\chi_{ij}(\varpi(\zeta))$ is singular at ζ_0 if $\mathbf{K}_0^+(i, j, \varpi(\zeta_0))$ fails to be in general position, we need to study the movement of the vertices of $\mathbf{K}_0^+(i, j, \varpi(\zeta))$ as ζ varies. Now, $\varphi_{ij}(\varpi(\zeta))(s, t)$ is the vertex p_l of $\mathbf{K}$ if and only if there is a triangle (z_1^*, z_2^*, z_3^*) of shape $\varpi(\zeta)$ with z_1^* at $p_i + sw_i$, z_2^* at $p_j + tw_j$ and z_3^* at p_l. This occurs if and only if there is a triangle $(\tilde{z}_1^*, \tilde{z}_2^*, \tilde{z}_3^*)$ of shape $\varsigma(\varpi(\zeta))$ with $\tilde{z}_1^*$ at p_l, $\tilde{z}_2^*$ at $p_i + sw_i$ and $\tilde{z}_3^*$ at $p_j + tw_j$, where, for fixed i, j and l, we regard s and t as functions of ζ. Then, by (8.25), we have

$$v_{ij}(\varsigma(\varpi(\zeta)))\, s(\zeta) + w_{lij}(\varsigma(\varpi(\zeta))) = 0$$

and so the first coordinate $s(\zeta)$ of $\varphi_{ij}(\varpi(\zeta))^{-1}(p_l)$ is the quotient of two real harmonic functions of (x, y), the imaginary parts of complex analytic functions of ζ. Non-constant harmonic functions are open mappings and so the mapping $\zeta \mapsto s(\zeta)$ is also open unless it is constant. However, then the two complex analytic functions

$$\frac{w_i\{1 + \sqrt{3}\varsigma(\varpi(\zeta))\}}{2w_j}$$

and

$$\frac{p_l\{1 - \sqrt{3}\varsigma(\varpi(\zeta))\} + p_i\{1 + \sqrt{3}\varsigma(\varpi(\zeta))\} - 2p_j}{2w_j}$$

would have the same imaginary part for all ζ and so themselves would differ by a real constant independent of ζ. However, this is easily seen to be impossible. Similarly, for the second coordinate $t(\zeta)$ of $\varphi_{ij}(\varpi(\zeta))^{-1}(p_l)$, we find

$$u_{ji}(\varsigma^2(\varpi(\zeta)))\, t(\zeta) + w_{jli}(\varsigma^2(\varpi(\zeta))) = 0$$

and, again, $\zeta \mapsto t(\zeta)$ is an open mapping.

It follows that $\zeta \mapsto \varphi_{ij}(\varpi(\zeta))^{-1}(p_l)$ is also an open mapping unless there is a constant c such that $s(\zeta) = ct(\zeta)$. Then, since we have already excluded the possibility that $s(\zeta) \equiv 0, 1$ or $t(\zeta) \equiv 0, 1$, the locus of inverse images of p_l is a line transverse to the boundary of the unit square. Thus, in all cases, when a vertex of $\mathbf{K}_0^+(i, j, \varpi(\zeta_0))$ lies on the boundary of the unit square, there are, arbitrarily close to ζ_0, both ζ for which the corresponding vertex of $\mathbf{K}_0^+(i, j, \varpi(\zeta))$ lies outside the unit square and ζ for which that vertex lies inside the square. Thus, we do indeed get a singularity of $\chi_{ij}(\varpi(\zeta))$ at ζ_0 when a vertex of $\mathbf{K}_0^+(i, j, \varpi(\zeta_0))$ lies on the boundary of the unit square, and similar arguments show that such a singularity also arises when a vertex $[0, 1]^2$ lies on an edge of $\mathbf{K}_0^+(i, j, \varpi(\zeta_0))$.   ∎

Rather than specifying when a certain $\mathbf{K}_0^+(i, j, \zeta)$ is in general position, we shall characterise, both algebraically and geometrically, the set of points ζ for which there exist i, j and ϖ such that $\mathbf{K}_0^+(i, j, \varpi(\zeta))$ fails to be in general position. That set will turn out to be a tessellation of the ζ-plane by segments of lines and arcs of circles. So, in view of Lemma 8.1, we make the following definition.

Definition 8.2. The set $\mathcal{J}(\mathbf{K})$ of points ζ at which there exist $1 \leqslant i \neq j \leqslant n$ and $\varpi \in \Omega$ such that the contribution $\chi_{ij}(\varpi(\zeta))$ to $\tilde{m}_{\mathbf{K}}$ is not smooth at ζ is called the singular tessellation of $\tilde{m}_{\mathbf{K}}$.

Clearly, it is necessary for ζ to be in $\mathcal{J}(\mathbf{K})$ for it to be a singularity of $\tilde{m}_{\mathbf{K}}$. However, after the full analysis of the relevant contributions to $\tilde{m}_{\mathbf{K}}$ in the next section, it will be clear that they do not cancel each other's singularities, so that this necessary condition is also a sufficient condition.

To describe $\mathcal{J}(\mathbf{K})$ we first note that Equation (8.25) implies that there is a triangle (z_1^*, z_2^*, z_3^*) of shape ζ with its first vertex z_1^* at the vertex p_i of $\mathbf{K}$, z_2^* at p_j and z_3^* on the extended edge $\mathbf{L}_l$ if and only if $w_{ijl}(\zeta) = 0$. Thus, if we write $\tilde{e}_{ijl}$ for the lth edge of the polygon in the ζ-plane bounded by the n lines

$$w_{ijl}(\zeta) = 0, \quad 1 \leqslant l \leqslant n,$$

and write

$$\tilde{e}_{ijl}^{\varpi} = \{\zeta : \varpi(\zeta) \in \tilde{e}_{ijl}\},$$

then the union of the $\tilde{e}_{ijl}$, $1 \leqslant l \leqslant n$, forms a copy of $\partial\mathbf{K}$, shifted, rotated and rescaled so that the ith and jth vertices are located at the special shape points $\mp 1/\sqrt{3}$, respectively, and, similarly, the union of all the $\tilde{e}_{ijl}^{\varpi}$ forms its inverse image under ϖ, which we shall denote by $\partial\tilde{\mathbf{K}}_{ij}^{\varpi}$.

Theorem 8.9. *The singular tessellation* $\mathcal{J}(\mathbf{K})$ *of* $\tilde{m}_{\mathbf{K}}$ *is*

$$\mathcal{J}(\mathbf{K}) = \bigcup \{\tilde{e}_{ijl}^{\varpi} : \varpi \in \{1, \varsigma, \varsigma^2\}, \quad 1 \leqslant i, j, l \leqslant n \quad and \quad i \neq j\}$$
$$= \bigcup \{\partial \tilde{\mathbf{K}}_{ij}^{\varpi} : \varpi \in \{1, \varsigma, \varsigma^2\}, \quad 1 \leqslant i, j \leqslant n \quad and \quad i \neq j\}.$$

Proof.   The failure of condition (i) in the definition of general position is equivalent to the existence of a triangle (z_1^*, z_2^*, z_3^*) of shape $\varpi(\zeta)$ with each of z_1^* and z_2^* at an extremity of the edge of $\mathbf{K}$ on which it lies and with z_3^* also on an edge of $\mathbf{K}$. Similarly, the failure of condition (ii) is equivalent to there being a triangle (z_1^*, z_2^*, z_3^*) of shape $\varpi(\zeta)$ with z_3^* at a vertex of $\mathbf{K}$ and with one of z_1^* and z_2^* at an extremity of the edge, e_i or e_j, respectively, on which it lies. Thus, given ϖ and ζ, the polygon $\mathbf{K}_0^+(i, j, \varpi(\zeta))$ fails to be in general position for some i and j when there exists a triangle of shape $\varpi(\zeta)$ with its vertices on $\partial \mathbf{K}$ and at least two of them coinciding with the vertices of $\mathbf{K}$ itself. However, that occurs if and only if there is a triangle Δ of shape ζ with the same property. Then, either Δ

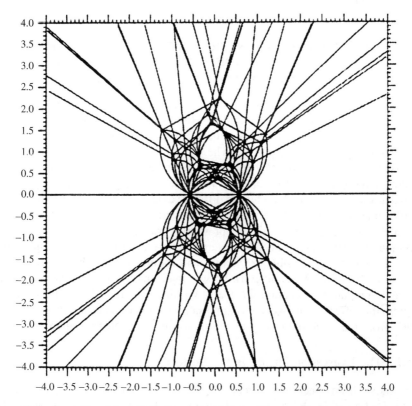

Figure 8.9   Reproduced from D.G. Kendall and H. Le, The structure and explicit determination of convex-polygonally generated shape-densities, *Advances in Applied Probability* **19** (1987), 896–916, by permission of the Applied Probability Trust

itself, $\varsigma(\Delta)$ or $\varsigma^2(\Delta)$ has its first two vertices coinciding with vertices of $\mathbf{K}$ and so ζ lies on $\tilde{e}_{ijl}$, $\tilde{e}_{ijl}^{\varsigma}$ or $\tilde{e}_{ijl}^{\varsigma^2}$, for an appropriate choice of i, j and l in each case. Taking the union over all possible i, j and l, and observing that the two vertices common to the triangle and to $\mathbf{K}$ cannot coincide, since we are excluding the special shape points, we obtain the stated results.   ∎

Figure 8.9 shows the singular tessellation $\mathcal{J}(\mathbf{K})$ for the case when $\mathbf{K}$ is a certain irregular pentagon.

When we come to discuss the differential order rather than the position of the singularities, the subset $\mathcal{J}_0(\mathbf{K})$ of $\mathcal{J}(\mathbf{K})$, consisting of those points at which $\psi_{ij}(\varpi(\zeta))$ is singular for some triple (i, j, ϖ), will be important. This subset is given by

$$\mathcal{J}_0(\mathbf{K}) = \{\tilde{e}_{i-1,i,i}^{\varpi}, \tilde{e}_{i,i+1,i-1}^{\varpi} : \varpi \in \Omega, \quad 1 \leqslant i \leqslant n\} \tag{8.26}$$

and consists of some half lines in the ζ-plane with finite endpoints at one of the special points $\mp 1/\sqrt{3}$ and some circular arcs with endpoints at both of the special points.

8.8 THE SHAPE-MEASURE ON Σ_2^3 INDUCED BY THREE LABELLED iid UNIFORM DISTRIBUTIONS IN A CONVEX POLYGON. II: THE EXPLICIT FORMULA

We close this chapter with a description of a so-called *stepping-stone* method to obtain an explicit formula for the Radon–Nikodým derivative (8.17) of the shape-measure of random triangles whose labelled vertices are iid uniformly distributed in a compact convex polygon $\mathbf{K}$. The reason for introducing this method of description is that, as we saw in the previous section, the singularities of the Radon–Nikodým derivative of this shape-measure split the whole space into irregular tiles on which it has entirely different expressions. Moreover, the number of tiles increases rapidly with the number of vertices of $\mathbf{K}$ and the change in the singular tessellation is generally abrupt when $\mathbf{K}$ changes, so that it is prohibitively laborious to work out the shape-measure in every tile from first principles for a given $\mathbf{K}$, and it is impossible to get a general formula for the shape-measure that is suitable for all convex polygons. So, we shall first identify a 'basic' reference tile and compute the function $\tilde{m}_{\mathbf{K}}$ there. We then find the 'jump functions' that express the difference between its expression on pairs of ajacent tiles and, finally, 'step' from the basic tile to any given tile to find its expression there.

8.8.1 The Expression for $\tilde{m}_{\mathbf{K}}$ in the Basic Tile

We know from Section 8.6 that $\tilde{m}_{\mathbf{K}}$ is a constant on the real segment $[-1/\sqrt{3}, 1/\sqrt{3}]$ of the ζ-plane, which we shall call *the basic segment*. The argument there also implies that, when ζ is on this segment, $\mathbf{K}^+(i, j, \zeta)$ and $\mathbf{K}^+(i, j, \tau(\zeta))$ are $[0, 1]^2$ for all $i \neq j$ and the polygons $\mathbf{K}^+$ corresponding to the other relabelling transformations are all void or degenerate. Hence, the constant value $c_{\mathbf{K}}$ of $\tilde{m}_{\mathbf{K}}$ on the basic segment can be expressed as

$$c_{\mathbf{K}} = \frac{1}{96|\mathbf{K}|^3} \sum_{i \neq j} c_i a_i a_j \int_0^1 \int_0^1 f(s,t) g(s) \, ds \, dt.$$

To describe our stepping-stone method we need at least to find the expression for $\tilde{m}_{\mathbf{K}}$ in one of the tiles of the singular tessellation. To do so, we note that it is a property of the singular tessellation that the basic segment is always an edge of exactly two tiles and that these tiles are congruent triangles. Since $\tilde{m}_{\mathbf{K}}$ is real-analytic in each tile, we are able to obtain its expression in these two tiles by examining it at any ζ sufficiently close to the basic segment and, since the relabelling operation τ yields the symmetry $\tilde{m}_{\mathbf{K}}(\zeta) = \tilde{m}_{\mathbf{K}}(-\zeta)$, it will be enough for us to consider the expression for $\tilde{m}_{\mathbf{K}}$ in the one, of these two tiles, that lies in the upper half-plane. In all that follows this tile will be called *the basic tile*.

Looking from within $\mathbf{K}$, it is clear that, if e_i and e_j are neither contiguous nor have a single edge of $\mathbf{K}$ between them, then, for ζ sufficiently close to the basic segment, $\mathbf{K}^+(i, j, \varpi(\zeta))$ remains as it was for ζ in the basic segment and so $\chi_{ij}(\varpi(\zeta))$ will remain constant. This will be the case until the choice of ζ forces the third vertex to lie on $\partial \mathbf{K}$, necessarily for (s, t) at one corner of $[0, 1]^2$, or the third vertex to coincide with a vertex of $\mathbf{K}$, for (s, t) at some point of $\partial([0, 1]^2)$. Thus, each such summand $\chi_{ij}(\varpi(\zeta))$ remains constant until ζ meets the appropriate edge of $\mathcal{J}(\mathbf{K})$, where $\mathbf{K}_0^+(i, j, \varpi(\zeta))$ fails to be in general position. So, these summands certainly remain constant throughout the basic tile.

On the other hand, when $j = i - 2$, as ζ moves away from the basic segment into upper half-plane, the set $\mathbf{K}^+(i, j, \zeta)$ loses an increasing triangular area near the $(0, 1)$-corner. However, $\mathbf{K}^+(i, j, \tau(\zeta))$ remains equal to $[0, 1]^2$ and, for $\varpi \in \Omega$, $\varpi \neq 1, \tau$, the set $\mathbf{K}^+(i, j, \varpi(\zeta))$ remains empty. When $j = i - 1$, $\mathbf{K}^+(i, j, \zeta)$ loses two increasing congruent triangular areas containing the $(0,0)$-corner and $(1,1)$-corner, respectively. Again, $\mathbf{K}^+(i, j, \tau(\zeta))$ remains equal to $[0, 1]^2$ and, for $\varpi = \varsigma, \varsigma^2$, $\mathbf{K}^+(i, j, \varpi(\zeta))$ remains empty. However, in this case, both the previously empty sets $\mathbf{K}^+(i, j, \varsigma\tau(\zeta))$ and $\mathbf{K}^+(i, j, \varsigma^2\tau(\zeta))$ begin to grow out from the $(0,1)$-corner that maps to the common vertex. Similar results hold when $j = i + 1, i + 2$, except that then the roles of ζ and $\tau(\zeta)$ are interchanged. This discussion shows that $\tilde{m}_{\mathbf{K}}$ can be expressed in the basic tile as

$$\tilde{m}_{\mathbf{K}}(\zeta) = \tilde{m}_{\mathbf{K}}^{(1)}(\zeta) + \tilde{m}_{\mathbf{K}}^{(2)}(\tau(\zeta)),$$

where

$$\tilde{m}_{\mathbf{K}}^{(1)}(\zeta) = \frac{1}{2} c_{\mathbf{K}} + \frac{1}{192|\mathbf{K}|^3} \sum_{i=1}^{n} c_i a_i \left\{ - \sum_{j=i-2, i-1} a_j \int \int_{\mathbf{K}_c^+(i,j,\zeta)} f(s,t) \, g(s) \, ds \, dt \right.$$

$$+ a_{i+1} \sum_{\varpi = \varsigma, \varsigma^2} \left| \frac{d(\varpi(\zeta))}{d\zeta} \right|^2 \int \int_{\mathbf{K}^+(i,i+1,\varpi(\zeta))} f(s,t) \, g(s) \, ds \, dt \right\},$$

$$\tilde{m}_{\mathbf{K}}^{(2)}(\zeta) = \frac{1}{2}c_{\mathbf{K}} + \frac{1}{192|\mathbf{K}|^3}\sum_{i=1}^{n} c_i a_i \left\{ -\sum_{j=i+1,i+2} a_j \int\int_{\mathbf{K}_c^+(i,j,\zeta)} f(s,t)g(s)\,ds\,dt \right.$$

$$\left. +a_{i-1}\sum_{\varpi=\varsigma,\varsigma^2} \left| \frac{d(\varpi(\zeta))}{d\zeta} \right|^2 \int\int_{\mathbf{K}^+(i,i-1,\varpi(\zeta))} f(s,t)g(s)\,ds\,dt \right\}$$

and $\mathbf{K}_c^+$ denotes the complement of $\mathbf{K}^+$ in $[0,1]^2$.

Clearly, for each fixed i there are eight non-constant contributions to $\tilde{m}_{\mathbf{K}}(\zeta)$ associated with $z_1^* \in e_i$. However, the non-constant contributions to $\tilde{m}_{\mathbf{K}}(\zeta)$ in the expression for $\tilde{m}_{\mathbf{K}}^{(2)}(\tau(\zeta))$ may be found directly from appropriate ones in $\tilde{m}_{\mathbf{K}}^{(1)}(\zeta)$. For example, the resultant expression for

$$c_i a_i a_{i+1} \int\int_{\mathbf{K}_c^+(i,i+1,\tau(\zeta))} f(s,t)g(s)\,ds\,dt$$

may be found from that for

$$c_{i+1} a_{i+1} a_i \int\int_{\mathbf{K}^+(i+1,i,\zeta)} f(s,t)g(s)\,ds\,dt$$

by substituting i for $i+1$, $i+1$ for i and $\tau(\zeta)$ for ζ. The analysis summarised above also tells us that the domains of the corresponding $\mathbf{K}^+$ are determined by the intersection with the unit square of at most two bounding lines of $\mathbf{K}_0^+$. After some computation, with these comments kept in mind, we get the following result.

Theorem 8.10. *The expression for $\tilde{m}_{\mathbf{K}}$ in the basic tile is given by*

$$c_{\mathbf{K}} + \frac{1}{192|\mathbf{K}|^3}\sum_{i=1}^{n} c_i \{ -\sin(\beta_{i+1}-\beta_{i-1})F_i(\zeta) + \sin(\beta_{i-1}-\beta_{i-2})F_{i-1}(\zeta)$$

$$+ \sin(\beta_{i+2}-\beta_{i+1})F_{i+1}(\zeta) \},$$

where

$$F_i(\zeta) = -\frac{a_i^5}{15}G_i(\zeta)G_{i+1}(-\bar{\zeta})\{6 + 4[\cos(\beta_i-\beta_{i-1})G_i(\zeta)$$

$$+ \cos(\beta_{i+1}-\beta_i)G_{i+1}(-\bar{\zeta})] + G_i(\zeta)^2$$

$$+ \cos(\beta_{i+1}-\beta_{i-1})G_i(\zeta)G_{i+1}(-\bar{\zeta}) + G_{i+1}(-\bar{\zeta})^2\}$$

and where

$$G_i(\zeta) = \frac{\sqrt{3}\,y}{(1+\sqrt{3}x)\sin(\beta_i-\beta_{i-1}) - \sqrt{3}\,y\cos(\beta_i-\beta_{i-1})}.$$

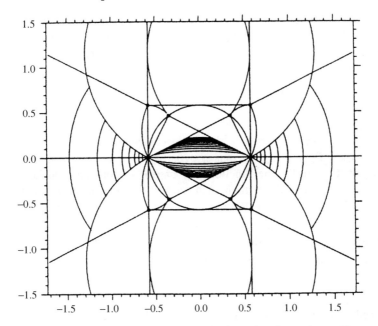

Figure 8.10 Reproduced from H. Le, Explicit formulae for polygonally generated shape-densities in the basic tile, *Mathematical Proceedings of the Cambridge Philosophical Society*, **101** (1987), 313–21 by permission of Cambridge University Press

In Figure 8.10 we show the singular tessellation for **K** being a rectangle, in which the contours for $\tilde{m}_\mathbf{K}$ are drawn on the basic tile and its five equivalents.

8.8.2 The Jump-Functions

The jump-functions for $\tilde{m}_\mathbf{K}$ that we shall give will be defined, one on a neighbourhood of each open edge of the singular tessellation $\mathcal{J}(\mathbf{K})$, and will link the local forms of $\tilde{m}_\mathbf{K}$ in the two tiles that lie either side of that edge. The 'primary' edges $\tilde{e}_{ijl}^\varpi$ of $\mathcal{J}(\mathbf{K})$ can overlap one another, but we shall need to distinguish them in order to describe the jump-functions. Thus, if the intersection of $\tilde{e}_{i_1j_1l_1}^{\varpi_1}$ and $\tilde{e}_{i_2j_2l_2}^{\varpi_2}$ is an arc γ of positive length, when we discuss the jump of $\tilde{m}_\mathbf{K}$ with respect to $\tilde{e}_{i_1j_1l_1}^{\varpi_1} \bigcap \gamma$, we temporarily ignore the jump of $\tilde{m}_\mathbf{K}$ arising from $\tilde{e}_{i_2j_2l_2}^{\varpi_2} \bigcap \gamma$.

When identifying the singular tessellation in Theorem 8.9, each edge $\tilde{e}_{ijl}^\varpi$ accounted for several summands of $\tilde{m}_\mathbf{K}$. We now need to make that correspondence precise. To that end we recall that a point ζ_0 lies on the open edge $\overset{\circ}{e}_{ijl} = \tilde{e}_{ijl} \setminus \{\text{end points}\}$ if and only if there is a triangle (z_1^*, z_2^*, z_3^*) of shape ζ_0 with z_1^* at p_i, z_2^* at p_j and z_3^* in the interior of e_l. That will cause $\mathbf{K}_0^+(l_1, l_2, \zeta_0)$ not to be in general position, and so $\chi_{l_1l_2}(\zeta_0)$ to be singular, whenever

$$(l_1, l_2) = (i, j), (i-1, j), (i, j-1) \text{ or } (i-1, j-1).$$

However, since, for each $\varpi \in \Omega$, the triangle (z_1^*, z_2^*, z_3^*) may also be regarded as a triangle of shape $\varpi(\zeta_0)$ with $z_{\varpi(1)}^*$ at p_i, $z_{\varpi(2)}^*$ at p_j and $z_{\varpi(3)}^*$ in the interior of e_l, we see that the full set of summands of $\tilde{m}_K$ that are singular at ζ_0 on account of ζ_0 lying on $\mathring{e}_{ijl}$, is

$$\{\chi_{l_1l_2}(\varpi(\zeta_0)) : \varpi \in \Omega; (l_1, l_2) = \pi_{12}(\varpi(i', j', l)); i' = i, i-1; j' = j, j-1\},$$
(8.27)

where $\pi_{12} : \mathbb{N} \times \mathbb{N} \times \mathbb{N} \mapsto \mathbb{N} \times \mathbb{N}$ is the projection on the first two factors.

Suppose now that a part of $\tilde{e}_{ijl}^{\varpi_0} \in \mathcal{J}(\mathbf{K})$ contributes to the boundary γ that separates tiles $\mathbf{T}_1$ and $\mathbf{T}_2$, so that $w_{ijl}(\varpi_0(\zeta)) = 0$ on γ. Then, for ζ in the interiors of $\mathbf{T}_1$ and $\mathbf{T}_2$, the function $w_{ijl}(\varpi_0(\zeta))$ is non-zero and has different signs that are constant throughout each set. Let the sum of all the contributions (8.27) to $\tilde{m}_K$ be $\hat{f}_1$ in the tile $\mathbf{T}_1$, where $w_{ijl}(\varpi_0(\zeta)) \leqslant 0$, and be $\hat{f}_2$ in the tile $\mathbf{T}_2$, where $w_{ijl}(\varpi_0(\zeta)) \geqslant 0$. Then each of $\hat{f}_1$ and $\hat{f}_2$ can be continued as real-analytic functions into a two-dimensional neighbourhood $\mathbf{N}_{ijl}$ of the open arc $\mathring{\gamma}$. If these continuations are called $\hat{f}_1^*$ and $\hat{f}_2^*$, then

$$J_{ijl}^{\varpi_0}(\zeta) = \hat{f}_2^*(\zeta) - \hat{f}_1^*(\zeta)$$

is defined to be the jump-function for $\tilde{m}_K$ with respect to $\tilde{e}_{ijl}^{\varpi_0}$. Then, if γ is the intersection of $\tilde{e}_{i_b,j_b,l_b}^{\varpi_b}$, $1 \leqslant b \leqslant b_0$, the total jump of $\tilde{m}_K$ along γ will be given, on the intersection $\mathbf{N}_\gamma$ of the neighbourhoods $\mathbf{N}_{i_b,j_b,l_b}^{\varpi_b}$, by the composite jump-function:

$$J_\gamma(\zeta) = \sum_{b=1}^{b_0} \text{sign}(w_{i_b,j_b,l_b}(\varpi_b(\zeta))) J_{i_b,j_b,l_b}^{\varpi_b}(\zeta),$$

where $\text{sign}(t)$ is the function that is 1 if $t > 0$, -1 if $t < 0$, and 0 if $t = 0$.

Thus, once we know either one of $f_1 = \tilde{m}_K|_{\mathbf{T}_1}$ or $f_2 = \tilde{m}_K|_{\mathbf{T}_2}$, say, f_1, we are able to construct the other, f_2, in $\mathbf{N}_\gamma \bigcap \mathbf{T}_2$ by adding the *total* jump-function of $\tilde{m}_K$ along $\mathring{\gamma}$ to the continuation f_1^* of f_1: that is, we have

$$f_2(\zeta) = f_1^*(\zeta) + J_\gamma(\zeta)$$

in $\mathbf{N}_\gamma \bigcap \mathbf{T}_2$. Then, since each of the summands of $\tilde{m}_K$ has a unique expression in the interior of each tile, the expression found for J_γ in $\mathbf{N}_\gamma$ remains valid for its analytic continuation throughout $\mathbf{T}_1 \bigcup \mathbf{T}_2$. Hence, the expression we found for f_2 in $\mathbf{N}_\gamma \bigcap \mathbf{T}_2$ actually remains valid throughout $\mathbf{T}_2$.

The structure of the tessellation also shows that the jump-functions for $\tilde{m}_K$ with respect to $\tilde{e}_{ijl}^\varsigma$ and $\tilde{e}_{ijl}^{\varsigma^2}$ can be deduced from the jump-functions for $\tilde{m}_K$ with respect to the segments $\tilde{e}_{ijl}^1 = \tilde{e}_{ijl}$ by making use of the transformation operators ς and ς^2 and applying the appropriate absolute Jacobian factors to allow for the difference between the complex differentials $d\zeta$ and $d(\varpi(\zeta))$. Hence, in what follows it is sufficient to find the jump-function for $\tilde{m}_K$ with respect to each segment $\tilde{e}_{ijl}$.

The set (8.27) of contributions to $\tilde{m}_{\mathbf{K}}$ that are singular along $\tilde{e}_{ijl}$ is composed of two distinct subsets. First, there is the subset, in which $\varpi = 1$ or τ, corresponding to the polygons $\mathbf{K}_0^+(l_1, l_2, \zeta)$ and $\mathbf{K}_0^+(l_1, l_2, \tau(\zeta))$ that fail to satisfy condition (i) when ζ lies on $\tilde{e}_{ijl}$. For each such polygon it is its lth edge that contains a vertex of $[0, 1]^2$ and so breaks the analyticity of the associated integral terms. Then, there is the complementary subset of eight summands corresponding to the set of polygons that fail to satisfy condition (ii) on $\tilde{e}_{ijl}$. In this case, one of the suffices (l_1, l_2) is equal to l and it is the other suffix that determines the vertex of the appropriate polygon that lies on an edge of $[0, 1]^2$ and so accounts for the lack of analyticity of the corresponding summand of $\tilde{m}_{\mathbf{K}}$. In this second subset, ϖ takes the values $\varsigma, \varsigma^2, \tau\varsigma$ or $\tau\varsigma^2$. The terms in the jump-function corresponding to the four members of the first subset that involve the same value of ϖ are all very similar and depend only on the choice of the suffixes (l_1, l_2), and the same is true for each pair of members of the second subset that involve the same value of ϖ. In addition, for a given choice of (l_1, l_2), the term corresponding to $\tau(\varpi)$ is directly deducible from that corresponding to ϖ in a similar manner to that described in the computation for the formula for $\tilde{m}_{\mathbf{K}}$ in the basic tile. Thus, it is sufficient to carry out the explicit computation only in the following three special cases.

(i) The lth edge of $\mathbf{K}_0^+(i, j, \zeta)$ passes through $(0, 0)$ in the (s, t)-plane when ζ is on $\tilde{e}_{ijl}$. Therefore, the change in the type of shape of $\mathbf{K}^+(i, j, \zeta)$ is associated with the inequalities

$$u_{il}(\zeta)\, s + v_{jl}(\zeta)\, t + w_{ijl}(\zeta) \geqslant 0$$

and $s, t \geqslant 0$. It follows that the integral formula for the associated jump term is

$$\frac{1}{192|\mathbf{K}|^3} c_i a_i a_j \int_0^{s_0} ds \int_0^{t_0} f(s, t)\, g(s)\, dt,$$

where

$$s_0 = -\frac{w_{ijl}(\zeta)}{u_{il}(\zeta)} \quad \text{and} \quad t_0 = -\frac{w_{ijl}(\zeta) + u_{il}(\zeta)\, s}{v_{jl}(\zeta)}.$$

(ii) The jth vertex of $\mathbf{K}_0^+(l, i, \varsigma(\zeta))$ lies on the edge $t = 0$ of $[0, 1]^2$ when ζ is on $\tilde{e}_{ijl}$. Therefore, the change in the type of shape of $\mathbf{K}^+(l, i, \varsigma(\zeta))$ is associated with the inequalities

$$-\frac{a_l}{a_{j-1}} \left| \frac{2}{1 + \sqrt{3}\zeta} \right|^2 v_{j-1,l}(\zeta)\, s + v_{i,j-1}(\varsigma(\zeta))\, t + w_{l,i,j-1}(\varsigma(\zeta)) \geqslant 0,$$

$$-\frac{a_l}{a_j} \left| \frac{2}{1 + \sqrt{3}\zeta} \right|^2 v_{jl}(\zeta)\, s + v_{ij}(\varsigma(\zeta))\, t + w_{lij}(\varsigma(\zeta)) \geqslant 0$$

and $t \geqslant 0$, where we have used the relation

$$a_j \left| \frac{1 + \sqrt{3}\zeta}{2} \right|^2 u_{lj}(\varsigma(\zeta)) = -a_l v_{jl}(\zeta).$$

Because the t-coordinate of the jth vertex of $\mathbf{K}_0^+(l, i, \varsigma(\zeta))$ is $u_{il}(\zeta)\, t_0 = -w_{ijl}(\zeta)$, it follows that the integral formula for the associated jump term is

$$\frac{1}{192|\mathbf{K}|^3} c_l a_l a_i \left| \frac{2}{1+\sqrt{3}\zeta} \right|^4 \int_0^{t_0} dt \int_{s_1}^{s_2} f(s, t)\, g(s)\, ds,$$

where

$$t_0 = -\frac{w_{ijl}(\zeta)}{u_{il}(\zeta)},$$

$$s_1 = 1 + \frac{a_{j-1}}{a_l} \left| \frac{1+\sqrt{3}\zeta}{2} \right|^2 \frac{w_{l+1,i,j-1}(\varsigma(\zeta)) + v_{i,j-1}(\varsigma(\zeta))\, t}{v_{j-1,l}(\zeta)},$$

and

$$s_2 = 1 + \frac{a_j}{a_l} \left| \frac{1+\sqrt{3}\zeta}{2} \right|^2 \frac{w_{l+1,i,j}(\varsigma(\zeta)) + v_{ij}(\varsigma(\zeta))\, t}{v_{jl}(\zeta)}.$$

(iii) The ith vertex of $\mathbf{K}_0^+(j, l, \varsigma^2(\zeta))$ lies on the edge $s = 0$ of $[0, 1]^2$ when ζ is on $\tilde{e}_{ijl}$. Therefore, the change in the type of shape of $\mathbf{K}^+(j, l, \varsigma^2(\zeta))$ is associated with the inequalities

$$u_{j,i-1}(\varsigma^2(\zeta))\, s - \frac{a_l}{a_{i-1}} \left| \frac{2}{1-\sqrt{3}\zeta} \right|^2 u_{i-1,l}(\zeta)\, t + w_{j,l,i-1}(\varsigma^2(\zeta)) \geq 0,$$

$$u_{ji}(\varsigma^2(\zeta))\, s - \frac{a_l}{a_i} \left| \frac{2}{1-\sqrt{3}\zeta} \right|^2 u_{il}(\zeta)\, t + w_{jli}(\varsigma^2(\zeta)) \geq 0$$

and $s \geq 0$, where we have used the relation

$$a_i \left| \frac{1-\sqrt{3}\zeta}{2} \right|^2 v_{li}(\varsigma^2(\zeta)) = -a_l u_{il}(\zeta).$$

Because the s-coordinate of the ith vertex of $\mathbf{K}_0^+(j, l, \varsigma^2(\zeta))$ is $v_{jl}(\zeta)\, s_0 = -w_{ijl}(\zeta)$, it follows that the integral formula for the associated jump term is

$$\frac{1}{192|\mathbf{K}|^3} c_j a_j a_l \left| \frac{2}{1-\sqrt{3}\zeta} \right|^4 \int_0^{s_0} ds \int_{t_1}^{t_2} f(s, t)\, g(s)\, dt,$$

where

$$s_0 = -\frac{w_{ijl}(\zeta)}{v_{jl}(\zeta)},$$

$$t_1 = \frac{a_{i-1}}{a_l} \left| \frac{1-\sqrt{3}\zeta}{2} \right|^2 \frac{w_{j,l,i-1}(\varsigma^2(\zeta)) + u_{j,i-1}(\varsigma^2(\zeta))\, s}{u_{i-1,l}(\zeta)}$$

and

$$t_2 = \frac{a_i}{a_l} \left| \frac{1 - \sqrt{3}\varsigma}{2} \right|^2 \frac{w_{jli}(\varsigma^2(\zeta)) + u_{ji}(\varsigma^2(\zeta))\ s}{u_{il}(\zeta)}.$$

After calculating and simplifying the integrals, we obtain an expression for the jump-function for $\tilde{m}_\mathbf{K}$ as follows.

Theorem 8.11. *The jump-function J_{ijl} for $\tilde{m}_\mathbf{K}$ at ζ with respect to $\tilde{e}_{ijl}$ is given by:*

$$-\frac{a_{i-1}a_i a_{j-1}a_j}{288|\mathbf{K}|^3} \frac{w_{ijl}^4}{u_{i-1,l}u_{il}v_{j-1,l}v_{jl}} \sin(\beta_i - \beta_{i-1})\sin(\beta_j - \beta_{j-1})$$

$$\times \sum_{l_1,l_2=i}^{j-1} a_{l_1}a_{l_2}\cos(\beta_{l_1} - \beta_{l_2}) + \frac{1}{192|\mathbf{K}|^3}\{F_{ijl}(w_{ijl}, -u_{il}, -u_{i-1,l}, v_{jl}, i, j)$$

$$- F_{ijl}(w_{ijl}, -u_{il}, -u_{i-1,l}, v_{j-1,l}, i, j-1) - F_{ijl}(w_{ijl}, v_{jl}, v_{j-1,l}, -u_{il}, j, i)$$

$$+ F_{ijl}(w_{ijl}, v_{jl}, v_{j-1,l}, -u_{i-1,l}, j, i-1)\}, \tag{8.28}$$

where

$$F_{ijl}(w, u_1, u_2, v, i', j') = F_{ijl}^{(1)}(w, u_1, u_2, v, i', j')$$

$$\times \{F_{ijl}^{(2)}(w, u_1, u_2, v, i', j') + 5F_{ijl}^{(3)}(w, u_1, u_2, v, i', j')\},$$

$$F_{ijl}^{(1)}(w, u_1, u_2, v, i', j') = \frac{a_{i'}a_{i'-1}}{15}\{c_{j'} - c_l\cos(\beta_{j'} - \beta_l)\}\sin(\beta_{i'} - \beta_{i'-1})\frac{w^2}{u_1 u_2},$$

$$F_{ijl}^{(2)}(w, u_1, u_2, v, i', j') = a_{j'}^3\frac{w^3}{v^3} + a_{j'}^2 a_{i'}\frac{w^3}{v^2 u_1}\cos(\beta_{j'} - \beta_{i'})$$

$$+ a_{j'}^2 a_{i'-1}\frac{w^3}{v^2 u_2}\cos(\beta_{j'} - \beta_{i'-1})$$

$$+ a_{j'}a_{i'}a_{i'-1}\frac{w^3}{v u_1 u_2}\cos(\beta_{i'} - \beta_{i'-1})$$

$$+ a_{j'}a_{i'}^2\frac{w^3}{v u_1^2} + a_{j'}a_{i'-1}^2\frac{w^3}{v u_2^2},$$

and

$$F_{ijl}^{(3)}(w, u_1, u_2, v, i', j') = a_{j'}^2\frac{w^2}{v^2}\sum_{l'=i}^{j-1} a_{l'}\cos(\beta_{l'} - \beta_{j'})$$

$$+ a_{j'}a_{i'}\frac{w^2}{v u_1}\sum_{l'=i}^{j-1} a_{l'}\cos(\beta_{l'} - \beta_{i'})$$

$$+ a_{j'}a_{i'-1}\frac{w^2}{v u_2}\sum_{l'=i}^{j-1} a_{l'}\cos(\beta_{l'} - \beta_{i'-1}).$$

We now examine the order of the first discontinuous derivative at a singularity of $\tilde{m}_K$. Theorem 8.11 shows that the jump-function J_{ijl} for $\tilde{m}_K$ with respect to the component $\tilde{e}_{ijl}$ of $\mathcal{J}(\mathbf{K})$ can be expressed as a finite sum of quotients of binary polynomials in (x, y) in which all the denominators of the summands are products of powers of $u_{il}(\zeta)$, $u_{i-1,l}(\zeta)$, $v_{jl}(\zeta)$ and $v_{j-1,l}(\zeta)$, where $\zeta = (x, y)$. Hence, the denominators occurring in the summands of $J_{ijl}^{\varpi}(\zeta)$, as i, j, l and ϖ vary, can be split into powers of factors of the following forms:

$$(1 \pm \sqrt{3}x) \sin(\beta_i - \beta_j) + \sqrt{3}y \cos(\beta_i - \beta_j),$$

$$(1 - 3x^2 - 3y^2) \sin(\beta_i - \beta_j) + 2\sqrt{3}y \cos(\beta_i - \beta_j)$$

and

$$\{(1 \pm \sqrt{3}x)^2 + 3y^2\}^2,$$

where the last factor arises from the Jacobian $\left|\frac{d\varpi(\zeta)}{d\zeta}\right|^2$. The way in which the above factors are involved in the summands of the jump-functions means that the type of singularity of a jump-function will be determined by whether or not the relevant edge belongs to the set $\mathcal{J}_0(\mathbf{K})$, defined at the end of Section 8.7, in the following manner.

Theorem 8.12. *The order of differentiability of the jump of $\tilde{m}_K$ with respect to $\tilde{e}_{ijl}^{\varpi}$ is three when $\tilde{e}_{ijl}^{\varpi} \in \mathcal{J}_0(\mathbf{K})$, and otherwise it is at least four.*

Proof.   The analyticity of the jump-function $J_{ijl}(\zeta)$ in a neighbourhood of $\mathring{e}_{ijl}$ asserts that none of the singularity lines of $J_{ijl}(\zeta)$,

$$u_{il}(\zeta) = 0, \quad u_{i-1,l}(\zeta) = 0, \quad v_{jl}(\zeta) = 0 \quad \text{and} \quad v_{j-1,l}(\zeta) = 0, \qquad (8.29)$$

can intersect $\tilde{e}_{ijl}$ unless $\tilde{e}_{ijl}$ is part of one of these lines. The open arc $\mathring{e}_{ijl}$ is part of the line determined by $w_{ijl}(\zeta) = 0$. So, if $\tilde{e}_{ijl}$ is not part of one of the lines (8.29), it follows from (8.28) that $J_{ijl}(\zeta)$ has a zero of order four and hence that the order of differentiability of the jump of $\tilde{m}_K$ with respect to $\tilde{e}_{ijl}$ is at least four. On the other hand, $\tilde{e}_{ijl}$ is part of one of the lines (8.29) if and only if one of the following conditions holds:

$$j = i + 1, l = i + 1; \quad j = i - 1, l = i - 2;$$
$$j = i - 1, l = i; \quad j = i + 1, l = i - 1.$$

Then, the corresponding functions $w_{ijl}(\zeta)$ can be rewritten as

$$-u_{il}(\zeta), \quad u_{i-1,l}(\zeta), \quad -v_{jl}(\zeta) \quad \text{and} \quad v_{j-1,l}(\zeta),$$

respectively, and, on these segments, the singularity is removable and then $J_{ijl}(\zeta)$ is $O(w_{ijl}^3(\zeta))$ and is not $O(w_{ijl}^4(\zeta))$. Thus, if we substitute $\varpi(\zeta)$ for ζ in (8.29) and compare it with (8.26), we find that $\tilde{e}_{ijl}^{\varpi}$ is part of one of loci (8.29) if and only if $\tilde{e}_{ijl}^{\varpi} \in \mathcal{J}_0(\mathbf{K})$, as required. ■

We observe that each jump-function for $\tilde{m}_{\mathbf{K}}$ with respect to a component of $\mathcal{J}(\mathbf{K})$ is real-analytic away from a natural singularity set consisting of either infinite lines through one of the special shape points $\mp 1/\sqrt{3}$, or complete circles through both of these special points, or both of such infinite lines and complete circles. We also note that the union of all the singularity sets of the jump-functions for $\tilde{m}_{\mathbf{K}}$ coincides with the union of the x-axis and the set

$$\{\zeta : \varphi_{ij}(\varpi(\zeta)) \text{ is a singular mapping, } \varpi \in \Omega \text{ and } 1 \leqslant i \neq j \leqslant n\}.$$

8.8.3   The Stepping-Stone Principle and an Explicit Formula for $\tilde{m}_{\mathbf{K}}$

We are now in a position to describe our stepping-stone method to obtain an explicit formula for $\tilde{m}_{\mathbf{K}}$, whatever the convex polygon $\mathbf{K}$ may be. This will allow our evaluation of $\tilde{m}_{\mathbf{K}}$ to spread out from the basic tile and eventually to cover the whole of the plane using our knowledge of the singular tessellation $\mathcal{J}(\mathbf{K})$, the formula for $\tilde{m}_{\mathbf{K}}$ in the basic tile and the formulae for the jump-functions for $\tilde{m}_{\mathbf{K}}$, together with the fact that $\tilde{m}_{\mathbf{K}}(\zeta) = \tilde{m}_{\mathbf{K}}(-\zeta)$.

We proceed as follows. Let $\mathbf{T}_{i_0}$ be a tile in the upper half-plane in which we wish to find an explicit formula for $\tilde{m}_{\mathbf{K}}$. There are many ways of stepping from the basic tile $\mathbf{T}_0$ to $\mathbf{T}_{i_0}$ in the upper half-plane and, from our present point of view, it does not matter which route we choose, although obviously some routes will be more convenient than others. Suppose we have decided on the route $\{\mathbf{T}_i : i = 0, 1, \ldots, i_0\}$. Let $\tilde{m}_{\mathbf{K}} = f_j$ in the tile $\mathbf{T}_j$ for each j and suppose that we already know the functions $f_0, f_1, \ldots, f_i$. To get a formula for f_{i+1} we recall that, if f_i^* is the real-analytic continuation of f_i, then

$$J_i^{i+1} = f_{i+1}^* - f_i^*$$

will obviously be real-analytic, at least throughout an open neighbourhood of the open arc $\overset{\circ}{\gamma}$ of the boundary separating $\mathbf{T}_i$ and $\mathbf{T}_{i+1}$, and at most differ from our jump-function J_γ for $\tilde{m}_{\mathbf{K}}$ by a sign: that is, $J_i^{i+1} = \pm J_\gamma$. The sign is totally determined by the equations of the bounding lines of $\mathbf{K}_0^+$ together with the route we have chosen, so that J_i^{i+1} is known to us by Theorem 8.11, and we are then able to express f_{i+1} in $\mathbf{T}_{i+1}$. Thus, we have established the following result.

Theorem 8.13. *For any tile $\mathbf{T}_{i_0}$ in the upper half-plane we have*

$$f_{i_0}^* = f_0^* + \sum_{i=0}^{i_0-1} J_i^{i+1},$$

whenever the tiles $\mathbf{T}_0, \mathbf{T}_1, \ldots, \mathbf{T}_{i_0}$ form a chain in which each pair of adjacent tiles has a boundary-arc in common.

The decomposition formula given in Theorem 8.13 as an algebraic identity can be used, at least theoretically, to obtain the explicit form for $\tilde{m}_{\mathbf{K}}$ in any named tile by starting with its form in the basic tile and adding to it certain jump-functions describing the switches in analytic form when crossing tile boundaries, this sum being formed following any desired stepping-stone route from the basic tile to the target tile via a stepwise continuous sequence of intermediate tiles. However, there is a problem that might arise in a practical computation based on this approach. The existence of the singularities of the jump-functions makes it possible that some terms in the decomposition formula are singular at some points of the tile $\mathbf{T}_{i_0}$. Then, the theorem would imply that there must be more than one such singular term and the singularities viewed algebraically must cancel out. On the other hand, when we work numerically, the unwanted terms would appear as $\infty - \infty$ and then the numerical computation will fail. Similarly, when there is a removable singularity, this would appear as $0/0$ and straightforward numerical computation would fail to evaluate it. Nevertheless, since, with the aid of the formulae for the jump-functions, we know exactly where the singularities of each term lie, it would usually be possible to examine alternative stepping-stone routes from the basic tile to the target tile and to try to choose one so that no term in the decomposition formula is singular at a given point. This, however, may not always be possible: sometimes there is no stepping-stone route from the basic tile such that no term in the decomposition formula is singular at every point in the target tile. For example, the points on the lines $x = \pm 1/\sqrt{3}$ all have this pathological character when $\mathbf{K}$ is a square. However, as such a numerical value is usually rarely wanted to more than, say, nine-figure accuracy, we can first attempt a direct evaluation at the given point and then, if that fails, attempt one at a slight perturbation of the given point. The direction of the perturbation can always be chosen after inspecting the union of the global singularity curves for all jump-functions in the decomposition formula, which consists of a finite number of lines and circles. Such an approximation technique will also deal with the removable singularities.

CHAPTER 9

Mean Shapes and The Shape of the Means

In any classical statistical analysis the estimation of the mean of a sample is an important first step. In the case of the statistical analysis of shape it is not even clear what the mean should mean and different circumstances may require different definitions. Further confusion can arise when, as is often the case, we are considering the shapes of configurations of random vertices in a Euclidean space. Then, it is quite natural to choose the shape of the means of the vertices to be the mean. However, it is not obvious, and indeed may not be the case, that this is the mean of the shapes in any sense that can be defined directly on the appropriate shape space. Neither is it clear that such an intrinsically defined mean might not be a more appropriate statistic for any particular problem.

In this chapter we shall describe various concepts of mean shape, by which we understand a mean that can be defined directly on shape space, and discuss the relations both among them and between them and the shape of the means. We shall also discuss practical problems that arise in their application, such as associated Laws of Large Numbers and algorithmic methods of computation.

9.1   CONCEPT OF MEANS IN NON-LINEAR SPACES

As we have seen in earlier chapters, shape spaces are not linear spaces and most of them are not even manifolds, which would be the next best possibility. The most we can say, in general, is that they are all metric spaces with a natural stratification in which all the strata are Riemannian manifolds. To understand the problems that can arise when we try to define a mean in the absence of a given linear structure, it is enough to consider the simplest non-linear manifolds. For a probability measure on an arc of a circle we could map the arc isometrically onto an interval of the real line, perform our calculation of the mean there in the usual way and then transfer it back onto the arc. The result would surely accord with our intuitive preconception of where the mean should lie. What, however, if the probability measure were supported on an entire circle? There is no way to map that isometrically into the real line. We might, rather artificially and certainly non-intrinsically, choose an isometric embedding of the circle in the plane and carry out the classical computation for a planar distribution. However, that would give us a mean that does not lie on the circle. If this were a shape calculation, then we would have a mean shape that is not a shape! We could recover the situation by projecting the planar mean from the centre back onto the circle. Provided the planar mean is not at the centre of the circle, that will give us a well-defined mean on the circle itself. However, this approach fails, at least if we want to obtain a unique well-defined mean, not only when the planar mean is at the centre of the circle but also for less regular simple closed curves for which there is no obvious preferred projection of the interior back onto the curve. It could also fail more fundamentally if the mean falls outside the curve or if the interior of the curve has no point from which the projection onto the curve is continuous, which is surely a necessary pre-requisite for a sensible theory.

The problems that can arise when similar embedding techniques are applied to probability measures in higher dimensional non-linear spaces are even more intractable, so clearly there is a need for an intrinsic definition of a mean, where the calculations, and the solution, lie entirely within the space on which the probability measure was originally defined. However, the potential non-uniqueness of means is a feature we shall have to accept in general since, as we shall see below, the intrinsic methods of calculation that do exist do not guarantee to give a unique answer. Once again, simple examples will show that we should not expect them to do so. Regarding the unit circle S^1 as the set of points of unit modulus in the complex plane, consider a distribution with equal weights at $+1$ and -1. Where is its mean? Any reasonable approach will give $+i$ and $-i$ as equally valid answers. In fact, it is easy to construct examples where the set of means has dimension greater than zero. Consider, for example, a uniform distribution on the part of the sphere lying in the 'tropics', that is, between latitudes 23.5°N and 23.5°S. Then, almost any approach will lead to the conclusion that every point of the equator is a mean. In general, the set of means could occupy any submanifold or more general subspace and it makes sense to ask for topological or geometric invariants of the set of means. At the very crudest level, probability measures whose sets of means had different dimensions could be expected to be significantly different in other ways.

To obtain an intrinsic definition for the mean of random variables or probability measures on general metric spaces or on manifolds where there are no linear structures, there are various non-linear operators we may use to replace the usual linear one. Three of the most successful ones are the notions of Fréchet means of random variables (cf. Ziezold, 1977), of barycentres of measures (cf. Emery, 1989) and of Riemannian centres of mass (cf. Karcher, 1977). These means are all defined on a metric space (**M**, dist) and it will be clear from the definitions that follow that none of them is necessarily unique.

Definition 9.1. Let (**M**, dist) be a metric space and ξ be an **M**-valued random variable with probability measure μ on **M**.

(i) The point x_0 is said to be a Fréchet mean of ξ with respect to 'dist' if the function

$$F_\mu(x) = \tfrac{1}{2} \int_{\mathbf{M}} \text{dist}(x, y)^2 \, d\mu(y) \tag{9.1}$$

attains its global minimum at x_0, provided $F_\mu(x) < \infty$ for some $x \in \mathbf{M}$.

Suppose further that $(\mathbf{M}, \text{dist})$ is a Riemannian manifold.

(ii) The point x_0 is said to be the barycentre of ξ if

$$f(x_0) \leqslant \int_{\mathbf{M}} f(x) \, d\mu(x)$$

for all bounded convex functions $f : \mathbf{U} \mapsto \mathbb{R}$, where $\mathbf{U} \subset \mathbf{M}$ is open and convex, $x_0 \in \mathbf{U}$ and range$(\xi) \subset \mathbf{U}$ a.s.

(iii) The point x_0 is said to be a Cartan mean of ξ with respect to 'dist' if x_0 is a local minimum of the function F_μ in (9.1).

The Fréchet mean could be generalised by replacing the metric in the expression (9.1) for F_μ by a member of a wider class of functions on $\mathbf{M} \times \mathbf{M}$ (cf. Le, 1998). Note, however, that to obtain results such as the Law of Large Numbers in Proposition 9.2 below we need to use a metric, while for Proposition 9.1 we need to have the specific metric induced by the Riemannian metric. Many results concerning Cartan means, as is also the case for barycentres, are related to random variables concentrated on domains that can be described geometrically in terms of convex geometry. The corresponding uniqueness results that can be obtained relate also to those domains, rather than the entire manifold. However, it is easy to construct examples similar to those described above, where even a Fréchet mean, defined as minimum for the function F_μ restricted to an appropriate convex domain $\mathbf{U}$, is no longer a Fréchet mean for F_μ defined on the entire space $\mathbf{M}$. It is, in general, a non-trivial matter to establish that a Fréchet mean for $\mathbf{U}$, which a priori is only a Cartan mean for $\mathbf{M}$, is indeed a Fréchet mean for $\mathbf{M}$, since this involves taking into account the global topological nature of the space $\mathbf{M}$.

The sufficient conditions for uniqueness of Cartan means referred to above generally involve the curvature of a manifold. To specify such conditions we follow Hildebrandt (1985) in calling a geodesic ball of radius a *regular* if the supremum of the sectional curvatures upon it is less than $(\pi/2a)^2$. This bound is required for the following results. Note that the restriction on μ therein is not very severe since, for example, on a sphere, a regular geodesic ball could be almost a hemisphere and, on a space of non-positive curvature, it could be the entire space.

Proposition 9.1. *Suppose that μ is a probability measure on a Riemannian manifold $(\mathbf{M}$, dist$)$ and that $\mathcal{B}_a(x_0)$ is a regular geodesic ball contained in the manifold with centre x_0 and radius a.*

(i) *If μ is supported on $\mathcal{B}_a(x_0)$, then there is one and only one Cartan mean of μ on $\mathcal{B}_a(x_0)$.*

(ii) *If μ is supported on the concentric ball $\mathcal{B}_{a/2}(x_0)$ of half the radius, then F_μ is convex and has one and only one critical point, necessarily a Cartan mean, on $\mathcal{B}_{a/2}(x_0)$.*

The first of these results was obtained by Kendall (1990b) and the second by Karcher (1977). Karcher's hypothesis is, of course, strictly stronger. However, the conclusion is more precise and it remains important as a practical method of finding the mean.

As already noted, to estimate such means in practice we need a related Law of Large Numbers and, in fact, an appropriate generalisation to random variables on metric spaces of the classical Strong Law of Large Numbers has been obtained by Ziezold (1977). To state his result we introduce the analogue of the Fréchet mean for a sample of n points.

For a given, determinate, set of n points $\{x_j \in \mathbf{M} : 1 \leqslant j \leqslant n\}$, we can define a discrete uniform probability measure μ_0 supported on these points. Then, a Fréchet mean of such a probability measure is a global minimum of the function

$$F_{\mu_0}(x) = \frac{1}{2n} \sum_{j=1}^{n} \text{dist}\,(x, x_j)^2.$$

Analogously, if we assume that the n given points are iid random variables ξ_i on $\mathbf{M}$ with common probability measure μ on $\mathbf{M}$, then we may define the set of Fréchet means of samples of size n from μ to be

$$\mathbf{M}(\xi_1, \ldots, \xi_n) = \left\{ x_0 \in \mathbf{M} : \sum_{j=1}^{n} \text{dist}(x_0, \xi_j)^2 = \min_{x \in \mathbf{M}} \sum_{j=1}^{n} \text{dist}\,(x, \xi_j)^2 \right\}.$$

Then, the relation that Ziezold obtained between the set of Fréchet means of samples and the set of Fréchet means of μ is the following.

Proposition 9.2. *Let $\xi_1, \xi_2, \ldots$ be iid random variables with common probability measure μ, having values in a separable metric space $(\mathbf{M}, \text{dist})$ and such that $E[\text{dist}(x, \xi_1)^2] < \infty$ for some $x \in \mathbf{M}$. Let $\mathbf{M}_\mu$ be the set of Fréchet means of μ with respect to 'dist' and $\mathbf{M}(\xi_1, \ldots, \xi_n)$ be defined as above. Then*

$$\bigcap_{n=1}^{\infty} \overline{\bigcup_{j=n}^{\infty} \mathbf{M}(\xi_1, \ldots, \xi_j)} \subseteq \mathbf{M}_\mu \quad \text{a.s.}$$

9.2   METRICS ON SHAPE SPACE

Of the means introduced in the previous section, we shall now primarily be concerned with Fréchet means. However, we shall also need to consider the more general Cartan means at some stages of our discussion. Both concepts require that we select metrics, or possibly more general functions, on shape space. In fact, most of our results will make use of three particular metrics. The first two of these, which we have already met in Section 6.4, are induced from metrics on the pre-shape sphere. We recall that, since shape space is the orbit space of the pre-shape sphere under the action of a compact group with quotient map π, the natural way to induce a metric on shape space from one on the pre-shape sphere is to define

$$\text{dist}(\pi(X), \pi(Y)) = \min \ \text{dist}(X', Y'),$$

where the minimum is taken over all X' in the orbit $\pi^{-1}(\pi(X))$ of X and all Y' in $\pi^{-1}(\pi(Y))$.

Applying this procedure to the standard Riemannian metric or great circular arc distance d on the pre-shape sphere, we obtained the metric ρ given by Equation (6.4). In the special case $m = 2$, if we use the complex row vectors instead of matrices to represent the pre-shapes, then the distance between two points z and w on the pre-shape sphere is given by

$$\cos d(z, w) = \Re(\langle z, \ w \rangle),$$

where $\langle z, \ w \rangle = z\overline{w}^t$, and the induced distance between the corresponding shapes by

$$\cos \rho(\pi(z), \pi(w)) = |\langle z, \ w \rangle|. \tag{9.2}$$

Similarly, from the chordal metric $\hat{d}$ on the pre-shape sphere, we obtained the procrustean metric $\hat{\rho}$ on Σ_m^k, given by Equation (6.3). For the complex representation of the case $m = 2$, $\hat{d}(z, w)$ is given by $\|z - w\|$ on the pre-shape sphere and

$$\hat{\rho}(\pi(z), \pi(w))^2 = 2\{1 - |\langle z, \ w \rangle|\} \tag{9.3}$$

on shape space.

A useful variant of the second of these metrics arises by defining

$$\tilde{d}(X, Y)^2 = 1 - (X \cdot Y)^2 = 1 - \{\text{tr}(XY^t)\}^2$$

on the pre-shape sphere. Thus,

$$\tilde{d}(X, Y) = \sin d(X, Y),$$

which is the length of the perpendicular from Y onto OX in the Euclidean space containing the pre-shape sphere. Its square may also be expressed as

$$\tilde{d}(X, Y)^2 = \min_{a>0} \text{tr}\{(X - a Y)(X - a Y)^t\}.$$

As before, on shape space we may define

$$\tilde{\rho}(\pi(X), \pi(Y))^2 = \min_{T \in \mathbf{SO}(m), a>0} \text{tr}\{(X - a TY)(X - a TY)^t\},$$

which also gives

$$\tilde{\rho}(\pi(X), \pi(Y)) = \sin \rho(\pi(X), \pi(Y)).$$

For the complex representation when $m = 2$, the corresponding formulae are

$$\tilde{d}(z, w)^2 = 1 - \{\Re(\langle z, w \rangle)\}^2$$

on the pre-shape sphere and

$$\tilde{\rho}(\pi(z), \pi(w))^2 = \min_{\alpha \in [0, 2\pi), \, a > 0} ||z - a e^{i\alpha} w||^2$$

$$= 1 - |\langle z, w \rangle|^2 = \sin^2 \rho(\pi(z), \pi(w)) \qquad (9.4)$$

on shape space. Although $\tilde{d}$ is not a metric on the pre-shape sphere since $\tilde{d}(X, -X) = 0$, nevertheless $\tilde{\rho}$ defined on shape space is a metric. To see that, note that ρ takes values in the interval $[0, \pi/2]$ on which sine is an increasing function. So, $\tilde{\rho}(\pi(X), \pi(Y)) = 0$ if and only if $\rho(\pi(X), \pi(Y)) = 0$ and, writing s_1 and s_2, respectively, for $\rho(\pi(X), \pi(Z))$ and $\rho(\pi(Z), \pi(Y))$, we have

$$\tilde{\rho}(\pi(X), \pi(Y)) \leqslant \sin(s_1 + s_2) = \sin s_1 \cos s_2 + \cos s_1 \sin s_2$$

$$\leqslant \sin s_1 + \sin s_2 = \tilde{\rho}(\pi(X), \pi(Z)) + \tilde{\rho}(\pi(Z), \pi(Y)),$$

provided $s_1 + s_2 \leqslant \pi/2$. When $s_1 + s_2 > \pi/2$, we have

$$\sin s_1 + \sin s_2 > \sin \left(\tfrac{\pi}{2} - s_2\right) + \sin s_2 = \cos s_2 + \sin s_2 \geqslant 1 \geqslant \tilde{\rho}(\pi(X), \pi(Y)).$$

All three of these metrics have been used in various statistical analyses of shape, generally via the minimising procedures that give rise to them. We should emphasise that here, and throughout this chapter, we use z and w to denote points on the pre-shape sphere $\mathcal{S}_2^k$. This contrasts with our previous use of such symbols to denote general points in $\mathbb{C}^{k-1}$, for which the above formulae would not remain valid.

9.3 UNIQUENESS OF FRÉCHET MEANS OF SHAPE-MEASURES

The Strong Law of Large Numbers due to Ziezold, which we mentioned in Section 9.1, is most easily applied when the probability measure itself has a unique Fréchet mean and, from a practical point of view, this is also the most important case. However, as we made clear in the first section of this chapter, we cannot, in general, expect there to be a unique Fréchet mean. Although Proposition 9.1 gives what are, in fact, unique Fréchet means as far as the relevant geodesic balls are concerned, those results do not address the question as to whether they are global minima, that is, whether they remain Fréchet means on the entire space. Similarly, although a regular geodesic ball can be arbitrarily large in a Riemannian manifold of non-positive curvature, that is not the case for shape spaces since they have positive curvature, which is even unbounded above for $m > 2$. This means that those results, which require the distribution to be supported on a geodesic ball, cannot be applied to most shape-measures induced from distributions of vertices which, as we saw in Chapter 8, are commonly supported by the entire shape space. In this section we shall use our explicit knowledge of shape space firstly to show that, for shape-measures supported on suitable geodesic balls, their Fréchet means will also lie in that ball. This will enable us to translate results on the uniqueness of Cartan means for such shape-measures into uniqueness theorems for their Fréchet means. Secondly, we shall obtain conditions for the uniqueness of Fréchet means that hold for a large class of shape-measures and that, in particular, do not require any restriction on their support.

To describe these results we shall now, and throughout the remainder of this chapter, restrict ourselves to the case $m = 2$, although some of the results we shall obtain can easily be generalised to the case $m > 2$.

The basic metric on shape space is ρ and, with this metric, Σ_2^k is a Riemannian manifold. We shall use several of the properties of this metric starting with the fact, which is clear from the expression (9.2) for it given above, that it is invariant under the group induced by the unitary group $U(k-1)$ of isometries. Indeed, Σ_2^k is homogeneous with respect to ρ since the action of the unitary group on the pre-shape sphere is transitive and commutes with the action of $SO(2)$. Moreover, since this induced action of $U(k-1)$ is its standard action on CP^{k-2}, the stabiliser in $U(k-1)$ of each shape $\pi(z)$ is transitive on each set of shapes at a given distance from $\pi(z)$. Thus, given two shapes whose Riemannian distance apart is s, we may map them to the standard shapes $\pi((1, 0, \ldots, 0))$ and $\pi((\cos s, \sin s, 0, \ldots, 0))$. Then, the reflection

$$\begin{pmatrix} \cos s & \sin s \\ \sin s & -\cos s \end{pmatrix} \oplus I_{k-3}$$

in $U(k-1)$ induces an isometric involution of shape space that interchanges the latter shapes and hence determines an isometric involution that interchanges the two given shapes.

We consider first the question of the location of Fréchet means.

Lemma 9.1. *If μ is a shape-measure on Σ_2^k supported on a geodesic ball of radius $\pi/8$, then all the Fréchet means of μ with respect to ρ, to $\tilde{\rho}$ or to $\hat{\rho}$ lie in that ball.*

Proof. Writing $\mathcal{B}_{\pi/8}(\pi(z_0))$ for the given geodesic ball, we show that, whichever of ρ, $\tilde{\rho}$ or $\hat{\rho}$ is involved, the integrand in $F_\mu(\pi(z))$ is increasing as $\pi(z)$ moves along the outward normal to the boundary of $\mathcal{B}_s(\pi(z_0))$ for $\pi/8 \leqslant s \leqslant \pi/4$. Since ρ^2, $\tilde{\rho}^2$ and $\hat{\rho}^2$ are all increasing functions of ρ, it is sufficient to prove that, for $\pi(w)$ in $\mathcal{B}_{\pi/8}(\pi(z_0))$, $\rho(\pi(z), \pi(w))$ is increasing along such normals. To establish this we use the fact that Σ_2^k is homogeneous to take z_0 in the standard position $(1, 0, \ldots, 0)$ and to take any given geodesic starting from $\pi(z_0)$ to be the image $\pi(z_s)$ of the horizontal geodesic $(\cos s, \sin s, 0, \ldots, 0)$ through it (cf. Chapter 6). Then, for $0 \leqslant s \leqslant \pi/2$, the metric distance $\rho(\pi(z_s), \pi(z_0))$ is equal to s. Since the subset of Σ_2^k determined by the pre-shapes with $w_1 = 0$ does not meet $\mathcal{B}_{\pi/8}(\pi(z_0))$, we may represent $\pi(w)$ in $\mathcal{B}_{\pi/8}(\pi(z_0))$ by the standard inhomogeneous coordinates $\zeta_j = w_{j+1}/w_1$ for $1 \leqslant j \leqslant k-2$. In terms of these coordinates and writing r_j for $|\zeta_j|$, the Riemannian distance between $\pi(z_0)$ and $\pi(w)$ is given by

$$\cos^2 \rho(\pi(z_0), \pi(w)) = |w_1|^2 = \frac{1}{1 + r_1^2 + \cdots + r_{k-2}^2} > \cos^2 \tfrac{\pi}{8} \qquad (9.5)$$

and, for $0 \leqslant s \leqslant \pi/2$, that between $\pi(z_s)$ and $\pi(w)$ is given by

$$\cos^2 \rho(\pi(z_s), \pi(w))$$
$$= \cos^2 \rho(\pi(z_0), \pi(w)) \{(\cos s + \zeta_1 \sin s)(\cos s + \bar{\zeta}_1 \sin s)\}. \qquad (9.6)$$

Since the geodesic $\pi(z_s)$ hits the boundary of $\mathcal{B}_{s_0}(\pi(z_0))$ when $s = s_0$, and does so orthogonally, and since $\cos^2 s$ is a strictly decreasing function of s for $0 \leqslant s \leqslant \pi/2$, it follows that, in order to show that, for each $\pi(w)$ in $\mathcal{B}_{\pi/8}(\pi(z_0))$, $\rho(\pi(z), \pi(w))$ is increasing as $\pi(z)$ moves along the outward normal to the boundary of $\mathcal{B}_{s_0}(\pi(z_0))$, it suffices to show that

$$\frac{d}{ds} \cos^2 \rho(\pi(z_s), \pi(w)) < 0$$

for $\pi/8 \leqslant s \leqslant \pi/4$. However, since

$$\frac{1}{1 + r_1^2} > \cos^2 \tfrac{\pi}{8}, \quad \text{that is,} \quad r_1 < \tan \tfrac{\pi}{8},$$

for $\pi/8 \leqslant s \leqslant \pi/4$ we have

$$\frac{d}{ds} \cos^2 \rho(\pi(z_s), \pi(w)) = \cos^2 \rho(\pi(z_0), \pi(w)) \{(r_1^2 - 1) \sin 2s + (\zeta_1 + \bar{\zeta}_1) \cos 2s\}$$
$$\leqslant \cos^2 \rho(\pi(z_0), \pi(w)) \{(r_1^2 - 1) \sin 2s + 2 r_1 \cos 2s\}$$
$$< \cos^2 \rho(\pi(z_0), \pi(w)) \{(\tan^2 \tfrac{\pi}{8} - 1) \sin 2s$$
$$+ 2 \tan \tfrac{\pi}{8} \cos 2s\}$$
$$= \cos^2 \rho(\pi(z_0), \pi(w)) \cos^{-2} \tfrac{\pi}{8} \sin \left(\tfrac{\pi}{4} - 2s\right) \leqslant 0,$$

as required.

It follows that, since each value of the integrand of F_μ, for each of ρ, $\tilde{\rho}$ or $\hat{\rho}$, is increasing in all radial directions throughout $\overline{\mathcal{B}_{\pi/4}(\pi(z_0))} \setminus \mathcal{B}_{\pi/8}(\pi(z_0))$, the same must be true for F_μ itself. Thus, the minimum values of F_μ on the compact set $\overline{\mathcal{B}_{\pi/4}(\pi(z_0))}$ must all be taken inside $\mathcal{B}_{\pi/8}(\pi(z_0))$. However, that implies that these minima must, in fact, be global minima of F_μ on Σ_2^k. For if $\pi(z)$ is any point outside $\overline{\mathcal{B}_{\pi/4}(\pi(z_0))}$ distant $\varepsilon > 0$ from the boundary of $\mathcal{B}_{\pi/4}(\pi(z_0))$, then, for all $\pi(w)$ in $\mathcal{B}_{\pi/8}(\pi(z_0))$, we have

$$\rho(\pi(z), \pi(w)) > \varepsilon + \tfrac{\pi}{8} > \varepsilon + \rho(\pi(z_0), \pi(w)).$$

Thus, $F_\mu(\pi(z))$ is strictly greater than $F_\mu(\pi(z_0))$ and so $\pi(z)$ cannot be a Fréchet mean of μ with respect to any of ρ, $\tilde{\rho}$ or $\hat{\rho}$. ∎

We recall that in Theorem 7.3 we computed the sectional curvatures of shape spaces and, in particular, we saw that with the metric ρ the maximal sectional curvature at any point of Σ_2^k is equal to four. It follows that any geodesic ball of radius $\pi/4$ is regular, so we may combine Proposition 9.1 (ii) with Lemma 9.1 to give the following result.

Theorem 9.1. *If μ is a shape-measure on Σ_2^k that is supported on a geodesic ball $\mathcal{B}_{\pi/8}(\pi(z_0))$, then μ has a unique Fréchet mean with respect to the Riemannian metric ρ and that mean lies in $\mathcal{B}_{\pi/8}(\pi(z_0))$.*

Our more general uniqueness results will depend on the Radon–Nikodým derivative of the shape-measure, with respect to the uniform measure $d\omega_2^k$ on Σ_2^k, being a function of the Riemannian distance ρ from a fixed point. We first give a sufficient condition for that point to be the unique Fréchet mean, calculated with respect to any of the metrices ρ, $\hat{\rho}$ or $\tilde{\rho}$. To establish that we require the following lemma.

Lemma 9.2. *Let f_1 and f_2 be two strictly decreasing functions on the non-negative real line and $\pi(z_1)$ and $\pi(z_2)$ be distinct points in Σ_2^k. Then, for any $\pi(z_0)$ in Σ_2^k,*

$$\int_{\Sigma_2^k} f_1(\rho(\pi(z_1), \pi(w)))\, f_2(\rho(\pi(z_2), \pi(w)))\, d\omega_2^k(\pi(w))$$

$$< \int_{\Sigma_2^k} f_1(\rho(\pi(z_0), \pi(w)))\, f_2(\rho(\pi(z_0), \pi(w)))\, d\omega_2^k(\pi(w)).$$

Proof. We show first that the integral on the right-hand side of this inequality is independent of the choice of $\pi(z_0)$. By transitivity we may choose g in the group induced by $U(k-1)$ such that $g(\pi(z_0)) = \pi(z_1)$. Then, since g is an isometry, we have

$$\int_{\Sigma_2^k} f_1(\rho(\pi(z_0), \pi(w)))f_2(\rho(\pi(z_0), \pi(w)))\, d\omega_2^k(\pi(w))$$

$$= \int_{\Sigma_2^k} f_1(\rho(g^{-1}(\pi(z_1)), \pi(w)))\, f_2(\rho(g^{-1}(\pi(z_1)), \pi(w)))\, d\omega_2^k(\pi(w))$$

$$= \int_{\Sigma_2^k} f_1(\rho(\pi(z_1), g(\pi(w))))\, f_2(\rho(\pi(z_1), g(\pi(w))))\, d\omega_2^k(\pi(w)).$$

However, Σ_2^k is metrically homogeneous, which, in particular, implies that the uniform measure $d\omega_2^k$ is invariant with respect to the induced $U(k-1)$-action. Using these two facts, we see that the final expression above is equal to

$$\int_{\Sigma_2^k} f_1(\rho(\pi(z_1), g(\pi(w)))) f_2(\rho(\pi(z_1), g(\pi(w)))) d\omega_2^k(g(\pi(w)))$$

$$= \int_{\Sigma_2^k} f_1(\rho(\pi(z_1), \pi(w))) f_2(\rho(\pi(z_1), \pi(w))) d\omega_2^k(\pi(w)).$$

Now let $\hat{\jmath}$ be an isometric involution in the group induced by $U(k-1)$ that interchanges $\pi(z_1)$ and $\pi(z_2)$; let $\mathcal{A}$ be the subset of Σ_2^k that consists of all points of Σ_2^k that are closer to $\pi(z_1)$ than to $\pi(z_2)$ and write $\hat{f}_i(\pi(w))$ for $f_i(\rho(\pi(z_1), \pi(w)))$. Then, taking $\pi(z_0)$ to be at $\pi(z_1)$ and observing that the fixed point set of $\hat{\jmath}$ has measure zero, we see that the difference between the right-hand and left-hand sides of the inequality in the lemma is

$$\int_{\Sigma_2^k} \hat{f}_1(\pi(w))(\hat{f}_2(\pi(w)) - \hat{f}_2(\hat{\jmath}(\pi(w)))) d\omega_2^k(\pi(w))$$

$$= \int_{\mathcal{A}} \hat{f}_1(\pi(w))(\hat{f}_2(\pi(w)) - \hat{f}_2(\hat{\jmath}(\pi(w)))) d\omega_2^k(\pi(w))$$

$$+ \int_{\hat{\jmath}(\mathcal{A})} \hat{f}_1(\pi(w))(\hat{f}_2(\pi(w)) - \hat{f}_2(\hat{\jmath}(\pi(w)))) d\omega_2^k(\pi(w))$$

$$= \int_{\mathcal{A}} (\hat{f}_1(\pi(w)) - \hat{f}_1(\hat{\jmath}(\pi(w)))) (\hat{f}_2(\pi(w)) - \hat{f}_2(\hat{\jmath}(\pi(w)))) d\omega_2^k(\pi(w)),$$

which is strictly positive since $\mathcal{A}$ has positive ω_2^k-measure.   ∎

We now observe that since $\int_{\mathbf{M}} d\mu = 1$ for a probability measure μ on $\mathbf{M}$, a Fréchet mean of μ with respect to 'dist' is a global *maximum* of

$$\tfrac{1}{2}\delta(\mathbf{M}) - F_\mu(x) = \tfrac{1}{2} \int_{\mathbf{M}} \left\{ \delta(\mathbf{M}) - \text{dist}(x, y)^2 \right\} d\mu(y),$$

where $\delta(\mathbf{M})$ is the diameter of $\mathbf{M}$ with respect to 'dist'. Once we note that Σ_2^k has finite diameter with respect to each of ρ, $\hat{\rho}$ and $\tilde{\rho}$ and that these metrics are all strictly increasing functions of ρ, Theorem 9.2 below, which simultaneously identifies the Fréchet mean and proves its uniqueness, is a direct consequence of Lemma 9.2. It may be worth noting that our results lend themselves to some obvious generalisations. For example, the hypotheses of Lemma 9.2 may obviously be weakened: it is sufficient to assume that the functions $\hat{f}_i$ in the proof are non-increasing and are strictly decreasing on a subset of $\mathcal{A}$ of positive measure. Similarly, although our current applications only involve Fréchet means with respect to the metrics ρ, $\hat{\rho}$ and $\tilde{\rho}$ explicitly mentioned in the theorem, the point $\pi(z_0)$ from which the distance is measured would also be the unique 'generalised

Fréchet mean' with respect to any strictly increasing function of ρ for which Σ_2^k has finite 'diameter'.

Theorem 9.2. *Suppose that $f \, d\omega_2^k$ is a shape-measure on Σ_2^k, where f can be expressed as a non-increasing function of the distance ρ from a fixed point $\pi(z_0)$ that is strictly decreasing on a set of positive measure. Then, $\pi(z_0)$ is the unique Fréchet mean of the given shape-measure with respect to ρ, to $\hat{\rho}$ or to $\tilde{\rho}$.*

Given that the Radon–Nikodým derivative of the shape-measure is a function of Riemannian distance from a fixed shape, the sufficient condition of Theorem 9.2 for that shape to be the unique Fréchet mean is not a necessary condition. However, in the case of the metric $\tilde{\rho}$ it is possible to give a necessary and sufficient condition as follows.

Theorem 9.3. *Suppose that $f \, d\omega_2^k$ is a shape-measure on Σ_2^k. If f is a function of the distance ρ from a fixed point $\pi(z_0)$, then $\pi(z_0)$ is the unique Fréchet mean of the given shape-measure with respect to $\tilde{\rho}$ if and only if*

$$\int_{\Sigma_2^k} \cos^2 \rho(\pi(z_0), \pi(w)) \, f(\pi(w)) \, d\omega_2^k(\pi(w)) > \frac{1}{k-1}.$$

Proof. As in the observation that precedes Theorem 9.2, it follows from the relation between ρ and $\tilde{\rho}$ that a point $\pi(z)$ is a Fréchet mean of the shape-measure $f(\pi(w)) \, d\omega_2^k(\pi(w))$ with respect to $\tilde{\rho}$ if and only if it is a global maximum of the function defined by

$$\Psi(\pi(z)) = \int_{\Sigma_2^k} \cos^2 \rho(\pi(z), \pi(w)) \, f(\pi(w)) \, d\omega_2^k(\pi(w)). \qquad (9.7)$$

Since the uniform measure $d\omega_2^k(\pi(w))$ is invariant with respect to the induced $U(k-1)$-action, our hypothesis on f implies that for any such induced isometry g that fixes $\pi(z_0)$, we have

$$\Psi(g(\pi(z))) = \int_{\Sigma_2^k} \cos^2 \rho(g(\pi(z)), \pi(w)) \, f(\pi(w)) \, d\omega_2^k(\pi(w))$$

$$= \int_{\Sigma_2^k} \cos^2 \rho(\pi(z), g^{-1}(\pi(w))) \, f(\pi(w)) \, d\omega_2^k(\pi(w))$$

$$= \int_{\Sigma_2^k} \cos^2 \rho(\pi(z), g^{-1}(\pi(w))) \, f(g^{-1}(\pi(w))) \, d\omega_2^k(g^{-1}(\pi(w)))$$

$$= \int_{\Sigma_2^k} \cos^2 \rho(\pi(z), \pi(w)) \, f(\pi(w)) \, d\omega_2^k(\pi(w)) = \Psi(\pi(z)).$$

Since the stabiliser of $\pi(z_0)$ in $U(k-1)$ is transitive on each set of points at a given distance from $\pi(z_0)$, it follows that Ψ is a function of the distance from the given shape $\pi(z_0)$. Thus, $\pi(z_0)$ is a global maximum of Ψ if and only if it is a global maximum along any particular geodesic through $\pi(z_0)$.

As in the proof of Lemma 9.1, the homogeneity of $\mathcal{S}_2^k$ means that we may take z_0 in the standard position $(1, 0, \ldots, 0)$ and consider the horizontal geodesic $z_s = (\cos s, \sin s, 0, \ldots, 0)$ through it. As the subset of Σ_2^k determined by the preshapes with $w_1 = 0$ has ω_2^k-measure zero, it makes no contribution to Ψ and again we may work with the standard inhomogeneous coordinates $\zeta_j = w_{j+1}/w_1 = r_j e^{i\theta_j}$ for $1 \leqslant j \leqslant k - 2$. We recall that, in terms of these coordinates, for any s such that $0 \leqslant s \leqslant \pi/2$ and any w with $w_1 \neq 0$, the Riemannian distance ρ between $\pi(z_s)$ and $\pi(w)$ is given by (9.5) and (9.6). We also know from Chapter 8 that the uniform measure has the expression

$$d\omega_2^k(\pi(w)) = \frac{(k-2)!}{\{1 + r_1^2 + \cdots + r_{k-2}^2\}^{k-1}} \prod_{j=1}^{k-2} d\left(\frac{\theta_j}{2\pi}\right) d(r_j^2). \tag{9.8}$$

Now, for any s such that $0 \leqslant s \leqslant \pi/2$ and any w with $w_1 \neq 0$, (9.6), (9.7) and (9.8) imply that we can express Ψ along the above geodesic as

$$\Psi(\pi(z_s)) = (k-2)! \int \left\{ \left[\int_0^{2\pi} \frac{1}{2\pi} (\cos s + \bar{\zeta}_1 \sin s)(\cos s + \bar{\zeta}_1 \sin s) d\theta_1 \right] \right.$$

$$\left. \times \cos^{2k} \rho(\pi(z_0), \pi(w)) f(\pi(w)) \prod_{j=1}^{k-2} d(r_j^2) \right.$$

$$= (k-2)! \int \left\{ \cos^2 s + r_1^2 \sin^2 s \right\}$$

$$\times \cos^{2k} \rho(\pi(z_0), \pi(w)) f(\pi(w)) \prod_{j=1}^{k-2} d(r_j^2). \tag{9.9}$$

The metric homogeneity implies that (9.9) is equal to the similar expression with any r_j in place of r_1 and hence we can express $\Psi(\pi(z_s))$ in the following homogeneous manner.

$$\Psi(\pi(z_s)) = (k-2)! \int \left\{ \cos^2 s + \frac{1}{k-2} \sin^2 s \tan^2 \rho(\pi(z_0), \pi(w)) \right\}$$

$$\times \cos^{2k} \rho(\pi(z_0), \pi(w)) f(\pi(w)) \prod_{j=1}^{k-2} d(r_j^2)$$

$$= \int \left\{ \cos^2 s \cos^2 \rho(\pi(z_0), \pi(w)) + \frac{1}{k-2} \sin^2 s \sin^2 \rho(\pi(z_0), \pi(w)) \right\}$$

$$\times f(\pi(w)) d\omega_2^k(\pi(w)).$$

Hence, we have for all $0 \leqslant s \leqslant \pi/2$

$$\frac{\mathrm{d}\Psi(\pi(z_s))}{\mathrm{d}s} = \frac{\sin 2s}{k-2} \int \{-(k-1)\cos^2 \rho(\pi(z_0), \pi(w)) + 1\} \, f(\pi(w)) \, \mathrm{d}\omega_2^k(\pi(w))$$

and so $\Psi(\pi(z_s))$ attains the unique global maximum at $s = 0$, that is, at $\pi(z_0)$, if and only if the inequality in the theorem holds. ∎

There is some overlap between our Theorems 9.2 and 9.3. The case $f \equiv 1$ of Theorem 9.2, that is, when the given shape-measure on Σ_2^k is uniform, shows that for any fixed point $\pi(z_0) \in \Sigma_2^k$ we have

$$\int_{\Sigma_2^k} \cos^2 \rho(\pi(z_0), \pi(w)) \, \mathrm{d}\omega_2^k(\pi(w)) = \frac{1}{k-1}.$$

From this we can deduce that, if f is a non-increasing function of the distance ρ of $\pi(z)$ from a given point $\pi(z_0)$ and f is strictly decreasing on a set of positive measure, then the inequality required for Theorem 9.3 holds and Theorem 9.3 then coincides with the case when the metric is $\tilde{\rho}$ in Theorem 9.2.

However, Theorem 9.2 is not implied by Theorem 9.3, since not only does the former apply to Fréchet means defined with respect to any of three metrics rather than just to one, but it is clear from the proof that it also applies to such means defined with respect to any strictly increasing function of the Riemannian metric ρ.

Conversely, let f satisfy the hypotheses of Theorem 9.2 and so, as noted above, also those of Theorem 9.3. If h is a function of distance from $\pi(z_0)$ having a positive jump at a distance for which f does not have a negative one and if h is normalised so that $h \, \mathrm{d}\omega_2^k$ is a shape-measure on Σ_2^k, then, for sufficiently small $a > 0$, $(1-a)f + ah$ will satisfy the hypotheses of Theorem 9.3 but not those of Theorem 9.2.

9.4 FRÉCHET MEANS AND THE SHAPE OF THE MEANS

The results of the previous section hold for a broad range of shape-measures induced from distributions of vertices, for any of which we are naturally interested in knowing the relation between the shape of the configuration that is the mean of the joint distribution of the vertices, that is, the shape determined by the means of the marginal distributions of the vertices, and the Fréchet mean of the induced shape-measure. In this section we shall describe some of these measures and investigate the optimal case in which not only is there a unique Fréchet mean, but it also coincides with the shape of the means. First, since the Radon-Nikodým derivative of the induced shape-measure of k labelled independent Gaussian distributions $\mathcal{N}(z_{0j}^*, \sigma^2 I)$ on $\mathbb{R}^2$, with z_{0j}^* not all equal, is a strictly decreasing function of distance ρ from the shape of the means (cf. Chapter 8), the following result follows directly from Theorem 9.2.

Theorem 9.4. *The shape of the means of k labelled independent Gaussian distributions $\mathcal{N}(z^*_{0j}, \sigma^2 I)$ on $\mathbb{R}^2$, provided those means are not all equal, is the unique Fréchet mean shape of the corresponding induced shape-measure with respect to ρ, to $\hat{\rho}$ and to $\tilde{\rho}$.*

That, of course, is a rather special case. However, using Theorems 9.2 and 9.3, we can extend it to other joint distributions of k vertices, which, like that of Theorem 9.4, are isotropic on $\mathbb{R}^{2k}$. These extensions depend on the following result, which gives us a significant class of induced shape-measures on Σ^k_2 that satisfy the main hypothesis of those two theorems with distance measured to the shape of the means. In the proof of this and later results we shall follow the convention we have used in the general case by denoting points in $\mathbb{C}^{k-1}$ by $\tilde{z}$, $\tilde{w}$, etc. and the corresponding points to which they project on the pre-shape sphere by z, w, respectively.

Proposition 9.3. *Suppose that k labelled random variables $z^*_1, \ldots, z^*_k$ in $\mathbb{R}^2$ have means $z^*_{01}, \ldots, z^*_{0k}$, which are not all equal, and suppose that the joint distribution on $\mathbb{R}^{2k}$ of $z^*_1 - z^*_{01}, \ldots, z^*_k - z^*_{0k}$ is isotropic. Then, the Radon–Nikodým derivative, with respect to the uniform measure, on Σ^k_2 of the induced shape-measure is a function of the distance ρ of $\pi(z)$ from $\pi(z_0)$, the shape of the means.*

Proof. For a random vector $x \in \mathbb{R}^{2k}$ to follow an isotropic distribution means that, when written in polar coordinates $x = sy$, where $s > 0$ and $y \in \mathbf{S}^{2k-1}$, the radial part s follows an arbitrary distribution on $[0, \infty)$ independently of y, which follows a uniform distribution on $\mathbf{S}^{2k-1}$. This is equivalent to the density function of x being a function of distance to the origin. Hence, if k labelled points in $\mathbb{R}^2$ jointly follow an isotropic distribution and if we remove the effects of translation by a projection onto to the hyperplane orthogonal to $(1, 1, \ldots, 1)$, then the resulting $\tilde{z}$ in $\mathbb{C}^{k-1}$ also follows an isotropic distribution.

With the above considerations, we suppose that $k - 1$ labelled random variables $\tilde{z}_1, \ldots, \tilde{z}_{k-1}$ in $\mathbb{R}^2$ have means $\tilde{z}_{01}, \ldots, \tilde{z}_{0,k-1}$, respectively, and that the joint density of $\tilde{z}_1 - \tilde{z}_{01}, \ldots, \tilde{z}_{k-1} - \tilde{z}_{0,k-1}$ is a function of distance to the origin. We may express the joint density as a function f of the squared distance to the origin. That is, the joint distribution of $\tilde{z}_1, \ldots, \tilde{z}_{k-1}$ is

$$f(||\tilde{z} - \tilde{z}_0||^2) \, d\tilde{z}_1 \cdots d\tilde{z}_{k-1}. \tag{9.10}$$

This implies that z has an offset uniform distribution on the pre-shape sphere (cf. Kent and Mardia, 1997). Without loss of generality, we may assume that $\tilde{z}_{01} = a > 0$ and $\tilde{z}_{0j} = 0$ for $2 \leqslant j \leqslant k - 1$. To obtain the induced shape-measure on shape space we write $\tilde{z}_1 = r_0 e^{i\theta_0}$ and we then have

$$\cos^2 \rho(\pi(z_0), \pi(z)) = \frac{|\langle \tilde{z}_0, \tilde{z} \rangle|^2}{||\tilde{z}_0||^2 ||\tilde{z}||^2} = \frac{r_0^2}{||\tilde{z}||^2}$$

and

$$\|\tilde{z} - \tilde{z}_0\|^2 = \|\tilde{z}\|^2 + \|\tilde{z}_0\|^2 - \langle \tilde{z}_1, \tilde{z}_{01} \rangle - \langle \tilde{z}_{01}, \tilde{z}_1 \rangle$$
$$= a^2 + r_0^2 \cos^{-2} \rho(\pi(z_0), \pi(z)) - 2a\, r_0 \cos \theta_0.$$

We recall that, when using the inhomogeneous coordinates $(\zeta_1, \ldots, \zeta_{k-2})$ at $\pi(z)$ on shape space, where $\zeta_j = \tilde{z}_{j+1}/\tilde{z}_1 = z_{j+1}/z_1$, scaling effects can be represented by r_0 and rotation effects can be represented by θ_0. Thus, to obtain the shape-measure on shape space induced by (9.10), we need to integrate out r_0 and θ_0. However, the uniform measure on Σ_2^k has the expression (9.8) and

$$d\tilde{z}_1 \cdots d\tilde{z}_{k-1} = r_0^{2k-4} d\tilde{z}_1 \, d\zeta_1 \cdots d\zeta_{k-2}.$$

Hence, the Radon–Nikodým derivative, with respect to the uniform measure, in Σ_2^k is

$$\cos^{-2(k-1)} \rho(\pi(z_0), \pi(z))$$

$$\times \frac{1}{\pi} \int_0^{2\pi} \int_0^{\infty} f\left(a^2 + r_0^2 \cos^{-2} \rho(\pi(z_0), \pi(z)) - 2a\, r_0 \cos \theta_0\right) r_0^{2k-3}\, dr_0\, d\theta_0$$

$$= \frac{1}{\pi} \int_0^{2\pi} \int_0^{\infty} f\left(a^2 + \hat{r}^2 - 2a\, \hat{r} \cos \rho(\pi(z_0), \pi(z)) \cos \theta_0\right) \hat{r}^{2k-3}\, d\hat{r}\, d\theta_0$$

$$= \frac{2}{\pi} \int_0^{\pi/2} \int_0^{\infty} \left\{ f\left(a^2 + \hat{r}^2 - 2a\, \hat{r} \cos \rho(\pi(z_0), \pi(z)) \cos \theta_0\right)\right.$$
$$\left. + f\left(a^2 + \hat{r}^2 + 2a\, \hat{r} \cos \rho(\pi(z_0), \pi(z)) \cos \theta_0\right) \right\} \hat{r}^{2k-3}\, d\hat{r}\, d\theta_0,$$

where $\hat{r} = r_0/\cos \rho(\pi(z_0), \pi(z))$. This is clearly a function of ρ as required. ∎

To proceed from this result to a proof that the shape of the mean of a joint distribution of the vertices is the unique Fréchet mean of the induced shape-measure, there are two routes we may pursue. On the one hand, if the function f in the proof of this proposition is differentiable, then the condition required for Theorem 9.2 that the Radon–Nikodým derivative, with respect to the uniform measure, of the induced shape-measure be a decreasing function of the distance ρ is satisfied if and only if

$$\frac{4a}{\pi} \int_0^{\pi/2} \int_0^{\infty} \left\{ f'\left(a^2 + \hat{r}^2 + 2a\, \hat{r} \cos \rho(\pi(z_0), \pi(z)) \cos \theta_0\right) \right.$$
$$\left. - f'\left(a^2 + \hat{r}^2 - 2a\, \hat{r} \cos \rho(\pi(z_0), \pi(z)) \cos \theta_0\right) \right\} \hat{r}^{2k-2} \cos \theta_0\, d\hat{r}\, d\theta_0 > 0. \qquad (9.11)$$

Although this inequality looks complex, it is frequently straightforward to verify in practice. It holds, for example, if f is a C^1 convex function. For then f' is increasing and so

$$f'\left(a^2 + \hat{r}^2 + 2a\, \hat{r} \cos \rho(\pi(z_0), \pi(z)) \cos \theta_0\right)$$
$$- f'\left(a^2 + \hat{r}^2 - 2a\, \hat{r} \cos \rho(\pi(z_0), \pi(z)) \cos \theta_0\right) \geqslant 0$$

for all $\hat{r} > 0$, for all $\theta_0 \in [0, \pi/2]$ and for all $\cos\rho$. The class of convex $\mathcal{C}^1$ functions includes the following functions that often arise in practice:

(i) $f(s) = (1 + s)^c, c < -1,$
(ii) $f(s) = e^{-cs}, c > 0,$
(iii) $f(s) = (1 + s)^c e^{-bs}, c < 0$ and $b > 0.$

Whenever we are able to verify the necessary and sufficient condition (9.11), we deduce, from Theorem 9.2, that the shape of the mean of the joint distribution of the vertices is the unique Fréchet mean of the induced shape-measure whether this is calculated with respect to ρ, $\hat{\rho}$ or $\tilde{\rho}$ or, indeed, with respect to the more general functions mentioned before Theorem 9.2.

On the other hand, for the random variables in Proposition 9.3, the shape of the mean of the joint distribution of the vertices is always the Fréchet mean with respect to $\tilde{\rho}$ of the induced shape-measure since the hypotheses of Theorem 9.3 are always satisfied, as was shown by Kent and Mardia (1997).

Theorem 9.5. *Suppose that k labelled random variables $z_1^*, \ldots, z_k^*$ in $\mathbb{R}^2$ are given as in Proposition 9.3. Then, the shape of the means, $\pi(z_0)$, is the unique Fréchet mean of the induced shape-measure with respect to $\tilde{\rho}$.*

Proof. Rather than a complete proof, we shall give a summary of Kent and Mardia's proof that ties it in with our present point of view. By the results of Theorem 9.3 and Proposition 9.3, we only need to show that the induced shape-measure satisfies the necessary and sufficient condition given in Theorem 9.3, which, in turn, is equivalent to showing that $\pi(z_0)$ is the unique global maximum of the function Ψ defined in the proof of Theorem 9.3. However, if we pull back the induced shape-measure onto the pre-shape sphere, we have

$$\Psi(\pi(w)) = w \ E[\bar{z}^t z] \ \overline{w}^t.$$

It is easy to check that $E[\bar{z}^t z]$ is invariant with respect to $\mathbf{U}(k-1)$ and so, by the spectral decomposition, $E[\bar{z}^t z]$ must be of the form:

$$E[\bar{z}^t z] = a I_{k-1} + b \bar{z}_0^t z_0.$$

Hence, $\pi(z_0)$ is the global maximum of Ψ if and only if b is greater than zero. However, we have

$$\Psi(\pi(w)) = a + b \cos^2 \rho(\pi(w), \pi(z_0)),$$

where $a > 0$ and $(k-1)a + b = 1$, so that our necessary and sufficient condition, which is now $a + b > 1/(k-1)$, is equivalent to $b > 0$. However, in Kent and Mardia (1997) it is proved that, when z_j^* satisfy the condition given in the theorem, b is greater than zero. ∎

We should note that the hypotheses of Theorem 9.2 are much weaker than those of Theorems 9.3 and 9.4, which require, in particular, that the distributions on $\mathbb{C}^{k-1}$ be isotropic. There is indeed a large class of distributions that satisfy the former, but not the latter, for which, therefore, we know that there is a unique Fréchet mean of the induced shape-measures with respect to ρ, $\hat{\rho}$ or $\tilde{\rho}$, but for which Theorems 9.4 and 9.5 are unable to tell us whether or not it is the shape of the means. The following is such an example of a *non-isotropic* distribution on $\mathbb{C}^{k-1}$ whose marginal distribution on $\mathbf{S}^{2k-3}$, nevertheless, induces a shape-measure on Σ_2^k that satisfies the hypotheses of Theorem 9.2.

Define a function f on the pre-shape sphere $\mathbf{S}^{2k-3}$ by

$$f(z) = f((z_1, \ldots, z_{k-1})) = c\, e^{|z_1|^2},$$

where $c > 0$ is a constant such that

$$\int_{\mathbf{S}^{2k-3}} f(z)\, dv_{\mathbf{S}^{2k-3}}(z) = 1.$$

As before, $dv_{\mathbf{S}^{2k-3}}$ is the volume element of $\mathbf{S}^{2k-3}$. Consider the distribution $d\mu$ on $\mathbb{C}^{k-1}$ defined by

$$d\mu(\tilde{z}) = \tilde{c}\, f\left(\frac{\tilde{z}}{\|\tilde{z}\|}\right) e^{-\|\tilde{z}\|^2} \prod_{j=1}^{k-1} d\tilde{z}_j,$$

where $\tilde{c}$ is another normalising constant. Then, $f\, dv_{\mathbf{S}^{2k-3}}$ is the marginal distribution of $d\mu$ on $\mathbf{S}^{2k-3}$. Now, it is clear that the density function of $d\mu$ is not a function of the distance from a fixed point on $\mathbb{C}^{k-1}$, so that $d\mu$ is not an isotropic distribution. On the other hand, $f(z) = c\, e^{\cos^2 \rho(\pi(z_0), \pi(z))}$, where $z_0 = (1, 0, \ldots, 0)$ in $\mathbf{S}^{2k-3}$, so that f is the composite of the projection with a function defined on Σ_2^k and, for any function h on Σ_2^k, we have

$$\int_{\mathbf{S}^{2k-3}} h(\pi(z))\, f(z)\, dv_{\mathbf{S}^{2k-3}}(z) = \hat{c} \int_{\Sigma_2^k} h(\pi(z))\, e^{\cos^2 \rho(\pi(z_0), \pi(z))}\, d\omega_2^k(\pi(z)).$$

Thus, $f\, dv_{\mathbf{S}^{2k-3}}$ on $\mathbf{S}^{2k-3}$ induces the shape-measure on Σ_2^k whose Radon–Nikodým derivative, with respect to $d\omega_2^k$, is $\bar{c}e^{\cos^2 \rho(\pi(z_0), \pi(z))}$ and, since this is a decreasing function of ρ, this shape measure has $\pi(z_0)$ as its unique Fréchet mean with respect to ρ, $\hat{\rho}$ or $\tilde{\rho}$.

9.5   UNIQUENESS OF FRÉCHET MEANS OF *n* GIVEN SHAPES

Suppose that $\{\pi(z_j) \in \Sigma_2^k : 1 \leqslant j \leqslant n\}$ are the n given shapes. Then, as explained in Section 9.2, by a Fréchet mean of the n shapes with respect to the metric 'dist' we understand any $\pi(z^\dagger) \in \Sigma_2^k$ at which the function

$$F_{\mu_0}(\pi(z)) = \frac{1}{2n} \sum_{j=1}^{n} \text{dist}(\pi(z), \pi(z_j))^2$$

defined on Σ_2^k attains its global minimum.

To find uniqueness results for such Fréchet means with respect to two of our three metrics, it will be more convenient to work on the pre-shape sphere. For example, since the set of points on the pre-shape sphere with the same shape as w is $\{e^{i\alpha}w : 0 \leqslant \alpha < 2\pi\}$, the metric $\hat{\rho}$ on shape space can be expressed in terms of pre-shapes by

$$\hat{\rho}(\pi(z), \pi(w))^2 = \min_{\alpha \in [0, 2\pi)} ||z - e^{i\alpha}w||^2. \qquad (9.12)$$

So, we see that $\pi(z^\dagger)$ is a Fréchet mean of the n given shapes with respect to $\hat{\rho}$ if and only if $z^\dagger \in S^{2k-3}$ realises the minimum of the function

$$G_{\mu_0}(z) = \min_{\alpha_j \in [0, 2\pi)} \sum_{j=1}^{n} ||z - e^{i\alpha_j}z_j||^2 \qquad (9.13)$$

on the pre-shape sphere.

Similarly, we can pull the F_{μ_0} associated with $\tilde{\rho}$ or ρ back to the pre-shape sphere to obtain analogous expressions. In particular, it follows from (9.4) that $\pi(z^\dagger)$ is a Fréchet mean of the n given shapes with respect to $\tilde{\rho}$ if and only if $z^\dagger \in S^{2k-3}$ realises the minimum

$$1 - z \left\{ \sum_{j=1}^{n} \bar{z}_j^t z_j \right\} \bar{z}^t,$$

that is, if and only if $z^\dagger \in S^{2k-3}$ is an eigenvector corresponding to the maximum eigenvalue of the matrix $\sum_{j=1}^{n} \bar{z}_j^t z_j$ (cf. Kent, 1992). Hence, we can already see that the uniqueness of the Fréchet mean of the n given shapes with respect to $\tilde{\rho}$ corresponds to the maximum eigenvalue of this matrix having geometric multiplicity one.

Similarly, for the Fréchet means of the n given shapes with respect to the Riemannian metric ρ we already have the uniqueness result, Theorem 9.1: if the n given shapes are contained in an open geodesic ball of radius $\pi/8$, then they have a unique Fréchet mean with respect to ρ and this mean lies inside the ball. If the n given shapes are only known to lie in a geodesic ball of radius $\pi/4$, then we still have the weaker result of Proposition 9.1(i) that there is a unique Cartan mean on that ball. However, in that case, we do not know that it is a Fréchet mean, nor that there are no other Fréchet means outside the ball.

In view of these results for ρ and $\tilde{\rho}$, we shall devote the rest of this section to obtaining a similar condition for the uniqueness of Fréchet means of the n given shapes with respect to $\hat{\rho}$. So, from now on, the function F_{μ_0} whose global minima we shall be seeking on shape space will be given by

$$F_{\mu_0}(\pi(z)) = \frac{1}{2n} \sum_{j=1}^{n} \hat{\rho}(\pi(z), \pi(z_j))^2.$$

For this we need to bring into play the size-and-shape space, which, we recall from Chapter 1, in the case $m = 2$ is the quotient space of $\mathbb{C}^{k-1}$ by $\mathbf{SO}(2)$ acting on the left. We shall denote the size-and-shape space by $S\Sigma_2^k$ and the quotient map $\mathbb{C}^{k-1} \to S\Sigma_2^k$ by $\tilde{\pi}$. Since the pre-shape sphere lies in $\mathbb{C}^{k-1}$ and the $\mathbf{SO}(2)$ action preserves size, we also have $\Sigma_2^k \subset S\Sigma_2^k$ and $\tilde{\pi}\,|_{S_2^k} = \pi$. Moreover, the norm metric on $\mathbb{C}^{k-1}$ induces a metric $\hat{\rho}$ on $S\Sigma_2^k$ that extends the similarly named metric on Σ_2^k. This extension is given by a similar formula to (9.12), but with $\tilde{\pi}(\tilde{z})$ replacing $\pi(z)$, etc.

We now extend the above function F_{μ_0} to $\tilde{F}_{\mu_0}$ given by the same expression on the size-and-shape space. Since $\pi(z^\dagger)$ is a global minimum of F_{μ_0} if and only if $z^\dagger$ is a global minimum of G_{μ_0} on the pre-shape sphere, we also extend G_{μ_0} to the similarly defined function $\tilde{G}_{\mu_0}$ on the entire space $\mathbb{C}^{k-1}$. Note that both G_{μ_0} and $\tilde{G}_{\mu_0}$ are constant on $\mathbf{SO}(2)$-orbits so that $G_{\mu_0} = F_{\mu_0} \circ \pi$ and $\tilde{G}_{\mu_0} = \tilde{F}_{\mu_0} \circ \tilde{\pi}$ and the values, in particular, the minimum values, taken by F_{μ_0} and $\tilde{F}_{\mu_0}$ are the same as those taken by G_{μ_0} and $\tilde{G}_{\mu_0}$, respectively. It also follows that the critical points of F_{μ_0} and $\tilde{F}_{\mu_0}$ are the images of those of G_{μ_0} and $\tilde{G}_{\mu_0}$, respectively, since the partial derivatives of the latter functions along the $\mathbf{SO}(2)$-orbits are always zero.

It will be convenient, for $\underline{\alpha} = (\alpha_1, \ldots, \alpha_n) \in [0, 2\pi)^n$, to write

$$M(\underline{\alpha}) = \frac{1}{n} \sum_{j=1}^{n} e^{i\alpha_j} z_j,$$

the mean of the corresponding n points in $\mathbb{C}^{k-1}$, taken one from each of the n fibres $\{e^{i\alpha_j} z_j : \alpha_j \in [0, 2\pi)\}$ lying above the shape points $\pi(z_j)$ for $1 \leqslant j \leqslant n$. We also write

$$\mathbb{C}_0^{k-1} = \{M(\underline{\alpha}) : \underline{\alpha} \in [0, 2\pi)^n\} \subseteq \mathbb{C}^{k-1}$$

for the set of all such means, which will play an important role in our analysis. Then,

$$\tilde{G}_{\mu_0}(\tilde{z}) = \min_{\underline{\alpha} \in [0, 2\pi)^n} H(\underline{\alpha}, \tilde{z}),$$

where

$$H(\underline{\alpha}, \tilde{z}) = \sum_{j=1}^{n} ||\tilde{z} - e^{i\alpha_j} z_j||^2$$

and, writing $h(\underline{\alpha})$ for $H(\underline{\alpha}, M(\underline{\alpha}))$, which, for fixed $\underline{\alpha}$, is the minimum value of $H(\underline{\alpha}, \tilde{z})$ as $\tilde{z}$ varies in $\mathbb{C}^{k-1}$, we see that

$$\min_{\tilde{z} \in \mathbb{C}^{k-1}} \tilde{G}_{\mu_0}(\tilde{z}) = \min_{\tilde{z} \in \mathbb{C}^{k-1}} \min_{\underline{\alpha} \in [0, 2\pi)^n} H(\underline{\alpha}, \tilde{z})$$

$$= \min_{\underline{\alpha} \in [0, 2\pi)^n} \min_{\tilde{z} \in \mathbb{C}^{k-1}} H(\underline{\alpha}, \tilde{z}) = \min_{\underline{\alpha} \in [0, 2\pi)^n} h(\underline{\alpha}).$$

Since $[0, 2\pi)^n$, which is essentially the product of n copies of the unit circle, is compact, this minimum will be attained in $[0, 2\pi)^n$. In particular, any minimum point $\tilde{z} = M(\underline{\alpha})$ of $\tilde{G}_{\mu_0}$ lies in $\mathbb{C}_0^{k-1}$.

To obtain our result for Fréchet means with respect to $\hat{\rho}$ we shall first correlate the global minima of $\tilde{G}_{\mu_0}$, or, equivalently, those of H, with those of G_{μ_0}, which map under the quotient map π to the Fréchet means that we seek, the global minima of F_{μ_0}. We then characterise the critical points of $\tilde{G}_{\mu_0}$ and the related function h and, in the latter case, we obtain a sufficient condition for such a point to be a local minimum. Each critical point of $\tilde{G}_{\mu_0}$ will determine a critical point of h, which, provided the corresponding shape is sufficiently close to the n given shapes, will satisfy this condition to be a local minimum. Then, if the n given shapes lie in a sufficiently small geodesic ball, we shall be able to show that F_{μ_0} has a unique global minimum and that it lies in that ball.

First, then, we correlate the global minima of G_{μ_0} with those of $\tilde{G}_{\mu_0}$.

Lemma 9.3. *Let $\{z_j \in \mathbf{S}^{2k-3} : 1 \leqslant j \leqslant n\}$ be given. If $\tilde{z}^\dagger \in \mathbb{C}^{k-1}$ is a global minimum of $\tilde{G}_{\mu_0}$, then the corresponding $z^\dagger$ is a global minimum of G_{μ_0}. Conversely, if $z^\dagger \in \mathbf{S}^{2k-3}$ is a global minimum of G_{μ_0}, then there exists an $s^\dagger > 0$ such that $\tilde{z}^\dagger = s^\dagger z^\dagger$ realises the global minimum of $\tilde{G}_{\mu_0}$.*

Proof. Since we are assuming that $||z_j|| = 1$ for each j, on expanding $H(\underline{\alpha}, M(\underline{\alpha}))$ we find that

$$h(\underline{\alpha}) = H(\underline{\alpha}, M(\underline{\alpha})) = n(1 - ||M(\underline{\alpha})||^2).$$

Similarly,

$$H\left(\underline{\alpha}, \frac{M(\underline{\alpha})}{||M(\underline{\alpha})||}\right) = 2n(1 - ||M(\underline{\alpha})||).$$

We have already seen that $\tilde{z}$ realises the minimum of $\tilde{G}_{\mu_0}$ if and only if $\tilde{z} = M(\underline{\alpha})$, where $\underline{\alpha}$ realises the minimum of $h(\underline{\alpha})$, so that $\tilde{z}$ must be a point of maximum norm in $\mathbb{C}_0^{k-1}$. On the other hand, the minimum value of G_{μ_0} on the pre-shape sphere is

$$\min_{\underline{\alpha} \in [0, 2\pi)^n, \, z \in \mathbf{S}^{2k-3}} H(\underline{\alpha}, z)$$

$$= \min_{\underline{\alpha} \in [0, 2\pi)^n, \, z \in \mathbf{S}^{2k-3}} \sum_{j=1}^n ||z - e^{i\alpha_j} z_j||^2$$

$$= 2\left\{ n - \max_{\underline{\alpha} \in [0, 2\pi)^n, \, z \in \mathbf{S}^{2k-3}} \Re\left(\sum_{j=1}^n \langle z, e^{i\alpha_j} z_j \rangle \right) \right\}$$

$$= 2n\left\{ 1 - \max_{\underline{\alpha} \in [0, 2\pi)^n, \, z \in \mathbf{S}^{2k-3}} \Re(\langle z, M(\underline{\alpha}) \rangle) \right\}. \tag{9.14}$$

However, writing $M(\underline{\alpha}) = (a_1 e^{i\beta_{11}}, \ldots, a_{k-1} e^{i\beta_{1k-1}}) \in \mathbb{C}_0^{k-1}$ with $a_j \geqslant 0$ and $z = (b_1 e^{i\beta_{21}}, \ldots, b_{k-1} e^{i\beta_{2k-1}})$ with $b_j \geqslant 0$, then, as the arguments β_{2j} are allowed to vary,

$$\Re(\langle z, M(\underline{\alpha})\rangle) = \sum_{j=1}^{k-1} a_j b_j \cos(\beta_{1j} - \beta_{2j})$$

achieves its maximum value $\sum_{j=1}^{k-1} a_j b_j$ when $\beta_{2j} = \beta_{1j}$. Thus, to find $z^\dagger$ that realises the maximum value of $\Re(\langle z, M(\underline{\alpha})\rangle)$ as z varies in $\mathbf{S}^{2k-3}$ is equivalent to solving

$$\max_{b_j \geqslant 0} \sum_{j=1}^{k-1} a_j b_j \quad \text{subject to} \quad \sum_{j=1}^{k-1} b_j^2 = 1.$$

That is attained at $b_j^\dagger = a_j / \left\{ \sum_{j=1}^{k-1} a_j^2 \right\}^{1/2}$ with the maximal value $\left\{ \sum_{j=1}^{k-1} a_j^2 \right\}^{1/2}$. This implies that the minimum value (9.14) of G_{μ_0} is

$$2n \left\{ 1 - \max_{\underline{\alpha} \in [0,2\pi)^n} \|M(\underline{\alpha})\| \right\} = \min_{\underline{\alpha} \in [0,2\pi)^n} H\left(\underline{\alpha}, \frac{M(\underline{\alpha})}{\|M(\underline{\alpha})\|} \right).$$

The stated relation between the global minima of $\tilde{G}_{\mu_0}$ and G_{μ_0} is now clear, since both are determined by points of maximum norm in $\mathbb{C}_0^{k-1}$. ∎

It follows from this lemma that the global minima of $\tilde{G}_{\mu_0}$, which correspond to those of h, also determine those of G_{μ_0} and hence those of F_{μ_0} that we require. However, rather than looking directly for global minima of $\tilde{G}_{\mu_0}$ or h, we shall need to study their general critical points. For this purpose, we shall need an alternative expression for the metric $\hat{\rho}$ on size-and-shape space. As we showed in Chapter 6 for pre-shapes, it follows similarly that, for any $\tilde{z} = (\tilde{z}_1, \ldots, \tilde{z}_{k-1})$ and $\tilde{w} = (\tilde{w}_1, \ldots, \tilde{w}_{k-1})$ in $\mathbb{C}^{k-1}$, $\alpha^\dagger$ realises the minimum

$$\min_{\alpha \in [0,2\pi)} \|\tilde{z} - e^{i\alpha} \tilde{w}\|^2 = \|\tilde{z}\|^2 + \|\tilde{w}\|^2 - 2 \max_{\alpha \in [0,2\pi)} \Re(\langle \tilde{z}, e^{i\alpha} \tilde{w}\rangle)$$

if and only if $\langle \tilde{z}, e^{i\alpha^\dagger} \tilde{w}\rangle$ is real and non-negative, which implies that

$$\hat{\rho}(\tilde{\pi}(\tilde{z}), \tilde{\pi}(\tilde{w}))^2 = \|\tilde{z}\|^2 + \|\tilde{w}\|^2 - 2|\langle \tilde{z}, \tilde{w}\rangle|.$$

This expression for $\hat{\rho}$ on size-and-shape space enables us to find the critical points of $\tilde{G}_{\mu_0}$ as follows.

Lemma 9.4. *A point $\tilde{z}^\dagger \in \mathbb{C}^{k-1}$ is a critical point of $\tilde{G}_{\mu_0}$ if and only if $\tilde{z}^\dagger$ is a solution of the equation*

$$\tilde{z}^\dagger = \frac{1}{n} \sum_{j=1}^{n} \frac{\langle \tilde{z}^\dagger, z_j \rangle}{|\langle \tilde{z}^\dagger, z_j \rangle|} z_j. \tag{9.15}$$

Proof. Since $\tilde{z}^{\dagger}$ is a critical point of $\tilde{G}_{\mu_0}$ if and only if $\tilde{\pi}(\tilde{z}^{\dagger})$ is a critical point of $\tilde{F}_{\mu_0}$, we may work on the size-and-shape space $S\Sigma_2^k$. If we restrict to $\tilde{z} \in \mathbb{C}^{k-1}$ having one particular component real and positive, then there is a local one-to-one correspondence between such $\tilde{z}$ and the corresponding $\tilde{\pi}(\tilde{z})$ in $S\Sigma_2^k$. This gives us local coordinate systems on $S\Sigma_2^k$. We differentiate $\hat{\rho}(\tilde{\pi}(\tilde{z}), \tilde{\pi}(\tilde{w}))^2$ as a function of $\tilde{\pi}(\tilde{z})$ on $S\Sigma_2^k$ by using such local coordinate systems. In the case when $\tilde{z}_1$ is real and positive we get

$$\frac{\partial}{\partial \tilde{z}_l} \hat{\rho}(\tilde{\pi}(\tilde{z}), \tilde{\pi}(\tilde{w}))^2 = 2 \left\{ \bar{\tilde{z}}_l - \bar{\tilde{w}}_l \frac{\langle \tilde{w}, \tilde{z} \rangle}{|\langle \tilde{w}, \tilde{z} \rangle|} \right\}, \quad 1 \leqslant l \leqslant k-1,$$

and

$$\frac{\partial}{\partial \bar{\tilde{z}}_l} \hat{\rho}(\tilde{\pi}(\tilde{z}), \tilde{\pi}(\tilde{w}))^2 = 2 \left\{ \tilde{z}_l - \tilde{w}_l \frac{\langle \tilde{z}, \tilde{w} \rangle}{|\langle \tilde{z}, \tilde{w} \rangle|} \right\}, \quad 2 \leqslant l \leqslant k-1.$$

Using this to differentiate the expression

$$\sum_{j=1}^{n} \hat{\rho}(\tilde{\pi}(\tilde{z}), \pi(z_j))^2$$

with respect to $\tilde{\pi}(\tilde{z})$ in $S\Sigma_2^k$, we have the required result. ∎

A straightforward consequence of Lemma 9.4 is that all the critical points of $\tilde{G}_{\mu_0}$ lie in $\mathbb{C}_0^{k-1}$ and hence those of $\tilde{F}_{\mu_0}$ must be contained in $\pi(\mathbb{C}_0^{k-1})$.

Next, we look at the critical points of h. Since $h(\underline{\alpha}) = n(1 - ||M(\underline{\alpha})||^2)$ and $||M(\underline{\alpha})|| = ||M(\underline{\alpha}')||$ whenever $\underline{\alpha} - \underline{\alpha}'$ has all n of its components equal, we see that h is constant along the line segment

$$\mathbf{L}_{\underline{\alpha}} = \{(\alpha_1 + \alpha, \ldots, \alpha_n + \alpha) : \alpha \in \mathbb{R}\} \bigcap [0, 2\pi)^n,$$

corresponding to the fact that $\tilde{G}_{\mu_0}$ and G_{μ_0} are constant along **SO(2)**-orbits. Accordingly, the nature of a critical point of h is determined by the behaviour of h restricted to $\mathbf{H}_{\underline{\alpha}}$, the intersection with $[0, 2\pi)^n$ of the hyperplane perpendicular to $\mathbf{L}_{\underline{\alpha}}$.

Lemma 9.5. $\underline{\alpha}^{\dagger} = \left(\alpha_1^{\dagger}, \ldots, \alpha_n^{\dagger} \right)$ *is a critical point of* h *if and only if*

$$\left\langle e^{i\alpha_j^{\dagger}} z_j, \sum_{l \neq j} e^{i\alpha_l^{\dagger}} z_l \right\rangle \in \mathbb{R}, \quad 1 \leqslant j \leqslant n. \tag{9.16}$$

If, in addition,

$$\Re \left(e^{i(\alpha_j^{\dagger} - \alpha_l^{\dagger})} \langle z_j, z_l \rangle \right) \geqslant 0, \quad 1 \leqslant l, j \leqslant n, \tag{9.17}$$

then it is a local minimum of h. *If these inequalities are all strict, then* $\underline{\alpha}^{\dagger}$ *is a strict local minimum of the restriction of* h *to* $\mathbf{H}_{\underline{\alpha}}$.

Proof.   The first statement follows from the fact that

$$\frac{\partial h}{\partial \alpha_j} = \frac{i}{n} \sum_{l \neq j} \left\{ e^{i(\alpha_l - \alpha_j)} \langle z_l, z_j \rangle - e^{i(\alpha_j - \alpha_l)} \langle z_j, z_l \rangle \right\}, \quad 1 \leqslant j \leqslant n.$$

Then, since

$$\frac{\partial^2 h}{\partial \alpha_j^2} = \frac{1}{n} \sum_{l \neq j} \left\{ e^{i(\alpha_j - \alpha_l)} \langle z_j, z_l \rangle + e^{i(\alpha_l - \alpha_j)} \langle z_l, z_j \rangle \right\}, \quad 1 \leqslant j \leqslant n,$$

which, at critical points of h, is equal to

$$\frac{2}{n} \left\langle e^{i\alpha_j} z_j, \sum_{l \neq j} e^{i\alpha_l} z_l \right\rangle \in \mathbb{R}, \quad 1 \leqslant j \leqslant n,$$

it follows that, if h attains a local minimum at $\underline{\alpha}^\dagger$, then the n real numbers in (9.16) are all non-negative. For $l \neq j$,

$$\frac{\partial^2 h}{\partial \alpha_j \partial \alpha_l} = -\frac{1}{n} \left\{ e^{i(\alpha_j - \alpha_l)} \langle z_j, z_l \rangle + e^{i(\alpha_l - \alpha_j)} \langle z_l, z_j \rangle \right\} = -\frac{2}{n} \Re \left(e^{i(\alpha_j - \alpha_l)} \langle z_j, z_l \rangle \right).$$

As the product space $[0, 2\pi)^n$ is flat, the matrix Φ of the Hessian of h with respect to the tangent vectors $\left\{ \frac{\partial}{\partial \alpha_j} : 1 \leqslant j \leqslant n \right\}$ is

$$\Phi = \left(\frac{\partial^2 h}{\partial \alpha_j \partial \alpha_l} \right) = 2 \{ \Phi_1 + \Phi_2 \},$$

where

$$\Phi_1 = -\frac{1}{n} \Re \left\{ \begin{pmatrix} e^{i\alpha_1} z_1 \\ \vdots \\ e^{i\alpha_n} z_n \end{pmatrix} \left(e^{-i\alpha_1} \overline{z}_1^t \quad \cdots \quad e^{-i\alpha_n} \overline{z}_n^t \right) \right\}$$

and

$$\Phi_2 = \frac{1}{n} \Re \left(\operatorname{diag} \left\{ \sum_{j=1}^n e^{i(\alpha_1 - \alpha_j)} \langle z_1, z_j \rangle, \ldots, \sum_{j=1}^n e^{i(\alpha_n - \alpha_j)} \langle z_n, z_j \rangle \right\} \right).$$

Then, at the critical point $\underline{\alpha}^\dagger \in [0, 2\pi)^n$, for any $(a_1, \ldots, a_n) \in \mathbb{R}^n$,

$$\begin{pmatrix} a_1 & \cdots & a_n \end{pmatrix} \Phi \begin{pmatrix} a_1 \\ \vdots \\ a_n \end{pmatrix}$$

$$= -\frac{2}{n} \left\| \sum_{j=1}^n a_j e^{i\alpha_j^\dagger} z_j \right\|^2 + \frac{1}{n} \sum_{j,l=1}^n \left\{ a_j^2 + a_l^2 \right\} \langle e^{i\alpha_j^\dagger} z_j, e^{i\alpha_l^\dagger} z_l \rangle$$

$$= \frac{2}{n} \sum_{j,l=1}^n (a_j - a_l)^2 \Re \left(\langle e^{i\alpha_j^\dagger} z_j, e^{i\alpha_l^\dagger} z_l \rangle \right). \tag{9.18}$$

If condition (9.17) holds, then this will always be non-negative and hence $\underline{\alpha}^\dagger$ will be a local minimum. Moreover, if the inequalities in (9.17) are all strict, the expression (9.18) is equal to zero if and only if all a_j are equal. However, a tangent vector to $\mathbf{H}_{\underline{\alpha}^\dagger}$ never has all its components equal and so, with strict inequalities in (9.17), the restriction of h to $\mathbf{H}_{\underline{\alpha}^\dagger}$ will have a strict local minimum at $\underline{\alpha}^\dagger$.   ∎

In the following lemma we obtain a relation between critical points of $\tilde{G}_{\mu_0}$ and those of h, and also a sufficient condition for a critical point of $\tilde{G}_{\mu_0}$ to determine a local minimum of h. For that purpose we define a function $\underline{\alpha}$ from $\mathbb{C}^{k-1}$ to $[0, 2\pi)^n$ by

$$\underline{\alpha}(\tilde{z}) = (\alpha_1(\tilde{z}), \ldots, \alpha_n(\tilde{z})) = (\arg\{\langle \tilde{z}, z_1 \rangle\}, \ldots, \arg\{\langle \tilde{z}, z_n \rangle\}).$$

Lemma 9.6. *If $\tilde{z}^\dagger$ in $\mathbb{C}^{k-1}$ is a critical point of $\tilde{G}_{\mu_0}$, then $\underline{\alpha}^\dagger = \underline{\alpha}(\tilde{z}^\dagger)$ is a critical point of h. If, in addition, for $1 \leqslant j \leqslant n$*

$$\rho(\pi(z^\dagger), \pi(z_j)) < \pi/4,$$

then $\underline{\alpha}^\dagger$ is a local minimum of h, which is strict when h is restricted to $\mathbf{H}_{\underline{\alpha}^\dagger}$.

Proof.   Lemma 9.4 says that $\tilde{z}^\dagger$ is a critical point of $\tilde{G}_{\mu_0}$ if and only if $\tilde{z}^\dagger = M(\underline{\alpha}(\tilde{z}^\dagger))$. For such $\tilde{z}^\dagger$, since

$$\alpha_j(\tilde{z}^\dagger) = \arg\{\langle \tilde{z}^\dagger, z_j \rangle\} = -\arg\{\langle z_j, \tilde{z}^\dagger \rangle\},$$

we have

$$\left\langle e^{i\alpha_j(\tilde{z}^\dagger)} z_j, \tilde{z}^\dagger \right\rangle = |\langle \tilde{z}^\dagger, z_j \rangle| \in \mathbb{R}$$

and so

$$\left\langle e^{i\alpha_j(\tilde{z}^\dagger)} z_j, \sum_{l \neq j} e^{i\alpha_l(\tilde{z}^\dagger)} z_l \right\rangle = \left\langle e^{i\alpha_j(\tilde{z}^\dagger)} z_j, n\tilde{z}^\dagger - e^{i\alpha_j(\tilde{z}^\dagger)} z_j \right\rangle$$

$$= n|\langle \tilde{z}^\dagger, z_j \rangle| - \|z_j\|^2 \in \mathbb{R}.$$

Thus, $\underline{\alpha}(\tilde{z}^\dagger)$ satisfies the necessary and sufficient condition (9.16) for it to be a critical point of h.

Assuming now that $\rho(\pi(z^\dagger), \pi(z_j)) < \pi/4$, since, for $\alpha_j^\dagger = \arg\{\langle z^\dagger, z_j \rangle\}$, we have $\langle \tilde{z}^\dagger, e^{i\alpha_j^\dagger} z_j \rangle$ real and non-negative, it follows that

$$\langle z^\dagger, e^{i\alpha_j^\dagger} z_j \rangle = \cos(\rho(\pi(z^\dagger), \pi(z_j))) > \frac{1}{\sqrt{2}}.$$

Let

$$\tilde{z}_0^\dagger = \frac{1}{\sqrt{2}} z^\dagger.$$

Then,

$$||\tilde{z}_0^\dagger - e^{i\alpha_j^\dagger}z_j||^2 = \hat{\rho}(\tilde{\pi}(\tilde{z}_0^\dagger), \tilde{\pi}(z_j))^2 = 1 + \tfrac{1}{2} - \sqrt{2}\cos\rho(\pi(z^\dagger), \pi(z_j)) < \tfrac{1}{2}.$$

Thus, by the triangle inequality, we have, for each pair (j, l),

$$||e^{i\alpha_j^\dagger}z_j - e^{i\alpha_l^\dagger}z_l|| \leqslant ||e^{i\alpha_j^\dagger}z_j - \tilde{z}_0^\dagger|| + ||e^{i\alpha_l^\dagger}z_l - \tilde{z}_0^\dagger||$$

$$= \hat{\rho}(\tilde{\pi}(z_j), \tilde{\pi}(\tilde{z}_0^\dagger)) + \hat{\rho}(\tilde{\pi}(z_l), \tilde{\pi}(\tilde{z}_0^\dagger)) < \sqrt{2}$$

and it follows that

$$\Re\left(\langle e^{i\alpha_j^\dagger}z_j, e^{i\alpha_l^\dagger}z_l\rangle\right) > \tfrac{1}{2}\left\{||z_j||^2 + ||z_l||^2\right\} - 1 = 0.$$

By Lemma 9.5, this implies that $\underline{\alpha}^\dagger$ is a local minimum of h, which is strict when h is restricted to $\mathbf{H}_{\underline{\alpha}^\dagger}$. ■

We are now ready to discuss the Fréchet means of our n given shapes. Of course, since shape space is compact, Fréchet means will always exist. However, as already mentioned in Section 9.3, in practice we need to know rather more than that. Firstly, if, as we commonly do, we work on a geodesic ball or other submanifold containing the given shapes, then we would like to know whether any of the Fréchet means also lie in that ball. Secondly, it is very desirable to know when there is a unique Fréchet mean. This is particularly relevant in practice when we have found an explicit mean by algorithms or other methods. We are now able to answer these questions under sufficient hypotheses on the n given shapes, which are similar to some of those we have used earlier for general shape-measures.

Theorem 9.6. *If the set of n given shapes, $\left\{\pi(z_j) \in \Sigma_2^k : 1 \leqslant j \leqslant n\right\}$, is contained in a geodesic ball $\mathcal{B}_{\pi/8}(\pi(z_0))$ with centre $\pi(z_0)$ and radius $\pi/8$, then those shapes will have a unique Fréchet mean with respect to $\hat{\rho}$. This Fréchet mean will lie in $\mathcal{B}_{\pi/8}(\pi(z_0))$ and may be identified as the unique point $\pi(z^\dagger)$ in that ball such that there exists a real positive $s^\dagger$ for which $s^\dagger z^\dagger$ is a solution of (9.15).*

Proof. Since Σ_2^k is compact, Fréchet means exist and by Lemma 9.1, given the hypotheses of this theorem, they all lie in $\mathcal{B}_{\pi/8}(\pi(z_0))$. To establish uniqueness we show that such Fréchet means are characterised as stated in the theorem. Granted, then, that $\pi(z^\dagger)$ is any global minimum of F_{μ_0}, $z^\dagger$ will be a global minimum of G_{μ_0} and Lemma 9.3 shows that there is $s^\dagger > 0$ such that $s^\dagger z^\dagger$ is a global minimum and hence a critical point of $\tilde{G}_{\mu_0}$, which, by Lemma 9.4, is a solution of Equation (9.15).

Conversely, to show that any such critical point of $\tilde{G}_{\mu_0}$ projects to a Fréchet mean, we may assume, without loss of generality, that $\tilde{z}^\dagger$ is a solution of (9.15) with $\pi(z^\dagger)$ in $\mathcal{B}_{\pi/8}(\pi(z_0))$. Since all the given shapes also lie in $\mathcal{B}_{\pi/8}(\pi(z_0))$, the hypotheses of Lemma 9.6 are satisfied and hence $\underline{\alpha}^{\dagger} = \underline{\alpha}(\tilde{z}^{\dagger})$ is a local minimum of h, which is strict when h is restricted to $\mathbf{H}_{\underline{\alpha}^{\dagger}}$. It follows that $\tilde{G}_{\mu_0}$ and, similarly, G_{μ_0} when restricted to a local codimension one submanifold transverse to the $\mathbf{SO}(2)$-orbit through $\tilde{z}^{\dagger}$, respectively $z^{\dagger}$, have strict minima at those points. Hence, $\tilde{\pi}(\tilde{z}^{\dagger})$ is, in fact, a strict global minimum of $\tilde{F}_{\mu_0}$ and $\pi(z^{\dagger})$ is a strict global minimum of F_{μ_0}.

We note that the argument of the previous paragraph in fact shows that any critical point of $\tilde{F}_{\mu_0}$ with image in $\mathcal{B}_{\pi/8}(\pi(z_0))$ must be a strict global minimum, since it must be the image of a critical point of $\tilde{G}_{\mu_0}$, which, in turn, will satisfy Equation (9.15). However, the pre-image in $S\Sigma_2^k$ of the geodesic ball $\mathcal{B}_{\pi/8}(\pi(z_0))$ is connected: in fact, it is homeomorphic with a cone on $\mathcal{B}_{\pi/8}(\pi(z_0))$. Hence, if all the critical points of F_{μ_0} are isolated and all are global minima, there must be precisely one of them and so there is also precisely one Fréchet mean on $\mathcal{B}_{\pi/8}(\pi(z_0))$.   ∎

9.6 PROCRUSTEAN MEAN SHAPES

In the final section of this chapter we show that so-called procrustean means are special cases of Fréchet means and use our results to answer some questions that naturally arise in procrustean analysis. We shall continue, as for most of this chapter, to work with the case of configurations in $\mathbb{R}^2$, where we shall mainly discuss the two most commonly used means, which are generally referred to as the 'partial' and 'full' procrustean mean shapes.

Procrustean methods are a much used practical means for comparing two configurations in terms of their vertices. The basic principle involved is to use as a measure of the difference between two configurations of k labelled points in $\mathbb{R}^m$ the square-root of the sum of the squares of the Euclidean distances between corresponding points after an optimal matching of the two configurations under such operations as translation, rotation and scale change. This is, in effect, just the way in which we obtained induced metrics on shape, or size-and-shape, space from the norm metric on the configuration space $\mathbb{R}^{mk}$. In particular, the partial and full procrustean mean shapes implicitly involve the metrics on shape space, which we have labelled $\hat{\rho}$ and $\bar{\rho}$, respectively, (cf. Goodall, 1991; Kent, 1992 and Le, 1995a) and we shall show that they are, in fact, Fréchet means with respect to these metrics.

Specialising to the case $m = 2$ and writing, as usual, z^* for the complex k-ad representing the vertices of a configuration, a partial procrustean mean shape of the n points $z_1^*, \ldots, z_n^*$ in the configuration space $\mathbb{C}^k$ is the shape of a configuration $(z^*)^{\dagger}$ of norm one that realises

$$\min \left\{ \sum_{j=1}^{n} \left\| z^* - c_j \mathbf{1}_k - e^{i\alpha_j} \frac{z_j^*}{||z_j^* - z_{j,c}^* \mathbf{1}_k||} \right\|^2 : c_j \in \mathbb{C}, \alpha_j \in [0, 2\pi), ||z^*|| = 1 \right\},$$

$$(9.19)$$

where $z_{j,c}^*$ denotes the centroid of the components of z_j^*, and $\mathbf{1}_k$ denotes the row vector in $\mathbb{C}^k$ with all its components equal to one. Similarly, a full procrustean mean shape, defined on the configuration space, is the shape of a configuration $(z^*)^\dagger$ of norm one that realises

$$\min\left\{\sum_{j=1}^n ||z^* - c_j\mathbf{1}_k - a_je^{i\alpha_j}z_j^*||^2 : c_j \in \mathbb{C}, a_j > 0, \alpha_j \in [0, 2\pi), ||z^*|| = 1\right\}.$$

(9.20)

It follows that the partial and full procrustean means may be calculated on the pre-shape sphere as the shape of any $z^\dagger$ that realises

$$\min\left\{\sum_{j=1}^n ||z - e^{i\alpha_j}z_j||^2 : \alpha_j \in [0, 2\pi), ||z|| = 1\right\}$$

(9.21)

and the shape of any $z^\dagger$ that realises

$$\min\left\{\sum_{j=1}^n ||z - a_je^{i\alpha_j}z_j||^2 : a_j > 0, \alpha_j \in [0, 2\pi), ||z|| = 1\right\},$$

respectively.

If in (9.21) we minimise over the α_j first, we see from (9.12) and (9.13) that $z^\dagger$ is the minimum of G_{μ_0} defined there on the pre-shape sphere. Thus, the partial procrustean mean shapes of the n given configurations are, in fact, the Fréchet means of the corresponding shapes defined with respect to $\hat{\rho}$. Similarly, from the expression (9.4) for $\tilde{\rho}$ we see that their full procrustean means are the corresponding Fréchet means with respect to $\tilde{\rho}$.

Having identified the various procrustean means as special cases of Fréchet means, we may now use our work on the latter to answer questions about the former. We consider first the practical computation of procrustean means. As pointed out at the beginning of the previous section, a Fréchet mean of the n given shapes $\{\pi(z_j) : 1 \leqslant j \leqslant n\}$ with respect to the metric $\tilde{\rho}$ is the shape of an eigenvector corresponding to the maximum eigenvalue of $\sum_{j=1}^n \bar{z}_j^t z_j$. However, there is generally no closed form for Fréchet means of the n given shapes with respect to $\hat{\rho}$. To compute such means we denote the composition $M \circ \alpha$ by g, that is,

$$g(z) = \frac{1}{n}\sum_{j=1}^n u_j(z)z_j,$$

where $u_j(z) \in \mathbf{S}^1$ are given by

$$u_j(z) = \begin{cases} \dfrac{\langle z, z_j\rangle}{|\langle z, z_j\rangle|} & \text{if } \langle z, z_j\rangle \neq 0, \\ 1 & \text{if } \langle z, z_j\rangle = 0. \end{cases}$$

We denote the set of fixed points of g by $\mathbb{C}_*^{k-1}$ so that $\mathbb{C}_*^{k-1}$ is necessarily contained in the image $\mathbb{C}_0^{k-1}$ of M and, by Lemma 9.4, we see that it is just the set of critical points of $\tilde{G}_{\mu_0}$. Thus, $\pi(\mathbb{C}_*^{k-1})$ is the set of critical points of $\tilde{F}_{\mu_0}$ and, in particular, contains all its local minima. On the other hand, for any given w_0, the sequence $\{w_{n+1} = g(w_n) : n \geqslant 0\}$ is actually the same as the sequence obtained by the well-known generalised procrustean algorithm or GPA. In practice, we tend to take the shape of any stable point of this algorithm to be 'the' Fréchet mean of the n given shapes with respect to $\hat{\rho}$, that is, their procrustean mean. We can now establish conditions under which this assumption is justified. Theorem 9.6 gives us the following uniqueness result.

Proposition 9.4. *If the shapes $\pi(z_j)$ of the n configurations z_j^* all lie in a geodesic ball $\mathcal{B}_{\pi/8}(\pi(z_0))$, then the intersection of that ball with the projection onto Σ_2^k of the quotient set of $\mathbb{C}_*^{k-1}$ by $\mathbf{SO}(2)$ acting on the left contains exactly one element, and that element is the unique partial procrustean mean shape of the n given configurations.*

Reinterpreting Proposition 9.4 using the definition of $\mathbb{C}_*^{k-1}$, we get the following result on fixed points of GPA.

Theorem 9.7. *Suppose that the shapes $\pi(z_j)$ of the n configurations z_j^* all lie in a geodesic ball $\mathcal{B}_{\pi/8}(\pi(z_0))$. If, for any given starting point w_0, the generalised procrustean algorithm has a fixed point $\tilde{z}^\dagger$ such that $\pi(z^\dagger)$ lies in $\mathcal{B}_{\pi/8}(\pi(z_0))$, then $\pi(z^\dagger)$ is the unique partial procrustean mean shape of the n given configurations.*

We turn finally to the question of the consistency of the procrustean mean shapes defined by (9.18) or (9.19) as estimators of the shape of the means under various statistical models. By Theorem 9.2 and Ziezold's Strong Law of Large Numbers, we have the following theorem, which shows consistency of both estimators under certain conditions on one type of simple statistical model.

Theorem 9.8. *Suppose that $\{z_j^* : 1 \leqslant j \leqslant n\}$ is a set of independent configurations of k labelled points in $\mathbb{R}^2$ each obtained from the model:*

$$z_j^* = c_j(1, \ldots, 1) + a_j e^{i\alpha_j}\{z_0^* + \varepsilon_j\}, \quad 1 \leqslant j \leqslant n,$$

where z_0^* is a fixed configuration, $\{\varepsilon_j\}$ are iid errors in $\mathbb{R}^{2k}$, and $c_j \in \mathbb{C}$, $\alpha_j \in [0, 2\pi)$ and $a_j > 0$ are unknown nuisance parameters. If the induced Radon–Nikodým derivative, with respect to $d\omega_2^k$, of $z_0^* + \varepsilon_1$ in Σ_2^k is a non-increasing function of the distance ρ from $\pi(z_0)$, the shape of the means, which is strictly decreasing on a set of positive measure, then both their partial and full procrustean mean shapes will tend to $\pi(z_0)$ as n tends to infinity.

An important special case of this theorem is the consistency of these means when $\varepsilon_1 \sim \mathcal{N}(0, \sigma^2 I_{2k})$ for, in that case, the hypotheses are satisfied, as was remarked before the statement of Theorem 9.4. More generally, Proposition 9.3 and the ensuing discussion imply that, if in Theorem 9.8 the errors ε_j are isotropic and satisfy the conditions mentioned in that discussion, then the partial and full procrustean mean shapes will both tend to the shape of z_0^* as n tends to infinity.

It also follows from Theorem 9.8 that, when its hypotheses are satisfied, we can in practice use either the partial or full procrustean mean shapes to estimate the shape of the means. In addition, in those circumstances and for large sample size, we can use the partial procrustean mean shapes to approximate the full procrustean mean shapes or vice versa. For then both the procrustean mean shapes tend to the same limit, the shape of the means, as sample size tends to infinity.

Further results may be deduced similarly from Theorems 9.3 and 9.5. The latter shows that, for the consistency of the full procrustean mean, it is sufficient that the ε_j in the model considered in Theorem 9.8 be isotropic, while the former gives necessary and sufficient conditions on the induced shape-measure for consistency of the full procrustean mean.

CHAPTER 10

Visualising The Higher Dimensional Shape Spaces

In this chapter we discuss the problem of trying to visualise what is happening in a shape space that is not only of a higher dimension than those with which we are familiar but, even more crucially, is also non-Euclidean. We shall illustrate the problem, and our approach to its solution, by considering the representation of the space Σ_3^4 that was developed by Kendall (1994a,b, 1995). Since the projective spaces Σ_2^k may be considered well known and since Σ_3^4 is a five-dimensional manifold with singularities homeomorphic, but not isometric, with S^5, this may be considered the first non-standard space in the family of shape spaces. Of course, as the dimension and the topological complexity increase, the problem rapidly, in some sense exponentially, becomes more complicated and difficult. For example, to represent the eight-dimensional shape space Σ_3^5 in a similar manner to that which we propose for Σ_3^4 would require 672 diagrams, corresponding to that number of eight-dimensional cells. Obviously, there is no perfect or final solution to the problem. However, we shall attempt to describe how we may 'look at' stochastic phenomena in Σ_3^4 sufficiently clearly to get some feeling for what is happening. We hope thereby to persuade the reader that 'even when the desirable is unattainable, a second best can be quite startlingly informative'.

10.1 THE TWO-DIMENSIONAL REPRESENTATION OF Σ_3^4

Since a two-dimensional representation of a five-dimensional space certainly cannot be faithful, our technique for retaining as much fidelity as possible will be to break the space up into a number of sizeable chunks and represent each chunk on a two-dimensional diagram, together with an indication in terms of these diagrams of how the corresponding chunks fit together to form the shape space. Our 'chunks' will, in fact, be topological cells and there will be 24 of them. They arise as follows.

We recall that the pre-shape of four points in a 3-space is represented by a 3×3 matrix of norm one. If it has a pseudo-singular values decomposition $U\Lambda V$, then the diagonal matrix Λ has entries $\lambda_1, \lambda_2, \lambda_3$ such that $\sum_{i=1}^{3} \lambda_i^2 = 1$. When the λ_i are distinct, the corresponding shape lies in the non-singular part of the shape space and we can make a unique choice by restricting Λ to lie in $\mathbf{S}_0^2 = \{(x_1, x_2, x_3) \in \mathbf{S}^2 : x_1 > x_2 > |x_3|\}$. Then, the passage from pre-shape to shape corresponds to omitting the special orthogonal matrix U. The matrices V, which lie in $\mathbf{SO}(3)$, and Λ are uniquely determined by the shape up to multiplication by matrices in $\mathbf{D}$, the centre of $\mathbf{SO}(3)$. This group $\mathbf{D}$ is comprised of the diagonal matrices with entries ± 1, of which an even number are -1. Thus, the part of Σ_3^4 where the corresponding pre-shape matrices have distinct pseudo-singular values, which is a one-codimensional subset of the non-singular part, is parameterised by

$$\mathbf{S}_0^2 \times \mathbf{SO}(3)/\mathbf{D}.$$

The set $\mathbf{S}_0^2$ is an open spherical triangle that we can most faithfully project onto a plane by rotating until its centroid is on a horizontal axis, projecting it horizontally onto an enveloping cylinder with a vertical axis and then flattening out that cylinder after cutting it along a suitable generator. The result is a bell-shaped triangle of the form displayed in Figure 10.1, which can also be seen in the figures that appear later in the chapter, starting at Figure 10.5. Here, the central vertical axis represents points where $\lambda_3 = 0$ and along which λ_1 ranges from $1/\sqrt{2}$ to 1. This gives us a bijective, conformal, though not isometric, representation of the factor $\mathbf{S}_0^2$. We note that these bells, which represent one twenty-fourth of the surface of the unit sphere are rather different from those we

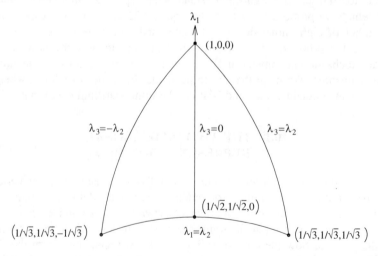

Figure 10.1 The projection of $\mathbf{S}_0^2$ with closure points: the indicated sets of coordinates are $(\lambda_1, \lambda_2, \lambda_3)$

used in Chapter 1 to represent one twelfth of the surface of the sphere of radius one-half. In particular, there is less distortion of the metric in these bells.

To represent shapes where some of the λ_i coincide we need the boundary of S_0^2, which is marked in Figure 10.1 with the corresponding coincidences. At these boundary points the second coordinate factor **SO**(3) has to be quotiented by a larger group than **D**, since now the matrix Λ also commutes with all rotations in the plane corresponding to the coincident λ_i. Since this extra quotient will not be explicitly included in our representation, it needs to be kept in mind when interpreting the pictures we obtain. In particular, these extra quotients do not correspond to singularities of the shape space, rather they are singularities of the representation. The singularities of Σ_3^4 occur at the points where the rank of $U\Lambda V$ is one, that is, where $\lambda_1 = 1$, $\lambda_2 = \lambda_3 = 0$, represented by the topmost vertices of our bell-diagrams.

The extra information contained in the factor **SO**(3)/**D** is only utilised discretely. In the next section we shall describe a cellular decomposition of **SO**(3) which has 96 3-cells that are freely permuted by **D**. Since $|\mathbf{D}| = 4$, this gives us 24 quotient 3-cells, each of which is contiguous with others across the three 2-cells that form its boundary. Our representation of Σ_3^4 then consists of 24 bell-diagrams, one for each cell of **SO**(3)/**D**, together with an indication of which cells are contiguous. Then, for a general point in the non-singular part of Σ_3^4, we may record its two-dimensional S_0^2-coordinate in the copy that corresponds to the 3-cell in which its remaining coordinates lie. Except, however, that, when two of the pseudo-singular values λ_i coincide, it will appear in more than one bell-diagram because of the necessary extra quotienting of **SO**(3) mentioned above.

10.2   THE CELL-DECOMPOSITION OF SO(3)

We represent an element of **SO**(3) by a 3×3 matrix with orthonormal rows and columns. Then, the cells in our decomposition are determined by the various special cases that can arise.

We have 24 vertices corresponding to matrices in which two entries are chosen to be ± 1. Since these cannot lie in the same row or column, there are six possible choices for the first row and then four for the second, after which the third is uniquely determined. Since we shall need to refer to these explicitly later, we adopt the notation V^{++} for the matrix diag$\{+1, +1, +1\}$, V^{+-} for diag$\{+1, -1, -1\}$, with V^{-+} and V^{--} defined similarly in terms of the first two diagonal entries. Then, we may define

$$V_{(12)}^{++} = \begin{pmatrix} 0 & +1 & 0 \\ +1 & 0 & 0 \\ 0 & 0 & 1 \end{pmatrix}, \quad V_{(123)}^{++} = \begin{pmatrix} 0 & +1 & 0 \\ 0 & 0 & +1 \\ 1 & 0 & 0 \end{pmatrix},$$

etc., where the additional lower suffix indicates the column permutation needed to obtain the matrix from the corresponding diagonal one.

Next, we have 72 edges or 1-cells lying, four at a time, on 18 circles. A circle here is the set of all matrices (of **SO**(3)) in which a particular entry is ± 1. For example

$$\left\{ \begin{pmatrix} 0 & 1 & 0 \\ \cos\alpha & 0 & \sin\alpha \\ -\sin\alpha & 0 & \cos\alpha \end{pmatrix} : \alpha \in [0, 2\pi) \right\}$$

and

$$\left\{ \begin{pmatrix} 0 & -1 & 0 \\ \cos\alpha & 0 & \sin\alpha \\ \sin\alpha & 0 & -\cos\alpha \end{pmatrix} : \alpha \in [0, 2\pi) \right\},$$

which we shall denote by S_{12}^{+} and S_{12}^{-}, respectively, with the lower suffix indicating the position of the special entry and the upper one its sign. The four open 1-cells, which, together with the relevant vertices, form a particular circle are determined by restricting α to lie in the four ranges $(0, \pi/2)$, $(\pi/2, \pi)$, $(\pi, 3\pi/2)$ and $(3\pi/2, 2\pi)$.

At the two-dimensional level we have 144 faces or 2-cells lying, 16 at a time, on nine tori, where a torus is formed by the set of all matrices with a zero entry in a given position. For example,

$$\left\{ \begin{pmatrix} 0 & \cos\alpha & \sin\alpha \\ \cos\beta & -\sin\alpha\sin\beta & \cos\alpha\sin\beta \\ \sin\beta & \sin\alpha\cos\beta & -\cos\alpha\cos\beta \end{pmatrix} : \alpha, \beta \in [0, 2\pi) \right\}$$

is clearly a torus, which we shall denote by T_{11}. It contains eight of the 18 circles: namely, the set, $S_{12}^{\pm}$ and $S_{13}^{\pm}$, of four disjoint β-circles and the set, $S_{21}^{\pm}$ and $S_{31}^{\pm}$, of four disjoint α-circles. Each α-circle meets each β-circle in a unique vertex and so the induced decomposition of the torus has 16 vertices, 32 edges and 16 faces arranged as in Figure 10.2. Once again, the 16 2-cells on this torus are determined by requiring each of α and β to lie in one of the four ranges $(0, \pi/2)$, $(\pi/2, \pi)$, $(\pi, 3\pi/2)$ and $(3\pi/2, 2\pi)$. However, for our purposes it is more convenient to note that, as α and β vary in any such pair of ranges, the signs of all the entries in the corresponding matrices of **SO** (3) retain a pattern characteristic of that 2-cell. Thus, each of the 16 2-cells above is determined by a choice of ε_1, ε_2, ε_3, ε_4 independently in $\{+, -\}$ and is then formed of all the matrices with the sign pattern

$$\begin{pmatrix} 0 & \varepsilon_1 & \varepsilon_2 \\ \varepsilon_3 & -\varepsilon_2\varepsilon_4 & \varepsilon_1\varepsilon_4 \\ \varepsilon_4 & \varepsilon_2\varepsilon_3 & -\varepsilon_1\varepsilon_3 \end{pmatrix}. \tag{10.1}$$

The three-dimensional components of our decomposition will also turn out to be 3-cells, although, since this is not so immediately obvious, we shall refer to them as 'compartments'. Once again, a compartment is determined by the sign pattern of the entries in the matrices that comprise it. Thus, by continuity,

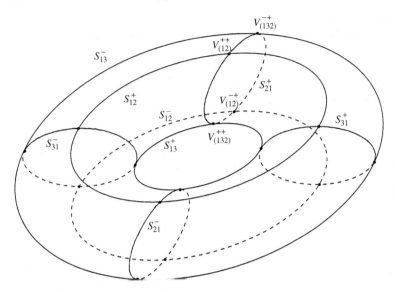

Figure 10.2   Decomposition of T_{11}

each 2-cell (10.1) above will be contiguous with the two compartments having
sign patterns

$$\begin{pmatrix} \varepsilon_0 & \varepsilon_1 & \varepsilon_2 \\ \varepsilon_3 & -\varepsilon_2\varepsilon_4 & \varepsilon_1\varepsilon_4 \\ \varepsilon_4 & \varepsilon_2\varepsilon_3 & -\varepsilon_1\varepsilon_3 \end{pmatrix},$$

where again $\varepsilon_0 \in \{+, -\}$.

   To count the compartments we need to know how many such 2-cells lie on the
boundary of each compartment. We consider the subgroup, **G**, of isometries of
SO(3) generated by those that interchange two rows or two columns and, at the
same time, change the sign of a row or a column. This group **G** is easily seen to
be transitive on each of the sets of vertices, edges, circles, 2-cells and tori. Thus,
it suffices for us to examine the faces of one particular compartment adjacent to
one particular 2-cell. Accordingly, we look at the 3-cell, with sign pattern

$$\begin{pmatrix} + & + & + \\ + & - & + \\ + & + & - \end{pmatrix} \tag{10.2}$$

determined by $\varepsilon_1 = \varepsilon_2 = \varepsilon_3 = \varepsilon_4 = +$ above, which, as we have just seen, has
the 2-cell boundary component

$$\begin{pmatrix} 0 & + & + \\ + & - & + \\ + & + & - \end{pmatrix}$$

on the torus T_{11} that we have been considering.

To find other 2-cell boundary components we note that the special form of sign pattern (10.1) in such 2-cells means that we cannot replace an arbitrary sign in the pattern (10.2) for a 3-cell by a zero. It is not difficult to check that we can do so if and only if the complementary 2×2 submatrix has determinant zero when the signs $\pm$ are replaced by the numbers ± 1. By this criterion we see that the compartment with sign pattern (10.2) above will also have the boundary 2-cells

$$
\begin{pmatrix}
+ & + & + \\
+ & - & 0 \\
+ & + & -
\end{pmatrix}
$$

on the torus T_{23} and

$$
\begin{pmatrix}
+ & + & + \\
+ & - & + \\
+ & 0 & -
\end{pmatrix}
$$

on the torus T_{32}. Since no other entry in the 3-cell matrix satisfies the necessary criterion, these three 2-cells, and their bounding edges and vertices, form the entire boundary of the compartment.

Let us now look at the vertices, and hence the edges, of these 2-cells. We find that they each have both of the vertices

$$
V_{(12)}^{++} = \begin{pmatrix} 0 & 1 & 0 \\ 1 & 0 & 0 \\ 0 & 0 & -1 \end{pmatrix} \quad \text{and} \quad V_{(13)}^{+-} = \begin{pmatrix} 0 & 0 & 1 \\ 0 & -1 & 0 \\ 1 & 0 & 0 \end{pmatrix},
$$

together with two of the three vertices

$$
V_{(123)}^{++} = \begin{pmatrix} 0 & 1 & 0 \\ 0 & 0 & 1 \\ 1 & 0 & 0 \end{pmatrix}, \quad V_{(132)}^{++} = \begin{pmatrix} 0 & 0 & 1 \\ 1 & 0 & 0 \\ 0 & 1 & 0 \end{pmatrix} \quad \text{and} \quad V^{+-} = \begin{pmatrix} 1 & 0 & 0 \\ 0 & -1 & 0 \\ 0 & 0 & -1 \end{pmatrix}.
$$

This is the classic picture of the double suspension of a triangle with each pair of triangles suspending the same edge of the basic triangle amalgamated to form a creased rectangle, as indicated in Figure 10.3, where the relevant parts of the standard picture, Figure 10.3(a), that appear on the boundary of the cell with sign pattern (10.2) are shown in Figure 10.3(b) with the vertices labelled. Hence, the boundary of the compartment is homeomorphic to a 2-sphere and it follows from the topological fact that $SO(3) \cong RP^3$ is indecomposable that the compartment itself must be a 3-cell.

It is now clear that the decomposition is completed by 96 compartments, each of which is a 3-cell. The number is determined by the facts that each of the nine tori has 16 2-cells, with no two tori ever sharing a common 2-cell, and each of these 2-cells is one face of two different compartments. As each compartment has three 2-cell faces, there must be $9 \times 16 \times 2/3 = 96$ compartments altogether.

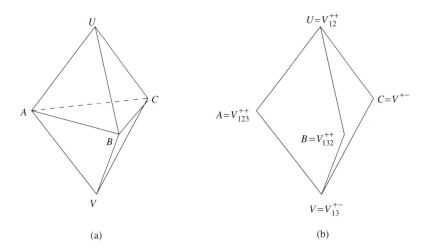

Figure 10.3 (a) Double suspension of the triangle *ABC*: comprising six triangles *AUB*, *BUC*, *CUA* and *AVB*, *BVC*, *CVA*; (b) Double suspension with amalgamations: comprising three creased rectangles *AUBV*, *BUCV*, *CUAV*

10.3   THE ACTION OF THE GROUP D

We recall that **D**, the centre of **SO**(3), acts on the left of $V \in$ **SO**(3) in a psuedo-singular values decomposition. Thus, each of the four elements of **D** simultaneously changes all the signs in two of the rows of V. Each such operation clearly preserves the above decomposition of **SO**(3) and has no fixed points. The orbits of vertices, edges, faces and 3-cells are all seen to have four elements and hence the induced decomposition of **SO**(3)/**D** has six vertices, 18 edges, 36 faces and 24 3-cells.

In Figure 10.4 we represent each quotient 3-cell in **SO**(3)/**D** by the sign pattern of the member of the orbit that has the signs '+' at the beginning of each of the first two rows. Then, we write A, B, C, D, E, F for the basic sign patterns

$$\begin{pmatrix} + & + & + \\ + & - & - \\ + & + & - \end{pmatrix}, \begin{pmatrix} + & + & + \\ + & - & + \\ + & + & - \end{pmatrix}, \begin{pmatrix} + & + & + \\ + & - & + \\ + & - & - \end{pmatrix},$$

$$\begin{pmatrix} + & + & - \\ + & - & + \\ + & - & - \end{pmatrix}, \begin{pmatrix} + & + & - \\ + & + & + \\ + & - & - \end{pmatrix}, \begin{pmatrix} + & + & - \\ + & + & + \\ + & - & + \end{pmatrix},$$

and then write $_iX_j$ for the matrix derived from X by changing all the signs in the ith row and jth column, so that the (i, j)th entry remains unchanged, and, similarly, write X_{ij} for the matrix obtained from X by changing all the signs in its ith and jth columns. Then, the complete set of 3-cells of **SO**(3)/**D** is represented by the 24 sign patterns $X, X_{23}, {}_3X_2$ and $_3X_3$, where $X \in \{A, B, C, D, E, F\}$. Since

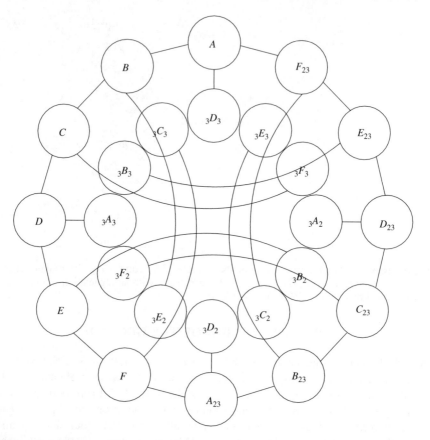

Figure 10.4 The complete set of adjacencies

each 3-cell has three facial 2-cells, it is contiguous with three other 3-cells. We need to identify and record which three.

From our previous discussion it will be clear that two 3-cells of **SO**(3)/**D** are contiguous if two of their representative 3-cells in **SO**(3) differ in their sign pattern at just one location that satisfies the criterion for it to determine a 2-cell when those differing signs are replaced by zero. It will not always be possible for the sign difference to occur between our chosen representatives. However, in Figure 10.4 we display our 24 chosen patterns in such a way that adjacent members of each circle of 12 patterns represent contiguous 3-cells as well as the four pairs $A - {_3}D_3$, $D - {_3}A_3$, ${_3}D_2 - A_{23}$ and ${_3}A_2 - D_{23}$. The remaining eight pairs of contiguous cells do not lie close together in the diagram and are indicated by the eight curved lines. For example, the leading diagonal entry in

$$B = \begin{pmatrix} + & + & + \\ + & - & + \\ + & + & - \end{pmatrix}$$

satisfies the criterion for an adjacency to occur. When we change it, we get

$$\begin{pmatrix} - & + & + \\ + & - & + \\ + & + & - \end{pmatrix},$$

which is not one of our representative patterns. However, it is in the same **D**-orbit as

$$\begin{pmatrix} + & - & - \\ + & - & + \\ - & - & + \end{pmatrix},$$

which is the cell $_3E_2$. In Figure 10.4 the eight adjacencies between cells B and $_3E_2$, C and $_3F_3$, etc. are indicated by the longer curved lines to show, for each given 3-cell, the complete set of three 3-cells with which it shares a face. Other arrangements of the cells are, of course, possible. If we flip the inner circle of cells about its vertical axis, we obtain a diagram in which alternate pairs, $A - _3D_3$, $E_{23} - _3B_3$, etc. have all the 3-cells that are contiguous with them in **SO(3)/D** placed adjacent to them in the diagram. There are then just six pairs of non-adjacent contiguous cells lying on the three diameters at angles 0, $\pi/3$, $2\pi/3$ to the x-axis. At the cost of increasing the number of extra lines to 12 we could arrange for all cells contiguous to the cells in the outer ring to be adjacent, but there is no way to arrange that all contiguous pairs of cells be placed adjacent to each other in the diagram.

This, then, is our representation of Σ_3^4. In each of the 24 circles we shall incribe a copy of our projection of $\mathbf{S}_0^2$, together with the sign pattern that labels the corresponding 3-cell in **SO(3)/D**. In the interests of clarity we shall not include the lines indicating the non-adjacent pairs that represent contiguous 3-cells, but the reader needs to bear their existence in mind when interpreting the results that we shall display. Note that the $\mathbf{S}_0^2$-factor means that each k-cell in **SO(3)/D** represents a $(k + 2)$-cell in Σ_3^4.

10.4 THE GEODESICS OF Σ_3^4

As a first application of our visualisation technique for Σ_3^4, we will 'look at' some geodesics, using the results produced by Kendall (1995). In Figure 10.5 we see the projection of a typical geodesic with 'jumps' between 3-cells of **SO(3)/D** indicated by dotted lines. It will be observed that, as we would expect, these jumps take place between contiguous 3-cells with a common face, including such pairs as $_3C_3 - F$, $_3B_3 - E_{23}$ and $_3F_2 - C_{23}$, which are not adjacent in the diagram. However, there are also a number of jumps between E_{23} and $_3C_2$ that do not share a common face. On closer inspection we see that these jumps in fact take place between points on the left-hand and right-hand boundaries of the relevant bells. These are points where the pseudo-singular values satisfy $\lambda_3 = \pm\lambda_2$. We also see, after changing the signs in the second and third rows of

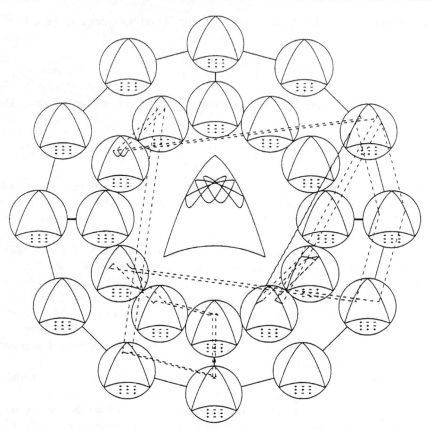

Figure 10.5 Reproduced with permission from D.G. Kendall, How to look at objects in a five-dimensional shape space: looking at geodesics, *Advances in Applied Probability* **27** (1995), 35–43, by permission of the Applied Probability Trust

$_3C_2$ that both E_{23} and $_3C_2$ have on their boundary the 1-cell of S_{23}^- specified by the pattern

$$\begin{pmatrix} + & - & 0 \\ 0 & 0 & -1 \\ + & + & 0 \end{pmatrix}.$$

To understand what is happening here we should recall that each 3-cell has six edges in our decomposition and, as there are 96 3-cells and 72 edges, each edge must lie on eight 3-cells. In the case of the edge of S_{23}^- specified by the above pattern we may easily check, on changing all the signs in the last two rows of the patterns $_3X_2$, that these eight cells are C_{23}, D_{23}, E_{23}, F_{23}, $_3C_2$, $_3D_2$, $_3E_2$ and $_3F_2$ in the cyclic order in which successive pairs share a common face. Clearly, by symmetry, the two faces of each of these 3-cells that meet along the common edge must do so at an angle of $\pi/4$, so that corresponding faces of E_{23} and $_3C_2$ meet at right angles, with a maximum angle of $3\pi/4$ between the curves that meet that edge from the two 3-cells. Since we are in the non-singular part of Σ_3^4 and geodesics cannot turn corners and since its full projection on the bell-diagram is not tangent to the edge at the point where it moves from one cell to the other, we must conclude that the Λ-coordinates of the geodesic remain constant for a while before the geodesic emerges in the different 3-cell. Moreover, since the geodesic is 'straight' in terms of the metric structure of Σ_3^4, for it to be possible for the geodesic to emerge from a different 3-cell, these eight 3-cells must be twisted since they are identified along their common edge. More precisely, this is true of the eight corresponding 5-cells in Σ_3^4 since they are identified along their common three-dimensional face.

The parameters λ_1, λ_2, λ_3 are continuous functions of shape, so, when we superimpose all the geodesic segments in the various bells onto a single bell, as we have done in the central, larger bell in Figure 10.5, we get a continuous image. Generally, this projection of the geodesic is also smooth. However, in Figure 10.6

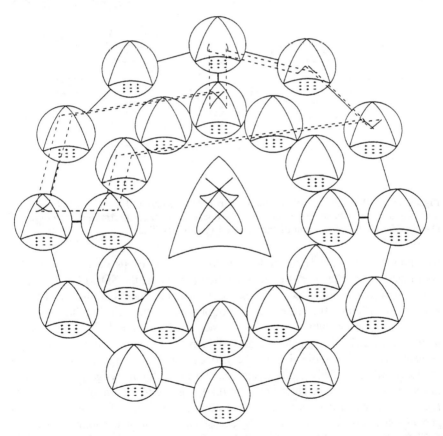

Figure 10.6 Reproduced with permission from D.G. Kendall, How to look at objects in a five-dimensional shape space: looking at geodesics, *Advances in Applied Probability* **27** (1995), 35–43, by permission of the Applied Probability Trust

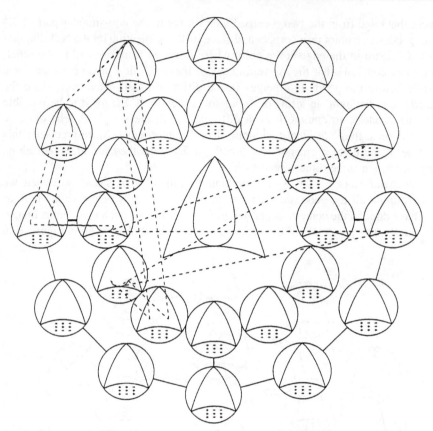

Figure 10.7   Reproduced with permission from D.G. Kendall, How to look at objects in a five-dimensional shape space: looking at geodesics, *Advances in Applied Probability* **27** (1995), 35–43, by permission of the Applied Probability Trust

we show the portrait of a geodesic with a pair of cusps caused by the S_0^2-coordinates along the geodesic retracing their path while the $SO(3)/D$-coordinates remain constant. Another possible source of non-smoothness is illustrated by the geodesic in Figure 10.7. Here, the geodesic passes through the singularity set of the shape space, which in Σ_3^4 is characterised by $\lambda_1 = 1$, $\lambda_2 = \lambda_3 = 0$. As it does so, the λ_3-coordinate changes sign, resulting in a discontinuity of the tangents to the full projection of the geodesic in the central bell representing the S_0^2-coordinates. This geodesic also displays two double 'edge jumps' similar to those in Figure 10.5. However, this time it goes, for example, from $_3A_3$ via E_{23} to $_3F_2$, which does have a face in common with $_3A_3$. In other words, the geodesic has moved from $_3A_3$ to $_3F_2$ across an edge of their common face.

These examples illustrate how it is possible to make inferences about the behaviour of the geodesics, and even the structure of shape space itself, beyond that which is explicitly contained in our representation.

10.5 SOME DISTRIBUTIONS ON Σ_3^4

As a second example of our visualisation process for Σ_3^4, we display the projections of two of the distributions of random shape points that we discussed in Chapter 8. The first of these, Figure 10.8, plots the shape points of tetrahedra associated with 5000 independent 3×4 Gaussian matrices. In the next diagram, Figure 10.9, we display the shape points associated with the independent random tiles of Poisson–Delaunay tessellations. Despite the apparent crudity of our representation, the different nature of these two distributions is clearly visible: the striking empty regions lying at the top of each bell and around its median vertical line in the Poisson–Delaunay case corresponds to the fact that a Delaunay tetrahedron is most unlikely to be nearly flat, in contrast to the Gaussian case where there is no bias against flatness.

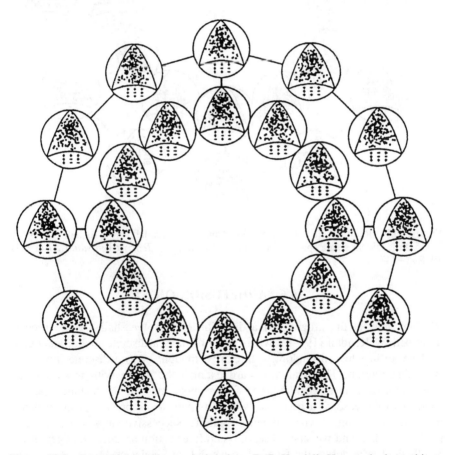

Figure 10.8 Reproduced with permission from D.G. Kendall, How to look at objects in a 5-dimensional shape space I: Looking at distributions, *Teoriya Veroyatnostel* (1994), **39**, 242–247

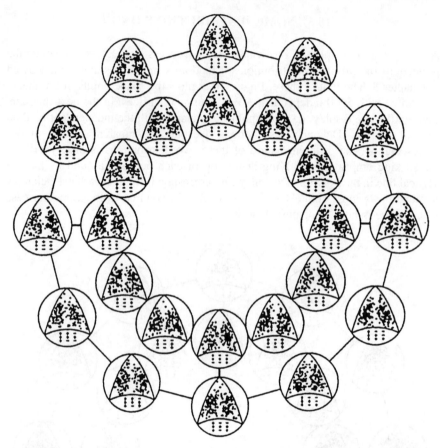

Figure 10.9 Reproduced with permission from D.G. Kendall, How to look at objects in a 5-dimensional shape space I: Looking at distributions, *Teoriya Veroyatnostel* (1994), **39**, 242–247

10.6   A DIFFUSION ON Σ_3^4

We look now at the progress of a diffusion on Σ_3^4. We shall use the process described by Kendall (1994b), where he constructs a discrete model analogous to the way in which a random walk can be thought of as a discrete model for Brownian motion. The straightforward example he works with is sufficiently representative and yet enables us to forget about most of the technicalities. In contrast to the case of a geodesic, where its path to its present position determines the direction in which it must continue, successive steps in our process are independent and we shall observe much freer action around the edges of the 3-cells, and even across the faces, than we did for geodesics.

We start by choosing four labelled iid Gaussian points in $\mathbb{R}^3$. We then displace these so that the centroid of the tetrad lies at the origin and then scale the configuration to have unit size in the usual sense of shape theory. We then record the shape of this standardised tetrad on the appropriate bell-diagram. At the next stage, we displace each of the four points of the standardised tetrad by independent three-dimensional Gaussian perturbations of linear standard deviation ε, re-standardise the resulting tetrad and plot the corresponding shape point. Continuing inductively in this manner, we generate a stochastic process whose only parameters are the value ε and the initial randomising seed.

The start of the resulting process is displayed in Figure 10.10. We see the process starting in the bell-diagram that is labelled $_3E_3$ in Figure 10.4. At first, it travels about that bell in a more or less Brownian manner, allowing for the discrete nature of our construction. However, after a while there is a jump, indicated by a dotted line, into the bell labelled B_{23} and, after some Brownian-like

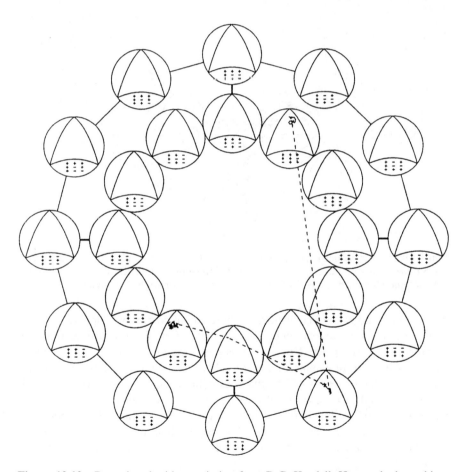

Figure 10.10 Reproduced with permission from D.G. Kendall, How to look at objects in a 5-dimensional shape space II: Looking at diffusions, in F.P. Kelly (ed), *Probability, Statistics and Optimization*, Wiley (1994), pp. 315–24. Copyright John Wiley & Sons Ltd

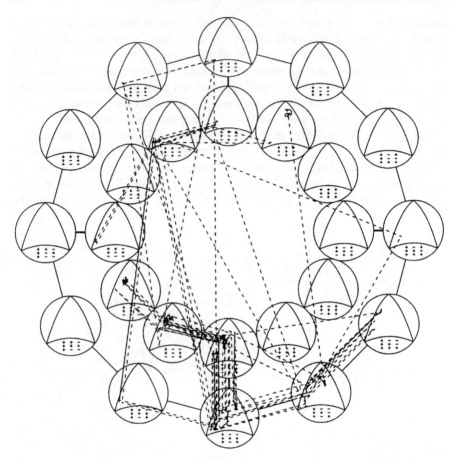

Figure 10.11 Reproduced with permission from D.G. Kendall, How to look at objects in a 5-dimensional shape space II: Looking at diffusions, in F.P. Kelly (ed), *Probability, Statistics and Optimization*, Wiley (1994), pp. 315–24. Copyright John Wiley & Sons Ltd

motion there, into the bell labelled $_3E_2$. These are, of course, only apparent jumps, not true ones, caused by our suppression of three of the five dimensions in which the process is taking place. However, it is possible to infer something of what is happening in these remaining dimensions. For example, the 3-cells $_3E_3$ and B_{23} share the common face formed by matrices with the sign pattern (10.1) in which $\varepsilon_1 = \varepsilon_2 = -$ and $\varepsilon_3 = \varepsilon_4 = +$. Obviously, the jump took place across that face between the two 3-cells. On the other hand, the 3-cells B_{23} and $_3E_2$ do not share a commom face. However, we notice that they do both have the same 1-cell of the circle S_{21}^+ on their boundary, namely, the 1-cell specified by the pattern

$$\begin{pmatrix} 0 & - & - \\ 1 & 0 & 0 \\ 0 & - & + \end{pmatrix}.$$

In fact, looking more closely, we see that the jump did not occur directly between B_{23} and $_3E_2$ but paused briefly at the 3-cell $_3D_2$, which also has that 1-cell on its boundary. So, it is clear that in the unrecorded dimensions the coordinates remain on or close to that 1-cell as the process moves between the three 3-cells.

In Figure 10.11, which gives a later stage of the diffusion, as well as the further diagrams in Kendall (1994b), we see that these observations remain true: the jumps take place between 3-cells with a common face or a common edge. Moreover, it is clear from the later development that, as we would expect, most jumps take place between two 3-cells with a common face and relatively few between those with just a common edge. We also note that, again as might be expected, after a jump across a common face, the process will either remain in the new cell or jump back to the one whence it came, whereas, after moving to a new 3-cell sharing an edge, it is equally likely, as in the example above, to pass on to a third 3-cell sharing that edge.

CHAPTER 11

General Shape Spaces

11.1 SHAPE SPACES FOR GENERAL MANIFOLDS

In Chapter 1 we considered the shapes formed by a k-ad of vectors in the Euclidean space $\mathbb{R}^m$. Two k-ads have the same shape if there is a Euclidean similarity that maps one k-ad on to the other. The set of Euclidean similarities forms a Lie group, which acts on the set of k-ads. The orbits of this group action are the shapes in the space Σ_m^k. Later chapters showed how we could study the geometry of the shape space by using the simpler properties of the space of k-ads. In this chapter we wish to examine a more general situation that will allow us to consider shapes for k-ads of points in other manifolds, such as spheres or hyperbolic spaces.

The general situation we wish to consider is where a Lie group $\mathbb{G}$ acts isometrically on a manifold $\mathbf{E}$. Thus, $\mathbf{E}$ is a smooth manifold with a metric that we will denote by d. Each g in the group gives an isometry

$$\mathbf{E} \longrightarrow \mathbf{E}; \ x \mapsto g(x).$$

We will say that two points x and x' are the same *modulo* $\mathbb{G}$ if there is an isometry g in the group $\mathbb{G}$ with $g(x) = x'$. This is an equivalence relation on $\mathbf{E}$ and the equivalence class containing x is the orbit $\{g(x) : g \in \mathbb{G}\}$. The set of equivalence classes will be denoted by $\mathbf{E}/\mathbb{G}$ and is called the quotient of $\mathbf{E}$ by $\mathbb{G}$. The quotient map

$$\pi : \mathbf{E} \longrightarrow \mathbf{E}/\mathbb{G}; \ x \mapsto \{g(x) : g \in \mathbb{G}\}$$

sends each point of $\mathbf{E}$ to its equivalence class. We wish to study the geometry that the quotient $\mathbf{E}/\mathbb{G}$ inherits from $\mathbf{E}$.

We can define the distance in $\mathbf{E}/\mathbb{G}$ from one point $\pi(x)$ to another $\pi(x')$ as the shortest distance between the orbits of x and x' in $\mathbf{E}$. More precisely, this is

$$\rho(\pi(x), \pi(x')) = \inf\{d(g(x), g'(x')) : g, g' \in \mathbb{G}\}.$$

Since each $g \in \mathbb{G}$ is an isometry, we have $d(g(x), g'(x')) = d(x, g^{-1}g'(x'))$ and so

$$\rho(\pi(x), \pi(x')) = \inf\{d(x, g(x')) : g \in \mathbb{G}\}.$$

It is clear that ρ is symmetric and satisfies the triangle inequality, so it is always a pseudo-metric on $\mathbf{E}/\mathbb{G}$. Furthermore, the distance is zero precisely when x is in the closure of the orbit of x'. Consequently, ρ is a metric if and only if all the orbits are closed. We will only consider cases where this is true.

The situation described above does include the shape spaces Σ_m^k for k-ads of points in the Euclidean space $\mathbb{R}^m$. By translating and enlarging we can map any k-ad of points in $\mathbb{R}^m$, which are not all equal, to a k-ad in the set

$$\mathbf{E} = \left\{ (\boldsymbol{x}_1, \boldsymbol{x}_2, \ldots, \boldsymbol{x}_k) : \sum_{j=1}^k \boldsymbol{x}_j = \mathbf{0} \quad \text{and} \quad \sum_{j=1}^k ||\boldsymbol{x}_j||^2 = 1 \right\}.$$

This set $\mathbf{E}$ is the pre-shape sphere and, being a subset of $(\mathbb{R}^m)^k$, has the Euclidean metric:

$$d((\boldsymbol{x}_1, \boldsymbol{x}_2, \ldots, \boldsymbol{x}_k), (\boldsymbol{y}_1, \boldsymbol{y}_2, \ldots, \boldsymbol{y}_k)) = \left\{ \sum_{j=1}^k ||\boldsymbol{x}_j - \boldsymbol{y}_j||^2 \right\}^{1/2}.$$

Two k-ads $(\boldsymbol{x}_1, \boldsymbol{x}_2, \ldots, \boldsymbol{x}_k)$ and $(\boldsymbol{y}_1, \boldsymbol{y}_2, \ldots, \boldsymbol{y}_k)$ in $\mathbf{E}$ have the same shape if there is a Euclidean similarity $S : \mathbb{R}^m \to \mathbb{R}^m$ that has $S(\boldsymbol{x}_j) = \boldsymbol{y}_j$ for $j = 1, 2, \ldots, k$. This similarity must send the centroid $\frac{1}{k} \sum_{j=1}^k \boldsymbol{x}_j$ to the centroid $\frac{1}{k} \sum_{j=1}^k \boldsymbol{y}_j$ so S fixes the origin. Similarly, S must preserve length because $\sum_{j=1}^k ||\boldsymbol{x}_j||^2 = 1 = \sum_{j=1}^k ||\boldsymbol{y}_j||^2$. Therefore, S is in the group $\mathbf{SO}(m)$ of rotations of $\mathbb{R}^m$ about the origin. The quotient $\mathbf{E}/\mathbf{SO}(m)$ is then the shape space that we called Σ_m^k. The metric defined on the quotient

$$\rho(\pi(\boldsymbol{x}_1, \boldsymbol{x}_2, \ldots, \boldsymbol{x}_k), \pi(\boldsymbol{y}_1, \boldsymbol{y}_2, \ldots, \boldsymbol{y}_k))$$

$$= \inf \left\{ \left(\sum_{j=1}^k ||\boldsymbol{x}_j - S(\boldsymbol{y}_j)||^2 \right)^{1/2} : S \in \mathbf{SO}(m) \right\}$$

is the procrustean metric.

In a similar way, we can consider the shape spaces for k-ads of points in any Riemannian manifold $\mathbf{M}$. Let $\mathbb{G}$ be a group of isometries of $\mathbf{M}$ and let $\mathbf{E}$ be the set of all k-ads from $\mathbf{M}$. Then, the product metric

$$d((x_1, x_2, \ldots, x_k), (y_1, y_2, \ldots, y_k)) = \left\{ \sum_{j=1}^k d(x_j, y_j)^2 \right\}^{1/2}$$

is a metric on $\mathbf{E}$ and the group $\mathbb{G}$ acts isometrically on $\mathbf{E}$ by

$$g : (x_1, x_2, \ldots, x_k) \mapsto (g(x_1), g(x_2), \ldots, g(x_k)).$$

We will say that two k-ads $(x_1, x_2, \ldots, x_k)$ and $(y_1, y_2, \ldots, y_k)$ have the same *shape modulo* $\mathbb{G}$ if there is an isometry $g \in \mathbb{G}$ with $g(x_j) = y_j$ for $j = 1, 2, \ldots, k$. Then, the quotient $\mathbf{E}/\mathbb{G}$ has one point for each shape of k-ads modulo $\mathbb{G}$. In the final part of this chapter we will consider such shape spaces when $\mathbf{M}$ is the sphere or the hyperbolic plane. It will also be useful to consider the situation where $\mathbf{E}$ is a proper subset of $\mathbf{M}^k$ and the metric on $\mathbf{E}$ is not the product metric. To include all of these cases we will study the general quotient and try to understand its geometry in terms of the geometry of $\mathbf{E}$.

Where possible, we would like to make the quotient $\mathbf{E}/\mathbb{G}$ into a manifold so that the quotient map $\pi : \mathbf{E} \to \mathbf{E}/\mathbb{G}$ is a submersion. This means that the derivative

$$\pi_*(x) : \mathcal{T}_x(\mathbf{E}) \longrightarrow \mathcal{T}_{\pi(x)}(\mathbf{E}/\mathbb{G})$$

is a linear projection *onto* the tangent space at $\pi(x)$. If this is the case, the orbits $\{g(x) : g \in \mathbb{G}\}$ must be submanifolds of $\mathbf{E}$ with constant dimension equal to $\dim(\mathbf{E}) - \dim(\mathbf{E}/\mathbb{G})$, since they are the inverse images of points under the submersion. We have already seen in the case of Euclidean shape spaces that there can be singular points where $\mathbf{E}/\mathbb{G}$ is not a manifold. If this occurs we can restrict our attention to a smaller subset of $\mathbf{E}$ that excludes these singularities. We can also reverse the above argument. Suppose that each of the orbits is a submanifold of $\mathbf{E}$ with fixed dimension n'. Then, the implicit function theorem shows that, in a neighbourhood $\mathbf{U}$ of each point $x \in \mathbf{E}$, we can find a chart $\phi : \mathbf{U} \to \mathbb{R}^n \times \mathbb{R}^{n'}$ that maps $\mathbb{G}$-orbits into the sets $\{u\} \times \mathbb{R}^{n'}$ for $u \in \mathbb{R}^n$. Projection onto the first coordinate then gives a chart for $\mathbf{E}/\mathbb{G}$ at $\pi(x)$ and this shows that $\mathbf{E}/\mathbb{G}$ is a manifold.

When $\mathbf{E}$ is a Riemannian manifold, we can go further and make the quotient $\mathbf{E}/\mathbb{G}$ into a Riemannian manifold also. For each $x \in \mathbf{E}$, let $\mathcal{V}_x$ be the tangent space to the orbit through x. We are assuming that the orbit is a submanifold of $\mathbf{E}$, so $\mathcal{V}_x$ is a vector subspace of the tangent space $\mathcal{T}_x(\mathbf{E})$. We call it the *vertical* tangent space at x. The Riemannian metric on $\mathbf{E}$ gives us an inner product on each tangent space, so we can define the *horizontal* tangent space $\mathcal{H}_x$ at x to be the orthogonal complement of $\mathcal{V}_x$ in $\mathcal{T}_x(\mathbf{E})$. The derivative $\pi_*(x)$ has $\mathcal{V}_x$ as its kernel and maps $\mathcal{H}_x$ bijectively onto $\mathcal{T}_{\pi(x)}(\mathbf{E}/\mathbb{G})$. We can then define an inner product on $\mathcal{T}_{\pi(x)}(\mathbf{E}/\mathbb{G})$ so that the bijection is an isometry from $\mathcal{H}_x$ onto $\mathcal{T}_{\pi(x)}(\mathbf{E}/\mathbb{G})$. This inner product does not depend on the choice of x. For, if $\pi(x) = \pi(y)$, then $y = g(x)$ for some $g \in \mathbb{G}$. Since g is an isometry, the derivative $g_*(x) : \mathcal{T}_x(\mathbf{E}) \to \mathcal{T}_y(\mathbf{E})$ maps $\mathcal{V}_x$ onto $\mathcal{V}_y$ and $\mathcal{H}_x$ onto $\mathcal{H}_y$ isometrically. Thus, we have constructed a Riemannian metric on the quotient $\mathbf{E}/\mathbb{G}$ so that $\pi : \mathbf{E} \to \mathbf{E}/\mathbb{G}$ is a Riemannian submersion (see Chapter 6 and O'Neill, 1966, 1983 for further details).

This Riemmanian metric is closely related to the distance ρ on $\mathbf{E}/\mathbb{G}$ defined earlier. For, suppose that d is the distance on $\mathbf{E}$ derived from a complete Riemannian metric. For any two points $x, x' \in \mathbf{E}$, the distance $\rho(\pi(x), \pi(x'))$ is the length of the shortest path γ in $\mathbf{E}$ from the orbit $\{g(x) : g \in \mathbb{G}\}$ to the point x'. Since γ is the shortest path, it must be orthogonal to $\{g(x) : g \in \mathbb{G}\}$ at x. Hence, the derivative of γ at x is a tangent vector orthogonal to the orbit $\{g(x) : g \in \mathbb{G}\}$, and so is a horizontal tangent vector at x. A similar argument applies at each point of γ, so γ is a geodesic in $\mathbf{E}$ with its derivative always horizontal. This implies that the Riemannian length of $\pi \circ \gamma$ is the same as the Riemannian length of γ. So, the distance from $\pi(x)$ to $\pi(x')$ for the Riemannian metric we constructed on $\mathbf{E}/\mathbb{G}$ is the same as the distance $\rho(\pi(x), \pi(x'))$.

It will be useful later to consider symmetries of the quotient $\mathbf{E}/\mathbb{G}$. Suppose that $f : \mathbf{E} \to \mathbf{E}$ is an isometry. This will induce an isometry

$$\overline{f} : \mathbf{E}/\mathbb{G} \longrightarrow \mathbf{E}/\mathbb{G}; \quad \pi(x) \mapsto \pi(f(x)),$$

provided that $fgf^{-1} \in \mathbb{G}$ for each $g \in \mathbb{G}$: that is, $f\mathbb{G}f^{-1} = \mathbb{G}$. Therefore, if $\mathbb{G}$ is a normal subgroup of a larger group $\mathbb{N}$ of isometries, then each $f \in \mathbb{N}$ induces an isometry $\overline{f} : \mathbf{E}/\mathbb{G} \to \mathbf{E}/\mathbb{G}$. Two elements f and f' have $\overline{f} = \overline{f'}$ if and only if $f' = fg$ for some $g \in \mathbb{G}$. So the group $\mathbb{N}/\mathbb{G}$ acts isometrically on $\mathbf{E}/\mathbb{G}$. Moreover, the quotient $(\mathbf{E}/\mathbb{G})/(\mathbb{N}/\mathbb{G})$ is naturally identified with $\mathbf{E}/\mathbb{N}$.

Once we have defined a Riemannian metric on the shape space $\mathbf{E}/\mathbb{G}$ in this way, it is straightforward to calculate the metric and other geometric invariants in terms of those of $\mathbf{E}$, although, as we saw in Chapter 7, the results can be quite complicated. First, consider a tangent vector $v(\pi(x))$ at a point $\pi(x)$ of $\mathbf{E}/\mathbb{G}$. The definition of the metric shows that there is a unique horizontal tangent vector $\tilde{v}(x)$ in $\mathcal{H}_x$ that $\pi_*(x)$ maps onto $v(\pi(x))$. If v is a vector field on $\mathbf{E}/\mathbb{G}$, then these horizontal tangent vectors give a vector field $\tilde{v}$ on $\mathbf{E}$ that is everywhere horizontal. We call this the *horizontal lift* of v. For vector fields v_1 and v_2 we denote by $\langle \tilde{v}_1, \tilde{v}_2 \rangle$ the function $x \mapsto \langle \tilde{v}_1(x), \tilde{v}_2(x) \rangle$. Then, the way the Riemannian metric on $\mathbf{E}/\mathbb{G}$ was defined ensures that $\langle \tilde{v}_1, \tilde{v}_2 \rangle$ is equal to $\langle v_1, v_2 \rangle \circ \pi$. Also, for any smooth function $f : \mathbf{E}/\mathbb{G} \to \mathbb{R}$, we have $vf = \tilde{v}(f \circ \pi)$. The Koszul formula allows us to calculate the covariant derivative of these horizontal lifts in terms of inner products and Lie brackets, so we find that $\tilde{\nabla}_{\tilde{v}_1} \tilde{v}_2$ and $(\nabla_{v_1} v_2)^{\sim}$ differ by a vector field that is vertical, where $\tilde{\nabla}$ and ∇ are the covariant derivatives on $\mathbf{E}$ and $\mathbf{E}/\mathbb{G}$, respectively. Set

$$V(v_1, v_2) = \tilde{\nabla}_{\tilde{v}_1} \tilde{v}_2 - (\nabla_{v_1} v_2)^{\sim}.$$

It is easy to check that V is a skew-symmetric tensor field. From this we can calculate the Riemannian curvature tensor $R_{v_1 v_2} v_3$:

$$\langle \tilde{v}_4, R_{\tilde{v}_1 \tilde{v}_2} \tilde{v}_3 \rangle = \langle v_4, R_{v_1 v_2} v_3 \rangle \circ \pi + 2 \langle V(v_4, v_3), V(v_1, v_2) \rangle$$
$$- \langle V(v_4, v_1), V(v_2, v_3) \rangle + \langle V(v_4, v_2), V(v_1, v_3) \rangle.$$

This shows how the curvature $R_{v_1 v_2} v_3$ in the shape space can be found in terms of the curvature $R_{\tilde{v}_1 \tilde{v}_2} \tilde{v}_3$ in $\mathbf{E}$, as was the case for the Euclidean shape space. These formulae simplify when we consider the sectional curvature $K(v_1, v_2)$. This is defined by

$$K(v_1, v_2) = \frac{\langle R_{v_1 v_2} v_1, v_2 \rangle}{||v_1||^2 ||v_2||^2 - \langle v_1, v_2 \rangle^2}.$$

So, we obtain

$$K(\tilde{v}_1, \tilde{v}_2) = K(v_1, v_2) - \frac{3||V(v_1, v_2)||^2}{||v_1||^2||v_2||^2 - \langle v_1, v_2 \rangle^2}.$$

For further details see O'Neill (1966).

The geodesics in the shape space $\mathbf{E}/\mathbb{G}$ are curves γ with tangent vectors $\frac{\mathrm{d}\gamma}{\mathrm{d}s}$ that are parallel along γ: that is,

$$\nabla_{\frac{\mathrm{d}\gamma}{\mathrm{d}s}} \frac{\mathrm{d}\gamma}{\mathrm{d}s} = 0.$$

If γ is a geodesic through $\pi(x)$, the vector field $\frac{\mathrm{d}\gamma}{\mathrm{d}s}$ along γ extends to a vector field on $\mathbf{E}/\mathbb{G}$ that lifts to a horizontal vector field. As for the special case we described in Chapter 6, the properties of Riemannian submersions ensure that the integral curve Γ of this horizontal vector field, which passes through x, remains over γ and, at each point, the tangent vector $\frac{\mathrm{d}\Gamma}{\mathrm{d}s}$ is then a horizontal lift of $\frac{\mathrm{d}\gamma}{\mathrm{d}s}$. Now,

$$\tilde{\nabla}_{\frac{\mathrm{d}\Gamma}{\mathrm{d}s}} \frac{\mathrm{d}\Gamma}{\mathrm{d}s} = \left(\nabla_{\frac{\mathrm{d}\gamma}{\mathrm{d}s}} \frac{\mathrm{d}\gamma}{\mathrm{d}s} \right)^{\tilde{}} + V\left(\frac{\mathrm{d}\gamma}{\mathrm{d}s}, \frac{\mathrm{d}\gamma}{\mathrm{d}s} \right)$$

and V is skew-symmetric, so

$$\tilde{\nabla}_{\frac{\mathrm{d}\Gamma}{\mathrm{d}s}} \frac{\mathrm{d}\Gamma}{\mathrm{d}s} = 0.$$

Thus, Γ is a geodesic in $\mathbf{E}$. This shows that every geodesic in the shape space $\mathbf{E}/\mathbb{G}$ is the image under the quotient map $\pi : \mathbf{E} \to \mathbf{E}/\mathbb{G}$ of a geodesic in $\mathbf{E}$ that has all its tangent vectors horizontal.

Finally, we wish to consider probability distributions on the quotient $\mathbf{E}/\mathbb{G}$ related to the metric. We will concentrate on the distributions associated with Brownian motion. The Riemannian metric on $\mathbf{E}$ gives rise to a Laplacian Δ and then we can define Brownian motion $(x_t)_{t \geq 0}$ on $\mathbf{E}$ to be a Markov process with infinitesimal generator $\frac{1}{2}\Delta$. The image of this $(\pi(x_t))_{t \geq 0}$ then gives a random process on the quotient $\mathbf{E}/\mathbb{G}$. It is, in fact, a Markov process. For suppose that f is a smooth function on $\mathbf{E}/\mathbb{G}$. Since each $g \in \mathbb{G}$ acts isometrically on $\mathbf{E}$, it preserves the Laplacian, so $\Delta(f \circ \pi)$ is constant on each orbit. Thus, there is a differential operator $\mathcal{L}$ on $\mathbf{E}/\mathbb{G}$ with $\Delta(f \circ \pi) = (\mathcal{L}f) \circ \pi$. Then, $\frac{1}{2}\mathcal{L}$ is the infinitesimal generator of the process $(\pi(x_t))_{t \geq 0}$, which is therefore a Markov process. For example, suppose that the k vectors $x_1, x_2, \ldots, x_k$ in $\mathbb{R}^m$ follow independent Brownian motions. Then, their size-and-shape will give a Markov process in the size-and-shape space $S\Sigma_m^k$.

Since $\mathbf{E}/\mathbb{G}$ is already a Riemannian manifold, it has a Laplacian Δ and $\frac{1}{2}\Delta$ generates a Brownian motion on $\mathbf{E}/\mathbb{G}$. However, $\mathcal{L}$ and Δ are not usually the same and consequently the process $(\pi(x_t))_{t \geq 0}$ is not usually a Brownian motion. The following well-known proposition explains the connection between $\mathcal{L}$ and Δ. (See, for example, Helgason, 1984, Theorem 3.7 and Equation (33').)

Proposition 11.1. *Let $\mathbb{G}$ be a compact Lie group of isometries of the Riemannian manifold $\mathbf{E}$ with $\pi : \mathbf{E} \to \mathbf{E}/\mathbb{G}$ a Riemannian submersion. For each $\sigma \in \mathbf{E}/\mathbb{G}$, the orbit $\pi^{-1}(\sigma)$ is a compact submanifold of $\mathbf{E}$ with fixed dimension, say, d. Let $v(\sigma)$ be the d-dimensional volume of $\pi^{-1}(\sigma)$ and H the vector field $\nabla \log v$. Then,*

$$\mathcal{L}f = \Delta f + Hf,$$

where Δ is the Laplacian on $\mathbf{E}/\mathbb{G}$.

Proof. Consider two smooth functions f and g on $\mathbf{E}/\mathbb{G}$ with compact support. If we denote the volume elements on $\mathbf{E}$ and $\mathbf{E}/\mathbb{G}$ by $dv_{\mathbf{E}}$ and $dv_{\mathbf{E}/\mathbb{G}}$, respectively, then the divergence theorem gives

$$\int_{\mathbf{E}} \Delta(f \circ \pi) \cdot g \circ \pi \, dv_{\mathbf{E}} = - \int_{\mathbf{E}} \langle \nabla(f \circ \pi), \nabla(g \circ \pi) \rangle \, dv_{\mathbf{E}}$$

$$= - \int_{\mathbf{E}} \langle \nabla f, \nabla g \rangle \circ \pi \, dv_{\mathbf{E}}$$

$$= - \int_{\mathbf{E}/\mathbb{G}} \langle \nabla f, \nabla g \rangle \cdot v \, dv_{\mathbf{E}/\mathbb{G}}$$

$$= \int_{\mathbf{E}/\mathbb{G}} (\mathrm{div}(v \cdot \nabla f)) \cdot g \, dv_{\mathbf{E}/\mathbb{G}}.$$

However, the first integral can also be written as $\int_{\mathbf{E}/\mathbb{G}} \mathcal{L}f \cdot g \cdot v \, dv_{\mathbf{E}/\mathbb{G}}$, so

$$\mathcal{L}f = v^{-1}\mathrm{div}(v \cdot \nabla f) = \Delta f + v^{-1}\langle \nabla v, \nabla f \rangle = \Delta f + Hf.$$

This is the desired formula.   ■

11.2   SIZE-AND-SHAPE SPACES

We will now show how to apply the results of the previous section to shape spaces by considering the size-and-shape space for k points in Euclidean space $\mathbb{R}^m$. These size-and-shape spaces have arisen earlier in Chapter 9. They have similar properties to the shape spaces but have a simpler geometry. Two k-ads $(x_1, x_2, \ldots, x_k)$ and $(y_1, y_2, \ldots, y_k)$ of points in $\mathbb{R}^m$ will have the same size-and-shape if there is an orientation-preserving isometry $g : \mathbb{R}^m \to \mathbb{R}^m$ with $g(x_j) = y_j$ for $j = 1, 2, \ldots, k$. The orientation-preserving isometries are the maps

$$g : \mathbb{R}^m \longrightarrow \mathbb{R}^m; \quad x \mapsto R(x) + b$$

for $R \in \mathbf{SO}(m)$, a rotation, and b, a translation vector. We can translate any k-ad $(x_1, x_2, \ldots, x_k)$ so that its centroid $x_c = \frac{1}{k} \sum_{j=1}^{k} x_j$ is moved to the origin. Therefore, the size-and-shape space $S\Sigma_m^k$ can be thought of as the quotient of

$$\mathbf{E} = \{(x_1, x_2, \ldots, x_k) \in (\mathbb{R}^m)^k : x_c = \mathbf{0}\}$$

by the group $\mathbf{SO}(m)$. Each rotation acts isometrically on $\mathbf{E}$ for the product metric, so we can apply the results of the previous section. In the size-and-shape spaces we distinguish between k-ads that have the same shape but different sizes. If we restrict attention to k-ads $(x_1, x_2, \ldots, x_k)$ with $\sum_{j=1}^{k} ||x_j - x_c||^2 = 1$, we obtain the shape space Σ_m^k as a subset of the size-and-shape space $S\Sigma_m^k$.

There is a slightly different way of thinking about k-ads of points in $\mathbb{R}^m$ that will prove useful later. First, fix a standard k-ad $(u_1, u_2, \ldots, u_k)$ of points in $\mathbb{R}^{k-1}$. This will have its centroid u_c at the origin and will be specified more precisely in a moment. Then, any linear map $T : \mathbb{R}^{k-1} \to \mathbb{R}^m$ will map $(u_1, u_2, \ldots, u_k)$ to a k-ad $(T(u_1), T(u_2), \ldots, T(u_k))$ of points in $\mathbb{R}^m$ with its centroid at the origin. Two such maps T and T' give k-ads with the same size and the same shape when $T' = RT$ for some rotation $R \in \mathbf{SO}(m)$. Thus, we can identify the size-and-shape space with the quotient $\mathrm{Hom}(\mathbb{R}^{k-1}, \mathbb{R}^m)/\mathbf{SO}(m)$ of the space $\mathrm{Hom}(\mathbb{R}^{k-1}, \mathbb{R}^m)$ of linear maps from $\mathbb{R}^{k-1}$ to $\mathbb{R}^m$ by the group $\mathbf{SO}(m)$.

We now need to be more precise in defining the standard k-ad. Let $e_1, e_2, e_3, \ldots, e_k$ be the standard unit vectors,

$$\begin{pmatrix} 1 \\ 0 \\ 0 \\ \vdots \\ 0 \end{pmatrix}, \quad \begin{pmatrix} 0 \\ 1 \\ 0 \\ \vdots \\ 0 \end{pmatrix}, \quad \begin{pmatrix} 0 \\ 0 \\ 1 \\ \vdots \\ 0 \end{pmatrix}, \ldots, \begin{pmatrix} 0 \\ 0 \\ 0 \\ \vdots \\ 1 \end{pmatrix},$$

in $\mathbb{R}^k$ and $\mathbf{1}$ the vector $\sum_{j=1}^{k} e_j$ with all components equal to 1. Then, the orthogonal complement $\mathbf{V}$ of $\mathbf{1}$ is a $(k-1)$-dimensional vector space and so it is isometric to $\mathbb{R}^{k-1}$ as we may see by choosing an orthonormal basis for it. Let u_j be the orthogonal projection of e_j onto $\mathbf{V}$, so $u_j = e_j - \frac{1}{k} \sum_{i=1}^{k} e_i$. These form the standard k-ad $(u_1, u_2, \ldots, u_k)$ in $\mathbf{V}$ or, equivalently, in $\mathbb{R}^{k-1}$. Note that

$$u_c = \frac{1}{k} \sum_{j=1}^{k} u_j = \mathbf{0}; \quad ||u_j|| = \left(\frac{k-1}{k}\right)^{1/2}; \quad ||u_i - u_j|| = \sqrt{2} \quad \text{for } i \neq j.$$

So, the k-ad is regular. For any k-ad $(x_1, x_2, \ldots, x_k)$ in $\mathbb{R}^m$ with $x_c = \mathbf{0}$, the $m \times k$ matrix X with columns $x_1, x_2, \ldots, x_k$ gives a linear map $X : \mathbb{R}^k \to \mathbb{R}^m$ that maps e_j to x_j. The restriction of X to $\mathbf{V}$ is then a linear map $T : \mathbf{V} \to \mathbb{R}^m$ with $T(u_j) = x_j$. We can give the vector space $\mathrm{Hom}(\mathbf{V}, \mathbb{R}^m)$ a Euclidean norm by setting $||T|| = \{\mathrm{tr}(T^t T)\}^{1/2}$. The corresponding inner product is $\langle T, T' \rangle = \mathrm{tr}(T^t T')$.

Let $(x_1, x_2, \ldots, x_k)$ be a k-ad in $\mathbb{R}^m$ with centroid x_c. This corresponds to the linear map $X : \mathbb{R}^k \to \mathbb{R}^m$ with $Xe_j = x_j - x_c$. The restriction of X to $\mathbf{V}$ is the linear map $T : \mathbf{V} \to \mathbb{R}^m$. Let $(x'_1, x'_2, \ldots, x'_k)$ be another k-ad with X' and T' the corresponding maps. Then, $X^t X'$ agrees with $T^t T'$ on $\mathbf{V}$ and is zero on $\mathbb{R}\mathbf{1}$. So,

$$\langle T, T' \rangle = \mathrm{tr}(T^t T') = \mathrm{tr}(X^t X') = \sum_{j=1}^{k} \langle x_j - x_c, x'_j - x'_c \rangle.$$

Therefore, the metric on the size-and-shape space is identical to that on the quotient $\mathrm{Hom}(\mathbf{V}, \mathbb{R}^m)/\mathbf{SO}(m)$. This metric is

$$\rho(\pi(T), \pi(T'))^2 = \inf_{R \in \mathbf{SO}(m)} ||T - RT'||^2$$

$$= ||T||^2 + ||T'||^2 - 2 \sup_{R \in \mathbf{SO}(m)} \mathrm{tr}(T^t R T').$$

We can also relate this to the metric on the shape space Σ_m^k. The size of the k-ad $(x_1, x_2, \ldots, x_k)$ is

$$s(T) = \left\{ \sum_{j=1}^{k} ||x_j - x_c||^2 \right\}^{1/2} = \left\{ \mathrm{tr}(X^t X) \right\}^{1/2} = \left\{ \mathrm{tr}(T^t T) \right\}^{1/2} = ||T||.$$

It is clear that the set $\{\pi(T) : s(T) = 1\}$ is the shape space Σ_m^k and that the metric is the same as the procrustean metric considered in Chapter 6, where ρ is denoted by $\hat{\rho}$. Any linear map $T : \mathbf{V} \to \mathbb{R}^m$ can be written as $s(T) \cdot \hat{T}$ for some map $\hat{T}$ of unit norm. Consequently, the size-and-shape space $S\Sigma_m^k$ can be regarded as a cone on the shape space Σ_m^k with $\pi(T) \in S\Sigma_m^k$ corresponding to $(s(T), \pi(\hat{T}))$ in $\mathbb{R} \times \Sigma_m^k$ with all the points $(0, \pi(\hat{T}))$ identified together to represent the k-ad with all points equal. The metric satisfies

$$\rho(\pi(T), \pi(T'))^2 = s(T)^2 + s(T')^2 - 2s(T) \, s(T') \sup_{R \in \mathbf{SO}(m)} \mathrm{tr}(\hat{T}^t R \hat{T}')$$

$$= s(T)^2 + s(T')^2 + s(T) \, s(T') \left\{ \rho(\pi(\hat{T}), \pi(\hat{T}'))^2 - 2 \right\}$$

$$= (s(T) - s(T'))^2 + s(T) \, s(T') \rho(\pi(\hat{T}), \pi(\hat{T}'))^2.$$

This is the usual relationship between the metric on a cone and the metric on its cross-section at unit radius from the vertex.

We now wish to describe coordinates for the size-and-shape space and calculate the Riemannian metric relative to these. This is very similar to the calculations for the shape space in Chapter 6, so we will be brief.

Let $(x_1, x_2, \ldots, x_k)$ be a k-ad of points in $\mathbb{R}^m$ with $x_c = \mathbf{0}$ and X the corresponding $m \times k$ matrix. Let $P = X^t X$. The entries in P are $p_{ij} = \langle x_i, x_j \rangle$ and these inner products are clearly unaltered when we replace $(x_1, x_2, \ldots, x_k)$ by

$(Rx_1, Rx_2, \ldots, Rx_k)$ for any of rotation $R \in \mathbf{SO}(m)$. We thus obtain a well-defined map

$$q : S\Sigma_m^k \longrightarrow \mathrm{Hom}(\mathbb{R}^k, \mathbb{R}^k); \ \pi(x_1, x_2, \ldots, x_k) \mapsto P = X^t X$$

on the size-and-shape space. The matrix $P = X^t X$ is symmetric, non-negative and has $P\mathbf{1} = \mathbf{0}$, because $x_c = X\mathbf{1} = \mathbf{0}$. Moreover, the rank of P is $\mathrm{rank}(P) = \mathrm{rank}(X)$, which is at most m. Therefore, q maps into the set $\mathcal{P}_m(k)$ of all symmetric, non-negative $k \times k$ matrices P with $P\mathbf{1} = \mathbf{0}$ and $\mathrm{rank}(P) \leq m$. We will show that q maps onto this set. For, each $P \in \mathcal{P}_m(k)$ has a symmetric square root S with $S^t S = S^2 = P$. Since $P\mathbf{1} = \mathbf{0}$, we see that $S\mathbf{1} = \mathbf{0}$. Also, $\mathrm{rank}(S) = \mathrm{rank}(P) \leq \min(m, k)$, so we can choose an orthogonal map U that sends the image of S into $\mathbb{R}^{\min(m,k)}$, which we regard as a subspace of $\mathbb{R}^k$. Now, $X = US : \mathbb{R}^k \to \mathbb{R}^m$ has $X\mathbf{1} = \mathbf{0}$, so X gives a point in $S\Sigma_m^k$ with $X^t X = P$. This shows that q is surjective. Moreover, if X and X' satisfy $X^t X = X'^t X' = P$, we see that $X' = RX$ for some orthogonal matrix $R \in \mathbf{O}(m)$. If $\det(R) = +1$, then $R \in \mathbf{SO}(m)$ and X, X' have the same size-and-shape. However, when $\det(R) = -1$, the matrices X and X' may have different shapes. Let J be a fixed reflection of $\mathbb{R}^m$. Then, $R \in \mathbf{O}(m)$ with $\det(R) = -1$ is equal to UJ with $U \in \mathbf{SO}(m)$. Consequently, X and $X' = RX$ have the same size-and-shape if and only if X and JX do. This happens precisely when all the points $x_1, x_2, \ldots, x_k$ lie in an $(m-1)$-dimensional subspace of $\mathbb{R}^m$. Thus, X and RX have the same shape, for $R \in \mathbf{O}(m) \setminus \mathbf{SO}(m)$, if and only if $\mathrm{rank}(X) < m$. This means that the map

$$q : S\Sigma_m^k \longrightarrow P \in \mathcal{P}_m(k)$$

sends two distinct points to each $P \in \mathcal{P}_m(k)$ with $\mathrm{rank}(P) = m$ and maps only one point to each $P \in \mathcal{P}_m(k)$ with $\mathrm{rank}(P) < m$.

There are three different cases to consider, depending on the relative sizes of k and m.

(i) $k - 1 < m$. In this case, let $\mathcal{P}(k)$ be the set of all symmetric, non-negative $k \times k$ matrices P with $P\mathbf{1} = \mathbf{0}$. Every such matrix has $\mathrm{rank}(P) \leqslant k - 1 < m$, so $\mathcal{P}_m(k) = \mathcal{P}(k)$ and the map $q : S\Sigma_m^k \to \mathcal{P}_m(k) = \mathcal{P}(k)$ is a bijection. The set $\mathcal{P}(k)$ is readily seen to be a cone with dimension $k(k-1)/2$ homeomorphic to a closed half-space of the same dimension. This identifies $S\Sigma_m^k$ up to homeomorphism.

(ii) $k - 1 = m$. Since $q : S\Sigma_{k-1}^k \to \mathcal{P}(k)$ is two-to-one on the shapes X with $\mathrm{rank}(X) = m$, we see that $S\Sigma_{k-1}^k$ consists of two copies of the cone $\mathcal{P}(k)$ joined along their boundary. It is therefore homeomorphic to $\mathbb{R}^{k(k-1)/2}$. This should be compared with Casson's theorem identifying the shape space Σ_{k-1}^k with $\mathbf{S}^{(k+1)(k-2)/2}$.

(iii) $k - 1 > m$. As in (ii) we see that $S\Sigma_m^k$ consists of two copies of $\mathcal{P}_m(k)$ joined along the boundary, which consists of matrices P with $\mathrm{rank}(P) < m$.

Let us now investigate the Riemannian metric on the size-and-shape space. Choose a linear map $T : \mathbf{V} \to \mathbb{R}^m$ and let $(x_1, x_2, \ldots, x_k)$ be the image of the standard k-ad in $\mathbf{V}$ under this map. The orbit of T is the image of the smooth map

$$\rho_T : \mathbf{SO}(m) \longrightarrow \mathrm{Hom}(\mathbf{V}, \mathbb{R}^m); \ R \mapsto RT.$$

So, the derivative of ρ_T at the identity I will map the tangent space to $\mathbf{SO}(m)$ at I onto the vertical tangent space $\mathcal{V}_T$. The tangent space to $\mathbf{SO}(m)$ at I is the Lie algebra

$$so(m) = \{A \in \mathrm{Hom}(\mathbb{R}^m, \mathbb{R}^m) : A^t + A = 0\}.$$

So, the vertical tangent space is

$$\mathcal{V}_T = \{AT \in \mathrm{Hom}(\mathbf{V}, \mathbb{R}^m) : A^t + A = 0\}.$$

This has dimension $r(2m - r - 1)/2$, where r is the rank of T: that is, the dimension of the space spanned by $(x_1, x_2, \ldots, x_k)$. So, we see that we obtain a manifold structure on the size-and-shape space at those points where this dimension is locally constant. When $k - 1 \geqslant m$, this means we have a manifold when rank(T) is m or $m - 1$ and singular points otherwise.

The horizontal tangent space at T is the orthogonal complement of $\mathcal{V}_T$, so it is

$$\mathcal{H}_T = \{H \in \mathrm{Hom}(\mathbf{V}, \mathbb{R}^m) : \langle H, AT \rangle = 0 \text{ for all } A \text{ with } A^t + A = 0\}.$$

Now, $\langle H, AT \rangle = \mathrm{tr}(H^t AT) = \mathrm{tr}(ATH^t)$ and this is zero for all A with $A^t + A = 0$ precisely when TH^t is symmetric. Thus,

$$\mathcal{H}_T = \{H \in \mathrm{Hom}(\mathbf{V}, \mathbb{R}^m) : TH^t = HT^t\}.$$

To describe the Riemannian metric on $S\Sigma_m^k$ more exactly it is convenient to change coordinates in $\mathbf{V}$ and $\mathbb{R}^m$ so that T has a simple form. We can choose a unit vector $v_1 \in \mathbf{V}$ with $\|Tv_1\|$ maximal. Then, $Tv_1 = \tau_1 f_1$ for $\tau_1 \geqslant 0$ and a unit vector $f_1 \in \mathbb{R}^m$. Since $\|Tv_1\|$ is maximal, we see that T maps the orthogonal complement of v_1 into the orthogonal complement of f_1. Repeating this process for the restriction of T to the orthogonal complement of v_1, we obtain an orthonormal basis $(v_1, v_2, \ldots, v_{k-1})$ of $\mathbf{V}$, an orthonormal basis $(f_1, f_2, \ldots, f_m)$ of $\mathbb{R}^m$ and scalars $\tau_1 \geqslant \tau_2 \geqslant \tau_3 \geqslant \ldots \geqslant 0$ with

$$T = \sum_{j=1}^{m} \tau_j f_j v_j^t.$$

So, T is diagonal relative to these bases. The numbers $\tau_1, \tau_2, \tau_3, \ldots$ are called the *approximation numbers* of T. Note that τ_j must be 0 for $j > \min(k - 1, m)$. This should be compared with the pseudo-singular values decomposition in Chapters 1 and 6. Note that we may assume that the basis $(v_1, v_2, \ldots, v_{k-1})$ is positively oriented, because we may replace v_{k-1} by $-v_{k-1}$ if necessary. However, the basis $(f_1, f_2, \ldots, f_m)$ may then not be positively oriented.

Changing orthonormal bases in $\mathbf{V}$ or in $\mathbb{R}^m$ does not change the metric in the size-and-shape space $\mathrm{Hom}(\mathbf{V}, \mathbb{R}^m)/\mathbf{SO}(m)$. This is clear for $\mathbb{R}^m$, since T and RT have the same size-and-shape for each $R \in \mathbf{SO}(m)$. If we have two orthonormal bases for $\mathbf{V}$, then there is an orthogonal linear map $U : \mathbf{V} \to \mathbf{V}$ that maps one to the other. The corresponding change of bases transforms $T \in \mathrm{Hom}(\mathbf{V}, \mathbb{R}^m)$ to

TU. Now, this transformation commutes with $T \mapsto RT$ for any $R \in \mathbf{SO}(m)$, so, as we saw in the previous section, there is an isometry

$$\mathrm{Hom}(\mathbf{V}, \mathbb{R}^m)/\mathbf{SO}(m) \longrightarrow \mathrm{Hom}(\mathbf{V}, \mathbb{R}^m)/\mathbf{SO}(m); \quad \pi(T) \mapsto \pi(TU).$$

Consequently, we may assume that T is diagonal in our calculations.

For $T = \sum_{j=1}^{m} \tau_j f_j v_j^t$ we have

$$\mathcal{V}_T = \left\{ \sum_{i,j=1}^{m} a_{ij}\tau_j f_i v_j^t : a_{ij} = -a_{ji} \text{ for } i, j = 1, 2, \ldots, m \right\},$$

$$\mathcal{H}_T = \left\{ \sum_{i,j=1}^{m} h_{ij} f_i v_j^t : h_{ij}\tau_j = h_{ji}\tau_i \text{ for } i, j = 1, 2, \ldots, m \right\}.$$

Consider any tangent vector at T represented by a matrix $S \in \mathrm{Hom}(\mathbf{V}, \mathbb{R}^m)$ with $S = \sum_{i,j=1}^{m} s_{ij} f_i v_j^t$. Then, we can write $S = V + H$ with V vertical and H horizontal. Thus,

$$s_{ij} = a_{ij}\tau_j + h_{ij} \quad \text{with } a_{ij} = -a_{ji} \text{ and } h_{ij}\tau_j = h_{ji}\tau_i \text{ for } i, j = 1, 2, \ldots, m.$$

We can solve these equations to find H:

$$
\begin{aligned}
(\tau_i^2 + \tau_j^2) h_{ij} &= \tau_i^2 h_{ij} + \tau_i \tau_j h_{ji} \\
&= \tau_i^2 s_{ij} - \tau_i^2 \tau_j a_{ij} + \tau_i \tau_j s_{ji} - \tau_i^2 \tau_j a_{ji} \\
&= \tau_i^2 s_{ij} + \tau_i \tau_j s_{ji}.
\end{aligned}
$$

Therefore, the orthogonal projection of S onto the horizontal tangent vectors is

$$H = \sum_{i,j=1}^{m} \frac{\tau_i^2 s_{ij} + \tau_i \tau_j s_{ji}}{\tau_i^2 + \tau_j^2} f_i v_j^t.$$

The Riemannian metric for $S\Sigma_m^k$ is given by making the length of $\pi_*(S)$ equal to $\|H\|$. This is

$$
\begin{aligned}
\|H\|^2 &= \sum_{i,j=1}^{m} \left(\frac{\tau_i^2 s_{ij} + \tau_i \tau_j s_{ji}}{\tau_i^2 + \tau_j^2} \right)^2 \\
&= \sum_{i,j=1}^{m} \frac{\tau_i^4 s_{ij}^2 + \tau_i^2 \tau_j^2 s_{ij}^2 + 2\tau_i^3 \tau_j s_{ij} s_{ji}}{(\tau_i^2 + \tau_j^2)^2}.
\end{aligned}
$$

Interchanging the roles of i and j and averaging gives

$$
\begin{aligned}
\|H\|^2 &= \sum_{i,j=1}^{m} \frac{(\tau_i^4 + \tau_i^2 \tau_j^2) s_{ij}^2 + (\tau_i^3 \tau_j + \tau_i \tau_j^3) s_{ij} s_{ji}}{(\tau_i^2 + \tau_j^2)^2} \\
&= \sum_{i,j=1}^{m} \left\{ \frac{\tau_i^2}{\tau_i^2 + \tau_j^2} s_{ij}^2 + \frac{\tau_i \tau_j}{\tau_i^2 + \tau_j^2} s_{ij} s_{ji} \right\}.
\end{aligned}
$$

Note that this is well-defined unless two of the approximation numbers τ_i are zero, when we are at a singular point of the size-and-shape space.

To calculate the curvature and other geometric invariants of $S\Sigma_m^k$ we need to find the covariant derivative $\nabla_{v_1} v_2$ of vector fields v_1, v_2 on $S\Sigma_m^k$. For simplicity, we will concentrate on the case where the approximation numbers are non-zero. For each symmetric linear map $S : \mathbf{V} \to \mathbf{V}$, the composite $H = TS$ has $HT^t = TST^t$ symmetric, so it is a horizontal tangent vector at T. Therefore,

$$\tilde{v} : \text{Hom}(\mathbf{V}, \mathbb{R}^m) \longrightarrow \text{Hom}(\mathbf{V}, \mathbb{R}^m); T \mapsto TS$$

is the horizontal lift of a vector field v on $S\Sigma_m^k$. Let $\tilde{v}_j : T \mapsto TS_j$ be two such vector fields. The vector space $\text{Hom}(\mathbf{V}, \mathbb{R}^m)$ is flat, so the covariant derivative is given by

$$\nabla_{\tilde{v}_1} \tilde{v}_2 : T \mapsto \tilde{v}_2'(T)\{\tilde{v}_1(T)\} = TS_1 S_2.$$

However, we know from the previous section that $\nabla_{\tilde{v}_1} \tilde{v}_2 = (\nabla_{v_1} v_2)^{\sim} + V(v_1, v_2)$, where $(\nabla_{v_1} v_2)^{\sim}$ is the horizontal lift of the vector field $\nabla_{v_1} v_2$ and $V(v_1, v_2)$ is a vertical vector field. Hence, we can find these by taking the horizontal and vertical parts of $T \mapsto TS_1 S_2$. Suppose that $TS_1 S_2 = H + AT$ with H horizontal and AT vertical, so that $HT^t = TH^t$ and $A + A^t = 0$. Then,

$$TS_1 S_2 T^t = HT^t + ATT^t$$

and transposing gives

$$TS_2 S_1 T^t = TH^t - TT^t A.$$

Subtracting these gives

$$T[S_1, S_2]T^t = ATT^t + TT^t A,$$

where $[S_1, S_2]$ is the commutator $S_1 S_2 - S_2 S_1$. We can solve this by using the diagonal form of $T = \sum_{j=1}^{m} \tau_j f_j v_j^t$. For, if $A = \sum_{i,j=1}^{m} a_{ij} f_i f_j^t$ and $[S_1, S_2] = \sum_{i,j=1}^{k-1} [S_1, S_2]_{ij} v_i v_j^t$, then

$$\tau_i \tau_j [S_1, S_2]_{ij} = (\tau_i^2 + \tau_j^2) a_{ij}.$$

Therefore,

$$V(v_1, v_2) : T \mapsto AT = \sum_{i,j=1}^{m} \frac{\tau_i \tau_j^2}{\tau_i^2 + \tau_j^2} [S_1, S_2]_{ij} f_i v_j^t.$$

This determines the curvature of the size-and-shape space at T. We can explicitly determine the sectional curvature $K(v_1, v_2)$ by

$$K(v_1, v_2) = \frac{3\|V(v_1, v_2)\|^2}{\|v_1\|^2 \|v_2\|^2 - \langle v_1, v_2 \rangle^2}.$$

A straightforward calculation gives

$$||V(v_1, v_2)||^2 = \frac{1}{2} \sum_{i,j=1}^{m} \left(\frac{\tau_i^2 \tau_j^2}{\tau_i^2 + \tau_j^2} \right) [S_1, S_2]_{ij}^2,$$

$$||v_1||^2 ||v_2||^2 - \langle v_1, v_2 \rangle^2 = \frac{1}{2} \sum_{i,j=1}^{m} (\tau_i^2 + \tau_j^2)(S_1 - S_2)_{ij}^2.$$

This certainly shows that the curvature is non-negative everywhere on the size-and-shape space.

Having calculated the covariant derivative, it is easy to see that the geodesics through a shape $\pi(T)$ are given by

$$t \mapsto \pi(T + tH)$$

for a horizontal tangent vector H. We can also interpret this in terms of the k-ad $(x_1, x_2, \ldots, x_k)$. Consider k particles, each of unit mass, positioned at the points $x_1, x_2, \ldots, x_k$ and with velocities $\dot{x}_1, \dot{x}_2, \ldots, \dot{x}_k$. Since we want the centroid always to be at the origin, we will insist that the initial centroid $x_c = \frac{1}{k} \sum_{j=1}^{k} x_j$ is there and that the momentum $\sum_{j=1}^{k} \dot{x}_j$ is also zero. At each time t, the vectors $x_j + t\dot{x}_j$ form the columns of a $m \times k$ matrix $X + t\dot{X}$. The restriction of this to the subspace $\mathbf{V}$ of $\mathbb{R}^k$ gives a linear map $T + tH \in \text{Hom}(\mathbf{V}, \mathbb{R}^m)$. Now, H is horizontal at T when $HT^t = TH^t$. This is equivalent to $\dot{X}X^t = X\dot{X}^t$. Thus, for any two vectors $a, b \in \mathbb{R}^m$, we must have $a^t(\dot{X}X^t - X\dot{X}^t)b = 0$. Expanding this, we obtain

$$\sum_{j=1}^{k} \left\{ \langle x_j, b \rangle \langle \dot{x}_j, a \rangle - \langle \dot{x}_j, b \rangle \langle x_j, a \rangle \right\} = 0,$$

which is the condition that the angular momentum of the particles in the plane spanned by a and b is zero. Thus, the particles $(x_j + t\dot{x}_j)$ trace out a geodesic in the size-and-shape space when their angular momentum about their centroid is zero.

Finally, we may apply Proposition 11.1 to find the operator $\mathcal{L}$ on $S\Sigma_m^k$. Proposition 11.1 shows that $\mathcal{L} = \Delta + H$, where Δ is the Laplacian induced by the Riemannian metric and H is the gradient of $\log v$. In this expression, $v(\pi(T))$ is the volume of the orbit

$$\{RT : R \in \mathbf{SO}(m)\}$$

in $\text{Hom}(\mathbf{V}, \mathbb{R}^m)$. This orbit is the image of the map

$$J : \mathbf{SO}(m) \longrightarrow \text{Hom}(\mathbf{V}, \mathbb{R}^m); \ R \mapsto RT.$$

We will find its volume by computing how much the map J alters the volume of $\mathbf{SO}(m)$. For simplicity, we will assume that $k > m$.

The tangent space to $\mathbf{SO}(m)$ at the identity is the set $so(m)$ of skew-symmetric $m \times m$ matrices, and the derivative of J at the identity is

$$J_*(I) : so(m) \longrightarrow \text{Hom}(\mathbf{V}, \mathbb{R}^m); \; A \mapsto AT.$$

This is a linear map that maps $so(m)$ onto a vector subspace of $\text{Hom}(\mathbf{V}, \mathbb{R}^m)$. We need to find the factor δ by which it changes the volume. First, observe that the transpose of $J_*(I)$ is

$$J_*(I)^t : \text{Hom}(\mathbf{V}, \mathbb{R}^m) \longrightarrow so(m); \; S \mapsto \tfrac{1}{2}(ST^t - TS^t).$$

The composite

$$J_*(I)^t J_*(I) : so(m) \longrightarrow so(m); \; A \mapsto \tfrac{1}{2}(ATT^t + TT^t A)$$

then changes volumes by a factor δ^2. For $T = \sum_{j=1}^m \tau_j f_j v_j^t$ we see that

$$J_*(I)^t J_*(I) : f_i f_j^t - f_j f_i^t \mapsto (\tau_i^2 + \tau_j^2)(f_i f_j^t - f_j f_i^t).$$

Therefore, it changes volumes by $\prod_{i<j}(\tau_i^2 + \tau_j^2)$. A similar argument applies to the tangent space at any other point $R \in \mathbf{SO}(m)$, so the $\tfrac{1}{2}m(m-1)$-dimensional volume of the orbit $J(\mathbf{SO}(m))$ is

$$v(\pi(T)) = \left\{ \prod_{i<j}(\tau_i^2 + \tau_j^2) \right\}^{1/2} \times \text{Volume}(\mathbf{SO(m)}).$$

Consequently, the vector field H is the gradient of

$$\pi(T) \mapsto \frac{1}{2} \sum_{i<j} \log(\tau_i^2 + \tau_j^2).$$

11.3   SIZE-AND-SHAPE SPACES FOR THE PLANE

When $m = 2$ we may identify $\mathbb{R}^m$ with the complex plane $\mathbb{C}$. This significantly simplifies the arguments of the previous section in certain cases. Since the plane is an important source of examples, we will describe the situation briefly.

Suppose that $(z_1, z_2, \ldots, z_k)$ is a k-ad of points in $\mathbb{C}$. We think of this vector as defining a real linear map

$$X : \mathbb{R}^k \longrightarrow \mathbb{C}; \; e_j \mapsto z_j.$$

As in the previous section, we are concerned with the restriction of this map to the $(k-1)$-dimensional subspace $\mathbf{V}$. By choosing an orthonormal basis for $\mathbf{V}$

we see that this corresponds to a vector $\boldsymbol{w} = (w_1, w_2, \ldots, w_{k-1}) \in \mathbb{C}^{k-1}$. Each component w_j is a linear combination of the points z_j. It is simpler to work directly with the vector $\boldsymbol{w}$. A rotation in $\mathbf{SO}(2)$ acts on $\mathbb{C}$ by multiplication by a complex number ω with modulus 1. So the size-and-shape space $S\Sigma_2^k$ is the quotient $\mathbb{C}^{k-1}/\{\omega \in \mathbb{C} : |\omega| = 1\}$. We will denote the quotient map by π. Two vectors $\boldsymbol{w}$ and $\boldsymbol{w}'$ give the same size-and-shape if and only if $\boldsymbol{w}' = \omega \boldsymbol{w}$ for some $\omega \in \mathbb{C}$ with unit modulus. More generally, the distance in the size-and-shape space is

$$\rho(\pi(\boldsymbol{w}), \pi(\boldsymbol{w}'))^2 = \inf_{|\omega|=1} ||\boldsymbol{w} - \omega \boldsymbol{w}'||^2 = ||\boldsymbol{w}||^2 + ||\boldsymbol{w}'||^2 - 2 \sup_{|\omega|=1} \Re(\langle \boldsymbol{w}, \omega \boldsymbol{w}' \rangle)$$

$$= ||\boldsymbol{w}||^2 + ||\boldsymbol{w}'||^2 - 2|\langle \boldsymbol{w}, \boldsymbol{w}' \rangle|,$$

where $\langle \, , \, \rangle$ is the complex inner product: $\langle \boldsymbol{w}, \boldsymbol{w}' \rangle = \sum_{j=1}^{k-1} \overline{w}_j w_j'$. This is the metric on size-and-shape space that we used in Chapter 9.

For the Riemannian metric on $S\Sigma_2^k$ we note that at any non-zero point $\boldsymbol{w} \in \mathbb{C}^{k-1}$ a tangent vector $d\boldsymbol{w}$ is vertical when $d\boldsymbol{w} = i\lambda\boldsymbol{w}$ for some real number λ. Consequently, $d\boldsymbol{w}$ is horizontal when $\langle \boldsymbol{w}, d\boldsymbol{w} \rangle$ is real. It follows that a horizontal geodesic in $\mathbb{C}^{k-1}$ is of the form

$$\gamma : t \mapsto \boldsymbol{w} + t d\boldsymbol{w} \qquad \text{where } \langle \boldsymbol{w}, d\boldsymbol{w} \rangle \in \mathbb{R}.$$

Then, $||\gamma(t)||^2 = ||\boldsymbol{w}||^2 + 2t\langle \boldsymbol{w}, d\boldsymbol{w} \rangle + t^2 ||d\boldsymbol{w}||^2$, so there is a unique point on the geodesic with minimal norm. If we choose $\boldsymbol{w}$ as this point, then $\langle \boldsymbol{w}, d\boldsymbol{w} \rangle = 0$ and so $||\gamma(t)||^2 = ||\boldsymbol{w}||^2 + t^2 ||d\boldsymbol{w}||^2$. This describes the size of k-ads along the geodesic; the shapes trace out a geodesic in the shape space.

Finally, let us consider the probability distribution on $S\Sigma_2^k$ given by a k-ad of points that are independently normally distributed in $\mathbb{C}$. An isotropic normal random variable with mean z_0 and variance σ^2 has density

$$\frac{1}{2\pi\sigma^2} \exp\left\{ -\frac{|z - z_0|^2}{2\sigma^2} \right\}.$$

If the points $(z_1, z_2, \ldots, z_k)$ are independently distributed in $\mathbb{C}$, each with an isotropic normal distribution with variance σ^2, then the components of the corresponding vector $\boldsymbol{w} \in \mathbb{C}^{k-1}$ will also be independent isotropic normal distributions with variance σ^2. If the mean of $\boldsymbol{w}$ is $\boldsymbol{w}_0$, then the density for $\boldsymbol{w}$ is

$$\frac{1}{(2\pi\sigma^2)^{k-1}} \exp\left\{ -\frac{||\boldsymbol{w} - \boldsymbol{w}_0||^2}{2\sigma^2} \right\}.$$

To compute the corresponding density on the size-and-shape space we need to average this over all rotations, so we obtain

$$\frac{1}{(2\pi\sigma^2)^{k-1}} \int_0^{2\pi} \exp\left\{-\frac{||e^{i\theta}\boldsymbol{w} - \boldsymbol{w}_0||^2}{2\sigma^2}\right\} \frac{d\theta}{2\pi}$$

$$= \frac{1}{(2\pi\sigma^2)^{k-1}} \int_0^{2\pi} \exp\left\{-\frac{||\boldsymbol{w}||^2 + ||\boldsymbol{w}_0||^2 - 2\Re(e^{-i\theta}\langle\boldsymbol{w}, \boldsymbol{w}_0\rangle)}{2\sigma^2}\right\} \frac{d\theta}{2\pi}$$

$$= \frac{1}{(2\pi\sigma^2)^{k-1}} \exp\left\{-\frac{||\boldsymbol{w}||^2 + ||\boldsymbol{w}_0||^2}{2\sigma^2}\right\} J_0\left(\frac{|\langle\boldsymbol{w}, \boldsymbol{w}_0\rangle|}{\sigma^2}\right),$$

where

$$J_0(x) = \int_0^{2\pi} \exp(x\cos\theta)\frac{d\theta}{2\pi}$$

is the Bessel function of order 0. This should be compared with the results obtained by Mardia and Dryden in (1989a) and Section 8.5.

Closely related to this is the Markov process on $S\Sigma_2^k$ obtained when the k points $(z_1, z_2, \ldots, z_k)$ execute independent Brownian motion in $\mathbb{C}$. Then, the vector $\boldsymbol{w}$ will follow a Brownian motion in $\mathbb{C}^{k-1}$. Since the size-and-shape space is a cone, we obtain a skew-product process on it. The size $||\boldsymbol{w}||$ is clearly a Bessel process of dimension $2(k-1)$, while the shape follows a time-changed Brownian motion on $\mathbf{CP}^{k-2}$. We can prove this analytically by applying Proposition 11.1.

11.4 SPHERES AND HYPERBOLIC SPACES

In the next three sections we will use the hyperbolic plane and in the final section we will need hyperbolic 3-space. It is usually simplest to think of the hyperbolic plane as the upper half-plane $\mathbb{R}_+^2 = \{z \in \mathbb{C} : \Im(z) > 0\}$ with the Riemannian metric

$$ds = \frac{|dz|}{\Im(z)}$$

or the unit disc $\mathbf{B} = \{z \in \mathbb{C} : |z| < 1\}$ with the Riemannian metric

$$ds = \frac{2|dz|}{1 - |z|^2}.$$

The hyperbolic distance between two points z and z' is then

$$\rho(z, z') = \log\frac{1 + |\mu|}{1 - |\mu|}, \tag{11.1}$$

where

$$\mu = \frac{z - z'}{\bar{z} - z'} \quad \text{for } \mathbb{R}_+^2 \quad \text{and} \quad \mu = \frac{z - z'}{1 - \bar{z}z'} \quad \text{for } \mathbf{B}.$$

Every Möbius transformation $z \mapsto \frac{az+b}{cz+d}$ for $a, b, c, d \in \mathbb{C}$ with $ad - bc \neq 0$ that maps $\mathbb{R}_+^2$ to $\mathbb{R}_+^2$, or $\mathbf{B}$ to $\mathbf{B}$, is an isometry for the hyperbolic metric. All of the results we require in Sections 11.5 and 11.6 follow readily for these models. However, in studying hyperbolic 3-space in Section 11.7 it will be easiest to use the hyperboloid model for hyperbolic space, which views it as one sheet of a hyperboloid in a space with an indefinite inner product. Therefore, we will develop the properties of the hyperbolic spaces in this context.

To show the analogy between hyperbolic spaces and the spheres we will recall the properties of the spheres. The sphere S^n is the subset

$$\{(x_0, x_1, \ldots, x_n) \in \mathbb{R}^{n+1} : x_0^2 + x_1^2 + \cdots + x_n^2 = 1\}$$

of $\mathbb{R}^{n+1}$. We will write $\langle\ ,\ \rangle$ for the standard inner product

$$\langle x, y \rangle = x_0 y_0 + x_1 y_1 + \cdots + x_n y_n.$$

So, $S^n = \{x \in \mathbb{R}^{n+1} : \langle x, x \rangle = 1\}$. This is a submanifold of $\mathbb{R}^{n+1}$ and inherits a Riemannian metric d with

$$d(x, y) = \arccos \langle x, y \rangle,$$

which measures distances on the sphere rather than the chordal distance through $\mathbb{R}^{n+1}$. The group of rotations $SO(n+1)$ acts as a group of isometries of S^n and acts transitively. We can map S^n onto $\mathbb{R}^n$, plus an extra point ∞, by stereographic projection. This was described in Chapter 1, but it will be more convenient for us to project from the south pole rather than the north. Thus, the point $x \in S^n$ is projected radially outwards from $(-1, 0, 0, \ldots, 0)$ until it hits the set $\{(0, y_1, y_2, \ldots, y_n) \in \mathbb{R}^{n+1}\}$, which we identify with $\mathbb{R}^n$. It hits at the point $\left(\frac{x_1}{1+x_0}, \frac{x_2}{1+x_0}, \ldots, \frac{x_n}{1+x_0}\right)$. The metric on S^n is then transformed to the metric

$$ds = \frac{2\|dy\|}{1 + \|y\|^2},$$

$$\sin(\tfrac{1}{2}d(y, y')) = \frac{\|y - y'\|}{\sqrt{(1 + \|y\|^2)(1 + \|y'\|^2)}} \quad \text{for } y, y' \in \mathbb{R}^n \cup \{\infty\}.$$

We can also consider the real projective space $\mathbf{RP}^n$, which consists of all the one-dimensional vector subspaces of $\mathbb{R}^{n+1}$. Each such one-dimensional subspace cuts S^n at two antipodal points. So we may think of $\mathbf{RP}^n$ as the space obtained from S^n by identifying together every pair of antipodal points.

The hyperbolic spaces $\mathbb{H}^n$ are defined in a similar way to the spheres, or, more accurately, to the projective spaces, by replacing the inner product $\langle\ ,\ \rangle$ on $\mathbb{R}^{n+1}$ by an indefinite bilinear form. Let $\mathbb{R}^{1,n}$ be the vector space $\mathbb{R}^{n+1}$ with the indefinite, symmetric bilinear form

$$\langle x, y \rangle = -x_0 y_0 + x_1 y_1 + x_2 y_2 + \cdots + x_n y_n.$$

Then, $\mathbb{H}^n$ is the set

$$\mathbb{H}^n = \{x \in \mathbb{R}^{n,1} : \langle x, x \rangle = -1 \text{ and } x_0 > 0\}.$$

This is one of the two sheets of a hyperboloid. It is a manifold of dimension n. The hyperbolic metric d is given by

$$d(x, y) = \text{arccosh} \, (-\langle x, y \rangle).$$

It is often more convenient to use different models for hyperbolic space due to Poincaré. These allow us to identify the hyperbolic space $\mathbb{H}^n$ with the unit ball $\mathbf{B}^n = \{y \in \mathbb{R}^n : \|y\| < 1\}$ or with the upper half-space $\mathbb{R}^n_+ = \{y \in \mathbb{R}^n : y_n > 0\}$. Stereographic projection gives us a map from $\mathbb{H}^n$ to the ball $\mathbf{B}^n$. We map each point $x \in \mathbb{H}^n$ to the point $y \in \mathbb{R}^n = \{(0, y_1, y_2, \ldots, y_n) : y_j \in \mathbb{R}\}$, where the straight line through $(-1, 0, 0, \ldots, 0)$ and x cuts $\mathbb{R}^n$. This point is $\left(\frac{x_1}{1+x_0}, \frac{x_2}{1+x_0}, \ldots, \frac{x_n}{1+x_0} \right)$. The image point y lies in the unit ball $\mathbf{B}^n$. The hyperbolic metric on $\mathbb{H}^n$ gives a Riemannian metric on $\mathbf{B}^n$ with

$$ds = \frac{2\|dy\|}{1 - \|y\|^2},$$

$$\sinh(\tfrac{1}{2}d(y, y')) = \frac{\|y - y'\|}{\sqrt{(1 - \|y\|^2)(1 - \|y'\|^2)}} \quad \text{for } y, y' \in \mathbf{B}^n.$$

In a similar way, the mapping

$$\mathbb{H}^n \longrightarrow \mathbb{R}^n_+; \quad (x_0, x_1, x_2, \ldots, x_n) \mapsto \left(\frac{x_1}{x_0 + x_n}, \ldots, \frac{x_{n-1}}{x_0 + x_n}, \frac{1}{x_0 + x_n} \right)$$

enables us to identify the hyperbolic space $\mathbb{H}^n$ with the upper half-space $\mathbb{R}^n_+$. The corresponding Riemannian metric on $\mathbb{R}^n_+$ is

$$ds = \frac{\|dy\|}{y_n},$$

$$\sinh(\tfrac{1}{2}d(y, y')) = \frac{\|y - y'\|}{\sqrt{y_n y_n'}} \quad \text{for } y, y' \in \mathbb{R}^n_+.$$

The hyperbolic spaces are highly symmetric with a group of isometries that maps any point to any other. To see this we will consider 'reflections' in hyperplanes in $\mathbb{H}^n$. Let u be a vector in $\mathbb{R}^{1,n}$ with $\langle u, u \rangle = +1$ and set

$$\mathbf{P}_u = \{x \in \mathbb{H}^n : \langle x, u \rangle = 0\}.$$

This is a subset that is isometric to the $(n-1)$-dimensional hyperbolic space $\mathbb{H}^{n-1}$. Reflection in this subspace is given by

$$R_u : x \mapsto x - 2\langle x, u \rangle u.$$

It is easy to check that R_u is a linear map that sends $\mathbb{H}^n$ into itself. Also, $\langle R_u x, R_u x' \rangle = \langle x, x' \rangle$, so R_u is an isometry of the hyperbolic space. These reflections generate the group

$$\mathbf{O}^+(1, n) = \{ T \in \mathrm{Hom}(\mathbb{R}^{1,n}, \mathbb{R}^{1,n}) : \langle Tx, Tx' \rangle = \langle x, x' \rangle \quad \text{and} \quad T(\mathbb{H}^n) = \mathbb{H}^n \}.$$

Within this group the maps have determinant ± 1, depending on whether they are the product of an even number or an odd number of reflections. Those with determinant $+1$ form the subgroup $\mathbf{SO}^+(1, n)$, which consists of all of the orientation-preserving isometries of hyperbolic space. Those with determinant -1 preserve distances but reverse orientation.

In the ball or the upper half-space models, the hyperbolic hyperplane $\mathbf{P}_u$ corresponds to a spherical cap orthogonal to the boundary. Reflections correspond to inversions in such spheres orthogonal to the boundary. These generate the group of Möbius transformations of $\mathbb{R}^n \cup \{\infty\}$ that generalise the Möbius transformations $z \mapsto \frac{az+b}{cz+d}$ from $\mathbb{C} \cup \{\infty\}$ to itself.

We will also need to consider the boundary of hyperbolic space. For the ball $\mathbf{B}^n$ the boundary is the sphere $\mathbf{S}^{n-1} = \{ y : \|y\| = 1 \}$, and for the upper half-space $\mathbb{R}^n_+$ the boundary is $\{ y \in \mathbb{R}^n : y_n = 0 \} \cup \{\infty\}$. However, the boundary of the hyperboloid model $\mathbb{H}^n$ is a little more difficult to describe. Let x be a point of $\mathbb{H}^n$ and y the point of $\mathbf{B}^n$ that corresponds to it under stereographic projection. As y tends to a boundary point in $\mathbf{S}^{n-1}$, so the direction vector x converges to a direction in the cone

$$\mathbb{K}^n = \{ u \in \mathbb{R}^{1,n} : \langle u, u \rangle = 0 \text{ and } u_0 > 0 \},$$

the vectors of which we call *null vectors*. So, we will consider the half-lines $\{ \lambda u : \lambda > 0 \}$ in $\mathbb{K}^n$ as the boundary points of $\mathbb{H}^n$.

11.5 RELATIVE METRICS

In this section we wish to consider a different metric on the shape space Σ_2^3 that measures the relative displacement between triangles. This is the metric considered in much more detail by Bookstein (1978a, 1991). As we shall see, this gives no useful information for the shapes of triangles with collinear or coincident vertices. Indeed, it will have the property that all other triangles are infinitely far from such degenerate ones. Thus, this model of shape space is only apposite for a context in which it is natural to place such a constraint on the shapes we consider.

It is convenient to identify $\mathbb{R}^2$ with the complex plane $\mathbb{C}$. We will translate all triangles so that their centroid is at the origin 0. Fix a standard triangle Δ in the plane with vertices u_1, u_2, u_3 that are not collinear and with its centroid at the origin. For example, we might take u_1, u_2, u_3 to be the three cube roots of 1.

Then, any triangle with its centroid at 0 is the image of Δ by a real linear map $T : \mathbb{R}^2 \to \mathbb{R}^2$. Any such map is of the form

$$T : x + iy \mapsto w_1 x + w_2 y$$

for two complex numbers w_1 and w_2. We will think of the set of all triangles with centroid at the origin as the set $\mathrm{Hom}(\mathbb{R}^2, \mathbb{R}^2)$ of real linear maps. The shape of the triangle is unchanged when we multiply w_1 and w_2 by the same non-zero complex number. So, the ratio $\tau = w_2/w_1 \in \mathbb{C} \cup \{\infty\}$ determines the shape of the triangle. This is the way we identified the shape space Σ_2^3 with the extended complex plane in Chapter 1. (See also Section 11.3.) The triangle is flat, with collinear vertices, when T is singular or, equivalently, when $\tau \in \mathbb{R} \cup \{\infty\}$. If the triangle is oriented in the same way as Δ, then τ is in the upper half-plane $\mathbb{R}_+^2 = \{\tau \in \mathbb{C} : \Im(\tau) > 0\}$ and, if it is oppositely oriented, then $\Im(\tau) < 0$. In the previous chapters we have used the procrustean metric on the shape space to measure the distance $\hat{\rho}(\tau, \tau')$ between two shapes τ and τ' as

$$\hat{\rho}(\tau, \tau')^2 = 2 \left\{ 1 - \frac{|\overline{w}_1 w_1' + \overline{w}_2 w_2'|}{\sqrt{(|w_1|^2 + |w_2|^2)(|w_1'|^2 + |w_2'|^2)}} \right\}$$

$$= 2 \left\{ 1 - \frac{|1 + \overline{\tau}_2 \tau'|}{\sqrt{(1 + |\tau|^2)(1 + |\tau'|^2)}} \right\}.$$

This metric depends on the choice of the standard triangle Δ. For suppose that we chose a different triangle, say, $S(\Delta)$, where S is the linear map

$$S : \mathbb{R}^2 \longrightarrow \mathbb{R}^2; \quad \begin{pmatrix} x \\ y \end{pmatrix} \mapsto \begin{pmatrix} a & b \\ c & d \end{pmatrix} \begin{pmatrix} x \\ y \end{pmatrix} \quad \text{with } a, b, c, d \in \mathbb{R}.$$

For $S(\Delta)$ not to be flat we need S to be non-singular, so the determinant $\delta = ad - bc$ is non-zero. For this new standard triangle, the map T is replaced by TS^{-1}. Therefore, the shape $\tau = T(i)/T(1)$ is replaced by

$$\tilde{\tau} = \frac{T((d - bi)/\delta)}{T((-c + ai)/\delta)} = \frac{dw_1 - bw_2}{-cw_1 + aw_2} = \frac{-b\tau + d}{a\tau - c}.$$

Thus, $\tilde{\tau}$ is the image of τ under the Möbius transformation

$$\tau \mapsto \frac{-b\tau + d}{a\tau - c}.$$

Since $a, b, c, d \in \mathbb{R}$, all of these transformations map $\mathbb{R} \cup \{\infty\}$ into itself and, consequently, map the complement $\mathbb{C} \setminus \mathbb{R}$ into itself.

We now wish to consider a different metric ρ that is unaltered when we change the standard triangle. Thus, we should have

$$\rho(\tau, \tau') = \rho \left(\frac{-b\tau + d}{a\tau - c}, \frac{-b\tau' + d}{a\tau' - c} \right) \qquad (11.2)$$

for any $a, b, c, d \in \mathbb{R}$ with $ad - bc \neq 0$. It will measure the relative displacement of one triangle shape from another rather than the absolute displacement. Such a metric would be uninteresting on $\mathbb{R} \cup \{\infty\}$, which represents the flat triangles. For we would have

$$\rho(0, \infty) = \rho(-d/c, -b/a), \quad \text{whenever } ad - bc \neq 0.$$

So, all distances between distinct points of $\mathbb{R} \cup \{\infty\}$ are equal and we have a discrete metric. Also, the metric on the upper half-plane $\mathbb{R}^2_+$ determines the metric on the lower half-plane since

$$\rho(\tau, \tau') = \rho(\tau^{-1}, \tau'^{-1}).$$

Consequently, we need only consider the metric on the upper half-plane. This corresponds to restricting our attention to positively oriented triangles.

On the upper half-plane $\mathbb{R}^2_+$ we know that the hyperbolic metric does have the invariance property (11.2). Indeed, the only Riemannian metrics on $\mathbb{R}^2_+$ that satisfy (11.2) are constant multiples of the hyperbolic metric. Therefore, we will take ρ as the hyperbolic metric

$$\rho(\tau, \tau') = \log \left(\frac{|\tau' - \overline{\tau}| + |\tau' - \tau|}{|\tau' - \overline{\tau}| - |\tau' - \tau|} \right)$$

as in (11.1).

For certain results about the probability distributions on the shape space, this hyperbolic metric, the Bookstein metric, is more appropriate than the procrustean metric. Consider two probability distributions of triangles in the plane. Let x_1, x_2, x_3 have independent normal distributions with means u_1, u_2, u_3 and covariance matrix a multiple σ^2 of the identity. Then, the density for (x_1, x_2, x_3) is

$$\frac{1}{(2\pi\sigma^2)^3} \exp \left\{ -\frac{1}{2\sigma^2} \sum_{j=1}^{3} ||x_j - u_j||^2 \right\}.$$

This density depends only on the distance $d(x, u) = \left\{ \sum_{j=1}^{3} ||x_j - u_j||^2 \right\}^{1/2}$ and so is unchanged when we apply any isometry of $\mathbb{R}^2$ to all of the points. However, if we change the shape of the initial triangle $\triangle$, the density alters. It is clear that this probability distribution is intimately connected with the procrustean metric on the shape space.

Now, consider another distribution where we choose x_1, x_2, x_3 independently and uniformly from within the triangle $\triangle$. This distribution has very different symmetries, as we saw in Chapter 8. The differences $x_j - u_j$ no longer have the same distributions. However, if $S : \mathbb{R}^2 \to \mathbb{R}^2$ is any non-singular linear map, it will map the triangle $\triangle$ to another triangle $S(\triangle)$ with vertices Su_1, Su_2, Su_3. A point x_j uniformly distributed within $\triangle$ is mapped to Sx_j, which is uniformly distributed within $S(\Delta)$. So S transforms the uniform distribution on Δ to the uniform distribution on $S(\Delta)$. Although we can study, and have studied, such distributions on the shape space Σ_2^3, it is more natural to consider the hyperbolic metric that has the same symmetries as this distribution.

A more general setting for this type of distribution is as follows. Let T be a random variable that takes values in the space $\mathbf{SL}(2, \mathbb{R})$ of 2×2 real matrices with determinant 1. Then, $T(\Delta)$ is a random triangle derived from Δ. In a similar way, $ST(\Delta)$ is a random triangle derived from any other triangle $S(\Delta)$. We can now construct a Markov chain of triangles. Let $\{T_j : 1 \leqslant j < \infty\}$ be iid random variables taking values in $\mathbf{SL}(2, \mathbb{R})$. Then, the triangles

$$T_1 T_2 T_3 \cdots T_{n-1} T_n(\Delta)$$

form a Markov chain. We can use Furstenberg's (1993) work on random products of matrices to describe the behaviour of this chain as $n \to \infty$.

We wish to examine the shapes of the triangles in this chain. The standard triangle Δ has shape i. Let

$$T = \begin{pmatrix} a & b \\ c & d \end{pmatrix} \in \mathbf{SL}(2, \mathbb{R}).$$

Then,

$$\begin{pmatrix} T(1) \\ T(i) \end{pmatrix} = \begin{pmatrix} a + ci \\ b + di \end{pmatrix} = \begin{pmatrix} a & c \\ b & d \end{pmatrix} \begin{pmatrix} 1 \\ i \end{pmatrix} = T^t \begin{pmatrix} 1 \\ i \end{pmatrix},$$

so the shape τ of $T(\Delta)$ is

$$\frac{T(i)}{T(1)} = \frac{b + di}{a + ci}.$$

The distance $\rho(i, \tau)$ in the hyperbolic metric is then given by

$$\cosh \rho(i, \tau) = \frac{1 + |\tau|^2}{2\Im(\tau)} = \frac{|b + di|^2 + |a + ci|^2}{2}$$

$$= \frac{1}{2} \left\| \begin{pmatrix} a & c \\ b & d \end{pmatrix} \begin{pmatrix} 1 \\ i \end{pmatrix} \right\|^2 = \frac{1}{2} \left\| T^t \begin{pmatrix} 1 \\ i \end{pmatrix} \right\|^2.$$

Consequently, the shape τ_n of the nth triangle $T_1 T_2 T_3 \cdots T_{n-1} T_n(\Delta)$ in the Markov chain satisfies

$$\cosh \rho(i, \tau_n) = \frac{1}{2} \left\| T_n^t T_{n-1}^t \cdots T_2^t T_1^t \begin{pmatrix} 1 \\ i \end{pmatrix} \right\|^2.$$

Furstenberg (1963, Theorems 8.5 and 8.6) proved a Law of Large Numbers for such random products. He considered iid random variables $\{X_j : 1 \leqslant j < \infty\}$ taking values in $\mathbf{SL}(2, \mathbb{R})$ with a common distribution μ. If the distribution μ satisfies

$$\mathrm{E}(\log \|X_j\|) = \int \log \|X_j\| \mathrm{d}\mu < \infty$$

and if the closed subgroup generated by the support of μ must act irreducibly on $\mathbb{R}^2$, then there is a strictly positive constant α with

$$\frac{1}{n} \log \|X_n X_{n-1} \cdots X_2 X_1 u\| \longrightarrow \alpha \quad \text{a.s. as } n \longrightarrow \infty$$

for each non-zero vector $u \in \mathbb{R}^2$. By dividing u into real and imaginary parts we see that this also holds for $u \in \mathbb{C}^2$. We now apply Furstenberg's theorem to the case where $X_j = T_j^t$ and $u = \binom{1}{i}$. Provided that the conditions for μ are satisfied, we obtain

$$\frac{1}{2n} \log(2 \cosh \rho(i, \tau_n)) \longrightarrow \alpha \quad \text{a.s. as } n \longrightarrow \infty.$$

This certainly shows that $\rho(i, \tau_n) \to \infty$, so $\log(2 \cosh \rho(i, \tau_n))$ is asymptotic to $\rho(i, \tau_n)$. Thus,

$$\frac{\rho(i, \tau_n)}{n} \longrightarrow 2\alpha \quad \text{a.s. as } n \longrightarrow \infty.$$

Therefore, the shapes τ_n converge to the boundary $\mathbb{R} \cup \{\infty\}$ of $\mathbb{R}_+^2$ as $n \to \infty$. Thus, the triangles $T_1 T_2 T_3 \cdots T_{n-1} T_n(\Delta)$ converge to the set of flat triangles.

This type of argument was used by Mannion (1988) to examine the behaviour of triangles, where we choose the vertices of the nth triangle independently and uniformly from within the $(n-1)$th triangle. He explicitly computed the value of α for this case in Mannion (1990a). Another application is given in Bárány et al. (1996). Further results on random products of matrices are described in Bongerol and Lacroix (1985) and Ledrappier (1984).

A particularly simple application of the above ideas arises when we consider the random triangles where two vertices are fixed and the third is chosen uniformly from within the triangle. In this case we can see explicitly how convergence occurs. Suppose that we begin with a triangle A with vertices $-1, 1$ and σ for some $\sigma \in \mathbb{R}_+^2$. For simplicity, we will assume that $-1 \leq \Re(\sigma) \leq 1$. A new triangle $A^{(1)}$ is produced by choosing $\sigma^{(1)}$ uniformly from within A and taking $A^{(1)}$ to have vertices $-1, 1, \sigma^{(1)}$. Clearly, the imaginary part of $\sigma^{(1)}$ is no bigger than the imaginary part of σ. Also, the real part $\sigma_1^{(1)}$ of $\sigma^{(1)}$ has density

$$K(x \mid \sigma_1) = \begin{cases} \dfrac{x+1}{\sigma_1 + 1} & \text{for } -1 \leq x \leq \sigma_1, \\[2ex] \dfrac{x-1}{\sigma_1 - 1} & \text{for } \sigma_1 \leq x \leq 1 \end{cases}$$

conditional on the value σ_1 of $\Re(\sigma)$. So, if σ_1 has density f on $[-1, 1]$, then $\sigma_1^{(1)}$ has density Kf, where

$$Kf(x) = \int_{-1}^{1} K(x \mid \sigma_1) f(\sigma_1) d\sigma_1.$$

If we repeat this process, choosing the third vertex $\sigma^{(n)}$ independently and uniformly from within the triangle $(-1, 1, \sigma^{(n-1)})$, then we see that the imaginary part of $\sigma^{(n)}$ decreases monotonically to 0. So, $\sigma^{(n)}$ converges to the boundary of $\mathbb{R}_+^2$. The real part $\sigma_1^{(n)}$ of $\sigma^{(n)}$ has density $K^n f$. Since K is a well-known integral operator, we can evaluate the limit. Von Neumann's ergodic theorem shows that $K^n f \to \phi$ almost everywhere with ϕ a continuous solution of $K\phi = \phi$ having integral $\int_{-1}^{1} \phi(x)\,dx = 1$. Solving this we obtain $\phi(x) = \frac{3}{4}(1 - x^2)$. This gives the limiting density for the flat triangles to which the Markov process converges.

We can also find similar results in higher dimensions for the shapes of $(m + 1)$-ads in $\mathbb{R}^m$ (cf. Le and Small, 1997 and Small, 1996). First, we wish to produce a Riemannian metric on $\mathbf{E} = \mathbf{SL}(m, \mathbb{R})$ that is invariant under changes to the standard $(m + 1)$-ad Δ_{m+1}. Replacing Δ_{m+1} by $S(\Delta_{m+1})$ for $S \in \mathbf{SL}(m, \mathbb{R})$ transforms the linear map representing a $(m + 1)$-ad from T to TS^{-1}. So, we seek a metric d with

$$d(T_1, T_2) = d(T_1 S, T_2 S).$$

This is a right-invariant metric on the group $\mathbf{SL}(m, \mathbb{R})$. It is easy to construct such a metric. For we choose any inner product $\langle \,,\, \rangle_I$ on the tangent space $T_I(\mathbf{SL}(m, \mathbb{R}))$ at the identity and use the right-invariance to define the inner product at S by

$$\langle A_1, A_2 \rangle_S = \langle A_1 S^{-1}, A_2 S^{-1} \rangle_I.$$

The tangent space at I is the Lie algebra $sl(m, \mathbb{R})$, which is

$$sl(m, \mathbb{R}) = \{A \in \mathrm{Hom}(\mathbb{R}^m, \mathbb{R}^m) : \mathrm{tr}(A) = 0\}.$$

On this we may use our usual inner product $\langle A_1, A_2 \rangle_I = \mathrm{tr}(A_1^t A_2)$. This gives us a right-invariant Riemannian metric d on $\mathbf{SL}(m, \mathbb{R})$.

Each rotation $R \in \mathbf{SO}(m)$ gives a map

$$\lambda_R : \mathbf{SL}(m, \mathbb{R}) \longrightarrow \mathbf{SL}(m, \mathbb{R}); \quad T \mapsto RT$$

by left-multiplication. This is an isometry for d since, at any $S \in \mathbf{SL}(m, \mathbb{R})$, we have $(\lambda_R)_*(S) : A \mapsto RA$, so

$$\begin{aligned}
\langle (\lambda_R)_*(S)A_1, (\lambda_R)_*(S)A_2 \rangle_{RS} &= \langle RA_1, RA_2 \rangle_{RS} \\
&= \langle RA_1 S^{-1} R^{-1}, RA_2 S^{-1} R^{-1} \rangle_I \\
&= \mathrm{tr}\{(R^t)^{-1}(S^t)^{-1} A_1^t R^t RA_2 S^{-1} R^{-1}\} \\
&= \mathrm{tr}\{(S^t)^{-1} A_1^t A_2 S^{-1}\} = \langle A_1, A_2 \rangle_S.
\end{aligned}$$

Therefore, we obtain a metric ρ on the quotient $\mathbf{SL}(m, \mathbb{R})/\mathbf{SO}(2)$ by taking the shortest distance between $\mathbf{SO}(m)$-orbits in $\mathbf{SL}(m, \mathbb{R})$. We will call this the *relative metric* on $\mathbf{SL}(m, \mathbb{R})/\mathbf{SO}(m)$. As in Section 11.2, we can calculate geometric properties of this metric in terms of the metric on $\mathbf{SL}(m, \mathbb{R})$.

Let $q : \mathbf{SL}(m, \mathbb{R}) \to \mathbf{SL}(m, \mathbb{R})/\mathbf{SO}(m)$ be the quotient map that sends each $T \in \mathbf{SL}(m, \mathbb{R})$ to its orbit $q(T) = \{RT : R \in \mathbf{SO}(m)\}$. We constructed the metric

d on $\mathbf{SL}(m, \mathbb{R})$ precisely so that it would be highly symmetric. Indeed, for each $S \in \mathbf{SL}(m, \mathbb{R})$, we know that right-multiplication

$$\rho_S : \mathbf{SL}(m, \mathbb{R}) \to \mathbf{SL}(m, \mathbb{R}); T \mapsto TS$$

is an isometry. Therefore, the induced map

$$\overline{\rho_S} : \mathbf{SL}(m, \mathbb{R})/\mathbf{SO}(m) \longrightarrow \mathbf{SL}(m, \mathbb{R})/\mathbf{SO}(m); \ q(T) \mapsto q(TS)$$

is well-defined and is an isometry. In particular, $\overline{\rho_S}$ is an isometry that maps the orbit $q(I)$ to $q(S)$. So, the entire group $\mathbf{SL}(m, \mathbb{R})$ acts as a group of isometries on the quotient $\mathbf{SL}(m, \mathbb{R})/\mathbf{SO}(m)$ and acts transitively. This shows, in particular, that the curvature tensor at each point is the same.

The quotient $\mathbf{SL}(m, \mathbb{R})/\mathbf{SO}(m)$ is a symmetric space and its geometry has been extensively investigated, for example in Helgason (1978). Analogues of Furstenberg's Law of Large Numbers exist for random products of matrices in $\mathbf{SL}(m, \mathbb{R})$, so we can extend the convergence results to Markov chains of shapes in $\mathbf{SL}(m, \mathbb{R})/\mathbf{SO}(m)$ (cf. Furstenberg, 1963 and Bougerol and Lacroix, 1985).

11.6 ELLIPTIC FUNCTIONS

The classical theory of elliptic functions, as described, for example, in Ahlfors (1996), is related in various ways to the shape of triangles in the plane. The simplest connection uses the shape of a fundamental parallelogram, but there is a more complicated argument that considers double covers of the sphere ramified over infinity and over the vertices of the triangle.

Let ω_1 and ω_2 be two complex numbers, not both 0, and set $\tau = \omega_2/\omega_1 \in \mathbb{C}_\infty$. Then the three points ω_1, ω_2 and $\omega_3 = -\omega_1 - \omega_2$ are the vertices of a plane triangle $(\omega_1, \omega_2, \omega_3)$ with centroid at the origin. This triangle has the same shape as the one with vertices $1, \tau, -1 - \tau$, so the point τ determines the shape of $(\omega_1, \omega_2, \omega_3)$. When $\tau \in \mathbb{R} \cup \{\infty\}$, the triangle is flat with collinear vertices. In all other cases, ω_1 and ω_2 generate a lattice $\Lambda = \mathbb{Z}\omega_1 + \mathbb{Z}\omega_2$. The fundamental parallelogram for ω_1, ω_2 is

$$\mathbf{P} = \{\lambda_1\omega_1 + \lambda_2\omega_2 : 0 \le \lambda_1, \lambda_2 \le 1\}.$$

Each point of $\mathbb{C}$ is equivalent under Λ to a point of $\mathbf{P}$, so we can think of the quotient $\mathbb{C}/\Lambda$ as the space we obtain by joining together the opposite sides of $\mathbf{P}$. This is a torus and τ is called its modulus. Note that the modulus depends on the generators ω_1, ω_2 and not just on the lattice. The line segments $[0, \omega_1]$ and $[0, \omega_2]$ give closed loops in the torus that generate the fundamental group $\pi_1(\mathbb{C}/\Lambda)$. So, τ classifies tori with marked generators for the fundamental group. It is usual in the study of elliptic function to insist that τ lies in the upper half-plane $\mathbb{R}_+^2 = \{\tau \in \mathbb{C} : \Im(\tau) > 0\}$, which we can do by interchanging ω_1 and ω_2 if necessary. This corresponds to insisting that the triangle $(\omega_1, \omega_2, \omega_3)$ is positively oriented. The set $\mathbb{R}_+^2$ of possible values for τ is called the Teichmüller space for tori. Each point τ corresponds to a conformal equivalence class of tori with marked generators.

Now, we may consider the hyperbolic metric on $\mathbb{R}_+^2$. Given two triangles $(\omega_1, \omega_2, \omega_3)$ and $(\omega_1', \omega_2', \omega_3')$, there is a unique real linear map $T : \mathbb{C} \to \mathbb{C}$ with $T(\omega_j) = \omega_j'$ for $j = 1, 2, 3$. This map must be of the form

$$T : z \mapsto k(z + \mu\bar{z}) \quad \text{for some } k \in \mathbb{C} \setminus \{0\} \text{ and } \mu \in \mathbb{C}.$$

Elementary algebra shows that

$$\mu = -\left(\frac{\omega_1}{\bar{\omega}_1}\right)\left(\frac{\tau' - \tau}{\tau' - \bar{\tau}}\right),$$

so the hyperbolic distance $\rho(\tau, \tau')$ is

$$\log\left(\frac{1 + |\mu|}{1 - |\mu|}\right) = \log\left(\frac{|\tau' - \bar{\tau}| + |\tau' - \tau|}{|\tau' - \bar{\tau}| - |\tau' - \tau|}\right).$$

Thus, the hyperbolic distance between τ and τ' in the upper half-plane is the same as the hyperbolic distance between 0 and μ in the disc. The real linear map T maps the lattice $\Lambda = \mathbb{Z}\omega_1 + \mathbb{Z}\omega_2$ onto $\Lambda' = \mathbb{Z}\omega_1' + \mathbb{Z}\omega_2'$, so it induces a mapping $\mathbb{C}/\Lambda \to \mathbb{C}/\Lambda'$ between the corresponding tori. This is a quasi-conformal map with complex dilatation μ and the hyperbolic metric corresponds to the Teichmüller metric on the upper half-plane. Thus, the hyperbolic metric on the shape space and the Teichmüller metric on the Teichmüller space classifying tori are identical. Lehto in (1994) gives further details on the Teichmüller space for tori.

For the second connection, consider three distinct points z_1, z_2, z_3 in the complex plane. Then, we may construct a Riemann surface $\mathcal{R}$ that consists of two sheets and is ramified of order two at z_1, z_2, z_3 and infinity, but nowhere else. Then, $\mathcal{R}$ is an analytic torus, so it is equal to $\mathbb{C}/\Lambda$ for some lattice Λ. The covering map $\mathcal{R} \to \mathbb{C}$ then gives an elliptic function $f : \mathbb{C} \to \mathbb{C}_\infty$ that has period lattice Λ and degree two. Furthermore, f has critical values z_1, z_2, z_3 and ∞. By translating $\mathbb{C}$ we may ensure that the poles of f occur at the points of the lattice Λ and nowhere else. The only elliptic functions of degree two with poles at the points of Λ are those of the form

$$f(z) = A\wp(z) + B \quad \text{for some } A \neq 0, \; B \in \mathbb{C}.$$

Here, $\wp$ is the Weierstrass $\wp$-function for Λ. Each of these functions has critical points at $\omega_1/2, \omega_2/2, \omega_3/2, 0$ and equivalent points modulo the lattice. By relabelling the points $\omega_1, \omega_2, \omega_3$, if necessary, we may assume that $f(\omega_j/2) = z_j$ for $j = 1, 2, 3$. Then $z_j = f(\omega_j/2) = A\wp(\omega_j/2) + B$ for $j = 1, 2, 3$. The values $\wp(\omega_j/2)$ are usually denoted by e_j and satisfy $e_1 + e_2 + e_3 = 0$. So the triangle (z_1, z_2, z_3) has the same shape as (e_1, e_2, e_3). The lattice Λ is the period lattice of f, so it is uniquely determined by (z_1, z_2, z_3). However, the choice of generators ω_1, ω_2 or, equivalently, the choice of τ, is not unique. For we could choose a different set of generators ω_1', ω_2', provided that $f(\omega_j'/2) = f(\omega_j/2)$ for $j = 1, 2$. This requires that

$$\tfrac{1}{2}\omega_j' = \tfrac{1}{2}\omega_j + \lambda \quad \text{for some } \lambda \in \Lambda.$$

So,

$$\omega_1' = a\omega_1 + b\omega_2, \quad \omega_2' = c\omega_1 + d\omega_2$$

for integers a, b, c, d with

$$\begin{pmatrix} a & b \\ c & d \end{pmatrix} \equiv \begin{pmatrix} 1 & 0 \\ 0 & 1 \end{pmatrix} \quad (\text{mod } 2).$$

Since ω_1', ω_2' must also generate Λ, we must have $ad - bc = 1$. Therefore,

$$\begin{pmatrix} a & b \\ c & d \end{pmatrix}$$

is in the principal congruence subgroup

$$\Gamma(2) = \left\{ \begin{pmatrix} a & b \\ c & d \end{pmatrix} \in \mathbf{SL}(2, \mathbb{Z}) : \begin{pmatrix} a & b \\ c & d \end{pmatrix} \equiv \begin{pmatrix} 1 & 0 \\ 0 & 1 \end{pmatrix} \quad (\text{mod } 2) \right\}.$$

The triangle (z_1, z_2, z_3) thus determines a point τ in the quotient $\mathbb{R}_+^2/\Gamma(2)$. The value of τ depends only on the shape of (z_1, z_2, z_3). For, any Euclidean similarity $S : \mathbb{C} \to \mathbb{C}$ that sends z_j to z_j' will induce a conformal map from $\mathbb{C}/\Lambda$ to $\mathbb{C}/\Lambda'$, so the modulus τ of Λ and Λ' are the same.

Finally, note that the shaded region in Figure 11.1 is a fundamental region for $\Gamma(2)$. So, the quotient $\mathbb{R}_+^2/\Gamma(2)$ is obtained by sticking together the sides of the

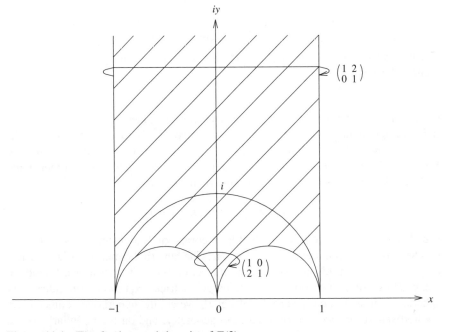

Figure 11.1 The fundamental domain of $\Gamma(2)$

shaded region as shown. This gives a sphere with three punctures, corresponding
to the points -1, 1 and ∞ in $\mathbb{R}^2_+$. This gives us again the shape space Σ^3_2 as
a sphere with the three exceptional points representing triangles with two equal
vertices. However, the hyperbolic metric on $\mathbb{R}^2_+/\Gamma(2)$ makes these exceptional
points infinitely far away and so differs from the Riemannian metric discussed
in previous chapters.

11.7   SHAPE SPACES FOR TRIANGLES IN THE SPHERE AND THE HYPERBOLIC PLANE

We now wish to consider shape spaces for triangles in the sphere, the Euclidean
plane and the hyperbolic plane. We will do this geometrically in a way that
describes all three similarly. To do this we will work in the three-dimensional
hyperbolic space $\mathbb{H}^3$ and refer to the general discussion and notation introduced
at the beginning of Section 11.4. As we shall see, $\mathbb{H}^3$ contains subsets that are
isometric to each of the sphere, the Euclidean plane and the hyperbolic plane.

For each vector $y \in \mathbb{R}^{1,3}$ with $\langle y, y \rangle = 1$, the hyperbolic plane

$$\mathbf{P}_y = \{x \in \mathbb{H}^3 : \langle x, y \rangle = 0\}$$

divides $\mathbb{H}^3$ into two half-spaces:

$$\mathbf{P}^+_y = \{x \in \mathbb{H}^3 : \langle x, y \rangle > 0\} \quad \text{and} \quad \mathbf{P}^-_y = \{x \in \mathbb{H}^3 : \langle x, y \rangle < 0\}.$$

We will orient the planes by choosing the normal to $\mathbf{P}_y$ to point outwards into
$\mathbf{P}^+_y$, so that the same plane with the opposite orientation is given by $\mathbf{P}_{-y}$. Every
oriented hyperbolic plane in $\mathbb{H}^3$ is $\mathbf{P}_y$ for a unique vector y with $\langle y, y \rangle = 1$.
Hence, the set

$$\mathbb{L} = \{y \in \mathbb{R}^{1,3} : \langle y, y \rangle = 1\}$$

corresponds to the set of all oriented hyperbolic planes in $\mathbb{H}^3$. Recall that a
point of the boundary of the hyperbolic space $\mathbb{H}^3$ is identified with a half-
line $\{\lambda u \in \mathbb{R}^{1,3} : \lambda > 0\}$ in the cone $\mathbb{K} = \{x \in \mathbb{R}^{1,3} : \langle x, x \rangle = 0 \text{ and } x_0 > 0\}$. See
Figure 11.2, in which the sets $\mathbb{K}$ and $\mathbb{L}$ are, in fact, connected three-dimensional
surfaces. If we choose any non-zero null-vector u, the set

$$\mathbf{h}_u = \{x \in \mathbb{H}^3 : \langle x, u \rangle = -1\}$$

is called a *horosphere* at u. In the ball $\mathbf{B}^3$ it corresponds to a sphere inside $\mathbf{B}^3$ that
touches $\partial \mathbf{B}^3$ at the point corresponding to u. The hyperbolic metric on $\mathbb{H}^3$ restricts
to give a metric on this horosphere and the set $\mathbf{h}_u$ with this metric is a Euclidean
plane. Thus, we obtain copies of all three geometries, hyperbolic, Euclidean and
spherical, within $\mathbb{H}^3$: on hyperbolic planes $\mathbf{P}_y$ we get the hyperbolic geometry; on
the horospheres $\mathbf{h}_u$ we get the Euclidean geometry; and on the boundary sphere
$\partial \mathbf{B}^3$ of $\mathbb{H}^3$ we have the spherical geometry. We will show that different subsets

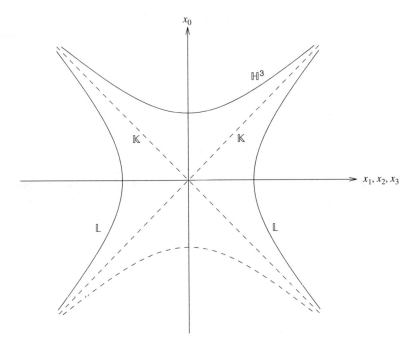

Figure 11.2 The hyperboloid model for hyperbolic 3-space

of $\mathbb{R}^{1,3}$ give shape spaces of triangles in each of these three geometries. The points of $\mathbb{H}^3$ represent the shapes of triangles in the sphere; points of $\partial\mathbb{H}^3 \equiv \mathbf{S}^2$ represent the shapes of triangles in the Euclidean plane; and some of the points in $\mathbb{L}$ represent the shapes of triangles in the hyperbolic plane. For the Euclidean triangles, we have known from Chapter 1 that the shape space for triangles is the sphere $\mathbf{S}^2$.

To prove these results we need to consider the group $\mathbf{SO}^+(1, 3)$ of orientation-preserving isometries of the hyperbolic 3-space. This consists of the linear maps with determinant $+1$ in the group $\mathbf{O}^+(1, 3)$ described in Section 11.4. Each isometry in this group maps $\mathbb{H}^3$ into itself, but also maps $\mathbb{L}$ into itself and the cone $\mathbb{K}$ into itself. So, each isometry gives us a map from $\mathbf{S}^2$ into itself. These maps of $\mathbf{S}^2$ are the Möbius transformations: if we identify $\mathbf{S}^2$ with the extended complex plane $\mathbb{C}_\infty$, then they are given by maps

$$z \mapsto \frac{az + b}{cz + d}; \quad a, b, c, d \in \mathbb{C}, \ ad - bc = 1.$$

This enables us to identify the isometry group of $\mathbb{H}^3$ with the Möbius group. In particular, we know that for any two triads of points (a_1, a_2, a_3) and (b_1, b_2, b_3) in $\mathbf{S}^2$, with a_1, a_2, a_3 distinct and b_1, b_2, b_3 distinct, there is a unique Möbius transformation sending a_j to b_j for $j = 1, 2, 3$. If $\mathbf{P}_y$ is a hyperbolic plane in $\mathbb{H}^3$

and the isometry T of $\mathbb{H}^3$ fixes y, then T will map $\mathbf{P}_y$ into itself, preserving the orientation, and so give an isometry of this hyperbolic plane. If $\mathbf{h}_u$ is a horosphere in $\mathbb{H}^3$ and the isometry T of $\mathbb{H}^3$ fixes u, then T will map $\mathbf{h}_u$ into itself and will be an isometry for the Euclidean metric on $\mathbf{h}_u$.

We will use the ball $\mathbf{B}^3$ as our model for $\mathbb{H}^3$ and think of the sphere $\mathbf{S}^2$ as its boundary. Choose three distinct points u_1, u_2, u_3 in $\mathbf{S}^2$. For example, we might take the points that correspond to $(1, 1, 0, 0)$, $(1, 0, 1, 0)$, $(1, 0, 0, 1)$ in $\mathbb{K}$. We will take these three points as the standard points and measure positions relative to them. Note that changing the three points corresponds to applying an isometry of $\mathbb{H}^3$. For each point $w \in \mathbb{H}^3$ we can draw hyperbolic geodesics γ_j from w to u_j. The three tangent vectors to γ_j at w are then unit vectors and so determine a spherical triangle. Conversely, suppose that we are given a spherical triangle with distinct vertices x_1, x_2, x_3. These are unit vectors giving a triangle in the sphere. Draw geodesics β_j from the origin to each x_j. Since these are geodesics from the origin, they are radial straight lines. There is a unique isometry T of $\mathbb{H}^3$ that maps x_j to u_j for $j = 1, 2, 3$ and this sends $\mathbf{0}$ to a point $w \in \mathbb{H}^3$. Then, $\gamma_j = T(\beta_j)$ are three geodesics from w to u_j, and their direction vectors at w clearly determine a spherical triangle with the same shape as (x_1, x_2, x_3), because the mapping T is conformal.

Suppose that (x_1', x_2', x_3') is another triad of distinct points in $\partial \mathbb{H}^3$ that yields the same point w in $\mathbb{H}^3$. Then, there is an isometry T' of $\mathbb{H}^3$ with $T'(x_j') = u_j$ and $T'(\mathbf{0}) = w$. The composite $S = (T')^{-1} T$ is then another isometry of $\mathbb{H}^3$ with $S(x_j) = x_j'$ and $S(\mathbf{0}) = \mathbf{0}$. Since S is an isometry, it must map the set of points at a fixed hyperbolic distance from zero into itself and preserve angles subtended at $\mathbf{0}$. This set is a Euclidean sphere about $\mathbf{0}$, so S is a rotation, that is, $S \in \mathbf{SO}(3)$. Consequently, (x_1, x_2, x_3) and $(x_1', x_2', x_3') = (S(x_1), S(x_2), S(x_3))$ have the same spherical shape. Thus, we have shown that $\mathbb{H}^3$ represents the shapes of triangles in the sphere $\mathbf{S}^2$ with three distinct vertices.

The same procedure, when we replace the point $w \in \mathbb{H}^3$ either by a boundary point $w \in \partial \mathbb{H}^3$ or else by a hyperbolic plane $\mathbf{P}_y$, will give the shape space for triads in the Euclidean plane or else the hyperbolic plane.

Consider first the Euclidean case. For each point $w \in \partial \mathbb{H}^3$, except u_1, u_2, u_3, we draw hyperbolic geodesics $\gamma_1, \gamma_2, \gamma_3$ from w to u_1, u_2, u_3. These will cut a horosphere $\mathbf{h}_w$ at three distinct points that form a triangle in the Euclidean plane $\mathbf{h}_w$. Conversely, suppose that we are given a triangle in the Euclidean plane. Choose any horosphere $\mathbf{h}_e$ and represent the triangle by three points x_1, x_2, x_3 in $\mathbf{h}_e$. Draw geodesics β_j from e through x_j and extend them until they hit the boundary $\partial \mathbb{H}^3$ at points ξ_j. These three points are distinct since x_1, x_2, x_3 are. So, there is an isometry T of $\mathbb{H}^3$ with $T(\xi_j) = u_j$ for $j = 1, 2, 3$. This sends e to a boundary point w and x_1, x_2, x_3 to points $T(x_1), T(x_2), T(x_3)$ in $T(\mathbf{h}_e)$, which is a horosphere at $T(e)$. Since T is an isometry of $\mathbb{H}^3$, it will preserve distances on $\mathbf{h}_e$, so the triangle $(T(x_1), T(x_2), T(x_3))$ is isometric to the Euclidean triangle (x_1, x_2, x_3).

Suppose that (x_1', x_2', x_3') is another triad of distinct points in the Euclidean plane $\mathbf{h}_e$ that yields the same point $w \in \partial\mathbb{H}^3$. Then, there is an isometry T' of $\mathbb{H}^3$ with $T'(\beta_j') = \gamma_j = T(\beta_j)$ and $T'(e) = w$. The composite $S = (T')^{-1}T$ is then another isometry of $\mathbb{H}^3$ with $S(\beta_j) = \beta_j'$ and $S(e) = e$. Then, S must map the horosphere $\mathbf{h}_e$ into another horosphere at e. Such a mapping is a Euclidean similarity. If the horospheres are not equal, then S enlarges or contracts Euclidean lengths. Hence, the triangles (x_1, x_2, x_3) and (x_1', x_2', x_3') have the same shape. Thus, $\partial\mathbb{H}^3 \setminus \{u_1, u_2, u_3\}$ represents the shapes of Euclidean triangles with distinct vertices. It is easy to see that the three omitted points u_1, u_2, u_3 represent those triangles with two vertices coincident. Thus, we obtain the full sphere $\partial\mathbb{H}^3 = \mathbf{S}^2$ as the shape space Σ_2^3 for Euclidean triangles that are not totally degenerate.

Finally, we consider the hyperbolic case. Suppose that $y \in \mathbb{L}$ is a point with $u_1, u_2, u_3 \in \mathbf{P}_y^+$. So, all three points u_1, u_2, u_3 lie on one side of the plane $\mathbf{P}_y$. Draw geodesics γ_j normal to this plane from $\mathbf{P}_y$ to u_j. These cut $\mathbf{P}_y$ at points $x_j \in \mathbf{P}_y$ that form a triangle in the hyperbolic plane $\mathbf{P}_y$. Since u_1, u_2, u_3 are distinct, the geodesics γ_j must meet $\mathbf{P}_y$ at distinct points, so x_1, x_2, x_3 are distinct. Conversely, suppose that we are given any hyperbolic triangle with distinct vertices, say, $x_1, x_2, x_3 \in \mathbf{P}_z$. Draw geodesics β_j orthogonal to $\mathbf{P}_z$ through x_j and going in the positive direction into $\mathbf{P}_z^+$. These geodesics will meet $\partial\mathbb{H}^3$ at three distinct points ξ_j. Then, there is an isometry T of $\mathbb{H}^3$ with $T(\xi_j) = u_j$ for $j = 1, 2, 3$ and $T(z)$ is some point $y \in \mathbb{L}$. Now, T maps the hyperbolic triangle (x_1, x_2, x_3) in $\mathbf{P}_z$ isometrically to a triangle $(T(x_1), T(x_2), T(x_3))$ in the hyperbolic plane $\mathbf{P}_y$. So, these triangles have the same hyperbolic shape. Moreover, ξ_1, ξ_2, ξ_3 lie in $\mathbf{P}_z^+$, so u_1, u_2, u_3 must lie in $\mathbf{P}_y^+$. Thus, every hyperbolic triangle corresponds to a point $y \in \mathbb{L}$.

Suppose that (x_1', x_2', x_3') is another hyperbolic triangle in the plane $\mathbf{P}_z$ that yields the same point $y \in \mathbb{L}$. Then, there is an isometry T' of $\mathbb{H}^3$ with $T'(\xi_j') = u_j$ for $j = 1, 2, 3$ and $T'(z) = y$. Consequently, $S = (T')^{-1}T$ is an isometry with $S(x_j) = x_j'$ for $j = 1, 2, 3$ and $S(z) = z$. This means that S maps the hyperbolic plane $\mathbf{P}_z$ into itself, so it is an isometry from (x_1, x_2, x_3) to (x_1', x_2', x_3'). Hence, these two triangles have the same hyperbolic shape. This shows that the shape space for triangles of distinct points in the hyperbolic plane is part of $\mathbb{L}$. It is the part consisting of those y where u_1, u_2, u_3 lie in $\mathbf{P}_y^+$. When we take $u_1 = (1, 1, 0, 0)$, $u_2 = (1, 0, 1, 0)$, $u_3 = (1, 0, 0, 1)$, this gives us the set

$$\{(y_0, y_1, y_2, y_3) \in \mathbb{L} : y_0 < y_1, \ y_0 < y_2, \ y_0 < y_3\}.$$

It is interesting to consider the significance of the remaining part of $\mathbb{L}$. Consider a point $y \in \mathbb{L}$ with $u_1, u_2, u_3 \in \mathbf{P}_y^+$ and the corresponding hyperbolic triangle (x_1, x_2, x_3). If we move y so that the plane $\mathbf{P}_y$ approaches u_1, then the vertex x_1 approaches the boundary of the hyperbolic plane. When u_1 lies in the plane $\mathbf{P}_y$, the vertex x_1 becomes an 'ideal vertex' on the boundary of the hyperbolic plane. As the plane $\mathbf{P}_y$ moves across u_1 so that u_1 moves into $\mathbf{P}_y^-$, the two sides of the triangle, x_1x_2 and x_1x_3, fail to meet, so the triangle has no vertex x_1. It is a

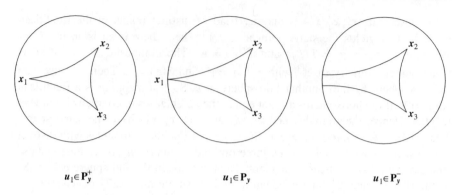

$$u_1 \in \mathbf{P}_y^+ \qquad\qquad u_1 \in \mathbf{P}_y \qquad\qquad u_1 \in \mathbf{P}_y^-$$

Figure 11.3   Hyperbolic trilaterals

trilateral rather than a triangle. This is illustrated in Figure 11.3, where we have used the disc model for the hyperbolic plane. Similar results hold for the other vertices. So, the points of $\mathbb{L}$ represent triangles that may have 'virtual vertices'. These are trilaterals with sides that are hyperbolic geodesics, but those sides may not meet at any point in the hyperbolic plane to give a triangle.

Note that there is a duality between vertices and edges for triangles. In the sphere or the plane, this duality associates any triangle described by its vertices with the dual triangle described by its edges. However, in the hyperbolic plane, this is no longer true. There are trilaterals described by three sides where the sides do not meet in vertices.

The shape spaces for triangles can also be described entirely algebraically. The group $\mathbf{SO}^+(1,3)$ is the isometry group for $\mathbb{H}^3$. This group acts on points in $\mathbb{R}^{1,3}$ and there is a natural bijection from the orbit of any point $y \in \mathbb{R}^{1,3}$ to the quotient $\mathbf{SO}^+(1,3)/\mathrm{Stab}(y)$ by the stabiliser

$$\mathrm{Stab}(y) = \{T \in \mathbf{SO}^+(1,3) : T(y) = y\}.$$

For $y \in \mathbb{H}^3$, the orbit is all of $\mathbb{H}^3$, so $\mathbf{SO}^+(1,3)/\mathrm{Stab}(y)$ is the shape space for spherical triangles. For $y \in \mathbb{L}$, the orbit is all of $\mathbb{L}$, so $\mathbf{SO}^+(1,3)/\mathrm{Stab}(y)$ contains the shape space for hyperbolic triangles. Finally, if we let $\mathbf{U}$ be a half-line $\{\lambda u : \lambda > 0\}$ in $\mathbb{K}$, then the orbit of $\mathbf{U}$ is the set of all half-lines in $\mathbb{K}$, which corresponds to $\partial\mathbb{H}^3$. Thus, $\mathbf{SO}^+(1,3)/\mathrm{Stab}(\mathbf{U})$ is the shape space for triangles in the Euclidean plane.

It is also interesting to consider the metric on the shape spaces that we have found above. Observe that changing the choice of points u_1, u_2, u_3 changes the point that represents the triangle by some isometry T of $\mathbb{H}^3$. Thus, the hyperbolic metric on $\mathbb{H}^3$ itself is unchanged and gives a canonical metric for spherical triangles. The isometry T acts as a Möbius transformation of the sphere $\partial\mathbb{H}^3 = \mathbf{S}^2$ and this can indeed change the metric. So, we have a family of metrics on $\mathbf{S}^2$. These metrics are all conformally equivalent and so do give a canonical conformal structure on the shape space for triangles in the Euclidean plane. However, they do not give the full strength of the metric results described in Chapter 1 and thereafter. Finally, on $\mathbb{L}$ the indefinite bilinear form $\langle \, , \, \rangle$ gives an indefinite metric that is not positive definite. This is invariant under T. So, we obtain a canonical indefinite metric on the shape space for hyperbolic triangles.

Appendix

In this appendix we shall outline some of the general results from homological algebra, as well as the more specific duality results for manifolds, which we have taken for granted in the main body of the book.

We shall restrict attention to the category of finitely generated abelian groups, which we shall write additively, so that the identity element is 0 and, for an integer n, ng is the nth 'power'. Similarly, the direct 'product' of two groups, $\mathbb{G}$ and $\mathbb{H}$, will be written $\mathbb{G} \oplus \mathbb{H}$. We shall continue to write $\mathbb{Z}_n$ for the cyclic group of order n, which others might denote by $\mathbb{Z}/n\mathbb{Z}$ or by C_n. Most modern texts describe the results for modules over an arbitrary commutative, or in some cases non-commutative, ring, whereas abelian groups are just the modules over $\mathbb{Z}$. The extra generality does not require much extra effort, but it has the effect of making the results look unfamiliar.

Before describing the main results, we first need to introduce some natural unary and binary operators on groups.

A.1 UNARY OPERATORS ON GROUPS

For any abelian group $\mathbb{G}$ we define

$$n\mathbb{G} = \{ng : g \in \mathbb{G}\},$$
$$^n\mathbb{G} = \{g \in \mathbb{G} : ng = 0\},$$
$$\tau\mathbb{G} = \{g \in \mathbb{G} : \text{order of } g \text{ is finite}\},$$
$$F\mathbb{G} = \mathbb{G}/\tau\mathbb{G}.$$

Note that $n\mathbb{G}$, $^n\mathbb{G}$ and $\tau\mathbb{G}$ are all subgroups of $\mathbb{G}$. However, although $\mathbb{G}$ has subgroups isomorphic with $F\mathbb{G}$, there is no canonical choice, unless $\mathbb{G}$ is equal to $F\mathbb{G}$ itself. Except for $n\mathbb{G}$, which is fairly common, this is not standard notation for these groups: $\tau\mathbb{G}$ is more usually denoted $\text{tors}(\mathbb{G})$ and otherwise there is no standard.

Recall that every finitely generated, abelian group is a direct sum of cyclic groups. If we look at a fixed such direct sum decomposition of $\mathbb{G}$, then $n\mathbb{G}$

has an infinite cyclic summand for every one that $\mathbb{G}$ has and, for every cyclic summand of $\mathbb{G}$ of order n', there is one in $n\mathbb{G}$ whose order is n' divided by the h.c.f. of n and n'. The subgroup $^n\mathbb{G}$ has a cyclic summand of order n for every summand of $\mathbb{G}$ of order a multiple of n. The subgroup $\tau\mathbb{G}$ is the direct sum of all the finite cyclic summands of $\mathbb{G}$ from a given decomposition, and the quotient $F\mathbb{G}$ is the direct sum of those that are of infinite order and so each isomorphic to $\mathbb{Z}$. Thus, $\mathbb{G} \cong \tau\mathbb{G} \oplus F\mathbb{G}$.

A.2 BINARY OPERATORS ON GROUPS

In addition to the direct sum already mentioned, there are four basic operators that produce a new group from two given ones.

A.2.1 Hom

For two abelian groups $\mathbb{G}$ and $\mathbb{H}$ we have (cf. MacLane, 1963, p. 21)

$$\mathrm{Hom}(\mathbb{G}; \mathbb{H}) = \{f : \mathbb{G} \longrightarrow \mathbb{H} : f \text{ is a homomorphism}\}.$$

This is made into an abelian group by defining addition of homomorphisms via addition of the images in the usual way. To make it look more like a binary operation analogous to $\mathbb{G} \otimes \mathbb{H}$ below, it is sometimes denoted $\mathbb{G} \pitchfork \mathbb{H}$. However, unlike $\otimes$ it is not symmetric.

There are isomorphisms (cf. MacLane, 1963, pp. 21, 23)

$$\mathrm{Hom}(\mathbb{Z}; \mathbb{G}) \cong \mathbb{G},$$
$$\mathbb{G}^* = \mathrm{Hom}(\mathbb{G}; \mathbb{Z}) \cong F\mathbb{G},$$
$$\mathrm{Hom}(\mathbb{G}_1 \oplus \mathbb{G}_2; \mathbb{H}) \cong \mathrm{Hom}(\mathbb{G}_1; \mathbb{H}) \oplus \mathrm{Hom}(\mathbb{G}_2; \mathbb{H}),$$
$$\mathrm{Hom}(\mathbb{G}; \mathbb{H}_1 \oplus \mathbb{H}_2) \cong \mathrm{Hom}(\mathbb{G}; \mathbb{H}_1) \oplus \mathrm{Hom}(\mathbb{G}; \mathbb{H}_2),$$
$$\mathrm{Hom}(\mathbb{Z}_n; \mathbb{H}) \cong {}^n\mathbb{H}.$$

Thus, for example, if $\mathbb{G} = \tau\mathbb{G}$ and $\mathbb{H} = F\mathbb{H}$, that is, if all the elements of $\mathbb{G}$ and none of the elements of $\mathbb{H}$ are of finite order, then $\mathrm{Hom}(\mathbb{G}; \mathbb{H}) = 0$.

A.2.2 Tensor

The tensor product $\mathbb{G} \otimes \mathbb{H}$ is the abelian group generated by the elements

$$\{g \otimes h : g \in \mathbb{G}, h \in \mathbb{H}\}$$

subject to the relations

$$(g_1 + g_2) \otimes h = g \otimes h_1 + g \otimes h_2 \text{ and } g \otimes (h_1 + h_2) = g \otimes h_1 + g \otimes h_2$$

(cf. MacLane, 1963, p. 138). In other words, it is the free abelian group generated by $\{g \otimes h : g \in \mathbb{G}, h \in \mathbb{H}\}$ quotiented by the free subgroup generated by all the elements

$$\{(g_1 + g_2) \otimes h - g \otimes h_1 + g \otimes h_2\} \text{ and } \{g \otimes (h_1 + h_2) - g \otimes h_1 + g \otimes h_2\}.$$

The tensor product is also characterised uniquely, up to isomorphism, by the fact that the group of homomorphisms from $\mathbb{G} \otimes \mathbb{H}$ to $\mathbb{Z}$, $\text{Hom}(\mathbb{G} \otimes \mathbb{H}; \mathbb{Z})$, is isomorphic with the group $\text{Bihom}(\mathbb{G}, \mathbb{H}; \mathbb{Z})$ of 'bihomomorphisms' or bi-additive maps from $\mathbb{G} \times \mathbb{H}$ to $\mathbb{Z}$. The basic facts are as follows (cf. MacLane, 1963, pp. 139–142).

$$\mathbb{G} \otimes \mathbb{H} \cong \mathbb{H} \otimes \mathbb{G},$$

$$\mathbb{G} \otimes \mathbb{Z} \cong \mathbb{G},$$

$$\mathbb{G} \otimes (\mathbb{H}_1 \oplus \mathbb{H}_2) \cong \mathbb{G} \otimes \mathbb{H}_1 \oplus \mathbb{G} \otimes \mathbb{H}_2,$$

$$\mathbb{G} \otimes \mathbb{Z}_n \cong \mathbb{G}/n\mathbb{G}.$$

A.2.3   Ext

An extension of a group $\mathbb{G}$ by a group $\mathbb{H}$ is any group $\mathbb{K}$ equipped with a homomorphism from $\mathbb{K}$ onto $\mathbb{H}$ with kernel $\mathbb{G}$. Thus, the group that is 'extended' is a subgroup of its extension and the quotient is the group 'by which it has been extended'. The extensions $\mathbb{K}$ for a given $\mathbb{G}$ and $\mathbb{H}$ can themselves be made into an abelian group, denoted $\text{Ext}(\mathbb{H}, \mathbb{G})$: note the rather unnatural order. Details of this, together with the following facts, can be found on pp. 64–71 of MacLane (1963).

$$\text{Ext}(\mathbb{Z}, \mathbb{G}) = 0,$$

$$\text{Ext}(\mathbb{G}, \mathbb{Z}) \cong \tau\mathbb{G},$$

$$\text{Ext}(\mathbb{H}, \mathbb{G}_1 \oplus \mathbb{G}_2) \cong \text{Ext}(\mathbb{H}, \mathbb{G}_1) \oplus \text{Ext}(\mathbb{H}, \mathbb{G}_2),$$

$$\text{Ext}(\mathbb{H}_1 \oplus \mathbb{H}_2, \mathbb{G}) \cong \text{Ext}(\mathbb{H}_1, \mathbb{G}) \oplus \text{Ext}(\mathbb{H}_2, \mathbb{G}),$$

$$\text{Ext}(\mathbb{Z}_n, \mathbb{G}) \cong \mathbb{G}/n\mathbb{G},$$

in particular, $\text{Ext}(\mathbb{Z}_n, \mathbb{Z}) \cong \mathbb{Z}_n$.

A.2.4   Tor

Finally, we have the 'torsion product', $\text{Tor}(\mathbb{G}, \mathbb{H})$ of $\mathbb{G}$ and $\mathbb{H}$, not to be confused with the torsion subgroup, which is why we are using τ for the latter. This product is the quotient of the set

$$\{(g, n, h) : g \in \mathbb{G}, n \in \mathbb{Z}, h \in \mathbb{H}, ng = 0 = nh\}$$

by the equivalence relation generated by $(gn, n', h) \sim (g, nn', h) \sim (g, n, n'h)$ and bi-additivity on $\mathbb{G} \times \mathbb{H}$: $(g_1 + g_2, n, h) \sim (g_1, n, h) + (g_2, n, h)$, etc. The following facts, analogous to those just given for Ext, can be found on p. 150 of MacLane (1963).

$$\text{Tor}(\mathbb{H}, \mathbb{G}) \cong \text{Tor}(\mathbb{G}, \mathbb{H}),$$

$$\text{Tor}(\mathbb{Z}, \mathbb{G}) = 0,$$

$$\text{Tor}(\mathbb{H}, \mathbb{G}_1 \oplus \mathbb{G}_2) \cong \text{Tor}(\mathbb{H}, \mathbb{G}_1) \oplus \text{Tor}(\mathbb{H}, \mathbb{G}_2),$$

$$\text{Tor}(\mathbb{Z}_n, \mathbb{G}) \cong {}^n\mathbb{G}.$$

A.2.5 Alternative Definitions of Tor and Ext

If we write the group $\mathbb{H}$ as the quotient $\mathbb{F}/\mathbb{R}$, where $\mathbb{F}$ is the free group generated by the generators of $\mathbb{H}$ and $\mathbb{R}$ is the free subgroup of $\mathbb{F}$ generated by the relations that determine $\mathbb{H}$, then there are induced homomorphisms

$$\iota_* : \quad \mathbb{R} \otimes \mathbb{G} \to \mathbb{F} \otimes \mathbb{G}; \quad r \otimes g \mapsto \iota(r) \otimes g$$

and

$$\iota^* : \quad \mathbb{F} \pitchfork \mathbb{G} \to \mathbb{R} \pitchfork \mathbb{G}; \quad \theta \mapsto \theta \circ \iota,$$

where $\iota : \mathbb{R} \to \mathbb{F}$ is the inclusion. Then, $\mathrm{Tor}(\mathbb{H}, \mathbb{G}) = \mathrm{Ker}(\iota_*)$ and (cf. MacLane, 1963, p. 100)

$$\mathrm{Ext}(\mathbb{H}, \mathbb{G}) = \mathrm{Coker}(\iota^*) = \mathrm{Hom}(\mathbb{R}; \mathbb{G})/\iota^*(\mathrm{Hom}(\mathbb{F}; \mathbb{G})).$$

This gives a method for computing some of the above results. For example, when $\mathbb{H} = \mathbb{Z}$, then $\mathbb{F} = \mathbb{H}$ and $\mathbb{R} = 0$, so $\mathrm{Hom}(\mathbb{R}; \mathbb{G}) = 0$ and $\mathrm{Ext}(\mathbb{H}, \mathbb{G}) = 0$.

A.3 THE UNIVERSAL COEFFICIENT THEOREMS

A.3.1 The General Theorems

We are now in a position to describe the theorems that relate the homology and cohomology of a space with standard integer coefficients to that with arbitrary coefficients. These theorems work at the level of the chain complex, irrespective of its provenance: it need not arise from a cellular decomposition of a topological space. So, we let

$$(\mathbb{K}, d) = \cdots \mathbb{K}_n \xrightarrow{d} \mathbb{K}_{n-1} \cdots \mathbb{K}_1 \xrightarrow{d} \mathbb{K}_0$$

be a chain complex of free abelian groups. Then, the Universal Coefficient Theorems are expressed by the following isomorphisms, which may be found on pp. 171 and 77, respectively, of MacLane (1963):

$$H_q(\mathbb{K}, \mathbb{G}) \cong H_q(\mathbb{K}) \otimes \mathbb{G} \oplus \mathrm{Tor}(H_{q-1}(\mathbb{K}), \mathbb{G})$$

and

$$H^q(\mathbb{K}, \mathbb{G}) \cong \mathrm{Hom}(H_q(\mathbb{K}), \mathbb{G}) \oplus \mathrm{Ext}(H_{q-1}(\mathbb{K}), \mathbb{G}),$$

where, as usual, $H_q(\mathbb{K})$, the qth homology group of $\mathbb{K}$, is the quotient $(\ker(d|\mathbb{K}_q))/d(\mathbb{K}_{q+1})$ and $H_q(\mathbb{K}, \mathbb{G})$ is the qth homology group of the complex $(\mathbb{K} \otimes \mathbb{G}, d \otimes 1_\mathbb{G})$. The cohomology of $\mathbb{K}$ with coefficients in $\mathbb{G}$, $H^q(\mathbb{K}, \mathbb{G})$, is the homology of the cochain complex $(\mathbb{K} \pitchfork \mathbb{G}, d^*)$, where $(\mathbb{K} \pitchfork \mathbb{G})_q = \mathbb{K}_q \pitchfork \mathbb{G}$ and $d^*(\theta) = \theta \circ d$ as before. $(\mathbb{K} \pitchfork \mathbb{G}, d^*)$ is called a *cochain* complex since d^* raises the degree, mapping $\mathbb{K}_q \pitchfork \mathbb{G}$ to $\mathbb{K}_{q+1} \pitchfork \mathbb{G}$.

When $\mathbb{K}$ is the chain complex associated with, for example, a cellular decomposition of a space Σ, then the homology and cohomology groups of $\mathbb{K}$ are, by definition, those of Σ.

A.3.2 The Shape Space Example

Suppose, as is the case for shape spaces, that $H_q(\mathbb{K})$ is the direct sum of r copies of $\mathbb{Z}$ and s copies of $\mathbb{Z}_2$ for suitable r and s. Then, $H_q(\mathbb{K}) \otimes \mathbb{Z}_2 \cong H_q(\mathbb{K}) \pitchfork \mathbb{Z}_2$ is a direct sum of $r + s$ copies of $\mathbb{Z}_2$, and

$$\mathrm{Tor}(H_q(\mathbb{K}), \mathbb{Z}_2) \cong \tau H_q(\mathbb{K}) \cong \mathrm{Ext}(H_q(\mathbb{K}), \mathbb{Z}_2)$$

is a direct sum of s copies of $\mathbb{Z}_2$. Thus, if there are t summands isomorphic with $\mathbb{Z}_2$ in H_{q-1}, each of $H_q(\mathbb{K}, \mathbb{Z}_2)$ and $H^q(\mathbb{K}, \mathbb{Z}_2)$ is a direct sum of $r + s + t$ copies of $\mathbb{Z}_2$. This agrees with what we obtained by computing directly with the complexes with $\mathbb{Z}_2$ coefficients since in that case all boundary maps are zero.

The above, very unnatural, isomorphisms are special cases of the following, which may be proved using the listed properties of the various operations. If $\mathbb{G}$ and $\mathbb{H}$ are finitely generated abelian groups, and so direct sums of cyclic groups of various prime power or infinite orders, and $\mathbb{H}$ is finite, then

$$\mathbb{G} \otimes \mathbb{H} \cong \mathbb{G} \pitchfork \mathbb{H},$$

$$\mathrm{Tor}(\mathbb{G}, \mathbb{H}) \cong \mathrm{Ext}(\mathbb{G}, \mathbb{H}).$$

A.4 DUALITY IN MANIFOLDS

We have had cause to refer to the duality between the homology and cohomology groups of a manifold, both for the limited extent to which it does hold for shape spaces and for the more general extent to which it does not.

A.4.1 Poincaré Duality

When $\mathbf{M}$ is a compact, *orientable* manifold-without-boundary of dimension n, or, more generally, if it is such a homology manifold, then we have the following Poincaré duality isomorphisms:

$$D : H^r(\mathbf{M}, \mathbb{Z}) \xrightarrow{\cong} H_{n-r}(\mathbf{M}, \mathbb{Z}).$$

If, instead of the integers, we take coefficients $\mathbb{Z}_2$, similar isomorphisms are valid for any homology n-manifold that is compact and without boundary, whether it is orientable or not:

$$D : H^r(\mathbf{M}, \mathbb{Z}_2) \xrightarrow{\cong} H_{n-r}(\mathbf{M}, \mathbb{Z}_2).$$

These results may be found on p. 181 of Maunder (1970). The proof rests on finding geometrically 'dual' cell decompositions E and F, and corresponding chain complexes $\mathbb{K}$, $\mathbb{L}$, of $\mathbf{M}$, where $\mathbb{K}$ is chain isomorphic to the dual of $\mathbb{L}$.

Thus, $\mathbb{K}$ will have basis elements e_r^i corresponding to cells E_r^i of dimension r in E, and $\mathbb{L}$ will have basis elements f_s^j corresponding to cells F_s^j in F. There is a one-to-one correspondence between the cells E_r^i of the first decomposition and F_{n-r}^i of the second, determined geometrically by the fact that corresponding cells meet transversally in a single point and, otherwise, that cells of complementary dimensions from the two decompositions are disjoint. Moreover, the relations between the cells of the two decompositions and their chosen orientations are such that the coefficient of e_r^j in the boundary $d(e_{r+1}^i)$ of e_{r+1}^i is $(-1)^{r+1}$ times the coefficient of f_{n-r-1}^i in $d(f_{n-r}^j)$. In other words, if $d(e_{r+1}^i) = \sum_j a_{ij} e_r^j$, then $d(f_{n-r}^j) = (-1)^{r+1} \sum_i a_{ij} f_{n-r-1}^i$.

So, with respect to these bases of the chain complexes determined by the respective decompositions of the manifold, $d : \mathbb{K}_{r+1} \to \mathbb{K}_r$ has matrix A, while $d : \mathbb{L}_{n-r} \to \mathbb{L}_{n-r-1}$ has matrix $(-1)^{r+1} A^t$. On the other hand, if we construct the dual cochain complex $\mathbb{L}^* = \mathbb{L} \pitchfork \mathbb{Z}$ of $\mathbb{L}$ for which the sth cochain group is $\mathbb{L}^s = \mathbb{L}_s \pitchfork \mathbb{Z}$ and

$$d^* : \mathbb{L}^{s-1} \longrightarrow \mathbb{L}^s; \quad \theta \mapsto \theta \circ d,$$

then $d^* : \mathbb{L}^{n-r-1} \to \mathbb{L}^{n-r}$ has matrix $(-1)^{r+1}(A^t)^t = (-1)^{r+1}A$ with respect to the dual basis (ϕ_i^s) of $\mathbb{L}^s$, which is defined by $\phi_i^s(f_s^k) = \delta_{ik}$. Thus, the correspondence between the basis elements e_r^i in $\mathbb{K}_r$ and $(-1)^{r+1}\phi_i^{n-r}$ in $\mathbb{L}^{n-r}$ induces a *chain isomorphism* $\alpha : \mathbb{K} \to \mathbb{L}^*$. That is, the diagrams

$$
\begin{array}{ccc}
\mathbb{K}_{r+1} & \xrightarrow{\ \alpha\ } & \mathbb{L}^{n-r-1} \\
\downarrow{\scriptstyle d} & & \downarrow{\scriptstyle d^*} \\
\mathbb{K}_r & \xrightarrow{\ \alpha\ } & \mathbb{L}^{n-r}
\end{array}
$$

commute for all r and so induce isomorphisms between the cohomology groups $H_r(\mathbb{K})$ of $\mathbb{K}$ and $H_{n-r}(\mathbb{L}^*)$ of $\mathbb{L}^*$. However, both $\mathbb{K}$ and $\mathbb{L}$ are chain complexes corresponding to cell decompositions of the manifold $\mathbf{M}$, so their homology is, by definition, that of $\mathbf{M}$ and the homology of $\mathbb{L}^*$ is, again by definition, the *cohomology* of $\mathbf{M}$. Thus, we have the required duality isomorphisms. Of course, we are implicitly using here the fact that different cell decompositions of the manifold lead to isomorphic homology groups. This can be proved using the Eilenberg–Steenrod axioms for a homology theory given in Chapter 3.

The easiest way to obtain the geometrically dual cell decompositions E and F of $\mathbf{M}$ required for the above proof is to assume that $\mathbf{M}$ is presented via a *handle decomposition*. That is, it is built up by successively adding *r-handles*, $\mathbf{B}^r \times \mathbf{B}^{n-r}$ attached along $\mathbf{S}^{r-1} \times \mathbf{B}^{n-r}$, starting from a set of 0-handles, $\mathbf{B}^0 \times \mathbf{B}^n = \{point\} \times \mathbf{B}^n$. Then, the cells of E may be obtained as natural extensions of the *cores* $\mathbf{B}^r \times \{0\}$ of these handles, and the cells of F may be obtained similarly from the *cocores* $\{0\} \times \mathbf{B}^{n-r}$.

The orientability of $\mathbf{M}$ is used in the above to relate the orientations of the cells of F with those of the cells of E, and hence correlate the boundary maps in the two complexes. If $\mathbf{M}$ is not orientable it is not possible to correlate the orientations in this way and then it is only possible to obtain the chain isomorphism when the chain complexes have $\mathbb{Z}_2$ coefficients. Hence, we have the restricted version of the theorem in that case.

A.4.2   Duality via Linking and Intersection

The natural duality isomorphisms are between the cohomology and homology of the manifold. However, by means of the Universal Coefficient Theorems we may re-interpret them as isomorphisms between subgroups and quotient groups of homology groups as follows.

From the isomorphisms

$$H^q(\mathbf{M}, \mathbb{Z}) \cong \text{Hom}(H_q(\mathbf{M}), \mathbb{Z}) \oplus \text{Ext}(H_{q-1}(\mathbf{M}), \mathbb{Z})$$
$$\cong F(H_q(\mathbf{M})) \oplus \tau(H_{q-1}(\mathbf{M}))$$

and

$$H^q(\mathbf{M}, \mathbb{Z}) \cong H_{n-q}(\mathbf{M}, \mathbb{Z}) \cong H_{n-q}(\mathbf{M})$$
$$\cong F(H_{n-q}(\mathbf{M})) \oplus \tau(H_{n-q}(\mathbf{M})),$$

we get

$$F(H_q(\mathbf{M})) \cong F(II_{n-q}(\mathbf{M})) \tag{I}$$

and

$$\tau(H_{q-1}(\mathbf{M})) \cong \tau(H_{n-q}(\mathbf{M})). \tag{L}$$

The isomorphism (I) may be re-interpreted in terms of intersection numbers and (L) may be re-interpreted in terms of linking numbers. An element, h_q, of $H_q(\mathbf{M})$ is represented by a cycle γ_q, that is, an element of $\ker(d|\mathbb{K}_q)$ and, similarly, an element, h_{n-q}, of $H_{n-q}(\mathbf{M})$ is represented by a cycle γ_{n-q}. Provided these cycles are in *general position* with respect to each other, which in this case means that they meet only in isolated points, and provided $\mathbf{M}$ is orientable, these points of intersection may be allotted a sign and then their sum is an invariant of the pair h_q and h_{n-q}. That is, it is independent of our choice of representative cycles. It is called their *intersection number*, $h_q \cdot h_{n-q} \in \mathbb{Z}$. The content of this aspect of Poincaré duality is that this pairing $H_q(\mathbf{M}) \otimes H_{n-q}(\mathbf{M}) \to \mathbb{Z}$ is zero if either of h_q or h_{n-q} is a torsion element and it determines a non-singular bilinear form on the free quotients. Hence, it induces the required isomorphism. This should be clear, in terms of the natural generators, from the above outline proof of duality.

The isomorphism (L) is obtained similarly, except that in this case the pairing is by linking numbers that are defined in $\mathbb{Q}/\mathbb{Z}$. For this, if a cycle γ_{q-1} represents a homology element h_{q-1} of order n, then $n\gamma_{q-1}$ is the boundary of some cycle γ_q. Then, if γ_{n-q} is a cycle representing another torsion element h_{n-q}, the quotient of the intersection number $\gamma_q \cdot \gamma_{n-q}$ by the order n of the first torsion element is a rational number that is well-defined modulo the integers. This defines the linking number $h_{q-1} \cdot h_{n-q}$ in the quotient group $\mathbb{Q}/\mathbb{Z}$. This is not so easy to see directly from the geometry and the algebraic proof requires the Bockstein boundary homomorphism arising from the exact sequence of coefficients

$$0 \longrightarrow \mathbb{Z} \longrightarrow \mathbb{Q} \longrightarrow \mathbb{Q}/\mathbb{Z} \longrightarrow 0.$$

When we take the coefficients in a field $\mathbb{F}$, such as the real numbers or the rational numbers, the isomorphism (I) can be re-interpreted as

$$H^q(\mathbf{M}, \mathbb{F}) \cong H^{n-q}(\mathbf{M}, \mathbb{F}). \tag{H}$$

This follows from Poincaré duality and the Universal Coefficient Theorems, in a similar manner to (I), since the cohomology with coefficients in a field has no torsion and so is equal to its free quotient. In the case of an orientable differentiable manifold $\mathbf{M}$ the cohomology with real coefficients $\mathbb{R}$ is the de Rham cohomology, obtained from the complex of exterior forms on the manifold and exterior differentiation. Then, the analogue of the intersection pairing is the pairing between q-forms θ_q and $(n-q)$-forms ϕ_{n-q}, given by

$$\int_{\mathbf{M}} \theta_q \wedge \phi_{n-q} \, \mathrm{d}v_{\mathbf{M}},$$

where the volume form $\mathrm{d}v_{\mathbf{M}}$ is determined by the orientation and a choice of metric. Given such choices, each de Rham class is represented by a unique *harmonic* form and then (H) is the Hodge duality between such forms.

There is a similar simplification of the duality theorem with $\mathbb{Z}_2$-coefficients, for which the manifold need not be oriented. Then, the isomorphisms

$$H_r(\mathbf{M}) \pitchfork \mathbb{Z}_2 \cong H_r(\mathbf{M}) \otimes \mathbb{Z}_2$$

and

$$\mathrm{Ext}(H_{r-1}(\mathbf{M}), \mathbb{Z}_2) \cong \mathrm{Tor}(H_{r-1}(\mathbf{M}), \mathbb{Z}_2),$$

which were mentioned at the end of Section A.3, together with the Universal Coefficient Theorems, allow us to re-interpret the duality as the, very unnatural, isomorphism

$$H_q(\mathbf{M}, \mathbb{Z}_2) \cong H_{n-q}(\mathbf{M}, \mathbb{Z}_2).$$

A.5   THE SPLITTING OF EXACT SEQUENCES

In our calculations of the homology groups of shape spaces we mentioned how very nearly our exact sequence of such groups splits, and how much simpler our calculations would have been had it done so. We recall now what these terms mean and derive the necessary and sufficient condition for a sequence to split to which we referred.

We say that a sequence of homomorphisms of abelian groups or, more generally, of modules, is *exact* if the kernel of each is the image of its predecessor in the sequence. Then the short exact sequence

$$0 \longrightarrow \mathbb{A}_1 \overset{\imath}{\longrightarrow} \mathbb{A}_2 \longrightarrow \mathbb{A}_3 \longrightarrow 0$$

splits if the image of $\mathbb{A}_1$ in $\mathbb{A}_2$ is a direct summand. If $\mathbb{K}$ is a direct complement, so that $\mathbb{A}_2 = \imath(\mathbb{A}_1) \oplus \mathbb{K}$, the exact sequence implies that $\mathbb{K}$ is isomorphic with

A_3. Since $\imath$ is injective, $\imath(A_1)$ is isomorphic with A_1 and so altogether we get an isomorphism $A_2 \cong A_1 \oplus A_3$. This implies that there is a homomorphism, $p : A_2 \to A_1$, the composition of the projection from A_2 onto $\imath(A_1)$ and the identification of $\imath(A_1)$ with A_1, such that $p, \circ \imath$ is the identity of A_1. In fact, the existence of such a homomorphism p is also sufficient for the sequence to split: its kernel will be the required direct complement of $\imath(A_1)$ in A_2.

More generally, we say that the long exact sequence

$$\cdots \longrightarrow A_1 \xrightarrow{\imath} A_2 \xrightarrow{J} A_3 \longrightarrow \cdots$$

splits at A_2 if it breaks up into two exact sequences

$$\cdots \longrightarrow A_1 \xrightarrow{\imath} \mathbb{K} \longrightarrow 0$$

and

$$0 \longrightarrow \mathbb{K} \longrightarrow A_2 \xrightarrow{J} A_3 \longrightarrow \cdots,$$

where $\mathbb{K}$ is the image of $\imath$ and, by exactness, hence also the kernel of J. As for the short exact sequence, the necessary and sufficient condition for this is that there exists a homomorphism $p : A_2 \to A_1$ such that $p \circ \imath$ is the identity of A_1.

Bibliography

Ahlfors, L.V. (1996) *Complex Analysis*, 2nd edn. McGraw-Hill, New York.

Ambartzumian, R.V. (1982) Random shapes by factorisation. In: Ranneby, B. ed., *Statistics in Theory and Practice*. Swedish University of Agricultural Science, Umea.

Ambartzumian, R.V. (1985) A Sylvester-type problem for homogeneous Poisson processes. *Izv. Nauk. Armyaskoi SSR* **20**, 284–288.

Ambartzumian, R.V. (1990) *Factorization Calculus and Geometric Probability*. Cambridge University Press, Cambridge.

Bárány, I., Beardon, A.F. and Carne, T.K. (1996) Barycentric subdivision of triangles and semigroups of Möbius maps. *Mathematika* **43**, 165–171.

Ben-Israel, A. and Greville, T.N.E. (1974) *Generalized Inverses*. John Wiley & Sons, New York.

Bookstein, F.L. (1978a) *The Measurement of Biological Shape and Shape Change*. Lecture Notes in Biomathematics **24**. Springer-Verlag, New York.

Bookstein, F.L. (1978b) Linear machinery for morphological distortion. *Comput. Biomed. Res.* **11**, 435–458.

Bookstein, F.L. (1986) Size and shape spaces for landmark data in two dimensions (with discussion). *Stat. Sci.* **1**, 181–242.

Bookstein, F.L. (1989) Principal warps: thin plate splines and the decomposition of deformations. *IEEE Trans. Pattern Anal. Machine Intell.* **11**, 567–585.

Bookstein, F.L. (1991) *Morphometric Tools for Landmark Data*. Cambridge University Press, Cambridge.

Bougerol, P. and Lacroix, J. (1985) *Products of Random Matrices with Applications to Schrödinger Operators*. Progress in Probability and Statistics **8**. Birkhäuser.

Bower, F.O. (1930) *Size and Form in Plants*. Macmillan, London.

Broadbent, S.R. (1980) Simulating the ley hunter (with discussion). *J. Roy. Stat. Soc.* (A) **143**, 109–140.

Bru, M.F. (1989) Processus de Wishart. *C.R. Acad. Sci. Paris, Ser.I Math.* (A) **308**, 29–52.

Carne, T.K. (1990) The geometry of shape spaces. *Proc. London Math. Soc.* (3) **61**, 407–432.

Dieudonné, J. (1970–4) *Treatise on Analysis*, II–IV. Academic Press, New York.

Dryden, I.L. (1989) *The Statistical Analysis of Shape Data*. Ph.D. dissertation, University of Leeds.

Dryden, I.L. and Mardia, K.V. (1991) General shape distributions in a plane. *Adv. Appl. Probab.* **23**, 259–276.

Dryden, I.L. and Mardia, K.V. (1998) *Statistical Shape Analysis*. John Wiley & Sons, Chichester.

Emery, M. (1989) *Stochastic Calculus in Manifolds*. Springer-Verlag, Berlin.

Furstenberg, H. (1963) Noncommuting random products. *Trans. Amer. Math. Soc.* **108**, 377–428.

Gallot, S., Hulin, D. and Lafontaine, J. (1987) *Riemannian Geometry*. Springer-Verlag, Berlin.

Goodall, C.R. (1991) Procrustes methods in the statistical analysis of shape (with discussion). *J. Roy. Stat. Soc.* (B) **53**, 285–339.

Goodall, C.R. and Mardia, K.V. (1991) A geometrical derivation of the shape density. *Adv. Appl. Probab.* **23**, 496–514.

Goodall, C.R. and Mardia, K.V. (1992) The non-central Bartlett decomposition, and shape densities. *J. Multivar. Anal.* **40**, 94–108.

Goodall, C.R. and Mardia, K.V. (1993) Multivariate aspects of shape theory. *Ann. Stat.* **21**, 848–866.

Gower, J.C. (1975) Generalized procrustes analysis. *Psychometrika* **40**, 33–51.

Helgason, S. (1978) *Differential Geometry, Lie Groups, and Symmetric Spaces*. Academic Press, New York.

Helgason, S. (1984) *Groups and Geometric Analysis, Integral Geometry, Invariant Differential Operators and Spherical Functions*. Academic Press, Orlando.

Hermann, R. (1960a) A sufficient condition that a mapping of Riemannian manifolds be a fibre bundle. *Proc. Amer. Math. Soc.* **11**, 236–242.

Hermann, R. (1960b) On the differential geometry of foliations. *Ann. Math.* (2) **72**, 445–457.

Hildebrandt, S. (1985) Harmonic mappings of Riemannian manifolds. In: Giusti, E. ed., *Harmonic Mappings and Minimal Immersions*. Lecture Notes in Mathematics **1161**. Springer-Verlag, Berlin, pp. 1–117.

Hill, M.O. (1974) Correspondence analysis: a neglected multivariate method. *Appl. Stat.* **23**, 340–355.

Hilton, P.J. and Wylie, S. (1960) *Homology Theory*. Cambridge University Press, Cambridge.

Icke, V. and van de Weygaert, R. (1987) Fragmenting the universe, I. Statistics of 2-dimensional Voronoi foams. *Astron. Astrophysics* **184**, 16–32.

Karcher, H. (1977) Riemannian center of mass and mollifier smoothing. *Commun. Pure Appl. Math.* **30**, 509–541.

Kendall, D.G. (1971a) Construction of maps from 'odd bits of information'. *Nature* **231**, 158–159.

Kendall, D.G. (1971b) Maps from marriages: an application of non-metric multidimensional scaling to parish register data. In: Hodson, F.R., Kendall, D.G. and Tautu, P. eds., *Mathematics in the Archaeological and Historical Sciences*. Edinburgh University Press, Edinburgh, pp. 303–318.

Kendall, D.G. (1975) The recovery of structure from fragmentary information. *Phil. Trans. Royal Soc. London* (A) **279**, 547–582.

Kendall, D.G. (1977) The diffusion of shape. *Adv. Appl. Probab.* **9**, 428–430.

Kendall, D.G. (1983) The shape of Poisson–Delaunay triangles. In: Demetrescu, M.C. and Iosifescu, M. eds., *Studies in Probability and Related Topics: Papers in Honour of Octav Onicescu on His 90th Birthday*. Nagard, Montreal, pp. 331–339.

Kendall, D.G. (1984) Shape manifolds, procrustean metrics, and complex projective spaces. *Bull. Lond. Math. Soc.* **16**, 81–121.

Kendall, D.G. (1985) Exact distributions for shapes of random triangles in convex sets. *Adv. Appl. Probab.* **17**, 308–329.

Kendall, D.G. (1986a) Contribution to the discussion following Bookstein (1986).

Kendall, D.G. (1986b) Further developments and applications of the statistical theory of shape. *Theory Probab. Its Appl.* **31**, 407–412.

Kendall, D.G. (1989) A survey of the statistical theory of shape. *Stat. Sci.* **4**, 87–120.

Kendall, D.G. (1990) Random Delaunay simplexes in $\mathbb{R}^m$. *J. Stat. Plan. Infer.* **25**, 225–234.

Kendall, D.G. (1991a) The Mardia–Dryden shape distribution for triangles: a stochastic calculus approach. *J. Appl. Probab.* **28**, 225–230.

Kendall, D.G. (1991b) Contribution to the discussion following Goodall (1991).

Kendall, D.G. (1992) Spherical triangles revisited. In: Mardia, K.V. ed., *The Art of Statistical Science.* John Wiley & Sons, Chichester, pp. 105–113.

Kendall, D.G. (1994a) How to look at objects in a 5-dimensional shape space I: Looking at distributions. *Teoriya Veroyatnostei* **39**, 242–247.

Kendall, D.G. (1994b) How to look at objects in a 5-dimensional shape space II: Looking at diffusions. In: Kelly, F.P. ed., *Probability, Statistics and Optimization.* John Wiley & Sons, Chichester, 315–324.

Kendall, D.G. (1995) How to look at objects in a 5-dimensional shape space III: Looking at geodesics. *Adv. Appl. Probab.* **27**, 35–43.

Kendall, D.G. and Kendall, W.S. (1980) Alignments in 2-dimensional random sets of points. *Adv. Appl. Probab.* **12**, 380–424.

Kendall, D.G. and Le, H. (1986) Exact distributions for shapes of random triangles in convex sets. *Adv. Appl. Probab. (Suppl.)* 59–72.

Kendall, D.G. and Le, H. (1987) The structure and explicit determination of convex-polygonally shape-densities. *Adv. Appl. Probab.* **19**, 896–916.

Kendall, W.S. (1988) Symbolic computation and the diffusion of shapes of triads. *Adv. Appl. Probab.* **20**, 775–797.

Kendall, W.S. (1990a) The diffusion of Euclidean shape. In: Grimmett, G. and Welsh, D. eds., *Disorder in Physical Systems.* Oxford University Press, Oxford, pp. 203–217.

Kendall, W.S. (1990b) Probability, convexity, and harmonic maps with small image I: uniqueness and fine existence. *Proc. London Math. Soc.* **61**, 371–406.

Kendall, W.S. (1998) A diffusion model for Bookstein triangle shape. *Adv. Appl. Probab.* **30**, 317–334.

Kent, J.T. (1992) New directions in shape analysis. In: Mardia, K.V. ed., *The Art of Statistical Science.* John Wiley & Sons, Chichester, pp. 115–127.

Kent, J.T. and Mardia, K.V. (1997) Consistency of procrustes estimators. *J. Roy. Stat. Soc.* (B) **59**, 281–290.

Kristof, W. and Wingersky, B. (1971) Generalization of the orthogonal Procrustes rotation procedure for more than two matrices. *Proc. 79th Annu. Conv. Amer. Psychol. Assoc.* 89–90.

Le, H. (1987a) Explicit formulae for polygonally generated shape densities in the basic tile. *Math. Proc. Cambridge Philos. Soc.* **101**, 313–321.

Le, H. (1987b) Singularities of convex-polygonally generated shape-densities. *Math. Proc. Cambridge Philos. Soc.* **102**, 587–596.

Le, H. (1988) *Shape Theory in Flat and Curved Spaces, and Shape Densities with Uniform Generators.* Ph.D. dissertation, University of Cambridge.

Le, H. (1989a) Random spherical triangles, I. Geometrical background. *Adv. Appl. Probab.* **21**, 570–580.

Le, H. (1989b) Random spherical triangles, II. Shape densities. *Adv. Appl. Probab.* **21**, 581–594.

Le, H. (1990) A stochastic calculus approach to the shape distribution induced by a complex normal model. *Math. Proc. Cambridge Philos. Soc.* **109**, 221–228.

Le, H. (1991) On geodesics in Euclidean shape spaces. *J. London Math. Soc.* (2) **44**, 360–372.

Le, H. (1992) The shapes of non-generic figures, and applications to collinearity testing. *Proc. Royal Soc. London* (A) **439**, 197–210.

Le, H. (1994) Brownian motions on shape and size-and-shape spaces. *J. Appl. Probab.* **31**, 101–113.

Le, H. (1995a) Mean size-and-shapes and mean shapes: a geometric point of view. *Adv. Appl. Probab.* **27**, 44–55.

Le, H. (1995b) The mean shape and the shape of the means. In: Mardia, K.V. and Gill, C.A. eds., *Proc. Int. Conf. Curr. Issues Stat. Shape Anal.* Leeds University Press, Leeds, pp. 34–39.

Le, H. (1998) On consistency of procrustean mean shapes. *Adv. Appl. Probab.* **30**, 53–63.

Le, H. and Bhavnagri, B. (1997) On simplifying shapes by subjecting them to collinearity constraints. *Math. Proc. Cambridge Phil. Soc.* **122**, 315–323.

Le, H. and Kendall, D.G. (1993) The Riemannian structure of Euclidean shape spaces: a novel environment for statistics. *Ann. Stat.* **21**, 1225–1271.

Le, H. and Small, C.G. (1999) Multidimensional scaling of simplex shapes. *Patt. Recog.* **32**, 1601–1613.

Ledrappier, F. (1984) Quelques propriétés des exposants caractéristiques. In: Hennequin, P.L. ed., *École d'été de Saint-Flour, XII.* Lecture Notes in Mathematics **1097**. Springer-Verlag, Berlin.

Lehto, O. (1994) *Introduction to Teichmüller Space.* Springer Graduate Texts in Mathematics. Springer-Verlag, Berlin.

Lele, S. (1993) Euclidean distance matrix analysis (EDMA): estimation of mean form and mean form difference. *Math. Geol.* **25**, 573–602.

MacLane, S. (1963) *Homology.* Springer-Verlag, Berlin.

Magnus, J.R. and Heudecker, H. (1988) *Matrix Differential Calculus.* John Wiley & Sons, New York.

Mannion, D. (1988) A Markov chain of triangle shapes. *Adv. Appl. Probab.* **20**, 348–370.

Mannion, D. (1990a) Convergence to collinearity of a sequence of random triangle shapes. *Adv. Appl. Probab.* **22**, 831–844.

Mannion, D. (1990b) The invariant distribution of a sequence of random collinear triangle shapes. *Adv. Appl. Probab.* **22**, 845–865.

Mardia, K.V. and Dryden, I.L. (1989a) Shape distributions for landmark data. *Adv. Appl. Probab.* **21**, 742–755.

Mardia, K.V. and Dryden, I.L. (1989b) The statistical analysis of shape data. *Biometrika* **76**, 271–281.

Mardia, K.V. and Dryden, I.L. (1994) Shape averages and their bias. *Adv. Appl. Probab.* **26**, 334–340.

Maunder, C.R.F. (1970) *Algebraic Topology.* van Nostrand Reinhold, London.

Miles, R.E. (1970) On the homogeneous planar Poisson point process. *Math. Biosci.* **6**, 85-127.

Muirhead, R.J. (1982) *Aspects of Multivariate Statistical Theory.* John Wiley & Sons, New York.

Newman, M.H.A. (1966) The engulfing theorem for topological manifolds. *Ann. Math.* **84**, 555-571.

O'Neill, B. (1966) The fundamental equations of a submersion. *Michigan Math. J.* **13**, 459-469.

O'Neill, B. (1967) Submersions and geodesics. *Duke Math. J.* **34**, 363-373.

O'Neill, B. (1983) *Semi-Riemannian Geometry.* Academic Press, New York.

Reinhart, B.L. (1959) Foliated manifolds with bundle-like metrics. *Ann. Math.* (2) **69**, 119-132.

Rogers, L.C.G. and Williams, D. (1987) *Diffusions, Markov Processes, and Martingales: Ito Calculus.* John Wiley & Sons, Chichester.

Rohlf, F.J. and Bookstein, F.L. eds. (1990) *Proc. Michigan Morphomet. Workshop.* University of Michigan Museum of Zoology. Special publication 2.

Small, C.G. (1981) *Distribution of Shape and Maximal Invariant Statistics.* Ph.D. dissertation, University of Cambridge.

Small, C.G. (1982) Random uniform triangles and the alignment problem. *Math. Proc. Cambridge Philos. Soc.* **91**, 315-322.

Small, C.G. (1983) Characterisation of distributions from maximal invariant statistics. *Z. Wahrsch. Verw. Gebiete* **63**, 517-527.

Small, C.G. (1984) A classification theorem for planar distributions based on the shape statistics of independent tetrads. *Math. Proc. Cambridge Philos. Soc.* **96**, 543-547.

Small, C.G. (1988) Techniques of shape analysis on sets of points. *Int. Stat. Rev.* **56**, 243-257.

Small, C.G. (1996) *The Statistical Theory of Shape.* Springer-Verlag, New York.

Spanier, E.H. (1966) *Algebraic Topology.* McGraw-Hill, New York.

Stoyan, D., Kendall, W.S. and Mecke, J. (1987) *Stochastic Geometry and its Applications.* John Wiley & Sons, Chichester.

Ten Berge, J.M.F. (1977) Orthogonal procrustes rotation for two or more matrices. *Psychometrika* **42**, 267-276.

Thompson, D'A.W. [1917] (1942) *On Growth and Form.* Cambridge University Press, London. Originally published in 1917.

van de Weygaert, R. (1991) *Voids and the Geometry of Large Scale Structure.* Ph.D. dissertation, Rijksuniversiteit Leiden.

von Neumann, J. (1937) Some matrix-inequalities and metrization of matrix-space. *Tomsk Univ. Rev.* **1**, 286-300. (Republished in *John von Neumann: Collected Works*, vol. IV, 205-219. MacMillan (1992).)

Ziezold, H. (1977) On expected figures and a strong law of large numbers for random elements in quasi-metric spaces. *Trans. 7th Prague Conf. Inf. Theory, Stat. Dec. Func, Random Processes. Vol. A.* Reidel, Dordrecht, 591-602.

Ziezold, H. (1990) Mean figures and mean shapes in the plane. *Math. Schrift.* Kassel.

Ziezold, H. (1994) Mean figures and mean shapes applied to biological figure and shape distributions in the plane. *Biom. J.* **36**, 491-510.

Index

WILEY SERIES IN PROBABILITY
AND STATISTICS

ESTABLISHED BY WALTER A. SHEWHART AND SAMUEL S. WILKS
Editors
*Vic Barnett, Noel A.C. Cressie, Nicholas I. Fisher, Iain M. Johnstone, J.B. Kadane,
David G. Kendall, David W. Scott, Bernard W. Silverman, Adrian F.M. Smith, Jozef
L. Teugels, Ralph A. Bradley, Emeritus, J. Stuart Hunter Emeritus*

Probability and Statistics Section
*ANDERSON • The Statistical Analysis of Time Series
ARNOLD, BALAKRISHNAN, and NAGARAJA • A First Course in Order Statistics
BACCELLI, COHEN, OLSDER, and QUADRAT • Synchronization and Linearity: An
  Algebra for Discrete Event Systems
BASILEVSKY • Statistical Factor Analysis and Related Methods: Theory and Appli-
  cations
BERNARDO and SMITH • Bayesian Statistical Concepts and Theory
BILLINGSLEY • Convergence of Probability Measures
BOROVKOV • Asymptotic Methods in Queuing Theory
BOROVKOV • Ergodicity and Stability of Stochastic Processes
BRANDT, FRANKEN, and LISEK • Stationary Stochastic Models
CAINES and DALANG • Sequential Stochastic Optimization
CONSTANTINE • Combinatorial Theory and Statistical Design
COOK • Regression Graphics
COVER and THOMAS • Elements of Information Theory
CSÖRGŐ and HORVÁTH • Weighted Approximations in Probability Statistics
CSÖRGŐ and HORVÁTH • Limit Theorems in Change Point Analysis
DETTE and STUDDEN • The Theory of Canonical Moments with Applications in
  Statistics, Probability, and Analysis
*DOOB • Stochastic Processes
DRYDEN and MARDIA • Statistical Analysis of Shape
DUPUIS and ELLIS • A Weak Convergence Approach to the Theory of Large Devi-
  ations
ETHIER and KURTZ • Markov Processes: Characterization and Convergence
FELLER • An Introduction to Probability Theory and Its Applications, Volume 1, *Third
  Edition*, Revised; Volume II, *Second Edition*
FULLER • Introduction to Statistical Time Series, *Second Edition*
FULLER • Measurement Error Models
GHOSH, MUKHOPADHYAY, and SEN • Sequential Estimation
GIFI • Nonlinear Multivariate Analysis
GUTTORP • Statistical Inference for Branching Processes
HALL • Introduction to the Theory of Coverage Processes
HAMPEL • Robust Statistics: The Approach Based on Influence Functions
HANNAN and DEISTLER • The Statistical Theory of Linear Systems
HUBER • Robust Statistics
HUŠKOVÁ, BERAN, and DUPAČ • Collected Works of Jaroslav Hájek - With Com-
  mentary
IMAN and CONOVER • A Modern Approach to Statistics
JUREK and MASON • Operator-Limit Distributions in Probability Theory
KASS and VOS • Geometrical Foundations of Asymptotic Inference

*Now available in a lower priced paperback edition in the Wiley Classics Library

KAUFMAN and ROUSSEEUW • Finding Groups in Data: An Introduction to Cluster Analysis
KELLY • Probability, Statistics, and Optimization
LINDVALL • Lectures on the Coupling Method
McFADDEN • Management of Data in Clinical Trials
MANTON, WOODBURY, and TOLLEY • Statistical Applications Using Fuzzy Sets
MORGENTHALER and TUKEY • Configural Polysampling: A Route to Practical Robustness
MUIRHEAD • Aspects of Multivariate Statistical Theory
OLIVER and SMITH • Influence Diagrams, Belief Nets, and Decision Analysis
*PARZEN • Modern Probability Theory and Its Applications
PRESS • Bayesian Statistics: Principles, Models, and Applications
PUKELSHEIM • Optimal Experimental Design
RAO • Asymptotic Theory of Statistical Inference
RAO • Linear Statistical Inference and Its Applications, *Second Edition*
RAO and SHANBHAG • Choquet–Deny Type Functional Equations with Applications to Stochastic Models
ROBERTSON, WRIGHT, and DYKSTRA • Order Restricted Statistical Inference
ROGERS and WILLIAMS • Diffusions, Markov Processes, and Martingales, Volume I: Foundations, *Second Edition;* Volume II: Itô Calculus
RUBINSTEIN and SHAPIRO • Discrete Event Systems: Sensitivity Analysis and Stochastic Optimization by the Score Function Method
RUZSA and SZEKELEY • Algebraic Probability Theory
SCHEFFÉ • The Analysis of Variance
SEBER • Linear Regression Analysis
SEBER • Multivariate Observations
SEBER and WILD • Nonlinear Regression
SERFLING • Approximation Theorems of Mathematical Statistics
SHORACK and WELLNER • Empirical Processes with Applications to Statistics
SMALL and McLEISH • Hilbert Space Methods in Probability and Statistical Inference
STAPLETON • Linear Statistical Models
STAUDTE and SHEATHER • Robust Estimation and Testing
STOYANOV • Counterexamples in Probability
TANAKA • Time Series Analysis: Nonstationary and Noninvertible Distribution Theory
THOMPSON and SEBER • Adaptive Sampling
WELSH • Aspects of Statistical Inference
WHITTAKER • Graphical Models in Applied Multivariate Statistics
YANG • The Construction Theory of Denumerable Markov Processes

Applied Probability and Statistics Section
ABRAHAM and LEDOLTER • Statistical Methods for Forecasting
AGRESTI • Analysis of Ordinal Categorical Data
AGRESTI • Categorical Data Analysis
ANDERSON, AUQUIER, HAUCK, OAKES, VANDAELE, and WEISBERG • Statistical Methods for Comparative Studies
ARMITAGE and DAVID (editors) • Advances in Biometry
*ARTHANARI and DODGE • Mathematical Programming in Statistics
ASMUSSEN • Applied Probability and Queues
*BAILEY • The Elements of Stochastic Processes with Applications to the Natural Sciences

*Now available in a lower priced paperback edition in the Wiley Classics Library

BARNETT and LEWIS • Outliers in Statistical Data, *Third Edition*
BARTHOLOMEW, FORBES, and McLEAN • Statistical Techniques for Manpower Planning, *Second Edition*
BATES and WATTS • Nonlinear Regression Analysis and Its Applications
BECHHOFER, SANTNER, and GOLDSMAN • Design and Analysis of Experiments for Statistical Selection, Screening, and Multiple Comparisons
BELSLEY • Conditioning Diagnostics: Collinearity and Weak Data in Regression
BELSLEY, KUH, and WELSCH • Regression Diagnostics: Identifying Influential Data and Sources of Collinearity
BHAT • Elements of Applied Stochastic Processes, *Second Edition*
BHATTACHARYA and WAYMIRE • Stochastic Processes with Applications
BIRKES and DODGE • Alternative Methods of Regression
BLOOMFIELD • Fourier Analysis of Time Series: An Introduction
BOLLEN • Structural Equations with Latent Variables
BOULEAU • Numerical Methods for Stochastic Processes
BOX • Bayesian Inference in Statistical Analysis
BOX and DRAPER • Empirical Model-Building and Response Surfaces
BOX and DRAPER • Evolutionary Operation: A Statistical Method for Process Improvement
BUCKLEW • Large Deviation Techniques in Decision, Simulation, and Estimation
BUNKE and BUNKE • Nonlinear Regression, Functional Relations, and Robust Methods: Statistical Methods of Model Building
CHATTERJEE and HADI • Sensitivity Analysis in Linear Regression
CHOW and LIU • Design and Analysis of Clinical Trials
CLARKE and DISNEY • Probability and Random Processes: A First Course with Applications, *Second Edition*
*COCHRAN and COX • Experimental Designs, *Second Edition*
CONOVER • Practical Nonparametric Statistics, *Second Edition*
CORNELLL • Experiments with Mixtures, Designs, Models, and the Analysis of Mixture Data, *Second Edition*
*COX • Planning of Experiments
CRESSIE • Statistics for Spatial Data, *Revised Edition*
DANIEL • Applications of Statistics to Industrial Experimentation
DANIEL • Biostatistics: A Foundation for Analysis in the Health Sciences, *Sixth Edition*
DAVID • Order Statistics, *Second Edition*
*DEGROOT, FIENBERG, and KADANE • Statistics and the Law
DODGE • Alternative Methods of Regression
DOWDY and WEARDEN • Statistics for Research, *Second Edition*
DUNN and CLARK • Applied Statistics: Analysis of Variance and Regression, *Second Edition*
ELANDT-JOHNSON and JOHNSON • Survival Models and Data Analysis
EVANS, PEACOCK, and HASTINGS • Statistical Distributions, *Second Edition*
FLEISS • The Design and Analysis of Clinical Experiments
FLEISS • Statistical Methods for Rates and Proportions, *Second Edition*
FLEMING and HARRINGTON • Counting Processes and Survival Analysis
GALLANT • Nonlinear Statistical Models
GLASSERMAN and YAO • Monotone Structure in Discrete-Event Systems
GNANADESIKAN • Methods for Statistical Data Analysis of Multivariate Observations, *Second Edition*
GOLDSTEIN and LEWIS • Assessment: Problems, Development, and Statistical Issues

*Now available in a lower priced paperback edition in the Wiley Classics Library

LEPAGE and BILLARD • Exploring the Limits Bootstrap
LINHART and ZUCCHINI • Model Selection
LITTLE and RUBIN···Statistical Analysis with Missing Data
MAGNUS and NEUDECKER • Matrix Differential Calculus with Applications in Statistics and Econometrics, *Revised Edition*
MALLER and ZHOU • Survival Analysis with Long Term Survivors
MANN, SCHAFER, and SINGPURWALLA • Methods for Statistical Analysis of Reliability and Life Data
McLACHLAN and KRISHNAN • The EM Algorithm and Extensions
McLACHLAN • Discriminant Analysis and Statistical Pattern Recognition
McNEIL • Epidemiological Research Methods
MILLER • Survival Analysis
MONTGOMERY and PECK • Introduction to Linear Regression Analysis, *Second Edition*
MYERS and MONTGOMERY • Response Surface Methodology: Process and Product in Optimization using Designed Experiments
NELSON • Accelerated Testing, Statistical Models, Test Plans, and Data Analyses
NELSON • Applied Life Data Analysis
OCHI • Applied Probability and Stochastic Processes in Engineering and Physical Sciences
OKABE, BOOTS, and SUGIHARA • Spatial Tesselations: Concepts and Applications of Voronoi Diagrams
PANKRATZ • Forecasting with Dynamic Regression Models
PANKRATZ • Forecasting with Univariate Box–Jenkins Models: Concepts and Cases
PIANTADOSI • Clinical Trials: A Methodologic Perspective
PORT • Theoretical Probability for Applications
PUTERMAN • Markov Decision Processes: Discrete Stochastic Dynamic Programming
RACHEV • Probability Metrics and the Stability of Stochastic Models
RÉNYI • A Diary on Information Theory
RIPLEY • Spatial Statistics
RIPLEY • Stochastic Simulation
ROUSSEEUW and LEROY • Robust Regression and Outlier Detection
RUBIN • Multiple Imputation for Nonresponse in Surveys
RUBINSTEIN • Simulation and the Monte Carlo Method
RUBINSTEIN and MELAMED • Modern Simulation and Modeling
RYAN • Statistical Methods for Quality Improvement
SCHUSS • Theory and Applications of Stochastic Differential Equations
SCOTT • Multivariate Density Estimation: Theory, Practice, and Visualization
*SEARLE • Linear Models
SEARLE • Linear Models for Unbalanced Data
SEARLE, CASELLA, and McCULLOCH • Variance Components
STOYAN, KENDALL, and MECKE • Stochastic Geometry and Its Applications, *Second Edition*
STOYAN and STOYAN • Fractals, Random Shapes, and Point Fields: Methods of Geometrical Statistics
THOMPSON • Empirical Model Building
THOMPSON • Sampling
TIJMS • Stochastic Modeling and Analysis: A Computational Approach
TIJMS • Stochastic Models: An Algorithmic Approach

*Now available in a lower priced paperback edition in the Wiley Classics Library

TITTERINGTON, SMITH, and MAKOV • Statistical Analysis of Finite Mixture Distributions

UPTON and FINGLETON • Spatial Data Analysis by Example, Volume I: Point Pattern and Quantitative Data

UPTON and FINGLETON • Spatial Data Analysis by Example, Volume II: Categorical and Directional Data

VAN RIJCKEVORSEL and DE LEEUW • Component and Correspondence Analysis

WEISBERG • Applied Linear Regression, *Second Edition*

WESTFALL and YOUNG • Resampling-Based Multiple Testing: Examples and Methods for *p*-Value Adjustment

WHITTLE • Systems in Stochastic Equilibrium

WOODING • Planning Pharmaceutical Clinical Trials: Basic Statistical Principles

WOOLSON • Statistical Methods for the Analysis of Biomedical Data

*ZELLNER • An Introduction to Bayesian Inference in Econometrics

Texts and References Section

AGRESTI • An Introduction to Categorical Data Analysis

ANDERSON • An Introduction to Multivariate Statistical Analysis, *Second Edition*

ANDERSON and LOYNES • The Teaching of Practical Statistics

ARMITAGE and COLTON • Encyclopedia of Biostatistics. 6 Volume set

BARTOSZYNSKI and NIEWIADOMSKA-BUGAJ • Probability and Statistical Inference

BERRY, CHALONER, and GEWEKE • Bayesian Analysis in Statistics and Econometrics: Essays in Honor of Arnold Zellner

BHATTACHARYA and JOHNSON • Statistical Concepts and Methods

BILLINGSLEY • Probability and Measure, *Second Edition*

BOX • R. A. Fisher, the Life of a Scientist

BOX, HUNTER, and HUNTER • Statistics for Experimenters: An Interoduction to Design, Data Analysis, and Model Building

BOX and LUCEÑO • Statistical Control by Monitoring and Feedback Adjustment

BROWN and HOLLANDER • Statistics: A Biomedical Introduction

CHATTERJEE and PRICE • Regression Analysis by Example, *Second Edition*

COOK and WEISBERG • An Introduction to Regression Graphics

COX • A Handbook of Introductory Statistical Methods

DILLON and GOLDSTEIN • Multivariate Analysis: Methods and Applications

DODGE and ROMIG • Sampling Inspection Tables, *Second Edition*

DRAPER and SMITH • Applied Regression Analysis, *Third Edition*

DUDEWICZ and MISHRA • Modern Mathematical Statistics

DUNN • Basic Statistics: A Primer for the Biomedical Sciences, *Second Edition*

FISHER and VAN BELLE • Biostatistics: A Methodology for the Health Sciences

FREEMAN and SMITH • Aspects of Uncertainty: A Tribute to D.V. Lindley

GROSS and HARRIS • Fundamentals of Queueing Theory, *Third Edition*

HALD • A History of Probability and Statistics and their Applications Before 1750

HALD • A History of Mathematical Statistics from 1750 to 1930

HELLER • MACSYMA for Statisticians

HOEL • Introduction to Mathematical Statistics, *Fifth Edition*

JOHNSON and BALAKRISHNAN • Advances in the Theory and practice of Statistics: A Volume in Honor of Samuel Kotz

JOHNSON and KOTZ (editors) • Leading Personalities in Statistical Sciences: From the Seventeenth Century to the present

*Now available in a lower priced paperback edition in the Wiley Classics Library

JUDGE, GRIFFITHS, HILL, LÜTKEPOHL, and LEE • The Theory and Practice of Econometrics, *Second Edition*

KHURI • Advanced Calculus with Applications in Statistics

KOTZ and JOHNSON (editors) • Encyclopedia of Statistical Sciences: Volumes 1 to 9 with Index

KOTZ and JOHNSON (editors) • Encyclopedia of Statistical Sciences: Supplement Volume

KOTZ, REED,and BANKS (editors) • Encyclopedia of Statistical Sciences: Update Volume 1

KOTZ, REED,and BANKS (editors) • Encyclopedia of Statistical Sciences: Update Volume 2

LAMPERTI • Probability: A Survey of the Mathematical Theory, *Second Edition*

LARSON • Introduction to Probability Theory and Statistical Inference, *Third Edition*

LE • Applied Survival Analysis

MALLOWS • Design, Data, and Analysis by Some Friends of Cuthbert Daniel

MARDIA • The Art of Statistical Science: A Tribute to G. S. Watson

MASON, GUNST,and HESS • Statistical Design and Analysis of Experiments with Applications to Engineering and Science

MURRAY • X-STAT 2.0 Statistical Experimentation, Design Data Analysis, and Nonlinear Optimization

PURI, VILAPLANA, and WERTZ • New Perspectives in Theoretical and Applied Statistics

RENCHER • Methods of Multivariate Analysis

RENCHER • Multivariate Statistical Inference with Applications

ROSS • Introduction to Probability and Statistics for Engineers and Scientists

ROHATGI • An Introduction to Probability Theory and Mathematical Statistics

RYAN • Modern Regression Methods

SCHOTT • Matrix Analysis for Statistics

SEARLE • Matrix Algebra Useful for Statistics

STYAN • The Collected Papers of T. W. Anderson: 1943–1985

TIERNEY • LISP-STAT: An Object-Oriented Environment for Statistical Computing and Dynamic Graphics

WONNACOTT and WONNACOTT • Econometrics, *Second Edition*

WILEY SERIES IN PROBABILITY
AND STATISTICS

ESTABLISHED BY WALTER A. SHEWHART AND SAMUEL S. WILKS

Editors
Robert M. Groves, Graham Kalton, J.N.K. Rao, Norbert Schwarz, Christopher Skinner

Survey Methodology Section

BIEMER, GROVES, LYBERG, MATHIOWETZ, and SUDMAN • Measurement Errors in Surveys

COCHRAN • Sampling Techniques, *Third Edition*

COX, BINDER, CHINNAPPA, CHRISTIANSON, COLLEDGE, and KOTT (editors) • Business Survey Methods

*DEMING • Sample Design in Business Research

DILLMAN • Mail and Telephone Surveys: The Total Design Method

GROVES • Survey Errors and Survey Costs

*Now available in a lower priced paperback edition in the Wiley Classics Library

*Now available in a lower priced paperback edition in the Wiley Classics Library